ANNALS OF THE NEW YORK ACADEMY OF SCIENCES

VOLUME 282

December 30, 1976

CHRONIC CANNABIS USE*

Editors and Conference Chairmen
RHEA L. DORNBUSH, ALFRED M. FREEDMAN, AND MAX FINK

CONTENTS

* This series of papers is the result of a conference entitled Chronic Cannabis Use, held on
January 26, 27, and 28, 1976, and sponsored by The New York Academy of Sciences, National
Institute on Drug Abuse, and New York Medical College.

ANNALS OF THE NEW YORK ACADEMY OF SCIENCES

Volume 282

CHRONIC CANNABIS USE

Edited by Rhea L. Dornbush, Alfred M. Freedman, and Max Fink

The New York Academy of Sciences
New York, New York
1976

Library of Congress Cataloging in Publication Data

Main entry under title:

Chronic cannabis use.

(Annals of the New York Academy of Sciences; v. 282)
Papers from a conference held Jan. 26–28, 1976, sponsored by The New York Academy of Sciences, National Institute on Drug Abuse, and New York Medical College.

1. Cannabis—Congresses. 2. Drug abuse—Congresses. I. Dornbush, Rhea L. II. Freedman, Alfred M. III. Fink, Max. IV. New York Academy of Sciences. V. National Institute on Drug Abuse. VI. New York Medical College, Flower and Fifth Avenue Hospitals. VII. Series: New York Academy of Sciences. Annals; v. 282. [DNLM: 1. Cannabis —Congresses. 2. Drug abuse—Congresses. W1 AN626Y1 v. 282/ WM276 C557 1976]

Q11.N5 vol. 282 [RC568.C2]   508'.1s [616.8'63]
ISBN 0-89072-028-2   76-58481

PCP

Printed in the United States of America
ISBN 0–89072–028–2

Part VII. Central Nervous System Functioning: Does Brain Damage Result from Long-Term Use?

Neurophysiologic Studies

Part VIII. Social Policy and Marijuana Use

Paper presented at the conference but not submitted for publication:

Psychophysiologic Changes Associated with Chronic Cannabis Use. *By* FRANK KNIGHT

Financial assistance was received from:

- DRUG ABUSE COUNCIL, INC.
- NATIONAL INSTITUTE ON DRUG ABUSE

INTRODUCTION

Rhea L. Dornbush * and Alfred M. Freedman

Department of Psychiatry
New York Medical College
New York, New York 10029

The use of marijuana increased dramatically in the 1960s, particularly among middle-class youths. Because marijuana was classified as a narcotic by the United States Government, and its effects were poorly understood and subject to political and emotional misrepresentations, a large-scale national effort was undertaken to investigate its pharmacology. In 1972, it was reliably estimated that 24 million people in the United States had tried marijuana and that 8 million were using it with some regularity.[1] The rate of increase of use was estimated at 20–30% per year. In 1976, the National Institute on Drug Abuse reported that 53% of Americans aged 18–25 had tried marijuana, while 25% were currently using it.[2]

Although the problem of marijuana use in the United States is not new,[3] its urgency is of recent origin, and it continues to be of universal concern. In 1970, as interest in marijuana use was reaching its height, the President established a commission to study the problem of marijuana and drug abuse. Concern about increasing marijuana use, particularly in the under-30 population, and its long-term effects was not limited to the United States. In 1969, Canada established a Commission of Inquiry into the Non-Medical Use of Drugs. Preceding the interest of the United States and Canada about the effects of marijuana, other countries were already involved in the study of long-term cannabis users, notably India and Egypt.

Support for marijuana research in this country was mainly for the study of acute effects and the effects of limited periods of daily administration (21–90 days) in young adults (21–30 years). The typical user in the United States is drawn from the most achievement-oriented classes, and use reaches a peak during college years. Because users in the United States who had smoked for long periods (10 or more years) and had limited themselves to marijuana could not be identified, studies were undertaken abroad. Three studies of long-term heavy cannabis use were performed in the foreign populations of Jamaica, Greece, and Costa Rica. The populations studied limited themselves to cannabis, using no other abuse substances except tobacco and alcohol, socially. In contrast to the United States' studies, these users were derived from the lowest, least productive strata of society.

This Conference was organized as a forum to review and evaluate the data from long-term users, to provide a cohesive body of knowledge about the effects of cannabis, and to attempt an extrapolation of these data to casual use and project the outcome for relatively short-term users.

The Conference was organized around five major areas of concern: central nervous system functioning, health implications, cannabis psychosis, the amoti-

---

* Present address: Reproductive Biology Research Foundation, St. Louis, Mo. 63108.

vational syndrome, and tolerance, dependence, and withdrawal. Several laboratory studies of daily administration in short-term users (performed mainly in the United States and Canada) were also included to provide a comparison with the studies in populations of long-term users. The recent interest in hormonal and immunologic effects of cannabis, while touched on in this monograph, is not assayed here since the present studies were not designed with these concerns in mind.

Some of the data presented here has been reported previously. Parts of studies have been presented independently of the contexts in which they were obtained, occasionally leading to distorted impressions of the data and of the effects of cannabis. When the data are presented in the context of the studies in which they were obtained, with particular attention to the subject samples, and are compared to those obtained in other similar studies, a different perspective of the effects of marijuana emerges.

There are two ways to read this monograph: by the questions of concern, which is the way the monograph is organized, or by studies. The Jamaican studies are represented by the papers of Knights and Grenier, Knight, Cruickshank, Comitas; the Greek studies by the papers of Dornbush *et al.*, Liakos *et al.*, Fink, Boulougouris *et al.*, and Stefanis *et al.*; the Costa Rican studies by Satz *et al.*, Karacan *et al.*, Coggins and Carter; the Egyptian studies by Soueif; and the Indian studies by Chopra and Jandu. The Conference sequence differed from the order of this monograph.

We wish to extend our gratitude to both the National Institute on Drug Abuse and the Drug Abuse Council, Inc. for their support of this Conference.

REFERENCES

1. NATIONAL COMMISSION ON MARIHUANA AND DRUG ABUSE. 1972. First Report. Marihuana: A Signal of Misunderstanding. United States Government Printing Office. Washington, D.C.
2. NATIONAL COMMISSION ON MARIHUANA AND DRUG ABUSE. 1976. Fifth Report. Marihuana and Health. United States Government Printing Office. Washington, D.C.
3. MAYOR'S COMMITTEE ON MARIHUANA. 1944. The Marihuana Problem in the City of New York. Jaques Cattell Press. Tempe, Ariz.

INTRODUCTION: WHAT IS THE EVIDENCE FOR AN AMOTIVATIONAL SYNDROME IN CANNABIS USERS?

Dana L. Farnsworth *

*Harvard University
Cambridge, Massachusetts 02138*

Very few issues of public interest have given rise to so many strongly expressed differences in every aspect of its nature and consequences as have the effects of cannabis on those who ingest it, whether by smoking or otherwise. Indeed, one is reminded of the minister's wife who was reading her husband's sermon for delivery the following Sunday and wrote a note in the margin where a questionable point was being discussed: "Weak point—shout loud." Intensity of emotion frequently prevails over accuracy of observations. Our task today is to examine the evidence as to whether an amotivational syndrome does, in fact, exist.

An entirely different question, but one that has at least a tenuous relationship to this one, is whether ingestion of cannabis, or any other drug, truly increases one's ability in intellectual, artistic, or religious pursuits. I have thus far failed to convince myself that claims of such new insights are valid. Shortcuts to wisdom have not been developed by the rapid accumulation of knowledge that is constantly occurring. Indeed, wisdom is not something that can be acquired by any form of wishful thinking or by any form of chemical reaction within the brain cells. It can only be acquired by attainment of a rich mixture of knowledge, competence, compassion, intellectual flexibility, objectivity, and patience. Whatever else may be needed, drugs are not the answer.

The arguments for an amotivational syndrome from the use of cannabis were more numerous and persuasive in the late 1960s than at present. There probably is considerable evidence that any excessive use of drugs for pleasure may decrease the individual's motivation. However, it is now our task to examine the data we' presently have, confusing as they may be, to determine whether cannabis has any specific capacity for inhibition of motivation not possessed by other drugs.

---

* Henry K. Oliver Professor of Hygiene, Emeritus.

SOCIAL AND CULTURAL ASPECTS OF CANNABIS USE IN COSTA RICA *

William E. Carter and Paul L. Doughty

Department of Anthropology
University of Florida
Gainesville, Florida 32611

The history of cannabis introduction and use in Costa Rica is not well documented. It seems likely, however, that cannabis was introduced into the country about 100 years ago. Groups of railroad construction laborers were brought from Panama in the 1880s after de Lesseps had abandoned the French plans for the isthmus canal. It was reported that the Chinese and Jamaicans who were among these laborers planted and smoked cannabis. During the same period, there were some scattered attempts to establish a fiber industry based on hemp, but these projects never flourished.

Cannabis use as a psychotropic drug thus appears to go back about a century. There is little use of cannabis as a medicinal plant, although its use to relieve asthma has been reported. Presently, the drug is used, mainly in cigarette form, by a broad cross section of the working-class population in urban areas and, to some extent, in the banana plantations in coastal areas.

Most of the marijuana used in Costa Rica is grown in the country itself, but an undetermined amount is imported from Panama, Colombia, and Mexico. Production occurs in scattered plots in the tropical lowlands of the country, generally in remote areas. The crop is brought to market in a variety of ways, usually in small and large quantities of *picadura,* the chopped leaves and flowers of the plants. The *picadura* is later rolled into cigarettes by urban wholesalers and retailers. Yellow wheat paper is most commonly used for this purpose.

Marijuana is readily available to users despite attempts of the Costa Rican government, dating back to the 1920s, to control the substance. Attempts at control since 1970 have included the establishment of a special narcotic police unit. Confiscations and arrests have not produced any notable deterrent to cannabis production or use but have caused the price of marijuana to consumers to fluctuate at times.

The potency of Costa Rican marijuana was tested by sending 13 street samples to United States' laboratories for analysis under special permit from both Costa Rican and United States' governments. The analyses showed that the tetrahydrocannabinol (THC) content of the marijuana varied from 1.27 to 3.72% by weight. The cigarettes are generally sold in "rolls" of 25, which have an average weight close to 5 g. The standard marijuana cigarette in Costa Rica thus contains about 200 mg of marijuana. The users in our sample smoked a mean of 9.6 cigarettes per day (median of seven). The reported range of cigarettes smoked regularly on a daily basis by members of the sample was from 2.5 to 40 per day. Some persons were observed to smoke up to 80 cigarettes daily on occasion.

The average Costa Rican user in the sample has smoked regularly for 16.9

* The work upon which this publication is based was performed pursuant to Contract NO1–MHE–0233 with the National Institute on Drug Abuse.

years. Because he smokes about 10 cigarettes per day, he is exposed to less Δ^9-THC (about 40 mg) than is his Moroccan, Indian, or Egyptian counterpart, who consumes 60–90 mg. The heaviest user in our sample, who smokes an average of 40 cigarettes per day, has a level of Δ^9-THC exposure on a par with heavy hashish smokers in Morocco and India and as reported among United States military personnel in Europe at 160 mg per day. Figures for the heavy Egyptian hashish smokers are somewhat higher, 200 mg per day. This figure approaches what we found in the user who on occasion consumes 80–100 cigarettes in a single day and who probably is exposed to more than 350 mg of Δ^9-THC.

Costa Rican interest and knowledge about marijuana have risen sharply since 1968. This concern coincides with the general pattern of interest that developed elsewhere in Europe and North America at the same time and is related to it. Prior to this time, the most pressing drug problem in Costa Rica was considered to be alcoholism and the illegal production of alcohol. Given the rise in newspaper publicity covering marijuana since 1968, public interest has turned to the topic.

The change in public interest coincides with a perceived increase in marijuana use by the educated middle- and upper-class youth on an occasional recreational basis. Fears about possible deleterious effects of marijuana smoking have been encouraged by sensationalist newspaper reports that are widely read by all social classes in Costa Rica. Middle- and upper-class preoccupation stems largely from the fact that what was traditionally assumed to be just a lower-class trait and associated with undesirable behavior is now being more widely accepted.

Despite the creation of a special police unit and great publicity given to their activities, neither the supply of marijuana nor the level and extent of its use has demonstrably changed since 1950, when the earliest data on confiscations became available. There has been no particular change in the pattern of heavy alcohol consumption or production, both legal and illegal, over the same period. Thus, the change in public concern seems to stem largely from recent efforts at publicizing aspects of cannabis use and police activity. Once public perception heightened, and fears arose about possible social and biologic effects of marijuana use, drugs became a national issue in Costa Rica.

There is little evidence that heroin, cocaine, and similar substances are much used in Costa Rica. Police and Ministry of Health records show that 98% of all arrests and drug seizures, aside from those related to illegal alcohol, concern marijuana. With respect to alcohol, estimates and studies show that clandestine production and consumption of unlicensed cane alcohol equal those officially sanctioned and that alcoholism is a major social and economic problem, especially among the working-class population. Tobacco use in Costa Rica is also very widespread, and the vast majority of Costa Rican men are tobacco smokers.

Long-time marijuana users, who consider its use as harmless and acceptable behavior, regard the recently developed public attitudes about marijuana use as unjust. In contrast, nonusers accept, without question, the pejorative assertions made in the news media about the drug.

STUDY SAMPLE

Our research was conducted in the metropolitan area of the city of San José, capital of Costa Rica. The subjects studied were selected from the 437,000 inhabitants of the city in accord with their residential, employment, social class, and educational characteristics. They were all male, lived in 45 of the city's working-class residential barrios and constituted a stratified and purposive sample. It was impossible to use random selection techniques, because marijuana use is illegal.

Eighty-four users and 156 nonusers were chosen and studied during the first year of the study. Sociocultural and biomedical interviews and examinations were conducted with each subject. During the second year, a subsample of 41 users and 41 matched nonusers was chosen from this population for in-depth studies in several areas of inquiry. These pairs of individuals were matched on the basis of six characteristics: occupation, educational level, marital status,

TABLE 1

RESULTS ON AGE, MARITAL STATUS, EDUCATION, OCCUPATION, ALCOHOL
CONSUMPTION, AND TOBACCO CONSUMPTION FOR BASE AND FINAL SAMPLES

	Base Sample		Final Sample	
Variable and Categories	Users ($n=84$)	Nonusers ($n=156$)	Users ($n=41$)	Nonusers ($n=41$)
Mean age	31.07	30.68	29.95	28.98
Marital status (%)				
Formal and consensual marriage	53.5	68.0	61.0	73.2
Single	42.8	28.8	36.6	22.0
Education (%)				
None	1.2	5.1	2.4	0.0
Incomplete primary	52.4	35.9	46.3	39.0
Complete primary	27.4	33.3	31.7	39.0
Incomplete secondary	16.7	21.8	19.5	22.0
Complete secondary	1.2	3.8	0.0	0.0
Occupation (%)				
Unskilled	41.7	41.0	34.1	26.8
Skilled	58.3	59.0	65.9	73.2
Mean alcohol consumption *	9.68	8.92	8.512	8.829
Tobacco consumption				
Mean number of pack-years	19.30	13.79	16.21	15.27

* On a 17-point scale.

age, and levels of tobacco and alcohol consumption. In this fashion, we controlled many environmental and social factors so as to delineate, as exactly as possible, the dimensions and effects of chronic marijuana use (cf. TABLE 1).

In terms of socioeconomic status, the sample population is representative of all except the lowest and highest deciles of San José's population and, on the average, ranks in the middle of the working class. The variety of occupations found in the sample population are typical of urban economic life: 24 were employed in commerce, 32 in transportation, 129 were in artisanal or building trades, and the rest were in service occupations. As a group, the subjects tended to earn a little less than the average incomes projected for their barrios, but their incomes fell entirely within normal ranges.

The study was designed to reveal the character and effects of chronic, long-term heavy marijuana use in a natural (as opposed to clinical or laboratory) population. The study population was typical of the urban area and was selected through their participation in a series of tight social networks, forming a socially connected, geographically disperse, and economically active group.

The base sample of 240 persons showed a great similarity among their social characteristics. Users and nonusers were significantly differentiated from one another in only 10 of 54 variables examined in the initial phase of the study. In the base sample, there were no significant differences found between users and nonusers with respect to religion, political activity, educational level achieved, involvement in work as children, family structure, unemployment, family size, or number of children produced. Significant initial differences in the base sample occurred with respect to the nonusers earning slightly more in wages, being arrested less often because they were not involved in marijuana use, being in jail and reformatory less often, and being less likely to have been raised by surrogate parents.

The matched-pair subsample, derived from the original base sample, largely reflected the patterns established in the larger group. In the detailed matched-pair study, the meanings of the differences noted above and others that eventually emerged were explored in depth and are summarized below. In general, we concluded from our examination of both base and matched samples that the subject population is highly representative of the Costa Rican working-class man and his life experience.

FINDINGS

Our subjects in the matched-pair subsample of 82 individuals originally came in almost equal numbers from urban and rural areas. At the time of the study, practically all were living in urban areas and had been for many years. As a group, however, the users who migrated to the city (either with or without their parents) came at an earlier age than did nonusers.

Childhood and Family

In broad outline, the family structure was very similar for both groups during the subjects' period of socialization. The rural origins of such working-class families were evident in behavioral patterns, particularly those associated with early work for children and general kinship relations. The small, independent farmer or farm laborer family focuses largely on the nuclear family unit and kinsmen who contribute to their lives in some manner. In the city, social life concentrates on extended family ties rather than on neighbors and other barrio residents. The system of godparentage (*padrinazgo*) and godsiblings (*compadrazgo*), so commonly reported elsewhere in both rural and urban areas of Latin America, is little developed in San José. Very few of the subjects from either group had much to do with fictive kinsmen and rarely received assistance from them at any stage in their lives.

On the other hand, relatives often lived in the same or adjacent barrios and even next door to one another. The average family size for both groups was about five, a number that generally included both parents of the subject. Although many kinsmen were present, our subjects' families of orientation remained economically independent, receiving assistance in crisis situations from relatives, and then in limited extent. Although most fathers of all subjects regularly worked and supported their families, the mothers tended to be the dominant social figures during childhood, and many of them worked, especially those whose sons later became marijuana users. In general, most subjects of both groups felt that their childhood and homelife were satisfactory and that they were fairly treated, even spoiled. Most children were working to some degree by the age of 12.

The typical family of both groups was not involved in community affairs, showed little interest in religion, and was seldom concerned with politics. Families of these men socialized and celebrated their kinship and common life to only limited degrees. Normally, few meals were eaten together, friends were seldom brought home, and family parties occurred only at Christmas or an occasional birthday. Instead, men concentrated on developing their lives outside the home, and their social networks were largely independent of family ties. On the other hand, female members of the family, especially mothers, were expected to be present in the home. Mothers were idolized and revered. Most subjects remembered their childhood period as being one of stability and adequacy, although not free of problems.

Despite these many similarities in families of orientation, several significant differences did exist, which separated future users from future nonusers. More users grew up in the city. More users abandoned home, and, when they did, they abandoned home earlier. Users had less adequate diet and housing as children. More users had mothers who worked full or part time outside the home and who either controlled or helped control the family finances. Users' mothers were more likely to be puritanical in their behavior, being nondrinkers. More users' fathers failed to assume any role of leadership or even be active in community activities. More users came from families that gave unequal treatment to their offspring, especially favoring other children in the family. More users came from families that were downwardly mobile.

Users related more poorly to the institutions of socialization than did nonusers. Significantly more users engaged in mischievous behavior in school; they had a higher rate of school absences and were more frequently expelled from school. During adolescence, more users than nonusers engaged in delinquency, such as petty theft, and significantly fewer users worked full time. Although not a single nonuser was sentenced to the reformatory, sentencing occurred with 36.6% (15) of the users.

The fact that this sizable percentage of marijuana users had at some time or other served a reformatory sentence, whereas not a single nonuser had done so, would seem to be one of the most significant findings of our study. One could argue that the reformatory has served as a school, both for marijuana smoking and for other delinquent behavior. Noteworthy in this regard is that although 17.1% of the nonusers speak of their delinquent acts during adolescence, not a single one was taken to the reformatory. By contrast, 83.3% of the users who committed delinquent acts were sentenced. A reasonable hypothesis would be that young marijuana users were, because of their use, pursued by the authorities. Once designated as "marijuanos," they became more vulnerable, both because of continued marijuana smoking and for other reasons, whether related to marijuana or not. Having abandoned home, their primary groupings were other street youth, and this, too, could have made them more vulnerable.

Thus, by the time users entered adolescence, they had already, as a group, developed along different lines than did nonusers. By and large, they were individuals who came from weakly constituted families, who had absent and moralistic mothers and weak fathers, who suffered from disciplinary inconsistencies and sibling rivalry, who lived in poverty, and who had begun to have serious problems with the major institutions of society. There is no clear pattern that indicates that marijuana led to these problems, however. In fact, the opposite would seem to be the case. Of nine users who left home at age 12 or earlier, eight began smoking after leaving home, and one began at the same age. Of those who left home between 13 and 16 years of age, six were already smoking, six began at the time they left home, and three began smoking later. None said that their reason for leaving home was marijuana use; most cited economic problems.

Whereas only 29% of users stayed with their parents until marriage or never left their parental home, 66% of nonusers did so. A significant number of users were therefore on their own by the time they were in their late teens, independent of family ties and responsible only to themselves. Closely related to this situation would seem to be the fact that, in contrast to nonusers, the users seldom married in their teens.

During the adolescence of all subjects, whether users or nonusers, peer groups constituted important social alternatives to both home and school life. Most boys "ran" with street gangs and cliques at one time or another, but users were more committed to such activity. Generally, such peer groups assumed great importance among those who left home; they literally became the "school of hard knocks."

Among peers, most boys acquired social habits and experience not taught in other institutional arrangements. Drinking behavior, sexual relations, marijuana smoking, street survival techniques, and occupations were learned in this context. Experimentation in employment, sex, and personal "style" was encouraged among peers. Teenagers often migrated together on leaving home to work in the coastal banana plantations or even to travel to neighboring countries. Street trades, such as shoe shining, theft, gambling, and vending, were learned. Such activity often led to reform school for those who became chronic users.

Many of the differences cited here appear again when, instead of marijuana use, we consider alcohol consumption. In controlling for various social attributes, we devised an alcohol use scale that divided all 82 subjects into categories of abstemious or light drinkers, moderate drinkers, and heavy drinkers. Childhood experiences and performance of the subjects in each of these categories showed that the childhood experiences of men who at present are moderate and heavy drinkers resembled those of the marijuana user population. Heavy and moderate drinkers as children were significantly more inclined to be unruly in school, fight, be absent from school, be indulged at home, and consider their childhood in either a fair or bad light. In general, those who became heavy drinkers showed an early hostility to authority and institutional controls and, together with future moderate drinkers, abandoned their parental home significantly earlier than did those who became light drinkers or abstainers.

Adulthood

Despite the tendency of nonusers to gain regular employment earlier, the work profile of the subjects in both groups during adulthood was, in some ways, similar. For both groups, the average age at the onset of regular work, either full-time or part-time, was 12 years. The need to work in the support of their families was the principal reason given by both groups for leaving school. All of the subjects were involved as workers in a variety of trades and jobs through time.

Several significant differences in job histories did exist, however. Users more frequently changed jobs than did nonusers; more had part-time, temporary, or no employment; users had more frequent periods of unemployment and had longer unemployment periods. They had fewer salary raises and promotions and were significantly more likely to engage in extralegal activities to supplement their income. Users had fewer debts, saved less money, and were less likely to own substantial material goods than were nonusers.

Although users are slightly different with respect to their greater involvement in consensual unions, families of procreation of the subjects are, in general, similar in structure for both users and nonusers. Paradoxically, users in the matched sample tend to have somewhat longer lasting relationships with their wives or consensual mates than do nonusers. Both users and nonusers have the same average number of children, 2.6.

The spouses of our subjects exercise roles much like those of their mothers; they rear the children, instill the moral and ethical values, and work part-time on a frequent basis. The subjects as fathers express affection for their children.

Users tend to help their spouses in the home more than do nonusers. In general, both hope that their offspring will enjoy an equal or better socioeconomic status than their own. Upward striving does not characterize the majority of the men of either group.

By and large, the children of the subjects appear to be passing through sets of experiences very much like those of their parents. They have few alternatives or life choices that differ from those faced by either group of subjects as children and youth.

The housing of users and nonusers is virtually identical in character, although more users than nonusers live in apartments. The users also tend to move their residences more often than do nonusers, although the frequencies are not significantly different. In overall character, the houses, services, and physical quality of the home are the same for both groups and reflect the level of income of the subjects' families. The overall standard of living for the two groups is approximately equal.

As a general rule, users continue to be less involved in formal institutions than do nonusers. They are less likely to become leaders in any kind of organization, are less likely to participate in political clubs, and are less likely to attend church. This reluctance to become involved is congruent with their earlier problems in dealing with authority.

As a group, users spend more free time with their friends and less with their families than do nonusers. Because users have longer-lasting unions with their spouses, this fact does not seem to have affected their marital relationship.

During their adult life, users have been detained more, jailed more, and involved in other legal entanglements more than have nonusers. This involvement with the law would seem to be related, at least in part, to the fact that their police records and their drug use make them more visible, and therefore more vulnerable, to the police. Understandably, more users than nonusers view the legal system as unjust and express a general distrust of other people.

The overall picture that emerges with respect to users is one of an accumulation of negative experiences: childhood problems with authority, unhappy home lives, early entry into street life, reform school, arrests, increased vulnerability to police activity, lack of regular employment and advancement, and a haunting sense of inferiority vis-à-vis their siblings.

The pattern these men develop in their adult life replicates, in large part, that from which they suffered as children. They offer weak role models for their own offspring, take little part in civic and community life, and tend to delegate the management of household finances to their wives. They also spend more of their free time outside the home than do nonusers, preferring to be with friends rather than family.

Users, however, do not present a uniform pattern in all of these respects. Major differences appear among them that have led us to classify them into three distinct types. Those who continue the adolescent pattern of street life into later life have been classified as "street movers" if they are open, public smokers, and as "pastoralist-escapists" if they are careful, clandestine smokers. As a composite type, these "street people" are the ones who diverge most sharply from the nonusers in the factors mentioned above. The remaining users have been classified as "stable smokers." They constitute the majority and are characterized by stable adult family situations, with patterns of employment, income, debt, and accumulation of material possessions practically identical to those of the nonusers.

Marijuana Use

In examining the effects and circumstances of marijuana use among the user population, we found that the typology outlined above was an important one. Stable smokers were the oldest, with a mean age of 33.9; street movers had a mean age of 28.1, and pastoralist-escapists, the youngest of all, had a mean age of only 22.5.

In speaking of the environments in which they smoked marijuana, each of the three types favored certain ones. In all, 578 different context accounts were given by the subjects, classifiable into 13 specific, discrete types of environment. The most commonly cited smoking environment (22.1%) was smoking at home alone. Following in order of popularity were street group, workshop with group, bar, boarding house-brothel, vehicle, countryside alone, dance hall, and prison.

Stable smokers were responsible for only 9% of all described street group environments, whereas street movers accounted for nearly 90% of such descriptions. In general, street movers and stable smokers smoked in polar opposite environments; only in the "work alone" category did the two groups report similar levels of practice.

Street movers were the only ones in the sample to cite smoking experience in prison. In this regard, it seems significant that "street group" was the most commonly cited smoking environment for street movers, that is, the environment most openly exposing a user's marijuana habits to the police and to the rest of the community.

With pastoralist-escapists, "countryside alone" was the most commonly cited smoking environment, thus confirming the need to set these individuals apart from the other two types of users.

When asked with whom they smoked most of the time, users in the matched-pair sample responded as follows: 9.8% said that they preferred to smoke with relatives, 48.8% preferred to be with friends, 19.5% with work companions, and only 9% alone.

Most appear to be reclusive and timid, not defiant in their use. At most, 39% of the sample may be identified as open flaunters of Costa Rican societal and legal conventions. For the most part, users are cautious about people and places around which they smoke.

Thirty-nine different effects were described by one or another of the users. Each tended to be associated with a specific type of environment and a specific type of user. For example, "physical effects" tended to be associated with "home alone" environments and "stable smokers."

In general, the effects perceived by the marijuana smoker were closely linked to the character of the setting and what he found close at hand. Thus, increased appetite was often mentioned for home or boarding house environments and rarely for open or social environments and *"muerte blanca,"* or panic reaction, with the insecurity and fear of open street smoking.

A few effects seem to be universally experienced, regardless of user type. Generally, users said that marijuana smoking helps them get to sleep. Most also said that marijuana increases their appetite for food and enjoyment of sex. Approximately three-fourths reported that marijuana always helps them work better.

Uncontrollable mirth, so often described by other user populations, was cited only infrequently: roughly 2% of all 516 effect citations. Euphoria was mentioned 27 times, generally in connection with the most popular smoking environments: street alone, home alone, and street group. Passive spectatorship, so common among United States' smokers, was seldom mentioned. When asked what they liked to do best while smoking, 27 of the 41 in the user group spoke of active sports, recreation, or work, seven spoke of being with friends, and only seven mentioned passive behavior.

When users compared marijuana with alcohol, they overwhelmingly claimed that marijuana was superior. They stated that, in contrast to alcohol, marijuana is not physically harmful and that, rather than making them more aggressive, it calms their nerves. The general consensus was not only that marijuana is more benign than alcohol but also that it improves conversation and that it leads to clearer thought and deeper insights.

Just as there appears to be a clear relationship between context and effect, so is there one between effect and user type. Physical effects were cited in significantly higher frequencies by the stable smokers. Appetite and bad trip effects were cited more frequently by street movers. Street movers seemed to consider marijuana a way or simple organic escape, something to take them out of the ordinary routine. In contrast, stable smokers appeared to have established a way of life that included the drug in their everyday routine; instead of using marijuana to escape their responsibilities, they saw it as an amenity that makes their routine more bearable.

All three types of users agreed that the mixture of marijuana with alcohol generates effects that are very different from those of either alone. Such a mixture is known as "crossing the cables"; the general consensus was that it usually leads to unpleasant experiences.

Most users began regular smoking of marijuana during late childhood or adolescence. The mean age for beginning regular use was 15.2 years. Seventy-five percent of the users were initiated to the drug by persons older then themselves, in most cases older members of their street-side peer groups.

The fact that many users had bad trips with their first marijuana experiences did not discourage them from trying again or from developing into chronic users. Not a single user claimed that marijuana has been harmful in his life. Nor did he see any relationship between his well-being and social mobility and his use of the drug.

Complete school records could be found for only seven of the 41 matched pairs in the subsample. These records showed no difference in school performance that could be related to marijuana use. Users who began smoking marijuana while still students claimed unanimously that it had helped them in school. In no case was marijuana usage a cause for school dropout or failure. Although users more consistently remembered that they had been unruly in school, this characteristic was not reflected in the documented performance of the seven matched pairs for whom records could be found. Nor was there a significant difference among these seven pairs with regard to the number of years of school attempted or completed.

If marijuana usage leads to poorer social adjustment, irresponsible behavior, and lack of motivation, one would expect that the heavier the usage, the greater such problems would be. The opposite, however, is the case. The heavier the usage, the more stable is the employment record. The heavier the usage, the fewer are the periods of unemployment. The heavier the usage, the shorter are these periods of unemployment. Users who have long-term full-time jobs smoke significantly more than do those who have temporary, part-time, or no work. Heavy users are more likely to engage in deficit spending than are light users, but they also have significantly more material goods, in this respect, paralleling the practices of the nonusing group and following a common pattern of ambitious working-class Costa Ricans. Heavier users are more involved in illegal or extralegal economic activity than are lighter users. Much of this illegal activity, however, involves the distribution of marijuana and is therefore a function of the heavy users' greater access to the drug.

From these facts, one cannot conclude that marijuana, as such, seriously interferes with an individual's functioning as a normal, productive member of society. Much more important determinants would seem to be his overall life-style, as established in childhood and adolescence and carried into adulthood.

When the three basic life-styles of users are cross tabulated with specific sociocultural variables, some highly significant correlations emerge. Street movers and pastoralist-escapists were on their own in childhood more than were other users. They claim to have been more rowdy in school than were stable smokers. They engaged more frequently in illegal and rebellious behavior, such as vandalism and theft. During adolescence, they were significantly less likely to have steady jobs than were stable smokers.

In adulthood, these "street people" have experienced significantly less upward mobility than have stable smokers, have had less full-time employment, more frequent unemployment, and longer periods of unemployment than have stable smokers.

Employment records of stable smokers resemble those of nonusers. Understandably, significantly more stable smokers claim that marijuana has positive effects on work than do street movers.

We have seen that chronic use begins in adolescence, and its initiation is usually related to periods of transition and stress. The vast majority of users had serious adjustment problems long before they began marijuana smoking. With future street movers, these problems were more serious than with future pastoralist-escapists or stable smokers. In fact, so overwhelmingly were the most serious problems experienced by the street mover group that we can say that most significant differences between users and nonusers in the work history are due to the inclusion of street movers in the matched subsample. Street movers, however, constitute less than 50% of the user sample. Most users are stable smokers, "invisible," solid, productive citizens. Their life-styles in no way can be construed as confirming hypotheses such as that of the amotivational syndrome. In fact, many of these people, while under the influence of marijuana, prefer to work.

CONCLUSIONS

The significant differences found in adult behavior between users and nonusers are highly correlated with different kinds of socialization experiences. The vast majority of these experiences antedate marijuana use and more adequately explain the significant differences found between users and nonusers than does marijuana use itself. This conclusion supports similar findings from studies of United States' populations.[1, 2]

Longitudinal studies of high-school and college youth in the United States indicate that initiation of marijuana use is predictable by such variables as attitudes that approve deviance, lack of religious participation and involvement, social support for drug use, friends' approval of use, deviant behavior, and more intensive "petting" behavior.[3] All of these variables, except possibly "petting" (the higher incidence of syphilis among users does suggest greater promiscuity), coincide strikingly with the preconditions observed in the childhood and adolescence of future chronic users in San José.

A common finding in United States' studies is that students who report delinquent behavior are more likely to use marijuana than are those who do not report such problems.[4] The Costa Rican data are superficially similar. However, delinquency and other antisocial behavior found in the life histories of the users can be explained solely by differences in their early life experiences, without need to introduce marijuana as an explanatory factor. For example, it was discovered that a decided differential existed in the intervention of law enforcement agents vis-à-vis adolescent delinquency between users and nonusers. Of users who reported adolescent delinquency, 83% were sentenced to the reformatory; of nonusers who reported such delinquency, not a single one was given a reformatory sentence. This comparison leads to the conjecture that rather than delinquency per se, it is society's response to that delinquency that helps determine whether an individual will become a chronic marijuana user.

Marijuana use among working-class males in San José is invariably learned in the streets, usually from older peers. This finding coincides with those of several studies previously reported; that is, that peers, rather than parents, are the more important influence on an individual's attitude toward marijuana.[1, 5] Among many Costa Rican users, peer groups continue to play important roles throughout adulthood. Yet, it cannot be said that, as in the United States, "the greater the involvement with marihuana, the greater the likelihood that those with whom one associates are also marihuana users, and, therefore, the more justified one is in expecting tolerance towards one's own marihuana use."[1, 6]

The style of use among Costa Ricans varies greatly. Some of the heaviest users are stable family men who live much by themselves and who smoke in solitude. The networks of all users contain many nonusers who play important roles in their lives. We did not find any trends among users to reduce such contacts.

Many studies have considered the issue of drug use proneness among marijuana smokers. Smith [7] found that children who were regular cigarette smokers were more likely than nonsmokers to later use marijuana. Also an earlier, nationwide, study of high-school students found that those who use marijuana were more likely to use alcohol and other psychoactive drugs than were their nondrug-using peers.[4] The 1974 National Institute on Drug Abuse report on Marijuana and Health repeatedly states that the more heavily a user smokes marijuana, the greater the probability he has used or will use other drugs.[1]

Among Costa Rican working-class men, we found similar relationships. Heavy marijuana users also tended to be heavy tobacco users, and many heavy marijuana users also used alcohol heavily. The fact that the users and nonusers were matched for tobacco and alcohol consumption meant that no significant differences were found between user and nonuser in this respect. In building the matched-pair sample, however, the field anthropologists had great difficulty finding nonmarijuana-using controls because of the heavy tobacco and alcohol consumption of many members of the user group.

One finding not confirmed by the Costa Rican data is the movement from marijuana to other drugs, such as amphetamines, barbiturates, heroin, lysergic acid diethylamide, and cocaine. These substances were available, but users showed little interest in them. Nor does there appear to have been much use of more potent cannabis substances. The reason given by users is that if they want a stronger effect, they can simply smoke more marijuana.

Another finding from United States' studies questioned by the Costa Rican data is that the greater the involvement with marijuana, the greater is the need to perceive others as involved, and therefore the greater is the likelihood to expect tolerant reactions from others.[1] The attitude of a sizable minority of Costa Rican users (39%) is definitely ambivalent. Although they continue to use the drug, they do not uncritically justify its use. Many clearly state that marijuana is preferable to alcohol but that it would be better to use neither. And their hope is that their children will never become involved.

Another finding from the United States' studies *not* confirmed by the Costa Rican data is that of parental influence on use. It was observed in the United States that the highest rates of marijuana usage were found among adolescents whose parents, and particularly mothers, were drug users.[5] We were unsuccessful in obtaining hard data on use of prescription drugs among the parents of our subject group. However, we did obtain data on use of tobacco, alcohol, and illicit drugs. No differences emerged with regard to fathers. In the case of mothers, however, there were two. There was a statistically significant trend ($p = 0.02$) for the mothers of future marijuana users to abstain totally from alcohol, and there was a nearly significant trend ($p = 0.07$) for them to also abstain from tobacco (only one mother was reported to have used marijuana). Other, possibly related, statistically significant trends were that mothers of future users were more likely to work full-time outside the home and to be capricious in rewards and sanctions to their children.

Reasons given for marijuana use by Costa Rican users are, to some degree, like those given by United States' users. As with their United States' counterparts, Costa Rican users tend to have low self-esteem and a high level of experience and adventure seeking.[8] And as in the United States, Costa Rican users seek, through the drug, attainment of a state of well-being, instant achievement, relaxation, easier social interaction, avoidance of boredom, psychologic support for dealing with pain and discomfort, rebellion or rejection of parental values, a search for purpose, a way for organizing experience, an aphrodisiac, and an adaptation to life.[1] One thing they do *not* seek is mystical or religious experience. However, there are many other benefits attributed by Costa Rican users to the drug: 39 in all. Each is differentially related to setting and user's lifestyle. In addition, the various effects are perceived in a very different order of popularity or hierarchy from those reported for United States' users.[9]

Many of the effects reported by users indicate selective perception of the world about them. Marijuana is said to enhance one's enjoyment of food, sex, work, music, conversation, and even involvement in physically active sports. This belief is consistent with many reports from the United States and with support coming from electroencephalographic studies to the idea of selective attention to particular aspects of the outside world.[1]

Although some users report that marijuana impairs their short-term memory processes, this notion was *not* confirmed by the neuropsychologic battery administered to the subjects.[10] The contradiction may be attributable to the fact that users were reporting their *acute* reactions, whereas the test battery was designed and administered to measure *chronic* effects.

No hard data were obtained regarding the effect of marijuana use on driving ability. However, some of the user subjects earn their living by driving trucks, buses, or taxis, and some prefer to drive while under the influence of the drug.

Although many subjects attribute greatly increased appetites to marijuana use, the nutritional studies uncovered *no* significant differences in food intake between users and nonusers.

Many other studies have dealt with the effect of marijuana on human aggression. The general conclusion is that, unlike alcohol, marijuana suppresses aggressiveness, dominance, and competition among all nonstressed animals, man included.[1] A large body of anecdotal material consistent with this conclusion was provided by user subjects in our San José study. Some turned from alcohol to marijuana specifically to become less aggressive. There appear to have been sociocultural precedents here, however. As a group, marijuana smokers had significantly fewer fights during adolescence than had moderate and heavy alcohol users.

Because no time-motion studies were made, it is impossible to say whether there was an increasing depression of work output at successively higher levels of marijuana use. However, a clear inverse relationship was found to exist between stability of work and level of use. The heaviest users have the highest incomes, the least unemployment, and the most stable job histories of the entire user group. They also more frequently report that their preferred activity while intoxicated is to work. These facts question the applicability of the amotivational syndrome concept among marijuana-using working-class Costa Ricans.[11]

As with Jamaicans who use the drug primarily as a work adjunct, Costa Rican users do not usually report the "high" sought by American recreational users. The specific effect is clearly conditioned by both setting and user's lifestyle. Not a single user reported hallucinations, although many did report a panic reaction known locally as "white death." This reaction was related not to level or potency of dosage but to the physical and psychologic state of the victim. Treatment was purely physical, a high-sugar content drink, and recovery was quick and assured. The quick recovery is reminiscent of that reported by Chopra and Smith for victims of "cannabis psychosis" in Calcutta, India.[12]

There was a great deal of anecdotal evidence for the buildup of tolerance. Well-experienced users never fall victim to "white death." Instead, they describe in considerable detail how they have learned to handle the drug. The heaviest user averages 40 marijuana cigarettes per day and yet manages a very successful business with eight employees.

No reports or observations of withdrawal symptoms were collected. Users categorically deny that they ever occur. They contrast the lack of such symptoms for marijuana with their presence for alcohol and tobacco. Many subjects have stopped marijuana use for varying periods of time because of lack of funds, travel, or imprisonment and so have a solid subjective basis for making such a judgment.

Overall, very few adverse effects of marijuana smoking were reported or observed over the 2-year period. Negrete has classified the various adverse effects as found in the literature as severe intoxication, pathologic intoxication, acute cannabis psychoses, subacute and chronic cannabis psychoses, and residual conditions, including flashbacks.[13] Only two such conditions were observed or self-reported by the user population: pathologic intoxication ("white death") and flashback (reported very rarely). There was absolutely *no* indication of severe intoxication, acute cannabis psychoses, or subacute and chronic cannabis psychoses, despite heavy, prolonged usage of fairly potent marijuana. Nor was there a single report of "freaking out," that is, being overcome by an outside force or will that was evil or hostile in intent.[14]

In areas of personal and social life, marijuana usage was not shown to result in behavior that impaired the individual's ability to function as a regular member of his society.[15] Significant differences between users and nonusers tended to antedate marijuana use and continue to be reflected in later life. Marijuana was not shown to have caused these differences, although its use was associated with them.

Marijuana use, as found among working-class men in San José, functions largely as a device that the individual feels aids him to cope with his daily routines and problems. In sociocultural terms, the basic problem derived from marijuana usage is police harrassment and possible imprisonment. Secondary problems are the financial drain caused by the cost of an illegal substance and the type of peer group with which one associates when he engages in illegal behavior. There is no other conclusive evidence of marijuana-caused interference in the normal functioning of an adult, working-class male, living in Costa Rica's capital city.

REFERENCES

1. NATIONAL INSTITUTE ON DRUG ABUSE. 1974. Marihuana and Health. Fourth Annual Report to the U.S. Congress from the Secretary of Health, Education, and Welfare. United States Government Printing Office. Washington, D. C.
2. HALIKAS, J. A., D. W. GOODWIN & S. B. GUZE. 1971. Marihuana effects—a survey of regular users. J. Amer. Med. Ass. **217:** 692–694.
3. JESSOR, R., S. L. JESSOR & J. FINNEY. 1973. A social psychology of marihuana use: longitudinal studies of high school and college youth. J. Personality Social Psychol. **26**(1)**:** 1–15.
4. JOHNSTON, L. 1973. Drugs and American youth. Institute for Social Research, University of Michigan. Ann Arbor, Mich.

5. KANDEL, D. B. 1973. Adolescent marihuana use: role of parents and peers. Science **181:** 1067–1070.
6. FISHER, G. 1972/1973. Personality characteristics ascribed to marihuana users by users and nonusers. Behav. Neuropsychiat. **4**(9–10): 5–12.
7. SMITH, G. 1974. Drugs and personality. Progress report to National Institute on Drug Abuse.
8. BASKETT, G. D. & R. W. NYSEWANDER. 1973. Drug use correlates. Psychol. J. Human Behav. **10**(1): 54–66.
9. CHEEK, F. E., M. SARRETT-BARRIE & C. N. HOLSTEIN, et al. 1973. Four patterns of campus marihuana use: Part I, drug use. Int. J. Addictions **8**(1): 13–31.
10. CAPPELL, H. D. & P. L. PLINER. 1973. Volitional control of marijuana intoxication: a study of the ability to "come down" on command. J. Abnormal Psychol. **82:** 428–434.
11. BURDSAL, C., G. GREENBERG & R. TIMPE. 1973. The relationship of marijuana usage to personality and motivational factors. J. Psychol. **85:** 45–51.
12. CHOPRA, G. D. & J. W. SMITH. 1974. Psychotic reactions following cannabis use in East Indians. Arch. Gen. Psychiat. **30:** 24–27.
13. NEGRETE, J. C. 1973. Psychological adverse effects of cannabis smoking: tentative classification. Can. Med. Ass. J. **108:** 195, 196.
14. TART, T. Marihuana intoxication: common experiences. Nature (London) **226:** 701–704.
15. BEAUBRUN, M. H. & F. KNIGHT. 1973. Psychiatric assessment of 30 chronic users of cannabis and 30 matched controls. Amer. J. Psychiat. **130:** 309–311.

SOCIAL TRAITS OF HEAVY HASHISH USERS
AND MATCHED CONTROLS *

J. C. Boulougouris, A. Liakos, and C. Stefanis

Department of Psychiatry
Athens University Medical School
Eginition Hospital
Athens, Greece

Because hashish use has been linked to antisocial behavior and mental illness,[1, 2] a thorough investigation of the family and personal characteristics of long-term and nonusers was conducted. In particular, an attempt was made to isolate any parent or peer influences on hashish usage during initiation, because such influences are partially responsible for hashish smoking in adolescents.[3, 4] Furthermore, one object of this investigation was to examine the drug history, reported experiences during intoxication, life charts of the subjects with some illustration of their family and social characteristics, and the effects of hashish on their work performance and everyday life. As an example, a decline in the subjects' occupational status could provide some support for the expressed view that long-term hashish use leads to the development of an "amotivational syndrome." [5] The importance of such a systematic and controlled inquiry has been urgently pointed out,[6] and in this paper, the results presented have been related to the personal, family, and social characteristics.

METHODS AND MATERIALS

A detailed description of the overall strategy for selecting hashish users and controls has been presented elsewhere.[7] The controls were matched for age, family origin, upbringing, education, and place of birth. All data presented in this paper were obtained by semistructured psychiatric interviews according to the Mayer-Gross, Slater, and Roth [8] format. A social history was compiled by a social worker in a standardized manner. The reported hashish data, that is, age of starting hashish smoking, frequency and quantity of smoking during the past and the present, and periods of abstinence, were obtained by a psychiatrist and the social worker. Past use was defined as the period before 1967; in that year, a more restricted law was enacted, and since then a considerable reduction in hashish consumption has been noted. The period from 1967 up to the day of the interview was defined as present use. During their psychiatric evaluation, hashish users were asked to report their usual experience or symptoms while intoxicated. Three main questions were addressed to all subjects: "In what way does cannabis smoking affect you?" "What do you feel after smoking?" "Does it have any unpleasant effect on you?" The subjects' reports were recorded and later analyzed under the headings of pleasant and undesirable effects of cannabis smoking.

* Supported in part by Contract HSM 42–70–98 from the National Institute on Drug Abuse to the International Association for Psychiatric Research.

17

A great part of the psychiatric interview focused on the family's mental health, family relationships, presence of broken homes, that is, loss of one or both parents by death or permanent separation before the subject reached the age of 15, and preexisting abnormal psychopathology prior to hashish smoking. In particular, an attempt was made to find any relationship between criminal behavior and hashish smoking.

The social worker systematically recorded the occupational status and the reasons for changes. Apart from the data on hashish smoking, she also recorded therein any use of other dependent substances, including alcohol. The psychiatrist's interview lasted an average of 1 hr, and that of the social worker usually took 45 min. Further, the social worker visited the homes of some hashish users ($n = 29$) and some controls ($n = 13$), interviewing the wives and occasionally other members of the families. In all, 60 hashish users and 64 controls were examined, but the comparison was eventually made between 47 hashish users and 40 controls. The reasons for excluding some individuals have been discussed elsewhere.[7]

In the final sample of 47 hashish users, 28 belonged to the previously studied group[9] referred to us for further study. Nineteen were recruited from the community by our social service.

RESULTS

Reported Hashish Data

The mean age of onset of cannabis smoking was 17, and subjects smoked nearly every day for a mean period of 23 years (TABLE 1). The mean frequency of smoking per day in the past was 4.5 times and at present 2.3 times. On a day that a patient smoked, a mean of 7.4 g of hashish were consumed in the past; 3.1 g was the average amount consumed in the present. The mean number of abstinence periods due to various reasons (imprisonment, difficulty to obtain, and so on) was 1.2, and the mean duration of abstinence was 10 months. Analysis of the hashish described by subjects as of "average strength" revealed a 4–5% content of Δ^9-tetrahydrocannabinol (Δ^9-THC), or a calculated mean intake of 200 mg of Δ^9-THC per day.

TABLE 1

REPORTED HASHISH DATA

	Starting Age	Years of Use	Times per Day on Day of Smoking		Quantity (g) on Day of Smoking		Abstinence Periods	
			Past Use	Current Use	Past Use	Current Use	Times	Total Duration (months)
Mean	17.61	23.10	4.5	2.32	7.48	3.13	1.21	10.06
SD	4.12	9.70	3.76	1.01	5.98	1.81	1.01	10.84

TABLE 2

PERSONAL HISTORY DATA

	Cannabis Users (n=47)		Controls (n=40)			
	Mean	SD	Mean	SD	*t*	p
Age	40.72	12.12	41.72	7.6	0.52	ns
Education	4.22	2.86	5.37	2.69	1.93	≫
No. of occupations	3.10	1.67	3.07	1.78	0.08	≫
No. of job changes	3.74	2.14	4.55	2.44	1.63	≫

The main reasons for initiation of smoking were curiosity (22), conformation and pressure (19), and therapeutic (6). Five of the latter six individuals started consuming hashish in an attempt to abstain from alcohol, which they succeeded in doing. No significant events were found to be associated with hashish initiation. The main reasons for continuation of smoking were relaxation (13), euphoric effect (12), to work better (9), habit (6), increase of sexual desire (2), and unknown (9). The chief reasons for reduction were fear of the law (17), financial (9), and difficulty of obtaining the drug (8). Six subjects smoked before going to work, two after work finished, 16 both before and after work, and 13 at any time, thereby not relating their smoking to work. The preferred ways of smoking were with company (30), alone (10), with company and alone (6), not stated (1). The main effects during intoxication were dry mouth (95%), increased sexual desire (88%), euphoria (77%), and overtalkativeness (68%). As undesirable effects, nine subjects (20%) reported panic attacks, persecutory ideas, and thought blocking. Depression and psychomotor retardation were reported by seven subjects (15%).

Personal and Family Characteristics

No significant differences were found between hashish users and controls with respect to age, education, number of occupations, and number of occupational changes (TABLE 2). Controls had 1 more year of schooling, but on the whole, both populations were of low education. Of the 47 hashish users, six were illiterate, 34 had between 1 and 6 years of primary schooling, and seven had a secondary education. Of the 40 controls, three were illiterate, 28 had primary schooling of between 1 and 6 years, and nine had received secondary education.

Hashish users and controls belonged to the lower socioeconomic classes, and the hashish users were mainly peddlers, street vendors of flowers or fruit, scrap metal collectors, and flayers in slaughter houses. The controls were largely skilled factory workers or small business owners. The main reasons for occupational changes reported by the hashish users were financial or personality conflicts with their employers. The controls changed occupations to find better working conditions or to obtain permanent positions.

The two populations did not differ in neurotic traits during childhood, and in marital status no differences were found.

TABLE 3

FAMILY HISTORY DATA

	Cannabis Users ($n=47$)		Controls ($n=40$)		χ^2	p
	No.	%	No.	%		
Refugee parents						
Father	20	42.55	24	60.0	0.31	ns
Mother	23	48.93	24	65.0	1.06	≫
Both	17	36.17	21	52.5	2.34	≫
Family history of mental illness						
Father	0	—	1	2.5	—	—
Mother	5	10.36	1	2.5	2.22	≫
Siblings	7	14.89	3	7.5	1.161	≫
Alcoholic father	14	29.78	9	22.5	0.59	≫
Cannabis-user father	3	6.38	1	2.5	—	—
Broken home	14	29.78	5	12.5	3.84	≫

The wives of 24 hashish users agreed to the husband smoking hashish because it calmed him down and improved their sexual life. Fifteen wives disagreed, because hashish smoking carried a social stigma and was expensive.

With respect to the migrancy factor, hashish users did not differ from controls (TABLE 3). The family histories of mental illness showed that more hashish users (5) had mentally ill mothers than did controls (1), but this difference was not significant. Although more hashish users had alcoholic or cannabis-using fathers, these differences were not significant. The presence of a broken home did not distinguish hashish users from controls.

Significant differences were found in the following personal history data (TABLE 4).

Previous Psychiatric Treatment. Nine hashish users (19%) had previous psychiatric treatment as inpatients or outpatients, compared to two (5%) of the controls ($\chi^2 = 3.94$, p < 0.05).

Regular Military Service. Only 26 of 47 cannabis users (55%) served in the army, compared with 38 of 40 controls (95%). This difference was signifi-

TABLE 4

PERSONAL HISTORY DATA: SIGNIFICANT DIFFERENCES

	Cannabis Users ($n=47$)		Controls ($n=40$)		χ^2	p
	No.	%	No.	%		
Previous psychiatric treatment	9	19.14	2	5.0	3.94	<0.05
Regular military service	26	55.31	38	95.0	17.49	<0.001
Imprisonments related to cannabis	25	53.19	1	2.5	26.49	<0.001
Other reasons	29	61.70	10	26.0	11.76	<0.001
Skilled workers	12	25.53	25	62.5	12.08	<0.001
Unemployed when examined	20	42.55	6	15.0	7.82	<0.01

cant at p < 0.001. The main reasons for exemption from service were cannabis use and antisocial behavior.

Imprisonment. Twenty five cannabis users (53%) had been in prison as a result of cannabis law violations, in comparison with one (2%) of the controls ($\chi^2 = 26.5$, p < 0.001). Additionally, 29 cannabis users (63%) were sentenced for reasons other than cannabis violations, as compared with 10 (26%) controls ($\chi^2 = 11.76$, p < 0.001).

Work Record. Although the two samples did not differ in number of occupations and changes therein, more cannabis users (42%) were unemployed when seen, as compared with controls (15%). This difference was significant ($\chi^2 = 7.82$, p < 0.01). Similarly, 12 (25%) cannabis users were skilled workers, as compared with 25 (62%) controls ($\chi^2 = 12.08$, p < 0.001).

The relationship between degree of hashish use and the social parameters was investigated by dividing the hashish users into heavy users, those who consumed at present more than the mean quantity (4 g), and moderate users, those who consumed less than the mean quantity. It was found that the amount of reported hashish smoking was not correlated with employment and work skill. Prison sentences, due to reasons other than cannabis law violations, were also unrelated to the severity of hashish smoking.

DISCUSSION

Because the data related to hashish smoking were reported by the subjects, their validity and reliability can be argued. It can be stated that the identified hashish users were confirmed chronic users and had not complicated their smoking with dependent substances. Such a statement derives from the fact that the hashish data were obtained from two sources, the psychiatrist and social workers, and no differences emerged. The amount of drug consumed in Δ^9-THC is difficult to estimate because of the variability in potency and in weight and size of hashish cigarettes. On the other hand, analyzed hashish samples revealed a high concentration of Δ^9-THC (4–5%), and such estimates cannot be discarded. They provide further evidence that these subjects were very heavy users, unlike those in the United States, who used materials with 1% of Δ^9-THC per day, clean weight of marijuana.[10, 11] The reported amount of hashish consumption is rather similar to that in Eastern countries.[12] In addition, the information obtained from home visits, to interview wives or close relatives, confirms the drug histories taken from the hashish users. Meeting the subjects and their cosmoking friends in the community, and having had the opportunity to see some of these subjects during the experimental studies, removes any reservations of the kind mentioned above. The reasons for the initiation of hashish smoking may not be entirely similar to those described in Western societies,[13] but curiosity and conformation are very powerful motives. The threat of the law was the main reason for reduction, and not changes due to marriage or entry into parenthood, as have been suggested,[13] and this finding is in agreement with those of others.[14] The validity of retrospective reports of experiences under intoxication has been discussed by Tart.[15] The experiences reported in this study cannot easily be compared with those found in Western studies, where the cultural and educational background of the individuals studied were different.

Further studies [16] showed that the individuals studied were representative of chronic hashish users in Greece. The two populations studied were well matched by the criteria chosen, and the observed differences were not due to chance but truly characterized the two populations. Therefore, the initiation of hashish smoking was not due to apparent environmental factors, because the controls were reared in the same area [7] and did not differ in their family characteristics. The view expressed that naive users [3] copy their parents in starting smoking was not supported by our findings. Our results on family characteristics agreed with observations on chronic hashish users in Jamaica,[17] in that family psychopathology probably was not a factor that contributed to hashish smoking.

The differences in employment of the subjects and their type of occupation may indicate the presence of an "amotivational syndrome" [5] in the cannabis smokers. Because hashish smoking carries a stigma and its discovery involves severe prison sentences, this difference in employment may be due to these factors. On the other hand, imprisonments due to other reasons were higher among hashish smokers than in controls. As has been shown elsewhere,[18] the greater incidence of prison sentences in hashish users is not related to antisocial behavior or to severity of hashish smoking. It can be postulated that this difference is due to the fact that such individuals were better known to the police because of their hashish smoking habits and thus were more liable to be arrested.

REFERENCES

1. BENABUD, A. 1957. Psychopathological aspects of the cannabis situation in Morocco. Statistical data for 1956. Bull. Narcotics **9:** 1–16.
2. NEGRETE, J. C. 1973. Psychological adverse effects of cannabis smoking. Can. Med. Ass. J. **108:** 159–196.
3. SMART, G. R. & D. FEJER. 1972. Drug use among adolescents and their parents: closing the generation gap in mood modification. J. Abnormal Psychol. **19**(2): 153–160.
4. KENDEL, D. B. 1973. Adolescent marihuana use: role of parents and peers. Science **181:** 1067–1069.
5. McGLOTHLIN, W. H. & L. J. WEST. 1968. The marihuana problem: an overview. Amer. J. Psychiat. **125:** 125–134.
6. NATIONAL COMMISSION ON MARIHUANA AND DRUG ABUSE. 1972. Marihuana: a Signal of Misunderstanding. Vol. I. United States Government Printing Office. Washington, D.C.
7. LIAKOS, A., J. BOULOUGOURIS, D. GEFOU & C. STEFANIS. 1976. Selection and definition of hashish users and controls. *In* Hashish! A Study of Long-Term Use. C. Stefanis, R. L. Dornbush & M. Fink, Eds. The Raven Press. New York, N.Y. In press.
8. MAYER-GROSS, W., E. SLATER & M. ROTH. 1970. Clinical Psychiatry. Cassell and Co., Ltd. London, England.
9. MIRAS, C. J. 1969. Experience with chronic hashish smokers. *In* Drugs and Youth. J. R. Wittenborn, H. Brill, Y. Smith & L. Wittenborn, Eds. Charles C Thomas. Springfield, Ill.
10. DONHER, V. A. 1972. Motives for drug use: adult and adolescent. Psychosomat. Med. **8**(5): 317–324.
11. JONES, R. T. 1971. Tetrahydrocannabinol and the marihuana induced social "high" or the effects of the mind on marihuana. Ann. N.Y. Acad. Sci. **191:** 155–165.
12. SOUEIF, M. I. 1967. Hashish consumption in Egypt with special reference to psychological aspects. Bull. Narcotics **19**(2): 1–12.

13. HENLEY, J. R. & L. D. ADAMS. 1973. Marihuana use in post-collegiate cohorts: correlates of use, prevalence patterns and factors associated with cessation. Social Problems 20(4): 514–520.
14. CHEEK, F. E., M. SARRETT-BARRIE, C. N. HOLSTEIN, *et al.* 1973. Four patterns of campus marihuana use: Part I. Drug use. Int. J. Addictions 8(1): 13–31.
15. TART, C. 1971. On Being Stoned: A Psychological Study of Marihuana Intoxication. Science & Behavior Books, Inc. Palo Alto, Calif.
16. STEFANIS, C., C. BALLAS & D. GEFOU. 1975. Sociocultural and epidemiological aspects of hashish use in Greece. *In* Cannabis and Culture. V. Rubin, Ed. Mouton. The Hague.
17. BEAUBRUN, M. & F. KNIGHT. 1973. Psychiatric assessment of 30 chronic users of cannabis and 30 matched controls. Amer. J. Psychiat. 130: 309–311.
18. STEFANIS, C., A. LIAKOS, J. BOULOUGOURIS, M. FINK & A. FREEDMAN. 1976. Chronic hashish use in mental disorder. Amer. J. Psychiat. 133: 225–227.

CANNABIS AND WORK IN JAMAICA:
A REFUTATION OF THE AMOTIVATIONAL
SYNDROME *

Lambros Comitas

Department of Philosophy and the Social Sciences
Teachers College, Columbia University
New York, New York 10027

The prestigious Canadian Commission of Inquiry on the Non-Medical Use of Drugs defined the amotivational syndrome as "a set of symptoms including apathy, ineffectiveness, and non-productiveness, considered to reflect a deficit in general motivation. It has been suggested that such a syndrome may result from the chronic use of certain drugs."[1] The commission also emphasized the inadequacy of clinical research on cannabis as it relates to amotivation, especially because this research has rarely dealt with questions of predrug personality, cause and effect relationships, and the social and cultural specifics of the subjects.[1] One could go further and claim with justification that these clinical studies seem to be based on an exaggeration of the medical model of inquiry, with the subject conceived of as a closed system despite obvious and important sociocultural parameters that beg for inclusion. The search and cure of cannabis-induced pathology seem to be a primary goal, and a research philosophy is operant, essentially deductive, which makes comparison and cross-cultural examinations an extraordinarily formidable task.

Research that supports the existence of the amotivational syndrome can be divided roughly into three categories: studies that assume that if an individual smokes cannabis, this fact is sufficient indication of some deep underlying psychologic problem regardless of whether cannabis has damaging properties of itself; studies that attempt to show that cannabis has catalytic properties that trigger off psychoses; and studies that claim cannabis use as a direct cause of psychosis. A single-factor determinism pervades all three categories, to which Becker, in commenting on LSD research, provides a valid social scientific riposte:

> If the drug does prove to be the cause of a bona fide psychosis, it will be the only case in which anyone can state with authority that they have found *the* unique cause of any such phenomenon; a similar statement applies to causes of crime and suicide. Whatever the ultimate findings of pharmacologists and others now studying the drug, sociologists are unlikely to accept such an asocial and unicausal explanation of any form of complex social behavior.[2]

Becker could just as easily have been referring to certain categories of cannabis research. In any case, although clinical research on amotivation is open to serious question, it is obvious that one cannot dismiss the stereotypic or perhaps false relationships in the public's mind that link indolence, passivity,

* The basic study from which the data for this paper were drawn was supported by National Institute of Mental Health Contract 42–70–97 to the Research Institute for the Study of Man.

and withdrawal directly to cannabis use. A majority of the members of the Canadian commission state:

> When they think of the social harm caused by drug use the majority of the people seem to be chiefly concerned with its effect on the leading of reasonably normal and productive lives. They more or less accept the drug use in which people engage in order to help them to function effectively in conventional lines of endeavour. But it is the presumed effect of certain kinds of drug use on the motivation and attitudes required for conventional patterns of living which is the chief concern of the majority of people. They fear that certain kinds of drug use will sap the will and capacity for functioning in a socially acceptable manner. They very much fear the development of a widespread passivity and withdrawal from responsibility for the everyday work required to make the society function effectively. We have to face this attitude squarely. Whatever our personal views may be of the cultural conflict which underlies it, it cannot be brushed aside in a spirit of lofty detachment. It is a very real fear. It is this fear which is reflected in the concern with the "amotivational syndrome."[1]

The thrust of this paper, consequently, will be an attempt to alleviate unwarranted fears of social collapse by providing examples from a society in which cannabis has been in widespread use among the working class for a long time but where passivity and withdrawal from everyday work does not exist and where the amotivational syndrome does not pertain. In fact, it is a society in which cannabis use is thought by many to have motivational effects: to arouse or initiate socially productive activity, to sustain activity in progress, and to channel activity within a prescribed course.

From June 1970 through February 1972, the Research Institute for the Study of Man, in collaboration with the University of the West Indies, performed a multidisciplinary study of the effects of marijuana, or *ganja,* on chronic users in Jamaica, a new nation in the Caribbean. Simply put, two distinct but integrated methodologic thrusts were implemented: a social scientific and field-based one, with ethnohistoric, anthropologic, and sociologic components; and a clinical and hospital-based one, with medical, psychiatric, and psychologic components. The social science team was responsible for determining the patterns of ganja use among the Jamaican working classes, selecting the samples of smokers and nonsmokers for clinical study and documenting the behavioral context within which clinical findings could be fully explored. To reach these objectives, seven communities were studied by this team, each for approximately 6 months. One was in the southwestern parish of Westmoreland, one in the central parish of Manchester, another in a working-class neighborhood of Kingston, and four others in the southeastern parishes.

The clinical studies were undertaken by the Faculty of Medicine of the University of the West Indies and by the staff of the University Hospital. Sixty adult working-class males were selected by the social scientists from among hundreds of users and nonusers from four of the seven study communities. Thirty were ganja smokers with 10 or more years of cannabis experience, and 30 were nonsmokers, matched carefully for age, socioeconomic status, and residence. These 60 males were admitted to University Hospital for 6 consecutive days of wide-ranging medical, psychiatric, and psychologic examinations, the results of which form the basic clinical data bank of the project.

The Jamaican study was pathbreaking in cannabis research, in that, for the first time, it combined in-depth social scientific examination of cannabis users *in vivo,* that is, in their natural environments, in tandem with systematic clinical studies of individuals drawn from these settings. The general design of the project provided a framework for the interplay of social science and medicine and of concepts and data derived from these two quite different traditions of research. Because a full report on the project has been published,[3] I do not propose to review here the specifics or even the central arguments of the report but will deal only with the data generated by the Jamaican study that might shed light on the relationship between cannabis use and motivation or amotivation.

Two types of evidence or data are relevant. The first can be classified as self-reported, or the verbal statements of respondents, with regard to ganja. This category of data falls well within a major anthropologic tradition, which holds "that information about cultural behavior must be gathered as much as possible from 'the actors' point of view. That is, the meanings and interpretations that 'the natives' give to cultural happenings are of great importance for untangling their patterns of behavior."[4] Consequently, this type of data for Jamaica, which include life histories, illuminates the folk wisdom concerning ganja through the stated motives, beliefs, attitudes, and thoughts of informants. The second category of evidence on ganja-related behavior is based on observations and measurements by scientists, in this case anthropologists, whose statements can be verified by independent observers utilizing similar operations. This body of data includes comparisons of individual work performance with or without ganja through the analysis of videotapes collected in customary work settings and comparisons of productivity over time of groups of ganja users and nonusers on sugar plantations. Combining and analyzing these two bodies of information allows us to assess the veracity of informants' statements and to contribute constructively to the debate about the "amotivational syndrome."

Fundamental to the belief system that shapes and supports the Jamaican ganja complex is the conviction held by the using population that ganja is a beneficial substance. The belief system permits discrimination concerning the diversity of benefits and effects and the various methods of use. For example, nonsmokers usually draw a sharp distinction between the effects of ganja tea drinking and those of smoking ganja. Teas and tonics, according to these individuals, are absorbed into the bloodstream, strengthen the blood, and enable it to ward off disease, whereas smoked ganja goes directly from the lungs to the brain, where it sometimes may have unpredictable consequences. Among users, there exists a range of beliefs related to the potential effect of ganja on most emotional and physical states. Quite importantly, descriptions of these effects by users are often modified by mention of necessary prior conditions. For example, if the user is in a mood for sleep, the smoking of ganja will help produce the desired effect. If he is not, other effects, situationally prescribed, may result.

There is little diversity, however, in beliefs about ganja that relates to work. Almost uniformly, users in the study communities maintain that ganja enhances the ability to perform hard work, and they regularly consumed it with this objective in mind. In this regard, ganja is believed to take effect in two ways: one is the cumulative benefits that come with "building" one's blood and strength with regular doses; the other is that ganja has the immediate effect of producing a burst of energy sufficient for completing laborious tasks. There is no doubt in users' minds that cannabis, particularly when smoked, enables them to work harder, faster, and longer. "Dem c'yan keep up to the work me do when we smoke it," would not be an atypical comment nor would the respondent who claimed that ganja made him work "like holy hell" be unusual. Nevertheless, unanimity among users about the positive relation of ganja to work does not mean that there are no differences of opinion about the ways and conditions under which it should be consumed for optimum effectiveness. "Is not fe smoke in de hot sun, it will cramp your body and make you sleepy." Or, as put by a user discussing why one should not smoke ganja in a chillum pipe before working, "it would give you an amount of revolution in your stomach and jerk your structure. For work purposes, a spliff is a better t'ing." Of the 27 of 30 smokers in the clinical phase of the study who were asked about their alcohol/ganja preferences, 25 indicated that they preferred cannabis to alcohol; the major reasons given for this preference were that ganja enabled them to do their work and that, unlike alcohol, it is not socially disruptive. Significantly, even nonusers note an increase in work drive among smokers. As one such individual put it: "After they smoke it and they decide to work you have to come out of their way, they don't stop work. They can't tire, you get more work out of them." It is not unusual, therefore, for nonsmoking cultivators to provide ganja for smokers who join them in cooperative field labor or for sugar plantation managers to make it available to their field hands.

As reflected in their verbal responses, the belief and attitudes of lower-class users about ganja and work are not at all ambiguous. Ganja is universally perceived as an energizer, a motive power—never as an enervator that leads to apathy and immobility. In Jamaica, ganja, at least on the ideational level, permits its users to face, start, and carry out the most difficult and distasteful manual labor.

The widely reported perception in Jamaica that cannabis stimulates work activity is a significant datum in and by itself but insufficient to demonstrate that this relationship objectively holds. Without other evidence, one could conclude, given the negative thrust of some of the clinical literature on the amotivational syndrome, that the beliefs and attitudes voiced by users are, at best, systematic lies that attempt to rationalize a debasing habit or, at worst, hallucinations of deranged minds. Consequently, we turn to the next category of self-reported data: 60 lengthy life histories collected from the 30 users and 30 controls involved in the clinical phase of the Jamaican study. These data, which were subjected to verification by the field-based anthropologists, were transcribed, content analyzed, and coded for computer, and the results underwent statistical examination. By in-depth comparison of users and controls in the several dimensions generated from the life histories that indicate, directly and indirectly, the presence or lack of motivation, such as education, occupational history, job changes, property ownership, and income, we are able to perceive differences, if any, between the subsamples.

With reference to education, the mean number of years completed by the total sample was 4.5, and the mean grade level, or standard, was 3.0, with no differences between smokers and controls on either variable. Current occupation and occupational history data also showed no significant differences between the groups. Most sample subjects held multiple occupations, a not too uncharacteristic pattern of the Jamaican lower class.[5] The primary occupations reported were, in descending order of importance, farming, fishing, masonry, and carpentry, semiskilled work, produce vending, "scuffling" or odd jobs, and ganja vending. Two smokers were active ganja dealers at the time of the study; 11 had been dealers at other times. Interestingly, three controls also reported such illegal activity in the past. In the words of one, this illegal activity was undertaken "to raise a penny to send the children to school." Smokers were more likely to have had work experience as fishermen, and controls showed a slight tendency to have had more experience as artisans.

No significant differences emerged in the patterning of job changes or in the reason given for this change, although controls were slightly more inclined to report that they changed employment to better themselves, and smokers were more likely to say that they quit because they disliked the job or their coworkers. Perhaps most importantly, no differences exist in ownership and control of property, such as house, land, vehicles, fishing canoes, and fishing pots, or in income, calculated on a weekly basis. In sum, none of these measures indicate any statistically significant differences. It would appear, in fact, that the socio-economic profiles of smokers and controls generated by these data are virtually indistinguishable from each other and, I would argue on the basis of long field experience in Jamaica, from that of the general laboring population of that island. From the self-reported but verified life histories, we are led to at least one conclusion: no negative effect on work history and, therefore, on work motivation due to chronic cannabis use is discernible in this sample.

Next, we move to objective rather than self-reported subjective evidence, specifically to an assessment of the widely held Jamaican belief that because ganja enhances energy, it has a positive effect on work. As one part of the project, the acute effects on actual work performance and productivity were systematically probed. To accomplish this task, a sample of ganja-using rural cultivators were individually and collectively videotaped over several time periods during work under controlled circumstances.[6] All cannabis consumed in these sessions was weighed, and samples were later analyzed for tetrahydro-cannabinol and other properties; work completed was meticulously measured; the nutritional status of subjects was documented; and the expenditure of subjects' kilocalories while at work was monitored by a Kofrani-Michaelis gas collection device and a Lloyd gas analyzer. After intensive analyses of these extensive data, Joseph Schaeffer, the anthropologist who conducted this aspect of the research, came to four tentative conclusions:

Ganja Smoking Is Related to Changes in the Rate and Organization of Body Movement and the Expenditure of Energy. To elaborate, the data indicate considerable individual variation, but it appears demonstrable that the internal organization of major body movements of laborers who use ganja during work is less complex, that there are greater numbers and/or variations in numbers of movement per unit of time after smoking, and that the workers' thoughts are more concentrated on the task itself at a cost, on the average, of a higher kilocaloric expenditure per task. At one level of abstraction, it can be argued that the objective measures obtained and the subjective views of the users are not at all contradictory. The user firmly believes that ganja helps him to perform arduous work better; the observations demonstrate that behavior during work changes, giving at a very minimum the appearance of determined effort.

Both Moderate and Heavy Smoking Reinforce Social Cohesiveness During Work in Group Situations. The following example succinctly illustrates this point:

On February 7, 1971, he [the subject] and eleven other farmers plowed a field together with iron forks. Just after arriving, most men shared some of the *ganja* provided by the host farmer. For a short period (10 to 15 minutes) they 'worked like demons', talking and laughing as they moved up the hill, forks pounding the earth in a close, straight line. Then, gradually, a quiet, dogged concentration replaced the gaiety. The sharply lineal work formation changed, as one, then another man dispersed to carry out his task in seeming solitude. The work pace, highly varied at first, became steady during the extended period of concentration and then slackened as evident fatigue set in. A farmer called for more 'herb'. Skliff (*ganja cigars*) were rolled and passed and the acute effects began. Again, animation in social concert was followed by concentration, gradual dispersal, and fatigue. The process was repeated twice (a total of four times) during the day. Finally, after a filling lunch served in the field by the host's wife and a late afternoon hour of work, the party ended—the happy host satisfied with a 'fine piece of forking'.

As the behavioral patterns varied in concert among the men throughout the day, one had the impression of togetherness—of social cohesiveness. It was a cohesiveness based on similarities of behavioral patterns in sequence rather than focused social involvement. Ellis [the subject], himself, felt the effects: 'Relations with other people are better when I smoke,' he said, 'I don't interrupt nobody . . . I feel good about everybody.' [6]

Again, the subjective impressions of many coincide with more objective observations.

Behavioral Changes Related to Light or Moderate Smoking (defined by either dose or frequency) Are Not Significant in Agricultural Work Over Extended Time Periods.

Behavioral Changes Related to Heavy Ganja Smoking Are Significant in Agricultural Work Over Extended Time Periods. From our cases, it seems that heavy use does alter the relationship between perception and action, thereby affecting the movement-energy-production pattern related to some agricultural tasks. Extrapolating from limited-time data, it appears that some heavy users work longer and expend more kilocalories to weed, hoe, and turn soil after smoking. It is hypothesized that such an individual without smoking could perhaps cultivate an additional acre with no increase in energy expenditure, even though the subject may believe he is working at full capacity. Nevertheless, we have argued elsewhere that there might well be a positive function to this phenomenon in situations where there are impoverished economic resources and where ethical codes include prescriptions for hard work. It has also been stressed that the productivity findings in specific cases not be misunderstood as a suggestion that a direct and constant relationship exists between heavy use of cannabis and decreased production.[3] Such work as sawing, for example, does not show this relationship, perhaps because the movement patterns linked to ganja smoking are those conducive to the successful completion of such work; nor does cane cutting, as we shall see. In any case, it is abundantly evident from all aspects of this detailed research that heavy ganja smoking does nothing to curtail the motivation to work.

While the movement-energy expenditure studies concentrated on acute ganja effects on individual work over short time periods, another project anthropologist, Melanie Dreher, compared work productivity to ganja-using and nonusing cane cutters on a large Jamaican sugar estate over an entire reaping season. There can be no doubt that cane cutting, a manual operation, is one of the most arduous energy-consuming tasks in all commercial agriculture. Consequently, if the chronic use of cannabis produces any physiologic, psychologic, or behavioral impairment to work, under the stress of such grinding, heavy labor, some indication of this damage should be apparent. To test this proposition, three work gangs of the estate, the gangs that regularly worked three topographically similar cane fields, were selected for study. Each gang included smokers and nonsmokers, for a total sample of 77 of the former and 82 of the latter. To ensure the most objective indicators of worker performance, two 3-week time periods were selected for detailed analysis, periods in which there was no inclement weather or labor disputes to prevent work crews from being out in full force. In addition to data collected through the use of standard anthropologic techniques, the records and accounts of the estate that pertain to productivity were made available by the corporation. The most useful information gleaned from these records were daily figures on tons of cane reaped per cutter, the weekly wages of workers for the first 12 weeks of the 30-week

TABLE 1 *

PRODUCTION OF CANE CUTTERS

			Field I		Field II		Field III	
			Smokers	Non-smokers	Smokers	Non-smokers	Smokers	Non-smokers
P e r i o d	A	Mean number of tons cut per man per week	50.2	50.5	31.3	33.4	34.2	32.5
		Median number of tons cut per man per week	50.7	46.6	30.3	32.5	32.6	34.3
P e r i o d	B	Mean number of tons cut per man per week	45.5	44.6	30.0	32.6	40.8	40.5
		Median number of tons cut per man per week	45.0	46.6	32.6	34.0	46.0	39.6
		N	30	26	28	20	19	36

* Adapted from tabulations provided by Melanie Dreher.

reaping season, the distribution of money from a strike settlement, and individual annual bonus figures based on productivity and paid after the harvest to those who worked at least 20 weeks of the season.

Of these data, the figures on tons of cane reaped are particularly relevant for purposes of this argument. TABLE 1 presents mean and median tons cut per individual per week by smokers and nonsmokers in each gang and for each 3-week time period.

Analysis of TABLE 1 reveals no statistically significant differences in the work productivity of ganja smokers and nonsmokers. Ganja use does not appear to be a factor in this kind of work, and the analysis of all other variables related to worker earnings fully supports this conclusion. This finding strongly reinforces a point made above, that no direct and constant relationship exists between heavy use of cannabis and decreased production.

What do these subjective and objective measures mean? Most importantly, it is abundantly clear that there are no signs of apathy, ineffectiveness, nonproductiveness, or deficits in general motivation among Jamaican laborers. This conclusion is also strongly confirmed by the results of scores of psychiatric and psychologic examinations given to the clinical sample of 60.[3] Quite the contrary, it is apparent that ganja is associated in the minds of users with what we have termed a "motivational syndrome," even though motivation to work need not be correlated objectively with exact levels of productivity. What we need to know, then, is how and why, and research along these lines is a necessary next step.

Jamaica is not unique in the patterns described and the beliefs voiced. From scattered data, it appears that these elements occur or have occurred in many cannabis-using agricultural societies with a long history of use. For example, the classic *Report of the Indian Hemp Drugs Commission,* originally published in 1894, makes the following observations about ganja on the Indian subcontinent:

The use of these drugs to give staying-power under severe exertion or exposure or to alleviate fatigue is very largely in evidence. Here it is ganja especially which is credited with these beneficial effects. For ganja is far more extensively used than bhang by the labouring classes. The latter is mainly used by persons like the Chaubes of Mathra, who are very frequently referred to, and professional wrestlers. Gymnasts, wrestlers and musicians, palki-bearers and porters, divers and postal runners, are examples of the classes who use the hemp drugs on occasions of especially severe exertion. Fishermen and boatmen, *singhara* cultivators working in tanks, dhobis and night watchmen, mendicants and pilgrims, are named among those who use them under severe exposure. All classes of labourers, especially such as blacksmiths, miners, and coolies, are said more or less generally to use the drugs as a rule in moderation to alleviate fatigue.[7]

Similar observations or studies about the relationship of cannabis to work and the alleviation of fatigue have been made about African miners early in this century, workers in the Southwest of the United States and Mexico, Black dock hands in New Orleans in the 1920s and 1930s, and about laborers in contemporary rural India.[8] More recent work has indicated the same phenomenon among the Khmers of Southeast Asia,[9] Colombian laborers,[10] and urban workers in Greece.† One may expect that this very incomplete list will grow considerably as cross-cultural field investigations of cannabis use increase. Such studies will enrich our understanding of both the specific linkage of cannabis to work and, more importantly, of the relationship between culture and the patterned use and patterned effects of cannabis.

As the French ethnobotanist Marie Alexandrine Martin observes:

. . . in Southeast Asia, distrust regarding hemp appears among individuals having cultural and social attitudes patterned after those of the West. As for the peasants, they experiment with everything that belongs to their universe, often have complete knowledge of all the elements that compose it, and how to use them in moderation. There is thus nothing surprising in the fact that they consider cannabis to be a plant that is socially beneficial.[6]

---

† The inclusion of this group in this statement is based on unpublished field reports of a Greek anthropologic team, supervised by this author, who are currently studying chronic hashish use.

What is surprising is the meager effort Western science has made to test the validity or invalidity of such contentions.

ACKNOWLEDGMENTS

My coprincipal investigator in this study was Vera Rubin. I am grateful to Melanie Dreher, University of Massachusetts, a member of our Jamaica Marihuana Project team, for permitting the use of as yet unpublished data on productivity of Jamaican cane cutters, and to Ansley Hamid, Teachers College, Columbia University, for his able research assistance.

REFERENCES

1. CANNABIS: A REPORT OF THE COMMISSION OF INQUIRY INTO THE NON-MEDICAL USE OF DRUGS. 1972. Information Canada. Ottawa, Ontario, Canada.
2. BECKER, H. S. 1967. History, culture and subjective experience: an exploration of the social bases of drug-induced experiences. J. Health Social Behav. 8(3): 163–176.
3. RUBIN, V. & L. COMITAS. 1975. Ganja in Jamaica: A Medical Anthropological Study of Chronic Marihuana Use. Mouton. Paris, France.
4. PELTO, P. J. 1970. Anthropological Research: The Structure of Inquiry. Harper & Row, Publishers. New York, N.Y.
5. COMITAS, L. 1973. Occupational multiplicity in rural Jamaica. In Work and Family Life: West Indian Perspective. L. Comitas & D. Lowenthal, Eds. : 157–173. Anchor Books, Anchor Press/Doubleday. Garden City, N.Y.
6. SCHAEFFER, J. 1975. The significance of marihuana in a small agricultural community in Jamaica. In Cannabis and Culture. V. Rubin, Ed. : 355–388. Mouton. Paris, France.
7. KAPLAN, J. (Ed.) 1969. Marijuana: Report of the Indian Hemp Drugs Commission 1893–1894. Thomas Jefferson Publishing Company. Silver Spring, Md.
8. GRINSPOON, L. 1971. Marihuana Reconsidered. Harvard University Press. Cambridge, Mass.
9. MARTIN, M. A. 1975. Ethnobotanical aspects of cannabis in southeast Asia. In Cannabis and Culture. V. Rubin, Ed. : 63–75. Mouton. Paris, France.
10. PARTRIDGE, W. L. 1975. Cannabis and cultural groups in a Colombian municipio. In Cannabis and Culture. V. Rubin, Ed. : 147–172. Mouton. Paris, France.

THE AMOTIVATIONAL SYNDROME AND CANNABIS USE WITH EMPHASIS ON THE CANADIAN SCENE

Ian Campbell

Faculty of Arts
Sir George Williams University
Concordia University
Montreal, Quebec, Canada

Interest in the amotivational syndrome appears to have been greatest in Canada from about 1968 to 1973. Since that time, there seems to have been a decreasing interest in the subject among scholars and among that diminishing part of the public involved in debates concerning drugs and their effects.

The subject was carefully reviewed by a Commission of Inquiry of the Canadian Government * on which I had the privilege to serve. We submitted a report on cannabis in 1972, the research findings and conclusions of which were sustained in our final report that was submitted 1 year later.

The commission reviewed all major studies of the effects of cannabis use. We were certainly aware that many foreign studies, particularly in the East, had led to a conclusion that heavy cannabis use produced a state of apathy, inactivity, and self-neglect. However, we were unable to accept their findings as either conclusive or necessarily applicable to the Canadian situation and were concerned about the adequacy of their methodologies. We noted the general absence of comparable control groups in these studies and the absence of data on the representativeness of the samples. We were aware of the dangers of making cross-cultural comparisons. North American studies were generally of little more help. Many, if not most, were found to be methodologically inadequate; moreover, in most cases the subjects were multiple drug users, and it was therefore difficult or impossible to reach conclusions about the effects of a particular drug. Within Canada, we found very few useful studies. The most impressive work in Canada was an incomplete study by the Addiction Research Foundation of Ontario. It attempted to examine the social and personal effects of cannabis use. During the study, the subjects were required to live in an experimental hospital ward. They were healthy young males without mental or physical illness and with about 2 years of marijuana experience prior to the study. In our report, we described the experiment in detail,† and because a final report has not yet been issued, it appears useful to review our statement here.

The project was organized around a model "microeconomy" system which approximated some aspects of normal socio-economic behaviour. Subjects were given

---

* The Commission of Inquiry into the Non-Medical Use of Drugs was established on May 29, 1969 and submitted its final report on December 14, 1973. The members of the Commission were Gerald LeDain (chairman), Marie-Andrée Bertrand, Ian Campbell, Heinz Lehmann, and Peter Stein.

† This work had not been reported at the time of the publication of the commission's report on cannabis and was therefore reported in greater detail than usual. Unfortunately, the illness of the present principal investigator has so far prevented complete analysis of the data.

the opportunity to engage in productive behaviour in the ward for which they were paid in the form of cash value tokens which could be exchanged for everyday needs or desires. Certain minimal life-maintaining conditions were provided without charge; the bed and cleaning services, heat and light were free. All other items were paid for by the subjects with the . . . tokens. These tokens could be exchanged, for example, for food, candy, cigarettes, beverage alcohol, newspapers, records, baths, medical information about themselves, access to a gymnasium, to films and other recreational facilities, trips outside in the company of staff members and, in some conditions, marijuana cigarettes.

The costs of goods and services purchased in the ward were generally matched to realistic prices and, in turn, the subjects' earning potential was comparable to that which might occur with similar work in the outside world. . . . Subjects were paid on a piecework basis for completed items (woven woollen belts) which met strict quality standards. A subject might typically earn several hundred dollars per week. Unspent tokens could be saved and exchanged at the end of the experiment for the cash equivalent. Some subjects accumulated several thousand dollars. . . . Twenty subjects were employed in the first phase of the main study—10 each in experimental and placebo groups. . . . The experimental group was required to smoke marijuana cigarettes, while the control group was initially scheduled to smoke inactive placebo cigarettes only. The final experimental treatment regime was as follows:

(a) *Experimental group.* For the first eighteen days no cannabis was allowed. For the next week marijuana cigarettes (containing 8 mg of THC) were available for purchase. For the following fifty-one days a mandatory minimum dose was given, plus whatever marijuana subjects wished to purchase. During this period the mandatory dose of THC was increased in stages from 16 mg (two cigarettes) per day for 27 days, to 24 mg (three cigarettes) for fifteen days, and then finally to 30 mg (two cigarettes) for nine days. Then followed a twelve-day period when cannabis was again available only on purchase—no minimum dose was required. In the remaining ten days of the experiment, cannabis use was not allowed.

(b) *Control group.* After an initial base-line period, inactive placebo cigarettes were administered to the control group. After forty-three days of placebo, a small daily dose of 4 mg of THC was given (for six days) increasing abruptly to a high dose of 30 mg on each of two days. A twelve-day free-purchase period ensued, during which marijuana cigarettes containing 15 mg of THC were available. A final cannabis-free period followed.

The second phase of the main study was conducted under conditions generally similar to those described in phase 1, but, in addition, was designed to explore the effects of cannabis when it is freely available for purchase and consumed in quantities determined only by the individual's own desires.

Preliminary conclusions of the Addiction Research Foundation Team ‡ were set out in our report:

No gross behavioural changes appeared during the experiments. . . . No evidence was found of social deterioration, or a decline in concern over personal hygiene or general physical condition. . . . No significant alterations in intellectual functioning were detected. . . .

In general, subjects reported that mandatory consumption of large doses of marijuana for long periods of time were subjectively unpleasant (to the extent that some threatened to leave the experiment and thereby forfeit a high proportion of their earnings). . . .

When large mandatory doses of marijuana were introduced after long periods of abstinence in the laboratory, work productivity tended to be depressed. Discontinuation of marijuana use after a prolonged period of forced daily smoking of high doses

‡ C. G. Miles, G. Congreve, P. Devanyi, R. Gibbons, J. Marshman, and J. Rankin.

resulted in an increase in productivity. When the work output of subjects on a mandatory high dose was compared to that of subjects who consumed only the amounts they desired (which were, in fact, relatively small quantities) the forced-dose group showed dramatically lower average productivity, which was most pronounced in the first few weeks. Some behavioural adaptation or tolerance to this effect of the drug seemed to develop over the course of the experiment and differences between the mandatory and free-purchase groups were minimal towards the end of the experimental period. The researchers suspect that this productivity decrement is due more to a reduction in time spent working, rather than to inefficient performance.

Recognizing the relatively short period of this experiment and the highly repetitive nature of the work, the commission concluded that this study lends "support to the notion that cannabis, in certain circumstances, may reduce motivation for performing certain manually conducted tasks." However, we cautioned that work of greater "intellectual or artistic variety" might have yielded different results.

The commission did not find conclusive evidence to support the position that cannabis use produced changes of personality that could be termed an amotivational syndrome. We felt that many of the symptoms generally described under this term could be associated with changes in values that stemmed from other sources. However, we did not conclude that the question had been finally answered and argued that there was cause for continuing concern and research.

More than the other members of the commission, I was and remain concerned that a significant drop in motivation is a consequence that may, in some individuals, be associated with the continued use of several psychoactive drugs, including cannabis. I stress, however, that I do not find it as a unique consequence of cannabis use, because I have seen the same symptoms in a large number of chronic and heavy users of alcohol.

My concern about the possibility of a relationship between persistent cannabis intoxication and a deterioration in motivation derives in large part from my observations over a 4-year period, 1968–72. In 1972, I was able to identify, by name, 206 of the estimated 275 students who used cannabis during that year § and was able to hold tape-recorded interviews with 127 of them. A year by year analysis of final examination averages of these students showed that the greater their use of cannabis, the greater the tendency for a decline in final averages. Final averages dropped in 77% of the heaviest users and in 32% of the lightest users. The heavy users also had a higher failure rate and lower averages than did the light users. All of these facts could be attributed to many sources, including their heavy cannabis use, their participation in a subculture that did not tend to stress academic success or the acceptance of such values as planning, punctuality, concern with the future, and rationality, which tend to be associated with academic success, or to a general decline in motivation. My interviews with and observations of these students certainly suggested that apathy increased and vitality diminished as frequency of cannabis intoxication increased.

I was able to examine essays and examinations written by many students whose grades had been analyzed. In this exercise, I compared material written toward the end of the year prior to their heaviest use, at various points through the year of heaviest use, and early in the following year after a summer vacation

§ Total enrollment in the university was approximately 1000 students.

when cannabis had not been used or used only slightly. In examining this work, I was concerned with the way material was organized and handled rather than with its content. It seemed very clear that after periods in which the students had smoked cannabis four, five, or more times per week for 4–6 weeks, there was a lessening in the quality of abstracting and synthesizing. However, the quality of abstraction and synthesizing returned after the summer vacation when the students were free or largely free of cannabis use for as long as 4 months. It seems not unreasonable to hypothesize that a loss of synthesizing and abstracting capacity could yield a change in motivation and, at least in part, account for the apathy and other behavior that would be described as the amotivational syndrome. On reflection, it appears that what I had described as an impairment of abstracting and synthesizing ability could be better described as a lessening of the capacity to perceive relationships of appropriateness. Such an impairment would surely influence the use that these students made of their potential and could well affect their motivation. I am not persuaded, however, that this effect is related uniquely to cannabis but more likely to the use of several drugs, including, in some cases, alcohol.

Canadian research has not produced conclusive evidence to support the hypothesis of an amotivational syndrome associated with cannabis use, although there is some experimental evidence of a decline in productivity among heavy users in an experimental setting. My studies of university students suggest a loss of ability to synthesize and abstract, or to perceive appropriateness in some situations, after periods of frequent and heavy cannabis use.

THE AMOTIVATIONAL SYNDROME
AND THE COLLEGE STUDENT

Glen D. Mellinger, Robert H. Somers, Susan T. Davidson,
and Dean I. Manheimer

Institute for Research in Social Behavior
The Claremont Office Park
Berkeley, California 94705

INTRODUCTION

This longitudinal study is concerned with the extent to which men at a major public university are able to benefit from their academic experience and find self-fulfilling and socially useful roles in society. It has often been suggested that drug use impairs this process by producing an amotivational syndrome of apathy, mental confusion, and lack of goals. The investigators have been looking for evidence to support or refute the hypothesis that drug use produces amotivational symptoms that are serious and long lasting enough to be reflected in the academic and career progress of drug users as compared with nonusers. Such evidence would be especially significant, because respondents in this study represent a student population that provides a pool of exceptional talent for future leadership.

There are several important ways in which an amotivational syndrome that results from drug use might affect academic and career progress. One would be to reduce motivation to stay in school, especially in a competitive academic setting. This paper is concerned specifically with that issue. Drug use might also impair one's ability to maintain good grades and to establish clear occupational goals. Data that pertain to those issues have been reported elsewhere.[2, 3]

In earlier papers, we reported that multiple drug users were more likely than nonusers to drop out.[1, 3] Men who had used only marijuana also were somewhat more likely than nonusers to drop out, but the difference was not statistically significant. We discovered, however, that there was *no* relation at all between drug use and dropping out among the majority of men in the sample who, as entering freshmen, appeared to be committed to traditional academic goals and standards. These men accepted the importance of getting good grades and also expressed the intention (as entering freshmen) of pursuing an uninterrupted career at the university. However, multiple drug use (but not use of only marijuana) was associated with dropping out among men who expressed reservations on either grounds. In short, differences between users and nonusers with respect to academic motivation "explained" a great deal of the relation between drug use and dropping out.

The earlier paper left unresolved two important issues. First, although much of the bivariate relation between dropping out and prior drug use disappeared when we controlled for prior academic motivation, the fact remains that both marijuana use and multiple drug use were quite strongly and negatively related to academic motivation. It was possible, therefore, that drug use was *indirectly* related to dropping out through whatever effects it may have had on academic motivation. Because our data were obtained during the freshman year in college, we have no information about academic motivation during high school that would enable us to make causal inferences as to whether drug use tended to precede low motivation or vice versa. In our analyses, drug use and academic motivation are concomitant variables, both of which exist prior to dropping out.

Second, we were interested in the possibility that the relation of drug use to both dropping out and academic motivation can be explained by sociocultural factors, in particular the tendency of drug users to espouse broader social values that discourage conformity to conventional academic standards. We also wanted to consider the effects of such prior variables as parents' education and poor relationships with parents during high school (reported retrospectively) that may have contributed jointly to drug use and to low academic motivation in college.

Our analyses of the relation of drug use to dropping out, as well as to grades and career indecision, have explored these two possibilities. After extensive examination of the data available to us, our conclusion is that, in all three cases, sociocultural factors account for most of the relation of drug use to adverse outcomes *in this normal population*.[3] There is, however, a small residual relation that may be due to the amotivational syndrome, to other personality factors, or to some idiosyncratic combination of factors. This residual relation specifically involves multiple drug users and not those who used only marijuana. The methods we used and the findings upon which this conclusion is based will be described in later sections.

BACKGROUND

Drug Use and the Amotivational Syndrome

This paper directly addresses a question about the amotivational syndrome that was raised by the Secretary of the Department of Health, Education, and Welfare in The Second Annual Report to Congress on *Marihuana and Health*.[4] "Obviously," the report observes, "individuals in a state of chronic intoxication are unlikely to show conventional levels of motivation. . ." (p. 246). From many other studies,[6-9] including our own,[5] it is clear that most users in normal populations do not use drugs to this extent. "Therefore," as the secretary's report says, "The relevant question would seem to be whether or not the regular use of marihuana at a level below chronic intoxication may bring about personality changes through mechanisms other than the immediate pharmacological effects of the drug" (p. 246).[4]

The amotivational syndrome is described as a cluster of symptoms that include apathy, lack of clear goals, flattening of affect, and mental confusion.[10, 11] This syndrome is familiar to most clinicians who have treated cannabis users and, in controlled studies, seems to be associated (although not consistently) with long, continued use at high dosage levels.[11] Recent reviews by Maugh and Hollister suggest, however, that occasional use of the mild forms of marijuana that are generally available is unlikely to produce lasting symptoms associated with the amotivational syndrome.[10-12]

Serious discussion of the amotivational syndrome has been marked by controversy and by apparently conflicting results. We suggest that the controversy stems in part from the fact that different types of investigations are asking different questions. In particular, they are studying use of marijuana under widely different conditions (dosage levels, length of time used, and so on), in different settings, and with different types of subjects.

In controlled studies of marijuana use, investigators ask at what dosage levels marijuana produces symptoms of "toxicity." Important as they are, these studies are usually conducted under conditions that deviate in two important respects from conditions that typically prevail in actual practice.

First, to control dosage levels with precision, these investigators usually rely on oral administration of marijuana extracts or of synthetic tetrahydrocannabinol (THC), with doses that range from 10 to 70 mg. As Hollister has remarked, ". . . most doses were beyond those which might be obtained from smoking an ordinary marihuana cigarette" (p. 22).[12] * Second, oral administration introduces another important variation from the way in which marijuana is customarily used; that is, most marijuana smokers tend to titrate their rate of smoking to achieve a desired level of "high." Oral administration, of course, does not allow the subject to moderate the effects of use at his own volition. Thus, a subject in a controlled study who receives 70 mg of THC in one oral dose undoubtedly attains what must be a truly exceptional "high" by customary standards of use.

Clinical observations have also been useful in suggesting hazards that may be associated with use of marijuana. As with controlled studies, however, there are important limitations on the extent to which clinical observations can be generalized to the broader population of users. Those who have used marijuana frequently over prolonged periods of time are a small proportion of all drug users.[9] It is therefore likely that they are deviant in many respects, in addition to their heavy pattern of use. McGlothlin finds, for example, that they are also heavy users of other drugs (especially alcohol) and have a history of a relatively unstable life-style.[13] Thus, the frequent and prolonged use of marijuana is so intertwined with other deviant behavior and characteristics of such persons that it may be impossible to sort out probable causes and effects in any meaningful way.

Therefore, to complete a rounded and meaningful assessment of the personal and social implications of marijuana use, it is necessary to go beyond clinical observations and controlled studies and ask three additional questions:

How are marijuana and other drugs actually being used by persons in specified normal populations outside the laboratory?

What consequences are associated with use of these drugs under the conditions of use that prevail in the specified population?

To what extent can observed differences between drug users and nonusers (with respect to particular outcomes) be explained by background and other characteristics that differentiate users from nonusers?

Drug Use and the Drug Subculture

In this report, the "other characteristics" of particular interest are personal and social values that many investigators find to be associated with the "drug subculture." [6, 16, 17, 24] In contrast to the pharmacologically oriented amotivational syndrome theory, the "sociogenic" theory of drug use stresses the impor-

---

* In his studies, for example, Hollister uses doses of THC that range from 30 to 70 mg. He estimates that the minimum dose is equivalent to about four marijuana cigarettes of reasonable quality, and the maximum dose to about nine.

tance of interpersonal influences and of participation in an adolescent subculture that has a distinctive set of values that are at odds with the more conventional values of the adult or parent culture.[17] The values of the drug subculture appear, on the surface at least, to reject the conventional work-success ethic and to downgrade the importance of getting to work on time, getting good grades, and so on (see, for example, Slater [18]).

Our analyses may be regarded as one way of testing the subcultural theory of drug use. This theory is supported to the extent that the relation of drug use to dropping out and to academic motivation is "explained" by variables that represent subcultural values, in combination with family background factors. The test is not conclusive, however, because it does not contrast the predictive power of a sociogenic model of drug use with that of a pathogenic (or amotivational syndrome) model. Moreover, any residual relation of drug use to dropping out or to academic motivation, after controlling for values and background characteristics, does not necessarily support an amotivational syndrome theory. Other explanations may be possible, and we leave it to other investigators to examine the predictive utility of other models.

Drug Use and Academic Attrition

One difficulty with past research on dropouts is the lack of uniformity in the way the term has been defined. "A substantial proportion of so-called dropouts are dropouts only from the campus of original registration; many dropouts return to that campus after an interruption, and many others go on with their higher education at other colleges and universities" (p. 35).[14] In reporting on their study conducted at the University of California at Berkeley (UCB) in the early 1960s, Suczek and Alfert also pointed out that different personality factors appear to be associated with different patterns of dropping out.

> Students who return to the original campus are an unusually mature group with a high level of complexity at the time they first enter the university. Students who are "true" dropouts are somewhat less mature, less complex, and less flexible. Students who drop out from Berkeley and continue their education elsewhere resemble the students who continue without interruption at Berkeley, in relatively greater conventionality, control and compliance to authority (p. 35).[14]

Another difficulty in integrating findings from previous studies of dropouts is that a ". . . characteristic that may encourage withdrawal at one type of college may be irrelevant at another type, and may even promote persistence at a third" (p. 291).[15] In selective and competitive academic settings, attitudinal and motivational factors are likely to be of greater importance than in other academic settings.

Although less directly important than motivational factors, previous studies have found that background characteristics, such as socioeconomic status, also are related to dropping out.[15] Thus, coming from a home in which the parents are college graduates undoubtedly provides several advantages that are conducive to remaining in school. As we will see, this factor has an important part in the data we report here.

In this report, we focus attention on "permanent dropouts," that is, men who were not enrolled in college in Spring 1973 and who said either that they did not plan to return to any school or who expressed uncertainty about whether and when they would return. There were 57 men (7% of the total sample) who met this definition, and they comprise just under one-half of all the dropouts. We chose to concentrate on the permanent dropouts for two reasons. First, dropping out of college permanently is apt to have more serious consequences for the individual than is dropping out temporarily. Second, we have shown elsewhere [1] that permanent dropouts differed from temporary dropouts in important respects; for example, they were less likely to cite money problems as a reason for dropping out.

Until recently, little was known about the relation of drug use to dropping out, largely because it is difficult to obtain a sample of dropouts without the kinds of longitudinal studies that are now being conducted. In one such study of high school students, Johnston [8] found a definite association between dropping out and use of illicit drugs, as well as between use of alcohol and use of cigarettes. However, he notes that ". . . some or all of those differences would probably be eliminated by controlling for other factors" (p. 129).[8] With respect to drug use, dropouts differed most from those who went on to college, and the differences were apparent prior to dropping out.

In their longitudinal study at the University of California at Los Angeles (UCLA), Brill and Christie [19] found that marijuana users were more likely than nonusers to drop out, and the users who dropped out were more likely than other dropouts to say they left college "to reassess goals" and to report having difficulty in deciding on career goals.

STUDY METHODS

Study Setting

This report is based on data from a large-scale longitudinal study of probability samples of two groups of male students at UCB. The groups sampled were men who entered as freshmen in Fall 1970 and senior men who intended to graduate in Spring 1971. The present report is based on data from the freshman panel.

The university, along with other academically selective schools, was one of the centers of the newly emerging drug culture in the 1960s. By the early 1970s, UCB had a relatively long tradition of drug use, and prevalence rates were relatively high. Thus, drug use in this setting had become, at least statistically, normal rather than deviant behavior, a situation that prevailed more widely across the nation's campuses a few years later.

Consequently, this university provided an unparalleled opportunity to study the personal and social implications of drug use among an academically select group of men whose potential as individuals and as future leaders of society is great. Moreover, the drug user himself could suffer serious consequences if his drug use were to become a barrier to his own personal growth and self-fulfillment.

Sampling

Data from the freshman cohort were collected at two points in time. Time-1 (Fall 1970) data were obtained from 960 men early in their freshman year by means of personal interviews and self-administered forms. The completion rate, 92% of the originally designated probability sample, was exceptionally high.[20] The same men were resurveyed at time 2 (Spring 1973) by self-administered questionnaires. We again achieved a very high completion rate, 87% of the time-1 responders, or 80% of the originally designated sample. These response rates help greatly to reduce sampling biases that might be associated with non-participation.[5]

Data: Drug Use

In both waves of the study, drug use data were obtained from a self-administered questionnaire, and questions about drug use were asked in an identical fashion, with some additional questions at time 2. Questions were restricted to use of illicit drugs and to illicit use of drugs that can be obtained legally. The drug classes about which we asked questions were marijuana and/or hashish, psychedelics, cocaine, heroin, opium, other opiates, inhalants, amphetamines and other stimulants, and barbiturates and sedatives.† For the various classes, we supplied a short list of trade and street names of specific drugs to illustrate what was to be included in each class. It should be noted that only 2% of the men in this sample had ever used heroin by time 2; however, 14% had used opium, 19% had used cocaine, and 36% had used psychedelics.[5]

Respondents were first asked to indicate whether they had ever used any drug in each of the classes and were then asked other questions about each of the classes they had used. Three of the additional questions provide the basis for this report: How long ago did you first use it? How long ago did you last use it? How many days did you use it during the Fall quarter (time 1)?

FINDINGS

Drug Use

It is evident from Table 1 that use of illicit drugs was widely prevalent in this population. More than one-half had already used drugs before entering the university, and early in the freshman year men who had never used drugs were even more in the minority (41%). Almost one-half (47%) used drugs at least once during the Fall quarter.

Although these prevalence rates are high, there is evidence from other studies that they were not atypical. Data from a national study of college students conducted by Groves one year earlier [6] indicate that usage rates in our freshman

---

† The drug variables used in this report do not include use of stimulants and sedatives, because our questions at time 1 did not clearly identify recreational use. A question asked at time 2 indicated that, for the most part, these drugs were being used infrequently and were not being used to "get high." Most men who did use these drugs to get high were also using other drugs. Consequently, the number of possible misclassifications in the time-1 data was reduced by eliminating these drugs from consideration, and the time-2 classifications were not materially affected by the omission. Use of inhalants is excluded for similar reasons and also because there were very few men who reported using them.

panel at time 1 were not much higher than the average nationally at similar schools and were below the usage rates at some. More recent Gallup [21] data also show that prevalence of drug use among college students generally was about on a par, by 1974, with the prevalence we found at UCB in 1970.

Two comments about TABLE 1 help to explain our method of classifying users. One is that the distinction between men who had used only marijuana and the multiple drug users (MDU) who had also used other drugs, namely, psychedelics, cocaine, and opiates, is exceedingly important. Throughout our analyses, this distinction has consistently been the most useful basis for classifying drug users. One reason for this finding is that the multiple drug users as a group appeared to be substantially more involved in drug use and in the drug subculture than were men who restricted their use of illicit drugs to marijuana. As compared with the latter, multiple drug users tended to use marijuana more frequently, were more likely to have many friends who use drugs, and were more likely to identify with drug users.

A second important aspect of these data is that even though prevalence of use is high, levels of marijuana use generally suggest experimental, casual, and recreational use rather than habitual or compulsive use, especially among men who used only marijuana. Among the latter, 16% (47 men) had used marijuana 18 or more times during the Fall quarter, that is, on an average of about twice weekly or more. Thus, the majority of these men could be regarded as less than "regular" users.

At the same time, although it is difficult to compare the frequency of marijuana use with the frequency of using other drugs, our impression is that the latter was rather substantial given the greater potency of these drugs. Almost half of the men who had used drugs other than marijuana during the year before entering UCB had done so seven or more times.

In classifying drug users, our major goal was to identify characteristics or patterns of use most likely to produce amotivational symptoms. For reasons mentioned above, we first distinguished multiple drug users from men who used only marijuana. Within each group, we further identified subgroups of users whose patterns of use were relatively extreme. After many analyses exploring various ways of classifying users, we reached two conclusions. First, given the patterns of use in this population, there were very few individuals whose level of use could be regarded as substantial over any extended period of time. But second, both *continuity* of use (i.e., use during both the Fall quarter and during the year before entering UCB) and *multiple drug use* were strongly related to *frequency* of marijuana use. Continuity and multiple drug use thus provide convenient criteria for identifying groups of users whose frequency of use differs appreciably.

Accordingly, the classifications of drug users that we used in the analyses reported here are shown in the third column of TABLE 1. Among the multiple drug users, we distinguished those whose use was continuing from those who had stopped or just begun using other drugs during the Fall quarter. Among the marijuana-only users, we identified 71 "continuing-frequent" users who had used that drug at least four times during the Fall quarter and at least 14 times during the previous year. These criteria obviously do not signify substantial levels of use, but they do eliminate the experimental and more casual users. Because of the correlation between frequency and continuity of use, they also identify a group of users whose frequency of use was relatively "extreme" in this population, and more extreme than the criteria would suggest: 49% of the

TABLE 1

PREVALENCE AND FREQUENCY OF DRUG USE DURING YEAR BEFORE ENTERING UCB AND DURING FALL QUARTER 1970 (TIME 1)

Drug Use	Year Prior to Entering UCB — Number of Days Used	%	(n)	Time 1: Fall Quarter 1970 — Number of Days Used	%	(n)	Drug Use Status: Continuity/Frequency of Use from Year Prior to UCB through Fall Quarter	%	(n)
Never used	none	46	(381)	none	41	(344)		41	(344)
Used only marijuana	none	2	(14)	none	8	(70)			
	1–3	9	(76)	1–3	11	(93)			
	4–13	13	(105)	4–8	10	(82)	continuing frequent users *	9	(71)
	14–26	6	(50)	9–17	8	(67)			
	27–52	5	(42)	≥18	6	(47)	other users who did not meet frequency criteria both times	28	(231)
	≥53	4	(34)						
	[total]	[38]	[321]	[total] †	[43]	[359]			
Multiple drug users (MDU)	none	1	(5)	none	4	(32)			
	1–3	5	(40)	1–2	6	(50)	continuing MDU ‡	9	(77)
	4–6	3	(26)	3	5	(40)			
	≥7	7	(61)	≥4	1	(9)	MDU but not at both times	13	(111)
	[total]	[16]	[132]	[total]	[16]	[131]			
Grand totals §		100	(834)		100	(834)		100	(834)

* Continuing-frequent marijuana-only users are those who fall into both boxes defined by dashed lines.

† Includes 57 men who were multiple drug users before entering UCB.

‡ Continuing multiple drug users are those who fall into both boxes defined by dotted lines.

§ Percentages may add to slightly more or less than 100 due to rounding.

continuing-frequent marijuana-only users had used marijuana 27 or more times during the year before college, as compared with 2% of the remaining marijuana-only users who had used the drug during the previous year. Also, 61% of the former group had used marijuana nine or more times during the Fall quarter (about once per week or more), as compared with 24% of the latter.

Isolating the continuing multiple drug users also identifies men who tended to use both marijuana and other drugs relatively frequently. Thus, data not shown here indicate that 70% of the continuing multiple drug users reported using marijuana nine or more times (about once per week or more) during the

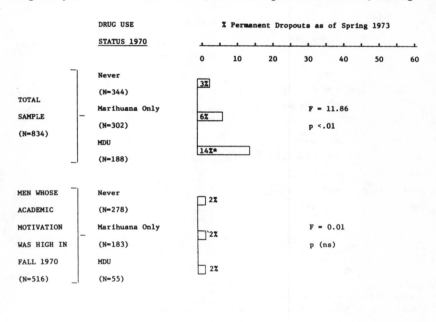

*Difference between specified subgroup of users and men who never used drugs is statistically significant, p <.01.

FIGURE 1a. Percentage of permanent dropouts as of Spring 1973 by drug use status as of Fall quarter 1970 (shown separately for total sample and for men whose academic motivation was high as of Fall 1970).

Fall quarter of the freshman year, as compared with 59% of the noncontinuing multiple drug users. And 57% of the former had used other drugs seven or more times during the year before college, as compared with 30% of the noncontinuing users who had used other drugs the year before.

Drug Use and Dropping Out

FIGURES 1a and 1b show the relation of drug use status early in the freshman year to subsequent dropping out of school. In the upper portion of FIGURE 1a, data based on the total sample indicate that 3% of the men who had never used drugs became permanent dropouts, as compared with 6% of the men who had used only marijuana and 14% of the multiple drug users. (The difference between the multiple drug users and men who had never used drugs is statistically significant, but the difference between the latter and the marijuana-only users is not.)

From the lower portion of FIGURE 1a, and from FIGURE 1b, we see that the differences between drug users and nonusers essentially disappeared (with one

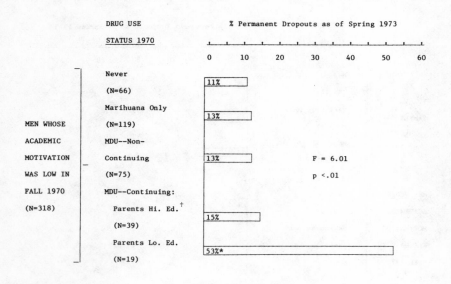

[†]High education means one or both parents were college graduates; low education means neither parent was a college graduate.

*Difference between specified subgroup of users and men who never used drugs is statistically significant, p <.01.

FIGURE 1b. Percentage of permanent dropouts as of Spring 1973 by drug use status as of Fall quarter 1970 among men whose academic motivation was low in Fall 1970 (shown separately for all men whose academic motivation was low and for subgroups of multiple drug users as defined by continuity of use and by parents' education).

important exception) when two other factors were taken into account: conventional academic motivation as a freshman and, among the continuing multiple drug users, whether one or both parents had a college degree.

Among freshmen whose academic motivation was high (62% of the sample), there was no relation between time-1 drug use and becoming a permanent dropout (lower portion of FIGURE 1a). Only 2% dropped out regardless of drug use status. Among freshmen whose academic motivation was low (38% of the sample), there were no statistically significant differences between men who had never used drugs and three of the four groups of users (FIGURE 1b). However, the percentage of persons dropping out was strikingly high (53%) in the small subgroup of 19 continuing multiple drug users whose academic motivation at time 1 was low and neither of whose parents was a college graduate. Although the number of cases is small, the differences between this group and men who had never used drugs (11% of whom dropped out) is both statistically significant and striking. An interaction term that represents this subgroup will be used in the multiple regression analyses below.

Multiple Regression Analyses

Earlier we noted that most of the apparent relation between drug use and dropping out could be explained by the lower academic motivation of the drug users, including users of only marijuana. This finding suggests that drug use may have an indirect effect on dropping out through its association with low academic motivation. The analyses reported in this section are addressed to that issue.

The strategy we used is based on the logic of path analysis. Although we made no attempt to develop and test a formal path model, the path analytic concept of partitioning a zero-order correlation into direct and indirect effects provides a convenient tool for dealing with this issue. In path analysis,[22] the *direct* effect of a predictor X_3 (e.g., drug use) on a criterion X_5 (e.g., dropping out) is the standardized partial regression coefficient after controlling for the effects of other predictors, X_1, X_2, and X_4. This coefficient (or "path") is represented by the symbol p_{53}. If predictor X_4 is academic motivation, its direct effect on dropping out is estimated by the coefficient p_{54}, again controlling for the other predictors, X_1–X_3. Then, the *indirect* effect of drug use on dropping out, via academic motivation, is the product of the two path coefficients p_{54} and p_{43}. Drug use may also have other indirect effects via other predictors, but these effects are not relevant to the issues of this report.

To estimate the direct effect of drug use on academic motivation (p_{43}), we calculated a regression equation in which the criterion variable was academic motivation at time 1; the predictors were drug use and six other variables that represent demographic background, closeness of relationships with parents during high school (reported retrospectively at time 1), and cultural values reported at time 1. These other predictors are listed in TABLE 2. To estimate the direct effects of drug use and academic motivation on dropping out (p_{53} and p_{54}, respectively), we used the latter variable (with dropouts coded 1, others coded 0) as a criterion in a regression equation that was otherwise the same as the first, except that academic motivation was added to the predictors. The three path coefficients obtained from the analysis thus provided the following information: estimated direct effect, p_{53}; estimated indirect effect (via academic motivation), $p_{54}p_{43}$; sum of direct and indirect effects, $p_{53} + p_{54}p_{43}$. No rigorous statistical meaning is attached to this sum of the two effects. It is simply a convenient way of estimating the combined effects of drug use on dropping out.

The preceding explanation has referred to a single variable, "drug use." In fact, our sample permitted us to analyze separately the effects of several distinctive patterns of drug use relative to nonuse. For this purpose, the estimation of direct and indirect effects described above was calculated in five separate regression analyses, one for each of the drug groups: continuing-frequent marijuana-only, all other marijuana-only, noncontinuing MDU, continuing MDU, and frequent marijuana-only year before UCB. For each estimation, drug use was entered as a dichotomous variable that represents the *main effect* of drug use in each equation. In one equation, for instance, the continuing marijuana users were coded 1 and contrasted with the nonusers (coded 0). All other types

TABLE 2

LIST OF PREDICTORS (OTHER THAN DRUG USE) EMPLOYED IN
MULTIPLE REGRESSION ANALYSES

Background and Social Factors

1. *Race/Religious/Ethnic Background.* A dichotomous variable with a high score that represents men from Catholic, Black, or Latin American families.
2. *Parents' Education.* A dichotomous variable with a high score that represents men, one or both of whose parents were college graduates.
3. *High School Grade Point Average.* Data obtained with prior written permission of respondents from university admission records.
4. *Closeness to Parents During High School.* A 17-point scale based on six items that elicit retrospective reports (at time 1) about relationships with parents before coming to UCB. High scores identify a respondent who said he felt close to both parents, felt that both parents approved his way of life and the way he spent his time, identified and felt a sense of solidarity with his family, and would like his own life to be similar to his father's.

Cultural Values and Academic Motivation

5. *Importance of Preparing for a Specific Occupation as a Reason for Being in College* (*time 1*). A four-category ordinal item with a high code that identifies respondents who answered "very important."
6. *Political/Social Alienation* (*time 1*). A 42-point scale based on responses to 10 items. High scores identify respondents who:
   ... believe that (1) political spokesmen who represent their views do not have much influence on national policy, (2) no influential officials in Washington give serious consideration to their views, (3) very few Americans share their views, and (4) American society is hopeless and needs complete change;
   ... (5) are not at all optimistic about the future of American society;
   ... describe themselves as (6) politically radical on most issues, (7) feeling that the world is absurd and meaningless, (8) critical of conventional moral practices and values, (9) being in conflict with almost all authority, and (10) *not* affiliated currently with one of the major religious institutions, that is, Protestant, Catholic, or Jewish.
7. *Academic Motivation.* A dichotomous variable with a high score that represents respondents who said (1) that it is very or fairly important to them to maintain good grades in college *and* (2) that they planned to work straight through 4 years to get their degree.

of users were excluded from that equation, which effectively isolated the effects of continuing use of marijuana.

In two of the above analyses, we also entered an *interaction term* that represents a specific subgroup of the larger group of users for which the equation was calculated. This interaction term, also a dichotomous variable, indicates the extent to which the *combination* of drug use with some other characteristic produces results that are different for the subgroup than for the group as a whole. Men with that combination are coded 1 for the variable; all others, including the other drug users, are coded 0. The two interaction terms used in these analyses represent two subgroups: continuing multiple drug users whose academic motivation was low at time 1 and neither of whose parents had a college degree and men who had used marijuana 53 or more times during the year before entering UCB and who became multiple drug users after entering UCB.‡

The formulation of regression equations in this way permitted us to contrast each particular type of drug use (and its interaction term) with the absence of drug use, while other differences between users and nonusers were statistically equated on the other variables that enter into the equation. The information produced by any one equation may be viewed as identical to results that would have been obtained had we deliberately selected for our probability sample only that particular type of user, together with a random sample of nonusers.

The results of the multiple regression analyses are summarized in TABLE 3. Complete results of all analyses in this report are available from the senior author on request. The first column shows the zero-order correlation between each of the prior drug use variables and becoming a permanent dropout. Six of the seven correlations are positive and statistically significant at the 0.05 level or better, indicating that, in general, men who were using (or had used) drugs as freshmen were more likely than nonusers to become permanent dropouts by time 2.

The first interaction term represents the subgroup of 19 continuing multiple drug users discussed previously, and the high dropout rate in this subgroup is indicated by the correlation of 0.401 between this term and dropping out. The other interaction term represents 20 of the 34 men who had used marijuana 53 or more times during the year before entering UCB. These 20 men, unlike the remaining 14, subsequently became multiple drug users. Although the correlation with dropping out is virtually identical for the subgroup (0.107) and the group as a whole (0.097), men in this small subgroup were somewhat more likely to drop out (14%) than were the others (7%) (data not shown). As we will see, the two variables operated differently in the regression analyses.

As can be seen in the second column of TABLE 3, the effect of introducing the background, social, and cultural predictors into the regression analyses was to reduce four of the relations to essentially zero, indicating that all of the relation between drug use and dropping out in these cases can be explained by these other predictors. In one other case (the continuing-frequent marijuana-only users), there is a small but *negative* and significant coefficient. As compared with nonusers, therefore, users were somewhat *less* likely to become permanent dropouts than one would expect, given their background, and so on.

One can therefore conclude that, for most of the drug users in this sample, the probability of becoming a dropout was no higher (and in one case was somewhat lower) than one would expect, given their background characteristics, value orientations, and academic motivation as freshmen.

There are two exceptions to this generalization. One involves the subgroup

‡ See Kerlinger and Pedhazur (chapter 10) for a discussion of methods for coding interaction terms in multiple regression analysis by use of dichotomous variables.[28] We are indebted to Professor Ira Cisin and Dr. Michael Tiktinsky for calling our attention to these procedures.

TABLE 3

EFFECTS OF DRUG USE ON DROPPING OUT: ZERO-ORDER CORRELATIONS, DIRECT EFFECTS, INDIRECT EFFECTS THROUGH ACADEMIC MOTIVATION, AND SUM OF DIRECT AND INDIRECT EFFECTS *

Drug Use Predictor (no. of cases)	Drug Use and Permanent Dropout		Indirect Effect		Sum of Direct and Indirect Effects
	Correlation	Direct Effect	Drug Use and Academic Motivation	Academic Motivation and Permanent Dropout	
	(r_{53})	(p_{53})	(p_{43})	(p_{54})	$(p_{53} + p_{43}p_{54})$
Drug Use Status, Time 1					
Continuous-frequent marijuana-only (71) vs never used (344)	−0.045	−0.106 †	−0.084 ‡ ×	−0.100 ‡ = 0.008	−0.098
All other marijuana-only (231) vs never used (344)	0.087 †	0.000	−0.082 † ×	−0.173 § = 0.014	0.014
Noncontinuing MDU (111) vs never used (344)	0.126 §	0.001	−0.211 § ×	−0.127 † = 0.027	0.028
Continuing MDU (77) vs never used (344)	0.268 §	0.008	−0.180 § ×	−0.116 † = 0.021	0.029
Interaction term (no. of cases in subgroup=19)¶	0.401 §	0.286 §	−0.137 § ×	−0.116 † = 0.016	0.302
Drug Use Year Before Entering UCB					
Frequent marijuana-only (34) vs. never used (381)	0.097 †	−0.006	−0.096 ×	−0.113 † = 0.011	0.005
Interaction term (no. of cases in subgroup=20)¶	0.107 †	0.081	−0.054 ×	−0.113 † = 0.006	0.087

* Data based on standardized partial regression (path) coefficients after controlling for background and social factors and cultural values in TABLE 2.
† p < 0.05.
‡ p < 0.10.
§ p < 0.01.
¶ See text (*Multiple Regression Analyses*) for definition of subgroups.

of 19 continuing multiple drug users with less educated parents. Although the relation of this predictor was reduced from 0.401 to 0.286, it is apparent that these men were definitely more likely than nonusers to drop out and that their higher rate of dropping out is not explained by the other predictors (including academic motivation) in the analysis.

The other exception is suggestive, even though the coefficient is low (0.081) and not statistically significant. This exception involves the subgroup of men who were using marijuana quite frequently during the year before entering college and who escalated to multiple drug use after entering college. Although this relation is based on a very small number of cases, these data suggest that the progression from frequent marijuana use during high school to multiple drug use during college may possibly increase the likelihood of dropping out. However, that increase (if any) is small.

Finally, the data in columns three to five suggest that drug use has little if any effect on dropping out by way of whatever effect it may have on academic motivation. Although all except two of the coefficients in columns three and four are statistically significant, they are all too low to produce any appreciable "indirect effects." Consequently, in the last column, the three estimated overall effects of any magnitude (−0.098, 0.302, and 0.087) are due almost entirely to the direct effects of drug use on dropping out.

TABLES 4 and 5 are included for the reader who is especially interested in knowing how various types of drug users differed from nonusers in this sample and how the various sociocultural characteristics we included in our regression equations are related to each other and to dropping out. Unlike TABLES 2–4, TABLE 5 is based on data for the entire sample.

Of particular interest are the interrelations among closeness to parents, political/social alienation, drug use, academic motivation, and dropping out of school. These findings have interesting implications that we will discuss briefly under DISCUSSION AND SUMMARY.

DISCUSSION AND SUMMARY

In earlier analyses of the relation of freshman drug use to becoming a permanent dropout over the next 2½ years, we found that much of that relation could be explained by differences between users and nonusers with respect to academic motivation. We also discovered that drug use was associated with low academic motivation, and with other characteristics that might explain the observed relations.

In this paper, we addressed two questions raised by the earlier analyses: Would multivariate analysis reveal that drug use has an indirect effect on dropping out by virtue of its relation to academic motivation? To what extent can the combined direct and indirect effects of drug use on dropping out be explained by social and cultural characteristics that differentiate users and nonusers?

With respect to the first question, the data showed that the indirect effects of drug use on dropping out were negligible. There remained in some cases a statistically significant and negative relation between drug use and academic motivation after controlling for other factors. However, these partial regression coefficients were too small to produce any appreciable indirect effect on dropping out.

TABLE 4

ZERO-ORDER CORRELATIONS BETWEEN THE VARIOUS DRUG USE PREDICTORS AND THE BACKGROUND AND SOCIAL FACTORS AND CULTURAL VALUES

Drug Use Predictor (no. of cases)	Catholic, Black or Latin American Background	One or Both Parents College Graduates	High School Grade Point Average	Closeness to Parents During High School	Importance of Preparing for Specific Occupation	Political/ Social Alienation
Drug Use Status, Time 1						
Continuous-frequent marijuana-only (71) vs never used (344)	−0.192	0.169	−0.079	−0.166	−0.257	0.316
All other marijuana-only (231) vs never used (344)	−0.191	0.122	−0.074	−0.185	−0.199	0.299
Noncontinuing MDU (111) vs never used (344)	−0.232	0.223	−0.123	−0.275	−0.415	0.520
Continuing MDU (77) vs never used (344)	−0.158	0.099	−0.192	−0.366	−0.363	0.516
Interaction term (no. of cases in subgroup=19)*	−0.048	−0.231	−0.091	−0.186	−0.227	0.250
Drug Use Year Before Entering UCB						
Frequent marijuana-only (34) vs never used (381)	−0.050	0.157	−0.091	−0.176	−0.163	0.329
Interaction term (no. of cases in subgroup=20)*	−0.107	0.166	−0.114	−0.127	−0.110	0.322

* See text (Multiple Regression Analyses) for definition of subgroups.

TABLE 5

ZERO-ORDER CORRELATIONS AMONG THE VARIOUS BACKGROUND AND SOCIAL FACTORS, CULTURAL VALUES, ACADEMIC MOTIVATION, AND DROPPING OUT PERMANENTLY BY TIME 2 *

Predictor	0	1	2	3	4	5	6
0. Permanent dropout	—	—	—	—	—	—	—
1. Catholic/Black/Latin American	−0.091	—	—	—	—	—	—
2. One/both parents college graduates	−0.094	−0.196	—	—	—	—	—
3. High school grade point average	−0.081	−0.011	−0.003	—	—	—	—
4. Closeness to parents during high school	−0.142	0.025	0.055	−0.029	—	—	—
5. Importance of preparing for specific occupation	−0.198	0.156	−0.090	0.077	0.223	—	—
6. Political/social alienation	0.178	−0.186	0.090	−0.053	−0.365	−0.458	—
7. Academic motivation	−0.257	0.164	−0.079	0.087	0.218	0.425	−0.409

The answer to the second question was that there were two instances in which a positive relation between drug use and dropping out was not entirely explained by the other predictors in the analysis, although one of the partial regression coefficients was not statistically significant. Both instances involved small subgroups of men who either continued to be or became multiple drug users after entering the university.

However, among men who had not used drugs other than marijuana, and even among the majority of multiple drug users, there was no evidence that drug use had any relation to dropping out that was independent of family background, relationships with parents in high school, and social values. For most users, then, it appeared to be these factors, rather than drug use per se, that accounted for dropping out of school. These data lend strong support to the subcultural theory of drug use espoused by Goode,[16] Johnson,[17] and others. Thus, there is no evidence that the generally moderate patterns of use among men in this sample produced amotivational symptoms that were sufficiently serious or long lasting to increase the risk of dropping out of school. Data on the relation of drug use to grades and to career indecision (reported elsewhere[3]) support this conclusion. Given these prevailing patterns of use, the findings would seem to argue for the wisdom of moderation in using drugs, if one chooses to use them at all.

The findings also leave open the possibility that some illicit drug users, like some users of alcohol, are less able than others to cope with drug use. For these persons, drug use may create problems or impair one's capacity to cope realistically and constructively with life. Further analyses are required to ascertain what factors differentiate users who seem to be able to cope with drugs from those who cannot do so.

Any interpretation of our findings should consider that they apply to an academically select group of men who were sufficiently motivated and competent to seek and obtain admission to a public university of high standing. Drug use may be more problematic for men who are less goal directed and less well equipped to achieve the goals they have set for themselves.

In closing, we are struck by the fact that poor relationships with family and alienation from the larger society are associated with academic motivation and dropping out of school, and with drug use. These findings suggest to us that relationships with parents may have important implications for efforts to find ways to minimize the destructive consequences of drug use. Perhaps the real question is how can parents, teachers, and other adults teach young people to cope realistically and responsibly with the realities of the society we live in. One of those realities is drug use.

REFERENCES

1. MELLINGER, G. D., R. H. SOMERS & D. I. MANHEIMER. 1976. Drug use and academic attrition among university men. *In* Proceedings of the Conference on the Social Psychology of Drug and Alcohol Abuse. In press.
2. SOMERS, R. H., G. D. MELLINGER & D. I. MANHEIMER. 1974. Drug use and academic decisions: a longitudinal analysis of the freshman panel. Unpublished paper.
3. MELLINGER, G. D., R. H. SOMERS, S. T. DAVIDSON & D. I. MANHEIMER. 1976. Drug use, academic performance and career indecision: longitudinal data in

search of a model. Paper presented at the Conference on Longitudinal Research on Drug Use, San Juan, Puerto Rico. To be published.

4. DEPARTMENT OF HEALTH, EDUCATION, AND WELFARE. 1972. Marihuana and Health: Report to the Congress from the Secretary, Department of Health, Education, and Welfare. Second annual report. United States Government Printing Office. Washington, D.C.

5. DAVIDSON, S. T., G. D. MELLINGER & D. I. MANHEIMER. 1976. Changing patterns of drug use among university men. Addictive Diseases Int. J. In press.

6. GROVES, W. E. 1974. Patterns of college student drug use and life-styles. *In* Drug Use: Epidemiological and Sociological Approaches. E. Josephson & E. E. Carroll, Eds. : 241–275. Hemisphere Publishing Corporation. Washington, D.C.

7. JOSEPHSON, E. 1974. Adolescent marijuana use, 1971–72: findings from two national surveys. Addictive Diseases Int. J. **1**(10): 55–72.

8. JOHNSTON, L. D. 1974. Drug use during and after high school: results of a national longitudinal study. Amer. J. Publ. Health Suppl. **64**: 29–37.

9. RESPONSE ANALYSIS CORPORATION. 1972. Public Attitudes Toward Marihuana. Part I. Response Analysis Corporation. Princeton, N.J.

10. MAUGH, T. H. 1974. Marihuana: the grass may no longer be greener. Science **185**(4152): 683–685.

11. MAUGH, T. H. 1974. Marihuana (II): does it damage the brain? Science **185** (4153): 775, 776.

12. HOLLISTER, L. E. 1971. Marihuana in man: three years later. Science **172**: 21–29.

13. McGLOTHLIN, W. H., D. O. ARNOLD & P. K. ROWAN. 1970. Marijuana use among adults. Psychiatry **33**(4): 433–442.

14. SUCZEK, R. F. & E. ALFERT. 1966. Personality characteristics of college dropouts. United States Department of Health, Education, and Welfare Cooperative Research Project 5–8232. University of California. Berkeley, Calif.

15. FELDMAN, K. A. & T. M. NEWCOMB. 1969. The Impact of College on Students. Jossey-Bass, Inc., Publishers. San Francisco, Calif.

16. GOODE, E. 1972. Drugs in American Society. Alfred A. Knopf, Inc. New York, N.Y.

17. JOHNSON, B. C. 1973. Marihuana Users and Drug Subcultures. John Wiley & Sons, Inc. New York, N.Y.

18. SLATER, P. E. 1970. The Pursuit of Loneliness: American Culture at the Breaking Point. Beacon Press. Boston, Mass.

19. BRILL, N. Q. & R. L. CHRISTIE. 1974. Marijuana use and psychosocial adaptation. Arch. Gen. Psychiat. **31**: 713–719.

20. MANHEIMER, D. I., G. D. MELLINGER, R. H. SOMERS & M. T. KLEMAN. 1972. Technical and ethical considerations in data collection. Drug Forum **1**(4): 323–333.

21. THE AMERICAN INSTITUTE OF PUBLIC OPINION. 1974. Gallup Opinion Index **109**: 14–30.

22. DUNCAN, O. D. 1966. Path analysis: sociological examples. Amer. J. Sociol. **72**(1): 1–16.

23. KERLINGER, F. N. & E. J. PEDHAZUR. 1973. Multiple Regression in Behavioral Research. Holt, Rinehart & Winston, Inc. New York, N.Y.

24. KANDEL, D. 1974. Interpersonal influence on adolescent drug use. *In* Drug Use: Epidemiological and Sociological Approaches. E. Josephson & E. E. Carroll, Eds. : 207–240. Hemisphere Publishing Corporation. Washington, D.C.

GENERAL DISCUSSION

Dana L. Farnsworth, *Moderator*

Harvard University
Cambridge, Massachusetts 02138

DR. A. WIKLER: Dr. Comitas, have you considered the possibility that the increased energy and work output during heavy ganja smoking is an example of state dependence? These Jamaican subjects had been smoking ganja for 7–20 years, I understand, and perhaps they could have acquired state-dependent effects that would work only under ganja. When they were not intoxicated with ganja, they could not work. I understand from your remarks about Bowman and Pihl's paper that patients reported that when they were not smoking ganja, they were disinclined to work; they could not do the heavy work. Is it conceivable that perhaps this situation is the amotivational syndrome? I was trying to recollect whether the descriptions of the amotivational syndrome in our own country were made on the basis of subjects who were seen when they were not intoxicated but had been smoking for years. Perhaps we're looking at this problem upside down.

DR. L. COMITAS: I didn't say that the ganja users when not using ganja did not work, nor that they were disinclined to work.

In fact, Dr. Knight reported that the use of ganja in Jamaica is endemic among the lower-class population; that is, we would estimate that on the order of 60–70% of the lower-class population uses ganja to a considerable extent. From our field observations, clearly there are situations in which ganja users do not use the drug to work; sometimes they do not use it on their own, that is, and it appears not to effect their work. I do not know of a situation where a ganja user will not work because he has no ganja. When ganja is available and can be bought, it is used.

DR. WIKLER: In Bowman and Pihl's paper, they quote reports of ganja smokers who cannot work when they do not use ganja. I'm asking whether this disinclination to work when not smoking may be the amotivational syndrome. In your comparisons, did you have some control subjects who were never ganja smokers? Did you compare their work output with those of ganja smokers who were not using ganja at the time they were working?

DR. COMITAS: We conducted a community study in a sugar plantation, in which the anthropologists got to know the workers quite well, the standard anthropologic material, but also managed to obtain the daily productivity records of the company itself. We were able to separate our ganja users from nonusers specifically with respect to production, and we found no difference in work output.

DR. WIKLER: When you refer to ganja users, were they smoking ganja when working in the plantations?

DR. COMITAS: The ganja users were smoking and not smoking.

DR. WIKLER: I wanted to know whether ganja users who were not smoking ganja were able to perform as much work.

DR. COMITAS: We couldn't determine that from these figures.

DR. WALTER CLARKE (*Andover Newton Theological School, Andover, Mass.*): There's an old adage: call a man a thief, and he will steal. I won-

56

dered whether we might paraphrase that adage: call a drug a drug of abuse, and it will be abused. Have any of you specifically planned research that would be concentrated on the possible creative uses of the drug? I know that this possibility has been mentioned, but I wondered whether any kind of research emphasizes this aspect of marijuana.

DR. G. D. MELLINGER: I guess I could speak for the group in saying that probably we have not emphasized that point. I would be interested in undertaking studies in which we would look at the factors that seem to be associated with moderate use as distinct from abuse, and that might be a step in the direction you're talking about.

DR. W. E. CARTER: The subjects with whom we worked in Costa Rica did not conceive that they were abusing the drug; they were simply using it. I mentioned that by the time we collected all of their descriptions of the drug, they listed 39 effects. To my memory, two effects were negative, and all of the rest were positive reasons for which people used the drug.

DR. JAMES HALIKAS (*Washington University, St. Louis, Mo.*): Both Dr. Carter and Dr. Boulougouris identified a substantial minority of the user population that has antisocial activities to a high degree, beginning very early in childhood. I would suggest that since in both cultures marijuana use is illegal, we're seeing deviant individuals who are willing to do deviant things. By analogy, if we studied bank robbers, we would find a high proportion of criminals among them.

Dr. Carter, were the street movers the group that had the high proportion of excess use of alcohol and tobacco? Were the stable users in those categories, in fact, similar to the controls?

DR. CARTER: We thought that we would find a difference in terms of alcohol and tobacco with the street movers. We checked for this difference and did not find it.

INCIDENCE OF MENTAL ILLNESS IN HASHISH USERS AND CONTROLS *

Costas Stefanis, Aris Liakos, and John C. Boulougouris

Department of Psychiatry
Athens University Medical School
Eginition Hospital
Athens, Greece

INTRODUCTION

Whether chronic cannabis use affects mental health still remains a highly controversial issue in the literature. Though it is widely recognized that, under certain conditions, an acute transitory psychotic state may occur immediately after use, the question of more lasting effects on mental health is still unresolved.

Several early reports that originated mainly from Eastern countries described an association of chronic cannabis use and mental disorders.[1-3] In some studies, it is claimed that cannabis use can produce a specific type of psychosis.[4-6] However interesting the above studies may be, they are easily disputed on the grounds that sampling and other sources of bias are present. Lack of controlled studies in this area of cannabis research is due to several methodologic difficulties. Representative samples of chronic cannabis users who do not use other addictive substances are difficult to obtain, and factors likely to influence the incidence of mental disorder are difficult to control. Moreover, considerable difficulties are encountered in establishing an accurate diagnosis of mental disorders on the basis of the currently employed clinical criteria. Despite these difficulties, three controlled studies were completed in the last few years.[7-9] In one of them [9] a higher incidence of personality disorders was noted in the user group, whereas the other two studies [7,8] showed no difference in the incidence of mental disorders between users and controls. In this paper, the results of a controlled study of a sample of Greek chronic cannabis users with regard to their mental state will be reported.

METHODS AND MATERIALS

The assessment of subjects' mental health and their final diagnosis was made by three psychiatrists who participated in the study. It was based on information obtained from structured social histories taken by a social worker, psychiatric examinations performed in a semistructured way according to the Mayer-Gross, Slater, and Roth [10] format, and data gathered from home visits, reports of local civil authorities, and finally from psychiatric records of subjects who received psychiatric treatment prior to the study. The diagnostic criteria of the American Psychiatric Association (1968) were used for the diagnostic evaluation of this information.

* Supported by National Institute of Mental Health Contract HSM 42–70–98 through the International Association for Psychiatric Research.

All cannabis users and controls were paid male volunteers. Controls were matched for age, family origin, education, residence at birth, and upbringing. Family origin was matched only for the factor "Greek refugee" from Asia Minor, because a large number of the cannabis users were from Greek families who emigrated from Turkey to Greece during the 1918 Greek-Turkish war. Upbringing was defined as the residence in which the subject spent most of his life during the first 15 years of age.

Matching was not performed on an individual basis. Controls were selected from the same residential areas as the users and were of the same socioeconomic background. We compared the groups for differences in the matching factors. We considered that satisfactory matching for a factor was obtained when there were no statistical differences between the samples.

The initial population of users consisted of individuals referred to us by Miras,[11] who had previously studied them. This population was enlarged by friends and acquaintances of these users and by users and controls recruited by our Social Service.

Subjects

Cannabis Users. Criteria for inclusion in the study were cannabis use for more than 10 years and no use of other addictive drugs. Social use of alcohol was not a reason for exclusion. Alcoholics, that is, subjects who reported being drunk regularly, who were addicted to alcohol, and whose drinking habits interfered with work performance, were excluded. Subjects older than 58 years or those suffering from incapacitating physical or neurologic illness were also excluded.

Sixty cannabis users were examined; 13 of them were excluded for the following reasons: three subjects for previous use of heroin, three for alcoholism, one for lysergic acid diethylamide use, one for inadequate current use of cannabis, and five who were older than 58 years.

The users reported cannabis consumption as follows: an average of 23 years of use, a smoking frequency of three times per day nearly every day, and an average daily amount of 5 g of hashish consumed. They started cannabis use at a mean age of 17 years.

Controls. The same criteria employed for cannabis users, excluding the first one, which was related to cannabis use, were utilized for selection of controls. Because all cannabis users were tobacco smokers, we excluded all controls who were not tobacco users.

Sixty-four controls were examined; 24 of them were excluded for the following reasons: eight smoked cannabis once or on several occasions, five were alcoholics, four were over 58 years of age, three were nontobacco users, two were suffering from central nervous system diseases, one used heroin, and one was a sibling of a cannabis user. The final control sample consisted of 40 males.

RESULTS

Comparisons of the two groups with respect to personal, family, and social characteristics have been presented in detail elsewhere.[12] Briefly, the users differed significantly from controls only on previous psychiatric illness, imprisonment records, regular military service, and work record.

The incidence of mental disorders is shown in TABLE 1. Significantly more users were diagnosed as suffering from a psychiatric abnormality (38%) in comparison to controls (17%). Twelve users were diagnosed as having "personality disorders" (25%) in comparison to three controls (7%). The difference in the incidence of personality disorders was significant. There was also a significant difference in the incidence of the subcategory of antisocial personality disorders. Five users were diagnosed as having antisocial personality disorders (10%) in comparison to none of the controls. All five exhibited pronounced antisocial maladjustive behavior typical of the antisocial personality disorders.

The differences in the incidence of other types of psychiatric abnormalities were not significant. Three cannabis users (6%) and three controls (7%) were neurotic, and one control was suffering from depression. Three users were diagnosed as paranoid schizophrenic psychotics. All three were found to have loosely organized paranoid delusions unrelated to their drug intake habits.

TABLE 1

INCIDENCE OF PSYCHIATRIC DISORDERS

Type of Disorder	Hashish Users ($n=47$)		Controls ($n=40$)		x^2	p
	No.	%	No.	%		
Personality disorders	12	25.53	3	7.5	4.94	<0.05
Antisocial type	5	10.63	0	—	4.51	<0.05
Other types	7	14.98	3	7.5	1.16	ns
Neurosis	3	6.38	3	7.5	0.04	ns
Depressive illness	0	—	1	2.5	—	ns
Schizophrenic disorder (paranoid)	3	6.38	0	—	—	ns
Total	18	38.28	7	17.50	4.56	<0.05

They neglected themselves and showed a lack of insight. One of the three reported visual and auditory hallucinations. Two of them had a positive family history of mental disorder. All three started using cannabis in their teens, and the formal onset of psychosis was many years later, except for one of the three subjects who reported possible psychotic symptoms at the age of 14.

To investigate a possible relationship between the incidence of psychiatric disorders and the amount of daily cannabis consumption, we divided the user sample into two groups according to their recent usage of hashish: heavy users, those who reported cannabis use above the mean daily consumption, and moderate users, those who reported present use lower than the mean daily consumption. Because the users were different from controls with respect to work record and imprisonment, we also tested for a relationship of degree of consumption to these parameters. TABLE 2 shows the results from comparisons between the two groups. No significant relationship between degree of consumption and incidence of psychiatric abnormality, employment, or imprisonment record was found. Regular military service was not included in the com-

TABLE 2

COMPARISON BETWEEN HEAVY SMOKERS
(ACCORDING TO PRESENT USE OF HASHISH)
AND MODERATE ONES

Item	Heavy ($n=14$)		Moderate ($n=32$)		χ^2	p
	No.	%	No.	%		
Skilled workers	1	7.14	10	31.25	3.11	ns
Imprisonments due to other reasons	7	50.00	22	68.75	1.46	≫
Employed when seen	9	64.28	18	56.25	0.26	≫
Mentally ill	3	21.42	14	43.75	2.08	≫

parison, because psychiatric disorder is a reason for exemption from service in the armed forces in Greece.

Regarding the relationship between degree of consumption and psychiatric abnormality, there was a tendency to a negative relationship; that is, more psychiatrically abnormal users were found among moderate users (43%) than heavy users (21%).

We also tested for differences between the psychiatrically ill and normal users in the parameters that discriminated users from controls. The only significant difference was with respect to prison sentences due to reasons other than cannabis offenses (TABLE 3). More psychiatrically abnormal cannabis users were sent to prison for reasons unrelated to cannabis offenses (83%) in comparison to psychiatrically normal subjects (48%).

DISCUSSION

The results of this study show a higher incidence of psychopathology in the population of chronic hashish users in comparison to controls. The difference is due mainly to the prevalence of personality disorders, particularly the antisocial type of personality. Because similar psychopathology has been noted by others,[9] the role of cannabis use in determining this difference must be considered. The possibility that individuals with an antisocial type of personality are more prone to cannabis use, especially in the particular social setting, is

TABLE 3

COMPARISON BETWEEN MENTALLY ILL HASHISH SMOKERS
AND NORMAL ONES

Item	Mentally Ill ($n=18$)		Normal ($n=29$)		χ^2	p
	No.	%	No.	%		
Imprisonments due to other reasons	15	83.33	14	48.27	5.77	0.02

the first to be considered. Hashish smoking in Greece is illegal and carries severe punishment and social stigma. In this setting, cannabis use may be considered as another form of antisocial behavior more likely to occur in people with a personality disorder. However, most of our subjects started smoking at a very early age, and, therefore, assessment of presmoking personality retrospectively at such an age is not possible. This point raises the possibility of chronic cannabis use exerting a modifying influence on the personality of the users.

We could not find a relationship between the incidence of psychiatric disorder and the degree of cannabis use. The lack of such a relationship is another reason to suspect that psychiatrically abnormal subjects are more likely to be found among cannabis users rather than cannabis use being responsible for the psychiatric abnormality. The difference in imprisonment records between psychiatrically abnormal and normal users can be explained by the prevalence of personality disorders among users.

The occurrence of three cases of psychosis among cannabis users, though not statistically significant, raises the question of prolonged chronic cannabis use leading to chronic psychotic states. The clinical features, however, of our three cases were indistinguishable from those of chronic schizophrenia, and the positive family history in two of them argues against this possibility.

Our sample of users belongs to a special cultural subgroup of the Greek population that mainly consists of Greek refugees from Asia Minor of low socioeconomic level and living in certain underprivileged areas. On the other hand, the investigated sample is considered representative of Greek chronic users, because it has been shown to be so by a study [13] that compared the present sample with the total sample of users in Greece from the Police records. We may, therefore, conclude from this study that long-term cannabis use is associated with a high incidence of personality disorders, a finding that may be related to the prevailing legal and social variables of hashish use in Greece.

REFERENCES

1. BENABUD, A. 1957. Psycho-pathological aspects of the cannabis situation in Morocco: statistical data for 1956. Bull. Narcotics 9(4): 1–16.
2. ASUNI, T. 1964. Socio-psychiatric problems of cannabis in Nigeria. Bull. Narcotics 16: 17–28.
3. BOROFFKA, A. 1966. Mental illness and Indian hemp in Lagos. East African Med. J. 43(9): 377–384.
4. STRIGARIS, M. G. 1933. Zur Klinik der Hashisch psychosen (Nach studien in Griechenland). Arch. Psychiatr. Nervenkr. 100: 522–532.
5. CHOPRA, G. S. 1971. Marihuana and adverse psychotic reactions. Bull. Narcotics 23: 15–21.
6. KOLANSKY, H. & T. W. MOORE. 1972. Toxic effects of chronic marihuana use. J. Amer. Med. Ass. 22: 35–41.
7. BEAUBRUN, M. D. & F. KNIGHT. 1973. Psychiatric assessment of 30 chronic users of cannabis and 30 matched controls. Amer. J. Psychiat. 130: 309–312.
8. HOFFMAN, J. S. & N. BRILL. 1973. Chronic marihuana use and psychosocial adaptation. Amer. J. Psychiat. 130: 132–140.
9. HALIKAS, J. A., P. W. GOODWIN & S. B. GUSE. 1972. Marihuana and psychiatric illness. Arch. Gen. Psychiat. 27: 162–165.
10. MAYER-GROSS, W., E. SLATER & M. ROTH. 1970. Clinical Psychiatry. Cassell and Co. Ltd. London, England.

11. MIRAS, C. J. 1972. Studies in the effects of chronic cannabis administration to man. *In* Cannabis and Its Derivatives. W. D. M. Paton & T. Crown, Eds. Oxford University Press. London, England.
12. BOULOUGOURIS, J. C., A. LIAKOS & C. STEFANIS. This monograph.
13. STEFANIS, C., C. BALLAS & D. MADIANOU. 1976. Sociocultural and epidemiological aspects of hashish use in Greece. *In* Hashish! A Study of Long-Term Use. C. Stefanis, R. L. Dornbush & M. Fink, Eds. The Raven Press. New York, N.Y. In press.

ROLE OF CANNABIS IN PSYCHIATRIC DISTURBANCE

Frank Knight

Department of Psychiatry
University of the West Indies
and Cornwall Regional Hospital
Montego Bay 1
Jamaica, West Indies

INTRODUCTION

This paper is based on two controlled studies of cannabis users in Jamaica [1,2] conducted between 1970 and 1972 and on several years of clinical observation before and after these studies were performed. It will present an account of some patterns of psychiatric illness and the relationship that cannabis may bear to them.

Jamaica is an island of slightly less than two million people, whose life-style is tropical and essentially Western. Jamaica is unusual for a Western country, in that cannabis is extensively cultivated, and its export in bulk has brought in a significant amount of foreign money, mainly from North America. The country is unusual, too, in that cannabis consumption has been endemic for decades. One survey [3] based on an indirect inquiry method of 78 nonhospitalized working-class males over the age of 15 concluded that 36 of them smoked more than once per day, while another five smoked less than once per day. The plant is believed to have been introduced to the country from India by indentured laborers about 100 years ago. The use of the drug in the form of *ganja* (the flowering tips and the young leaves of the plant) is widespread among the laboring classes. It is usually smoked but may be brewed as tea, and in this form it is commonly used by adults, and even given to young infants, for medicinal purposes. Laborers claim that it helps them to concentrate and to work harder.

In recent years, the use of ganja has spread to the middle classes, university students, and high school adolescents. In these three groups, its use generally reflects the pattern of use by comparable groups in North America.

Jamaica is also the home of the Rastafarian movement, whose adherents may be recognized by their freely growing locks of unshorn hair, their cultural use of ganja ("the holy weed of wisdom"), their belief in the godhead of the late Emperor Haile Selassie, and their view of Africa as the home to which all black people should return. [4] Members of this semireligious cult sometimes live in communities separate from the general population. This feature of their life-style, together with their dietary rules and their use of the Old Testament, makes their doctrine and way of life attractive to rebellious adolescents who may or may not also have borderline psychotic illness.

These features of Jamaican life and culture, in addition to its virtual freedom from hard drug users, make it the ideal location to study the effects of cannabis, because, although illegal, the drug is freely available at low cost, has wide cultural use, and is the only mind-altering or sedative drug used by a large sector of the population.

Despite its popularity among some of the middle class, there is a general attitude of disapproval and resistance among them toward the use of ganja,

64

which is associated in their minds with Rastafarians, teenage dropouts, crime, and madness. The association with madness is accepted in the island's one large psychiatric hospital, where the diagnosis of "ganja psychosis" has long had recognition among the staff.

This is a useful background against which to examine what relationships may exist between psychiatric illness and cannabis usage.

STUDIES OF CANNABIS USERS IN JAMAICA

Studies of Long-Term Use

A study of 30 chronic male cannabis users in Jamaica versus 30 matched controls did not reveal any active psychiatric disturbance or organic deficit, nor did it demonstrate any significant difference between the groups as measured by physical, physiologic, and psychometric tests or electroencephalographic examinations.[1] Chronic use was described as daily consumption for at least 7 years. Another study in Jamaica of 16 chronic smokers and 10 controls, and subsequently repeated with 28 subjects, looked at physiologic and psychologic funtioning and found no chronic effect in either area that could be attributed to cannabis usage.[2] In both of these studies, the subjects were required to abstain from the drug during the testing period. In the first study, the subjects, aged between 23 and 53 years, were admitted to the hospital for 1 week; in the second study, the subjects were required to not be "high" (i.e., not to have used cannabis in the 4 hr prior to the test).

Clinical Survey of Mental Hospital Patients

A survey of 106 of 112 consecutive male admissions to Bellevue Psychiatric Hospital in Kingston [3] showed that 26 of these patients were heavy ganja smokers (i.e., at least once per day), while another seven were light users (less than once per day). The authors' main theme is a suggestion that cannabis may be a cheaper alternative to alcohol for the poorer class of people. In addition to this suggestion, they conclude that there is no evidence to implicate cannabis use as a factor that contributes to psychiatric illness. However, the study lacks details of case histories or of diagnoses or symptoms and bases its findings on the patients' responses to questionnaires and the authors' clinical impression ["Notre expérience de deux années à Bellevue nous donne à penser que cela (ganja as a contributory factor in admission) est rarement le cas"]. It does not appear that there was enough evidence in this study on which to base this conclusion.

Clinical Findings in Psychiatric Patients in
Urban and Rural General Hospitals

At the University Hospital of the West Indies, of 74 males admitted to the psychiatric unit over a 12-month period in 1972, 29 (39%) gave a history of some past usage of cannabis. Ten of these patients (13.5% of the male admissions) who had smoked it within days or weeks of admission were diagnosed as "ganja psychosis," and a new diagnosis of "marijuana-modified mania" was coined for four others after their clinical picture changed from schizophreniform illness on admission to classic hypomania after a few days in the hospital.[5]

At another general hospital (see TABLE 1),[6] Cornwall Regional Hospital in Montego Bay, a total of 269 patients were admitted to the psychiatric unit in the 12 months that ended in March 1975, with 66 patients (24.2%) having a history of cannabis use, 35 of them (13%) within 2 months of admission (see TABLE 1). The functional psychoses, which were comprised of 223 patients, constituted the largest group, with 54 patients (24.2%) having a history of cannabis use.

The diagnoses given refer to diagnosis either on discharge or after several months of follow-up, by which time premorbid personality and family history could be taken into account and weighed against the acute clinical picture at the time of inpatient treatment. Schizophreniform characteristics were considered to be such features as blunted affect, primary delusional ideas, ideas of

TABLE 1

NUMBER OF PATIENTS WITH A HISTORY OF CANNABIS USE:
CORNWALL REGIONAL HOSPITAL, APRIL 1974 TO MARCH 1975

Diagnosis	Number	Recent Cannabis Use (last 2 months)	Past History Only of Cannabis Use	Total Number Who Used Cannabis
Hypomanic reaction	76	9	5	14 (18.4%)
Depressive reaction	59	1	6	7 (11.9%)
Schizophreniform reaction	88	25	8	33 (37.5%)
Total (functional psychoses)	223	35	19	54 (24.2%)
Other diagnoses	46	7	5	12 (26.1%)
Total	269	42	24	66 (24.2%)

reference, and alienation of thought. The term "schizophreniform reaction" (see below) was adhered to because it was thought that for a diagnosis of true schizophrenia to be made, the observer had to be certain that the clinical picture was not being influenced by cannabis use, and this certainly was not always possible once a habitual or occasional cannabis user was discharged from inpatient care.

At three other rural general hospitals over the same period of time, cannabis usage was thought to be a contributory factor in 11 of 51 (Falmouth Hospital), seven of 18 (Lucea Hospital), and 39 of 75 (Savanna-la-Mar Hospital) patients admitted for treatment of schizophreniform reactions.[6]

Findings on the Pathoplastic Effect of Cannabis

The description "marijuana-modified mania" was first applied to a particular clinical sequence when four male patients were admitted to the psychiatric unit of the University Hospital, Kingston over a period of time, with what at first appeared to be a schizophrenic reaction.[5] The common features of their reactions are described as follows: All patients were men aged 20–31. All had, for several years prior to their illness, used marijuana in moderate amounts without mishap. All displayed initial symptoms of a hypomanic nature, followed by a marked increase in marijuana usage. At the time of admission, an initial diagnosis of paranoid schizophrenia was made in three of the four patients based on the presence of withdrawal, persecutory delusions, auditory hallucinations, and disorder of thought. No patient displayed mood elevation at this stage, nor was there any evidence of toxic psychosis (all were normally orientated and lacked signs of clouding of consciousness). Within 3–4 days of admission, all developed symptoms and signs of manic or hypomanic illness. In addition, two patients had family histories of manic depressive psychosis, one suffered a subsequent episode of mania, and one developed a depressive illness.

The conclusion drawn was that "these patients were suffering from a primary affective illness (mania or hypomania) and that excessive use of marihuana was symptomatic of their illness (analogous to the excessive use of alcohol by some manic patients)." [5] These cases were seen as being distinguishable from mania with a paranoid flavor.

It commonly happens that, in certain stages mania exhibits features of paranoia and delusional thinking which are so prominent that a diagnosis of schizophrenia is in fact made. In a report on a longitudinal study on 20 manic patients Carlson and Goodwin (7) have emphasized the unreliability of cross-sectional observation in making a diagnosis. We believe that in the cases reported here marihuana was responsible not only for producing the schizophreniform picture, but also for making the episodes mimic schizophrenia as closely as they did by introducing features of withdrawn behaviour, echolalia, echopraxia, blunted affect, fragmentation of thought, and third person hallucinatory voices which generally are not encountered in manic illness that takes on a paranoid appearance.

Since these cases have been described, at least nine others that would fit into the same classification have been documented.[6]

In contrast to these cases that show the modifying effect of cannabis on hypomania are seven cases cited from the Cornwall Regional Hospital. These seven persons, of 59 with a depressive reaction, were diagnosed as having "cannabis involvement." This feature is thought to have modified the depressive picture, so that it included strong paranoid feelings and, in some instances, an aggressive excitability. (It is interesting to compare these features with the findings in depressed patients who, while being given tetrahydrocannabinol to help their symptoms, developed paranoid ideas of persecution.[8])

Individual Case Studies

One interesting case deserves special mention as showing only hypomanic features after cannabis use:

A 29-year-old unmarried male technician of rural working-class background, with a reputation for sobriety and an easygoing manner, was observed to be behaving oddly at work for a few days. One morning, he suddenly became short-tempered and assertive, threatening his boss verbally and disrupting the work of all of his colleagues. He was brought by force to the casualty department of the local hospital, where he presented with a typical hypomanic picture of distractibility, pressure of talk, and punning. Paranoid features were notably absent. He was persuaded to accept admission into a hospital, where he was treated with oral chlorpromazine, up to 800 mg/24 hr, and lithium carbonate, 250 mg four times daily. He improved rapidly within 3 days, although his discharge home was delayed for another 3 days to allow for full reassessment.

This man confessed to having started smoking cannabis 4 weeks previously, taking up to two "spliffs" daily. (A "spliff" or "skliff" is roughly the equivalent of a North American "joint.") He had done it partly for the experience and partly to help him forget the financial problems he anticipated with his forthcoming marriage. Long before his discharge from the hospital, he had regained full insight, was embarrassed by the incident, anxious that his fiancée should not be told the real cause, and certain that he would never use cannabis again.

Another interesting case is described:

A boy 16 years old experienced a "bad trip" on the first and only occasion that he smoked cannabis. Subsequent to that occasion, he had gone away to school but had to return home because of a series of experiences of unreality related to himself and to the passage of time. He also began to experience what was probably a form of sleep paralysis: near morning, he would dream that he was in his own bed and his own room (which he was) but was unable to move or call for help. Invariably, before the dream became distressing, he would have the experience of falling asleep, then would wake up in reality. This young man's symptoms went on for 3 years with periods of relapses and recovery, often with depressive episodes, before he started to remain consistently well.

EXPLANATION OF TERMS USED

Ganja Psychosis

The clinical features generally accepted by psychiatrists and nursing staff in psychiatric units in Jamaica as justifying a patient being placed into this category are a history of disturbed, sometimes aggressive, behavior after several days of unaccustomed cannabis use (either in persons who had not used it previously or had used it in smaller amounts); schizophrenic features, such as blunted affect, withdrawal, and bewilderment; other schizophrenic features, such as hallucinations and paranoid ideation; and the continuation of symptoms for a period of several weeks after the drug is presumed to have been eliminated from the body.

Schizophreniform Reaction

This term has come into use more and more as a provisional diagnosis at the Cornwall Regional Hospital, where it is considered that such a high proportion (37.5%) of patients admitted with symptoms of schizophrenia owe much of their symptomatology to cannabis. Sometimes for months after discharge, and despite the use of injectable depot fluphenazine, it is not possible to be certain that it is schizophrenia and not the continued use of cannabis that is responsible for the persistence of psychotic features.

It is convenient at this point to refer to a very useful classification suggested by Negrete [9] for adverse reactions to cannabis, which conforms to most of the syndromes seen in Jamaica. He recommends the adoption of severe intoxication, pathologic intoxication, acute cannabis psychoses, subacute and chronic cannabis psychoses, and residual conditions for the sake of clarity and uniformity in describing syndromes attributable to cannabis. The first of these classes is recognized in Jamaica as the response of a normal individual to an unusually large dose of cannabis, generally the result of a stronger than normal sample of the drug. No treatment is sought or given, and the subject who has been having hallucinations and a feeling of floating returns to normal when the concentration of the drug in the bloodstream falls. The second category ("panic and short-lasting paranoid states with fear of police arrests . . ., fear of death, of losing one's mind . . ., depersonalization . . . with consequent panic") is the well-known "ganja reaction" seen by casualty officers in hospitals all over the island. In our experience, the duration is less than 24 hr: the subject is usually given an intramuscular injection of about 200 mg of chlorpromazine and is allowed to sleep off his intoxication overnight.

Negrete's "acute cannabis psychosis" corresponds to the Jamaican "ganja psychosis," in which it is considered that the use of the drug has acted as a triggering mechanism in an individual who is vulnerable or susceptible to schizophrenic disorder. The psychotic reaction continues and requires treatment in its own right, much the same as may occur if it has been triggered off by obstetric confinement or a surgical operation. Our experience coincides with that of Murphy and of Bromberg, as quoted by Negrete,[9] that many of these cases are eventually diagnosed as schizophrenia.

Subacute and chronic cannabis psychosis as described in this classification matches approximately a picture most readily recognized in some Jamaican vagrants who bear the outward signs of the Rastafarian cult. In common with the Rastafarians, they sport the "dreadlocks" style of unshorn hair and use cannabis when it is available. But, unlike the true brethren, they wander the streets in a state of personal untidiness, often manifesting thought disorder and paranoid ideas if one stops to engage them in conversation. They do not really fit into the mainstream of Rastafarians. This author feels that they represent cases of schizoid personality or borderline psychosis who have been attracted to the Rastafarian cult and who, though they may gain some psychologic relief by use of cannabis, are pushed over into and kept in a state of mild psychosis. Some of them, no doubt, are true schizophrenics whose symptoms and bizarre behavior would be present even without their resorting to cannabis.

Into the category of "residual conditions," Negrete puts the amotivational syndrome. This category approximates a class of person in Jamaica who proves most difficult to manage. They are often represented by teenage rebels or dropouts from eminently respectable professional and middle-class families who adopt the Rastafarian style of speech (a characteristic of which is reference to one's self as "I man" or "I and I"). Possibly because of their middle-class background, and despite the change in language, hair style, and diet, their involvement with the doctrine of Rastafarianism is often more of a flirtation than a true commitment, leading one colleague to dub them "Rastoid" [10] (as contrasted with those who are truly Rastafarian). Our experience agrees with Negrete's view that their attitudes and behavior are related more to their changed beliefs than to cannabis usage. Their intelligence and convictions make them stubborn when they are not intoxicated, and when they do smoke, they become even more intransigent. The other residual condition included by Negrete, flashbacks, has been seen in Jamaica in several adolescents, occurring in them for many months after smoking cannabis. One of these cases was discussed above in the individual case studies.

GENERAL DISCUSSION

Planned studies have failed to reveal any evidence that cannabis is responsible for psychologic changes in long-term users. It is conventional and acceptable to refer to such studies when drawing conclusions about the effects of cannabis. However, the studies cited sought to identify permanent effects of cannabis use in subjects who were not under the acute influence of the drug at the time of testing. These subjects are really in a different category from those in whom clinical observation incriminates cannabis as a cause of psychiatric illness and adverse psychologic effects.

In any event, there will always be a discrepancy between what is observed during normal clinical activity and reported retrospectively, on the one hand, and what is found in planned controlled studies, on the other. For clinically reported episodes, the investigator is at a disadvantage in not knowing the potency of the cannabis used and in depending on the biased reports of the subject, his friends, and family. But the reporting of a large number of cases with a strong similarity in their histories would seem to go some way toward compensating for the absence of controls.

In considering the carefully controlled studies on long-term use, the question could arise as to the status of these users: whether, in fact, the samples may be biased from the beginning because the subjects chosen could be seen as the *survivors,* as it were, of many years of cannabis use.

Even controlled studies of acute consumption of cannabis may not present as unbiased a conclusion as we might think. For the sake of argument, it must be possible to subject 100 persons to the type of stress that is believed to lead to thyrotoxicosis or diabetes, without, in fact, producing a single case of either of these conditions. Such an approach neglects the factor of constitutional liability, which is accepted as operating in the causation of psychosomatic illness and which can be presumed to be present in the case of "ganja psychosis," to explain why, of the many persons known to expose themselves to the drug, only a small proportion suffers any serious adverse effects.

CONCLUSIONS

Despite the unlikelihood of being able to prove an association between cannabis usage and psychiatric disturbance, this author hopes that the examples presented will favor a reacceptance of the role of clinical observation in strengthening the validity of clinical theories. It is to be hoped that instead of a preoccupation as to whether cannabis is involved in the causation of psychiatric illness, more attention will be focused on the ways in which the disturbances are caused and on how they may be modified by the presence of the drug.

SUMMARY

Clinical observation suggests that cannabis is implicated in some types of psychiatric disturbance. A record of admissions to two urban and four rural hospitals in Jamaica is examined along with details of individual cases. One-third of male admissions to the psychiatric hospital have used cannabis. Of 74 males admitted to another psychiatric service over a 12-month period, 29 had used cannabis. Ten of these patients were diagnosed as "ganja psychosis," and four others were classified as "marijuana-modified mania." At another psychiatric service, 54 of 223 admissions (24.2%) for functional psychosis presented with cannabis usage as a contributory factor. These 54 patients included 14 and seven cases of hypomanic and depressive reactions, respectively. At three other rural general hospitals, psychiatric admissions for psychosis showed 11 of 51, seven of 18, and 39 of 75 patients, respectively, in whom cannabis was considered directly responsible. These findings lend support to the idea of causation of illness or modification of existing illness. The negative findings of controlled studies in the same country are not inconsistent. A suggested classification for adverse reactions to cannabis offered by one author is recommended, because it is in accord with common local clinical experience.

REFERENCES

1. BEAUBRUN, M. H. & F. KNIGHT. 1973. Psychiatric assessment of 30 chronic users of cannabis and 30 matched controls. Amer. J. Psychiat. **130:** 309–311.
2. BOWMAN, M. & R. O. PIHL. 1973. Psychological effects of chronic heavy use. A controlled study of intellectual functioning in chronic users of high potency cannabis. Psychopharmacologia **29:** 159–170.
3. PRINCE, R., R. GREENFIELD & J. MARRIOTT. 1972. Cannabis ou alcool? Observations sur la consommation de ces substances en Jamaïque. Bull. Stupéfiants **24:** 1.
4. SMITH, M. G., R. AUGIER & R. NETTLEFORD. 1960. The Rastafari movement in Kingston, Jamaica. Institute of Social and Economic Research. Kingston, Jamaica.
5. HARDING, T. & F. KNIGHT. 1973. Marihuana-modified mania. Arch. Gen. Psychiat. **29:** 635–637.
6. KNIGHT, F. 1976. Report from the Department of Psychiatry, Cornwall Regional Hospital. Montego Bay, Jamaica.
7. CARLSON, G. A. & F. K. GOODWIN. 1973. The stages of mania: a longitudinal analysis of the manic episode. Arch. Gen. Psychiat. **28:** 221–228.
8. KOTIN, J., R. M. POST & F. K. GOODWIN. 1973. Delta-9-tetra-hydro-cannabinol in depressed patients. Arch. Gen. Psychiat. **28:** 345–348.
9. NEGRETE, J. C. 1973. Psychological adverse effects of cannabis smoking: a tentative classification. Can. Med. Ass. J. **108:** 195–202.
10. ALLEN, E. A. 1971. Personal communication.

PSYCHIATRIC AND BEHAVIORAL OBSERVATIONS OF CASUAL AND HEAVY MARIJUANA USERS IN A CONTROLLED RESEARCH SETTING *

Isaac Greenberg, Jack H. Mendelson, John C. Kuehnle,
Nancy Mello, and Thomas F. Babor

Alcohol and Drug Abuse Research Center
Harvard Medical School–McLean Hospital
Belmont, Massachusetts 02178

Recent clinical reports have implicated marijuana in certain biochemical changes in the central nervous system,[25] cerebral atrophy,[6] depression and paranoia,[24] and in diminution of ambition and motivation.[29] Concern about possible persistent changes in mental status and behavioral patterns after marijuana use has stimulated considerable research on these issues.

Unfortunately, knowledge of marijuana effects has, until recently, been limited to case study reports and anecdotal accounts. Case study reports suffer from several serious methodologic complications, including the use of selective nonrepresentative samples [2] and the lack of an adequate control population. Grinspoon [18] has observed that the prevalence of "cannabis psychosis" does not differ significantly from the prevalence of psychosis found in general population surveys. Similarly, in a study of the amotivational syndrome, Kupfer *et al.*[27] concluded that impaired motivation may reflect depressive episodes rather than drug-induced changes. The role of preexisting depression in behavior often associated with chronic marijuana use has been more fully discussed by Halikas *et al.*[19]

Although data that implicate marijuana in psychiatric or behavioral disturbances are not compelling, evidence that suggests that marijuana has no adverse psychiatric effects also requires rigorous scrutiny. Questionnaires that specifically examine prior adverse drug effects may be selectively answered by subjects who enjoy the effects of marijuana and have positive attitudes about its use. Studies that assess neurophysiologic or psychiatric effects of marijuana on college students either implicitly [13, 35] or explicitly [28] select healthy subjects, in whom adverse reactions or residual drug effects are minimal. To complicate matters further, subjects who clearly enjoy the drug are most readily available as research subjects, a self-selection process that is often difficult to circumvent.

In the relatively few studies in which reasonable control group procedures were employed or where sampling bias was not a critical factor, the incidence of marijuana-related adverse reactions appeared to be very low. No impairment in abstract thinking, concentration, perception, or learning capacity was found in a prisoner population of heavy cannabis users given a battery of tests sensitive to brain dysfunction.[5] Kroll [26] treated only five patients who were psychiatrically incapacitated by marijuana use, of 45,000 troops in Thailand. Bialos [3] reports only one case of marijuana-related social breakdown during an entire year at a university mental health clinic.

* Supported by Grant DA 4RG010 from the National Institute on Drug Abuse.

In addition to the ambiguities that arise from methodologic problems, other variables may also mitigate against any clear conclusions about chronic marijuana effects. Psychotropic drugs have complex pharmacologic properties that may interact with nonpharmacologic variables, such as personality, social and cultural context,[8] prevailing mood coincident with drug use,[9] dose, quality, and route of administration of the drug, and expectations.[9] It is little wonder, then, that despite recent attempts to describe chronic effects of cannabis, there remains a significant lack of consensus among researchers in the area.

There is somewhat more agreement on the acute behavioral effects of the drug, although here, too, nonpharmacologic variables may play a significant role. Marijuana has been shown to influence short-term memory,[14] selective attention,[15] time estimation,[10] and pain perception.[20] Subjects have been described as apprehensive, euphoric,[1] sedated,[21] and dizzy[38] after acute marijuana doses. It is unclear whether such subjective states are "adverse" or are the reinforcing elements that ensure continued drug use.

In view of the confusion that still surrounds the status of marijuana, there seems to be a clear need for research under controlled conditions where subject history is available, where tetrahydrocannabinol (THC) concentration in the marijuana is known, and where data can be collected over a period of time in a relatively controlled environment.

The research design of the present project includes psychologic, physiologic, and social variables. Although there was no attempt to specifically examine or test an amotivational hypothesis, the data to be reported here are relevant to this issue. This report summarizes previous descriptions of individual[33] and group[34] operant behavior.

MATERIALS AND METHODS

Subjects

Twenty-seven young adult male volunteers were selected on the basis of "heavy" or "casual" marijuana use, defined in terms of reported smoking frequency. The two groups were closely matched for age and years of marijuana experience. The 12 "casual" users ($\overline{X}$ age = 23.6 years; range 21–26) reported a mean duration of marijuana use of 5.3 years (range 3–8 years) and a monthly smoking frequency of 11.5 (range ±6.5) marijuana cigarettes during the past year. The 15 "heavy" users ($\overline{X}$ age = 23.2 years; range 21–25) reported a mean duration of marijuana use of 5.6 years (range 3–9 years) and a monthly smoking frequency of 42 (range ±24.5) marijuana cigarettes during the previous year. All subjects were matched as closely as possible with regard to socioeconomic background, general intelligence, and level of educational achievement.

Subjects were recruited through advertisements placed in local periodicals and newspapers. The 27 men studied were selected from more than 300 applicants on the basis of complete psychiatric and medical evaluations. All subjects were in good health and showed no evidence of physical or mental abnormalities, as determined by appropriate clinical and laboratory examinations. Screen tests included a complete physical examination, mental status examination, chest x ray, electrocardiogram, timed vital capacity, intraocular pressure, and the following laboratory analyses: lactic acid dehydrogenase, serum glutamic-oxaloacetic transaminase, total bilirubin, total protein, albumin, globulin, A/G ratio, alkaline phosphatase, uric acid, blood urea nitrogen (BUN), creatinine, glucose, total cholesterol, total lipids, white blood cell, red blood cell, hemoglobin, hematocrit, and differential blood count.

Each subject was fully informed as to the nature and duration of each phase of the study and was told that he could withdraw at any time.

Research Ward

Subjects lived in a research ward throughout the 31-day study. The ward consisted of four individual bedrooms, a nursing station, examining and testing rooms, kitchen and lavatories, and a comfortably furnished dayroom area with television, high fidelity equipment, and a variety of other recreational materials. Subjects also had supervised access to gymnasium facilities and playing fields. Physicians, nursing personnel, and ward assistants were present 24 hr per day.

Procedural Sequence

Each subject was used as his own control in the three consecutive phases of the study: a 5-day baseline, a 21-day marijuana smoking period, and a 5-day postmarijuana control period. During all three phases of the study, subjects had an opportunity to work at a simple operant task to earn points that were exchangeable for money. Money earned could be used to buy marijuana or could be retained by the subject at the conclusion of the study. Subjects had no expenses during the course of the study. During the 21-day smoking period, subjects could buy and smoke marijuana at any time.

Blood samples were collected daily for analysis of testosterone and cortisol. These data have been reported separately.[31] Social interaction patterns, subjective mood reports, food ingestion and body weight, intraocular pressure, studies of chromosomes and white blood cells, hematocrit, reaction time, rotory pursuit, running digit span, visual-motor coordination, electrocardiogram, and cardio-pulmonary function tests were also studied and will be reported elsewhere.

Psychiatric Assessments

Clinical assessments were made by means of a standardized interview schedule in an attempt to minimize observer bias. The instrument chosen was the current section of the Current and Past Psychopathology Scales (CAPPS), developed by Endicott and Spitzer.[16] This instrument has proven sensitive to change over time when applied sequentially. The scale was modified to cover the 16 categories considered relevant to the live-in situation of the research setting. A series of scaled judgments were made for the categories involved and were recorded on the basis of a 6-point scale from none (1) to extreme (6). The period of time assessed was reduced from 30 days in the standard CAPPS to the previous 5 days in our assessments.

The interviews were performed jointly by two staff members who had received personal instruction and reliability training in the administration of the instrument.

The CAPPS assessments were made at the end of the initial 5-day baseline period and again toward the end of the 21-day marijuana acquisition period.

Behavioral Assessments

To earn points for marijuana or money, subjects pressed the response button on a portable operant manipulandum. The portable manipulandum was attached to a movable cable that could be connected to coded terminals located in the bedrooms and in the central dayroom. Consequently, subjects could work wherever and whenever they wished. Programming circuitry recorded correct responses and registered points earned, both in the central data station and in each subject's bedroom.

Response Requirements

To earn points, subjects had to button press on a fixed-interval 1-sec schedule of reinforcement. Only the first response after 1 sec elapsed was recorded as a point by the programming circuitry.

One marijuana cigarette cost 1800 points or 50 cents and could be obtained by 30 min of sustained operant work. In 1 hr, a subject could earn a maximum of 3600 points, which were worth $1.00. The price of marijuana in the research ward was chosen on the basis of the current price prevailing in the Boston metropolitan area at the time.

Whenever a subject purchased a marijuana cigarette, the points spent were immediately deducted from his reinforcement point accumulation. Subjects could work at any time, and a record of their total point accumulation was continuously available.

Marijuana Dosage

Cigarettes that contained approximately 1 g of marijuana were obtained from the National Institute of Drug Abuse (NIDA) in lot standard dosage form. Each 1-g cigarette contained approximately 1.8–2.3% tetrahydrocannabinol (THC), as assayed by the NIDA. Maximal standardization and equivalent dosage and "draw" characteristics of cigarettes were insured by machine rolling. Content analysis confirmed that the THC concentration of the cigarettes remained stable over many months. Actual content analysis of the marijuana by use of Soxhlet and modified Lerner extraction procedures was as follows (% ± SD): cannabidiol, $0.18 \pm 0.04\%$; Δ^8-THC, $0.002 \pm 0.002\%$; Δ^9-THC, $2.06 \pm 0.08\%$; cannabinol, $0.08 \pm 0.12\%$.

Smoking Controls

All marijuana smoking had to be done at the time of cigarette purchase, under the observation of a staff member. Unused portions of smoked marijuana cigarettes were returned to the staff to ensure that the "roaches" were removed by the inpatient hospital research ward; the staff were able to confirm that the subjects did not use drugs other than marijuana.

RESULTS

Marijuana Consumption

There was a clear difference between the smoking patterns of heavy and casual users, indicated by the number of marijuana cigarettes purchased during the 21-day period of marijuana availability (FIGURE 1). Casual users smoked an average of 2.6 cigarettes per day, whereas heavy users averaged 5.7 cigarettes daily. Both groups showed linear increases in consumption as a function of time. Casual users initially purchased an average of two cigarettes per day and increased to slightly less than three per day on Days 21–25. Marijuana purchases by heavy users rose from approximately four cigarettes per day during the initial smoking period to just over six per day on Days 21–25. On the last smoking day (Day 26), marijuana purchases were unusually elevated in both groups, and casual and heavy users consumed an average of 5.8 and 14.3 cigarettes, respectively.

Psychiatric Assessments

FIGURE 2 shows a selected portion of the CAPPS; "daily routine-leisure time impairment" and "retardation-lack of emotion" are two of the 16 categories

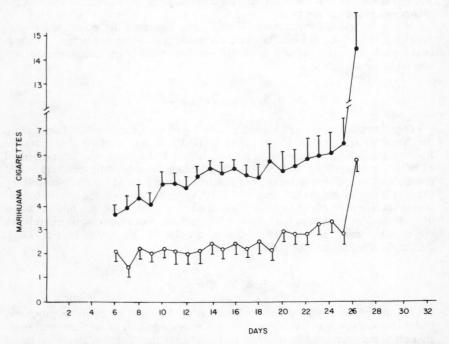

FIGURE 1. Mean (±SE) number of marijuana cigarettes smoked by heavy (●, $n=15$) and casual (○, $n=12$) user groups are presented for consecutive days. Days 1–5 and 27–31 are pre- and postsmoking baseline days, respectively, and are not shown in this Figure (From Mendelson et al.[33] By permission of The Raven Press.)

```
DAILY ROUTINE-LEISURE TIME IMPAIRMENT
The inability or refusal to perform his usual daily
routine activities or to carry through tasks which he
or others expect him to do, and impairment in
pleasure or ability to carry out leisure time activi-
ties. Examples: difficulty getting up or dressed,
can't feed self; confused while traveling, doesn't
enjoy TV anymore, can't concentrate when reading,
too nervous to sew, refuses to make bed. Do
not include impairment in the occupational roles
of student, housekeeper or wage earner.
```

?   1   2   3   4   5   6

```
RETARDATION-LACK OF EMOTION
Observed or reported overt slowing down or lack
of speech or movements; ignoring the surroundings;
lack of emotional expression or response in face,
speech, or gestures.
```

?   1   2   3   4   5   6

FIGURE 2. Two selected items from the Current and Past Psychopathology Scales (CAPPS). The top scale, "daily routine-leisure time impairment" (item 232 on the Psychiatric Evaluation Form—D), is related to the degree of interference of psychopathology in daily routine actvities. The bottom scale, "retardation—lack of emotion" (item 240), is concerned with slowing down of either motor or verbal behavior.

covered by the assessment. The descriptive standards range from mild to severe symptoms and are, therefore, applicable to a wide range of psychiatric disorders. Our objective was not only to define specific symptomatology in these subjects but also to measure any change in a category as a function of 21 days of marijuana use.

TABLE 1 presents the overall mean CAPPS scores of the marijuana users. The presmoking baseline scores are all below 2.00 on the CAPPS scale for both groups, which suggests that the subjects manifested no psychopathology on any of the 16 scales. This result was most probably a reflection of the careful screening procedures that excluded any subjects who showed evidence of psychopathology. In comparison with baseline measures, multiple t tests revealed that casual users showed somewhat more somatic concern toward the end of the marijuana phase, whereas heavy users tended to be more elated with an otherwise flatter affect. Subjects perceived that their ability to complete routine tasks was also somewhat impaired. Changes in categories were never greater than 1.2 scale units and never exceeded 2.50 units in absolute terms.

Operant Analysis

All subjects worked diligently on the operant task (FIGURE 3). Heavy users emitted between 35,000 and 39,000 reinforced responses per day during the baseline (Days 1–5) and marijuana phases (Days 6–26). During the predrug baseline period, casual users emitted reinforced responses at a rate well below that of the heavy user group and worked at even lower rates on initiation of the smoking phase. Casual user rates remained stable during the postdrug period. Heavy users exhibited a dramatic drop in response rate when only

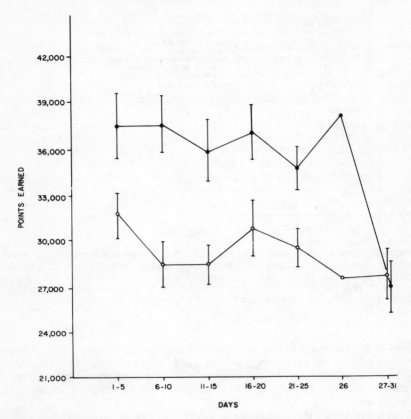

FIGURE 3. Mean (±SE) points earned by heavy (●,$n=15$) and casual (○, $n=12$) user groups are presented for consecutive 5-day periods. Study Day 26, the last day of marijuana availability, is plotted separately.

money was available. Rates for heavy users decreased to approximately 27,000 per day (73% of their initial baseline).

Heavy users saved between $10.00 and $11.00 per day during the predrug phase, as compared to savings of approximately $9.00 for the casual users (TABLE 2). During the 21-day drug phase, heavy user daily earnings gradually decreased from $8.00 saved per day on Days 6–10 to $6.00 per day on Days 21–25. Due to the heavy marijuana consumption on Day 26, heavy users could save only $3.00 of their operant points on that day. Casual users maintained a stable earning pattern from Days 6 to 25, with a drop in savings on Day 26. In the postdrug period, both groups saved approximately equal amounts of money. As seen in subsequent studies, marijuana use often resulted in depressed response rates. Such effects were transient, generally lasting no more than 30 min after marijuana use. Response rates, when affected, decreased as much as 10% from predrug local rates. Rates on Day 27, the first postdrug day, were often sporadic, with very low and high rates occurring throughout the day. By Day 28, local rates recovered to baseline levels.

DISCUSSION

The results of the present study reveal few significant chronic or acute behavioral disturbances in subjects with histories of long-term marijuana use.

Examination of the presmoking baseline scores of the psychiatric assessment scale (TABLE 1) shows that average scores for both groups were well within the range of a normal psychiatric profile. Within our selected sample of subjects with a 5-year smoking history, no significant signs of psychopathology were noted. However, the heavy user group scored higher than casuals on 11 of the 16 assessment categories in the predrug baseline, whereas the casual users scored higher than heavy users on only three of the categories (two were ties). This finding suggests that although the differences between the two groups were clinically minor, there was a trend toward greater psychopathology in subjects with a history of heavy sustained marijuana use. This finding may be even more significant, because subject selection criteria explicitly excluded applicants who had a history of prior psychiatric illness or who manifested grossly deviant behavioral symptoms during the initial interview.

Prolonged marijuana consumption resulted in few category changes in the CAPPS. Casual users showed a small significant change in somatic concern, possibly attributable to the relative lack of stimulation on the ward. Heavy users did not show this effect. The three statistically significant category changes in the heavy user group, increase in elated mood, increased routine-leisure time impairment, and increased lack of emotion, were small from a clinical viewpoint.

TABLE 1

CURRENT AND PAST PSYCHOPATHOLOGY SCALES (CAPPS)

	Moderate Marijuana Users (n=12)		Heavy Marijuana Users (n=15)	
	Presmoking Baseline	Last Week of Smoking	Presmoking Baseline	Last Week of Smoking
Somatic concern	1.13	1.75 *	1.20	1.40
Elated mood	1.38	2.21	1.47	2.27 *
Anxiety	1.25	1.71	1.17	1.27
Depression	1.58	1.96	1.20	1.37
Guilt	1.00	1.00	1.00	1.00
Suicide	1.08	1.21	1.00	1.00
Social isolation	1.88	1.67	1.00	1.03
Suspicion	1.42	1.83	1.03	1.17
Grandiosity	1.38	1.42	1.00	1.00
Hallucinations	1.17	1.00	1.00	1.00
Routine-leisure time impairment	1.42	2.50	1.07	2.17 *
Belligerence	1.33	1.67	1.07	1.47
Retardation-lack of emotion	1.71	1.92	1.23	2.43 *
Agitation	1.38	1.83	1.43	1.57
Disorientation	1.00	1.33	1.00	1.00
Delusion	1.17	1.17	1.00	1.00

* p <0.05.

TABLE 2

MEAN (± SE) DOLLARS SAVED PER DAY BY HEAVY AND CASUAL USER GROUPS PRESENTED IN 5-DAY BLOCKS

	Study Phase (5-day blocks)						
	1–5	6–10	11–15	16–20	21–25	26 *	27–31
Casual users	9.00±0.50	6.80±0.30	6.80±0.40	7.30±0.40	6.80±0.25	4.80	7.70±0.50
Heavy users	10.50±0.60	8.30±0.40	7.40±0.40	7.60±0.50	6.70±0.20	3.60	7.50±0.40

* Study Day 26, the last day of marijuana availability, is listed separately.

The changes in affect and leisure time impairment have also been noted by others. For example, in a 4-year longitudinal study of college student marijuana users, Brill and Christie [4] found that a small percentage of regular users sought advanced degrees as compared to nonusers or occasional users. Only 6% of nonusers reported a deterioration in their emotional state over the previous 4 years versus 10% of regular users and 20% of those who smoked 7 or more years. These findings suggest that either regular marijuana use results in effective problems or that people with emotional problems may use more marijuana than others. As in the present study, Brill and Christie [4] report that the changes were minor. They concluded that there was no general relationship between the degree of marijuana use and the emergence of impaired adaptability.

Examination of the operant data in the present report underscores the weak relationship between degree of use and earnings. Casual and heavy marijuana users continued to work for points for marijuana *and* money throughout the period of marijuana availability, and there appeared to be no exclusive preoccupation with marijuana acquisition and use. Subjects were keenly aware of the amount of money they had accumulated. All subjects earned points far in excess of the number required to purchase the marijuana actually smoked, and, consequently, all saved more dollars per day than were spent on marijuana cigarettes.

Heavy user point totals in the postdrug phase were significantly lower than at any other time in the study, but casual user earnings remained at stable levels. Although this finding appears to be evidence of a withdrawal effect in the heavy user group, other explanations are equally likely. No overt signs of withdrawal were reported by the staff or the subjects, and point earnings remained well above zero at levels similar to the casual users. This finding suggests that removal of marijuana as an available reinforcer for the heavy user subjects may have been a source of the performance decrement. When money alone served as the reinforcer that maintained operant behavior, heavy and casual users performed at similar levels.

Operant data obtained from casual and heavy marijuana users differed strikingly from operant data obtained from alcoholic subjects, physically dependent on alcohol. There was a dramatic dissociation between periods of working for alcohol on a comparable button-pressing manipulandum and periods of alcohol consumption.[30] Despite the simplicity of the operant task, alcoholic subjects abstained while working even to the point of uncomfortable partial withdrawal signs and symptoms, until they earned enough points to support a 2- or 3-day drinking spree. This pattern of alternate periods of working and drinking was then repeated over a 60-day alcohol available period.

It is difficult to determine whether the acute changes observed in local response rates reflect a deterioration in motor control, timing behavior, or some other psychologic function. Reports that ascribe a distorted time sense to marijuana use have been inconsistent. In some cases, errors of estimation were seen at only one of three durations tested,[22] whereas in other reports time judgment was distorted in only one of two testing procedures.[23] The general consensus now appears to be that in both humans [11] and chimpanzees,[12] administration of marijuana or Δ^9-THC results in overestimation of time; the effect is rather weak, however. Carlini *et al.*[10] report that when feedback is introduced into the session, time estimation under THC returns to control levels.

While the acute effects may be attributed to changes in a hypothetical internal timing mechanism, the data can be viewed in terms of drug-related suppression of high response rates. This concept is in agreement with many animal studies that indicate that THC administration results in accelerated responding when baseline rates are low and in depressed responding when baseline rates are high.[17] Procedures used to study timing behavior generally demand very low rates of responding, such as in discrete trial procedures or differential reinforcement of low rate (DRL) schedules (e.g., Reference 7); these procedures tend to result in premature responses that are interpreted as time overestimation. In the present study, high rates of responding occurred and were somewhat depressed after self-administration of the drug. Whether this result was related to timing behavior, motivation to respond, or other variables cannot be determined from the present results.

Although caution should be exercised in interpreting and generalizing from the data of the present report, prior experimental work in this area [32] and observations in natural uncontrolled settings [36, 37] suggest that marijuana-related deficits in work performance are short-lived when they are seen at all. The simple operant task employed in this study was not incompatible with smoking behavior; this was also most probably true of the work tasks measured in the Greek [37] and Jamaican [36] studies. As yet, it is unclear how work output would be affected if smoking and working were made incompatible. Moreover, the extent to which our results may be applicable to sustained performance on a more complex task remains to be determined.

REFERENCES

1. ADAMS, R. 1942. Marihuana. Bull. N.Y. Acad. Med. **18:** 705–730.
2. ALTMAN, H. & R. C. EVENSON. 1973. Marijuana use and subsequent psychiatric symptoms: a replication. Comp. Psychiat. **14:** 415–420.
3. BIALOS, D. 1970. Adverse marihuana reactions: a critical examination of the literature with selected case material. Amer. J. Psychiat. **127:** 819–824.
4. BRILL, N. Q. & R. L. CHRISTIE. 1974. Marihuana use and psychosocial adaptation. Arch. Gen. Psychiat. **31:** 713–719.
5. BRUHN, P. & N. MAAGE. 1975. Intellectual and neuropsychological functions in young men with heavy and long-term patterns of drug abuse. Amer. J. Psychiat. **132:** 397–401.
6. CAMPBELL, A. M. G., M. EVANS, J. L. G. THOMPSON & M. J. WILLIAMS. 1971. Cerebral atrophy in young cannabis smokers. Lancet **11:** 1219–1226.
7. CAPPELL, H., C. D. WEBSTER, B. S. HERRING & R. GINSBERG. 1972. Alcohol and marihuana: a comparison of effects on a temporally controlled operant in humans. J. Pharmacol. Exp. Ther. **182:** 195–203.
8. CAPPELL, H. & P. PLINER. 1973. Volitional control of marijuana intoxication: a study of the ability to "come down" on command. J. Abnormal Psychol. **82:** 428–434.
9. CARLIN, A. S., C. B. BAKKER, L. HALPERN & R. D. POST. 1972. Social facilitation of marijuana intoxication: impact of social set and pharmacological activity. J. Abnormal Psychol. **80:** 132–140.
10. CARLINI, E. A., I. G. KARNIOL, P. F. RENAULT & C. R. SCHUSTER. 1974. Effects of marihuana in laboratory animals and in man. Brit. J. Pharmacol. **50:** 299–309.
11. CLARK, L. D., R. HUGHES & E. N. NAKASHIMA. 1970. Behavioral effects of marihuana: experimental studies. Arch. Gen. Psychiat. **23:** 193–198.
12. CONRAD, D. G., T. F. ELSMERE & F. J. SODETZ. 1972. Δ^9-Tetrahydrocannabinol: dose-related effects on timing behavior in chimpanzee. Science **175:** 547–550.

13. CULVER, C. M. & F. W. KING. 1974. Neuropsychological assessment of undergraduate marihuana and LSD users. Arch. Gen. Psychiat. **31:** 707–711.
14. DARLEY, C. F., J. R. TINKLENBERG, W. T. ROTH & R. C. ATKINSON. 1974. The nature of storage deficits and state-dependent retrieval under marihuana. Psychopharmacologia **37:** 139–149.
15. DITTRICH, A., K. BÄTTIG & I. V. ZEPPELIN. 1973. Effetcs of (−) Δ⁹-trans-tetrahydrocannabinol (Δ⁹THC) on memory, attention and subjective state. Psychopharmacologia **33:** 369–376.
16. ENDICOTT, J. & R. L. SPITZER. 1972. Current and past psychopathology scales: rationale, reliability and validity. Arch. Gen. Psychiat. **27:** 678–684.
17. FRANKENHEIM, J. M., D. E. MCMILLAN & L. S. HARRIS. 1971. Effects of L-Δ⁹ and L-Δ⁸ trans-tetrahydrocannabinol and cannabinol on schedule-controlled behavior of pigeons and rats. J. Pharmacol. Exp. Ther. **178:** 241–252.
18. GRINSPOON, L. 1970. The psychiatric aspects of the use of marihuana. Paper presented at American Psychiatric Association, San Francisco, Calif.
19. HALIKAS, J. A., G. W. GOODWIN & S. B. GUZE. 1972. Marihuana use and psychiatric illness. Arch. Gen. Psychiat. **27:** 162–165.
20. HILL, S. Y., R. SCHWIN, D. W. GOODWIN & B. J. POWELL. 1974. Marihuana and pain. J. Pharmacol. Exp. Ther. **188:** 415–418.
21. HOLLISTER, L. E., R. K. RICHARDS & H. K. GILLESPIE. 1968. Comparisons of tetrahydrocannabinol and synhexyl in man. Clin. Pharmacol. Ther. **9:** 783–791.
22. HOLLISTER, L. & H. K. GILLESPIE. 1970. Marihuana, ethanol, and dextroamphetamine: mood and mental functions. Arch. Gen. Psychiat. **23:** 199–203.
23. JONES, R. T. & G. C. STONE. 1970. Psychological studies of marihuana and alcohol in man. Psychopharmacologia **18:** 108–117.
24. KEELER, M. H. 1967. Adverse reactions to marihuana. Amer. J. Psychiat. **124:** 674–677.
25. KOLANSKY, H. & W. T. MOORE. 1972. Toxic effects of chronic marihuana use. J. Amer. Med. Ass. **222:** 35–41.
26. KROLL, P. 1975. Psychoses associated with marihuana use in Thailand. J. Nervous Mental Disease **161:** 149–156.
27. KUPFER, D. J., D. DETRE, J. KORAL & P. FAJANS. 1973. A comment on the "amotivational syndrome" in marijuana smokers. Amer. J. Psychiat. **130:** 1319–1322.
28. MARCUS, A. M., H. KOLONOFF & M. LOW. 1974. Psychiatric status of the marihuana user. Can. Psychiat. Ass. J. **19:** 31–39.
29. MCGLOTHLIN, W. H. & L. J. WEST. 1968. The marihuana problem: an overview. Amer. J. Psychiat. **125:** 370–378.
30. MELLO, N. K. & J. H. MENDELSON. 1972. Drinking patterns during work contingent and non-contingent alcohol acquisition. Psychosomat. Med. **34:** 139–164.
31. MENDELSON, J. H., J. C. KUEHNLE, J. ELLINGBOE & T. F. BABOR. 1974. Plasma testosterone levels before, during and after chronic marihuana smoking. N. Engl. J. Med. **291:** 1051–1055.
32. MENDELSON, J. H., A. M. ROSSI & R. E. MEYER. (Eds.) 1974. The Use of Marihuana: A Psychological and Physiological Inquiry. Plenum Publishing Corporation. New York, N.Y.
33. MENDELSON, J. H., J. C. KUEHNLE, I. GREENBERG & N. K. MELLO. 1975. The effects of marihuana use on human operant behavior: individual data. *In* The Pharmacology of Marihuana. M. C. Braude & S. Szara, Eds. The Raven Press. New York, N.Y.
34. MENDELSON, J. H., J. C. KUEHNLE, I. GREENBERG & N. K. MELLO. 1976. Operant acquisition of marihuana in man. J. Pharmacol. Exp. Ther. In press.
35. ROBBINS, P. R. & R. H. TANCK. 1973. Psychological correlates of marihuana use: an exploratory study. Psychol. Rep. **33:** 703–706.

36. RUBIN, V. & L. COMITAS. 1975. Ganja in Jamaica. *In* A Medical Anthropological Study of Chronic Marihuana Use. Mouton. Paris, France.
37. STEFANIS, C., R. DORNBUSH & M. FINK. 1976. Hashish! A Study of Long-Term Use. The Raven Press. New York, N.Y. In press.
38. WASKOW, I. E., J. E. OLSSON, C. SALZMAN & M. M. KATZ. 1970. Psychological effects of tetrahydrocannabinol. Arch. Gen. Psychiat. **22:** 97–107.

CANNABIS AND ALCOHOL EFFECTS ON ASSAULTIVENESS IN ADOLESCENT DELINQUENTS *

J. R. Tinklenberg, W. T. Roth, B. S. Kopell, and P. Murphy

Department of Psychiatry and Behavioral Sciences
Stanford University School of Medicine
Stanford, California 94305
and Veterans Administration Hospital
Palo Alto, California 94304

INTRODUCTION

Over the past 10 years, an increase in the consumption of cannabis by young people in the United States has occurred concurrently with an increase in assaultive crimes and other forms of antisocial behavior. Because these two behaviors have a temporal relationship, the following question arises: Does cannabis directly contribute to assaultive behavior? To test this possibility empirically, we have systematically investigated drug use patterns among delinquents incarcerated in a California Youth Authority facility. These incarcerated youths have exhibited criminal behavior and have extensively used cannabis, alcohol, and many other psychoactive substances. Thus, any specific relationships between the use of cannabis, alcohol, or other drugs and aggressive or other forms of aberrant behavior might be discernible among this population. Alcohol, a drug frequently linked with assaultive behavior,[1] is included in this paper for particular comparison.

We will address the following possible interactions between specific drugs and deviant behavior:

In comparison to alcohol, how frequently was cannabis actually involved in fights, driving accidents, problems with family or friends, and other difficulties?

In comparison to alcohol, how did our subjects perceive cannabis to alter assaultive tendencies?

Was cannabis deliberately used to augment or to suppress aggressive behavior?

SUBJECTS

The subjects of this investigation were 248 male adolescents imprisoned during June 1973 to July 1975 at the moderate-security Northern California Youth Authority facilities. They were selected from three different inmate groups: physically assaultive delinquents, sexual offenders, and offenders who had never been charged with or convicted of any assaultive or sexual crimes but who had committed other offenses. Preliminary analyses indicated no

* Supported by the Drug Abuse Council, Inc., Washington, D.C., National Institute on Drug Abuse Contract 271–76–3113, National Institute of Mental Health Grant AA–00397, and the Veterans Administration.

marked differences among these groups in relation to the issues addressed in this paper, so they were consolidated into a single sample. These subjects are representative of the most serious youthful offenders in California. Most delinquents in the state are handled by probation or other community procedures, and severely psychiatrically disturbed youths or major security risks, who comprise about 2–3% of youths convicted of serious crimes, are ineligible for these facilities.

TABLE 1 shows that the median age of the subjects at the time of their present commitment offense was 17.1 years, with a range of 13–21 years. This age group uses many different types of psychoactive drugs and also contributes disproportionately to violent crime.[2] The ethnic composition of this sample was 37% Black, 34% Caucasian, 28% Mexican-American, and 2% other. Ethnic variables were not significant for most issues addressed in this paper. A majority of the subjects were from lower socioeconomic urban backgrounds and had spent most of their adolescence in California.

SOURCES

Data were obtained from two sources: a semistructured, private interview conducted by either an experienced psychiatrist or a professional interviewer and concurrent analyses of official documents, such as police records and laboratory reports. This form of corroboration, which permits immediate cross-validation and resolution of discrepancies, was used to maximize validity. Interview reports had to coincide closely with official records; if the two sources were discordant, these data were not used.

Respondents were told the purpose of the study and that the information they furnished was purely voluntary and completely anonymous. The youths

TABLE 1

DEMOGRAPHIC INFORMATION

(N=248)		n	%
Ethnic Background			
Caucasian		83	33.5
Black		91	36.7
Mexican-American		69	27.8
Other		5	2.0
Total		248	100.0
Age at Time of Offense (years)			
Median age	17.1		
Range	13–21		
Size of Hometown			
Central city		145	58.5
Urban fringe		43	17.3
Small town		51	20.6
Rural		5	2.0
Migrant		4	1.6
Total		248	100.0

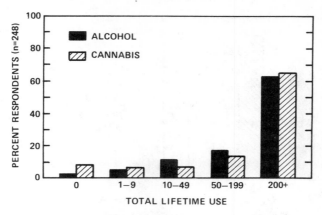

FIGURE 1. Frequency of alcohol and cannabis usage.

knew that the investigators were associated with Stanford University and could not influence treatment conditions or length of incarceration. Only two subjects refused to be interviewed. To further reduce possible distortion and denial, all interviews were conducted at least 6 months after arrest. Our experiences and those of others indicate that denial is often maximal immediately after arrest, especially regarding sexual offenses, and that initial verbal reports of drug use during criminal activities are sometimes erroneous.[3] However, denial usually dissipates during the first 4–6 months of incarceration, perhaps because inmates learn from each other that their crucial concern, the time of their release, is not determined by specific details of their commitment offense, such as drug involvement, but by the general nature of their crime, their performance within the institution, and the prevailing policies of the parole board. At the time of interview, our subjects seemed candid about their behavior and usually either confirmed the official records or described the official records as underreporting their drug use and the involvement of drugs in the commitment offense.

Throughout the study, we had excellent cooperation from the California Youth Authority, which was able to provide important ancillary information concerning the precise details of the offense. The personnel of the Youth Authority made it clear to the respondents that their participation was voluntary and would not influence their treatment.

RESULTS

FIGURE 1 shows the lifetime frequency of cannabis and alcohol use. Both of these drugs are illegal in California for individuals under the age of 21. These frequency figures are composed of the cumulative number of "episodes of use," which were defined as periods of being continuously "high," under the influence of the drug, without "coming down to your usual nondrug self." These data indicate that the subjects used cannabis and alcohol at approximately the same frequency.

FIGURE 2 buttresses the reliability of the cannabis and alcohol frequency data. Responses to a separate question, "Which have you used more times,

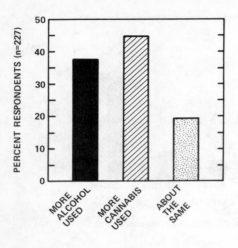

FIGURE 2. Comparative usage of alcohol and cannabis.

marijuana or alcohol—or did you use them about the same?" also indicate approximately equivalent use of each drug. From these two separate sets of information on lifetime frequency of drug use, one can infer an equal *potential* for the involvement of both cannabis and alcohol in the subjects' behavior. Useful perspectives can be obtained by juxtaposing these frequency of use data with the frequency of drug-related problems described next.

FIGURE 3 depicts the relative involvement of cannabis and alcohol in five types of behavioral problems: medical complications, substantial troubles with their friends or difficulties with their families, trouble at school or work, automobile accidents or arrests for intoxicated driving, and arrests for public intoxication or disorderly conduct. Although the lifetime frequencies of use are about equal, alcohol was more often linked with each of these problem areas. These

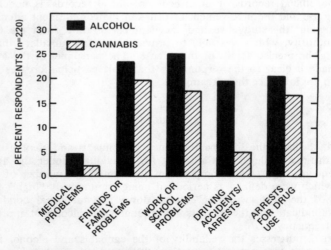

FIGURE 3. Problems that result from drug usage.

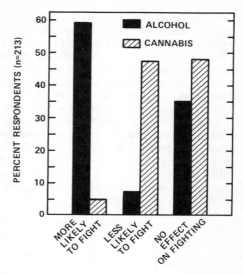

FIGURE 4. Perception of drug influence on fighting.

and other results were assessed by chi/square analysis with the level of significance set at $\alpha = 0.01$ because of the large samples. Alcohol was significantly more involved in driving difficulties ($\chi^2(2) = 28.5$, $p < 0.001$).

FIGURE 4 shows the response to the following questions: "When you were using marijuana (or drinking), would you be more likely to get into a fight than when you were sober (straight), less likely, or would using marijuana (drinking) have no effect whatever on whether you got into a fight?" To reduce any response set, the marijuana question and the alcohol question were asked in different parts of the interview. While alcohol was perceived to increase the probability of fighting, cannabis reportedly had no effect or reduced the likelihood. This difference between alcohol and cannabis was significant ($\chi^2(2) = 592$, $p < 0.001$).

These self-perceptions of drug effects and assaultiveness were consistent with the subjects' actual behavior. FIGURE 5 shows the reported number of times

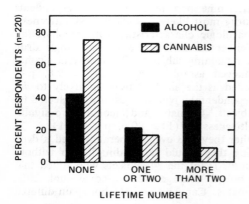

FIGURE 5. Actual fights during intoxication.

cannabis or alcohol was involved in actual fights during the individual's life. Again, the questions were asked at different parts of the interview so as to reduce response set. Fifty-nine percent of the 220 respondents reported one or more fights while under the influence of alcohol, whereas 25% reported one or more fights under the influence of cannabis ($\chi^2(2) = 107$, p < 0.001).

To enlarge the scope of comparison and assess internal reliability, we asked these delinquent subjects, most of whom had used a wide variety of drugs, how they expected other drugs they had used had altered their propensities for assaultive behavior. Specifically, they were asked: "Of all the drugs you have tried, which one drug made you the most likely to get into a fight or hit someone when you were mad or angry?" and "Of all the drugs you have tried, which one drug helped you calm down—'cool it'—when you got angry or mad, so you didn't get into a fight?" Those people who had had experience with only one drug were excluded from the analysis. The drugs identified by the multiple drug

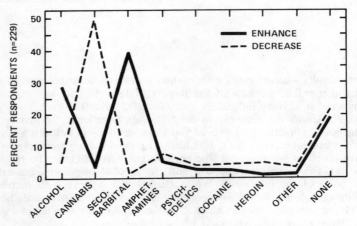

FIGURE 6. Drug identified as most likely to alter assaultiveness.

users are shown in FIGURE 6. Thirty-nine percent of the 229 respondents identified secobarbital as the single drug most likely to *enhance* assaultiveness. Alcohol, which shares many pharmacologic characteristics with secobarbital, was in second place, with 28%. Neither cannabis nor any other single drug was chosen by more than 5% of the remaining subjects. Cannabis and alcohol again differed significantly on enhanced assaultiveness ($\chi^2(1) = 45.8$, p < 0.001). Conversely, cannabis was cited as the single drug most likely to *decrease* assaultiveness (49% of the respondents). No other drug was selected by more than 7% of the remaining subjects. Cannabis and alcohol were significantly different on decreased assaultiveness ($\chi^2(1) = 80.6$, p < 0.001).

We also asked our subjects whether they had ever deliberately used a drug to "get up" courage to do something they would not ordinarily do without drugs. The results are shown in FIGURE 7: of the 84 subjects who stated that they had used drugs specifically to bolster courage, 42% used alcohol, 20% used secobarbital, and 16% used cannabis. Cannabis and alcohol again differed

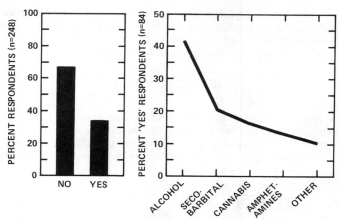

FIGURE 7. Drugs used to bolster courage.

statistically ($\chi^2(1) = 10.1$, $p < 0.005$). The converse information is provided in FIGURE 8, which shows data from the following questions: "Have you ever taken any drugs for the specific purpose of keeping you calm so that you wouldn't get into a fight" and "Have you ever used any drugs for the purpose of keeping you out of trouble?" Twenty-four subjects used cannabis for such tranquilizing purposes, and four used alcohol ($\chi^2(1) = 14.3$, $p < 0.001$).

The final measurement of drug involvement in assaultive behavior is shown in FIGURE 9. Unlike FIGURE 5, the question described in this Figure compared all drugs and focused on a specific 1-year period. The subjects were asked to recall each fight they had had in the year immediately prior to their present incarceration. Except for a few individuals who fought very frequently, most subjects could recall these fights with considerable clarity. Each subject was then asked to describe the drug involvement, if any, in each of those fights.

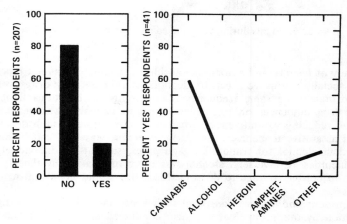

FIGURE 8. Drugs used for calming effects.

Twenty-nine percent of the fights were reported as involving only alcohol; 2% of the fights involved cannabis alone ($\chi^2(1) = 33.9$, $p < 0.001$). Of interest is the fact that alcohol-related fights were reported as more frequent than fights that occurred in a nondrug state, whereas with cannabis the opposite obtained.

COMMENT

In this study of California youth who had demonstrated both delinquent behavior and intensive use of a variety of psychoactive drugs, one finding is that, in comparison with alcohol, cannabis was underrepresented in a variety of behavioral problems: fights, difficulties with police and other authorities, trouble

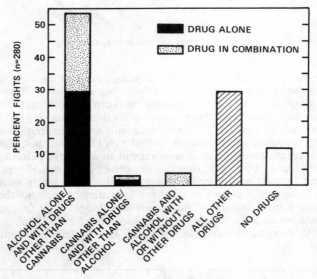

FIGURE 9. Fights during year immediately prior to incarceration.

with family or friends, and automobile accidents. Cannabis was not reported to have the socially disruptive effects of alcohol, even though both drugs were used at approximately the same frequency. On a range of questions designed to measure drug influences on aggressive behavior, cannabis was generally described as reducing assaultiveness, whereas alcohol either had little effect or increased assaultive tendencies. Similarly, cannabis was used much more frequently than alcohol for tranquilizing purposes, so that the individual would avoid difficulties. Conversely, alcohol was more often used by these youthful offenders to bolster courage to do something they would not do in a nondrug state.

The present findings are consistent with a previous 1971–1972 drug-crime investigation by our group that was also conducted at a Northern California Youth Authority facility.[4, 5] An assaultive group of 50 subjects convicted of crimes that involved actual tissue damage was compared for patterns of drug use with a matched group of 80 incarcerated subjects never charged or convicted of violent crimes. Fifty-six assaults committed by the 50 assaultive subjects were examined for specific drug involvement. Two (6%) of the 36 drug-related assaults involved cannabis alone or combined with drugs other than alcohol, whereas 19 (53%) of the drug-related assaults involved alcohol alone or in combination with drugs other than cannabis. The comparatively low incidence of cannabis involvement in criminal aggression among those 1971–72 subjects is emphasized by the fact that their median lifetime usage of cannabis for that group was greater than that of alcohol. Cannabis was also identified in that study as the single drug most likely to *decrease* the possibility of violence. Furthermore, because the nonassaultive subjects had used cannabis more often, the overall extent of cannabis use was not a positive predictor of assaultive crime, as would be expected if cannabis per se directly contributed to aggressiveness.

Several other field studies on the relationship between cannabis and various types of human aggression have been conducted in the last few decades; these studies have also indicated that cannabis is seldom associated with the augmentation of human aggression.[6] In a large-scale interview study of young men in West Philadelphia, there was no evidence that cannabis use directly contributed to criminal activity.[7] The 559 respondents generally denied any criminogenic effects from cannabis, and nearly all reported no aggressive behavior during cannabis intoxication. One extensive assessment of drug-crime interactions was made by Eckerman *et al.*,[3] who conducted interviews, urine analyses, and record searches on a systematic sample of 1889 individuals arrested during 1971 in six separate metropolitan areas of the United States. Unfortunately, alcohol was not included as a comparison drug in this study. Their results did indicate that cannabis users were less frequently arrested for aggravated assaults and other assaults than were noncannabis users.

Attempts to study the effects of cannabis on various components of human aggression in laboratory settings have obvious limitations. Nevertheless, it is worth noting that many findings in experimental laboratory investigations are consistent with the results from field research. Moderate doses of cannabis generally induce a reduction in inclination toward extreme physical effort,[8] a reduction in tendencies toward intense social interaction,[9] an increase in positive mood states,[10] a reduction in hostility,[11] and a reduction in tendencies toward inflicting pain on others.[12] In contrast, laboratory studies indicate that alcohol can augment human aggression.[13]

In summary, there is no evidence that an increase in violent crime is directly related to the increase in cannabis use; in fact, considerable evidence suggests that cannabis often decreases assaultive tendencies. In contrast, alcohol is frequently linked with aggressive behavior.

REFERENCES

1. TINKLENBERG, J. R. 1973. Alcohol and violence. *In* Alcoholism: Progress in Research and Treatment. P. G. Bourne & R. Fox, Eds., 195–210. Academic Press, Inc. New York, N.Y.
2. NATIONAL COMMISSION ON THE CAUSES AND PREVENTION OF VIOLENCE. 1970. Final report. To establish justice, to insure domestic tranquility. United States Government Printing Office. Washington, D.C.

3. ECKERMAN, W. C., J. D. BATES, J. V. RACHEL & W. K. POOLE. 1971. Drug usage and arrest charges among arrestees in six metropolitan areas of the United States. Department of Justice, Bureau of Narcotics and Dangerous Drugs. United States Government Printing Office. Washington, D.C.

4. TINKLENBERG, J. R. & K. M. WOODROW. 1974. Drug use among youthful assaultive and sexual offenders. Res. Publ. Ass. Res. Nervous Mental Disease 52: 209–224.

5. TINKLENBERG, J. R., P. L. MURPHY, P. MURPHY, C. F. DARLEY, W. T. ROTH & B. S. KOPELL. 1974. Drug involvement in criminal assaults by adolescents. Arch. Gen. Psychiat. 30: 685–689.

6. TINKLENBERG, J. R. 1974. Marijuana and human aggression. In Marijuana: Effects on Human Behavior. L. L. Miller, Ed. : 339–357. Academic Press, Inc. New York, N.Y.

7. GOODE, E. 1972. Appendix. In Marihuana: A Signal of Misunderstanding. The Technical Papers of the First Report of the National Commission on Marihuana and Drug Abuse. Vol. 1: 446–469. United States Government Printing Office. Washington, D.C.

8. HOLLISTER, L. E., R. K. RICHARDS & H. K. GILLESPIE. 1968. Comparison of tetrahydrocannabinol and synhexyl in man. Clin. Pharmacol. Ther. 9(6): 783–791.

9. BABOR, T. F. 1973. Studies of group behavior. Psychopharmacol. Bull. 9(4): 51, 52.

10. MENDELSON, J. H. & R. E. MEYER. 1972. Appendix. In Marihuana: A Signal of Misunderstanding. The Technical Papers of the First Report of the National Commission on Marihuana and Drug Abuse. Vol. 1: 68–246. United States Government Printing Office. Washington, D.C.

11. SALZMAN, C., G. E. KOCHANSKY & L. J. PORRINO. 1973. The effect of marijuana on hostility in an experimental group setting: preliminary observations. Psychopharmacol. Bull. 9(4): 54, 55.

12. BLOOM, R. 1972. The effects of tetrahydrocannabinol on aggression in humans. Ph.D. Dissertation. University of Georgia. Athens, Georgia.

13. BOYATZIS, R. E. 1974. The effect of alcohol consumption on the aggressive behavior of men. Quart. J. Studies Alc. 35: 959–972.

PSYCHOCLINICAL EFFECTS OF LONG-TERM MARIJUANA USE IN 275 INDIAN CHRONIC USERS. A COMPARATIVE ASSESSMENT OF EFFECTS IN INDIAN AND USA USERS

Gurbakhsh S. Chopra and Balwant S. Jandu

Drug Addiction Clinic & Hastings Research Center
Nabha and Patiala Field Centers
Calcutta 22, India

INTRODUCTION

The use of marijuana has aroused horror and rejection as well as adulation in the world. The present widespread use of the drug is a worldwide phenomenon. No caste, creed, nation, or country is free from its use. There are divergent views about its long-term effects. Despite keen public and professional interest in the adverse reactions and complications that result from chronic use of cannabis drugs, the description and documentation of associated medical and psychic effects have seldom gone beyond generalizations. This study will report on 275 chronic cannabis users and also on 17 alienated youths ("hippies") from America and Europe who had come from Nepal to India and smoked or consumed cannabis drugs regularly for periods of 6 months to several years. They volunteered information and submitted to examination. The studies were conducted in original settings at places of indulgence and work.

METHODOLOGY

The subjects were examined immediately after they had taken the drug and also after its effects had disappeared. Routine physical and neurologic examinations were performed, during which the individuals were subjected to intense interviews concerning the history of drug abuse, dose, frequency of use, duration, family, friends, interest in work, and their own assessment of the effects of marijuana. The subjects were also evaluated with respect to personality, mood, attitudes, and emotional stability.

Clinical Groups

Considering that the Indian and Nepali marijuana used in India is approximately equal in potency to the Mexican plant, which contains 1.47% Δ^9-tetrahydrocannabinol (Δ^9-THC), TABLE 1 lists the mean daily dose of the subjects as calculated in equivalents of Δ^9-THC content. The subjects were divided into four groups according to age, dose, and duration of use. Educational and vocational and income data are presented in TABLES 2 and 3, respectively.

95

TABLE 1

DOSE, AGE, AND DURATION

Group	Sample No.	Mean Age (years)	Mean Duration (years)	Mean Daily Dose of Δ^9-THC (mg)
I	56	48.5	27.1	350
II	58	29.7	7.0	150
III	72	19.1	3.5	75
IV	89	17.2	2.1	40

* *Bhang, ganja,* and *charas* were assessed and found to contain about 1, 3, and 5% by weight of Δ^9-THC, respectively.

TABLE 2

EDUCATIONAL LEVELS

Group	Sample No.	Uneducated No.	%	High School * No.	%	University No.	%
I	56	40	71.42	16	28.57	—	—
II	58	32	55.17	18	31.03	8	13.79
III	72	20	27.77	45	62.50	7	9.72
IV	89	17	19.10	30	33.70	42	47.19
Total	275	109	39.63	109	39.63	57	20.72

* Fifteen hippies were high-school dropouts, and two were high-school graduates.

TABLE 3

VOCATIONS AND INCOME

Vocation	Number	Percent	Average Monthly Income (US dollars)
No income, beggars	26	9.45	0
Religious mendicants	25	9.09	25
Priests	20	7.27	31
Laborers	80	29.09	40
Artisans	46	16.72	50
Semiskilled workers	35	12.72	40
Skilled workers	15	5.45	65
Students	22	8.01	dependent on parents
White-collar workers	6	2.18	75

RESULTS

Subjective Assessment of Physical Health

The subjects' assessments of the effects of marijuana on their general health and working capacity are listed in TABLE 4. The 29.09% from the younger groups who used smaller doses believed that the drug had no adverse effect on their health. In 23.60% of the cases, health was thought to be impaired to a minor degree, whereas 43.63% complained of a marked degree of impairment in their general health and working capacity. The remaining 10 (3.68%) thought that their health and working capacity had improved.

TABLE 4

SUBJECTIVE ASSESSMENT OF PHYSICAL HEALTH

Group	Number	Mean Daily Dose of Δ^9-THC (mg)	No Adverse Effect on Health	Minor Impairment	Marked Impairment	Improvement
I	56	350	26 (32.50) *	18 (27.69)	50 (41.56)	
II	58	150	13 (16.25)	28 (43.07)	35 (29.16)	
III	72	75	22 (27.50)	5 (7.5)	25 (20.88)	6 (60)
IV	89	40	19 (23.75)	14 (21.53)	10 (8.3)	4 (40)
Total	275		80 (29.09)	65 (23.6)	120 (43.63)	10 (3.63)

* Figures within parentheses are percentages.

Effects of habitual indulgence in cannabis drugs on general health (TABLE 5) were generally minor, taking into consideration the poor nutrition and insanitary health conditions in which the Indian marijuana users live, when compared to the effects of other psychotoxic drugs, including alcohol. The former included respiratory disorders, such as laryngitis, pharyngitis, asthma, irritation cough, and dyspnea. The gastrointestinal system was seldom involved, although there were instances of increased appetite, dyspepsia, and minor liver damage. In the long-standing cases, there was evidence of malnutrition, anemia, poor skin condition, and congestion of ciliary vessels, sometimes with discoloration of the conjunctiva due to prolonged congestion. All of the effects were more pronounced in the first two groups, which was comprised of older individuals taking large drug doses over prolonged periods.

TABLE 5

GENERAL SYSTEMIC EFFECTS (SAMPLE 275)

Effects	Group				Total
	I	II	III	IV	
Malnutrition, anemia, asthenia, sallow complexion	15 *	7	2	—	24
	(5.45)†	(2.54)	(0.72)	—	(8.62)
Conjunctival vessels, congestion, discloration of conjunctiva	38	13	5	—	56
	(13.81)	(4.72)	(0.18)	—	(20.25)
Respiratory disorders, pharyngitis, dryness of throat, chronic bronchitis	58	23	8	—	89
	(21.09)	(8.35)	(2.90)	—	(32.36)
Gastrointestinal disorders, indigestion, unduly increased appetite, diarrhea	17	8	4	—	29
	(6.18)	(2.90)	(1.45)	—	(10.54)
Poor condition of skin, sallow muddy complexion	51	30	23	6	110
	(18.54)	(10.9)	(8.36)	(2.18)	(40.0)

* Number.
† Percent.

Psychopharmacologic Effects of Daily Doses in Chronic Users

TABLE 6 summarizes the effects and symptoms observed in each group with controlled doses. Most of the subjects in our present series took the drug with the objective of attaining a mild sense of intoxication, a relaxation of feelings toward sociability. The environment had a pronounced effect on the general trend of the subjective symptoms. Even though the doses were regulated, adverse reactions occurred in some individuals. These reactions are listed in TABLE 6.

Adverse psychic effects were found to occur with a greater incidence in the younger groups, which included subjects with mean ages between 19.1 and 17.2 years. Some of these younger subjects had histories of childhood neurosis, psychopathic personality, deviancy, and anxiety. They took the drug to stabilize these conditions and to regain self-confidence.

Psychologic Reactions When the Daily Dose Was Exceeded

Numerous addicts were contacted in the same region. Eighty-five subjects were found who had taken the drug in larger than the usual doses and were in a state of acute intoxication. TABLE 7 shows the adverse psychiatric reactions that occurred and the mean doses necessary to elicit each reaction, with the durations and doses specified. It can be seen that the type and intensity of the reaction varied with the dosage. As previously reported, prolonged marijuana use in larger doses may induce psychosis in individuals with low psychotic thresholds. It may also produce hallucinations and psychomimetic effects, as seen in stage of acute intoxication. There were wide variations in reactions among different individuals and within the same individual. The variations can be attributed to dosage, mood, personality, and preexisting psychopathology.

In all cases, the reactions subsided when the individual was no longer under the influence of the drug. Abnormal reactions that occur after large doses are manifestations of a temporary effect on the cerebral cells, whose physiologic activities are either maintained at a status quo or are partially or totally disorganized. This distorted action of the cerebral cells causes the higher control centers to be activated, thus allowing the senses to be more easily influenced by the preexisting personality traits or external stimuli. When the drug is absorbed into the system, it does not add any new elements to the brain; it only removes the higher control activity and excites the preexisting trend of mental abberrations, if any.

Long-Term Effects

During these investigations, relatives, friends, and employers of these addicts were contacted. They gave information regarding the daily lives of the subjects, the extent of their family interest, their attitudes toward society, and their interest in work. The subjects were examined several times by a sociologist and a psychiatrist. TABLE 8 summarizes these observations.

It is obvious that persons from groups I and II were more involved with the drug. Those in groups III and IV were younger, had used marijuana for a shorter period, and were taking smaller doses. Continued states of intoxica-

TABLE 6

PSYCHOLOGIC REACTIONS WITH CONTROLLED DAILY DOSES (SAMPLE 275)

Reactions	Group				Total
	I	II	III	IV	
Prolonged sense of well-being with euphoria	50 *	34	59	24	167
	(18.18) †	(12.35)	(21.45)	(8.72)	(60.72)
Weakening of inhibitions, false sense of ability to perform physical and intellectual duties	20	12	8	9	49
	(7.27)	(4.35)	(2.90)	(3.27)	(17.81)
Amotivation, self-neglect, dirty habits	15	4	2	—	21
	(5.45)	(1.45)	(0.72)	—	(7.63)
Release of social inhibitions	50	30	23	21	124
	(18.18)	(10.90)	(8.35)	(7.63)	(45.09)
Amnesia	58	23	7	4	92
	(21.09)	(8.35)	(2.54)	(1.45)	(33.45)
Partial loss of sense of time and space, mild degree of confusion	5	4	6	—	15
	(1.8)	(1.45)	(2.18)	—	(5.45)
	18	2	2	—	22
	(6.54)	(9.72)	(0.72)	—	(8.0)
Increased sexual drive	30	15	8	15	68
	(10.90)	(5.45)	(2.90)	(5.45)	(24.72)
Hallucinations and delusions	5	4	—	—	9
	(1.80)	(1.45)	—	—	(3.27)

* Number.
† Percent.

TABLE 7

PSYCHOLOGIC REACTIONS WITH HIGHER DOSES

Reactions	Number	Percent	Mean Dose of Δ⁹-THC (mg)	Approximate Duration
Elation, feeling of happiness, weakening of inhibition, false sense of security	10	11.75	100	0.5–2 hr
Amnesia	6	7.05	100	0.5–6 hr
Release of repressed behavior, occasionally hostile and violent	16	18.82	105	2–3 hr
Mild degree of confusion	10	11.75	75	10–24 hr
Loss of control, staggering gait, loss of coordination of muscular movements, slurred speech, dizziness	7	8.23	175	1–2 hr
Disorientation, depersonalization	2	2.35	175	0.5–2 hr
Hallucinations and delusions	4	4.70	180	0.5–36 hr
Amotivation, lethargy, self-neglect, general apathy	10	11.75	110	4–24 hr
Schizophrenia	6	7.05	190	several days
Paranoia of a minor degree	1	1.17	100	several days
Depressions of short duration	4	4.70	90	4 days
Anxiety	3	3.52	110	a few to 36 hr
Agitation	1	1.17	150	2 days
Acute brain syndrome	1	1.17	200	4–6 days
Criminal and aggressive tendencies	4	4.70	85	more or less permanent change in personality

tion, present in some individuals at some times, led to a state of confusion, manifested by disturbances in performance of their physical and intellectual work or duties. Little or no gross damage was noticed in the last two groups. More individuals in groups I and II showed a lack of initiation, motivation, and interest in their work and family. The work performed by these individuals while under the influence of the drug was not up to normal standards, as compared with that of a control group composed of individuals from the same area and of same general characteristics.

Behavioral Changes

Amotivational Syndrome

Chronic cannabis use in heavy doses affects the central nervous system. The changes are related to the type of dose and the setting in which the drug is taken. Overall, the picture is one of depression and apathy, but continued repeatedly higher doses sometimes may produce increased locomotor activity and aggressive behavior. Subjects who take smaller doses tend to be quiet, apathetic, and disinterested in their surroundings; these changes are followed by permanent behavioral alterations, which are more marked under stress, starvation, poor health, and so on, resulting in an "amotivational syndrome." In the present studies, all of the subjects were extensively interviewed and questioned about their goals, interest in life and family, and their attitudes toward Indian society and the world in general. Eighty-two (29.81%) individuals showed behavioral changes (TABLE 8) concerning lack of interest in work and family, a happy-go-lucky attitude, and other personality traits. In addition, 30 (10.90%) individuals, who mostly belonged to lower social strata, such as religious mendicants and other beggars, exhibited an "amotivational syndrome." They were generally ill-nourished and neglectful of personal hygiene. Excessive use is associated with personality inadequacies. Persons who exhibit emotional immaturity, low frustration tolerance, and failure to assume responsibility tended to be overrepresented in groups I and II, the heavy cannabis users. In behavioral terms, these traits are manifested in an unrealistic emphasis on the present as opposed to the future, a tendency to drift along in a passive manner, failure to develop long-term abilities or skills, and a tendency to favor regressive and magical rather than rational thinking processes.

Crime

Cannabis drugs are generally used by the poorer sectors of society, which include a higher percentage of criminals and other disreputable individuals.

TABLE 8

LONG-TERM EFFECTS (SAMPLE 275)

Effects	Group				Total	
	I	II	III	IV	No.	%
Amotivational syndrome	14	12	3	1	30	10.90
Lazy habits, loss of drive	6	7	2	—	15	5.45
Instability and immaturity	7	1	6	2	16	5.81
Short-term amnesia	4	2	3	—	9	3.27
Impairment of intellectual faculties	5	3	—	—	8	2.90
Lack of interest in work and family	9	2	1	5	17	6.18
Change in goals, happy-go-lucky attitude toward life	10	2	6	4	22	8%
Slow breakdown of personality	4	1	1	—	6	2.18
Character changes	8	3	7	2	20	7.27
Suspicious and hypersensitive, easily excited, unreasonable, aggressive	4	5	7	1	17	6.18
Premature senility	2	3	1	1	7	2.54
Status intoxicatus	4	2	—	—	6	2.18
Dementia	2	—	—	—	2	0.72
Criminal tendency	9	5	1	—	15	5.45

Most of their earnings are used for the purchase of drugs at exorbitant prices, through the black market. Little money thus remains for food and daily necessities. In such a situation, some of the heavy and chronic addicts are impelled to steal and commit other crimes to sustain themselves. In such instances, cannabis addiction is indirectly associated with crime. Concerning premeditated crime, cannabis may actually act as a deterrent due to its stupefying and depressive effects. Unlike alcohol, there therefore is little or no feelings in such a mental state toward violence. Another category of chronic cannabis users have personality problems, and exhibit irritable and amotivational behavior, and want to live by themselves quietly, undisturbed, and not interested in violence. Such persons sometimes may become irritable and violent when they feel that their "quiet" life is being disturbed. We came across four such instances among the religious mendicants, who attacked their associates with rods when disturbed under the influence of the drug. They may have been hallucinating or suffering from delusions while performing the acts of violence. TABLE 9 provides an analysis of the statements regarding convictions.

Twenty-six (9.44%) persons, mostly ganja and charas users, admitted having been convicted once. Nineteen (6.88%) stated that they had been convicted more than once. These conviction figures are higher than those for the general population. Ganja and charas users predominated, because the effects are more intense and instantaneous when the drugs are smoked; also, ganja and charas smokers mostly come from the lower sections of society, which has a higher percentage of habitual criminals.

Homicide and Suicide

Cannabis drugs have been used from very ancient times by criminals to fortify themselves for committing premeditated crime and also to enable them to endure unusual fatigue or exposure to inclement weather. Cannabis drugs are rarely used for suicidal or homicidal purposes, in comparison to opium and barbiturates. There are, however, few cases on record in India where ganja or charas was used to stupefy the victims for purposes of theft. It is doubtful that cannabis alone can fulfill this objective, so it is mixed with *dhatura* or *stra-*

TABLE 9

DRUG CONVICTIONS

Drug	Sample No.	No Convictions	One Conviction	More Than One Conviction
Bhang (mean Δ^9-THC): dose, 150 mg; range, 75–200 mg	192	171 * (89.06) †	15 (7.82)	6 (3.12)
Charas and ganja (mean Δ^9-THC): dose, 300 mg; range, 200–350 mg	83	59 (71.08)	11 (13.26)	13 (15.66)
Totals	275	230 (83.63)	26 (9.44)	19 (6.98)

* Number.
† Percent.

TABLE 10

EFFECTS IN CHRONIC USERS

Drug Data	Stimulant	Depressant	Stimulant Earlier and Depressant Later	No Effect
Mostly bhang: mean dose, 150 mg; range, 75–200 mg (sample 83)	33 * (39.75) †	8 (9.36)	19 (22.88)	23 (27.74)
Mostly ganja and charas: mean dose, 300 mg; range, 200–300 mg (sample 192)	29 (15.10)	67 (34.89)	50 (26.06)	46 (23.98)

* Number.
† Percent.

monium to stupefy the victim. There is another preventive factor, in that ganja and charas can be readily detected by their pungent odor. Thus, it is difficult to mix them with tobacco or other substances for the purpose of smoking without fear of detection. Ganja and charas, however, have been employed to stupefy persons who are habituated to their use by secretly mixing potent drugs like dhatura with them. There were three such instances, in which prostitutes were stupefied in this manner and robbed of their jewelry. Similar cases have also been reported among children who were offered sweets that contained bhang or ganja to stupefy them and were robbed of their belongings. Such instances are, however, rare in adults because of easy detection and uncertain action.

In this connection, it may be stated that one of the authors came across an interesting case during his law practice, where the wife of a medical practitioner who was habituated to ganja smoking regularly gave dhatura mixed with ganja to her husband for several years to stupefy him and make him incapable of sexual performance, with the objective that she could enjoy illicit intercourse with her lover. The case is still pending in the court at Patiala.

Sexuality

Aphrodisiac use of cannabis drugs have been reported from very ancient times. It is claimed by younger users that sexual performance and enjoyment are enhanced when under the influence of the drug. The subjective impression of slowing of time might, indeed, confer on the performer a very unusual gratification in an orgasmic experience, if it is extended from 30 sec to 30 min. These effects are more common with a low dosage. When taken in moderate doses, the effects are somewhat similar to those of alcohol: the drug induces the desire but makes performance impossible. The chronic use of the drug leads to a sad condition, where the lack of desire may also be coupled with inability to perform. TABLE 10 summarizes the experience of chronic marijuana users.

Fecundity

The marital histories of 75 chronic marijuana users in the present series who were married and taking the drug prior to marriage and after it were carefully studied. The average duration of use was 10.2 years. Numbers of children and the mean doses are given in TABLE 11. The number of sterile marriages was higher with larger doses. Those who used smaller doses had more children than those who took large doses.

In addition to the information obtained above, the question of fertility was pursued further in 150 subjects in five villages of Patiala who were married or widowers and who were using cannabis prior to marriage or who began to use it soon afterward. The number of children per 100 families was compared to that found in opium users and in the general population. The figures obtained were 344, 273, and 396, respectively. Sterility was found in 2% of the marriages, or almost twice the percentage in the general population but much lower than the 8.4% found among families of opium addicts. It is concluded that the fertility rate is lower than normal among cannabis users but higher than in opium addicts. Also, there was a marked difference between the bhang and the ganja and charas users: 0.4% of the marriages of bhang users were sterile, as opposed to 5.7% of ganja and charas user marriages, and the proportion of families with five or more children was higher in the former than in the latter group. This finding was attributed to the fact that ganja and charas "are mostly taken by sadhus, fakirs, and low-class people with loose morals and high incidence of venereal disease."

Tolerance and Dependence

It was verbally ascertained that subjects acquired tolerance to each dosage within a few days after each increment. In several cases, it developed rapidly and was more marked. These subjects become refractory to the drug, even to the point when toxicity symptoms developed. On withdrawal of the drug, abstinence symptoms occurred, namely, irritability, yawning, loss of appetite, occasional tremors, twitching, cramps, insomnia, and photophobia. Withdrawal symptoms, though mild, developed within a few hours of abstinence and lasted

TABLE 11

CANNABIS AND MARITAL HISTORY

Drug Data	Sterile Marriages	One or Two Children	More Than Three Children
Bhang (mean Δ^9-THC): dose, 150 mg; range, 75–200 mg	1	31	18
Ganja and charas (mean Δ^9-THC): dose, 300 mg; range, 200–350 mg	7	9	9
Totals	8 (10.66)*	40 (53.33)	27 (36.01)

* Percent.

TABLE 12

NEUROLOGIC EFFECTS

Effects	No.	Average Duration
Partial numbness	4	0.5–1 hr
Lack of coordination of muscles, as seen in weakening of hand grip and staggering gait	18	1–2 hr
Increased sense of taste and smell	7	a few minutes
Romberg's sign was positive in individuals who took large doses, and there was difficulty in maintaining the balance	2	a few minutes
Impairment of muscular grip when measured with ergograph	4	0.5–2 hr

for 3–4 days. Tolerance was less marked than with opiates, barbiturates, and alcohol but was similar to that which occurs with other hallucinogenic drugs, such as amphetamines and lysergic acid diethylamide. The withdrawal symptoms of some subjects subsided on administration of alcohol or barbiturates, thus suggesting a cross-tolerance reaction among cannabis, alcohol, and barbiturates. Also, it cannot be excluded that a storage capacity for the drug might also be achieved in some individuals over prolonged periods of cannabis consumption. In judging the presence or absence of psychic dependence in an individual, it is important to ascertain to what extent the use of the drug is a life-organizing factor, to what extent it takes precedence over the use of other means for coping with personality problems, or whether both factors are important. Our studies indicate that a large percentage of heavy users developed dependence. Whereas most of those who used it a few times on an experimental basis, or casually on a few festive occasions, during one year did not show psychic or other forms of dependence.

Neurologic Reactions

With higher doses of cannabis drugs, intellectual and physical performances are affected. Four typists in the series were given a passage to type. At the same time, four other typists, of the same age and group, who had never used cannabis were given the same passage to type. There were significant differences in the time required to type the passage and in the number of mistakes made. Five to 10% more time was required, and 6–12% more mistakes were made by those under the influence of the drug. Tests that involved counting backward and recitation of the alphabet also demonstrated the adverse effects of cannabis. Work performed under the influence of cannabis showed decreased accuracy. With larger doses, there was a marked decline in coherence and clarity. The performance impairment of complex tasks appears to arise from difficulty in maintaining and a logical train of thought (TABLE 12).

Acute Toxicity

Acute somatic toxicity of cannabis drugs is low when compared with that of other simple chemical substances that are rapidly absorbed in their pure form in the gastrointestinal tract. This lower toxicity explains why marijuana is not used for suicidal purposes. It was observed that severe physical side effects of marijuana are poorly correlated with its psychotoxicity and its ability to disintegrate mental functions, a condition that secondarily may cause bodily harm to self and others.

Chronic Toxicity

Among the vital organs affected by cannabis are the brain, which is the primary target, the liver, lungs, where the active ingredients are metabolized, and the heart, which rapidly accelerates its rate in response to the drug. Despite the long history of use of this drug, as old as the history of man, it has not been possible to observe any structural changes in the brain. There appears to be no or little morphologic or structural changes in the brain. Apparently, however, alterations in sensitivity of brain cells, or distortions in their functions occur, which result in changes in performance of mental functioning. One cannot exclude the possibility that repetitive impairment of these processes by frequent and long-term cannabis intoxication in adolescent years might induce permanent changes in thinking patterns or behavior. Such permanent changes would be related to permanent organic alterations.

COMPARATIVE ASSESSMENT OF EFFECTS IN INDIAN AND USA CHRONIC CANNABIS USERS

The subjective effects varied widely among different individuals and within the same individual. These variations may be explained by the fact that the crude form of the drug, as used in India, is not always of the same potency. It consists of a mixture of stems, leaves, and flowering tops with varying psychoactive properties. This factor partially explains the differences in observations by researchers in India and in the West, where observations are based mostly on studies of occasional and comparatively smaller numbers of subjects using weaker preparations. It is thus difficult to judge even approximately what drug potency is being studied. In our study, we have used an approximately equivalent Δ^9-THC content for determining the mean daily dose. Other than information about the active ingredient, Δ^9-THC, knowledge about other elements of the plant is lacking. Because of the dramatic changes in the psychologic, environmental, and sociologic aspects of the world today, more knowledge is needed about the long-term effects of marijuana. The present studies are only a preliminary effort in this direction. The intensity of the chronic effects of marijuana usage, as observed in India and Africa, has not been reported by Western observers. The milder preparations of cannabis used in the West partially explain this comparative absence of such psychoses. In India, there has always been a popular belief that prolonged and excessive use of these drugs leads to certain types of mental disorder and crimes of a violent nature. In previous studies, we have discussed the relationship between hemp habituation and mental disease and crime. It became evident in these studies that excessive indulgence in these drugs by unstable and susceptible individuals was likely to produce states of confusion, characterized by hallucinations, delusions, and disorientation. Prolonged excessive use also appeared to lead to the development of toxic psychosis. This paper was based on a study of 200 cannabis dependents that took place from 1963 to 1968. Taken into consideration were age of onset, education, socioeconomic status, dosage, motivation, psychologic and general health, signs of malnutrition, personality type, and so on. The present study also suggests similar findings.

Motivation and the environment have important roles in inducing predominant psychic effects. Various individuals listed different reasons for using cannabis. Most commonly, it was used as a substitute for alcohol. Among the 275 persons studied, 20% used the drug as a substitute for opium or alcohol. The lower cost of cannabis drugs than hemp, and the fact that the withdrawal symptoms are milder, make it an attractive substitute in developing countries, such as India. The use of cannabis drugs by certain sectors of the population in developing countries can be compared to the use of alcohol in the West. However, a recent study conducted at a university campus in Punjab (India) revealed that 60% of the students were using cannabis drugs, mostly ganja. It appears that the younger generation in India is trying to rapidly "catch up" with their counterparts in the West. This phenomenon appears to be characteristic of the general widespread use of marijuana worldwide. Distinctions should thus be made among occasional, regular, and moderate users and those who indulge excessively. The latter category of users is obviously more prone to adverse psychoclinical effects. Users in the United States and Canada belong mostly to the first two categories. This fact, again, partly explains the low frequency of acute toxic reactions among users in the United States and Canada. Like alcohol, excessive cannabis use can be attributed to preexisting personality problems. This conclusion is supported by a Moroccan saying, which states that, "You are a kif addict before you smoke your first pipe." In India, the highest percentage of excessive hemp users comes from the unemployed, from low-income classes, and from the student community. These individuals are mostly passive and nonproductive and are more prone to psychosis than are normal individuals, who have a regular, daily vocation.

Cannabis has also played a central role in the religions of Africa and South America, and in India. In Africa, an entire village has sometimes experienced a situation of "madness" after indiscriminate indulgence of *dagga*. In India, the drug is commonly abused by religious mendicants in places of worship and in the *takyas* of Muslim fakirs.

Marijuana has also been, and is, used by persons in the arts; supposedly, it enables one to expand his creativity. It is likely that the drug enhances the emotional aspects of the art media. However, there is no proof that it helps in technical performance. This is true in certain chronic users who use the drug in moderation.

Marijuana is also used for the relief of fatigue, monotony, and boredom. Cannabis is smoked among the laboring and working classes in urban areas to relieve these conditions. Such usage is not frequently excessive and is similar to that of alcohol in Western society.

CONCLUSIONS AND SUMMARY

Despite the rapidly changing scene of cannabis drug usage, it is becoming more frequent among university students; however, the majority of users (41.8%) are still uneducated. A high school education had been attained by

34.57% of this majority, while the remaining 29.5% were university students. Adverse reactions were more common in the uneducated group. Again, a different situation exists in the United States, where many marijuana users are educated youth from college campuses. With regard to occupation, persons in lower income groups were more susceptible to adverse reactions. This finding, again, contrasts with marijuana users in the United States and other Western countries, where users are mostly from the middle classes.

The individuals studied were apparently healthy persons with little or no apparent personality problems and no history of mental disorder or neurosis. An invariable element was their history of drug use. The symptoms and the effects were so similar and uniform that they suggest that, simply, a definite effect follows a definite cause. The effects were mostly of a mental nature that simulated toxic psychosis. There were no other common factors beyond the use of the drug. This eliminated the possibility that the adverse toxic reactions observed were caused by other factors. Thus, cannabis may precipitate latent psychiatric disorders, may aggravate preexisting psychiatric problems, or may have both effects.

References

1. ADDICTION RESEARCH FOUNDATION. 1970. Nineteenth Annual Report, 1969, Toronto, Appendix III.
2. CANADA, COMMISSION OF INQUIRY. 1970. Interim report of the Commission of Inquiry into the Non-Medical Use of Drugs. Information Canada. Ottawa, Ontario, Canada.
3. CHOPRA, R. N., G. S. CHOPRA & I. E. CHOPRA. 1942. Cannabis sativa in relation to mental diseases and crime in India. Indian J. Med. Res. **30:** 155–171.
3a. CHOPRA, G. S. & P. S. CHOPRA. 1965. Studies on 300 Indian drug addicts with special reference to psychological aspects, etiology, and treatment. Bull. Narcotics **17**(2): 8.
4. CHOPRA, G. S. 1969. Man and marijuana. Int. J. Addictions 4(2): 215–247.
5. CHOPRA, G. S. 1971. Marijuana and adverse psychotic reactions, evaluation of different fatcors involved. Bull. Narcotics **23:** 15–22.
6. CHOPRA, R. N. & G. S. CHOPRA. 1939. The present position of hemp drug addiction in India. Indian J. Med. Res. Mem. **31:** 1–119.
7. EVANS, G. F. W. 1904. Hemp drug insanity. Indian Med. Gazette **39:** 401.
8. ISBELL, H., C. W. GORODETSKY, D. JASINSKI, U. V. CLAUSSEN, F. SPULAK & F. KORTE. 1967. Effects of (−) 9-trans-tetrahydrocannabinol in man. Psychopharmacologia **11:** 184–188.
9. MECHOULA, R. 1970. Marijuana chemistry. Science **100:** 1159–1166.
10. MAYOR'S COMMITTEE ON MARIJUANA. 1944. Report on the Marijuana Problem in the City of New York. Jaques Cattell Press. Tempe, Ariz.
11. WORLD HEALTH ORGANIZATION. 1971. Technical Report 478. Geneva, Switzerland.

GENERAL DISCUSSION

Henry Brill, *Moderator*

Nassau-Suffolk Regional Office
State of New York Department of Mental Hygiene
Hauppauge, New York 11787

DR. J. R. TINKLENBERG: Were creatinine phosphokinase measurements made?

DR. G. S. CHOPRA: No. My observations were not conducted with highly scientific techniques, just the subjective and objective clinical examinations that we do as psychiatrists. We just interview and then evaluate the patients.

DR. TINKLENBERG: Did you look at the generational characteristics of the people who were susceptible to psychiatric disturbances? Second-, third-, or fourth-generation marijuana users?

DR. CHOPRA: We just evaluated the individual when he came, and we inquired about history of insanity or any toxic manifestations after taking the drug.

DR. E. B. TRUITT, JR. (*George Washington University Medical Center, Washington, D.C.*): Dr. Tinklenberg, how would you correct for possible antialcohol procannabis bias in your subjects? This was a criticism of the Crancer study on driving with marijuana versus alcohol.

DR. TINKLENBERG: Dr. Truitt, I'm not sure we really can correct for such biases. I think it's really intrinsic to the design that the individuals might have influenced their responses to us. We attempted to reduce those biases by inter-jecting questions about any particular drug among questions about other drugs, so we can't entirely reduce that bias.

DR. M. FINK: I was impressed by Dr. Chopra's description of a toxic-type of psychosis occurring in India. I also recall that neither Dr. Knight nor Dr. Stefanis described a toxic or an organic psychosis, and I would like to know whether Dr. Knight and Dr. Stefanis could describe the incidence of organic mental changes, or organic psychoses, in their two samples.

DR. CHOPRA: Toxic psychosis has pathognomonic symptoms, such as con-fusion, disorientation, aggressiveness, talkativeness, but rarely an initial tendency toward violence.

DR. C. STEFANIS: In that sense, every marijuana smoker has an organic psychotic syndrome, because whenever he is intoxicated, he is "high" or "stoned." The smoker is bound to have some consciousness disorders; his level of consciousness will be low, and he is bound to show some disorientation and other manifestations. If we're talking about the steady-state condition, however, the mental condition that results from chronic use, which affects memory, orien-tation, or other mental functions, we didn't find any such evidence. We had three people who presented a mental picture of a schizophrenia-like illness or syndrome, and we think that this was a true schizophrenia. We had family histories for two of these three subjects; in one of them, the mental symptoms began even before they started smoking hashish, so we have no grounds on which to attribute this kind of psychosis to hashish usage.

DR. F. KNIGHT: I believe that we see probably what we are looking for and what we want to see. I think all clinicians have this fallacy. I would draw a comparison to an excited catatonic whose behavior after 1 min may be very reminiscent of an organic state, but if you study him for about 20 min or several hours, it will become clear that he is not suffering from an organic condition but from a functional condition. When we see people who appear to be disoriented, we are still suspicious, especially if they are young people. Most of our subjects are young, and we know that ganja is endemic in the country, so we inquire about it.

We do find something that you might consider organic, which is a memory impairment. However, on the clinicians' insistence and with the patients' attempt to concentrate and to attend, we find that we are able to satisfy ourselves that this condition is not really organic but is probably due to the drug.

Another comparison is a hypomanic person, who can be persuaded to sit quietly and give logical cooperative answers for a limited period of 2 min, and then he goes out of control, and it is difficult to assess his behavior in the latter state.

DR. FINK: Would it be fair to ask or to conclude, then, that neither in the Jamaican nor in the Greek studies was there a definite group of users who were categorized by psychiatric classifications as organic mental syndromes or organic psychoses?

DR. KNIGHT: Yes, that is correct.

DR. A. WIKLER: I should like to remind the audience that Isbell and Jasinski performed an experimental study in 1967 that demonstrated that the psychomimetic properties of Δ^9-THC are dose related and that higher doses of the drug in one-step increments regularly produced a psychosis, which was characterized by hallucinations, delusions, depersonalization, and occasional disorientation, and these psychoses could be considered schizophreniform, organic, or affective, anything you like, depending on the particular constellation of psychotic symptoms and signs the patient exhibited.

I would like to caution the speakers to refrain from invoking predispositions when they don't have hard data to support those contentions. To contend that marijuana merely modified or precipitated a psychosis in a person who is predisposed to have a psychosis is a very common practice. I have yet to see any evidence of the preexisting predisposition. And, in fact, in my experience with such patients, there is only one test that can answer that question: not retrospective analysis of a patient's history, which usually turns up nothing, nothing you couldn't find in a comparable group of controls, but simply time. One simply waits. If the psychosis disappears on its own accord without chlorpromazine, without any specific antipsychotic drug, but perhaps a barbiturate, pentobarbital if necessary, but preferably no drugs, one simply waits. If the psychosis disappears, it clearly was due to the drug and not to some predisposition. I'd therefore like to ask you to disregard the retrospective data or alleged data to support a predisposition in your cases of psychoses.

DR. STEFANIS: I am referring to only these three cases, which were characterized by a steady mental state that was steadily psychotic. Regarding the acute intoxication due to the drug, of course, this is another thing; it goes away in time. The three other patients had this steady state, which was of the schizophrenia type anyway, for 5 or 6 years.

DR. CHOPRA: To prove that there's a separate entity, there is a mental condition called hemp psychosis for which we have performed certain experiments. We had certain individuals suffering from toxic psychosis due to hemp abuse, and they had the disease for about one month, and after a few days it subsided. When we asked the patients to take hemp again, the psychosis appeared again.

That shows, then, that it is a specific condition called hemp psychosis which is triggered or stimulated or precipitated by hemp drugs. I agree with you, sir.

DR. R. T. JONES: I want to come back to Dr. Wikler's point, which I think is a very important one. We do not want to give the impression that almost everyone who develops a psychosis after cannabis usage is somehow predisposed. I think it's important to remember that cannabis was the first psychomimetic schizophrenia-type drug model. Moreau de Tours wrote a book about this subject 100 years ago that Dr. Nahas reviews very nicely in his book.

From our experience, almost anybody given the right dose and in the right setting can exhibit something that may look like a schizophrenia-like set of symptoms. On the other hand, this is not to say that there isn't a predisposition in some people. One case in our chronic studies was an individual who, through a mistake in our screening process, was selected and it turned out that he had a process schizophrenia. Every time we tried to exceed a fairly modest dose of cannabis, about 70 mg/day, which was tolerated by all of our other subjects, this young man would develop delusions, disturbed aspect, and visual distortions. If we decreased the dose by 5 mg, these symptoms all disappeared. The phenomenon was reliably reproducible for 5 weeks; no tolerance developed to the drug, and his subsequent course after leaving the hospital convinced us that he was the type of schizophrenic who never goes to a psychiatrist's office and has never been hospitalized. Two years later, he's still doing fine, but he had a particular sensitivity to cannabis that one doesn't usually see in normal people.

DR. KNIGHT: Dr. Wikler, regarding susceptibility, we have to assume that, for example, if we take two vessels and drop one, it breaks; if we drop another, it doesn't break. We discover that one was made of glass, and one is made of wood. We have to assume that due to the inherent quality of glass, the one that broke was glass, even though we can't prove it.

DR. D. X. FREEDMAN: The question concerns the kind of inference to be drawn from the doses and schedules of use of American weed used on the street versus the kinds of doses and schedules that are being used in the laboratory. Because I have worked on LSD tolerance since 1958, I will underscore one point: the dose you need across species is the dose required for a minimal effect. The doses follow the laws of half-life, but all species differ in their half-life of drug degradation, so we shouldn't discuss the tonnage argument but rather the dose and schedule for the species. The question that will come up tomorrow is how much would you have to increase the dosage of American pot? How heavy should the dosage schedule be in order to begin to see the phenomena that are observed in the laboratory? I think that that's what is really at issue.

DR. FINK: Drs. Wikler, Stefanis, and Soueif talked about the fact that high doses are given in these populations, either in monkeys or in man, and that tolerance seems to develop; that is, high doses can be taken, and yet we hear reports in America of sensitivity at very low doses in individuals.

In the Greek or Egyptian studies, was there any evidence of this reverse tolerance, described more or less anecdotally in the American literature?

DR. STEFANIS: As I mentioned in my paper, there is an indication that reverse tolerance might occur. The definition of reverse tolerance is like many other definitions, not clear-cut. The fact that in successive days these people used to smoke less might indicate the presence of reverse tolerance. Is this effect due to the fact that the material has been depleted during abstinence and the individual needs to compensate for this lack? Once the subject has reached a certain dosage, of course, a lower dosage is then required to maintain the same metabolic state. If that is what we call reverse tolerance, it does occur.

Dr. Wikler might be able to provide a better definition. I have just described the phenomenon. Dr. Wikler, does this situation comply with the definition of reverse tolerance?

DR. WIKLER: In my paper, I have a rather lengthy section on what I call residual reverse tolerance. All of these studies on reverse tolerance have been performed in individuals with previous histories of heavy, moderate, or non-use of marijuana, and the time lapse between their last use of marijuana and the study varied tremendously, so we're talking about residual reverse tolerance.

Dr. Jones essentially found that this so-called reverse tolerance applies only to the label "high" on smoking marijuana. When the same subjects are given an equivalent amount of Δ^9-THC orally, they don't show any evidence of reverse tolerance; they show evidence of tolerance to certain physiologic effects. Only when they smoke marijuana or a placebo do they give more placebo responses with check off on the objective checklist as marijuana-like responses, and this is their reverse tolerance.

DR. JONES: I might add, Dr. Wikler, that you state results nicely, but you can eliminate the so-called reverse tolerance from the smoked placebo by occluding ones nose and eyes so that the individual can't smell anything or see anything. It all points to something psychologic proceeding along set expectation lines.

DR. FREEDMAN: Let's avoid the use of the word psychologic. It's a mystery word, but it's a conditioning or placebo effect.

DR. WIKLER: I believe that reverse tolerance has become another mystery or slogan word.

The studies of Lemberger et al. have raised a great furor over reverse tolerance. Lemberger et al. speculate that the reverse tolerance observed with chronic use of marijuana could be the consequence of induction of enzymes that convert Δ^9-THC to a more active, or more stable, metabolite. The phenomenon could also be due to cumulative effects of repeated administration, to increase receptor sensitivity to Δ^9-THC metabolites or to a learned and heightened response to the effect of Δ^9-THC. They've covered the waterfront.

Regarding the conversion of Δ^9-THC to 11-OH-Δ^9-THC, which is a very active compound, it appears that no evidence has been presented to indicate that such conversion takes place faster or is quantitatively greater in long-term marijuana users than in nonusers. The shorter half-life of the slower phase of the decline of plasma radioactivity after intravenous administration of radioactive Δ^9-THC in long-term marijuana users could well be due to liver microsomal enzyme induction by marijuana or other drugs, because these heavy users have used all kinds of drugs in the past, including "downers," which induce such liver enzymes.

At any rate, such enzyme induction could just as well account in part for the residual tolerance that Dr. Jones has described in such users. In other words, although there is evidence of what is called dispositional tolerance in formerly heavy users of marijuana, this dispositional tolerance does not explain the so-called reverse tolerance. It could just as easily explain the residual tolerance that such subjects show when compared with nonusers.

EXPERIMENTAL OBSERVATIONS OF A 3-DAY HASHISH ABSTINENCE PERIOD AND REINTRODUCTION OF USE *

Costas Stefanis, Aris Liakos, John C. Boulougouris,
Rhea L. Dornbush,†‡ and C. Ballas

Department of Psychiatry
Athens University Medical School
Eginition Hospital
Athens, Greece
† Department of Psychiatry
New York Medical College
New York, New York 10029

INTRODUCTION

Several reports in the literature suggest that tolerance and physical withdrawal symptoms may develop in man after chronic use of cannabis. Actually, a variety of mental and physical withdrawal symptoms in cannabis users (restlessness, insomnia, anorexia, and increased perspiration) were reported in the past to occur after abrupt pyrahexyl withdrawal.[1] Furthermore, several cases of acute psychosis associated with cannabis withdrawal have been described.[2] Bensusen [3] has also reported that seven *ganja* smokers developed anxiety, restlessness, abdominal cramps, nausea, sweating, low blood pressure, and muscular aches after withdrawal of cannabis. In the technical paper of the National Commission on Marihuana and Drug Abuse,[4] a "psychosomatic abstinence syndrome" was cited, which consisted of physical weakness, intellectual apathy, loss of appetite, flatulence, constipation, insomnia, fatigue, abdominal cramps, nervousness, restlessness, and headache. Most of these reports on physical withdrawal symptoms, however, are either anecdotal or obtained under poorly controlled conditions with subjects who were not stated to be exclusive marijuana users. Most of the research on cannabis up to 1970 claimed that cannabis produces neither tolerance nor physical dependence in man.[5-7] The issue, though, was recently raised again and is currently at the center of cannabis research, where both tolerance to repeated administration of Δ^9-tetrahydrocannabinol (Δ^9-THC) and abstinence symptoms to its withdrawal have been reported to develop in various animal species.[8, 9]

Several recent studies with repeated administration and abrupt cannabis withdrawal in naive or experienced American users [10, 11] failed to demonstrate physical withdrawal symptoms after ad lib. cannabis administration. On the other hand, Jones and Benowitz [12] reported physical withdrawal symptoms in subjects of average marijuana experience who were given increasingly larger doses of cannabis.

* Supported by Contract HSM 42–70–98 from the National Institute on Drug Abuse to the International Association for Psychiatric Research.
‡ Present address: Reproductive Biology Research Foundation, St. Louis, Mo. 63108.

There is also increasing evidence in the literature to suggest that long-term cannabis users tolerate and consume large amounts of cannabis without severe side effects.[11, 13] It can, therefore, be argued that the development of physical withdrawal symptoms may be related to increased consumption, such as occurs in long-term users.

To investigate the possibility of a withdrawal syndrome developing in chronic users who consume large amounts of cannabis, we undertook a tolerance and withdrawal study in a sample of very long-term Greek users who used only hashish and no other addictive substances continuously for more than 20 years. The study was part of a 3-year investigation of the effects of chronic cannabis use. In this paper, only the findings related to the amount of material consumed and the presence of withdrawal clinical symptoms will be reported.

MATERIALS AND METHODS

Subjects

Sixteen long-term male cannabis users participated in the tolerance-withdrawal experiments. Their mean age was 40.8 (SD = 9.0), and they reported use of cannabis for a mean 24 years (SD = 9.0). The reported frequency of use was two to six cigarettes per day, and the estimated amount consumed was 3–8 g of hashish on the day of smoking.

None of them was suffering from incapacitating physical or neurologic illnesses or had a history of other addictive drug use, with the exception of social use of alcohol. All were tobacco smokers and participated in the experiments as paid volunteers.

Design

The experimental design provided for 6 days of hospitalization divided into 3 days of marijuana smoking and 3 days of placebo smoking in a double-blind sequence. All subjects claimed to be continuous hashish users, but to make sure that they had smoked before hospitalization, they came to the hospital for 2 days before the experiment to smoke marijuana ad lib. twice daily.

Smoking of Material

Smoking sessions were associated with a set of experimental and clinical observations. These sessions occurred twice daily, with an interval of 4.5 hr. Each session lasted 30 min, during which time the subjects smoked ad lib. prepared "cigarettes" that contained marijuana placebo or National Institute of Mental Health-provided marijuana of an estimated 2.6% Δ^9-THC content per gram of marijuana. Tobacco was mixed with the material in a way that was customary for Greek cannabis users.

Withdrawal Symptoms

The following symptoms reported in the literature were systematically investigated every day 2 hr after the first smoking session: anxiety, depression, restlessness, irritability, fatigue, sexual desire, constipation, flatulence, abdominal pain, cramps, and appetite and blood pressure changes.

Self-rating 10-point scales were used for anxiety, depression, fatigue, restlessness, irritability, and sexual desire. Appetite and constipation were assessed by a three-point scale. A clinical assessment by a psychiatrist of the team was made at the same time for the presence of flatulence, abdominal pain, and cramps. Lastly, blood pressure was taken in standing and supine positions.

TABLE 1

MEAN NUMBER (MN) AND STANDARD DEVIATIONS (SD) OF "CIGARETTES" SMOKED AND MEAN Δ^9-THC EQUIVALENTS

Sequence	Day					
	1	2	3	4	5	6
		Placebo			Marijuana	
	First smoking session					
MN	2.72	1.78	1.43	5.65	5.70	4.83
SD	1.08	0.92	1.02	1.66	1.52	0.89
THC				146.90	148.20	125.58
	Second smoking session					
MN	1.37	1.09	1.21	4.40	3.76	3.78
SD	0.79	0.63	0.52	1.15	1.03	1.15
THC				114.40	97.76	98.28
		Marijuana			Placebo	
	First smoking session					
MN	2.75	3.50	2.38	1.75	1.63	1.44
SD	0.71	1.85	1.19	1.04	1.19	1.12
THC	71.50	91.00	61.88			
	Second smoking session					
MN	2.06	2.38	2.69	1.50	1.38	1.19
SD	0.94	1.19	1.16	0.93	1.25	1.16
THC	53.56	61.88	69.94			

RESULTS

TABLE 1 shows the numbers of marijuana and placebo cigarettes consumed during the experiment. Subjects smoked an average of seven cigarettes per day (between 125 and 190 mg of Δ^9-THC). A three-way analysis of variance was performed on the amount of cigarettes consumed during the first smoking session of the day. The variables were (1) sequence one, placebo for the first 3 days, followed by marijuana for another 3 days; sequence two, the reverse order was followed; (2) drug against placebo; (3) days (first to third). Statistically significant effects were found for all three variables and also for the interaction of sequence and drugs (all $p < 0.05$). Subjects smoked more marijuana in sequence one in comparison to sequence two. They smoked more marijuana than placebo cigarettes; they also smoked a greater number of marijuana cigarettes on the first day of smoking and fewer on the third day of smoking. The sequence-drug interaction is shown in FIGURE 1. As can be seen in this Figure, subjects smoked significantly more marijuana when it was administered after 3 days of placebo than before placebo and after the 2-day outpatient marijuana administration.

A second three-way analysis of variance was performed to compare the first and second smoking sessions. In this analysis, the variables were sequence

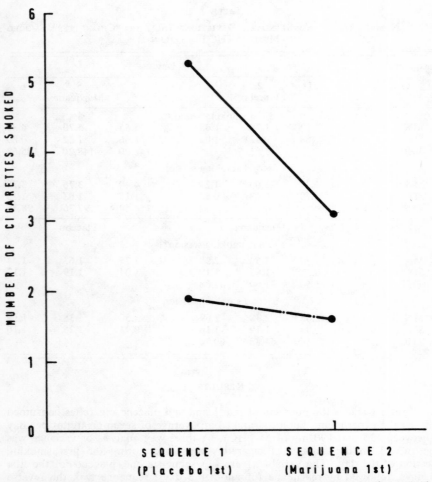

FIGURE 1. Sequence $\times$ drug interaction after first smoking session; marijuana (—), placebo (—·—).

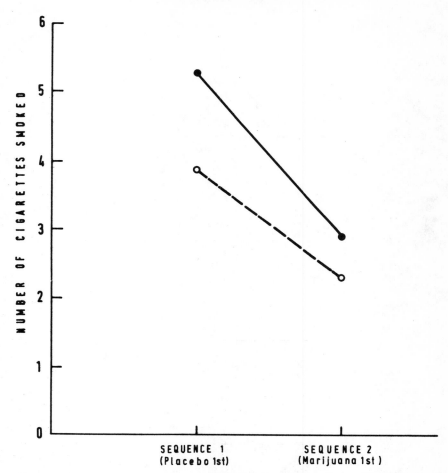

FIGURE 2. Amount of marijuana consumed during each smoking session as a function of sequence; first session (—), second session (- - -).

(marijuana preceding or following placebo), days (3), and smoking sessions (first or second of the day).

There was a statistically significant difference between the smoking sessions (p < 0.01). More marijuana was smoked during the first smoking session of the day than during the second session.

The sequence-smoking interaction was statistically significant (p < 0.01). More marijuana was smoked when the 3-day smoking period followed the 3-day withdrawal period. The sequence-smoking interaction is illustrated in FIGURE 2.

The analysis of symptom ratings showed no statistical difference between smoking and withdrawal periods. As shown in FIGURE 3, the 10-point scale ratings for all symptoms were quite low for both withdrawal and drug periods.

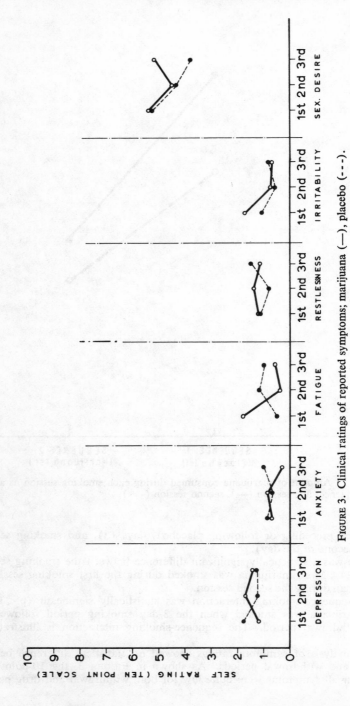

FIGURE 3. Clinical ratings of reported symptoms; marijuana (—), placebo (---).

Only sexual desire had an average rating for both periods. Only small and statistically insignificant differences between smoking and withdrawal periods were also noted in the clinical ratings of flatulence, constipation, cramps, headache, appetite, and standing and supine blood pressures.

DISCUSSION

The long-term cannabis users who participated in this tolerance-withdrawal experiment consumed under ad lib. smoking conditions a mean amount of between 125 and 190 mg of Δ^9-THC per day. This amount roughly coincides with the reported [14] dosages used, because estimates of Greek hashish samples by NIMH laboratories have shown a 4–5% Δ^9-THC content, and the doses employed by us ranged from 3 to 8 g of hashish per day. We may, thus, conclude that under our experimental conditions, users smoked amounts of Δ^9-THC similar to those consumed under a daily free-choice situation.

During the 3-day experimental smoking period, the amount of cannabis smoked decreased significantly from the first to the third day. Such a decrease might indicate the development of reverse tolerance, at least for the subjective effects. Under ad lib. administration, the users presumably smoke enough to reach a certain level of satisfaction. The mean subjective ratings of "feeling high" after smoking, which have not been described here, confirm this hypothesis, because they were similar during the 3 days of smoking.

Mendelson *et al.*[11] found, in a 21-day repeated ad lib. administration experiment, that the amount of marijuana consumed increased over the period of drug administration. Their results, however, are difficult to compare with ours, because they used a different experimental design, a longer smoking period, and subjects who had a shorter duration of previous smoking experience.

In our study, the subjects smoked significantly more marijuana when the smoking period followed the withdrawal period. This finding might indicate that there is a need for greater amounts of marijuana after withdrawal. Assuming that there exists a reverse tolerance due to the accumulation of the active material, we may attribute this finding to the need of the organism to compensate for the material depleted during the abstinence period.

The absence of withdrawal phenomena, reflected by the parameters investigated, is consistent with the failure of other systematic studies to demonstrate withdrawal symptoms after repeated cannabis administration and abrupt cessation.[10, 11, 15] However, our results appear to be at variance with those obtained by Jones and Benowitz,[12] who observed several withdrawal symptoms after repeated administration of high doses of marijuana in experienced users. In this study, however, the subjects ingested the material and had no way to control the dosage, as is the case with ad lib. smoking administration. Furthermore, the doses were gradually increased to levels that probably would not have been reached under natural free-choice conditions.

We may, therefore, conclude that very long-term marijuana users do not develop withdrawal symptoms after cessation of 3 days of smoking when conditions of dosage self-control occur prior to withdrawal.

REFERENCES

1. WILLIAMS, E. G., C. K. HIMMELSBACH, A. WIKLER, D. C. RUBLE & B. J. LLOYD. 1946. Studies on marihuana and pyrahexyl compound. Publ. Health Rep. **51:** 1059–1083.

2. FRASER, J. D. 1949. Withdrawal symptoms in Cannabis indica addicts. Lancet 2: 747, 748.
3. BENSUSEN, A. D. 1971. Marihuana withdrawal symptoms. Brit. Med. J. : 112 (Letter to editor).
4. NATIONAL COMMISSION ON MARIHUANA AND DRUG ABUSE. 1972. Marihuana: A Signal of Misunderstanding. Vol. 1.
5. MAYOR'S COMMITTEE ON MARIHUANA. 1944. The Marihuana Problem in the City of New York. Jaques Cattell Press. Tempe, Ariz.
6. EDDY, N. B., H. HALBACH, H. ISBELL & M. H. SEEVERS. 1966. Drug dependence: its significance and characteristics. Psychopharmacologia 3: 1–12.
7. JAFFE, J. H. 1975. Drug addiction and drug abuse. In The Pharmacological Basis of Therapeutics. L. S. Goodman & A. Gilman, Eds. 5th edit. : 284–324. The Macmillan Company, New York, N.Y.
8. FERRARO, P. P. & M. G. GRISHAM. 1971. Tolerance to the behaviour effects of marihuana in chimpanzees. Physiol. Behav. 9: 49–54.
9. KAYMAKCALAN, S. 1972. Physiological and psychological dependence on THC in rhesus monkeys. In Cannabis and Its Derivatives. W. D. M. Paton & J. Crown, Eds. : 142–149. Oxford University Press. London, England.
10. DORNBUSH, R. L., G. CLARE, J. FACKS, P. VOLAVKA, P. CROWN & M. FINK. 1972. Twenty one day administration of marihuana in male volunteers. In Current Research in Marihuana. M. F. Lewis, Ed. Academic Press, Inc. New York, N.Y.
11. MENDELSON, J. H., A. M. ROSSI & R. E. MEYER. 1974. Conclusions and implications. In The Use of Marihuana. A Psychological and Physiological Inquiry. J. H. Mendelson, A. M. Rossi & R. Meyer, Eds. : 175–190. Plenum Publishing Corporation. New York and London.
12. JONES, R. T. & N. BENOWITZ. 1976. The 30 day trip: clinical studies of cannabis tolerance and dependence. In The Pharmacology of Marihuana. M. C. Braude & S. Szara, Eds. : 627–642. The Raven Press. New York, N.Y.
13. BEAUBRUN, M. & F. KNIGHT. 1973. Psychiatric assessment of 30 chronic users of cannabis and 30 matched controls. Amer. J. Psychiat. 130: 309–311.
14. STEFANIS, C., A. LIAKOS, J. C. BOULOUGOURIS, M. FINK & A. FREEDMAN. 1976. Chronic hashish use in mental disorder. Amer. J. Psychiat. 133: 225–227.
15. COHEN, S., P. LESSIN, P. HAHN & E. TYRELL. 1976. The 94-day study. In The Pharmacology of Marihuana. M. C. Braude & S. Szara, Eds. : 621–626. The Raven Press, New York, N.Y.

CANNABIS-TYPE DEPENDENCE: THE PSYCHOLOGY OF CHRONIC HEAVY CONSUMPTION

M. I. Soueif

Psychology Department
Cairo University
Cairo, Egypt

INTRODUCTION

This paper presents an attempt at delineating the psychology of chronic heavy cannabis consumers (vs moderates) that might help to shed light on the concept of "cannabis-type dependence." [1] Heavy consumption is taken to mean self-administration of the drug on a regular basis, more than 30 times per month. This operational definition was chosen on sheerly empirical grounds. It is intended to facilitate communication and has no theoretical implications in itself.

Because of the multiplicity of difficulties involved in the use of the term "dependence" (let alone "psychic dependence"), we thought it would cause more confusion to give more weight to theoretical rather than empirical considerations. [2,3] Without lessening the importance of theoretical formulations (e.g., concepts, principles, and theories) in making an effort toward gathering new data, it is still believable that "the formulation of a definition or concept depends on the state of the experimental art." [2] By presenting some aspects of an empirical picture of the heavy user, we might be providing the concept of dependence with meaningful behavioral connotations. This done, we may in the future be in a position to infer some basic dimensions of cannabis-type dependence.

PROCEDURE

The Tool

A standardized interviewing schedule was constructed with the intention of administering it to various groups of regular cannabis users. Test retest reliability of the items was established. Several approaches for the ascertainment of validity were attempted. This yielded reasonable assurance that the kind of information we obtained was not exposed to anything like systematic distortion. A group of well-trained interviewers was employed to conduct the interviewing [4,5] (for a full English translation of the interview, see Soueif [6]).

Subjects

A detailed description of our subjects has been given elsewhere. [5,7] Only minimal relevant points will, therefore, be emphasized here. Our interviewees included the entire male population convicted exclusively for hashish use and

121

detained in Egyptian prisons during June 1967 to March 1968. The group comprised 577 heavy users and 273 moderate consumers. We could not detect any appreciable difference between the two subgroups on age, literacy, or urbanism. Also, the two subdivisions did not seem to differ much regarding socioeconomic status.

The Drug

The average Δ^9-tetrahydrocannabinol (Δ^9-THC) content in seven samples of cannabis seized on the illicit market, in various districts of the country, was found to be 3.04% by weight. The analysis was performed at the laboratory of the Biological Unit, at the National Centre for Social and Criminological Research (Cairo).

FINDINGS

Two types of data will be reported here: responses concerning the degree of attachment of heavy users to the drug, or the influence of the drug on heavy takers, and answers that describe behavioral aspects that are significantly associated with heavy usage.

Under the first type of responses, we found three subcategories that showed a powerful influence of cannabis on heavy consumers. When asked whether they had any desire to stop using hashish ($r = 0.57 \; \phi$), 75.3% of the heavy users versus 85.6% of moderate consumers replied "yes." This difference was statistically highly significant ($t = 3.4$). Asked whether at any time they stopped using hashish ($r = 72\%$ aggregate), the majority of heavy consumers said "no." They were differentiated from moderates at a very high level of statistical significance ($\chi^2 = 14.63$; 1 df). We found a relationship, though not significant, between dose and frequency. Of the heavy users, 18.2% versus 31.2% of moderates tended to consume less than 0.54 g at a time, whereas 13.2% of the heavy users versus 4.9% of the moderates consumed more than 1.08 g. In other words, the percentages of heavy users exceed the corresponding percentages of moderate consumers at high doses. And, finally, 63.3% of heavy users versus 38.5% of moderates reported that they would sometimes exceed their usual dose of the drug ($r_{11} = 0.97 \; \phi$). The difference, again, was statistically very highly significant ($t = 6.75$). Thus, under the first subcategory, four items characterized heavy users: they expressed a relatively weak desire to stop using cannabis, never tried before to stop using it, tended to consume large doses, and, more often than not, would exceed their usual doses.

The second subcategory included items that showed a high degree of reinforcement of drug-using behavior. Many more heavy users than moderates started to use the drug at an early age. Whereas 76% of those who began usage before the age of 22 became heavy consumers, only 56% of those who began after age 22 belonged to the same category ($r_{11} = 0.53$ Pearson). The discrepancy was statistically highly significant ($t = 6.1$). More heavy users (44.4%) than moderates (32.7%) had another family member who used drugs ($r_{11} = 0.80 \; \phi$). The disparity was statistically highly significant ($t = 3.2$). When asked whether when taking the drug they often jumped from one topic to another in conversation or in thought, more heavy users (67.7%) than moderates (56%) answered in the affirmative ($r_{11} = 82\%$ aggregate). The difference between the two percentages was statistically highly significant ($t = 3.28$). Under the second subcategory, therefore, three facts characterized heavy users. They began usage early, had another family member who used drugs (possibly involving a modeling effect, genetic influence, or both), and had a free flow of thought when under the influence of the drug (a fact that might have a rewarding effect).

The third subcategory comprised items about the use of other mood-modifying drugs over and above cannabis. Of the heavy users, 34.6% versus 25.9% of moderates admitted that they used opium ($r_{11} = 0.86 \; \phi$). The difference between the two groups was statistically significant ($t = 2.59$). Also, more heavy consumers (27%) than moderates (13.5%) used alcohol ($r_{11} = 0.83 \; \phi$). Again, the discrepancy was statistically highly significant ($\chi^2 = 18.77$; 1 df). When they resumed usage of hashish, after an unsuccessful attempt at stopping the practice, more heavy consumers than moderates added another drug (usually opium) to their menu ($r_{11} = 0.74 \; \phi$). Here, again, the disparity was statistically significant ($\chi^2 = 6.32$; 1 df). According to the third subcategory, then, heavy users exhibit an appetite for a wider range of drugs than do moderates.

Answers classified under the second type include a variety of items with various degrees of relatedness to drug behavior. A tentative subclassification that seems convenient for our purpose, here, would be dividing our data into two subdivisions: the first to include items directly (or explicitly) related to drug use and the second to cover items indirectly related (via some intervening variable, for example, an inferred motive or attitude) to such behavior.

An item that appears to be directly meaningful is one about passing leisure time ($r_{11} = 86\%$ aggregate). Two categories differentiate statistically highly significantly between our two groups. Heavy users spend much more time under the effect of the drug, or at cafes, than do moderates ($\chi^2 = 29.88$; 5 df).

Numerous other items are less directly meaningful. We found more loneliness among heavy users than among moderates. When asked about their marital status, the former indicated that a much larger percentage of them were bachelors, divorced, or widowers than were the latter ($r_{11} = 0.69\%$ c). The difference reached a high level of statistical significance ($\chi^2 = 12.19$; 3 df). We also found that heavy users gave more pathologic responses than moderates on three items selected from the Taylor Manifest Anxiety Scale. Heavy consumers had a higher incidence of fitful sleep ($t = 2.91$), insomnia ($t = 2.62$), and waking up very early in the morning and not being able to go back to sleep ($t = 2.94$). According to the system of psychiatric classification adopted by the Egyptian Association of Psychological Medicine,[8] such manifestations might denote some kind of a depressive neurosis. Heavy users were also found to work for longer hours, daily, than moderates ($r_{11} = 0.78$ Pearson). The difference between the two groups reached a very high level of statistical significance. When asked about the type of conversation they usually had in a hashish sitting, heavy consumers emphasized that it was not serious, that on the contrary it was merry and full of jokes ($r_{11} = 0.64 \; \phi$). The disparity between heavy users and moderates was statistically highly significant ($\chi^2 = 9.99$; 2 df).

In brief, heavy users were characterized by the following:

They express a rather weak desire to stop use of the drug and report few attempts at actually stopping the practice.

They take rather large quantities of the drug per sitting and frequently exceed their usual doses.

They show an appetite for a wide range of drugs.

They spend a sizable amount of their leisure time with the drug or exposed to a drug atmosphere.

They were introduced to the practice at an early age.

Somebody in their families was already using drugs before they were initiated into the practice.

When under the influence of the drug, they have a free flow of thought.

They emphasize having a merry atmosphere in their group hashish sitting.

They report manifestations of depressive neurosis.

They tend to lead a lonesome life.

They work for long hours daily.

DISCUSSION

Drug dependence has been defined as follows:

A state, psychic and sometimes also physical, resulting from the interaction between a living organism and a drug, characterized by behavioural and other responses that always include a compulsion to take the drug on a continuous or periodic basis in order to experience its psychic effects, and sometimes to avoid the discomfort of its absence. Tolerance may or may not be present. . . .[9]

Self-administration of the drug on a continuous or periodic basis seems to be the most tangible ingredient in that definition; by this statement, we mean that it can be externally observed with a reasonable degree of accuracy. Yet, it is not self-administration as such that is intended here. Rather, it is the insistence of the person on self-administration of the drug in the face of influences to the contrary.

The *Psychiatric Dictionary* defines compulsion "as an act contrary to the conscious will of the subject at the time the act is performed."[10] Though the net result of our statistical analysis shows a tendency toward more acceptance of the act among heavy users, a complementary fact still must be underlined. About 75% of the heavy users stated that they wanted to stop using the drug but that they could not, and 85.6% of the moderates expressed the same desire. Stated this way, it seems that cannabis users, in general, experience something like an overpowering desire to continue use of the drug. Some kind of taming of the will, however, occurs with heavy usage. We do not know which is the cause and which is the effect, or possibly both are effected through a very complex process that involves the drug, the organism, and the environment. We think that, in our work, we could obtain some factual data that might be treated as stepping-stones in an effort to construct a model with some heuristic value in this context. Facts such as spending a sizable amount of one's time using the drug, being introduced to the practice of drug consumption at an early age (before 16), having somebody in the family using drugs, and exhibiting an appetite for a wide range of mood-modifying drugs seem to indicate that heavy cannabis usage can be very deeply rooted in the organism. We have the impression that our consumers obtain tremendous reinforcement in their use of the drug: on the one hand, they are motivated by their lonesome life, depressive neurosis, and bad work conditions, and, on the other hand, they are rewarded by experiencing an enjoyable atmosphere at their hashish parties and a relaxing degree of freely flowing thought.

While working out such a model, several questions have to be considered; examples are: Is it a valid assumption that heavy cannabis users represent an extreme position on a continuum of regular consumption? And to what extent can data such as ours, with all their limitations, generate conclusions that may be validly generalized to other samples of subjects and cultural settings?

My contention is that we still need further investigation, but the type of investigation that permits comparison across workers, sociocultural settings, and research designs.

REFERENCES

1. WORLD HEALTH ORGANIZATION EXPERT COMMITTEE ON DEPENDENCE-PRODUCING DRUGS. 1965. Fourteenth Report. Tech. Rep. Ser. 312.
2. HALBACH, H. 1973. Defining drug dependence and abuse. In Psychic Dependence: Definition, Assessment in Animals and Man; Theoretical and Clinical Implications. L. Goldberg & F. Hoffmeister, Eds. : 17–21. Springer-Verlag. Berlin, Federal Republic of Germany.
3. EDDY, N. B. 1973. Prediction of drug dependence and abuse liability. In Psychic Dependence: Definition, Assessment in Animals and Man; Theoretical and Clinical Implications. L. Goldberg & F. Hoffmeister, Eds. : 192–198. Springer-Verlag. Berlin, Federal Republic of Germany.
4. COMMITTEE FOR THE INVESTIGATION OF HASHISH CONSUMPTION IN EGYPT. 1960. Hashish Consumption in Egypt; Research in Progress; Report I: The Interviewing Schedule; Construction, Reliability and Validity (in Arabic). Publications of the National Centre for Social and Criminological Research. Cairo, Egypt.
5. SOUEIF, M. I. 1967. Hashish consumption in Egypt, with special reference to psychosocial problems. Bull. Narcotics 19(2): 1–12.
6. SOUEIF, M. I. 1975. Chronic cannabis takers: some temperamental characteristics. Drug Alc. Depend. 1(2): 125–154.
7. SOUEIF, M. I. 1971. The use of cannabis in Egypt: a behavioural study. Bulletin on Narcotics 23(4): 17–28.
8. EGYPTIAN ASSOCIATION OF PSYCHOLOGICAL MEDICINE. 1972. Mimeographed report.
9. WORLD HEALTH ORGANIZATION EXPERT COMMITTEE ON DRUG DEPENDENCE. 1969. Sixteenth Report. Tech. Rep. Ser. 407.
10. HINSI, L. E. & R. J. CAMPBELL. 1960. Psychiatric Dictionary. Oxford University Press, Inc. New York, N.Y.
11. COMMITTEE FOR THE INVESTIGATION OF HASHISH CONSUMPTION IN EGYPT. 1964. Hashish Consumption in Egypt; Research in Progress; Report II: Hashish Users in Cairo City: A Pilot Study (in Arabic). Publications of the National Centre for Social and Criminological Research. Cairo, Egypt.

ASPECTS OF TOLERANCE TO AND DEPENDENCE ON CANNABIS *

Abraham Wikler

Departments of Psychiatry and Pharmacology
University of Kentucky Medical Center
Lexington, Kentucky 40506

INTRODUCTION

Three main issues appear to preoccupy investigators of tolerance to and dependence on cannabis: Is tolerance to cannabis "pharmacologic" or "learned"? Is there "tolerance" or "reverse tolerance" to cannabis? Is dependence on cannabis "psychic" or "physical"? Though seeking answers to these questions by experimentation can generate vast amounts of empirical "facts," the theoretical assumptions on which such questions are based require examination, because the uses to which the "facts" will be put depend on the *theories* that the "facts" allegedly illustrate. Therefore, before proceeding to a review of the literature on these issues, an attempt will be made to clarify their meaning.

The distinction between "pharmacologic" tolerance and "learned" tolerance seems to be based on lack of acquaintance with modern theories of pharmacologic tolerance. According to such theories, "tissue tolerance" (or "functional tolerance" [45]) is learned in the sense that as a consequence of the initial presence of a drug-produced disturbance in function, the organism, over time, may acquire the capacity to compensate for the disturbance in function through biochemical and/or neurophysiologic feedback mechanisms, regardless of the level of complexity at which such adaptations proceed. Thus, Goldstein and Goldstein [35] have suggested that the functionally active metabolites of a substrate, the metabolism of which is catalyzed by an enzyme (E) "repress" other enzymes that catalyze the synthesis of E. When the metabolism of the substrate is blocked by a drug, the concentration of functionally active metabolites of the substrate is reduced (producing a drug effect), and the enzymes that synthesize E are "derepressed"; with repetition of administration of the drug, such "derepression" results in a greatly increased concentration of E, which overcomes the drug-produced blockade (tolerance). Another modern theory of drug tolerance is the homeostatic and pharmacologic redundancy concept of Martin,[57] according to which, through negative feedback *drug-insensitive* neuronal loops that are normally only weakly active, the functional effect of a drug produced by its action on the normally active *drug-sensitive* neuronal pathway is partially opposed. On chronic administration of the drug, its action on the drug-sensitive pathway continues unaltered, but the activity of the negative feedback drug-insensitive loops increases, thereby overcoming the action of the drug on the drug-sensitive pathway (tolerance). It is also postulated that activity in the "redundant" drug-insensitive negative feedback neuronal loops is mediated by various neurotransmitters that differ, perhaps, from the neuro-

* Supported in part by Research Grant DA 00879 from the National Institute on Drug Abuse.

transmitter in the drug-sensitive pathway ("pharmacologic redundancy"). Other theories of tolerance that involve the acquisition of compensatory adaptations as a result of the functional consequences of drug actions are the pharmacologic denervation supersensitivity concept of Jaffe and Sharpless [42] and the receptor induction concept of Collier.[18]

In all of these theories, a biochemical-neurophysiologic mechanism is postulated that could account for how an enzyme, a cell, or an aggregate of neuronal circuits "learns" to compensate for a disturbance in function produced by a drug. In these theories, it is tacitly assumed that the initial disturbance in function produced by a drug is always present; for example, an animal must breathe, and it must maintain a constant body temperature. At the level of animal behavior, however, for example, lever pressing on some difficult task, the disturbance in function produced by a drug may not be present, unless the animal attempts to perform the function. Therefore, it is not surprising to find that tolerance to a drug develops more rapidly if the animal performs or attempts to perform the function while under the influence of the drug. Therefore, such a phenomenon will be referred to as "behaviorally augmented tolerance." [45] Definitive evidence for behaviorally augmented tolerance requires that the drug be given chronically *before* testing in one group of animals and *after* testing in another group, with comparison of the effects of the drug before testing on the last day of chronic administration.[3, 16, 33] Other tests for behaviorally augmented tolerance, such as the influence of prior training, in which the drug is given only before testing, constitute tentative evidence. It goes without saying that tolerance develops at different rates for different functions (or may not develop for some functions) because of differences in adaptive capacities of the brain with regard to disturbances produced by drugs on different functions. Also, the rate of development of tolerance may vary with the dose of drug; in a given period of chronic administration, tolerance may develop to a lower dose but not to a higher dose.

The role of "learning" is less clear in the case of "dispositional tolerance," [45] where certain drugs "induce" enzymes that increase the rate of their metabolism.[19]

Tolerance to a drug may develop with respect to some functions, no tolerance may develop with regard to other functions, and, at the same time, the subject may be more sensitive to the effects of the drug on still other functions ("reverse tolerance"), perhaps as a result of learning to recognize and label certain of its effects. Therefore, the issue of "tolerance" versus "reverse tolerance" is not an either-or question. Studies on "reverse" tolerance have utilized subjects with *previous* histories of chronic or occasional marijuana use with variable intervals between previous use and experimental investigation and variable (largely unknown) dosage of previous cannabis (and other drug) use. Therefore, these investigators are studying "residual tolerance" and "residual reverse tolerance," with little control of the presumably critical antecedent variables. It should therefore be expected that there would be wide discrepancies in the results of such studies.

The term "dependence" has two meanings: *The occurrence of abstinence phenomena:* if the abstinence phenomena are physiologic, the subject is said to be "physically dependent"; if they are behavioral, the subject is sometimes said to be "psychically" or "psychologically" dependent (a relic of traditional mind-body dualism). *The occurrence of drug-seeking (or self-administrating) behavior:* if this behavior occurs without abstinence signs, the subject is said to be "psychically" dependent; if abstinence signs do occur, the subject is said to be both "psychically" and "physically" dependent. Further, "psychic dependence" is offered as an explanation of drug-seeking (or self-administrating) behavior, with which, in one sense, it is synonymous. Apparently, the term "psychic" is used to refer to the unknown in terms of the undefined.[82] In this review, the problem to be explained will be designated "drug-seeking (or self-administering) behavior." From the standpoint of conditioning theory, it will be viewed as a consequence of reinforcement, which may derive from social sources (social reinforcement) and/or pharmacologic sources (pharmacologic reinforcement). The latter may be direct (interaction of the drug with as yet ill-defined or unknown organismic variables that were not produced by the drug) or indirect (interaction of the drug with organismic variables that had been generated by the drug, for example, abstinence phenomena). These concepts have been discussed in some detail elsewhere.[81]

No Tolerance

No tolerance to certain effects of cannabis appears to occur under the following conditions.

Lipparini et al.[53] report that in the rabbit and rat, Δ^9-tetrahydrocannabinol (Δ^9-THC), Δ^8-THC, and two methylated derivatives of Δ^8-THC induced "flattening" of the electroencephalogram (EEG) tracing, disruption of hippocampal θ waves, and trains of high-voltage spikes and waves. These EEG changes were accompanied by corneal areflexia and other signs of motor deficit. In one rabbit, 3 mg/kg of Δ^9-THC were administered daily for 6 days; no appreciable attenuation of the EEG or behavioral response to the drug was observed.

In rats, Pirch et al.[65] found that single doses of 20 or 40 mg/kg of Δ^9-THC (orally?) reduced the "integrated voltage" of the EEG and produced changes in "gross behavior" (catalepsy and hyperresponsiveness). On daily administration of these doses (20 mg/kg, 10–12 days; 40 mg/kg, 3–13 days), tolerance developed to these effects, but "spindle-like" activity in the EEG increased after 3–5 days and persisted throughout the period of drug treatment. These investigators conclude that although tolerance to the initial decrease in "integrated voltage" does develop, no tolerance develops to the spindle-like activity. This interpretation is open to question. One may argue that the decrease in integrated voltage is due to desynchronization of the EEG by Δ^9-THC, while spindle-like activity represents "compensatory" synchronization; in that case, the increase in spindle-like activity would be evidence of at least partial tolerance. On the other hand, one may ask whether increased spindle-like activity contributed to integrated voltage; if so, the degree of observed "tolerance" to the initial decrease in integrated voltage would be uncertain.

McMillan et al.[60] found equivocal evidence for tolerance to the analgesic effects (hot plate) of 40 mg/kg of Δ^9-THC in mice after five daily doses.

In mice and Chinese hamsters, ten Ham and van Noordwijk[74] observed no evidence of tolerance to the suppressive effects of Δ^8-THC or Δ^9-THC on aggressiveness during 30 days of daily administration of either of these drugs. These investigators speculate that THC metabolites produce effects to which tolerance occurs, whereas THC itself, to which no tolerance develops, suppresses aggressiveness.

Kaymakcalan[46] states that he and his coworkers observed slight or questionable evidence of tolerance to the bradycardic effect of daily THC administration for 16 days in the rat and only slight or partial tolerance to daily THC for 8 days on heart rate, respiration, and temperature in the dog.

In EEG sleep studies on human subjects who smoked 14 mg of Δ^9-THC-containing "joints" (number of "joints" and time smoked were not given) for 10 successive days, Barratt et al.[6] observed that during the first night, the percentage of time spent in slow-wave sleep increased and the percentage of time spent in rapid eye movement (REM) sleep decreased; thereafter, REM sleep returned to predrug control levels, but the percentage of time spent in slow-wave sleep decreased to levels well below those of predrug control baseline and remained at such low levels throughout the drug treatment period. Although it is clear that tolerance to the initial reduction of percentage of time spent in REM sleep does develop, interpretation of the persistent reduction of percentage of time spent in slow-wave sleep after the initial increase is more difficult. The investigators state there is a significant increase in REM sleep above predrug baseline levels in the 3-day postdrug recovery period; their data also show that the lowered levels of percentage of time spent in slow-wave sleep during the drug period fall to even lower levels during the 3-day postdrug recovery period. One might interpret these postdrug recovery data as indicative of a THC abstinence syndrome; in that case, the lowest levels of percentage of time spent in slow-wave sleep, observed during the last 4 days of the 10-day drug period, may represent a partial abstinence phenomenon after the development of some tolerance (to the initial decrease in percentage of time spent in REM sleep). Barratt et al.[6] hypothesize that "the *chronic* use of marijuana leads to a significant decrease in slow wave sleep (stage 3 and 4) which results in dysphoria, lethargy, and a less aggressive behavior in everyday life situations." The possible relationship of such dysphoric effects of *chronic* marijuana use (also of *chronic* opioid [36, 58, 78] and/or barbiturate [40] use) to possible between-dose abstinence periods will be discussed later (see DEPENDENCE, *Abstinence Phenomena*).

In an experimental study on human subjects with previous histories of "moderate" and "heavy" use of marijuana in which the subjects "worked" (button presses) for money with which they could purchase 1 g of marijuana cigarettes (containing 2.1% of Δ^9-THC) or which they could save, Babor et al.[4, 5] observed that "moderate" users smoked an average of 3.2 cigarettes per day over 21 consecutive days. Throughout this period, there was no diminution in ratings of intoxication or of duration of increased pulse rate (no tolerance). In contrast, previously "heavy" users smoked an average of 5.7 cigarettes per day and did show progressive diminution in ratings of intoxication and in duration of increased pulse rate. These investigators conclude that tolerance to marijuana does not develop unless large amounts are smoked daily.

TOLERANCE, UNDIFFERENTIATED

Carlini[14] reported that seven of 10 rats developed complete tolerance to the initial prolongation of rope-climbing time produced by "cannabis extract" given daily for 15 days; partial tolerance (designated "nontolerant") developed in the other three rats. In a group of rats on a variable-interval 24-sec (VI 24-sec) water reinforcement schedule, "cannabis extract" (25 mg/kg) blocked responses after the first dose, but complete tolerance developed by the 11th day of daily injections of the drug. In another study,[71] rats made tolerant to Δ^9-THC or "cannabis extract" on both rope-climbing time and the VI 24-sec water reinforcement schedule were found not to be cross-tolerant to lysergic acid diethylamide (LSD-25) or mescaline; conversely, rats made tolerant to LSD-25 or mescaline were not cross-tolerant to Δ^9-THC or "cannabis extract." On the other hand, rats tolerant to LSD-25 were cross-tolerant to mescaline and vice versa. Likewise, Isbell and Jasinski [41] found that human subjects tolerant to LSD-25 exhibited no cross-tolerance to a single dose of Δ^9-THC. These cross-tolerance studies indicate differences between LSD-25 or mescaline, on the one hand, and THC or cannabis extract, on the other, in the metabolism of these drugs and/or their central sites of action.

McMillan et al.,[60] Ford and McMillan,[31] and Harris [37] found evidence of tolerance to repeated doses of THC in several species of animals. In pigeons on a fixed-ratio, 30 responses, fixed-interval, 15-sec (FR 30, FI 15-sec) food reward schedule, 1.8 mg/kg of Δ^9-THC abolished all responses on the first day; there was less effect on the second day of drug administration, and full tolerance to this dose appeared by the sixth day; the dose was then progressively increased, and complete tolerance to 36 mg/kg of Δ^9-THC was observed by the 25th day; almost complete tolerance to 180 mg/kg of Δ^9-THC eventually developed (this dose was fatal to drug-naive pigeons). Tolerance to Δ^9-THC developed even when the drug was given at intervals of 7–9 days. Pigeons tolerant to Δ^9-THC were cross-tolerant to Δ^8-THC but not to morphine. Naloxone had no effect on pigeons tolerant to 48 mg/kg of Δ^9-THC. In rats on a FR 10 water reinforcement schedule, the first dose of 10 mg/kg of Δ^9-THC abolished responding, but tolerance to this effect eventually developed to 100 mg/kg of Δ^9-THC on daily administration of the drug. In mice, a single dose of 10 mg/kg of Δ^9-THC *shortened* the duration of loss of the righting reflex produced by 3.75 g/kg of ethanol, but when Δ^9-THC was given for 4 days prior to ethanol, no effect of Δ^9-THC was observed. In dogs, a 100-fold dose tolerance to the initial effects of 2 mg/kg of Δ^9-THC (ataxia, swaying, hypersensitivity to moving objects, and prancelike foot placement) was observed on daily administration. Dewey et al.[22] report further that such tolerance occurred even when Δ^9-THC or Δ^8-THC was given every eighth day and persisted for at least 23 days after the last dose of THC. In tolerant dogs, 161 mg/kg of Δ^9-THC produced less effect than did 0.5 mg/kg of Δ^9-THC in drug-naive dogs. In monkeys, 1 mg/kg of Δ^9-THC produced behavioral depression, hypothermia, and weight loss; on daily administration of this dose for 7 days, tolerance to these effects occurred (one tolerant monkey showed no effects after administration of 2 mg/kg of Δ^9-THC on the 11th day).

Similarly, Fernandes et al.[26] reported that in rats, Δ^8-THC (intraperitoneally) produced reduction of food intake, weight loss, hypothermia, and delayed excretion of orally administered tap water; partial tolerance to the hypothermic effect developed by the fifth day and more so by the 10th day and to the other effects by the 11th day.

Tolerance to the hypothermic effect of Δ^9-THC was also reported by Lomax.[55] This investigator found that single doses of marijuana extract distillate (MED), equivalent to 10 or 20 mg/kg of Δ^9-THC, produced a dose-related fall in body temperature. A lesser fall was observed on retesting the next day. After 6 days of daily administration of 20 mg/kg of Δ^9-THC, a *rise* in temperature was found. Lomax concludes that, like morphine, marijuana has a dual effect on thermoregulatory mechanisms in the rat: a depressant (temperature-lowering) one, to which tolerance develops, and a stimulant (temperature-elevating) one (to which, presumably, no tolerance develops). He speculates that in chronic marijuana users (in whom tolerance has developed to depressant effects), the stimulant effects predominate and may account for the "reverse tolerance" that has been reported [77] to occur in such subjects (see RESIDUAL TOLERANCE AND "REVERSE TOLERANCE").

In chicks 10 hr after hatching, Abel [1] observed that 10 mg/kg of Δ^9-THC markedly depressed locomotor activity, prolonged escape time from a heat stimulus, and produced profound hypothermia. On daily administration, almost complete tolerance developed within 16 days.

Potvin and Fried [67] compared the effects of parenterally administered Δ^9-THC (0.5 or 0.4 mg/kg; or the propylene glycol vehicle or handling and a "blank" injection) in rats that had received five or 25 injections (48 hr apart?) on a rotating rod, balance beam, time to enter a black or white choice box, open field, and swimming time. In rats that had received five previous injections, 0.5 mg/kg of Δ^9-THC had little effect, except on the open field test, whereas 4 mg/kg impaired all motor skills. In rats that had received 25 previous injections, performance on all motor tasks was equal or superior to that of control rats, indicating tolerance. The rats that had received 25 injections of Δ^9-THC showed evidence of "hyperemotionality," and both these rats and those that had received five injections developed a shift in preference for the white, instead of the black, choice boxes.

Davis et al.[20] reported that in rats, 25 mg/kg of Δ^9-THC (subcutaneously) increased locomotor activity for the first 2 hr but depressed it subsequently. On daily administration of Δ^9-THC, tolerance to the depressant effect developed by the 10th day and persisted up to 11 days after cessation of drug administration. Moreton and Davis [62] found that in rats, tolerance developed to the initial depressant effect of 10 mg/kg of Δ^9-THC on paradoxical sleep (REM sleep) on daily administration for 20 days; no "rebound" of paradoxical sleep occurred after withdrawal of Δ^9-THC, and partial tolerance to the depressant effect of the drug on paradoxical sleep remained on retesting on the 13th withdrawal day.

Kaymakcalan and Deneau [47] and Kaymakcalan [46] reported that in rats, tolerance develops rapidly to analgesic (hot plate and phenylquinone tests) and hypothermic effects and found reduction of ^{125}I uptake by the thyroid gland on daily administration of Δ^9-THC. Tolerance to the analgesic effect persisted for more than 1 month after a single injection of 10 mg/kg of Δ^9-THC. THC-tolerant rats were cross-tolerant to the analgesic effects of morphine (contrast with absence of cross-tolerance between THC and morphine in pigeons on a FR 30, FI 15-sec schedule, reported by McMillan et al.[60]).

In monkeys, Elsmore [25] observed partial tolerance to a decrease in accuracy of discrimination between duration of a visual stimulus and frequency of an auditory clicker on administration of 2–16 mg/kg of Δ^9-THC daily.

Deneau and Kaymakcalan [47] and Kaymakcalan [46] reported that in monkeys, on intravenous administration of 0.1 mg/kg of Δ^9-THC every 6 hr, the initial effects of the drug were ptosis, blank staring, scratching, and docility. The dose of Δ^9-THC was gradually increased to 4 mg/kg, and tolerance to these effects developed within a few days of each dose increment. Abrupt withdrawal of Δ^9-THC was followed by abstinence phenomena (see DEPENDENCE, Abstinence Phenomena).

Sassenrath and Chapman [70] studied the behavior of selected male and female monkeys living in either high-density caged or low-density outdoor groups. These selected animals were given 2.4 mg of Δ^9-THC in preferred food (said to be equivalent to smoking 0.4 mg/kg of Δ^9-THC cigarettes in man: "heavy" marijuana use) for various periods over 1 year. Initial effects included both sedation (increased frequencies and duration of sleep episodes and sitting or lying down; suppression or elimination of exploratory behavior; high arousal responses, such as cage shaking; decreased aggressive behavior of dominant group members, especially in the food competition situation, and reception of more aggression from nondrugged cagemates; more huddling with preferred cagemates and less grooming of others and self, play, and self-scratching) and activation (increased pacing and flipping; increased visual monitoring of cagemates). Tolerance to both the sedative and activation effects developed in 2 weeks to 2 months (no changes were observed in plasma testosterone, progesterone, or cortisol levels, in urinary excretion of cortisol, epinephrine, norepinephrine, or 3-methoxy-4-hydroxyphenylglycol, or of these catecholamine metabolites after administration of ACTH; conception and lactation were normal in females). Concurrently with the development of tolerance to the initial effects of Δ^9-THC, increased irritable responsiveness developed in drug-treated group members, which took the form of slightly increased aggression for most of the THC-treated subjects; drug-treated females (but not males) rose in the dominance hierarchy. These investigators state that: "In our own studies, initiating or increasing daily THC levels produced sedation and activation and depressed affect, while maintaining a constant daily dose level resulted in the development of tolerance to these effects and increased irritability." They note the resemblance of such a sequence of behavior to drug intoxication and withdrawal signs but doubt the latter, because the monkeys did not show increased aggressiveness after cessation of THC administration or preference for drugged food (however, these monkeys had not been operantly conditioned).

In chimpanzees pretrained for years on a differential reinforcement of low rates, 60–90 sec, fixed-ratio, 50 responses (DRL 60–90 sec, FR 50) food-reinforced schedule, Sodetz [72] observed that during a period of daily oral administration of 1 mg/kg of Δ^9-THC for 35 days, interresponse times were shortened (alterations of time sense), and reinforcements were forfeited initially, but tolerance eventually developed (fewer reinforcements were forfeited). "Rebound" lengthening of interresponse times (with forfeiture of reinforcements) occurred on the second to eighth withdrawal days, after which time interresponse times (and reinforcements) returned to control baselines.

Williams et al. [84] conducted studies on the effects of ad lib. ingestion of synhexyl (pyrahexyl compound, 60–2400 mg/day in one to eight divided doses for 26–31 days) and of smoked marijuana cigarettes (not assayed but considered "good weed" by the subjects, one to 26 cigarettes per day, average 17/day) for 39 days in groups of former marijuana users. In the synhexyl studies, the initial effects were drowsiness, euphoria, dryness of the mouth, injection of the scleral conjunctivae, increased appetite, swollen eyelids, spontaneous garrulity, pupillary dilatation, slowness of reaction, and difficulty in expressing thoughts. After 2 or 3 days, subjects lost interest in their surroundings and had a decreased ability to concentrate. After 4–6 days, all subjects increased their dosage, with reappearance of the initial effects to some degree. Again, tolerance to these effects developed, and thenceforth only progressive lethargy and irritability were observed. Tolerance was also observed to the initial increase in caloric intake and in hours of sleep. Changes suggestive of a withdrawal syndrome appeared on the third to fourth days after cessation of synhexyl administration (see DEPENDENCE, *Abstinence Phenomena*). In the marijuana cigarette smoking studies, much the same sequence of effects was observed, except that the increase in number of marijuana cigarettes smoked per day was small compared to the increase in ad lib. dosage of synhexyl. As in the synhexyl study, the initial euphoric-silly behavior soon changed to loss of interest in work, decreased activity, indolence, nonproductivity, and neglect of personal hygiene. Also, tolerance developed to the initial increase in pulse rate that persisted for the first 3 weeks of the smoking period, after which time the pulse rate was not significantly different from that in the premarijuana smoking period. All subjects reported they were "jittery" on the first day or two after abrupt cessation of smoking, but no objective concomitants were observed. Two subjects, one in this study and another in an ancillary study, displayed brief paranoid psychotic reactions after smoking marijuana.[79, 84]

Volavka et al.[75] and Dornbush et al.[24] also observed both the development of dysphoria and the paranoid thoughts and depression that appeared on the third to sixth days of a 21-day study on the effects of smoking two marijuana cigarettes, each of which contained 14 mg of Δ^9-THC, after the initial euphoric effects. Tolerance also developed to the initial impairment of short-term memory (recall of trigrams after 6-, 12-, and 18-sec delay) and increase in cardiac rate. The percentage of time occupied by α activity (α percentage) increased by 11 min, then returned to control values by 31 min on the first day of smoking marijuana cigarettes. Thereafter, the initial increase in α percentage persisted but by 31 min fell to values below the control level.

As already noted, Babor et al.[4, 5] observed tolerance to ratings of intoxication and duration of increased pulse rate in human subjects (previously "heavy" users of marijuana) smoking an average of 5.7 marijuana cigarettes per day for 21 days.

Barratt et al.[6] noted the development of tolerance to the initial depressant effect of marijuana cigarettes that contained 14 mg of Δ^9-THC on REM percentage of sleep in man over a 10-day smoking period. "Rebound" of REM percentage occurred on the third recovery day.

TOLERANCE, DIFFERENTIATED

Dispositional Tolerance

Dewey et al.[23] measured radioactivity in the plasma and plasma fractions of THC-tolerant and nontolerant pigeons after a single dose of 10 mg/kg of [^{3}H]Δ^9-THC; no differences were found. They concluded that tolerance to Δ^9-THC is not dependent on lowered blood levels of Δ^9-THC or its metabolites (including 11-OH-Δ^9-THC) in tolerant pigeons. McMillan and Dewey[59] measured brain radioactivity in "chronically" and "acutely" tolerant pigeons after seven daily injections of [^{3}H]Δ^9-THC (5.0 μCi). Brain radioactivity was higher in the "chronically" than in the "acutely" tolerant pigeons, and they concluded that "it seems unlikely that tolerance to Δ^9-THC depends on decreased penetration of total tetrahydrocannabinol in the brain." Noting the marked increase in lethal dose of THC in tolerant compared to nontolerant pigeons and the findings of Black et al.,[8] they also concluded that "by a process of elimination it appears that tolerance to Δ^9-THC occurs through pharmacodynamic mechanisms at the cellular level, rather than by learning or drug dispositional mechanisms."

On the other hand, Lemberger et al.[49, 51, 52] found that after intravenous injection of a single dose of 0.5 mg of $[^{14}C]\Delta^9$-THC in formerly "heavy" users of marijuana and in nonusers, the initial decline in plasma radioactivity was rapid in both groups of subjects ($t_{1/2} = 30$ min in nonusers), but this decrease was followed by a slower decline, the half-life of which was 28 hr in formerly "heavy" users and 50–60 hr in nonusers. The apparent volumes of tissue disposition were not significantly different for formerly "heavy" users and nonusers, so the shorter half-life in formerly "heavy" users may be the result of increased metabolism of Δ^9-THC. Whether such increased metabolism of Δ^9-THC can partially account for residual tolerance to the drug in "heavy" marijuana users, or for residual "reverse tolerance" in such subjects, will be discussed later (see RESIDUAL TOLERANCE AND "REVERSE TOLERANCE").

Behaviorally Augmented or Not

Definitive Evidence

Black et al.[8] found that the key-pecking rates of pigeons on a FR 30, FI 15-min schedule were depressed by intramuscular administration of 10 mg/kg of Δ^9-THC, 0.3 mg/kg of dimethylheptyl-substituted tetrahydrocannabinol (DMHP), or 10 mg/kg of synhexyl. Tolerance to these effects developed when the drugs were given once every 7 days for 7 weeks, regardless of whether the pigeons performed while under the influence of the drug, indicating that the tolerance was of pharmacologic origin. Cross-tolerance was also demonstrated between Δ^9-THC and synhexyl and between Δ^9-THC and DMHP at the dose levels mentioned.

In a one-way shock avoidance study on rats, Newman et al.[63] reported that in single doses, 20 mg of Δ^9-THC or 3.2 g/kg of ethanol (parenterally) depressed the percentage of avoidance responses. When given daily before or after testing, tolerance developed to the depressant effect of this dose of Δ^9-THC at a mean of 13.1 days, and then a single dose of 3.2 g/kg of ethanol had much less effect. In rats made tolerant to 3.2 g/kg of ethanol, a single dose of 20 mg/kg of Δ^9-THC had less effect than before the development of tolerance to ethanol. The investigators conclude that there is cross-tolerance between THC and alcohol, at least with regard to avoidance performing, and that such tolerance to these drugs is not due to increased training or state-dependent learning (during the tolerance trials).

Webster et al.[76] established a discriminated Sidman avoidance procedure in rats, so that a shock was delivered every 10 sec in the presence of a continuous light and a clicker unless the animal pressed a lever that terminated the shock, light, and clicker and that initiated a 20-sec delay, after which time the light and clicker were presented briefly, indicating that 10 sec later, it would appear again, accompanied by a shock. If the animal failed to respond during the latter 10-sec interval, the light and clicker continued, and shocks were delivered every 10 sec. By responding appropriately, the rats could avoid the shocks. One group of rats received 12 mg/kg of Δ^9-THC intraperitoneally daily *before* each session (DR group) and another group *after* each session (RD group), except on test days, when all rats received the drug before the session. The initial effect of Δ^9-THC was to increase total responding, premature responding, and number of shocks received. However, by the ninth day, tolerance was evident in both the DR and RD groups. Such tolerance was lost within 9 days after Δ^9-THC was replaced by the vehicle, propylene glycol.

Adams and Barratt [2] investigated the performance of monkeys on the following multiple schedule: time-out 10 sec (TO 10 sec) accompanied by a flashing light; fixed ratio 2–15 sec (FR 2–15 sec); hold lever 2–15 sec (HL 2–15 sec) accompanied by a steady white light; and release lever within 1 sec (RL 1 sec) in the presence of a red light. Correct sequential responses were rewarded by access to sucrose. Reaction times (RT) were measured from the onset of the red light to release of the lever. By oral intubation, 0.34, 0.68, and 1.36 mg/kg of Δ^9-THC were given *after* testing daily for 21 days, except every fifth day, when the Δ^9-THC was given *before* testing (the vehicle, Tween® 80 and saline, was given before testing, except every fifth day, when it was given after testing). At least 30 days without the drug elapsed between these three dose levels. On the first fifth day (Δ^9-THC *before* testing), the percentage of correct responses was decreased, and RTs were prolonged; on succeeding fifth days, tolerance was observed to these effects of 0.68 mg/kg of Δ^9-THC but not to 1.36 mg/kg of Δ^9-THC. On the intervening days (Δ^9-THC *after* testing), comparison with predrug treatment control data revealed that on 0.68 mg/kg of Δ^9-THC, RTs were prolonged, whereas on 1.36 mg/kg of Δ^9-THC, RTs were shortened. The effects of THC on RT appear to be biphasic; the later acceleration of RT (more marked on the larger dose, 1.36 mg/kg of Δ^9-THC) accounts for the decrease in percentage of correct responses (monkeys fail to hold the lever down for the required time). The investigators point out that this effect is consonant with the attenuation of time sense by marijuana in man ("speeding up of the internal clock"). They conclude that (at least with regard to the 0.68-mg/kg dose of Δ^9-THC) their results are consonant with the evidence for tolerance reported in studies on lower animals.

On the other hand, evidence of behaviorally augmented tolerance was found by Carder and Olson.[11] Rats were pretrained on a continuous reinforcement lever-pressing schedule for food reward. One group of rats received parenteral injections of marijuana distillate extract equivalent to 0.3 mg/kg of Δ^9-THC before testing daily for 6 days, while another group received the same dose of Δ^9-THC after testing daily for 6 days (the vehicle, propylene glycol, was given after testing in the first group and before testing in the second group). The performance of the group that received Δ^9-THC before testing was about half the control rate throughout the 6 days, whereas that of the other group (Δ^9-THC after testing) declined steadily to that of the first group (Δ^9-THC before testing) by the sixth day. The order of administration of Δ^9-THC was then reversed for half of each of the two groups, and it was observed that the performance of the subgroup that had been switched from Δ^9-THC after testing to Δ^9-THC before testing was significantly below that of the other three subgroups. A similar study with similar results was performed on rats on a continuous reinforcement lever-pressing schedule for water reinforcement, with Δ^9-THC increasing in daily dosage from 8 to 32 mg/kg over 7 days. These results were interpreted as indicating that the development of tolerance to marijuana involves a learning process (e.g., state dependence).

Tentative Evidence

Olson and Carder [64] pretrained rats on a zig-zag runway after oral administration of propylene glycol (the vehicle for Δ^9-THC) 1 hr before each session for four sessions. Training continued every second day for an additional 23 sessions, but one group of rats received marijuana extract distillate equivalent to 6 mg/kg of Δ^9-THC orally 1 hr before each session. Another group continued to receive propylene glycol until the fifth day, when a subgroup began to receive 6 mg/kg of Δ^9-THC orally instead of propylene glycol, and until the 15th day, when 6 mg/kg of Δ^9-THC was substituted for propylene glycol in another subgroup, while the remainder of the group continued to receive propylene glycol. The rats on the propylene glycol placebo reached maximum starting speed on the 11th day, whereas it took 20 days to attain this speed in rats started on Δ^9-THC the first day, 17 days in rats started on Δ^9-THC the fifth day, and only 5 days in rats started on Δ^9-THC the 15th day. It was concluded that increased prior training increases the rate of behavioral tolerance development.

In monkeys on a DRL 60-sec food reinforcement schedule, Manning[56] reported that 0.5–16 mg/kg of Δ^9-THC (orally), given 3 hr before the session in single doses at least 1 week apart, increased the number of unreinforced responses and shortened interresponse times. However, performance improved during the second half of each session. No differences were found when Δ^9-THC was given 4 hr, instead of 3 hr, before the session. Assuming that the pharmacologic actions of orally administered Δ^9-THC peak at 3 hr or less and that at 4 hr, the action of Δ^9-THC would be less than at 3 hr, Manning concluded that "it is performance under the influence of THC rather than mere exposure to the drug that is responsible for the marked improvement in performance observed during the drug sessions."

Ferraro[27] reports that in two of three monkeys trained on DRL 10 sec for a food reward, 2 mg/kg of Δ^9-THC orally each day for 21 days initially decreased the number of reinforcements obtained, but partial tolerance eventually developed. In the third monkey, the same dose of Δ^9-THC did not reduce the number of reinforcements obtained, though the number of responses increased by the sixth day, and no tolerance to this effect was observed through the 21st day of drug administration. Similarly, in two of three other monkeys trained on a VI 45-sec LH 8-sec schedule, partial tolerance developed to the initial depression of responding and decrease in number of reinforcements obtained on daily oral administration of 2 mg/kg of Δ^9-THC for 14 consecutive days, but in the third monkey, the same schedule of Δ^9-THC administration resulted in increased responding above the control level and in no loss of reinforcements; no tolerance to this effect was observed. Ferraro concludes that tolerance to THC is the consequence of learning to compensate for adverse effects of the drug (decrease in reinforcements); if no adverse effects occur (or the subject cannot learn compensatory responses), no tolerance develops.

Similar conclusions were reached in studies on chimpanzees. Ferraro[27] and Ferraro and Grisham[30] reported that tolerance developed by the sixth day of oral administration of 3 mg/kg of Δ^9-THC for 14 days, after an initial decrease in percentage of correct responses and number of reinforcements obtained (interresponse times shortened) on a DRL 10-sec food reward schedule. Likewise, in chimpanzees pretrained on a DRL 20-sec food reward schedule, tolerance developed to the initial depression of percentage of correct responses (and shortened interresponse times) observed during daily oral administration of Δ^9-THC that increased from 1 to 4 mg/kg over a period of 14 days.[30]

In a delayed matching-to-sample task[27, 30] with a 20-sec delay, no tolerance was observed to the reduction of matching accuracy during oral administration of Δ^9-THC before testing (1 mg/kg for 21 days, then no drug for 21 days, followed by 4 mg/kg for 42 days, and finally no drug for 33 days). It may be remarked here that 1 and 4 mg/kg of Δ^9-THC in chimpanzees are equivalent to the enormous total doses of 70 and 280 mg in a 70-kg man; Ferraro and Grilly [28] state that effects on behavior controlled by reinforcement schedules have been observed with THC doses as low as 0.2 mg/kg (presumably, in chimpanzees). However, in other chimpanzees, after reducing the delay to 10 sec and the daily dose of Δ^9-THC to 0.75 mg/kg for 15 days, complete tolerance was observed to the initial depression of percentage of matching accuracy. Later, the delay was increased to 20 sec, and no tolerance occurred during 15 days of daily oral administration of Δ^9-THC (0.75 mg/kg); on reversion to the 10-sec delay, tolerance was again observed to develop. On alternate days of testing on matching-to-sample and oral Δ^9-THC administration, followed by testing on matching-to-sample with delays up to 40 sec, Ferraro et al.[29] found that tolerance did develop to the initial depression of matching accuracy. They attribute such tolerance to learning compensatory responses on nondrug days.

DISSOCIATED LEARNING (STATE DEPENDENCE)

Bueno and Carlini [10] found that rats made tolerant to "cannabis extract" on a rope-climbing test quickly learned to press the correct one of two levers for a food reward when injected intraperitoneally with cannabis extract but not when injected intraperitoneally with a "control solution." Such discrimination extended to 5.0 mg/kg of Δ^9-THC. These investigators concluded that though tolerant to the effects of cannabis on rope-climbing time, the rats were not tolerant to other (unknown) effects that served as a discriminative cue for state-dependent learning.

Glick and Milloy [34] adduced evidence for state-dependent learning on Δ^9-THC in mice by utilizing a passive avoidance test. Mice were given a training trial, retested the next day, and again after 7 days. Δ^9-THC (2 mg/kg, parenterally) was given to one group on the training trial day only, to a second group on the first retest day only, and to a third group on the first and seventh retest days only. On the first and seventh retest trials, none of the mice in the second and third groups entered the shock box (i.e., median latencies to enter were more than 600 sec). However, the mice in the first group (those that had received Δ^9-THC before the training trial only) entered the shock box with median latencies of 350.3 sec on the first retest day and 172.3 sec on the seventh retest day, which were significantly shorter than 600 sec (p < 0.05). Actually, these results are a demonstration of asymmetric dissociation ("one-way" state-dependent learning).

Rickles et al.[68] reported evidence of state-dependent learning in previously "light" marijuana users on testing of recall 10 days after paired associate learning under either placebo or marijuana intoxication conditions. In contrast, a similar study by Cohen and Rickles [17] in previously "heavy" marijuana users revealed no evidence of state-dependent learning. In the previously "light" users, significantly more trials to criterion were needed under marijuana intoxication than on placebo, whereas in previously "heavy" users, no significant differences were observed, which suggests that previously "heavy" users had residual tolerance to marijuana. Cohen and Rickles suggest that lack of "novelty" may explain the absence of the state-dependent effect in heavy users of marijuana.

Bowman and Pihl [9] state that adult Jamaican males who typically smoked high potency (4–5% Δ^9-THC) marijuana heavily (equivalent to 23 cigarettes per day) on frequent occasions for a mean of 16.6 years since the age of 12.5 years "often smoked marijuana specifically to provide energy and strength in order to accomplish particularly heavy tasks, and the drug is widely regarded as a stimulant for this purpose. . . ." One possible interpretation of such use of marijuana in such subjects is state-dependent learning.

RESIDUAL TOLERANCE AND "REVERSE TOLERANCE"

Jones [43, 44] compared the effects of an orally administered extract of marijuana (25 mg of THC) or placebo and of smoking marijuana cigarettes (9 mg of Δ^9-THC) or placebo cigarettes in previously frequent and infrequent marijuana users. After smoking marijuana, acceleration of pulse rate and decrease in salivary flow were significantly less in frequent than in infrequent users, and the decrease in number of responses on the digit substitution test and the increase in complex reaction time were nonsignificantly less in frequent than in infrequent users, indicating residual tolerance in the frequent users. Residual tolerance to the subjective "high" was also found in frequent users compared to infrequent users after administration of the marijuana extract orally but not on smoking, when a marked placebo effect was seen in frequent users. In the frequent users, specific symptoms on the Waskow 272-item checklist were different for marijuana and placebo, but the subjects labeled these symptoms as a "high" on both placebo and marijuana. No evidence of "reverse" tolerance, such as that reported by Weil et al.,[77] was seen. Jones notes that sedative effects were generally observed when marijuana was smoked individually, whereas elation, euphoria, uncontrolled laughter, and a marked lack of sedation were observed when the subjects smoked in a group situation.

Casswell and Marks [15] found that experienced and naive marijuana users showed equal impairment on the goal-directed serial alternation task (which requires integrity of short-term memory and logical sequence of thoughts) and on the serial subtraction of sevens task after smoking marijuana cigarettes (which contained 3.3 and 6.6 mg of Δ^9-THC) compared to placebo, indicating absence of residual tolerance to these effects of marijuana in experienced subjects. Likewise, no differences were observed between experienced and naive users in subjective rating of intoxication and on the Tart scale, but "after smoking the *placebo* material the experienced subjects reported a greater effect on the variables of visual imagery, auditory imagery, and thought processes than naive subjects, presumably reflecting the importance of past learning experiences on the induction of cannabis effects" (cf. Jones [43, 44]).

The role of "setting" in facilitating marijuana effects was investigated by Hollister et al.[39] in former marijuana smokers ("heavy" or "light" not specified) who smoked marijuana cigarettes (which contained 19 mg of Δ^9-THC) or a placebo in a "favorable" (apartment, incense, mystical pictures, background "meditation" music, and so on) and a "neutral" (laboratory) environment. Scores on a "linear euphoriant scale" and a cart-sort version of the Addiction Research Center Inventory of subjective effects of marijuana and hallucinogens revealed strong effects for the subjects and drugs but not for the environmental conditions.

Likewise, Carlin et al.[13] found no significant "modeling" effects (provided by a "hip-type" accomplice who played "up" or "down") on self-ratings of intoxication, the Linton-Lang questionnaire checklist, or performance on color naming, digit symbol substitution, hidden figures, and association tasks in *marijuana-naive* 21–34-year-old subjects who smoked marijuana cigarettes (which contained 7.5 mg of Δ^9-THC) or a placebo (compared to placebo, marijuana produced significant scores of intoxication and impaired functioning on the cognitive tasks). However, significant marijuana-modeling interactions were found for time spent playing with psychedelic toys and for impairment of short-term memory (Wechsler Associate Learning Task). Comparing these data with those obtained in a previous study on *experienced marijuana users*,[12] they found that self-ratings of intoxication were about twofold higher in experienced users than in naive users (both on marijuana) and, again, about twice as high in experienced than in naive users on placebo, though in both groups, placebo ratings were much less than marijuana ratings. On the symptoms checklist, no differences were observed between experienced and naive users 30 min after smoking marijuana. Likewise, no differences between experienced and naive users were found in impairment of cognitive task performance by marijuana (indicating no residual tolerance). Carlin et al.[13] conclude that performance, rather than self-rating, is a more sensitive index of drug-setting interaction and that "symptoms and impairment do not contribute directly to judgments of intoxication, but must be interpreted in the light of previous experience in order for an individual to consider himself intoxicated. The response to marijuana is at least partially pharmacologically based, but the *interpretation* of the symptoms making up that response is a vital factor in determining whether one is 'high' or whether one is just forgetful, lightheaded etc. Sensitization to marijuana intoxication, and experiences of 'reverse tolerance' seem to be a cognitive social rather than physiological process."

In their studies on metabolism and disposition of 0.5 mg of $[^{14}C]\Delta^9$-THC administered intravenously in long-term marijuana smokers, Lemberger et al.[52] found that, unlike nonsmokers,[51] these subjects reported marijuana-like effects that lasted about 30 min (environmental conditions were not controlled, and no placebo was given). Also, they found that the half-time of decline in plasma radioactivity during the slower phase in long-term marijuana users was about half of that in nonusers. Considerable quantities of Δ^9-THC metabolites, including the active metabolite 11-OH-Δ^9-THC,[50] were present as soon as 10 min after intravenous administration of $[^{14}C]\Delta^9$-THC, and lesser quantities of 11-OH-Δ^9-THC and more polar metabolites appeared in the phase of slower decline of plasma radioactivity (though their concentrations exceeded that of Δ^9-THC itself after the initial 10 min). In the urine, an unknown polar metabolite continued to be excreted for up to 1 week.

Lemberger et al. speculate that "the 'reverse tolerance' observed in chronic users of marijuana could be the consequence of induction of enzymes which convert Δ^9-THC to a more active or more stable metabolite. It could also be due to cumulative effects of repeated administration, to increased receptor sensitivity to Δ^9-THC or its metabolites, or to a learned and heightened response to the effects of Δ^9-THC." Insofar as conversion of Δ^9-THC to 11-OH-Δ^9-THC and more polar metabolites is concerned, it appears to this reviewer that no evidence has been presented to indicate that such conversion occurs more rapidly or is quantitatively greater in long-term marijuana users than in nonusers. The shorter half-life of the slower phase of decline in plasma radioactivity after intravenous administration of $[^{14}C]\Delta^9$-THC in long-term marijuana users could well be due to liver microsomal enzyme induction by marijuana or other drugs (e.g., "downers") that long-term marijuana users may also take, but such enzyme induction could just as well account, in part, for the residual tolerance found by Jones.[43, 44]

Evidence of "reverse tolerance" to the effects of smoking marijuana (600 mg of what, by assay, contained 1.0% Δ^9-THC) was found by Milstein *et al.*[61] in experienced users on a perceptual-motor task (moving or holding a stylus in horizontal or vertical grooves or in holes of progressively smaller diameters without contacting the edges). The degree of impairment (compared to smoking placebo cigarettes) was greater in experienced than in naive subjects. Also, retrospective identification of marijuana or placebo cigarettes was significant for both groups of subjects, but there was a significant drug-previous experience interaction.

As already stated, Lomax[55] suggests that on certain functions (e.g., temperature in rats) marijuana exerts dual effects, depression predominating at first. However, tolerance develops to such depressant effects, and then the stimulant effects predominate. Assuming that no tolerance develops to such stimulant effects, the long-term marijuana user could manifest what appears to be "reverse tolerance."

DEPENDENCE

Abstinence Phenomena

No abstinence phenomena have been described in animal research in which cannabis extract or Δ^9-THC or other active THCs have been administered *once* daily for a variable number of days. However, Deneau and Kaymakcalan[21] and Kaymakcalan[46] have reported that in monkeys that received automatic intravenous injections of Δ^9-THC *every 6 hr* for 1 month in doses that increased from 0.1 to 0.4 mg/kg, tolerance developed to the initial effects (ptosis, blank staring, scratching, and docility), and when injections were discontinued, abstinence signs appeared, beginning at about 12 hr and continuing for about 5 days. These abstinence signs consisted of yawning, anorexia, piloerection, hyperirritability, and increase in aggressiveness, scratching, biting and licking fingers, pulling hair, tremors, twitches, penile erections and masturbation with ejaculation, eating feces and other unusual things, slapping at the cage walls, staring in circles, and grasping as if catching flies (hallucinations?).

The every 6-hr injection schedule used by these investigators may be crucial in the development of physical dependence on THC, because "around-the-clock" chronic intoxication has been employed traditionally in experimental demonstration of *optimal* conditions for the emergence of abstinence phenomena on abrupt withdrawal from barbiturates and other sedative drugs[40, 69, 83] and from morphine.[38]

In man, *physiologic* cannabis abstinence phenomena have not been observed, although Fraser[32] stated that withdrawal hyperirritability, terrifying visual and auditory hallucinations, and incessant masturbation that lasted 3–5 weeks occurred in nine ganja smokers among Indian soldiers. Kielholz and Ladewig[48] described withdrawal sweating, disturbed sleep, fine tremors, hypotonia, and mild depression that lasted for 5–7 days after withdrawal of hashish in three juveniles who had smoked pure hashish daily. Likewise, Jones[43] states that five heavy marijuana or hashish smokers who were interviewed reported they had experienced irritability, restlessness, insomnia, increased perspiration, and salivation that occurred about 24–48 hr after cessation of regular use and that these effects were relieved by barbiturates, alcohol, or resumption of marijuana use. Williams et al.[84] reported that experimental subjects who had smoked one to 26 marijuana cigarettes per day (average 17/day) for 39 days complained of transient "jitteriness" after abrupt cessation of marijuana smoking, but no objective abstinence signs were observed. These investigators also reported that more definite abstinence signs appeared in experimental subjects on abrupt withdrawal of synhexyl after 26–31 days of ad lib. ingestion of 60–2400 mg of the drug daily (in one to eight divided doses): on the third day after withdrawal, most of the subjects became restless, slept poorly, had poor appetites, hot flashes, and perspired. One subject displayed a panic reaction (agitated, fearful, disoriented), and on the fourth day, another became hypomanic (overactive, euphoria, bowing to others, drowsy at times).

In experimental studies on chronic marijuana or synhexyl intoxication in man [24, 75, 84] and in the monkey,[70] it has been observed that with the development of tolerance, the subjects became hyperirritable and dysphoric (this is also true of experimental subjects tolerant to barbiturates,[40] morphine,[36, 78] and methadone [58]). Such hyperirritability and dysphoria subside when a dose of marijuana is taken or given but reappear shortly afterward and persist until the next dose.[70] Such "oscillation of temperament" has been well described by Soueif [73] in a discussion of hashish use in Egypt. Soueif regards this "oscillation of temperament" as "the behavioral core of a state of psychic dependence" and regards the ascendancy, seclusiveness, negativism, depression of mood, and pugnacity that hashish users exhibit some time after the last previous dose of hashish as "the main components of a psychic withdrawal syndrome." Dispensing with the obfuscating term "psychic," it appears quite possible that the hyperirritability and dysphoria displayed by chronic cannabis users are actually *behavioral* abstinence phenomena. Under conditions of ordinary marijuana use in the West, such behavioral abstinence phenomena subside rapidly after cessation of marijuana smoking and may not be noticed by the smokers or their observers. On the other hand, the "amotivational syndrome" that has been described in long-term marijuana users (who, presumably, were not intoxicated at the time they were studied) may be due to persistence of such a between-dose abstinence syndrome.

Drug-Seeking Behavior

Deneau and Kaymakcalan [21] and Kaymakcalan [46] report that drug-naive monkeys will not self-administer Δ^9-THC. Apparently, at least in monkeys, Δ^9-THC is not a primary *direct* reinforcer. However, these investigators found that two of the six monkeys studied did initiate and maintain intravenous self-injection of Δ^9-THC when they displayed abstinence phenomena following withdrawal of Δ^9-THC after they had been made tolerant by automatic intravenous injections of the drug (0.1–0.4 mg/kg every 6 hr for 1 month). Therefore, it appears that in monkeys at least, Δ^9-THC is a primary *indirect* reinforcer; that is, its reinforcing properties derive from its potency in suppressing Δ^9-THC abstinence phenomena. A third monkey, which did not self-inject Δ^9-THC, did self-administer cocaine when this drug was made available and then initiated and maintained self-injections of Δ^9-THC when this drug replaced cocaine.

In man, the much-vaunted "marijuana high" may, at first glance, be regarded as evidence of primary direct reinforcing effects of Δ^9-THC or other active THCs. However, as Becker[7] has pointed out, the previously marijuana-naive subject must first learn to recognize that he is intoxicated (e.g., the logical sequence of thoughts is impaired) and then learn from experienced marijuana smokers to label such intoxication as a "high." In the study by Weil et al.,[77] habitual smokers of marijuana reported that they were "high," whereas naive subjects reported only that "things seem to go slower," "a sense of the past disappearing," "fits of silliness," and "I would keep forgetting what I was doing." Obviously, these subjective changes were typical effects of marijuana, but the naive subjects did not label them as a "high," presumably because of lack of "education." Wikler[80] and Lewis[54] have suggested that although not a primary pharmacologic reinforcer, marijuana acquires secondary (conditioned) reinforcing properties through bringing about social reinforcement (e.g., acceptance into membership in the "antiestablishment" group) in the milieu of the "pot party." In consequence of such social reinforcement, the previously naive user learns to call the functionally disrupting effects of the drug a "high" and is then disposed to repeat the experience. Babor et al.[4, 5] have noted that the tendency of even nontolerant subjects to increase the number of cigarettes smoked per day in an experimental situation may be due to such "psychosocial" factors. It appears, therefore, that the current popularity of repeated smoking of marijuana with relatively low Δ^9-THC content in the West is due, not to the pharmacologic actions that the drug exerts, but to the social reinforcement provided by the "hang loose" marijuana-using subculture of the population.

SUMMARY

Tolerance at all levels of complexity in the brain involves "learning" in the sense of the acquisition of compensatory adaptations to the consequences of the *presence* of a drug-produced disturbance in function. Depending on the function, species, and dose of cannabis, "tissue tolerance," behaviorally augmented (to provide the *presence* of the disturbed function) or not, develops at different rates or not at all (e.g., to impairment of the logical sequence of thoughts, to which no tolerance has yet been demonstrated). "Dispositional tolerance" (increased rate of metabolism of Δ^9-THC due to enzyme induction) may play a role in the development of tolerance or "reverse tolerance" to cannabis in man. There is evidence that for the label "high," placebo effects may account for the "reverse tolerance" seen in experienced users on smoking (but not on ingestion of Δ^9-THC or placebo) along with evidence of residual tolerance to other not-so-labeled effects of the drug.

Dependence on cannabis, in the sense of abstinence phenomena on abrupt withdrawal of Δ^9-THC, has been demonstrated in monkeys made tolerant to Δ^9-THC given four times daily for about 1 month. In man, *physiologic* marijuana abstinence signs have not been demonstrated, but *behavioral* (and some physiologic) abstinence phenomena have been reported in heavy users of hashish or ganja. The between-dose hyperirritability and dysphoria reported to occur in experimental studies on chronic marijuana intoxication may actually be early and short-lived abstinence changes.

In the West, where marijuana with relatively low Δ^9-THC content is widely smoked, dependence in the sense of drug-seeking behavior appears to be less a function of any pharmacologic reinforcing properties the drug may have than of secondary (conditioned) reinforcement derived from the social milieu in which the marijuana is smoked. In cultures where marijuana of higher Δ^9-THC content, hashish, or ganja is used, pharmacologic reinforcement (through suppression of abstinence changes) may play a greater role in maintaining drug-seeking behavior.

REFERENCES

1. ABEL, E. L. 1972. Studies of tolerance to l-Δ^9-tetrahydrocannabinol (Δ^9-THC) in neonatal chicks. Fed. Proc. **31:** 505 (Abs.).
2. ADAMS, P. M. & E. S. BARRATT. 1974. Effects of acute and chronic marijuana on complex operant performance by the squirrel monkey. *In* Drug Addiction, Volume 3. Neurobiology and Influences on Behavior. J. M. Singh & H. Lal, Eds. : 169–180. Stratton Intercontinental Medical Book Corp. New York, N.Y.
3. ADAMS, W. J., S. Y. YEH, L. A. WOODS & C. L. MITCHELL. 1969. Drug-test interaction as a factor in the development of tolerance to the analgesic effect of morphine. J. Pharmacol. Exp. Ther. **168:** 251–257.
4. BABOR, T. F., A. M. ROSSI, G. SAGOTSKY & R. E. MEYER. 1974. Group behavior: patterns of smoking. *In* The Use of Marihuana: A Psychological and Physiological Inquiry. J. H. Mendelson, A. M. Rossi & R. E. Meyer, Eds. : 47–59. Plenum Publishing Corporation. New York, N.Y.
5. BABOR, T. F., J. H. MENDELSON, I. GREENBERG & J. C. KUEHNLE. 1975. Marijuana consumption and tolerance to physiological and subjective effects. Arch. Gen. Psychiat. **32:** 1548–1552.
6. BARRATT, E., W. BEAVER, R. WHITE, P. BLAKENEY & P. ADAMS. 1972. The effects of the chronic use of marijuana on sleep and perceptual-motor performance in humans. *In* Current Research in Marijuana. M. F. Lewis, Ed. : 163–193. Academic Press, Inc. New York, N.Y.
7. BECKER, H. S. 1968. Marihuana: a sociological overview. *In* The Marihuana Papers. D. Solomon, Ed. : 65–102. Signet Books. New York, N.Y.
8. BLACK, M. B., J. H. WOODS & E. F. DOMINO. 1970. Some effects of (−) Δ^9-*trans*-tetrahydrocannabinol and other cannabis derivatives on schedule-controlled behavior. Pharmacologist **12:** 258 (Abs.).
9. BOWMAN, M. & R. O. PIHL. 1973. Cannabis: psychological effects of chronic heavy use. A controlled study of intellectual functioning in chronic users of high potency cannabis. Psychopharmacologia **29:** 159–170.
10. BUENO, O. F. A. & E. A. CARLINI. 1972. Dissociation of learning in marihuana tolerant rats. Psychopharmacologia **25:** 49–56.
11. CARDER, B. & J. OLSON. 1973. Learned behavioral tolerance to marihuana in rats. Pharmacol. Biochem. Behav. **1:** 73–76.
12. CARLIN, A. S., C. B. BAKKER, L. HALPERN & R. D. POST. 1972. Social facilitation of marihuana intoxication: impact of social set and pharmacological activity. J. Abnormal Psychol. **80:** 132–140.
13. CARLIN, A. S., R. D. POST, C. B. BAKKER & L. M. HALPERN. 1974. The role of modeling and previous experience in the facilitation of marijuana intoxication. J. Nervous Mental Disease **159:** 275–281.
14. CARLINI, E. A. 1968. Tolerance to chronic administration of *Cannabis sativa* (marihuana) in rats. Pharmacology **1:** 135–142.
15. CASSWELL, S. & D. F. MARKS. 1973. Cannabis and temporal disintegration in experienced and naive subjects. Science **179:** 803–805.
16. CHEN, C. S. 1968. A study of the alcohol tolerance effect and an introduction of a new behavioral technique. Psychopharmacologia **12:** 433–460.

17. COHEN, M. J. & W. H. RICKLES. 1974. Performance on a verbal learning task by subjects of heavy past marijuana usage. Psychopharmacologia **37**: 323–330.
18. COLLIER, H. O. J. 1965. A general theory of the genesis of drug dependence by induction of receptors. Nature (London) **205**: 181, 182.
19. CONNEY, A. H. 1967. Pharmacological implications of microsomal enzyme induction. Pharmacol. Rev. **19**: 317–366.
20. DAVIS, W. M., J. E. MORETON, W. T. KING & H. B. PACE. 1972. Marihuana on locomotor activity: biphasic effect on tolerance development. Res. Commun. Chem. Pathol. Pharmacol. **3**: 29–35.
21. DENEAU, G. A. & S. KAYMAKCALAN. 1971. Physiological and psychological dependence to synthetic Δ^9-tetrahydrocannabinol (THC) in rhesus monkeys. Pharmacologist **13**: 246.
22. DEWEY, W. L., J. JENKINS, T. O'ROURKE & L. S. HARRIS. 1972. The effects of chronic administration of trans-Δ^9-tetrahydrocannabinol on behavior and the cardiovascular system of dogs. Arch. Int. Pharmacodyn. **198**: 118–131.
23. DEWEY, W. L., D. E. MCMILLAN & L. S. HARRIS. 1972. Blood levels of ^{3}H-Δ^9-tetrahydrocannabinol (Δ^9-THC) and its metabolites in tolerant and non-tolerant pigeons. Fifth International Congress on Pharmacology, Abstracts of Volunteer Papers. : 56.
24. DORNBUSH, R. L., G. CLARE, A. ZAKS, P. CROWN, J. VOLAVKA & M. FINK. 1972. 21-Day administration of marijuana in male volunteers. In Current Research in Marijuana. M. F. Lewis, Ed. : 115–128. Academic Press, Inc. New York, N.Y.
25. ELSMORE, T. F. 1972. Effects of delta-^{9}-tetrahydrocannabinol on temporal and auditory discrimination performances of monkeys. Psychopharmacologia **26**: 62–72.
26. FERNANDES, M., D. RATING & S. KLUWE. 1971. The influence of subchronic tetrahydrocannabinol and cannabis-treatment on food and water-intake, body weight and body temperature of rats. Acta Pharmacol. Toxicol. **29**(Suppl. 4): 89.
27. FERRARO, D. P. 1972. Effects of Δ^9-trans-tetrahydrocannabinol on simple and complex learned behavior in animals. In Current Research in Marijuana. M. F. Lewis, Ed. : 49–95. Academic Press, Inc. New York, N.Y.
28. FERRARO, D. P. & D. M. GRILLY. 1973. Lack of tolerance to Δ^9-THC in chimpanzees. Science **179**: 490–492.
29. FERRARO, D. P., D. M. GRILLY & M. G. GRISHAM. 1974. Δ^9-Tetrahydrocannabinol and delayed matching-to-sample in chimpanzees. In Drug Addiction, Volume 3. Neurobiology and Influences on Behavior. J. M. Singh & H. Lal, Eds. : 181–207. Stratton Intercontinental Medical Book Corp. New York, N.Y.
30. FERRARO, D. P. & M. G. GRISHAM. 1972. Tolerance to the behavioral effects of marihuana in chimpanzees. Physiol. Behav. **9**: 49–54.
31. FORD, R. D. & E. E. MCMILLAN. 1971. Behavioral tolerance and cross tolerance to 1-Δ^8-tetrahydrocannabinol (Δ^8-THC) and 1-Δ^9-tetrahydrocannabinol (Δ^9-THC) in pigeons and rats. Fed. Proc. **30**: 279 (Abs.).
32. FRASER, J. D. 1949. Withdrawal symptoms in cannabis-indica addicts. Lancet **257**: 747, 748.
33. GEBHART, G. G. & C. L. MITCHELL. 1972. The relative contributions of the testing cylinder and the heated plate in the hot plate procedure to the development of tolerance to morphine in rats. Eur. J. Pharmacol. **18**: 56–62.
34. GLICK, S. D. & S. MILLOY. 1972. Tolerance, state-dependency and long-term behavioral effects of Δ^9-THC. In Current Research in Marijuana. M. F. Lewis, Ed. : 1–24. Academic Press, Inc. New York, N.Y.
35. GOLDSTEIN, A. & D. B. GOLDSTEIN. 1968. Enzyme expansion theory of drug tolerance and physical dependence. In The Addictive States. A. Wikler, Ed. Vol. **46**: 265–267. The Williams & Wilkins Co. Baltimore, Md.
36. HAERTZEN, C. A. & N. T. HOOKS. 1969. Changes in personality and subjective

experience associated with the chronic administration and withdrawal of opiates. J. Nervous Mental Disease **148:** 606–614.

37. HARRIS, L. H. 1971. General and behavioral pharmacology. Pharmacol. Rev. **23:** 285–294.

38. HIMMELSBACH, C. K. 1942. Clinical studies of drug addiction: physical dependence, withdrawal and recovery. Arch. Intern. Med. **69:** 766–772.

39. HOLLISTER, L. E., J. E. OVERALL & M. L. GERBER. 1975. Marihuana and setting. Arch. Gen. Psychiat. **32:** 798–801.

40. ISBELL, H., S. ALTSCHUL, C. H. KORNETSKY, A. J. EISENMAN, H. G. FLANARY & H. F. FRASER. 1950. Chronic barbiturate intoxication: an experimental study. Arch. Neurol. Psychiat. **64:** 1–28.

41. ISBELL, H. & D. R. JASINSKI. 1969. A comparison of LSD-25 with (−) Δ^9-*trans*-tetrahydrocannabinol (THC) and attempted cross-tolerance between LSD and THC. Psychopharmacologia **14:** 115–123.

42. JAFFE, J. H. & S. K. SHARPLESS. 1968. Pharmacological denervation supersensitivity in the central nervous system: a theory of physical dependence. *In* The Addictive States. A. Wikler, Ed. Vol. **46:** 226–246. The Williams & Wilkins Co. Baltimore, Md.

43. JONES, R. T. 1971. Tetrahydrocannabinol and the marijuana-induced social "high" or the effects of the mind on marijuana. Ann. N.Y. Acad. Sci. **191:** 155–165.

44. JONES, R. T. 1971. Marihuana-induced "high": influence of expectation, setting and previous drug experience. Pharmacol. Rev. **23:** 359–369.

45. KALANT, H., A. E. LE BLANC & R. J. GIBBINS. 1971. Tolerance and dependence on some non-opiate psychotropic drugs. Pharmacol. Rev. **23:** 135–191.

46. KAYMAKCALAN, S. 1973. Tolerance to and dependence on cannabis. Bull. Narcotics **25:** 39–47.

47. KAYMAKCALAN, S. & G. A. DENEAU. 1971. Some pharmacological effects of synthetic Δ^9-tetrahydrocannabinol (THC). Pharmacologist **13:** 247 (Abs.).

48. KIELHOLZ, P. & G. LADEWIG. 1970. Über Drogenabhängigkeit bei Jugendlichen. Deut. Med. Wochschr. **95:** 101–105.

49. LEMBERGER, L., J. AXELROD & I. J. KOPIN. 1971. Metabolism and disposition of tetrahydrocannabinols in naive subjects and chronic marihuana users. Ann. N.Y. Acad. Sci. **191:** 142–154.

50. LEMBERGER, L., R. E. CRABTREE & H. M. ROWE. 1972. 11-Hydroxy-Δ^9-tetrahydrocannabinol: pharmacology, disposition and metabolism of a major metabolite of marihuana in man. Science **177:** 62–64.

51. LEMBERGER, L., S. D. SILBERSTEIN, J. AXELROD & I. J. KOPIN. 1970. Marihuana: studies in the disposition of delta-^{9}-tetrahydrocannabinol in man. Science **170:** 1320–1322.

52. LEMBERGER, L., N. R. TAMARKIN, J. AXELROD & I. J. KOPIN. 1971. Delta-9-tetrahydrocannabinol: metabolism and disposition in long-term marihuana smokers. Science **173:** 72–74.

53. LIPPARINI, F., A. SCOTTI DE CARLOS & V. G. LONGO. 1969. A neuropharmacological investigation of some trans-tetrahydrocannabinol derivatives. Physiol. Behav. **4:** 527–532.

54. LEWIS, M. F. 1972. Marijuana today: an overview. *In* Current Research in Marijuana. M. F. Lewis, Ed. : 215–219. Academic Press, Inc. New York, N.Y.

55. LOMAX, P. 1971. Acute tolerance to the hypothermic effect of marihuana in the rat. Res. Commun. Chem. Pathol. Pharmacol. **2:** 159–167.

56. MANNING, F. J. 1973. Acute tolerance to the effects of delta-^{9}-tetrahydrocannabinol on spaced responding by monkeys. Pharmacol. Biochem. Behav. **1:** 665–671.

57. MARTIN, W. R. 1968. A homeostatic and redundancy theory of tolerance to and dependence on narcotic analgesics. *In* The Addictive States. A. Wikler, Ed. Vol. **46:** 206–225. The Williams & Wilkins Co. Baltimore, Md.

58. MARTIN, W. R., D. R. JASINSKI, C. A. HAERTZEN, D. C. KAY, B. E. JONES, P. A. MANSKY & R. W. CARPENTER. 1973. Methadone—a reevaluation. Arch. Gen. Psychiat. **28:** 286–295.
59. MCMILLAN, D. E. & W. L. DEWEY. 1972. On the mechanism of tolerance to Δ^9-THC. *In* Current Research in Marijuana. M. F. Lewis, Ed. : 97–114. Academic Press, Inc. New York, N.Y.
60. MCMILLAN, D. E., W. L. DEWEY & L. S. HARRIS. 1971. Characteristics of tetrahydrocannabinol tolerance. Ann. N.Y. Acad. Sci. **191:** 83–99.
61. MILSTEIN, S. L., K. MACCANNELL, G. KARR & S. CLARK. 1975. Marijuana-produced impairments in coordination. Experienced and non-experienced subjects. J. Nervous Mental Disease **161:** 26–31.
62. MORETON, J. E. & W. M. DAVIS. 1973. Electroencephalographic study of the effects of tetrahydrocannabinols on sleep in the rat. Neuropharmacology **12:** 897–907.
63. NEWMAN, L. M., M. P. LUTZ, M. H. GOULD & E. F. DOMINO. 1972. Δ^9-Tetrahydrocannabinol and ethyl alcohol: evidence for cross-tolerance in the rat. Science **175:** 1022, 1023.
64. OLSON, J. & B. CARDER. 1974. Behavioral tolerance to marihuana as function of amount of prior training. Pharmacol. Biochem. Behav. **2:** 243–247.
65. PIRCH, J. H., P. A. COHN, P. R. BARNES & E. S. BARRATT. 1972. Effects of acute and chronic administration of marijuana extract on the rat electroencephalogram. Neuropharmacology **11:** 231–240.
66. PIVIK, R. T., V. ZARCONE, W. C. DEMENT & L. E. HOLLISTER. 1972. Delta-^{9}-tetrahydrocannabinol and synhexyl: effects on human sleep patterns. Clin. Pharmacol. Ther. **13:** 426–435.
67. POTVIN, R. J. & P. A. FRIED. 1972. Acute and chronic effects on rats of $(-)$ Δ^9-trans-tetrahydrocannabinol on unlearned motor tasks. Psychopharmacologia **26:** 369–378.
68. RICKLES, W. H., M. J. COHEN, C. A. WHITAKER & K. E. MCINTYRE. 1973. Marijuana induced state-dependent verbal learning. Psychopharmacologia **30:** 349–354.
69. ROSENBERG, H. C. & M. OKAMOTO. 1974. A method for producing maximal pentobarbital dependence in cats: dependency characteristics. *In* Drug Addiction, Volume 3. Neurobiology and Influences on Behavior. J. M. Singh & H. Lal, Eds. : 89–103. Stratton Intercontinental Medical Book Corp. New York, N.Y.
70. SASSENRATH, E. N. & L. F. CHAPMAN. 1975. Tetrahydrocannabinol-induced manifestations of the "marihuana syndrome" in group-living macaques. Fed. Proc. **34:** 1666–1670.
71. SILVA, M. T. A., E. A. CARLINI, U. CLAUSSEN & F. KORTE. 1968. Lack of cross-tolerance in rats among $(-)\Delta^9$-trans-tetrahydrocannabinol, cannabis extract, mescaline and lysergic acid diethylamide. Psychopharmacologia **13:** 332–340.
72. SODETZ, F. J. 1972. Δ^9-Tetrahydrocannabinol: behavioral toxicity in laboratory animals. *In* Current Research in Marijuana. M. F. Lewis, Ed. : 25–48. Academic Press, Inc. New York, N.Y.
73. SOUEIF, M. I. 1967. Hashish consumption in Egypt, with special reference to psychosocial aspects. Bull. Narcotics **19:** 1–12.
74. TEN HAM, M. & J. VAN NOORDWIJK. 1973. Lack of tolerance to the effect of two tetrahydrocannabinols on aggressiveness. Psychopharmacologia **29:** 171–176.
75. VOLAVKA, J., R. DORNBUSH, S. FELDSTEIN, G. CLARE, A. ZAKS, M. FINK & A. M. FREEDMAN. 1971. Marijuana, EEG, and behavior. Ann. N.Y. Acad. Sci. **191:** 206–215.
76. WEBSTER, C. D., A. E. LEBLANC, J. A. MARSHMAN & J. M. BEATON. 1973. Acquisition and loss of tolerance to l-Δ^9-trans-tetrahydrocannabinol in rats on an avoidance schedule. Psychopharmacologia **30:** 217–226.
77. WEIL, A. T., N. E. ZINBERG & J. M. NELSON. 1968. Clinical and psychological effects of marihuana in man. Science **162:** 1234–1242.

78. WIKLER, A. 1952. A psychodynamic study of a patient during self-regulated readdiction to morphine. Psychiat. Quart. **26:** 270–293.
79. WIKLER, A. 1970. Clinical and social aspects of marihuana intoxication. Arch. Gen. Psychiat. **23:** 320–325.
80. WIKLER, A. 1971. Some implications of conditioning theory for problems of drug abuse. Behav. Sci. **16:** 92–97.
81. WIKLER, A. 1971. Present status of the concept of drug dependence. Psychol. Med. (London) **1:** 377–380.
82. WIKLER, A. 1974. The marijuana controversy. *In* Marijuana. Effects on Human Behavior. L. L. Miller, Ed. : 25–44. Academic Press, Inc. New York, N.Y.
83. WIKLER, A. & C. F. ESSIG. 1970. Withdrawal seizures following chronic intoxication with barbiturates and other sedative drugs. *In* Modern Problems of Pharmacopsychiatry, Volume 4: Epilepsy. E. Niedermeyer, Ed. : 170–184. S. Karger. Basel, Switzerland.
84. WILLIAMS, E. G., C. K. HIMMELSBACH, A. WIKLER, D. C. RUBLE & B. J. LLOYD. 1946. Studies on marihuana and pyrahexyl compound. Public Health Rep. **61:** 1059–1083.

HEALTH STATUS OF CHRONIC HEAVY CANNABIS USERS *

W. J. Coggins, Edward W. Swenson, William W. Dawson,
Alvara Fernandez-Salas, Juan Hernandez-Bolanos,
C. Francisco Jiminez-Antillon, Joaquin Roberto Solano,
Rodolpho Vinocour, and Federico Faerron-Valdez

*Department of Community Health and Family Medicine
University of Florida
Gainesville, Florida 32610
and Hospital Mexico
Caja Costarriense de Seguro Social
San José, Costa Rica*

The purpose of this study was to survey the general health status of chronic cannabis users in comparison with that of a control group from the same sociocultural class. This survey was the initial stage of a more thorough study of neuropsychologic, visual, pulmonary function, and sleep electroencephalographic characteristics of chronic cannabis users in San José, Costa Rica. The results of other aspects of this study are included elsewhere in this monograph.

The research design and methodology will be presented in detail by Carter and Doughty.[1] In brief, this paper will present the general health characteristics of 84 marijuana smokers and 156 nonsmoking control subjects. Criteria for chronic marijuana use were a minimum of 10 years of regular use, at a level of three or more times per week. The upper age limit was set at 50 years to restrict, to some extent, the effects of aging on the results. Only males were studied. The sample can thus be characterized as stratified and purposive.

All subjects were given a standard medical history, a physical, and a neurologic examination, which included a mental status test. All medical examinations and tests were performed in the outpatient department of the *Hospital Mexico.*

On the same day or the morning after this examination, a series of clinical and laboratory tests were performed. These tests consisted of the following: blood count: hemoglobin, hematocrit, white blood cell count, white blood cell differential, and erythrocyte sedimentation rate; blood chemistries: fasting blood sugar, blood sugar 2 hr after a 100-g glucose load, serum glutamic-pyruvic transaminase, blood urea nitrogen, prothrombin time, alkaline phosphatase, and serum protein electrophoresis; urinalysis: standard urinalysis for pH, specific gravity, protein, sugar, and microscopic examination; serologic test for syphilis (VDRL); chest x ray: standard 14 × 17-in. posteroanterior and lateral views; electrocardiogram: standard 12-lead resting; visual function screening test: Snellen acuity, refraction, slit lamp examination, applanation tonometry, fundus inspection by ophthalmoscope, color vision by use of Ishihara test plates.

Certain tests in the second phase of this study required bilateral visual

* The work reported herein was performed pursuant to Contract NO1–MHE–0233 with the National Institute on Drug Abuse.

function correctable to 20/40 or better and ability to perceive color. For this reason, subjects with visual acuity of less than 20/40 corrected or with poor performance on the Ishihara color plates were excluded from further participation in the study.

All screening tests were performed single blind. The observer or examiner did not know whether the subject was one of the 84 marijuana users or one of the 156 nonusers. The physicians, laboratory and technical personnel, and other attendants at *Hospital Mexico* understood the need for anonymity of the subjects and for objectivity in evaluating the results of the screening tests. All subjects were assigned an identification number that was subsequently used as the only identification of subjects for all interviews, tests, and screening procedures throughout the study.

The medical screening examinations were designed for three purposes: to ascertain the general health status of the subjects; to identify those with serious or life-threatening illnesses that would prevent their continued participation in the study over the next 2 years; and to eliminate those with uncorrectable visual defects, mentioned above, that would impair their ability to perform the visual function tests in the second phase of the project.

RESULTS

Medical History

Responses to several questions on the standard medical history were significantly different between the two groups. Marijuana users more frequently reported episodes of involuntary weight loss than did the controls. The controls more frequently indicated concern about obesity. The users more often reported adverse reactions to drugs than controls.

In response to the questions about changes in appetite (for food), the users more often reported both increased and diminished appetite than did the nonusers. Responses to questions about gastrointestinal symptoms indicate that the users more frequently experienced indigestion, nausea, and abdominal pain than did the control subjects.

In the battery of questions not related to eating or the digestive tract, relatively few responses were different between the two groups. Users more often reported having had serious trauma to the head, to have suffered from jaundice, and to have experienced excessive frequency of urination than did the controls (TABLE 1). Users indicated more frequent use of barbiturates, tranquilizers, hallucinogens, and vaporizing intoxicants, such as gasoline, than did the controls.

Although these differences were significant, the overall use of these substances was very limited. Only two users and seven controls reported the use of barbiturates or tranquilizers as frequently as once per week. Fourteen users and 11 controls reported use of these drugs as often as once per month. Twenty-three users and three controls reported having used these drugs in the past, but they were not using them at the time of this study.

Hallucinogens, such as lysergic acid diethylamide or mescaline, had been taken by 15 individuals in the user group. Nine reported casual use in the past, and six reported use as often as once per month. All denied current use. One of the control group reported daily use of hallucinogens in the past but no current use.

TABLE 1

RESPONSES TO THE MEDICAL HISTORY
(N=240)

	User * (n=84)		Control * (n=156)	
	No.	%	No.	%
Weight loss	25	29.8	22	14.1
Obesity	4	4.8	30	19.2
Reaction to drug	21	25.0	26	16.7
Changes in appetite	22	26.2	10	6.4
Indigestion	11	13.1	5	3.2
Nausea	12	14.3	4	2.6
Abdominal pain	9	10.7	4	2.6
Jaundice	7	8.3	2	1.3
Frequent urination	12	14.3	1	0.6
Trauma to head	50	59.5	61	39.1

* p≤0.05 for each item.

Inhalation of gasoline or paint thinner to obtain a high was reported by 19 of the users and two of the controls. Three users claimed that they had used such vaporizing intoxicants as often as daily, eight as often as once monthly, and eight as occasional casual experiences. Two of the control group claimed past daily use of such intoxicants. All denied current use.

Physical Examination

Several abnormalities revealed by physical and eye examination were not of sufficient seriousness to exclude the subjects' continued participation in the study. Among the marijuana users, seven were noted to have unilateral testicular atrophy. Six of them attributed the condition to mumps or to trauma to the scrotum. One was unaware of the atrophy until the time of the examination. In the control group, only two individuals were found to have testicular atrophy, and it was unilateral in both instances.

Pterygium was present in eight (9.52%) of the users and in only three (1.92%) of the controls.

The marijuana users had significantly lower weights as a group than the nonusers, and their mean systolic blood pressure was lower. Mean diastolic blood pressure for the user group was not significantly lower.

The user group more frequently had abdominal surgical scars than did the controls. Hyperemia or injection of the conjunctival blood vessels was found in 40 (47.6%) of the marijuana users and in 56 (35.9%) of the controls. TABLE 2 summarizes these findings.

Laboratory Tests

The users had a lower mean hematocrit than did controls. The mean of prothrombin times was higher in the user group. Users had a lower conjugated

bilirubin level than did controls, but the difference was not statistically significant. Serum albumin levels tended to be lower in users than in controls but
not significantly so. Serum globulin levels were lower in the users (p = 0.02).

There was no significant difference in the results of the other laboratory tests
(TABLE 3).

Examination of a single stool for evidence of intestinal parasites revealed
no significant differences in the overall rate of infestation based on one stool
examination. Thirty-eight (45.8%) of the users and 80 (52.3%) of the controls
had positive stool examinations for parasites. Eleven (13.3%) users and 35
(19.1%) controls had more than one parasite in their stool. The difference
was not significant.

The laboratory results were analyzed to determine how well the presence
of eosinophilia in the stained blood smear correlated with the finding of intestinal parasites in the stool. Only 12 of the 38 users with positive stool examinations for parasites had eosinophilia, defined as 4% or more eosinophilia in the
blood smear. Twenty-three of the control group of 80 with intestinal parasites
had eosinophilia.

Eosinophilia was present in 13 users who did not have stools positive for
parasites; 18 of the controls were in this category (TABLE 4). The difference
was not significant.

Electrocardiography

Ten of the users and 22 of the nonusers had electrocardiographic abnormalities, but only three subjects were found to have a serious cardiovascular defect.
TABLE 5 shows the electrocardiographic findings in the two groups. No pattern
of abnormalities distinguishes them.

Standard measurements of the rate, P-R interval, QRST complex, the Q-T
interval, and the electrical axis in the frontal plane were made. They were
compared statistically, and no significant differences between the two groups
were found.

TABLE 2

COMPARATIVE FINDINGS ON THE PHYSICAL EXAMINATION
(N=240)

	User (n=84)		Control (n=156)	
	No.	%	No.	%
Body weight (kg)	60.29 *		63.43	
Systolic blood pressure (mm Hg)	115		118	
Pterygium	8	(9.5)	3	(1.9)
Abdominal scars	14	(16.7)	11	(7.1)
Testicular atrophy, unilateral	7	(8.3)	2	(1.3)

* p ≤ 0.05 for each item.

TABLE 3

RESULTS OF LABORATORY TESTS

$(N=240)$

	User $(n=84)$		Control $(n=156)$	
	Mean	SD	Mean	SD
Hemoglobin (g/dl)	14.60	1.08	14.82	1.05
Hematocrit (ml/dl)	45.39	2.81	46.35	3.00 *
Leukocytes (1000s/mm³)	9.42	2.65	8.99	2.33
Segmented neutrophils (%)	56	8.8	57	11.34
Lymphocytes (%)	36	8.4	34	8.9
Eosinophils (%)	4.7	3.5	5.4	5.1
Monocytes (%)	2.4	2.3	2.0	2.0
Juvenile neutrophils (%)	0.5	0.9	0.7	1.2
Metamyelocytes (%)	0	0	0	0
Myelocytes (%)	0	0	0	0
Basophils (%)	0.1	0.4	0.1	0.3
Prothrombin time (sec)	13.4	0.9	12.9	1.2 *
Red blood cell sedimentation rate (mm/hr)	10.4	8.2	9.0	7.0
Blood sugar, fasting (mg/dl)	73.6	11.0	75.5	11.0
2 hr postglucose (mg/dl)	66.3	18.0	65.4	23.7
Blood urea nitrogen (mg/dl)	15.3	3.5	14.6	2.9
Alkaline phosphatase	3.5	1.7	3.6	1.5
Pyruvic transaminase (U/ml)	16.3	18.3	20.8	33.5
Bilirubin, direct (mg/dl)	0.16	0.14	0.19	0.14
Bilirubin, total (mg/dl)	0.48	0.25	0.53	0.29
Total protein (g/dl)	7.72	0.79	7.77	0.50
Albumin	4.12	0.39	4.22	0.41
Globulin	3.42	0.39	3.54	0.39 *
α_1	0.43	0.09	0.52	0.09
α_2	0.85	0.18	0.87	0.16
β	0.87	0.18	0.94	0.20
γ	1.29	0.24	1.27	0.26

* $p \leq 0.05$.

TABLE 4

INTESTINAL PARASITES AND EOSINOPHILIA $(N=238)$

	Users $(n=83 *)$			Controls $(n=155 *)$		
	Parasites Present	Eosino-philia	Positive (%)	Parasites Present	Eosino-philia	Positive (%)
	38	12	31.6	80	23	28.8
	45	13	28.9	75	18	24.0
Total	83	25	30.1	155	41	26.5

* One user and one control failed to submit stool specimens.

Discussion

The cluster of positive responses from the medical history associated with upper alimentary tract symptoms and centered around food intake is noteworthy, because the users indicated more frequent past concern about the availability of food and have more often experienced outright hunger. Whether intermittent episodes of hunger led to more awareness of related gastrointestinal symptoms, such as nausea, indigestion, and abdominal pain, cannot be determined from these data.

The more frequent history of jaundice in the user group was not reflected by an increase in physical or laboratory findings of liver disease in the user group. The mean bilirubin level tended to be lower in the users. Liver enzymes were not different between the two groups.

The higher percentage of users who had increased frequency of urination may be related to the higher incidence of positive serologic tests for syphilis mentioned above. Gonococcal infections are common in Costa Rica. One would expect gonorrhea to be more prevalent in individuals with active or treated syphilis than in those with no evidence of syphilis. Although no subjects had active symptoms of gonorrhea at the time of examination, it is likely that the incidence of acute gonococcal urethritis, in addition to nonspecific urethritis, is higher in the user group than in the controls. If so, the difference could be explained on that basis.

We have no explanation for the difference in reports of blows to the head. The field workers did not report greater evidence of physical violence among the users. The medical history did not explain the causes of the reported trauma. One could conjecture that there is a correlation between this finding and the higher number of arrests for drug possession in the user group, but our data do not illuminate this finding further.

This difference was not found in comparing the histories of subjects selected for the matched pair study, where occupation was one of the variables controlled. It may be that head trauma was related to occupational hazards.

The use of drugs other than marijuana is higher in the user group. Although the use of hallucinogens is not high in Costa Rica, barbiturates and other hypnotic agents are readily available without prescriptions. One would expect that marijuana users in Costa Rica would more frequently take other drugs, as has been shown to be the case in other studies of drug use behavior.[1a, 2]

The significant difference in mean body weight between the smokers and the controls has not been observed in previous studies in the United States. This difference of 3.14 kg (6.9 lb) may be related to the lower income and more frequent bachelor status of users. They may simply have less food available to them on a regular basis. This explanation is in agreement with the fact that the difference in weight is not present in the matched pair groups, where occupation and marital status are controlled during sample selection. The mean weight for the marijuana users in the Jamaica study was 7 lb less than for the controls.[3]

Systolic blood pressure, but not diastolic or mean blood pressure, was lower in the user group (115 vs 118 mm Hg; $p = 0.04$). Although several studies have reported mild decreases in blood pressure as an acute pharmacologic effect of marijuana, this finding may be explained by the lower weight of the users rather than by a direct effect of the drug on the cardiovascular system. Mean blood pressures were not reported in the Jamaica study but were described as being "within the normal ranges" for both users and controls.

Hematocrit levels averaged less in the user group than in the controls, even though hemoglobin levels were not statistically different. Because these two tests should corroborate each other, we have no explanation for this discrepancy. Only one subject was severely anemic, and the mean levels for both groups were well within the normal limits. These findings contrast with those of the Jamaica study,[3] where higher hemoglobins and hematocrits were found in the users.

Although the prothrombin times were slightly longer in the user group than in the controls, the difference was minimal, although statistically significant. In the absence of other differentiating factors related to blood coagulation and liver function, we have no explanation for this difference.

The tendency toward lower bilirubin levels in the users is more salient when these levels are compared in the matched sample. Here, the users have lower total and conjugated bilirubin levels, with the latter difference being significant at a confidence level of 0.05. Dr. Reese Jones and coworkers [3a] in San Francisco have found that bilirubin levels decline in healthy young males who are given

TABLE 5

ELECTROCARDIOGRAPHIC ABNORMALITIES

	User ($n=84$)	Control ($n=156$)	Total ($N=240$)
Occasional A-V nodal extrasystoles	0	1	1
Isolated A-N nodal and ventricular extrasystoles	0	1	1
A-V nodal rhythm	1	0	1
Short P-R interval	0	1	0
Atrioventricular block, first degree	1	1	2
Wolf-Parkinson-White syndrome	0	1	1
Right-bundle branch block, complete	0	2	2
Right bundle branch block, incomplete	6	8	14
Left ventricular hypertrophy	0	2	2
T-wave changes suggestive of ischemia	1	5	6
Prolonged Q-T interval	1	0	1
Total abnormalities	10	22	32

oral doses of Δ^9-tetrahydrocannabinol as high as 240 mg per day in acute toxicity studies. These levels return to normal promptly after removal of the drug.

Although comparable data based on epidemiologic surveys are generally unavailable for Costa Rican populations, one such study allows us to compare the prevalence of roundworm infestation.[4] The nationwide survey conducted by Kotcher et al. studied adults in San Jose for several ecologic correlates of intestinal parasitism. Rates ranged from 43.4 to 62.6% for the four types of roundworm found. In this study, the range was from 2.9 to 14.8%. Improvements in sanitation in San Jose in the decade between the two studies accounts for some of this remarkable improvement. Most of our subjects' homes have running water and indoor plumbing. None of our subjects are primarily agricultural workers. Thus, they have limited chances of reinfestation with these soil-transmitted parasites.

Evaluation of intestinal parasites in relation to eosinophilia was performed as an indirect measure of immunologic responsiveness. There is increasing evidence that eosinophilia is dependent on cell-mediated immune responses.[5] There was no significant difference in the presence of eosinophilia between the user and control groups, irrespective of whether intestinal parasites were present. It is probable that some of the subjects with eosinophilia in the absence of intestinal parasites would show parasites in their stools if more than one specimen per subject had been examined.

If cell-mediated immunity were suppressed by marijuana use, as suggested by Nahas *et al.*,[6] one might expect this impairment to be reflected in suppression of the eosinophilic response in these long-term heavy users.

Evaluation of the electrocardiograms showed no detectable pattern of electrical abnormalities in either group. Minor electrocardiographic abnormalities are not necessarily indicative of heart disease. Only 10 of the 32 abnormalities found in these tracings are regularly associated with heart disease, and these 10 were more often found in the nonusers than in the user group. The numbers are too small to draw statistical inferences.

In a recent review of the cardiovascular effects of marijuana, Clark[7] found T-wave changes reported in studies of acute effects. One study reported transient P-wave changes. The Mendelson study[7a] reported "minimal" electrocardiographic effects. The Jamaica study found "minor" electrocardiographic abnormalities in 30% of both marijuana smokers and controls and suggested that this high incidence of abnormalities was related to cardiomyopathy in Jamaica rather than to marijuana use. One study has demonstrated decreased exercise tolerance in patients with angina pectoris after smoking one marijuana cigarette.[8] The present study, by excluding individuals above age 50, did not include subjects who would most likely have arteriosclerotic heart disease with symptoms of myocardial ischemia. Thus, our study provides no additional data on the possible effect of marijuana on individuals with coronary artery disease.

Further studies of the effect of marijuana smoking in experienced smokers with evidence of coronary disease are needed.

SCREENING FOR MATCHED PAIRS

One of the major matching conditions between users and nonusers was that both groups be free of general pathologies that might affect the results in projected specialized tests. The conditions that were excluded are not thought to be related to the possible effects of marijuana use itself but would have had the potential of distorting the interpretations if they had not been eliminated. The potential effect of tuberculosis on pulmonary function could cause abnormalities in the pulmonary test battery that could not reasonably be attributed to the effects of smoking marijuana. Because we were interested in subtle central nervous system functions and changes possibly attributable to marijuana use and measured by such tests, we were also concerned that syphilis not be present in the matched pair group. The well-recognized effects of central nervous system syphilis could distort the findings in the neuropsychologic test battery, the electroencephalogram, and the visual function tests.

Subjects with a history of alcoholism, who were found to have abnormalities that indicated liver disease, on the basis of their physical examination and laboratory studies, would be diagnosed as having alcoholic cirrhosis of the liver and therefore would not be continued in the study. Subjects with minor abnormalities of one or more laboratory tests that did not lead to a diagnosis of a specific disease process, or those with minor abnormalities of their chest x ray or electrocardiogram, were maintained in the study as potential subjects for the matched pair tests.

Conditions Diagnosed for Which Subjects Were Excluded from the Study

By use of the criteria listed above for exclusion of subjects, the following defects were identified, and diagnoses were made.

The most common abnormality found was a positive serologic test for syphilis. This abnormality occurred in 20 of the marijuana users and 17 of the controls. This difference was statistically significant ($p < 0.01$).

The next most frequent abnormality was a pulmonary lesion on chest x ray, which was compatible with tuberculosis. This abnormality occurred in eight users and 17 controls. This difference was not statistically significant.

TABLE 6

SUBJECTS EXCLUDED FROM MATCHED-PAIR STUDY

	User (n=84)	Control (n=156)	Total (N=240)
Defects in visual acuity	4	4	8
Defective color vision	3	13	16
Positive serologic test for syphilis	20	17	37
Pulmonary lesion	8	17	25
Other serious disease	3	9	12
Total excludable defects	38	60	98
Total excluded subjects	37	56	93

Three of the users and 13 controls were found to have defective color vision, for which they were removed from the study. Defects in visual acuity that were not correctable to 20/40 or better were found in four marijuana users and four controls. This difference was not statistically significant.

A diagnosis of serious disease was made in 12 of the total sample. Three of these subjects were marijuana users, and nine were controls. One of the users and four of the controls had two or more causes for exclusion from the study. A total of 37 of the 84 users and 56 of the 156 controls were excluded from further participation from the study because of these abnormalities. These data are summarized in TABLE 6.

The diseases diagnosed in the user group were as follows. One had a severe anemia, with hemoglobin of 9.4 g/100 ml and a hematocrit of 32 vol%. The cause of the anemia was not determined. The second subject had diffuse enlargement of his thyroid gland, with elevations of his white blood cell count and erythrocyte sedimentation rate. The third subject was diagnosed as having subnormal mentality by the neurologist on the basis of his mental status examination. This subject would have been excluded because of a positive sero-logic test for syphilis in addition to the above findings.

Among the nonusers, the following diseases were diagnosed. Two subjects were found to have chronic alcoholism with cirrhosis of the liver; both had low serum albumin with reversal of the albumin-globulin ratio. One had further evidence of liver impairment, with elevation of his blood sugar, serum glutamic-pyruvic transaminase, and serum bilirubin. This individual also was found to have an impaired performance on the mental status examination.

Three subjects were diagnosed as having impaired performance on the mental status examination. Two of these subjects were also excluded on the basis of an abnormal chest x ray suggestive of pulmonary tuberculosis.

Three of the subjects were found to have serious cardiovascular diseases. One had severe hypertension and electrocardiographic evidence of enlargement of the heart. A second had coarctation of the aorta that had been diagnosed previously. Both of these subjects had impaired color vision, which would have led to their exclusion from further participation in the study had they not had cardiovascular disease. A third subject had mitral insufficiency with x-ray evidence of secondary pulmonary complications of that disorder.

One subject was found to have severe renal disease with proteinuria, urinary casts, elevation of blood urea nitrogen, and hypoalbuminemia, with reversal of the albumin-globulin ratio.

All subjects with identified diseases were referred to appropriate clinics for further diagnostic study and treatment.

Subjects with impaired visual acuity correctable with eyeglasses were furnished with suitable corrective lenses so that they could continue to participate in the study.

PLASMA TESTOSTERONE LEVELS

In the second phase of this study, which was conducted on matched pairs of 41 users and controls selected from the base sample, plasma testosterone levels were measured.

The effect of marijuana use on sexual function had received little attention from the scientific community until the report of Kolodny *et al.*[9] in 1974. This study of 20 users showed significantly lower testosterone levels than those found in a matched control group who did not take marijuana, and plasma testosterone returned to higher normal levels in three of the 20 subjects who discontinued marijuana use for 2 weeks. The mean testosterone levels correlated with the frequency of marijuana use, which suggested a dose-response relationship. The mean of sperm counts in 17 of the subjects also supported a dose-response relationship between the use of 10 or more marijuana cigarettes per week and five to nine per week, with the heavier users having significantly lower sperm counts. Sexual functioning was judged adequate in all except two of these subjects.

A study of plasma testosterone levels conducted in a closed-ward setting by Mendelson *et al.*[9a] on a group of 27 young men did not demonstrate diminution of this hormone. These subjects were smoking marijuana at considerably higher levels than those reported by Kolodny *et al.*[9] but for only 21 days. In another closed-ward study of the effects of orally administered Δ^9-tetrahydrocannabinol, Jones has reported transient decrements in testosterone levels that returned to baseline levels when drug administration was discontinued.[10]

These observations led us to question what effect very long-term marijuana smoking might have on plasma testosterone levels in our subjects.

METHOD

Venous blood samples were collected with subjects in the fasting state at 7:00–8:00 AM. The plasma was immediately separated, frozen, and stored at 0° C. Two samples were collected from each subject, 3–7 days apart. Frozen samples were airmailed in batches of 40 in dry-ice packing to the laboratory of the Reproductive Biology Research Foundation in St. Louis, Missouri for determination of testosterone by use of a radioimmunoassay technique. The normal range reported in that laboratory was 380–980 ng/dl. Two samples were collected 3–7 days apart from each subject. Samples for six subjects, two users and four controls, were analyzed by Bioscience Laboratories, Van Nuys, California. Duplicate analyses were performed for two subjects, with samples sent to both laboratories. In these two instances, plasma testosterone levels were reported as 245 and 302 ng/dl higher from Bioscience Laboratories. The results from both laboratories were within the normal ranges of each. In all, 38 of the 41 matched pairs had satisfactory collection and shipment of two plasma samples for analysis.

RESULTS

The results were first analyzed by use of the paired t test for each user and his matched control. The mean value of the two testosterone determinations was used for each subject. The result was a t value of 0.39, with 37 degrees of freedom ($p > 0.10$). This analysis was repeated by use of the lowest testosterone value for each subject. The result was a t value of 0.75, with 37 degrees of freedom ($p > 0.10$).

The group mean value for the 38 users was 564.06 ng/dl (SD $\pm$ 159.42), and for the controls the value was 549.37 ng/dl (SD $\pm$ 166.07). This difference was not significant.

To determine whether a dose-related effect was present, users whose daily average was 10 or more marijuana cigarettes were compared with their matched controls. The mean testosterone level in these 13 users was 522.45 ng/dl (SD $\pm$ 175.71), and in the controls the value was 550.31 ng/dl (SD $\pm$ 117.82).

Four of the seven users in the original sample of 84 who had unilateral testicular atrophy were matched for the special test portion and were therefore included in this sample. The mean testosterone level for these four subjects was 592.8 ng/dl (range 485–715), while their matched controls had a mean of 593.0 ng/dl (range 415–698).

Testosterone is attached to a carrier protein, a β globulin, in the plasma, except for 1–3% that circulates in the free state. Because these subjects had a tendency toward lower β-globulin levels than did the control group, the plasma testosterone levels in marijuana users with β-globulin levels below the mean level of the group were compared with the plasma testosterone levels of those with β-globulin measurements higher than the mean for the group. There was no difference between testosterone levels in users with relatively low β globulin and those with β globulin above the group mean. FIGURE 1 shows the plasma testosterone levels for both groups.

DISCUSSION

These findings are difficult to reconcile with those of Kolodny *et al.*[9] Our subjects have smoked marijuana for longer periods of time, in larger quantities than those reported in the St. Louis study. The lack of correlation between higher levels of marijuana use and lower testosterone levels within our subject group further mitigates against a cause and effect relationship between marijuana

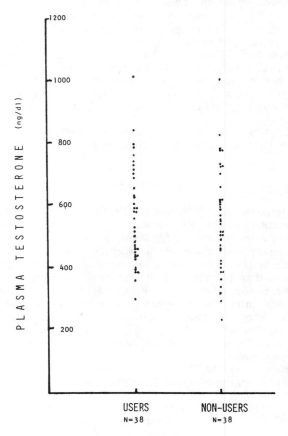

FIGURE 1. Plasma testosterone levels.

use and testosterone levels. It is possible that a tolerance to marijuana develops that overcomes some inhibitory action of marijuana on the hypothalamic-pituitary axis or on the end organ, the testis.

These results confirm and extend the findings of Mendelson mentioned above. The time interval between last marijuana smoking experience and sampling blood for testosterone may explain the discrepancy between our findings and those of the Mendelson study and of Jones,[10] where tetrahydrocannabinol was administered every 4 hr around the clock.

If marijuana smoking had a direct effect on Leydig cell function, one might expect plasma testosterone to be lower in users, with a marked decrement in their total mass of Leydig cells secondary to testicular atrophy. In the four users with unilateral testicular atrophy in this study, testosterone levels were not different from those of their fellow users or from those of the controls.

Transient decrements in plasma testosterone levels that remain within the normal range, as found by Kolodny et al.[9] and by Jones et al.,[10] would not be expected to affect sexual function, protein anabolism, or secondary sexual characteristics in the adult male. Such decrements would be of more concern in the adolescent male. The mean age at which our subjects began marijuana use was 15.2 years. The earliest use reported was at 9 years. The health screening examination did not reveal findings that suggested diminished masculine features in these subjects. Although measures of sexual function require more detailed and focused studies than were performed in this survey, procreative function was tested by asking each subject how many children he had fathered. The responses indicated a mean of 2.6 children and users and 2.6 for controls.

These findings cast serious doubt on a cause and effect relationship between marijuana smoking and plasma testosterone levels in long-term users.

CONCLUSIONS

Chronic marijuana users were found to have minimal differences in health status from nonusers of the same sociocultural class and age. Their medical histories showed more symptoms of gastrointestinal discomfort, and their body weights were lower than those of the control group, although none were markedly underweight. Marijuana users more often had positive serologic tests for syphilis than did the controls, but none were found to have active infection with syphilis. There was no other evidence of an increased incidence of past or present infections in the users suggestive of impaired immunologic responsiveness. Abnormal chest x rays were as frequent in controls as in marijuana users. Testosterone levels were no different in users than in their matched controls. There was no relationship between levels of marijuana use and testosterone levels.

Daily marijuana use for 10–28 years in this sample of men under the age of 50 years did not appear to impair their ability to function normally.

REFERENCES

1. CARTER, W. E. & P. L. DOUGHTY. This monograph.
1a. BLUM, R. H. 1970. Society and Drugs. Chap. XI: 245–275. Jossey-Bass, Inc. Publishers. San Francisco, Calif.
2. COGGINS, W. J. & J. LIPMAN. 1972. Use of illegal drugs in college. J. Florida Med. Ass. 59: 29–33.
3. RUBIN, V. & L. COMITAS. 19xx. Effects of chronic smoking of cannabis in Jamaica. Report to National Institute of Mental Health.
3a. JONES, R. T. Personal communication.
4. KOTCHER, C. V., G. VILLAREJOS, W. HUNTER, L. A. SHEARER, D. L. REDMOND, F. J. PAYNE & J. C. SCHWARZWALDER. 1964. An epidemiological study of four soil-transmitted nematodes in Costa Rica. International Center for Medical

Research and Training (L.S.U. School of Medicine) San Jose, Costa Rica. Unpublished.
5. ZUCKER-FRANKLIN, D. 1974. Eosinophil function and disorders. Advan. Intern. Med. **19:** 10–12.
6. NAHAS, G. G. 1974. Inhibition of cellular mediated immunity in marihuana smokers. Science **183:** 419, 420.
7. CLARK, S. C. 1975. Marihuana and the cardiovascular system. Pharmacol. Biochem. Behav. **3:** 299–306.
7a. MENDELSON, J. H., A. M. ROSSI & R. E. MEYER. (Eds.) 1974. The Use of Marihuana. A Psychological and Physiological Inquiry. : 159. Plenum Publishing Corporation. New York, N.Y.
8. ARNOW, W. S. & J. CASSIDY. 1974. N. Engl. J. Med. **291:** 65–67.
9. KOLODNY, R. C., W. H. MASTERS, R. M. KOLODNER & G. TORO. 1974. Depression of plasma testosterone levels after chronic marijuana use. N. Engl. J. Med. **290:** 872–874.
9a. MENDELSON, J. H., J. KUEHNLE, J. ELLINGBOE & T. F. BABOR. 1974. Plasma testosterone levels before, during and after chronic marihuana smoking. N. Engl. J. Med. **291:** 1051–1055.
10. JONES, R. 1975. Personal communication.
11. MARIJUANA: A SIGNAL OF MISUNDERSTANDING. 1972. First report of the National Commission on Marijuana and Drug Abuse. : 42. United States Government Printing Office. Washington, D.C.

PHYSICAL ASSESSMENT OF 30 CHRONIC CANNABIS USERS AND 30 MATCHED CONTROLS

E. K. Cruickshank

West of Scotland Committee
for Postgraduate Medical Education
The University of Glasgow
Glasgow G12 8QQ, Scotland

This study was initiated to assess the possible physical and mental effects of cannabis on adult males who had been heavy smokers for the last 7 years or more, in comparison with matched controls. These subjects were drawn from the lower social stratum of Jamaican society. They were mainly peasant farmers and fishermen from rural areas aged from 23 to 53 years, with an average of 34. Formal schooling ranged from less than 1 to 9 years; mean number of years of schooling completed was 4.5; the mean in educational attainment was the third grade of primary school. Primary occupations of the sample include farming, fishing, skilled and semiskilled crafts, and produce vending. Except for two, all subjects were gainfully employed either full or part-time.

SMOKING HISTORY

All except 12 subjects in the total sample had had an initial smoking experience. The age of the subjects at their first *ganja* smoking experience ranged from 8 to 36 years. Smokers, however, tended to have their first ganja smoking experience earlier than controls. The age at which regular use began for the smoker group ranged from 9 to 25; the average age was 15 years.

The 30 smokers have a history of regular ganja smoking that ranges from 7 to 37 years, with a mean of 17.5 years. The number of spliffs (ganja cigarettes) consumed per day at the time of the study ranged from one to 24, with an average of seven. Based on these frequencies, light use is defined as one to four spliffs per day, moderate use as four to seven per day, and heavy use as eight or more per day. Ganja smokers who use the chillum pipe consume from one to 25 pipeloads per week, with an average weekly consumption of 14 pipeloads. Ganja samples submitted by smoker subjects had a content of Δ^9-tetrahydrocannabinol that ranged from 0.7 to 10.3% (mean weight), with a mean of 2.96%. There were several grades of ganja; the potency of ganja smoked varies according to availability.

For smoking in spliffs and chillum pipes, ganja is customarily mixed with cigarette tobacco. In addition, 27 of the 30 ganja smokers in the sample also smoke tobacco cigarettes, while 11 of the controls do not smoke. Ganja is taken by both smokers and controls in tea and tonics for medicinal purposes and occasionally in food. Aside from ganja, no drugs (e.g., heroin, lysergic acid diethylamide, opiates, amphetamines, barbiturates, or datura) were taken by subjects in the sample. Smokers tend to drink less alcohol than do controls and tend to prefer ganja over alcohol for regular consumption. As a condition of

162

participation in the project, smokers agreed to abstain from ganja smoking while at the University Hospital. No withdrawal symptoms were reported.

These 60 subjects, 30 chronic ganja smokers and 30 controls, were admitted to the University Hospital for 6 days. The medical observers did not know whether the subjects examined were smokers or controls. A detailed medical history and examination, x rays of the heart and lungs, electrocardiograms, respiratory function tests, blood chemistry to determine liver and renal function, and hematologic and treponemal serology tests were performed. In addition to these tests, thorough psychologic and psychiatric assessments with electro-encephalograms, including sleep records in some subjects, were also undertaken. Blood and urine samples were sent to the Rockland State Research Center laboratory (USA) for analysis of peripheral thyroid hormone levels and steroid excretion study. The results of these tests are discussed separately.

Clinical Findings

These findings are summarized in TABLE 1.

No significant physical abnormality was in the subjects, except in two smokers. One had a long history of bronchial asthma, and one had "Jamaican neuropathy," a syndrome that presents with evidence of pyramidal tract damage and often posterior column damage with or without retrobulbar neuropathy and eighth nerve deafness. Its etiology is uncertain, but it may be an atypical form of neurosyphilis.[1] There was no reason to believe that these disabilities were in any way related to the use of cannabis. Blood pressures in both groups were within normal limits. X rays of the heart and lungs were normal in both groups, except for some scarring of the lungs in one of the controls.

The smokers and controls were well matched with respect to both height and age, but the smokers were an average of 7 lb lighter than the controls. This difference is probably not significant but might indicate that the chronic use of cannabis causes some suppression of appetite. Three of the ganja smokers and eight of the controls did not smoke tobacco, and alcohol consumption was approximately the same in both groups.

Serologic tests for treponematosis were positive in a higher proportion of the controls (57%) than smokers (37%). Both of these figures, however, are within the range of positive serology found in a random sample of the adult male population in various parts of Jamaica (20–40%); the upper value of this range is found in the rural areas of some parishes where clinical yaws used to be widespread. Even in recent years, surveys of treponemal serology in pre-pubertal school children in these rural areas give a positive rate of up to 25%, as compared with less than 1% in Kingston,[2] a difference that strongly suggests that treponemal infection (yaws) still occurs but at a subclinical level. As soon as any suspicious clinical lesion appears, effective penicillin therapy is undertaken, because florid clinical yaws is now exceptionally rare in these areas.

The minor electrocardiographic abnormalities in both groups (30%) may indicate the prevalence of cardiomyopathy, again of uncertain origin, that has been recognized in Jamaica.[3, 4] An obliterative disease of the small coronary vessels has been postulated as the immediate cause.[5] A high incidence of arteritis has been reported in Moroccan Kif users,[6] and this factor may contribute to the reputedly common finding of tropical foot ulcers in chronic users; however, heavy tobacco consumption so often associated with the use of cannabis can

TABLE 1

CLINICAL FINDINGS IN 30 CHRONIC CANNABIS USERS AND 30 MATCHED CONTROLS

Subjects	Average Age	Average Height (cm)	Average Weight (lb)	Daily Cigarette Consumption (tobacco)					Alcohol Consumption (rum and beer)		VDRL		Electrocardiographic Findings		Eosinophilia		Elevated SGOT SGPT	
				0	0–20	20–40	40+	ND*	Occasional	Moderate High	Neg.	Pos.	Neg.	Pos.	Neg.	Pos.	Neg.	Pos.
Smokers	33	168	135	3	13	8	2	2	21†	7	19	11	20	10	26	4	26	4
Controls	33	168	142	8	14	4	1	3	22‡	5	13	17	19	11	23	7	27	3

* Not determined.
† Not determined in two subjects.
‡ Not determined in three subjects.

precipitate or aggravate obliterative vascular disease. Of the heavy tobacco smokers (i.e., more than 20 cigarettes per day), two of the controls and two of the ganja smokers had electrocardiographic changes, while three controls and nine ganja smokers had normal electrocardiograms.

The hematologic findings revealed the presence of eosinophilia in 11 subjects, seven nonusers and four users, which is not statistically significant. No significant differences were found in the other hematologic tests, with the exception of hemoglobin and monocyte count values.

Elevation of the liver enzymes serum glutamic-oxaloacetic transaminase (SGOT) and serum glutamic-pyruvic transaminase (SGPT) was found in seven subjects, three nonusers and four users, but was not very high and does not indicate significant liver damage.

The major statistically significant differences between the 30 chronic smokers and the 30 controls were found in postexercise hemoglobin values and bicarbonate levels. Several trends of interest were noted in the respiratory function findings. The correlations indicate an association between frequency and duration of smoking per se (tobacco cigarettes and ganja spliffs and pipes) with these trends in respiratory function and differences in blood chemistry. Chronic heavy smokers (more than 20 cigarettes per day, plus chronic ganja smoking by spliff and/or pipe) are at greater risk of functional hypoxia. No other significant differences were established. We will, however, take a more detailed look at the data on respiratory function and blood chemistry, because every research variable was examined statistically and there were no significant differences, except in these two areas.

Lung Function

In general, no major statistically significant differences were found between ganja smokers and controls with respect to pulmonary function as measured by forced expiratory volume ($FEV_{1.0}$) and forced vital capacity (FVC) and arterial blood gas and pulse. However, several statistical trends are of interest.

Proportional decreases in $FEV_{1.0}/FVC$ in smokers mitigate against an obstructive ventilatory defect; possible causes of the reduced ratio include cardiomyopathy, pulmonary scars, and pulmonary fibroses.

There is a tendency for smokers' pO_2 at rest to be lower than that of controls, ruling out hypoventilation as a cause of resting hypoxia.

After exercise, there is a levelling of the tendency for differences between smokers and controls on pCO_2 values, with a postexercise persistency to a low pCO_2 in smokers.

Correlations between scores on indices of tobacco smoking, ganja smoking, and combined smoking rating show a decrease between $FEV_{1.0}$ and peak flow with number of years and quantity of ganja and cigarettes smoked.

Hematology

The results indicate significant differences between smokers and controls in hemoglobin and differences in packed cell volume (PCV) values. Five times as many smokers as nonsmokers were in the high-range (50–55%) group of

PCV values. Although not statistically significant, this finding reconfirms the hemoglobin results. Several explanations for this finding are possible, but the only data in the study that bear on these differences are arterial pO_2 values, which were lower in the smokers. Although carbonmonoxyhemoglobin values were not obtained, elevated carbonmonoxyhemoglobin values would be the most reasonable explanation for the elevated hemoglobin and PCV values noted. In other words, functional hypoxia has led to an increased demand on the bone marrow for red blood cell production. This suggestion is strengthened by the findings of Sagone et al.[7] on the relationship of cigarette smoking to tissue hypoxia.

Three further specialized studies were also undertaken.

Steroid Excretion Study

Comparison of the excretion of the major urinary metabolites of cortisol, the main corticosteroid secreted by the adrenal gland, in smokers and controls was undertaken to determine possible indications of marked changes in adrenal cortical function in chronic cannabis users. No statistically significant differences were found between the two groups.

Peripheral Thyroid Hormone Levels

Total and free thyroxine content was determined in 22 serum samples. No statistically significant differences were found. Chronic smoking of cannabis does not appear to affect these levels.

Chromosome Studies

Research was carried out on the 60 subjects by use of the microtechnique of Arakaki and Sparkes.[8] Twenty seven of the cultures failed to produce adequate results for analysis. The 33 successful cases were from 18 smokers and 15 controls. Chromatid breaks and gaps were found in 2.36% of cells in smokers and in 2.90% of cells in controls. The incidence of mild chromatid breakage was no higher than that found in random subjects studied in the University Hospital laboratory. It appears that chronic cannabis usage has no significant effect on the mitotic chromosomes of human peripheral blood lymphocytes in Jamaican adult males.

SUMMARY

Ganja is used extensively in the working-class population of Jamaica, particularly in certain agricultural and fishing communities. Ganja smoking is illegal but can be accepted as part of the culture in these areas. Sixty male subjects were chosen for assessment, 30 chronic smokers and 30 controls from comparable social, economic, and cultural backgrounds, and were matched for height and age. A chronic smoker had smoked a minimum of three spliffs per day for a minimum of 10 years. The subjects were admitted to the hospital for

1 week for psychologic and physical assessment. The physical assessment included a detailed medical history and examination, heart and lung radiography, electrocardiograms, respiratory, liver, and renal function tests, hematology, treponemal serology, and chromosomal studies. No significant physical abnormalities were found, except in two smokers, and there was no reason to suspect that these disabilities were related to ganja. No significant differences between the two groups were demonstrated in the wide range of tests administered.

REFERENCES

1. CRUICKSHANK, E. K., R. D. MONTGOMERY & J. D. SPILLANE. 1961. Obscure neurological disorders in Jamaica. World Neurol. **2:** 199–211.
2. ASHCROFT, M. T., W. E. MIALL, K. L. STANDARD & W. E. URQUHART. 1967. Treponemal serological tests in two Jamaican communities. Brit. J. Venereal Diseases **43:** 96–104.
3. STUART, K. L. & J. A. HAYES. 1963. A cardiac disorder of unknown aetiology in Jamaica. Quart. J. Med. **32:** 99–114.
4. FODOR, J., W. E. MIALL, K. L. STANDARD, Z. FEJFAR & K. L. STUART. 1964. Myocardial disease in a rural population in Jamaica. Bull. World Health Org. **31:** 321–335.
5. CAMPBELL, M., J. M. SUMMERELL, G. BRAS, J. A. HAYES & K. L. STUART. 1971. Pathology of idiopathic cardiomegaly in Jamaica. Brit. Heart J. Suppl. **30:** 193–202.
6. U.S. DEPARTMENT OF HEALTH, EDUCATION AND WELFARE. 1971. Marihuana and Health; A Report to Congress from the Secretary. United States Government Printing Office. Washington, D.C.
7. SAGONE, A. L., T. LAWRENCE & S. P. BALCERZAK. 1971. Smoking—a cause of "spurious" polycythemia. Blood **38**(6): 826 (Abs.).
8. ARAKAKI, D. T. & R. S. SPARKES. 1963. Microtechnique for culturing leukocytes from whole blood. Cytogenetics **2:** 57–60.

EFFECTS OF CHRONIC HASHISH USE ON
MEDICAL STATUS IN 44 USERS
COMPARED WITH 38 CONTROLS *

J. C. Boulougouris, C. P. Panayiotopoulos, E. Antypas,
A. Liakos, and C. Stefanis

Department of Psychiatry
Athens University Medical School
Eginition Hospital
Athens, Greece

Apart from the consistent physiologic and psychologic changes that occur during hashish intoxication,[1] severe medical hazards have been reported after long-term heavy hashish use. Respiratory ailments, such as bronchitis, asthma, and even pulmonary fibrosis,[2-4] arteritis,[5] endocarditis, and hepatotoxic effects [6, 7] have been reported. Dermatologic manifestations,[3] conjunctival injection, and neurologic changes consisted mainly of fine tremor of the fingers; [8, 9] nystagmus [9-11] and sluggish pupil reaction to light or accommodation [11] have also been described. All of these studies did not use controls and therefore failed to account for other factors, except for cannabis, likely to produce their results. Recent studies have failed to demonstrate significant physical abnormalities between chronic hashish users and controls,[12] and the liver dysfunction of hashish users has been attributed to persistent use of alcohol in the sample studied, rather than to the effects of cannabis.[13] In this paper, we report the findings of the routine medical and neurologic examinations that were included in the procedures for the selection of Greek hashish users and controls who were employed in later experimental studies.

METHODS AND MATERIALS

Subjects

Sixty cannabis users and 64 controls were examined. The final comparison was made between 44 long-term hashish users and 38 controls. We excluded subjects who suffered from incapacitating physical or neurologic illness or who had a history of other addictive substances, except for social use of alcohol. All subjects were tobacco smokers. Only two subjects from the control sample were excluded for having had central nervous system disease. Cannabis users had a mean age of 40.7 years (SD 10.12), and the mean duration in years of hashish use was 23 (SD 9.70). The controls were matched to users for age (mean, 41.7 years; SD, 41.72), family origin, education, residence at birth, and upbringing.

* Supported by National Institute of Mental Health Contract HSM 42–70–98 through the International Association for Psychiatric Research.

168

Examination

The physical status of each subject was assessed by a physician. A medical history was taken, and a clinical examination of the respiratory, cardiovascular, and alimentary systems was performed. Pulse rate, blood pressure in supine and erect positions, presence or absence of conjunctival injection, verbal hoarseness, and uvula edema were systematically recorded. A detailed neurologic examination was also performed by a neurologist. In view of the reported neurologic findings, special attention was paid to the following: corneal reflex, nystagmus, pupillary reaction to light and accommodation, tremor, finger to nose and heel to shin test, tendon reflexes, deep sensation, and grip strength.

RESULTS

Respiratory Tract

Thirteen hashish users and six controls were found by pulmonary auscultation to have high-pitched wheezing, indicating bronchitis. This difference was not statistically significant. In no case were the symptoms of bronchitis severe enough to prevent the patient from performing his everyday work. Two hashish users and one control had physical signs of emphysema. Cough and pharyngeal irritation were common among the users. Verbal hoarseness was detected in four hashish users and two controls. Uvula edema was observed in five hashish users and one control. Hashish users smoked more tobacco cigarettes per day (mean, 38.2; SD, 17.6) than did controls (mean, 26.7; SD, 14.4). This difference was statistically significant ($t = 3.34$, $p < 0.002$).

Cardiovascular System

The pulse rate was higher in hashish users (mean, 80.4 beats/min; SD, 10.1) than in controls (mean, 75.9 beats/min; SD, 7.4), but this difference was not statistically significant. No differences were found in blood pressure both in supine and erect positions. One hashish user had extrasystolic arrythmia. No signs of arteriosclerosis were found. Heart sounds were within normal limits. Conjunctival injection was observed in only four hashish users. The skin color was within normal limits in both groups, but four hashish users had scars.

Alimentary System

An enlarged spleen was found in one hashish user. No jaundice was detected, but enlarged livers (TABLE 1) were found in eight of 44 hashish users (18%), as compared with two of 38 controls (5%). This difference was statistically significant ($\chi^2 = 5.04$, $p < 0.025$).

Hashish users and controls were unaware of their hepatomegaly, because they had never shown clinical symptoms of liver dysfunction. To investigate the relationship between degree of cannabis use and enlarged liver, the cannabis users were divided into two groups (TABLE 2): heavy users, those who reported smoking amounts above the mean present use, and moderate users, those who

TABLE 1

INCIDENCE OF ENLARGED LIVER

| | Enlarged | | Normal | | | | |
	No.	%	No.	%	Total	χ^2	p
Hashish users	8	18.18	36	81.82	44		
						5.04	<0.025
Controls	1	2.5	37	97.5	38		

smoked amounts below the mean. No relationship was found between degree of current consumption of cannabis and enlarged liver. A similar investigation of hepatomegaly and hashish smoking with respect to past degree of smoking revealed no significant relationship.

Because alcohol consumption is frequently responsible for hepatomegaly, the correlation between alcohol use and enlarged liver was investigated. Subjects were rated for alcohol use by a 0–4 scale. Hashish users were divided into two subgroups according to the severity of drinking. Moderate drinkers were characterized as subjects who rated 0–2 on the scale, and heavy drinkers were classified as those who rated 3–4 (TABLE 3). Enlarged liver in hashish users was found to be related to the use of alcohol.

Neurologic Findings

The routine neurologic examination was within normal limits for both groups, but the following hashish users exhibited some neurologic findings: one subject complained of transitory vertigo when lying down or rising suddenly; two subjects had symptoms and/or signs that indicated lumbar spine disc; two had reduced grip strength; one had very brisk tendon reflexes and an impaired sense of vibration; one had mild tremors of the tongue; and one had no corneal

TABLE 2

RELATIONSHIP BETWEEN ENLARGED LIVER
AND DEGREE OF HASHISH USE

| | Enlarged Liver | | Normal Liver | | | | |
	No.	%	No.	%	Total	χ^2	p
Moderate users (below the mean daily consumption)	5	16.66	22	83.34	27		
						0.14	ns
Heavy users (above the mean daily consumption)	3	21.42	14	78.58	17		

reflex. No nystagmus, fine finger tremor, disturbance in coordination, or impairment of pupillary reaction to light and accommodation was found.

DISCUSSION

The hashish users studied were physically and neurologically healthy. Our negative findings are in agreement with those of other controlled studies and do not confirm reports on the deleterious effects of excessive use of cannabis preparations. All subjects, particularly the hashish users, were pleased to undergo a medical examination in order to be reassured that no harmful effects are produced by hashish smoking. The greater incidence of bronchitis in hashish users might be due to the increased number of tobacco cigarettes smoked.

Even an association between enlarged liver and degree of alcohol consumption was found: hashish users tended to drink more alcohol than did the controls, a trend opposite to that described by others.[12]

TABLE 3

ALCOHOL USE AND INCIDENCE OF ENLARGED LIVER

	Moderate Drinking (>2 points)	Enlarged Liver	%	Heavy Drinking (<2 points)	Enlarged Liver	%	χ^2	p
Present use								
Hashish users								
($n=44$)	39	5	12.82	5	3	60	6.63	<0.01
Control								
($n=38$)	37	2	5.40	1	0	—	—	—
Total	76	7	9.21	6	3	50.0	8.64	<0.005

On the other hand, in this study, we took into account only the effects of social use of alcohol, because alcoholics were excluded from the final comparison. In fact, most hashish users reported an aversion toward alcohol, and two of them who used to drink heavily reported that they stopped drinking after they had started hashish smoking. It may be that hashish smoking is incompatible with alcohol consumption, and differential patterns of the effects of cannabis and alcohol on some psychologic tests have been reported.[13] However, that cannabis may potentiate alcohol's hepatotoxic effect should not be disregarded. In cannabis users, the jaundice observed has been attributed to alcohol use, and not to hashish, in well-controlled studies [14] where liver function tests have been used. Enlarged livers were detected in the present study by clinical examination, and no liver function tests were performed. A series of liver function tests performed in 16 hashish users who cooperated in a withdrawal experiment proved to be negative, and one might postulate that enlargement of the liver is not necessarily accompanied by its physiologic dysfunction.

The absense of conjunctival injection in our subjects is difficult to explain, because it has been described very consistently in naive and experienced users, several days after smoking.[9]

Since grip strength was tested clinically, and the lack of a difference between hashish users and controls could be argued, further objective measurements of grip strength by the use of a hand dynamometer on 16 hashish users who cooperated in a withdrawal experiment also showed no difference between smoking and withdrawal conditions. It can therefore be stated that muscle weakness is most likely only a subjective complaint.[1] In conclusion, the clinical data obtained in this study do not support the opinion that chronic use of cannabis leads to physical deterioration.

REFERENCES

1. HOLLISTER, L. O. 1971. Status report on clinical pharmacology of marihuana. Ann. N.Y. Acad. Sci. **191:** 132–141.
2. GARY, N. E. & V. KEYLON. 1970. Intravenous administration of marihuana. J. Amer. Med. Ass. **211**(3): 501.
3. TENNANT, F. S., M. P. FREBLE, T. J. PRENDERGAST & P. VENTRY. 1971. Medical manifestations associated with hashish. J. Amer. Med. Ass. **211**(12): 1965–1969.
4. HENDERSON, L., F. S. TENNANT & R. GUERRY. 1972. Respiratory manifestations of hashish smoking. Arch. Otolaryngol. **95:** 248–251.
5. STEME, J. & C. DUCASTAING. 1960. Les arterites des cannabis indica. Arch. Maladies Coeur Vaisseaux **53:** 143–147.
6. LUNDERGEG, G. D., J. ADELSON & E. H. PROSNITZ. 1971. Marihuana induced hospitalization. J. Amer. Med. Ass. **215**(1): 121.
7. KEW, M. C., L. BERSOHN & S. SIEW. 1969. Possible hepatotoxicity of cannabis. Lancet **I:** 578, 579.
8. AMES, F. 1958. A clinical and metabolic study of acute intoxication with cannabis sativa and its role in the model psychoses. J. Mental Sci. **104**(437): 972–999.
9. BERNSTEIN, J. G., R. E. MEYER & J. H. MENDELSON. 1974. Psychological assessments: general medical survey. In The Use of Marihuana. A Psychological and Physiological Inquiry. J. H. Mendelson, A. M. Rossi & R. E. Meyer, Eds. Plenum Publishing Corporation. New York, N.Y.
10. ALLENTUCK, S. 1944. Organic and systemic functions. In Mayor's Committee on Marihuana. The Marihuana Problem in the City of New York. Sociological, Medical, Psychological and Pharmacological Studies. Jaques Cattell Press. Tempe, Ariz.
11. RODIN, E. & E. F. DOMINO. 1970. Effects of acute marihuana smoking in the electroencephalogram. Electroencephalogr. Clin. Neurophysiol. **29:** 321–324.
12. RUBIN, V. & L. COMITAS. 1974. Ganga in Jamaica. Mouton. The Hague.
13. RAFAELSEN, L., P. BECH, V. CHRISTRUP & O. J. RAFAELSEN. 1973. Cannabis and alcohol: effects on psychological tests. Nature (London) **242:** 117, 118.
14. HOCHMAN, J. S. & N. Q. BRILL. 1971. Chronic marihuana usage and liver function. Lancet **II:** 7728, 818.

CLINICAL STUDY OF FREQUENT MARIJUANA USE: ADRENAL CORTICAL RESERVE METABOLISM OF A CONTRACEPTIVE AGENT AND DEVELOPMENT OF TOLERANCE *

Mario Perez-Reyes

Department of Psychiatry
University of North Carolina at Chapel Hill
Chapel Hill, North Carolina 27514

Dolores Brine and Monroe E. Wall

Research Triangle Institute
Research Triangle Park
North Carolina 27709

In recent years, the frequent use of marijuana among segments of the American population has become a cause of concern as to whether the drug could significantly affect the health of the users. We will report the effects of marijuana as used by young Americans in a southeastern university town on three unrelated physiologic parameters: adrenal cortical reserve, liver metabolism of a contraceptive drug, and development of tolerance or sensitivity to Δ^9-tetrahydrocannabinol (Δ^9-THC).

In this report, we define frequency of marijuana use as the number of cigarettes smoked per year multiplied by the number of years of use. We recognize the faults of this method of measurement, in that it relies on subjective reporting, which might not be accurate, on mathematical averaging, which might not be appropriate, and on a total lack of knowledge of the potency of the marijuana used in terms of Δ^9-THC content. Whatever the disadvantages of the retrospective approach, it has produced significant results in the study of the health consequences of alcohol and tobacco use.

ADRENAL CORTICAL RESERVE

Chronic toxicity studies in rhesus monkeys by use of high doses of Δ^9-THC produced marked hyperplasia of the adrenal glands.[1] Our acute experiments in dogs showed that after intravenous injection of 10 mg of [^{3}H]Δ^9-THC, the radioactivity accumulated in the adrenal cortex at levels similar to those found in the liver, which were five to six times larger than the levels in any other tissue. These findings indicate the possibility that frequent use of marijuana might interfere with normal functioning of the adrenal cortex, such as the adrenocortical reserve.

To investigate this possibility, we compared the basal levels of cortisol and

* Supported by Contract HSM–42–71–95 between the National Institute on Drug Abuse and the Research Triangle Institute and by United States Public Health Service Research Grant RR–46.

the secretion of this hormone after intramuscular injection of synthetic cortico-tropin between two groups of volunteers with different patterns of marijuana use.

Twenty normal healthy male paid volunteers participated in the experiment. Ten had never smoked marijuana before, and 10 were frequent users of the drug. The experiments began at 10 AM with a venipuncture and the collection of a blood sample. Every subject was then intramuscularly injected with 250 μg of synthetic β^{1-24}-corticotropin (Cortrocyn®). Blood samples were collected at 15-min intervals for 90 min. In these samples, cortisol was determined by radioimmunoassay by use of the New England Nuclear Cortisol ^{3}H-Radio-immunoassay Pak.

The results of this experiment are illustrated in FIGURE 1. The graph at the top of the Figure shows the cortisol plasma levels that occurred in response to corticotropin stimulation at the specified times. The mean responses of the two groups studied were almost equal. At the bottom of the Figure, the char-acteristics of the subjects in terms of age, weight, and drug experience are listed.

To analyze the data in a different form, we have constructed TABLE 1 to indicate the basal levels of plasma cortisol, the maximal cortisol levels reached after corticotropin stimulation, the difference between these two values, and the percentage elevation over basal levels. The results show that there were

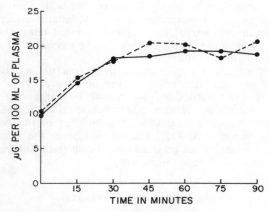

CHARACTERISTICS OF THE SUBJECTS

	NON-USERS N = 10	FREQUENT USERS N = 10	P
AGE	28.17± 5.57	21.3 ± 3.9	.01
WEIGHT (KG)	73.33 ±9.99	78.3 ± 8.9	.25 NS
AGE OF ONSET OF MJ USE		17.3 ± 2.72	.001
YEARS OF EXPERIENCE		4.9 ± 2.59	.001
MJ USE PER YEAR		671.4± 518.34	.001
TOTAL MJ USE		3101.6±2370.2	.001
HALLUCINOGENS*		64.1± 120.77	.001

The figures represent the mean of the groups ± the standard deviation

*The number of these drugs used during the life span of the subjects.

FIGURE 1. Cortisol plasma levels after intramuscular administration of β^{1-24}-cortico-tropin. Nonusers (—); frequent marijuana users (- - -).

TABLE 1

MAXIMAL SECRETION OF CORTISOL AFTER INTRAMUSCULAR ADMINISTRATION
OF β^{1-24}-CORTICOTROPIN

	Nonmarijuana Users	Frequent Marijuana Users	p
Basal level *	9.8±4.4	10.3±2.9	0.85, ns
Maximal levels *	21.0±6.8	24.7±3.9	0.25, ns
Total elevation *	11.2±4.9	14.5±3.8	0.20, ns
Elevation (%)	136±78	159±69	0.60, ns

* Figures represent the average micrograms per 100 ml of plasma ± the standard deviation.

only minor differences, which were not statistically significant, between the mean values of the two groups.

From the results of this experiment, we concluded that frequent use of marijuana did not alter the capacity of the adrenal cortex to respond to synthetic corticotropin stimulation.

RATE AND PATTERN OF [^{3}H]NORETHYNODREL METABOLISM

It is well known that certain drugs, such as barbiturates, are capable of inducing liver microsomal enzymes and increasing the metabolic activity of the organ. It is possible that frequent use of marijuana could produce the same effect. In this respect, we have studied the possible influence that frequent marijuana use might have on the rate and pattern of metabolism of a component of contraceptive "pills," norethynodrel. This drug is exclusively metabolized by the liver. We felt that this study was relevant, because the use of marijuana among young females has increased considerably in recent years, and many of them use contraceptive drugs.

Two groups that differed significantly in their frequency of marijuana use and that each consisted of five male and five female healthy paid volunteers participated in the experiment. The female subjects had never taken a contraceptive drug, used intrauterine devices for contraception, and were tested between the 18th and 23rd days of their menstrual cycles.

The volunteers were intravenously injected with a preparation that contained 2 mg of [^{3}H]norethynodrel, which contained 100 μCi of radioactivity and 50 μg of ethynylestradiol. The contraceptive agents were dissolved in 0.5 ml of 95% ethanol and then were suspended in 20 ml of 25% salt-free human serum albumin. Subjects did not experience any discomfort or side effects.

Blood samples were collected at 60, 90, 120, 150, and 180 min and at 6 and 24 hr after injection. Urine and feces were collected during the first 24 hr. In these samples, a determination of tritium-labeled norethynodrel and its metabolites was performed by the procedure of Cook *et al.*[2]

The results of this experiment are summarized in FIGURE 2. We have combined the values obtained for male and female subjects of both groups because they were not significantly different. Examination of the upper part of the Figure reveals that the free norethynodrel and its metabolites found in the plasma at the specified times did not differ between frequent and infrequent marijuana users despite the statistically significant differences in drug use, as indicated at the bottom of the Figure.

TABLE 2 illustrates the rate and pattern of metabolism of [³H]norethynodrel found in the plasma. The major metabolites found in the free fraction were norethindrone, 3α-hydroxy- and 3β-hydroxynorethynodrel, and polyhydroxy compounds derived from the primary metabolites. There were no significant

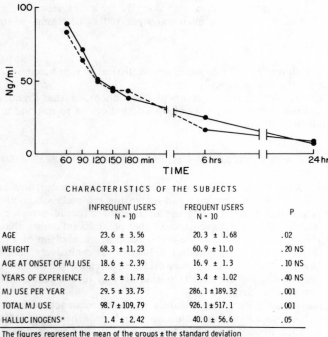

CHARACTERISTICS OF THE SUBJECTS

	INFREQUENT USERS N = 10	FREQUENT USERS N = 10	P
AGE	23.6 ± 3.56	20.3 ± 1.68	.02
WEIGHT	68.3 ± 11.23	60.9 ± 11.0	.20 NS
AGE AT ONSET OF MJ USE	18.6 ± 2.39	16.9 ± 1.3	.10 NS
YEARS OF EXPERIENCE	2.8 ± 1.78	3.4 ± 1.02	.40 NS
MJ USE PER YEAR	29.5 ± 33.75	286.1 ± 189.32	.001
TOTAL MJ USE	98.7 ± 109.79	926.1 ± 517.1	.001
HALLUCINOGENS*	1.4 ± 2.42	40.0 ± 56.6	.05

The figures represent the mean of the groups ± the standard deviation

*The number of these drugs used during the life span of the subjects.

FIGURE 2. Free norethynodrel and its metabolites found in the plasma after intravenous injection of [³H]norethynodrel. Infrequent marijuana users (—); frequent users (- - -).

differences in the rate and pattern of metabolism between frequent and infrequent marijuana users. Similar results were found for the conjugated material in the plasma and the free and conjugated compounds excreted in the urine and feces.

The results of this experiment indicate that frequent use of marijuana does not alter the metabolism of [³H]norethynodrel, and, therefore, it does not appear to alter liver metabolic activity.

TABLE 2

FREE NORETHYNODREL AND ITS METABOLITES FOUND IN THE PLASMA (ng/ml) *

Time	Polyhydroxy		3α-OH-Norethynodrel		3β-OH-Norethynodrel		Norethindrone		Norethynodrel		Total	
	Infrequent	Frequent	Infrequent	Frequent	Infrequent	Frequent	Infrequent	Frequent	Infrequent	Frequent	Infrequent	Frequent
60 min	10.2	10.8	5.9	7.1	6.0	6.8	12.5	15.5	4.5	4.1	39.1	44.3
90 min	9.7	9.2	4.3	4.5	5.5	5.7	9.2	12.5	3.0	3.7	31.7	35.6
120 min	7.9	8.1	2.8	3.2	4.1	4.2	6.6	7.6	2.0	2.3	23.4	25.4
150 min	7.3	7.8	2.1	2.1	3.5	3.5	5.9	6.2	2.0	2.0	20.8	21.6
180 min	8.0	7.9	2.2	1.9	2.3	3.2	6.5	5.1	2.2	1.8	22.1	19.9
6 hr	4.1	6.1	0.7	1.3	1.2	1.9	1.5	2.0	0.7	0.8	8.2	12.1
24 hr	2.5	1.8	0.5	0.3	0.4	0.4	0.8	0.7	0.4	0.5	4.6	3.7

* Figures represent the average values of 10 subjects.

Development of Tolerance to Δ⁹-THC

In the course of our investigations of the clinical pharmacology and metabolism of Δ⁹-THC, we have administered this compound intravenously to subjects who had different frequencies of marijuana use. We hypothesized that if either tolerance or sensitivity to the effects of marijuana had developed, frequent users would respond to the intravenous administration of Δ⁹-THC differently from infrequent users.

Of the many normal male healthy paid volunteers to whom we have administered [³H]Δ⁹-THC intravenously, we selected the eight subjects who had used marijuana most frequently and the eight subjects who had used marijuana least frequently. All were injected with a microsuspension of Δ⁹-THC in 25% salt-free human serum albumin.[3] The drug was injected at the rate of 0.2 mg/min. Heart rate was constantly monitored throughout the experiment, and the subjec-

TABLE 3

SELECTED GROUP OF MARIJUANA USERS

	Infrequent (n=8)	Frequent (n=8)	p
Age	24.88±1.96	21.50±1.50	0.005
Age of onset	23.88±1.96	17.88±1.62	0.001
Years of experience	1.13±0.78	3.75±1.48	0.001
Marijuana use per year	3.00±2.96	493.00±539.35	0.05
Total marijuana use	4.13±3.72	1598.00±1569.68	0.02
Hallucinogens	0	80.00±48.34	0.001
Perception of "high" (μg/kg)	20.76±8.01	21.36±9.66	0.90, ns
Heart acceleration (μg/kg)	26.33±8.06	24.67±14.38	0.80, ns
Total dose (μg/kg)	50.47±16.55	70.43±42.03	0.25, ns
Maximum level of "high"	38.13±16.37	35.50±14.51	0.70, ns
Maximum heart acceleration	64.13±18.34	76.63±27.00	0.30, ns
Heart acceleration at 15 min	41.50±18.49	58.25±28.69	0.20, ns

tive evaluation of drug effects was rated every 5 min by a technique described elsewhere.[4]

The subjects were instructed to report the moment they felt the action of the drug and to ask for the termination of the infusion as soon as they thought that they had arrived at their desired level of "high." The volunteers were encouraged to receive the largest amount of the drug that they could comfortably tolerate. By giving the subjects control as to the amount of the drug to be injected and by the constant recording of vital signs, we ensured the safety of the volunteers.

In TABLE 3, we have summarized the characteristics of the groups in terms of age, drug usage, and the amount of Δ⁹-THC (μg/kg) required to produce certain specific effects. Examination of this Table indicates that the groups differed significantly in age, age at which they started using marijuana, years of experience, marijuana use per year, total marijuana used (number of cigarettes smoked per year times number of years of experience), and total use of hallucinogens.[5]

Despite the different patterns of marijuana use, the groups did not differ significantly in the amount of Δ^9-THC necessary for its effects to be perceived, to accelerate the heart rate 25% above baseline levels, in total dose administered, maximum level of "high," maximum heart rate acceleration, and heart rate acceleration observed 15 min after the beginning of the infusion.

We believe that the results reported in this study are pharmacologically valid evidence that indicate that frequent use of marijuana does not alter the response qualitatively or quantitatively to the intravenous injection of Δ^9-THC.

It could be argued that the amount of marijuana cigarettes smoked by the frequent users is not large enough to elicit a change in the susceptibility to the effects of the drug. Although possible, we believe that smoking a mean of 493 cigarettes per year for almost 4 years should be enough exposure to any drug to induce the development of detectable tolerance or sensitivity changes. However, as we have demonstrated, no difference was found in several typical marijuana effects on the two groups studied.

Therefore, we conclude that marijuana, to the extent used by the young Americans we studied, does not produce tolerance or sensitivity to a challenge infusion of Δ^9-THC.

ACKNOWLEDGMENTS

We thank Drs. Monique Braude and Stephen Szara, National Institute on Drug Abuse, for their support and encouragement of this program. We also thank Donna Wagner and Mary Jane Simmons for their technical assistance.

REFERENCES

1. THOMPSON, G. R., R. W. FLEISCHMAN, H. ROSENKRANTZ & M. C. BRAUDE. 1974. Oral and intravenous toxicity of Δ^9-tetrahydrocannabinol in rhesus monkeys. Toxicol. Appl. Pharmacol. **27:** 648–665.
2. COOK, C. E., M. E. TWINE, C. R. TALLENT, M. E. WALL & R. C. BRESSLER. 1972. Norethynodrel metabolites in human plasma and urine. J. Pharmacol. Exp. Ther. **183:** 197–205.
3. PEREZ-REYES, M., M. C. TIMMONS, M. A. LIPTON, K. H. DAVIS & M. E. WALL. 1972. Intravenous injection in man of Δ^9-tetrahydrocannabinol and 11–OH–Δ^9-tetrahydrocannabinol. Science **177:** 633–635.
4. PEREZ-REYES, M., M. A. LIPTON, M. C. TIMMONS, M. E. WALL, D. R. BRINE & K. H. DAVIS. 1973. Pharmacology of orally administered Δ^9-tetrahydrocannabinol. Clin. Pharmacol. Ther. **14:** 48–55.
5. PEREZ-REYES, M., M. C. TIMMONS & M. E. WALL. 1974. Long-term use of marihuana and the development of tolerance or sensitivity to Δ^9-tetrahydrocannabinol. Arch. Gen. Psychiat. **31:** 89–91.

GENERAL DISCUSSION

J. R. Tinklenberg, *Moderator*

Department of Psychiatry and Behavioral Sciences
Stanford University School of Medicine
Stanford, California 94305
and Veterans Administration Hospital
Palo Alto, California 94304

DR. W. J. COGGINS: Dr. Boulougouris, was there a correlation between the finding of enlarged livers and elevations of serum bilirubin specifically?

DR. J. C. BOULOUGOURIS: We did not do these tests.

DR. COGGINS: Dr. Cruickshank, in analyzing the data on the pulmonary function studies and the evidence for hypoxia, I saw your figures on tobacco smoking but I couldn't quite understand the data as they were presented. I realize that tobacco and ganja are smoked together, but were the levels of tobacco use consistently higher in the ganja users than in the control group?

DR. E. K. CRUICKSHANK: I think the answer would be "yes," but I say I think because without looking at the data from that point of view, I couldn't give you an answer. There were smokers, of course, among the nonusers. But I think the users were heavier tobacco smokers than the nonusers who smoked.

DR. COGGINS: This was the case in our study, too. We would have had difficulty in matching for tobacco use in Costa Rica had we not used a control group that was larger than our marijuana group, because the marijuana group started smoking tobacco earlier and smoked larger amounts. We measured this parameter in three different ways, so we are quite confident that was the case.

DR. BOULOUGOURIS: Yes, we had some difficulty on that point, too.

DR. TINKLENBERG: I think the importance of trying to partition out the use of other drugs, especially tobacco, is important, not only in regard to possible additive or synergistic effects but also in regard to the findings that some components in marijuana, some of the cannabinoids, are in an acidic environment, such as what obtains in smoking tobacco, converted from inactive compounds into active compounds. Thus, the issue of trying to control for use of tobacco is certainly important.

Dr. Coggins, with regard to the finding of unilateral testicular atrophy, were there any other signs that suggested impairment along the gonadal axis? I'm thinking of decreased softening of testicular tissue, changes in hair pattern, or anything else that would suggest that your findings weren't a sampling type of situation.

DR. COGGINS: When the study was designed, we felt no need to look for testicular function or secondary sex characteristics in the males. We did look for evidence of gynecomastia, because that condition had been reported in the literature. I do not believe that we were looking carefully by performing general physical examinations at hairlines or examining for subtle differences in the palpation of the testicular mass. There was unilateral atrophy on one side. I don't think I said that six of the seven users who had unilateral testicular atrophy had a history of either mumps in adolescence or trauma to their testes. The situation was similar for the small number in the control group. We thought that we were seeing what one usually finds on examination of a male with unilateral testicular atrophy. However, we began to hypothesize, then, that we might be seeing a disproportionate representation in the marijuana user group because of two insults to testicular function, mumps or trauma, perhaps super-imposed, but I think that the testosterone studies laid that concern to rest.

DR. TINKLENBERG: When exactly did you measure plasma testosterone levels? Was this parameter measured in terms of time of day or a lapsed period of time after the last possible ingestion?

DR. COGGINS: For all of the studies, the subjects were asked to refrain from their marijuana smoking from bedtime on, and more specifically from midnight of the night before. Living patterns in Costa Rica are such that most people tend to go to bed early because they are very early risers. They are out of bed by 5 AM and are mostly at work by 7 AM. Our subjects were going into the hospital at 5:30 or 6:00 in the morning to begin their testing procedures. The rule, then, was no marijuana after midnight, so this parameter was generally measured 10 hr after their last marijuana use.

DR. G. G. NAHAS (*College of Physicians and Surgeons, Columbia University, New York, N.Y.*): Dr. Coggins, Dr. Kolodny reported that in addition to decreased testosterone levels he had observed oligospermia in six of 18 chronic marijuana users. A similar study at Columbia University on 11 marijuana smokers was just completed, but this study was performed under control conditions. Marijuana smokers smoked between five and 12 marijuana cigarettes per day for one month. Ten of 11 of these smokers showed a decrease in their sperm count that varied from 30 to 70%, with an average of 52%. In addition, there were some morphologic changes in the sperm. However, these changes occurred in the absence of any changes in testosterone, luteinizing hormone, or follicle-stimulating hormone, which were also measured, in as many as 75 samples for each subject. These samples were taken over a one-month period and the two control periods, of course. A possible explanation for this oligospermia stems from the known impairment of cell division that is observed *in vitro* in animals subjected to marijuana smoke. This point also brings me to another observation of Dr. Coggins. He seemed to discount somewhat the decrease in intestinal parasites in the marijuana smokers that he studied. In view of the knowledge that most of the marijuana products are eliminated through the gut and that these products contain a phenol that was used formerly to combat worms, it is quite possible that heavy marijuana smokers might also excrete more intestinal parasites than those who don't smoke.

DR. TINKLENBERG: Dr. Nahas, this is the first time that I heard you say anything positive about cannabis.

DR. NAHAS: I don't think that you have read carefully what I have written, then. Another interesting finding that fits pretty well with our own is the decrease in IgG or other immunoglobulins. I don't know whether you showed that IgG was significantly decreased, though not below normal when compared to controls. A similar observation was performed in our study. This observation brings us finally to the problem of possible impairment of cell division, which I think is central to the whole marijuana question. I would like to ask Dr. Cruickshank if in his chromosomal study he believes that he had enough samples. Indeed, if one looks at the table, it is obvious that the person who did that study examined between 12 and 25 cells and on that basis reported abnormalities in percentage. It's customary to examine at least 100 cells in most of the cytogenetic laboratories with which I am connected. I believe that this whole problem of marijuana and cell division is very central to the possible long-term health effects of this compound, and before this crucial area is clarified, I think that one should not make a statement like that made by Dr. Boulougouris, who seems to give a completely clean bill of health to chronic marijuana users.

Ms. P. J. Lessin (*National Institute on Drug Abuse, Rockville, Md.*): I would like to know what method you used to select the controls. What evidence do you have that those who were controls were not also smokers?

Dr. Cruickshank: This is the sociologic aspect of the investigation. Dr. Rubin is here, but I don't know if she is prepared to answer that question.

Dr. V. Rubin: The controls were selected to match the subjects on all of the significant socioeconomic status variables: age, sex, education, and so forth. The significant difference between them was that they had not smoked for at least 7 years before the study began.

Ms. Lessin: What was the evidence?

Dr. Rubin: The evidence? We had anthropologists working in the communities from which the subjects were selected. It seems to me that one of the significant points coming out of this conference is that you need to know a great deal about the subjects, their life-styles and their life histories, in addition to what they put on a questionnaire.

Dr. R. T. Jones: I want to return to the sampling issue. I still don't think it has been answered fully with respect to how random or how representative were both the controls and the drug users. Obviously, one could demonstrate that alcohol is a very dangerous drug or a very safe drug, depending on what group of alcohol drinkers one sampled, whether it was a city hospital clinic or your friends out in the suburbs. I haven't heard any of the speakers really address this issue of what criteria were used in sampling. On the testosterone issue, does marijuana affect testosterone levels? On the issue raised by Dr. Perez-Reyes, do smokers show tolerance in the laboratory? We've become increasingly surprised and almost astounded at the rapidity with which some of the cannabis effects disappear, even after high chronic dosage. For example, we see statistically significant but modest testosterone decreases while our subjects are on oral doses of THC, but 12 hr after the last oral dose, the effect had disappeared. The levels are back to normal and, in fact, are a bit above normal. If Dr. Perez-Reyes used subjects who smoked a lot of marijuana per year but didn't smoke during the day prior to testing, it would be quite reasonable to find no tolerance. I think one has to keep in mind basic pharmacologic principles before one launches into very complicated studies and interpretations.

Dr. M. Perez-Reyes: Actually, I think the subjects chose me rather than I chose them. They know that I pay good money, and it is well known in my town that you can make quite a bit of money if you participate in my experiments. They come and fill out a confidential questionnaire on which all drug usage is listed, and then on the basis of that questionnaire, I select who I will test next. In relation to the quick disappearance of marijuana effects, when we talk about tolerance, I think we are talking about tolerance to alcohol, to barbiturates, or to morphine. In that sense, marijuana has no tolerance level.

Dr. Coggins: I would like to respond to the sampling question in regard to the Costa Rican cannabis project. Sociocultural studies are not my forte. However, neither is it my forte to spend three years on a project in which we are not studying real phenomena. The technique used in our study was that of anthropologists going into the field in a community and spending 6 months before they announce their purpose of being there, getting to know a network of people. During that time, they had time to observe both the users and nonusers, get a feel for the ways and places in which marijuana was used, and hear the attitudes toward marijuana use. They then began to talk with people about participating in this study. I will say, though, that in our screening procedures during the first 12 months, we did identify some individuals who had misrepresented themselves; the number was small. We at least saw some daily, weekly, and monthly repetitive observational behavior, and we tested this behavior: two people in each group tried to misrepresent themselves and were discontinued from further participation in this study.

DR. TINKLENBERG: Would anyone like to comment on the sampling with regard to the Greek study?

DR. BOULOUGOURIS: The first hashish subjects were reported on by Professor Miras, who previously studied them. Then, we asked the hashish users to bring their friends. The first controls were through friends of the hashish users, and the rest came through the social service department. The criteria for matching users and nonusers were age, education, social culture, and area of residence.

DR. W. E. CARTER: I would like to add something about the Costa Rican sampling techniques, because I was directing the anthropologic studies. Dr. Coggins is quite right in stating that we had anthropologists in the field. We had three in the field who engaged in observation for months before any of the subjects were identified. Once we penetrated the neighborhoods in which we worked, we followed relational networks, which were networks of kinship, friendship, work, and recreation. We found eight major relational networks, each of which supplied us with both users and nonusers. These subjects were all members of the same social network. We also ended up with a sample from 45 differently designated neighborhoods in San José, and the sample represented all except the lowest and the highest income deciles of San José residents. I therefore think that we did have a very representative sample. When we determined our final control group, we discovered that we had problems, in that many of the users also drank alcohol and smoked tobacco in large quantities. We were matching for levels of tobacco and alcohol use and for education, marital status, occupation, and so forth. In particular, the levels of alcohol and tobacco use forced us to really search in the end to obtain the same levels in the control as in the user group.

DR. TINKLENBERG: I think that Dr. Jones' point is a good one. Dr. Carter, do you think you would have picked up the cannabis equivalent, if there is any, of the down and out skid-row alcoholic, the person for whom most social relationships have been entirely fragmented, perhaps for a period of years?

DR. JONES: Who has no kinship and no friends.

DR. CARTER: My answer is absolutely yes. We started our search in the worst bar in the lowest area of San José, an absolutely infamous place, and that, in fact, was one of our first networks. It was a key network that led into even middle-class networks in the city, because it was a distributional network for the drug.

DR. COGGINS: We deliberately excluded people who indicated difficulty in making and keeping appointments, for example, so the answer depends on how you characterize "down and out."

DR. CARTER: I think that we had to eliminate three users, because they were irresponsible in terms of making appointments. However, there were also two nonusers in the same category.

DR. JONES: I still keep using alcohol as a model for comparison, although it may turn out to be completely inappropriate. Alcoholics tend to break appointments, to be irresponsible, and to show the greatest evidence of brain damage, liver disease, and other problems. It is the exclusions that aren't always clearly stated that worry me. And it's hard to be sure that you're excluding on the same basis in your control group. Having a control group doesn't excuse all sins.

DR. CARTER: We had only these three people and the three people who were not responsible; that is, the users not responsible for making appointments were also very heavy alcohol users. I would have to go back and look into the life histories of the two nonusers who also failed to make appointments. I can certainly say that in the extensive life history materials that we obtained from all of these people, where they talked about all of their groups of friends who were users, we ended up with about 14,000 typed single-spaced pages. We did not find a single reference to an individual, either the person who was responding or friends of that person, who had been incapacitated in a social way through the use of marijuana. It simply wasn't there.

DR. CHRISTIAN: Can I bring the discussion back in the direction of hormones and testosterone for a minute? I would like to throw out some ideas about plasma testosterone. Most of you know that testosterone undergoes a small but significant diurnal variation in the normal male. It is also secreted in bursts rather than continuously. It's hard, then, to interpret a single value of it as being a reflection of the person's androgenicity. I think we should look at 24-hr urine values, or perhaps look at more points under the 24-hr curve, to get some estimation of total 24 hr testosterone levels. There are several papers in the literature, including one of ours, that seem to show essentially normal testosterone levels. There are some that are not yet published. Dr. Nahas referred to some at Presbyterian. Dr. Jones has information that suggests that marijuana use can lower testosterone levels, at least acutely. But the data indicate that the levels don't fall very much; indeed, they don't drop out of the normal range, which is quite broad. So what, then, might the significance be of a somewhat lower, but still normal, testosterone level? Are we correct in looking for such gross measurements of androgen function as recession of hairline, hair distribution, and libido? There are some other measurements of androgen-related functions, such as levels of thyroid hormone and cortisol in the blood. These hormones are transported by a binding protein. The binding protein is sensitive to androgen and to estrogen. Binding increases in estrogen-influenced states, such as pregnancy or the presence of birth control pills, and decreases when androgens are administered. It is therefore refreshing to hear that thyroid hormone levels were normal in Jamaica and that cortisol levels were normal in your study. These findings suggest that the baseline studies would reflect a significant change in cortisol-binding globulin or thyroxin-binding globulin and would push the cortisol levels up if there were a relative preponderance of estrogen effects and relatively less androgen effects. We therefore may not actually see a major swing, then, in androgen-related functions in marijuana smokers, if this information is fully corroborated.

DR. COGGINS: I wondered about the possible effect of binding globulins on testosterone levels in relation to our findings. We did not do immunoelectrophoresis in our study, because we didn't intend to examine immune mechanisms. However, we did perform a routine serum protein electrophoresis, and there were trends that suggested differences in globulins; in the matched pair study,

β globulin tended to be low. Testosterone-binding globulin is said to be in the β group. I simply selected individuals who had a high daily usage of marijuana, 10 or more cigarettes per day, and compared their β globulin with their plasma testosterone levels to see if there were correlations among marijuana dosage, β globulin, and plasma testosterone; I found no relationship. These comparisons were crude, but we did look at binding globulins.

DR. TINKLENBERG: Some groups have also found small but reproducible decreases in the levels of FSH, LH, and other hormones.

DR. E. B. TRUITT, JR. (*George Washington University Medical Center, Washington, D.C.*): The question of tolerance is still important in the triad of addiction, so we should clarify this point. Alcoholic tolerance, especially the tolerance accelerated in the metabolism of alcoholics, lasts about one month after heavy alcohol consumption. We have seen some evidence this morning about the acute tolerance of these chronic users to higher doses. Maybe these tolerance effects would disappear in the short time that Dr. Jones has mentioned or maybe they will last longer. I am referring particularly to Dr. Perez-Reyes' data. Unless there is a microsomal induction produced by heavy chronic use, I wouldn't expect to see any changes in metabolism. Were these subjects really heavy chronic users who were truly tolerant?

DR. PEREZ-REYES: Tolerance, for instance, to barbiturates, can be detected, and it lasts at least 60 days after the patient has stopped taking the drug. Dr. Truitt, you said that for alcohol, it would take about one month of abstinence for the tolerance to alcohol to begin to decrease. Then, in that case, marijuana doesn't appear to fall into that category.

DR. N. BENOWITZ: I have been involved with Dr. Reese Jones in studies of prolonged oral THC and crude marijuana extract administration in hospitalized volunteers. Very strikingly, we saw decreasing blood pressure, decreasing heart rate, and evidence of sympathetic insufficiency during administration of the drug, which did not produce tolerance after 2½ weeks; these phenomena returned to normal within 1 or 2 days. We also saw cardiographic changes in several subjects, but, again, these findings disappeared within 1 or 2 days after cessation of drug treatment. It is thus quite possible that just looking at subjects after 5 or 6 days would miss physiologic effects that persist throughout administration of cannabis. Concerning hormonal changes, we've looked at several hormonal functions, in particular, growth hormone and the cortisol response to insulin-induced hypoglycemia, and find that after 4 or 5 days in marijuana users, their response is normal or higher than normal; after 2 weeks of cannabis administration, however, there is marked suppression of both growth hormone and cortisol response to insulin-induced hypoglycemia. We haven't looked to see how long it takes to recover. It is clear, however, that these parameters are normal when the subjects come to the hospital and suppressed while taking cannabis. We have also seen a significant depression of thyroxin in these subjects, which, again, returns to normal within a few days after cessation of drug treatment.

BEHAVIORAL AND BIOLOGIC ASPECTS OF MARIJUANA USE *

Jack H. Mendelson, Thomas F. Babor, John C. Kuehnle, A. Michael Rossi, Jerrold G. Bernstein, Nancy K. Mello, and Issac Greenberg

Alcohol and Drug Abuse Research Center
Harvard Medical School-McLean Hospital
Belmont, Massachusetts 02178

INTRODUCTION

Before the current decade, only three comprehensive studies of the effects of repeat-dose marijuana administration had been conducted.[28, 45, 52] Our current data base has been expanded considerably and has been reviewed in part in several comprehensive publications.[25, 30, 35, 37, 47] Yet, despite an exponential increment in our fund of information about the effects of marijuana on human biologic function and behavior, we are still far from certain about the type and nature of any subtle, and perhaps disastrous, consequences that may be associated with long-term marijuana use.

Data presented in this paper reprint an overview of a series of multidisciplinary studies conducted in our laboratory. The major questions that we addressed in this research were similar to those we have posed in previous studies.[35] These questions were: "Does chronic use of marijuana systematically affect motivation to engage in a variety of social and goal-directed activities? Are there constant relationships between free-choice marijuana intake and antecedent and consequent mood states? What are the relationships between free-choice marijuana intake and patterns of verbal interaction? What are the relationships between free-choice marijuana intake and performance on psychologic tasks that assess such functions as problem solving and risk taking, memory, time estimation, and cognitive function? And, finally, are physiologic and biochemical changes associated with repeated doses of marijuana?" Some answers for these questions are provided in each of the topical sections of this manuscript.

This report is a summary of the current "state of science" for ongoing research in our laboratory and clinical research facility. More detailed presentations of data obtained in studies of behavorial and social reactions, group interaction, and tolerance will be published by Dr. Babor and his associates. Dr. A. Michael Rossi and his colleagues will report in subsequent publications on studies of mood, short-term memory, vigilance, and reaction time. Drs. Kuehnle and Bernstein have submitted data for publication on psychiatric aspects and cardiac and pulmonary function. Drs. Greenberg and Mello and their associates have presented a detailed description of studies of operant behavior elsewhere in this monograph.

One of the most important points we would like to emphasize is the

* Supported in part by Grant DA 4RG010 from the National Institute on Drug Abuse.

importance of the multidisciplinary nature of our study. An adequate understanding of the processes and potential hazards of any substance use or abuse
will likely require the contribution of many disciplines. At the present time,
it is not possible to specify a priority hierarchy for the contributions that can
be made by such disciplines as psychiatry, psychology, sociology, biochemistry,
and physiology. Rather, an integrated approach for hypothesis testing and
development should be carried out by a range of disciplines that utilize the
best techniques and methodologies that are currently available.

SUBJECTS

Subjects were recruited through advertisements placed in local newspapers.
More than 300 applicants responded to the advertisement and subsequently
visited the research facility to complete drug use questionnaires. Applicants
who most closely met the criteria of "heavy" or "casual" users of marijuana
were invited back to be interviewed by a psychiatrist; 28 men between the ages
of 21 and 26 years were selected from this group. One subject withdrew
from the experiment after 6 days, and his data were excluded from the analyses.
Twelve subjects with a mean age of 23.6 years (range 21–26) reported a mean
duration of marijuana use of 5.3 years (range 3–8 years) and a frequency of
use during the past year of 11.5 (± 6.5) times per month. These subjects were
designated as casual users. Fifteen subjects with a mean age of 23.2 years
(range 21–25) reported a mean duration of marijuana use of 5.6 years (range
3–9) and smoked 42 (± 24.5) marijuana cigarettes per month during the
previous year. These subjects were designated as heavy users.

All subjects selected for the study were in good health and showed no
evidence of physical or mental abnormalities, as determined by clinical and
laboratory examinations. Participation at all times was voluntary, and subjects
were free to leave at any time.

TABLE 1 describes the background data of the casual and heavy user groups.
With the exception of intelligence and military experience, the two groups
are comparable. Subjects tended to be middle and upper class, unmarried,
and with several years of college experience. Reasons most often cited for
participation were curiosity about marijuana and medical research and the
opportunity their participation afforded to earn money. TABLE 2 summarizes
information concerning the drug history of casual and heavy users.

RESEARCH DESIGN

The studies were conducted on a four-bed research ward of the Alcohol
and Drug Abuse Research Center at McLean Hospital. The ward consisted of
individual patient bedrooms, examining rooms, testing rooms, nursing station,
kitchen, and lavatories. The ward also contained a comfortably furnished
dayroom area with television, high-fidelity equipment, and a variety of other
recreational materials. The ward was staffed by physicians, nursing personnel,
and ward assistants on a 24-hr per day basis.

The study consisted of three phases: a baseline period of 5 days, a 21-day
period during which subjects could acquire and smoke marijuana cigarettes,
and a postmarijuana smoking period of 5 days' duration. During the entire 31-

TABLE 1

BACKGROUND AND PERSONAL DATA: CASUAL AND HEAVY USERS

	Casual Users (n=12)		Heavy Users (n=15)		Significance
Age					
$\overline{X}$	23.6		23.2		
SD	1.56		1.42		$t=0.43$, ns
Years of formal education					
$\overline{X}$	14.5		13.6		
SD	1.88		1.84		$t=1.25$, ns
Intelligence test score *					
$\overline{X}$	121.4		116.0		
SD	3.58		4.66		$t=2.81$, p <0.01
Marital status					
Single, % (n)	91.5%	(11)	100.0%	(15)	
Married, % (n)	8.3%	(1)	0.0%	(0)	
Father's socioeconomic level †					
Lower, % (n)	0.0%	(0)	6.7%	(1)	
Middle, % (n)	58.3%	(7)	20.0%	(3)	
Upper, % (n)	33.3%	(4)	33.3%	(5)	
Undetermined, % (n) ‡	8.3%	(1)	40.0%	(6)	
Military experience					
Yes, % (n)	0.0%	(0)	40.0%	(6)	
No, % (n)	100.0%	(12)	60.0%	(9)	
Reasons for participation					
Financial, % (n)	75.0%	(9)	60.0%	(9)	
Curiosity, % (n)	66.7%	(8)	73.3%	(11)	
Change of venue, % (n)	15.0%	(2)	33.3%	(5)	
Marijuana, % (n)	33.3%	(4)	13.3%	(2)	
No reason(s) given, % (n)	8.3%	(1)	6.7%	(1)	

* Intelligence level was assessed by means of the Shipley-Hartford IQ Scale, except for the first casual user study, where the Wechsler Adult Intelligence Scale was used. Unfortunately, intelligence tests were not given during the second casual user study. Therefore, the casual user mean is based on a sample of eight subjects.

† Father's socioeconomic status was estimated from information on father's occupation, which was coded according to Hollingshead's Occupational-Status Scale.[17a] The categories employed represent the following combinations of Hollingshead's seven categories: lower=categories 7 (unskilled), 6 (machine operators and semiskilled), and 5 (skilled manual); middle=categories 4 (clerical and sales, technicians, owners of little businesses) and 3 (administrative personnel, owners of small businesses, minor professionals); upper=categories 2 (business managers, proprietors, lesser professionals) and 1 (higher executives, proprietors, major professionals).

‡ Father's socioeconomic level could not be estimated for some subjects, because the father was deceased or data were not volunteered.

day study, subjects had an opportunity to work at a simple operant task to earn points that were exchangeable for either money or marijuana cigarettes (during the 21-day marijuana smoking period). Subjects were told that they could work at the task any time they wished and could purchase marijuana cigarettes and smoke any time they wished. However, all smoking of marijuana had to be performed under observation of a member of the staff to ascertain if the

TABLE 2

DRUG HISTORY INFORMATION: CASUAL AND HEAVY USERS

	Casual Users (n=12)		Heavy Users (n=15)		Significance of Difference
	$\overline{X}$	SD	$\overline{X}$	SD	
Marijuana: times per month	11.5	6.5	42.0	24.5	$U=0$, $p<0.002$
Age at first use	18.1	1.1	17.6	2.0	$t=0.74$, ns
Years using marijuana	5.3	1.7	5.6	1.7	$t=0.40$, ns
Alcohol: times per month	9.3	8.2	21.4	24.7	$U=52$, $p<0.10$
Age at first use	14.4	3.5	14.5	2.1	$t=0.14$, ns
Hallucinogens: lifetime use	45.4	53.6	33.8	36.3	$U=73$, ns
Amphetamines	28.1	40.4	30.9	35.8	$U=72.5$, ns
Barbiturates	*		21.3	37.3	—
Heroin	*		6.6	8.5	—

* Data unavailable.

material was smoked, when it was smoked, and the amount smoked. Subjects were also instructed that the unused portions of all smoked marijuana cigarettes were to be returned to the staff to ascertain that the remaining portions were not accumulated and smoked without staff knowledge.

Marijuana cigarettes were obtained from the National Institute of Mental Health in a lot-standard dosage form. The cigarettes were machine rolled to ensure maximal standardization and equivalent dosage and "draw" characteristics. Each cigarette contained approximately 1 g of marijuana with a tetrahydrocannabinol (THC) content of 1.8–2.3%, as assayed by the National Institute of Mental Health.

SMOKING PATTERNS

On a typical smoking occasion, one or more subjects would request marijuana by pressing the "purchase request" button on an individual console. The procedure required that the smoker punch in a mood report while a signal in the nursing station alerted the staff. All smoking occurred on the ward in the presence of a registered nurse. Subjects were free to smoke whenever they wished. No attempt was made to standardize the smoking procedure because this might have interfered with free-choice smoking behavior. Although the exact amount of THC consumed per cigarette varied within and between subjects, unsmoked portions of the cigarettes were weighed, and this weighing provided a basis for estimating the amount consumed.

Overall, casual users smoked about half as many marijuana cigarettes as did heavy users. On the average, casuals smoked 2.6 "joints" per day, while heavy users consumed 5.7. However, smoking patterns within days tended to be similar for both heavy and casual subjects. Both groups smoked most of their marijuana in the evening between 8 PM and midnight.

Smoking patterns across days were also similar. Casual users started at about two marijuana cigarettes per day and increased gradually to three per day over 20 days. On the last day of marijuana availability (Day 26), casual users averaged close to six cigarettes each.

The same pattern held true for the heavy users, who started at about 3.5 cigarettes per day and increased progressively to six per day over 20 days. Again, the last day of availability was atypical, with heavy users smoking an average of 14 marijuana cigarettes.

The smoking procedure itself occurred within a social context for all subjects. More than 90% of all marijuana was consumed in the public dayroom rather than in the subjects' private bedrooms. More than 80% of each subject's marijuana was consumed in the presence of at least one other subject. Furthermore, subjects were observed interacting with each other during more than 50% of their smoking occasions.

BEHAVIORAL AND SOCIAL REACTIONS

The studies provided an opportunity to answer questions about behavioral and social reactions to marijuana as it is smoked under conditions that approach typical social usage. What is the relationship between marijuana intoxication and physical activity? Does it affect ability and/or motivation to engage in work and recreation? How is social functioning affected during and after marijuana smoking? Are there characteristic changes in patterns of interaction and interpersonal behavior?

Data relevant to these questions were collected by means of the behavior inventory (BI) checklist, an observational system employed to obtain a representative sample of each subject's daily activity. Trained research aides observed each subject once every hour during 15-sec time intervals. The time at which hourly observations were initiated varied randomly from day to day. Immediately after observation, the subject's primary (predominant) and secondary (nonpredominant) activities were coded according to a list of 20 possible behaviors. The list included sleep, watching television, listening to music, watching others, reading, testing, vital signs, talking, stationary play (games), active play (sports), operant work, "no apparent activity," and several miscellaneous categories. In addition, social affiliation patterns were coded on a grid that represented subjects and staff in the immediate proximity of the smoker.

To evaluate changes in physical activity after marijuana smoking, each of the 20 BI activities was weighted according to the average energy expenditure (in kcal/m²/hr) estimated for that activity.[6] These weights were assigned to the primary activity observed before and after each smoking episode. Average before/after activity scores were then computed for each subject, based on the total number of marijuana smoking episodes sampled.

After the smoking episode, each group indicated a significant decrement in activity. By use of the "before" activity level as a baseline, it was estimated that energy expenditure after marijuana smoking was 17% lower for casual users and 15.5% lower for heavy users.

Changes in interpersonal behavior were analyzed by combining selected BI categories that reflected three levels of social interaction. Social isolation refers to situations where the subject was alone or in the presence of others but neither interacting nor coacting. Social interaction refers to situations where the subject's primary or secondary activity was a stimulus or response to the behavior of another, for example, conversation or ping pong. Social coaction applies to situations where the subject engages with others in some mutual task or activity (e.g., watching television, listening to music) but without direct communication or interaction.

After smoking, casual users were observed interacting significantly † less (32.2% before, 18.5% after) and coacting significantly more (44.5% before, 54.8% after). There was no significant change in amount of isolation. The heavy user data showed a slightly different pattern. No pronounced changes were observed in social coaction or interaction, but isolation decreased significantly after smoking (26.6% before, 22.3% after).

The systematic variations in physical activity and social interaction for both casual and heavy smokers suggested additional analyses to determine the specific types of activity and social behavior that could account for these changes. Casual users showed decrements in the primary activities of talking (8.9% before, 4.65% after) and active play (5.2% before, 1.1% after) and a significant increase in listening to the stereo (9.7% before, 15.6% after). No significant differences were noted in the remaining activities.

Heavy users showed significant decrements in active play (6.7% before, 2.9% after) and transit (1.9% before, 0.7% after) and a highly significant increase in watching television (27.3% before, 38.4% after).

The results show that marijuana smoking is definitely a group activity frequently engaged in to enhance recreational function. The most popular activity during smoking was watching television, followed by listening to music and talking. Marijuana was often the main organizing factor for the group. During the smoking session, social behavior was characterized by verbal interaction in response to a common purpose ("turning on") and as a result of the presence of other participants. These groups might be termed *interacting* groups. As the marijuana began to take effect, however, the character of the group changed from interaction to coaction. In these coacting groups, participants experienced common subjective effects and common external stimuli, but they were not interacting with one another in response to these stimuli.

The comparison of interaction patterns before and after smoking showed that both talking and the broader category of social interaction decrease significantly for casual users but not for heavy users. Thus, while the sociologic effect of marijuana seems to bring people together and "generate" interaction, the pharmacologic effect, at least for casual smokers, is to suppress social interaction. These findings suggest that although marijuana may be a "sociogenic" drug in the sociologic sense proposed by Goode,[14] the pharmacologic effect is quite different. These findings are consistent with the results of previous research [4, 5] in which social interaction was found to increase before marijuana smoking and decrease after intoxication.

The lack of a significant social effect in the heavy users is consistent with the concept of behavioral tolerance. As other researchers have reported in studies of psychomotor and cognitive performance,[18, 50] heavy users are more capable of accommodating themselves to the acute effects of marijuana.

One aspect of behavior that changed markedly for both types of user after marijuana smoking is physical activity. Activity level declined significantly, and this decline is reflected in the subjects' tendency to prefer more "passive" activities. Further analysis of the data, however, suggests that the relationship between marijuana and physical activity may be associational

---

† Differences between group means were determined by student's *t* test by use of the 0.05 level as the criterion of statistical significance.

rather than causative. Although marijuana intoxication may have contributed to a reduction in activity, there was also a tendency for subjects to smoke at those times when they would ordinarily be inactive. Subjects smoked the majority of their marijuana during the evening hours, when few research activities were scheduled. While it was not uncommon for a subject to smoke before or during various scheduled activities (e.g., group discussion, vital signs), there was a marked preference for smoking when research tasks would not interrupt recreational activities. Furthermore, subjects preferred to smoke after returning from off-ward recreation (most often scored as active play) rather than before.

These findings are in agreement with recent theoretical propositions developed by Orcutt and Biggs,[39] who propose that relaxation and internally oriented (intrapersonal) effects are major dimensions of the recreational effects of marijuana. An important question that demands further research attention is whether these reactions are primarily determined by social factors, as Orcutt and Biggs propose, or to pharmacologic factors. The present findings on behavioral tolerance in the heavy users suggest that at least some of the effects are pharmacologic. Further, the tendency to withdraw from social interaction has been noted in both recreational[4] and task-oriented situations.[5] This finding may indicate that contextual factors and socially learned expectations are less important than pharmacologic factors, which depend on dosage and prior tolerance.

GROUP INTERACTIONS

Each afternoon during the three phases of the study, subjects were convened for task-oriented discussions. The groups met in a small lounge located adjacent to the research ward. The lounge was equipped with a one-way mirror that permitted excellent visibility from an adjoining observation room. In addition to visual observation, sound monitoring and recording were also conducted. One-third of the discussions were based on a series of moral conflict problems, each of which involved a conflict between obligations to a friend and obligations to the larger society. In the remaining meetings, Charles Morris' "Ways to Live" was discussed. Each of the 13 ways to live contains a capsule summary of a different life-style common to the major religious or philosophical systems. After an initial reading of the topic, subjects were asked to express their opinions and then arrive at a group consensus regarding either the degree to which they liked or disliked the way to live or the manner in which they would resolve the conflict.

The discussion task was chosen because of its simplicity and comparability from one topic to another. No verbal or intellectual skills are required, and performance is affected minimally by repetition. Further, the discussion task resembles many employment situations where individuals meet to discuss practical, theoretical, or "human relations" problems.

Ongoing interaction ("who" speaks to "whom") and role behavior were observed according to procedures developed by Robert Bales. Following each group, an interpersonal rating form was employed to define the social role of each participant in terms of a three-dimensional model of group behavior. The rating scale yields scores on the following role dimensions: dominant-submissive, friendly-unfriendly, task oriented-nontask oriented.

The results indicated that during intoxication, moderate users were less task oriented and participated less in group discussion. No significant changes on any of the dependent measures were noted for the heavy users, although there was a trend (p < 0.10) toward less task orientation during intoxication. These findings are consistent with the results of previous research,[5, 50] in which decrements in the amount and quality of interaction were related to marijuana intoxication.

The results point to two conclusions concerning the influence of marijuana on social behavior. First, marijuana intoxication precipitates social withdrawal in casual users. In formal discussion groups, the intoxicated individual also changes his social role, in that he gives less attention to a specific task. Second, the effects of marijuana on verbal interaction may be mitigated by behavioral tolerance, because the tendency to withdraw was found to be nonexistent in heavy users.

TOLERANCE

Tolerance is said to develop when increasing doses of a drug are required to produce the same effect. There are numerous biologic, behavioral, and psychologic responses that a drug may influence, and tolerance to these different responses may have different implications for the chronic marijuana smoker.

Tolerance to the disruptive behavioral and physiologic effects would make it possible for experienced users to function at their "normal" level of efficiency, even after heavy consumption. On the other hand, the development of tolerance to the subjective effect, the psychologic "high," would increase the necessity of additional consumption to achieve previous levels of intoxication.

In the present research, pulse rate and subjective intoxication were consistently monitored before and after marijuana consumption over a 21-day smoking period. It was expected that these data would provide a basis for evaluating the relationship between marijuana consumption and the development of tolerance to both psychologic and physiologic effects.

Standing pulse rate was determined immediately before, immediately after, and 25 min after each marijuana cigarette was consumed. Ratings of subjective level of intoxication were obtained during written mood reports completed immediately before and 25 min after smoking. Subjects rated their level of intoxication on a seven-point bipolar adjective scale labeled "stoned vs. straight." To evaluate the development of tolerance, pulse rate changes were examined over the course of the 21-day smoking period. If tolerance was developing, one would expect to see a progressive decline over 21 smoking days in the pulse rate readings after smoking. Although the immediate effect of marijuana in pulse rate did not diminish over time for either group, the data indicated a tendency for heavy users' pulse rates to return to baseline levels after 25 min. This finding suggests that heavy users develop tolerance to the duration but not to the intensity of the physiologic effect.

Tolerance to the subjective effect was analyzed by plotting the high rating after the first cigarette of each day with the consecutive day of the study. The casual users' results indicate no significant degree of tolerance. However, heavy users demonstrated a strong tendency to rate themselves less high as they continued to smoke.

The results are consistent with those obtained in two recent studies of tolerance to marijuana in man [40, 42] and indicate very strongly that tolerance does not develop to the two most reliable indices of marijuana intoxication, the heart rate increase and subjective feelings of "highness," unless rather heavy doses of Δ^9-THC are self-administered repeatedly. Furthermore, the data indicate that the tendency to increase consumption over time, frequently cited as indirect evidence for pharmacologic tolerance,[29] is not necessarily associated with the development of tolerance. Both casual and heavy users indicated a progressive increase in consumption, but only heavy users developed tolerance to the physiologic and subjective effects. Thus, tolerance does not account for the consumption patterns of the casual users, and it is unlikely that it was related to the enormous amount of smoking by both groups on the final day of availability (Day 26).

In a poststudy follow-up questionnaire, subjects were asked why they smoked more than they initially expected. The reasons most frequently cited were boredom, availability, and the belief that "being stoned helped me better tolerate the ward routine." In addition, in a previous study [4] where small group smoking patterns were systematically observed, it was suggested that social influence and social reinforcement are important determinants of increased marijuana consumption. It is therefore likely that psychosocial factors were more important determinants of the casual user consumption patterns than was tolerance development.

These findings are also interesting in light of other aspects of the subjects' behavior and performance. Even though the casual users were consuming significantly less marijuana than were heavy users, only the former group indicated acute reactions on measures of informal social interaction and task-oriented interaction. Thus, tolerance may develop for many of the acute social-behavioral effects of marijuana, but only after a relatively heavy level of consumption is attained and maintained.

OPERANT BEHAVIOR

There has been considerable speculation about the behavioral effects of marijuana in man. Among the effects ascribed to marijuana are apathy, lethargy, diminished "drive" and ambition, decreased productivity and goal directedness, and indolence. These behavioral effects allegedly associated with chronic marijuana use are often referred to as an "amotivational syndrome." Data often interpreted to support a marijuana-induced "amotivational syndrome" hypothesis are not compelling,[33] and systematic criteria for establishing the presence or absence of such a syndrome have not been developed.[16] Clinical studies of marijuana effects have often used subjects with psychiatric problems who are not representative of average marijuana users and whose apparent motivational impairments may reflect problems unrelated to marijuana use.[21] For example, clinical depression may be synonymous with an "amotivational syndrome" in a college age population.[16, 23]

The notion that marijuana may produce an "amotivational syndrome" was not supported in one study of the effects of chronic use, in the absence of other drug use, on "motivation" as assessed by operant work.[35] Subjects worked on a fixed-ratio operant schedule where every 6000 points earned could be exchanged for one marijuana cigarette or 50¢. Subjects were limited to earning 60,000 points per day, which required about 5 hr of work. All subjects consistently earned the maximum number of points available and showed no evidence of a marijuana-induced impairment in work and/or in motivation.[35] However, it is possible that the 60,000-point limit on daily earnings may have been too low to be sensitive to any marijuana dose-related effects. The present study was designed to reexamine marijuana's purported amotivational properties on unrestricted operant work for money or marijuana reinforcement. "Motivation" could then be operationally defined by the number of points earned and the total time spent in operant work. Clearly, motivation cannot be directly observed and can only be inferred from some behavior.

Subjects were studied in groups of three or four, which consisted of all heavy *or* casual users. Subjects lived on a clinical research ward for 31 days, and each subject served as his own control. A 5-day baseline period was followed by a 21-day marijuana available period and a 5-day postmarijuana control period. Subjects could earn a 1-g marijuana cigarette (which contained 1.8–2.3% of Δ^9-THC) or 50¢ by 30 min of sustained performance on a simple operant task. To earn points exchangeable for money or marijuana, subjects had to press a button on a small portable operant manipulandum at a rate of at least one response per second. Only the first response after 1 sec had elapsed was recorded by the programming circuitry. Subjects could work whenever they wished and could purchase a marijuana cigarette at any time during the 21-day smoking period. Subjects smoked at the time of purchase and returned "roaches" to the staff supervisor. Points spent for marijuana were immediately deducted from the reinforcement point accumulations, and a record of accumulated points was continuously available to the subject.

The heavy users smoked more (4.3–6 cigarettes per day) than did the casual users (2–3 per day). On the final day of marijuana availability, the heavy users smoked an average of 14.3 cigarettes, and the casual users smoked 5.8 cigarettes. All of the casual and most of the heavy users gradually increased marijuana smoking through the 21-day period of drug availability.

Both groups worked between two and five times as many hours per day as was necessary to earn the number of cigarettes smoked and consequently earned and saved far more money than was spent on marijuana. The heavy users worked between 6.7 and 14.4 hr each day, even though only 2.2–3 hr of work were required to purchase the amount of marijuana smoked. Throughout the 21-day smoking period, the heavy users maintained an average work output of 36,000 points, which is equivalent to 10 hr of sustained work per day. The casual users worked between 5 and 11 hr per day, even though the number of cigarettes smoked required only 1–1.5 hr of steady work. These data indicate that motivation to work for both marijuana and money was maintained by both groups of subjects throughout the period of marijuana availability and heavy marijuana use.

Periods of maximum operant work coincided with periods of maximum marijuana smoking in both groups, that is, between 4 PM and 12 midnight each day. The temporal distribution of work periods within each day was comparable during the baseline, smoking, and postmarijuana periods for both groups. The temporal coincidence of peak operant responding and smoking shows that marijuana smoking did not interfere with operant work. This temporal pattern of drug acquisition and use is in marked contrast to that previously observed in alcohol addicts working for alcohol on a comparable operant task.[31]

The only data at all indicative of a dose-related marijuana effect on work output resulted from an analysis of the delayed effects of smoking. Because the half-life of Δ^9-THC has been estimated to be about 28 hr, and because most smoking occurred in the evening between 8 PM and midnight, effects on operant work could occur during the 24 hr after smoking. Delayed effects of marijuana on points earned the following day showed a dose-related decrement in operant work. Heavy users' earnings decreased sharply 24 hr after three cigarettes per day were smoked, then remained relatively stable after three to eight cigarettes on the preceding day. The largest 24-hr delayed changes in points earned by the casual users occurred after between one and two and between three and four marijuana cigarettes. The negative correlation between number of cigarettes smoked and points earned on the following day was significant only for the heavy user group (-0.25, $p < 0.05$). However, even after smoking eight marijuana cigarettes, these subjects still earned 36,000 points and worked 10 hr on the following day. Consequently, these data are not compelling evidence in support of an "amotivational syndrome" hypothesis.

Throughout the period of marijuana availability, heavy and casual users maintained operant work and earned points far in excess of the number required to purchase the marijuana actually smoked. The maximum work output for both casual and heavy users coincided with the period of maximum marijuana smoking each day. Although there were some dose-related delayed effects of marijuana on points earned, operant work was sustained at a high level and was never completely eliminated. These data are concordant with previous observations of sustained operant work during marijuana smoking.[35] These data are also consistent with findings that chronic marijuana use may not significantly affect work output in natural uncontrolled settings.[43, 46]

MOOD STUDIES

According to the results of numerous surveys, marijuana is used primarily to achieve a desired subjective mood state. This state is frequently described by the adjectives "stoned" or "high." Despite the almost universal agreement that it is a subjective effect that is sought by users, there has been very little laboratory research directly focused on the relationships between marijuana and mood. In previous work in our laboratory, we searched for evidence of consistent and characteristic patterns of mood states both before and after free-choice marijuana intake. Partial results of that research demonstrated that, contrary to anecdotal accounts, mood states after marijuana use were not consistently more euphoric than those that existed prior to the use of the drug. Indeed, in analyzing the results, there appeared to be little relationship of any kind between marijuana and either pre- or postmood states. In an attempt to understand the results, reference was made to the work of Schacter and Singer,[44] which demonstrated that the effect of a drug on mood is often determined by an interaction between the drug's pharmacologic effect and situationally determined cognitions. The present study was focused on the interaction among marijuana, individual mood states, and group mood states.

Four separate but identical studies were conducted with four male subjects in each study. One subject terminated his participation before the completion of a study, so the results reported here are based on 15 subjects. All subjects were defined as heavy users with a minimum of a 2-year history of marijuana use and a current average use pattern of 33 smoking sessions per month. Subjects lived on a hospital closed research ward for 31 days. During the first 5 days and the last 5 days, they did not have access to marijuana. During the intervening 21 days, they were permitted to purchase and smoke marijuana on a free-choice basis.

Subjects were required to report their moods three times per day at 10 AM, 2 PM, and 9 PM. In addition, they were required to report their moods just prior to and 30 min after smoking marijuana. These reports were in the form of self-ratings on eight seven-point scales that had paired adjectives as end-reference points. The paired adjectives were sad-happy, tense-relaxed, depressed-elated, confused-clear, worried-carefree, hostile-friendly, afraid-calm, and straight-stoned. Subjects indicated moods on an electronic apparatus, and results were automatically recorded.

The results were first analyzed for trends or changes in mood ratings made before and after smoking marijuana. These ratings were averaged for all subjects for each successive 5-day segment of the drug period, and the differences between the before and after ratings were also computed for each 5-day segment. Differences between the before and after ratings were negligible during all phases of the drug period for the adjective pairs worried-carefree, hostile-friendly, sad-happy, afraid-calm, confused-clear. During the early phases of the drug period, subjects tended to rate themselves as slightly more relaxed and elated after marijuana smoking, but these differences disappeared as the drug periods progressed. Differences between the before and after smoking marijuana ratings on the straight-stoned scale lessened as the study progressed, but this change apparently was due to subjects rating themselves as being more stoned before they smoked marijuana (as a consequence of a previous smoking session) rather than a consequence of subjects rating themselves as less stoned after smoking.

Thus, no consistent changes in mood occurred after marijuana smoking. This finding is a confirmation of the results obtained in earlier studies in our laboratory. However, although there apparently were no significant changes in the *differences* between before and after mood ratings, obvious variations in mood ratings occurred during the progress of each study.

The ratings obtained from each individual subject before and after smoking marijuana were averaged for each successive 5-day period. These averages were obtained separately for each adjective pair. Variations in these average ratings from one 5-day period to the next produced a mood pattern for each subject. In comparing these mood patterns, there apparently was far more similarity in the patterns obtained from subjects employed in the same study than in the patterns obtained from subjects employed in separate studies. It is possible that the prevailing mood of the group of subjects in a study may be such an important determinant that it may overshadow the pharmacologic effect of marijuana on mood of an individual subject.

Despite the fact that it is almost universally believed that people use marijuana to get "stoned" or "high" (i.e., to feel good), we have not yet been able to document a consistent euphoric effect related to marijuana use. Other investigators [19] are beginning to report results similar to ours. Thus, it appears that whatever pharmacologic effect marijuana has on mood, that effect must be limited and ancillary to other determinants of mood.

The results of the present study also suggest that one of these other determinants is the prevailing mood of others in the environment. While there is nothing novel about this suggestion, within the context of the total results of the study, it indicates that the marijuana "high" may be more a function of social variables than of the pharmacologic effect of THC. The replication of these results in future research would have obvious implications for social policy on marijuana.

Short-Term Memory, Vigilance, and Reaction Time

One of the most frequently cited effects of marijuana is its apparent interference with short-term memory. Early attempts to document this effect with controlled research led to inconsistent results. Some investigators [11] found such an effect, but others have not.[49] The inconsistency was attributed to variations in "set and setting" and to different measurement procedures employed from study to study. However, recent studies in this area were based on a more systematic analysis of the processes involved in short-term memory, and these studies have yielded more consistent results. In brief, these results suggest that it is the information and acquisition phases of short-term memory that are most susceptible to marijuana effects, the phases that are heavily dependent on attention.[1-3, 9, 10] In previous research in our laboratory, we found the effects of marijuana on short-term memory to be variable and susceptible to subject control. We concluded that when marijuana does affect short-term memory, it probably does so through an interference or change in attention rather than through a direct biochemical action in the memory storage system.

The equipment used in these assessments was a discriminate stimulus response (DSR) apparatus, which consists of a visual display screen, four response keys, capacity for programmed display of series of primary digits at controlled intervals, and automatic recording of both response times and correct responses. The DSR was used to make the following assessments:

Simple Reaction Time

Subject's Task: Press response key 1, 2, 3, or 4 as quickly as possible when the corresponding digit was visually displayed.

Stimulus Presentation: Digit 1 repeated 10 times, digit 2 repeated 10 times, digit 3 repeated 10 times, and digit 4 repeated 10 times. Digit display time was 1 sec; interstimulus time was 1 sec.

Vigilance

Subject's Task: Same as in previous assessment.

Stimulus Presentation: Digits 1–9 were displayed in random order with five displays of each digit. Digit display time was 1 sec; interstimulus time was 1 sec.

Short-Term Memory

Subject's Task: Same as in previous assessment, except that the effective stimulus digit was the digit displayed either two or three steps prior to the digit currently being displayed. Thus, subjects were required to retain the correct stimulus in memory before responding. They received 40 trials with a two-step delay, followed by 40 trials with a three-step delay.

Stimulus Presentation: Digits 1–4 in random order.

All subjects were scheduled for these assessments daily beginning at approximately 10 AM. In addition, during the drug period, one subject per day was scheduled on a rotating basis for a special assessment session to begin 30 min after the subject had smoked marijuana.

The data were analyzed by two procedures. First, a stepwise multiple regression analysis of variance was performed separately for each set of data that assessed short-term memory (two-step and three-step delays were combined for the statistical analyses), vigilance, and reaction time. The results of these analyses disclosed no statistically significant difference between daily (nonmarijuana related) and special (marijuana related) performances on any of the three assessment tasks. There also were no statistically significant differences in performance between the casual and heavy user groups.

Marijuana- and nonmarijuana-related performances on the reaction time task were remarkably similar. On the other hand, it appears that the lack of statistically significant differences between marijuana- and nonmarijuana-related performances on the short-term memory and vigilance tasks was not due so much to lack of differences between the two performances as to lack of consistency in the differences.

In the second procedure used to analyze the results, correlations between daily performances on the three tasks were computed for each subject. These correlations were computed separately for the marijuana- and nonmarijuana-related assessments performed during the 21-day drug period. To control for relationships in task performances due to practice effects, partial correlations were obtained with practice effects (i.e., "study day") partialled out. The obtained coefficients were transformed into Fisher's Z scores, which were then averaged across subjects, tested for statistical significance by Student's *t* test, and then retransformed back into an average correlation coefficient. This process was performed separately for the casual and heavy users.

During nonmarijuana-related assessments, performances on all three tasks were significantly correlated; however, during the marijuana-related assessments, only the performances on the short-term memory and vigilance tasks were significantly correlated. This pattern was present for both casual and heavy users. The lack of a significant correlation between performances on either of the other two tasks was related to the fact that there was little variation in reaction time performance between marijuana- and nonmarijuana-related assessments, whereas short-term memory and vigilance performances became more variable during marijuana-related assessments. The statistically significant correlation between the latter performances indicates that the variations occurred in concert.

The results of the present study disclosed no statistically significant marijuana effects on short-term memory. However, the lack of statistical significance appeared to be due to the lack of consistency in the differences between marijuana- and nonmarijuana-related performances rather than to the absence of differences per se. This large variability in marijuana-related performance on memory tasks has been reported by others.[41, 48]

The inclusion of a task in the present study that specifically assessed attention made it possible to demonstrate that the variability on a task that required short-term memory was related to the variability on a task that required attention. The fact that there was no correlation between performances on either of these tasks and performance on a task that assessed simple reaction time indicated the common variance on the attention and short-term memory tasks was not due to some general factor that affected all task performances during a given session.

In a study conducted by Kopell et al.,[22] it was found that a neurologic index of attention, the contingent negative variation (CNV), was enhanced by THC, which indicates that subjects' ability to sustain attention was increased rather than decreased by the drug. Similar results have been reported by Low et al.,[24] who also studied the effects of THC on the CNV. The results of these studies suggest that cannabis does not interfere with the basic neurologic processes involved in attention. These findings are consistent with results reported by Meyer et al.,[36] Weil et al.,[51] and Rafaelsen et al.,[41] which also indicated that marijuana did not impair performance on tasks that assessed attention.

If marijuana-related shifts in attention are not neurologically determined, this would suggest that the shifts are volitionally controlled (i.e., psychologically determined). Cappell and Pliner,[8] who conducted a study directly focused on subjects' ability to volitionally control some of the cognitive effects of marijuana, reported finding evidence for the existence of such control. The results of our earlier study in this area also suggested that some cognitive effects were susceptible to subject control. It is important that further research be conducted to arrive at a determination of the extent to which these effects are subject controlled.

This determination would be relevant to an evaluation of both the seriousness of marijuana-induced cognitive and motor decrements and the adequacy of research designs used in assessing the effects of marijuana on cognitive and motor functions. An evaluation of the seriousness of marijuana-related deficits in cognitive or motor performance would differ if the deficits were a function of a volitionally controlled change in attention rather than a direct impairment of the neurologic substrata of either attention or the cognitive and motor processes being assessed. Likewise, an evaluation of research designs in this area would be influenced if the reported "waxing and waning" of marijuana effects [15] is merely a reflection of volitional variables in subjects' attending to research task requirements.

PSYCHIATRIC ASSESSMENTS

It is generally accepted that marijuana use has greatly increased over the past decade compared to prior decades. The possible dangers involved in marijuana consumption remain an issue of controversy. Recent articles have again raised the question of possible risks.[26, 27] One of the critical questions is the effect of marijuana consumption on the psychiatric status of individuals who consume high doses over a prolonged period of time.[7, 12]

Changes in psychiatric status were determined as part of a larger multidisciplinary research program on the effects of prolonged marijuana consumption. Groups of four healthy male volunteer subjects lived on the clinical research ward for a 31-day period. The research ward was designed to be as "natural" a setting as possible, with television, stereo, and recreation available. A 5-day baseline control period preceded a 21-day period during which standardized (1.8–2.3% THC) United States Government marijuana cigarettes were freely available for purchase with points earned by performance on a simple operant task. Control data were obtained from a group of casual alcohol users, studied under the same conditions, but working for alcohol rather than marijuana. The three groups of subjects studied were 12 casual marijuana smokers who averaged 2.6 marijuana cigarettes per day, 15 heavy marijuana smokers who averaged 5.7 marijuana cigarettes per day, and eight minimal alcohol consumers who drank an average of less than 1 ounce of alcohol per day; no marijuana was available to these latter subjects. This group helped serve as a control group for the effects of living on a closed research ward.

Clinical assessments were made by means of a standardized interview schedule in an attempt to minimize behavior bias.[13] The instrument chosen was the current section of the current and past psychopathology scales (CAPPS) developed by Endicott and Spitzer.[17] This scale has proven sensitive to changes over time when given sequentially.[20] The scale was modified to cover the 16 categories considered relevant to the live-in situation of the research ward setting. A series of scaled judgments were made for the categories involved and were recorded on the basis of a six-point scale from none (1) to extreme (6). The period of time assessed was reduced from 30 days in the standard CAPPS to the previous 5 days in our assessments.

To further minimize possible observer bias, the interviews were conducted jointly by two psychiatrists who had received personal instruction and reliability training in the administration of the instrument.

The CAPPS assessments were made at the end of the initial 5-day baseline period and again toward the end of the 21-day marijuana or minimal alcohol acquisition period.

Interrater reliability between the two raters was demonstrated by a correlation coefficient of 0.72 or better for nine of the 16 categories. Correlation coefficients were not obtained on five categories (guilt, suicide, hallucinations, disorientation, and delusions), because these categories showed little or no variability. Scores in these categories were virtually all scored one, which indicated that no pathology was detected. The correlation coefficient for the category of grandiosity was 0.49.

Comparisons were made within each group between baseline assessments and the assessments made during the last week of minimal alcohol or marijuana consumption. Paired *t* tests were performed on each group. Among the three groups, no statistically significant change was found in most of the categories: 15 categories in the minimal alcohol-consuming group, 14 categories in the casual marijuana group, and 13 categories in the heavy marijuana user group. In the minimal alcohol-consuming group, only the category of depression showed a statistically significant ($p < 0.01$) increase. In the casual marijuana-consuming group, the categories of somatic concern and daily routine-leisure time impairment also showed a statistically significant ($p < 0.05$) increase. Among the heavy marijuana-consuming group, statistically significant increases occurred in elated mood ($p < 0.05$), daily routine-leisure time impairment, and retardation-lack of emotion ($p < 0.001$).

Marijuana consumed on a research ward under controlled conditions does not appear to produce significant change in a majority of categories of psychiatric assessments. Though multiple *t* tests can yield statistical significance in the absence of apparent clinical validity, the categories of daily routine-leisure time impairment and retardation-lack of emotion clearly are influenced by the heavy consumption of marijuana. Though of less statistical significance, the increase in depression in minimal alcohol consumers raises the possibility that living on a research ward may produce a mild depression over time. This possibility may account, in part, for the finding that casual users of marijuana failed to show an elated mood. Heavier marijuana use may have countered the mild depressant effect of living on a research ward, because these subjects did show increases in elated mood.

An increase in somatic concern in casual but not heavy marijuana users may also reflect an "overriding" euphoric effect at higher doses or tolerance for any possible side effects of marijuana in the heavy user group.

Despite statistically significant changes in some categories, the clinical degree of these changes all fall in the "mild" range (2–3) of the 1–6 scale. These mild changes in psychiatric status may reflect the fact that only physically and emotionally healthy subjects were selected. The minimal effects of marijuana in this group of casual and heavy users may not predict the potential psychiatric hazard for the population as a whole.

CARDIAC AND PULMONARY FUNCTIONS

All chest x rays were normal. No significant abnormalities were noted in blood chemistry profiles, blood counts, or urinalyses. Physical examinations, including neurologic examinations in all subjects, were normal throughout the study.

The heart rate generally increased after marijuana smoking, although bradycardia was occasionally observed. Subjects who consumed relatively large amounts of marijuana tended to have a persistent sinus tachycardia. No electrocardiographic abnormalities were found, nor were any disturbances in conduction of cardiac rhythm observed in electrocardiograms made at weekly intervals throughout the study. Blood pressure effects of marijuana tended to be variable, and both increases and decreases in systolic and diastolic blood pressures were observed throughout the period of study. Thus far, our data fail to show significant cardiovascular effects of marijuana smoked under research ward conditions other than the usual sinus tachycardia.

In studies of pulmonary function, we observed a significant reduction in baseline vital capacity (VC) in six of 28 subjects during the presmoking control period. The baseline vital capacity and 1-sec timed vital capacity measurements are shown in TABLE 3. Fifteen subjects showed an increase in 1-sec timed vital capacity measurements ($FEV_{1.0}$). When the ratio of $FEV_{1.0}/VC$ is calculated (TABLE 3, column 8), an increase can be readily noted in many subjects. In fact, 18 of our 28 experienced marijuana users had ratios of 90% or greater at the outset of our studies. This type of abnormality in pulmonary function testing is seen in patients with restrictive disease of the lung, such as interstitial fibrosis, which may be produced by chronic inhalation of irritating substances. In the absence of a prior history of pulmonary disease or other clinical abnormality in any subjects, these data strongly suggest that marijuana may have a significant local irritative effect on the lung. These observations further suggest that there may be a correlation between the subject's prior marijuana smoking and the pulmonary function changes observed. It is clearly necessary to conduct further extensive studies of the effects of long-term marijuana smoking on the lung, because the type of preliminary data reported here is highly suggestive of a potentially deleterious long-term effect of this substance.

Contrary to what appears to be a chronic effect of marijuana on lung function, there is also a separate and apparently distinct acute effect. In 12 of our 15 heavy user subjects, we observed increases in peak expiratory flow rate imme-

TABLE 3

VITAL CAPACITY AND 1-SEC TIMED VITAL CAPACITY ($FEV_{1.0}$)

Subject	Pre-dicted VC (L)	Actual * VC±SD	Devia-tion (%)	Pre-dicted $FEV_{1.0}$ (L)	Actual * $FEV_{1.0}$±SD	Devia-tion (%)	$FEV_{1.0}$/VC
Casual Users							
A1	5.32	4.86±0.25	−9	4.35	4.10±0.29	−6	84
A2 (T)†	5.22	4.60±0.69	−12	4.25	3.93±0.55	−8	85
A3	4.83	3.40±0.08 ‡	−30	4.05	3.38±0.34	−17	99
A4 (t)§	4.90	3.70±0.34 ‡	−25	4.10	3.60±0.25	−12	97
B1	5.40	5.13±0.20	−5	4.10	4.97±0.11	+21	97
B2	4.85	4.73±0.12	−3	4.05	4.58±0.18	+13	97
B3 (T)	4.90	4.61±0.64	−6	4.45	4.11±0.56	−8	89
B4	5.40	5.74±0.30	+6	4.45	5.13±0.15	+15	89
C1	4.54	3.82±0.23	−16	3.82	3.60±0.60	−6	94
C2	5.12	4.57±0.38	−11	4.22	3.64±0.29	−14	80
C3	5.21	5.18±0.39	+1	4.22	4.98±0.27	+18	96
C4	5.22	3.88±0.40 ‡	−26	4.32	3.72±0.27	−14	97
Heavy Users							
D1 (t)	5.54	5.77±0.18	+4	4.55	4.93±0.13	+8	85
D2	5.12	5.45±0.32	+6	4.26	5.20±0.12	+22	95
D3 (t)	4.26	4.13±0.17	−3	3.64	3.92±0.12	+8	95
D4	5.35	4.77±0.14	−11	4.40	3.97±0.39	−10	83
E1 (t)	5.30	5.52±0.21	+4	4.36	5.19±0.09	+19	94
E2 (T)	6.06	4.90±0.22 ‡	−19	4.90	4.80±0.20	−2	98
E3 (T)	4.98	4.80±0.16	−4	4.15	4.74±0.31	+14	99
E4	5.08	3.80±0.17 ‡	−25	4.24	3.70±0.13	−13	97
F1	5.64	5.43±0.25	−4	4.60	4.87±0.23	+6	90
F2 (t)	6.40	5.09±0.11 ‡	−20	5.10	5.09±0.36	0	100
F3(T)	5.60	5.64±0.40	+1	4.60	4.70±0.09	+2	83
F4 (t)	5.65	5.91±0.42	+5	4.60	5.08±0.35	+10	86
G1 (T)	4.02	3.66±0.40	−9	3.25	3.64±0.38	+12	99
G2 (t)	4.12	3.83±0.07	−7	3.35	3.65±0.14	+9	95
G3	4.96	4.86±0.27	−2	3.95	3.64±0.13	−8	75
G4 (T)	4.59	4.86±0.14	+6	3.65	4.84±0.12	+33	99

* Mean of measurements on five consecutive presmoking baseline days.

† Subjects who presently or previously smoked one or more packages of tobacco cigarettes daily.

‡ Values that differed by more than two standard deviations from predicted values.

§ Subjects who presently or previously smoked less than one package of tobacco cigarettes daily.

diately after marijuana smoking. This finding suggests a bronchodilator effect produced acutely by Δ^9-THC, the primary active ingredient of marijuana smoke. TABLE 4 documents the acute increases in peak expiratory flow rate that we observed in our subjects.

Our data suggest that long-term, moderate to heavy use of marijuana by smoking may induce clinically significant changes in pulmonary function. Because we failed to find abnormalities in chest x rays or in clinical examinations to suggest pulmonary disease, the changes produced may be rather insidious and not easily detectable by routine health examinations. Therefore, if our findings are confirmed in further studies, it would certainly be important to notify the population-at-risk of this potential health hazard of marijuana.

The acute increases in peak expiratory flow rate may be potentially beneficial, and, indeed, it is conceivable that pharmacologically active derivatives of

TABLE 4

PEAK EXPIRATORY FLOW RATE

Subject	Presmoking Mean±SD (liter/min × 100)	Postsmoking Mean±SD (liter/min × 100)	Statistical Significance
D1	623.81±45.11	670.95±58.30	p <0.001
D3	485.24±41.85	497.38±27.78	ns
D4	816.19±32.63	833.33±29.72	p <0.05
E1	533.10±36.55	553.81±55.11	ns
E2	536.67±24.10	574.05±59.83	p <0.02
E3	403.16±23.11	420.53±32.74	p <0.005
E4	459.05±36.08	472.86±33.90	p <0.02
F1	612.27±37.77	620.45±31.66	ns
F2	509.17±76.09	549.17±66.40	p <0.05
F3	488.00±39.42	522.50±24.47	p <0.001
F4	365.00±14.33	375.50±19.59	p <0.05
G1	365.24±31.84	392.62±24.73	p <0.005
G2	362.62±24.14	397.14±26.44	p <0.001
G3	425.48±19.62	450.48±26.36	p <0.001
G4	513.25±50.63	562.00±43.72	p <0.001

marijuana may eventually have some importance as therapeutic agents for the production of bronchodilatation. However, administered by the route of smoking, marijuana may itself produce or worsen pulmonary disease. Our studies fail to find any clinically significant beneficial or damaging effects of marijuana on cardiovascular functioning.

ANDROGEN HOMEOSTASIS

There is some controversy concerning both acute and chronic effects of marijuana on plasma testosterone and gonadotropin levels in human males. Much of the work in this area has been reviewed by Drs. Robert M. Rose, Robert C. Kolodny, and Jack H. Mendelson and his associates in their respective chapters (8–10) in *Marihuana and Health Hazards,* edited by Jared R. Tinklenberg.[47] These investigators pointed out that differences in findings obtained in studies of effects of chronic and acute marijuana use on plasma testosterone levels in adult males might be related to differences in dose and time factors plus enormous inter- and intraindividual variability in normal plasma testosterone levels. These investigators also stressed that both biologic and statistical significances in differences in plasma testosterone levels after marijuana smoking were a crucial issue. In many instances, statistically significant decrements in plasma testosterone levels associated with marijuana use were still well within the range of clinically normal values.

During most recent studies in our laboratory, we have attempted to examine episodic secretory rates of testosterone, luteinizing hormone (LH), and folliclestimulating hormone (FSH) in adult healthy males prior to, during, and after a period of intensive marijuana use. Samples of blood were obtained hourly during the 24 hr on the last day of the control period, the 21st day of marijuana smoking, and the third day after cessation of marijuana use. All samples were collected with a portable battery-operated pump device connected to an indwelling intravenous catheter placed in the subject's anticubital vein. While wearing this device, subjects were fully ambulatory, comfortable, and had no restriction of physical activity.

To date, we have completed analysis of plasma LH levels for five subjects. There were no significant differences in basal LH levels or episodic secretory pulses for any subject when presmoking, smoking, and postsmoking values were compared. Moreover, there appeared to be no relationship between dose of marijuana consumed and plasma LH levels.

The findings are different from those obtained on the effects of both alcohol and heroin administration on 24-hr episodic secretory rates of LH. Administration of 10 mg of heroin intravenously to healthy, normal male heroin addicts produced an almost immediate suppression of basal LH levels and abolished episodic secretory pulses for 4–6 hr. After LH levels fell after heroin administration, there was a subsequent drop in plasma testosterone levels.[38]

Acute alcohol administration produced a significant fall in plasma testosterone levels in healthy adult males.[32] Testosterone levels began to fall as blood alcohol levels rose, and the lowest plasma testosterone values were found when blood alcohol was at peak levels. Recovery of testosterone levels began to occur as blood alcohol levels fell. However, LH levels did not drop after acute alcohol administration and were significantly elevated at the same time testosterone levels were lowest (at the peak of the blood alcohol curve).

The effects of heroin on suppression of plasma testosterone levels probably are a consequence of inhibition of secretion of pituitary gonadotropins. Testosterone levels fell after a decrease in plasma LH levels. For alcohol, plasma testosterone levels are most likely suppressed as a consequence of a direct effect of ethanol on the biosynthesis and/or release of testosterone in the testes. The elevation in plasma LH levels after an initial decrease in plasma testosterone is due to feedback mechanisms that testosterone has on secretion of pituitary gonadotropins.

Because neither a rise nor a fall in plasma LH has been observed in our studies of marijuana self-administration, effects of marijuana on plasma testosterone levels (if they occur) could not be most parsimoniously explained by either inhibition of gonadotropin secretion or depression of biosynthesis or release of testosterone in the testes. However, marijuana could have an effect on plasma testosterone levels without any concomitant alterations in plasma LH levels. This effect could occur if marijuana use resulted in an enhanced rate of biotransformation of testosterone to estradiol in the liver. The basis for such a possibility would require the action of marijuana-induced enzyme alterations in the liver that regulate the biotransformation of steroids. If this action did occur, conversion of testosterone to estradiol would not result in an increased secretory rate of LH, because estradiol has also been shown to exert regulatory feedback control on LH output in males. However, if the ratios of estradiol to testosterone were significantly altered as a consequence of chronic marijuana use, adverse phenomena, such as gynecomastia, might be possible.

These hypotheses are speculations, which can only be substantiated by studies of 24-hr episodic secretory rates of LH, testosterone, and plasma estradiol levels in adult males after acute and chronic marijuana administration.

LONGITUDINAL STUDIES

Drug use patterns are complex, multidetermined behaviors. For this reason, the phenomenon has been a difficult one to study, and until recently, knowledge of drug use patterns has been derived primarily from epidemiologic studies. Techniques have now been developed to study changes that involve biologic, social, and psychologic functions in a research setting,[34] and while such research has become increasingly popular in the experimental study of drug abuse, several methodologic questions have been raised regarding the nature and scope of subchronic drug investigations. Among these questions are the following: How accurately do subjects replicate their regular drug use patterns in a research environment? How valid and reliable are the research data, and to what extent do they identify factors involved in the etiology and maintenance of drug use? In a related vein, what are the benefits or disadvantages of short-term institutionalization, and how do these factors affect subsequent attitudes, life-styles, and drug use patterns?

In an effort to evaluate these issues, a follow-up study was conducted on 27 research subjects who participated in an intensive multidisciplinary investigation of free-choice marijuana use over a 31-day period. Of special concern are the reported changes in drug use, attitudes, and adjustment during a 6-month poststudy follow-up period. We were also interested in the consistency of marijuana smoking behavior in different settings and with identifying factors that might be useful in predicting or explaining drug use patterns in both actual and experimental settings.

Subjects were middle- and upper-middle-class single males. A variety of research instruments and techniques were employed to gather the information reported here. Current drug use patterns and attitudes toward drugs were assessed by means of a drug use questionnaire given 1 or 2 weeks prior to admission to the research unit. On the day of admission, subjects were questioned about their reasons for participation and expected smoking behavior. They were also asked to complete Cattell's 16 personality factor test. During the 21-day inpatient phase of free access to marijuana, a careful record was made of the amount and patterning of marijuana smoking. On the last day of the study, subjects were asked to give a written evaluation and critique of the research experience. Finally, 6 months after the end of each study, a follow-up questionnaire was sent to all participants to assess their current attitudes, drug use patterns, and social adjustment.

To assess the long-term consequences, if any, of the research experience, a series of questions in the follow-up questionnaire dealt with personal and social adjustment, attitudes toward drug use, and current drug use patterns. Nine casual and 11 heavy users responded to the questionnaire.

In both groups, the overwhelming majority reported no change in legal and health status. Consistent with their high rate of employment, 80% of the casual users reported improvement in financial status and psychologic well-being. Only half of the percentage (40%) of heavy users reported improvement in these areas. In general, the category chosen most frequently by both groups to describe their current life adjustment was "no change." No respondent attributed any negative consequences to participation in the research program.

Several questions probed the subject's perceptions of the research experience. The response "I'm glad I participated" summarizes the favorable reaction given by 85% of the subjects. Many viewed it as a "pleasant, unique vacation" that was "educational and interesting." The main disadvantages cited were loss of contact with friends and isolation.

Changes in alcohol and marijuana consumption were evaluated by comparing frequency of use reported before and after the study with that observed during the study. On the average, casual users reported smoking 0.45 marijuana cigarettes per day before entering the study. Their daily consumption during the research increased more than fivefold (to 2.65) and then declined to 0.90 6 months after departure. The heavy users demonstrated a similar pattern of change. There was no significant change in daily consumption before and after the research period in either group. However, the differences between smoking behavior on the research ward and that reported before and after the research experience were highly significant ($p < 0.01$). As for marijuana use, the daily consumption of alcohol did not change significantly after the research.

Selected data on personality characteristics, demographic factors, and drug history were submitted to a correlational analysis to evaluate the consistency of marijuana smoking over time and to determine whether such behavior could be reliably predicted in different situations.

Demographic factors (age and educational level) and the 16 personality factors measured by Cattell's 16 PF inventory correlated minimally with marijuana consumption. The strongest predictors of research ward consumption were prior marijuana use ($r = 0.73$, $p < 0.01$), the subject's anticipated consumption before the smoking period began ($r = 0.63$, $p < 0.01$). Daily cigarette consumption ($r = 0.59$), prior alcohol use ($r = 0.48$), and subsequent marijuana smoking ($r = 0.49$) also correlated significantly ($p < 0.05$).

The results point to several conclusions concerning the validity and aftereffects of research on subchronic marijuana smoking in a research ward setting. First, the subjects' reports indicate that their participation in the research did not adversely affect subsequent adjustment, attitudes, psychologic well-being, or marijuana smoking patterns. Second, the findings suggest that free-choice drug use behavior in a research setting is consistent with such behavior in the natural environment. Despite a dramatic increase in overall consumption by all subjects, marijuana smoking under research conditions correlated significantly with smoking frequency prior to and after the research. Finally, the results show that marijuana smoking patterns, while highly labile, are nevertheless, predictable. Even though environmental circumstances (experimental vs natural setting) apparently exercised a profound influence on consumption, the magnitude of the increase could be reliably predicted on the basis of prior experience with marijuana, cigarettes, and alcohol.

REFERENCES

1. ABEL, E. 1970. Marijuana and memory. Nature (London) **227**: 1151, 1152.
2. ABEL, E. 1971. Marijuana and memory: acquisition or retrieval? Science **173**: 1038–1040.
3. ABEL, E. 1971. Effects of marijuana on the solution of anagrams, memory and appetite. Nature (London) **231**: 260, 261.
4. BABOR, T. F., A. M. ROSSI, G. SAGOTSKY & R. E. MEYER. 1974. Group behavior: patterns of smoking. In The Use of Marihuana: A Psychological and Physiological Inquiry. J. H. Mendelson, A. M. Rossi & R. E. Meyer, Eds. : 47–59. Plenum Publishing Corporation. New York, N.Y.
5. BABOR, T. F. A. M. ROSSI, G. SAGOTSKY & R. E. MEYER. 1974. Group behavior: verbal interaction. In The Use of Marihuana: A Psychological and Physiological Inquiry. J. H. Mendelson, A. M. Rossi & R. E. Meyer, Eds. : 61–72. Plenum Publishing Corporation. New York, N.Y.
6. BROWN, A. C. & G. BRENGELMANN. 1965. Energy metabolism. In Physiology and Biophysics. T. C. Ruch & H. D. Patton, Eds. : 1030–1045. W. B. Saunders Company. Philadelphia, Pa.
7. CANNABIS. 1968. Report by the Advisory Committee on Drug Dependence. Washington, D.C.
8. CAPPELL, H. D. & P. L. PLINER. 1973. Volitional control of marijuana intoxication: a study of the ability to "come down" on command. J. Abnormal Psychol. **82**: 428–434.
9. DITTRICH, A., K. BATTIG & I. VON ZEPPELIN. 1973. Effects of $(-)\Delta^9$-transtetrahydrocannabinol (Δ^9-THC) on memory, attention and subjective state; a double blind study. Psychopharmacologia **33**: 369–376.
10. DORNBUSH, R. L., M. FINK & A. M. FREEDMAN. 1971. Marihuana, memory and perception. Amer. J. Psychiat. **128**: 194–197.
11. DREW, W. G., G. F. KIPLINGER, L. L. MILLER & M. MARX. 1972. Effects of propranolol on marihuana induced cognitive dysfunctioning. Clin. Pharmacol. Ther. **13**: 526–533.
12. EDITORIAL. 1969. Cannabis. Lancet **1**: 139.
13. ENDICOTT, J. & R. L. SPITZER. 1972. Current and past psychopathology scales: rationale, reliability and validity. Arch. Gen. Psychiat. **27**: 678–687.
14. GOODE, E. 1969. Multiple drug use among marijuana smokers. Soc. Prob. **17**: 48–63.
15. GRINSPOON, L. 1971. Marihuana Reconsidered. Harvard University Press. Cambridge, Mass.
16. HALIKAS, J. A. 1974. Marijuana use and psychiatric illness. In Marijuana Effects on Human Behavior. L. L. Miller, Ed. : 265–302. Academic Press, Inc. New York, N.Y.
17. HERZ, M., J. ENDICOTT & R. L. SPITZER. 1971. Day versus inpatient hospitalization: a controlled study. Amer. J. Psychiat. **127**: 1371–1382.
17a. HOLLINGSHEAD, A. B. & F. C. REDLICH. 1958. Social Class and Mental Illness: A Community Study. John Wiley & Sons, Inc. New York, N.Y.
18. JONES, R. T. 1971. Marihuana-induced "high": influence of expectation, setting and previous drug experience. Pharmacol. Rev. **23**: 359–369.
19. JONES, R. T. 1971. Tetrahydrocannabinol and the marijuana social "high," or the effects of the mind on marijuana. Ann. N.Y. Acad. Sci. **191**: 155–165.
20. KENDELL, R. E. 1968. An important source of bias affecting ratings made by psychiatrists. J. Psychiat. Res. **6**: 135–141.
21. KOLANSKY, H. & W. T. MOORE. 1971. Effects of marihuana on adolescents and young adults. J. Amer. Med. Ass. **216**: 486–492.
22. KOPELL, B. S., J. R. TINKLENBERG & L. E. HOLLISTER. 1972. Contingent negative variation amplitudes: marijuana and alcohol. Arch. Gen. Psychiat. **27**: 809–811.

23. KUPFER, D. J., D. DETRE, J. KORAL & P. FAJANS. 1973. A comment on the "amotivational syndrome" in marijuana smokers. Amer. J. Psychiat. **130:** 1319–1344.
24. LOW, M. D., H. KLONOFF & A. MARCUS. 1973. The neurophysiological basis of the marijuana experience. Can. Med. Ass. J. **108:** 157–165.
25. NATIONAL INSTITUTE ON DRUG ABUSE. 1974. Marihuana and Health. Fourth Report to the U.S. Congress. United States Government Printing Office. Washington, D.C.
26. MAUGH, T. H., II. 1974. Marihuana: the grass may no longer be greener. Science **185:** 683.
27. MAUGH, T. H., II. 1974. Marihuana (II): does it damage the brain? Science **185:** 775.
28. MAYOR'S COMMITTEE ON MARIHUANA. 1944. The Marihuana Problem in the City of New York. Jacques Cattell Press. Tempe, Ariz.
29. McGLOTHLIN, W. H. 1971. The use of cannabis: east and west. *In* Biomedical and Pharmacological Aspects of Dependence and Reports on Marihuana Research. H. M. Van Praag, Ed. : 167–193. Deerven F. Bohn. Amsterdam, The Netherlands.
30. MECHOULAM R. (Ed.) 1973. Marihuana, Chemistry, Pharmacology, Metabolism and Clinical Effects. Academic Press, Inc. New York, N.Y.
31. MELLO, N. K. & J. H. MENDELSON. 1972. Drinking patterns during work-contingent and non-contingent alcohol acquisition. Psychosomat. Med. **34:** 139–164.
32. MENDELSON, J. H., J. C. KUEHNLE, J. ELLINGBOE & N. K. MELLO. 1976. Effects of acute alcohol administration on episodic secretory rates of testosterone and LH. In preparation.
33. MENDELSON, J. H., J. C. KUEHNLE, I. GREENBERG & N. K. MELLO. 1976. Operant acquisition of marihuana in man. J. Pharmacol. Exp. Ther. **198:** 42–53.
34. MENDELSON, J. H. & N. K. MELLO. 1966. Experimental analysis of drinking behavior of chronic alcoholics. Ann. N.Y. Acad. Sci. **133:** 828–845.
35. MENDELSON, J. H., A. M. ROSSI & R. E. MEYER. (Eds.) 1974. The Use of Marihuana: A Psychological and Physiological Inquiry. Plenum Publishing Corporation. New York, N.Y.
36. MEYER, R. E., R. C. PILLARD, L. M. SHAPIRO & S. M. MIRIN. 1971. Administration of marihuana to heavy and casual marihuana users. Amer. J. Psychiat. **128:** 198–204.
37. MILLER, L. L. (Ed.) 1974. Marihuana: Effects on Human Behavior. Academic Press, Inc. New York, N.Y.
38. MIRIN, S. M., J. H. MENDELSON, J. ELLINGBOE & R. E. MEYER. 1976. Acute effects of heroin and naltrexone on testosterone and gonadotrophin secretion: a pilot study. Psychoneuroendocrinology. In press.
39. ORCUTT, J. D. & D. A. BIGGS. 1975. Recreational effects of marihuana and alcohol: some descriptive dimensions. Int. J. Addictions **10:** 229–239.
40. PEREZ-REYES, M., M. C. TIMMONS & M. E. WALL. 1974. Long-term use of marihuana and the development of tolerance or sensitivity to Δ^9-tetrahydrocannabinol. Arch. Gen. Psychiat. **31:** 89–91.
41. RAFAELSEN, O. J., P. BECH, J. CHRISTIANSEN, H. CHRISTUP, J. NYBOE & L. RAFAELSEN. 1973. Cannabis and alcohol: effects on simulated car driving. Science **197:** 920–923.
42. RENAULT, P. F., C. R. SCHUSTER & D. X. FREEDMAN. 1974. Repeat administration of marihuana smoke to humans. Arch. Gen. Psychiat. **31:** 95–102.
43. RUBIN, V. & L. COMITAS. 1975. Ganja in Jamaica. A Medical Anthropological Study of Chronic Marihuana Use. Mouton. The Hague.
44. SCHACTER, S. & J. E. SINGER. 1962. Cognitive, social and physiological determinants of emotional state. Psychol. Rev. **69:** 379–399.
45. SILER, J. F., W. L. SHEEP, L. B. BATES, G. F. CLARK, G. W. COOK & W. A. SMITH. 1933. Marihuana smoking in Panama. Military Surg. **73:** 269–280.

46. STEFANIS, C., R. DORNBUSH & M. FINK. 1975. Chronic Hashish Use. The Raven Press. New York, N.Y. In press.
47. TINKLENBERG, J. R. (Ed.) 1975. Marihuana and Health Hazards. Academic Press, Inc. New York, N.Y.
48. TINKLENBERG, J. R., B. S. KOPELL, L. E. HOLLISTER & F. T. MELGES. 1970. A comparison of the effects of marihuana and ethanol on memory, evoked potential, and contingent negative variation. Paper presented at the American College of Neuropsychopharmacology meeting, San Juan, Puerto Rico.
49. TINKLENBERG, J. R., F. T. MELGES, L. E. HOLLISTER & H. K. GILLESPIE. 1970. Marihuana and immediate memory. Nature (London) 226: 1171, 1172.
50. WEIL, A. T. & N. E. ZINBERG. 1969. Acute effects of marihuana on speech. Nature (London) 222: 434–437.
51. WEIL, A. T., N. E. ZINBERG & J. M. NELSEN. 1968. Clinical and psychological effects of marihuana in man. Science 162: 1234–1242.
52. WILLIAMS, E. G., C. K. HIMMELSBACH, A. WIKLER, D. C. RUBLE & B. J. LLOYD. 1946. Studies on marihuana and pyrahexyl compound. Public Health Rep. 61: 1059–1083.

THE 94-DAY CANNABIS STUDY

Sidney Cohen

Neuropsychiatric Institute
School of Medicine
University of California at Los Angeles
Los Angeles, California 90024

For the past 4 years, a variety of investigations have been underway at this Institute into the human pharmacology of cannabis. Recently, we have been retaining volunteer subects for 94 days on the Marihuana Research Ward to study long-term effects in a controlled setting. This study will be described and a summary of the findings reported to you.

DESCRIPTION

Our subjects were required to be males, 21–35 years of age, with a history of moderate or heavy marijuana use. They were recruited in response to advertisements in local college papers from employment agencies and by word-of-mouth referrals (FIGURE 1).

They had to meet the following criteria before acceptance into the study. During the past 6 months, they must have smoked less than 10 tobacco cigarettes per day, taken no more than three drinks per week, or no more than four nonmedical exposures to drugs, and smoked at least three marijuana "joints" per week. They received $800.00 for completing the study and could earn an additional $1000.00 to $2000.00 for working at two tasks to be described. With the money, marijuana over and above the one free, compulsory daily cigarette could be purchased along with certain other amenities. It was hoped that motivation to work and desire to smoke cannabis might be measured in this modified token economy setting.

In excess of 2000 phone calls were received from potential applicants. More than 90% of the callers were rejected or withdrew after the phone interview because they were obviously ineligible (TABLE 1). A total of 206 came in for interviews (TABLE 2). Of these 206, 146 were rejected, 30 withdrew after being accepted, and 30 were accepted and entered the study. Two subjects did not complete the entire 94 days; one developed acute appendicitis and was transferred to the surgical service, and the other decompensated into a paranoid psychosis that required his termination. Chlorpromazine and psychotherapy over the next few weeks resulted in his recovery.

Standards for acceptance included no history or findings of a significant mental or physical illness, or MMPI scores more than 2 SD beyond the mean on the clinical scales. All drugs not provided by the staff, alcohol, and tobacco were not permitted during the 94-day period.

The 94 days were divided into, first, an 11-day preintoxication period, during which time all drugs were interdicted, baseline measurements were made, and the subject became familiar with the ward routines (TABLE 3). This period was followed by a 64-day intoxication phase during which the subjects smoked at least one joint [of 900 mg that contained 2.2%, or almost 20 mg, of tetrahydro-

```
MARIJUANA RESEARCH - Healthy males 21-35 to live

in hospital 94 consecutive days (pays $). UCLA

825-0094.
```

FIGURE 1. College newspaper advertisement for recruiting subjects.

cannabinol (THC)] and could buy as many more as they wished at 25 cents per joint during a 12-hr free period from noon to midnight. On the following 7 days, marijuana was withheld to study acute withdrawal effects and loss of tolerance. Finally, a second intoxication interval lasted 9 days, with the final 3 days used for detoxification and debriefing.

During the intoxication periods, subjects consumed a mean of 5.2 cigarettes (1.7–10) daily. Thus, their average daily exposure was 103 mg of THC, with individual ranges from 35 to 198 mg. The average street joint is said to contain about 5 mg of THC. Of course, the amount that enters the bloodstream under street and laboratory conditions is less by a factor of 50–75%.

The studies performed were so numerous that only some will be mentioned here (TABLES 4 & 5). They included echocardiography, chromosome investigations, skin testing for immune response, testicular and adrenal hormone assays, a complete battery of ophthalmologic examinations, multiple pulmonary function tests, including lung scans, sputum cytology, and respiratory dynamics.

An extensive battery of psychologic tests was completed at suitable intervals. These tests included verbal and nonverbal IQ, spatial orientation, tests of psychomotor skills, and personality inventories. Many tests for cerebral hemispheric dominance were performed. Blood, urine, and sputum tests were performed to assay cannabinoid content. Urine was collected randomly for drug screening determinations.

TABLE 1

RECRUITING PROCEDURES

Telephone Interview
  Drug use past 6 months (amount and frequency)
  Personal history
  Physical and mental health
If applicant fits these criteria, he is then scheduled for
Personal Interview
  To judge intelligence level, general attitude, and apparent suitability as a subject
  Detailed personal history
  Marijuana smoking history, to determine whether
    "Moderate," uses marijuana three to six times per week
    "Heavy," uses marijuana daily or several times per day
  If all above criteria fit, subject is then administered
    MMPI, applicants with profiles containing scores higher than two standard deviations above the mean for most clinical scales or with unusual profile configurations are eliminated
    Physical examination, including intense ophthalmologic examination
    Psychiatric interview, to assess mental status and acceptability of subject

TABLE 2

APPLICANTS: ACCORDING TO DRUG USE STATUS

Drug Use	Accepted	Rejected	Withdrew	Total
Heavy	13	68	14	95
Moderate	17	78	16	111
Total	30 *	146	30 †	206

* Two subjects did not complete the entire study. One due to acute appendicitis and another due to acute psychotic breakdown.
† Two subjects withdrew after being accepted onto the ward.

The two work assignments consisted of adding columns of figures on a calculator and of learning a foreign language to which the subject had no prior exposure. Wages were paid for correct answers at the rate of 10 cents per answer. Work was performed during both intoxication and nonintoxication periods to determine both speed and error levels under each condition.

RESULTS

A large number of individual studies have been completed during the past 4 years. The major findings can only be summarized here. It might be mentioned at this time that we learned a good deal, and not only about marijuana. The problems of keeping healthy, virile young men in a supervised situation for long periods of time were rediscovered by us. In this respect, marijuana appeared to act as a minor tranquilizer, reducing tensions, drives, and the frustrating restrictions placed on the subjects. The subjects who were only given placebos during their stay were generally more difficult for the staff to manage, especially because they were able to observe their fellow subjects "stoned."

Work Behavior

No general conclusions can be drawn regarding work output from our study.[1] Our volunteers cannot be considered at all typical of the universe of

TABLE 3

DISQUALIFICATIONS

Reason for Rejection	Drug Use	
	Moderate	Heavy
Unacceptable drug use	6	3
Abnormal MMPI	49	50
Psychiatrically unacceptable	9	10
Physically unacceptable	13	6
Total	77	69

marijuana users. Their prime motive for entering the study was "to make money"; second was "to smoke government pot." Piece-work wages were paid for correct answers to a psychomotor and a cognitive task. The psychomotor task was the addition of 10 sets of five-, six-, and seven-digit numbers on an electronic calculator. The cognitive task consisted of making correct responses after studying a foreign language to which the subject had never been exposed. A preprogrammed, self-learning language book was used, with the end of the chapter exercises being the test material.

The data analyzed to this point indicate that learning effects continued over the entire 94-day period. Total responses, total correct responses, responses per hour, correct responses per hour, and percentage of correct responses all continued to increase over the study period, regardless of whether the subjects were in an intoxication or a nonintoxication phase. Total errors, time worked, and errors per hour tended to remain unchanged throughout. Percentage of errors declined slightly from baseline to the end of the study. There were small, statistically nonsignificant decreases in correct responses on the day subjects went from a nonintoxication to an intoxication phase.

TABLE 4

INTOXICATION SCHEDULE

Days	Period
12–75 (64 days)	first intoxication
76–82 (7 days)	nonintoxication
83–91 (9 days)	second intoxication
92–94 (3 days)	detoxification

Pulmonary Function

The smoking of two to 10 National Institute on Drug Abuse (NIDA) cigarettes for 6–9 weeks produces a mild but significant narrowing of the smaller and larger airways, possibly due to chronic irritation. Despite this narrowing, the airways dilate after the acute smoking of a cannabis cigarette. Decreased airway resistance was also observed with oral Δ^9- and Δ^8-THC and to a much lesser extent with cannabinol and cannabidiol. Dose-response curves have been obtained with 0, 10, 15, and 20 mg of THC, with peak effects at 3 and persistent effects for 6 hr.[2]

Bronchospasm was induced in asthmatics by exercise or methacholine. In a single blind fashion, 10 mg of smoked THC was compared to 1.25 mg of aerosolized isoproterenol (Isuprel®) along with appropriate placebos. Bronchospasm was relieved promptly by both drugs and not by their placebos. The isoproterenol had a higher and earlier peak effect, but THC had a longer duration of action.[3] A degree of tolerance to the bronchodilating effect of THC occurs. An aerosolized THC has been tried, and the initial results are encouraging. The mean peak increase in specific airway conductance was 90% above baseline, much greater than when equivalent amounts (10 mg) of THC are smoked. Systemic effects, such as tachycardia and the "high," were not as pronounced with the aerosol.

TABLE 5

PHYSIOLOGIC STUDIES

Days	1–11	12–75	76–82	83–91	92–94
Echocardiography	2	13 16			92 93
Chromosomal studies	9	69		86	93
Routine blood and urine testing	5 10 11	40 43 46			
Hormone assays	5	12 18 25 32 37 39 46 53 60 66 67 72 74	81 81	83	
Immunologic studies					
In vivo	9	12 18 25 32 39 46 53 60 66 67 74	81		
In vitro	9	12 18 25 32 39 46 53 60 66 67 74			
Ophthalmologic studies					
Electroretinography	5	19 53 65	79	86	
Tonography		19 53			
Intraocular pressure	3	17 52 66	79	87	
Eye examination	3	17 52 66		87	
Orthoptics	4	19 53 74			
Doppler	3	17 52 66		87	
Pupillography	3	17 52 66		87	
Pulmonary studies					
Spirometry	8	15 22 25 29 71	82		
Body plethysmography	8	15 22 25 29 71	82		
Lung compliance	8	15 29 71			
Flow volume loop	8	15 71			
Single-breath O_2	8	15 71			
Closing volume	8	15 71			
Exercise study (VD–VT)		18 23 60 65 72			
Cardiopulmonary radioisotope	9				
Respiratory physiology	5	26 44 67 75			
Sputum cytology	5				92
Vital signs		12 13 14	76 77 78	83 84 85	92 93 94
	preintoxication 11 days	intoxication period 64 days	nonintoxication 7 days	intoxication 9 days	detoxification 3 days

The mechanism of the bronchodilator response remains obscure. Unlike isoproterenol, the THC-induced increase in specific airway conductance is not blocked by propanolol. In contrast to atropine, the THC-induced increase in bronchial diameter is not blocked by methacholine. Apparently, THC works over pathways independent of β adrenergic or muscarinic mechanisms.

Ophthalmic Studies

Early in these investigations, it was found that the generally accepted belief that cannabis dilated the pupils was incorrect. Under constant conditions of lighting and measurement, the pupils remain unchanged or constrict slightly after smoking cannabis.[5]

Of greater clinical interest was the observation that a dose-related clinically significant reduction in intraocular pressure (IOP) occurs in normal subjects.[6, 7] The IOP fell 30% in seven of 11 patients with wide-angle glaucoma after THC administration, and it lasts 4–5 hr. The IOP is also reduced with smoked marijuana and oral Δ^8-THC but only slightly with cannabinol and cannabidiol. Topically instilled THC in sesame oil produced a 40% reduction in IOP when compared to a group of rabbits given only sesame seed oil. So far, tolerance to the IOP reduction has not been established.

Cytogenetic Studies

Possible chromosomal impairment associated with marijuana use was studied by multiple sample analyses prior to and after 65 days of heavy smoking. No significant differences in the frequency of chromosomal breakage were found when comparing baseline and postsmoking samples of venous blood blind. The percentage of breaks before smoking was 1.78 (33/1850) and after smoking was 1.77 (23/1300). No other structural abnormalities were found. No relationship was discovered between the number of marijuana cigarettes smoked and chromosome breaks.[7] It should be noted that the baseline values cited above were for marijuana smokers who had abstained for at least 10 days. A comparison between smokers and matched nonsmokers is approaching completion.

Immunologic Studies

The cell-mediated immunity of 22 chronic, moderate, or heavy marijuana smokers showed no difference from that of nonsmoking controls when evaluated by in vivo skin testing with 2,5-dinitrochlorobenzene (DNCB). There was a marked difference in the immune response between the marijuana-using group, 100% of whom could be sensitized to DNCB, and age-matched cancer patients, who showed a decreased capacity to be sensitized.[8]

The immune system of 12 of our hospitalized marijuana subjects was evaluated. Enumeration of B- and T-cell subpopulations, lymphocyte proliferative responses to phytohemagglutinin (PHA) and to allogeneic cells, and serum immunoglobulin levels were studied. The baseline percentage of B cells and total B cells, determined either by surface immunoglobulins or complement receptors, was less than normal but increased to normal during the smoking phase. Baseline and percentage of T cells, initially low, also increased to normal by the end of the smoking period. *In vitro* lymphocyte responses to graded doses of PHA and to allogeneic cells were normal on baseline examination and did not change during the smoking period. Total IgG, IgA, and IgM were normal. Marijuana use does not appear to have a substantial adverse effect on the B or T cells of healthy young adults.[9]

Endocrinologic Studies

In cooperation with the Reproductive Biology Research Foundation, St. Louis, Missouri, 20 of our subjects were tested for acute changes in plasma testosterone level after smoking an NIDA joint. A significant depression occurred during the second and third hours. During the control day, the mean baseline reading was 725 ng/100 ml, and at 3 hr it was 711 ng/100 ml. On the test day, it fell from a mean of 754 to 533 ng/100 ml. Plasma luteinizing hormone levels were also significantly lower at 3 hr postsmoking.[10]

In a chronic study, the subjects were tested during the nonsmoking state. Their mean baseline plasma testosterone was 740 ng/100 ml. During the first 4 weeks before smoking, no significant changes in testosterone levels were recorded. From the fifth to the ninth weeks, the nonsmoking levels progressively decreased from 649, to 570, 524, and 509 ng/100 ml. After 1 week of abstention from marijuana, the mean level rose to 621 ng/100 ml, and after a final week of marijuana use, it fell again to 575 ng/100 ml. Plasma luteinizing hormone also fell after the fourth week. Plasma follicle-stimulating hormone was not significantly different from control levels until after the eighth week. Plasma prolactin and cortisol levels remained essentially unchanged throughout.

Cardiac Studies

The acute effects of marijuana produce an increase in cardiac output due to the well-known chronotropic effect. No change in stroke volume is found with indocyanine green or in echocardiographic studies. With chain smoking, the tachycardia disappears, indicating a complete tolerance to the chronotropic effect. Incidentally, tolerance to the euphoria parallels chronotropic tolerance fairly well. When smoking a cigarette every 2.5–5.5 hr, the heart rate change is about 90% of that expected from a single cigarette.

Fifteen subjects performed on a bicycle ergometer under control and marijuana conditions. Numerous measurements of cardiopulmonary function revealed that higher work loads could be performed before marijuana smoking than after smoking. The limiting factor during exercise may be that maximum heart rates are obtained at relatively low work loads. Electrocardiographic changes occur in a high percentage of subjects when marijuana and exercise are combined.

Hemispheric Dominance Studies

Marijuana may alter the relative roles of the right and left cerebral hemispheres during cognition. The drug was found to produce a differential effect on tasks that are lateralized to the right or left hemisphere. Performance on left lateralized, verbal-analytic tests was significantly impaired. Performance on right hemisphere, nonverbal-holistic tasks was significantly improved.

Subjects with a variable distribution of functions between their hemispheres seem to show significantly different patterns of response to marijuana intoxication. When the subject sample is split into "high-lateralized" and "low-lateralized" groups based on their nonintoxicated dichrotic listening performance, the high-lateralized group shows less impairment of verbal-analytic abilities and more enhancement of visual closure ability when intoxicated. In contrast, the low-lateralized group tends to show a pattern of general impairment. Visualization tasks thought to involve both hemispheres are markedly impaired by marijuana intoxication in both low and high lateralizers, whereas moderate lateralizers do not show impairment.

Electroencephalographic Studies

The computer-analyzed electroencephalogram can distinguish between abstinent marijuana smokers and age-matched nonusers. Marijuana users have greater δ (1–3 Hz) band power. In the θ band (4–7 Hz), the phase angle (lead/lag) relationship between wave forms is greater in nonsmokers between frontotemporal and parietooccipital linkages. In the α band (8–13 Hz), the nonsmokers show greater activity, while in the higher bands (14–25 Hz), the phase angles are similar to those in the θ band. Heavy smokers can, with lesser accuracy, be differentiated from moderate smokers. Moderate users have an electroencephalographic pattern that places them between heavy users and nonusers.[12]

Pronounced differences exist between pre- and postintoxication states. Smoking is associated with an α shift downward and a narrowing of bandwidth.

Radioimmunoassays

Utilizing a radioimmunoassay technique, urinary THC and 11-carboxy-THC peaks were determined 2–4 hr after smoking. Small amounts are detectable for 48 hr after the last use of marijuana. THC and 11-carboxy-THC plasma levels peak in 15–30 min, with a range of 50–150 ng/ml[13] (TABLE 6).

SUMMARY

The UCLA cannabis project has provided several interesting observations that contribute to our knowledge about this plant and its constituents. Some of the findings (reduction in intraocular pressure, bronchodilation) may have therapeutic significance in the future. Certain results (testosterone lowering, airway narrowing after heavy use) indicate that side effects are also a possibility. Other data (unchanged immune response, lack of chromosomal alterations) seem to controvert the reports of other investigators. Still other information obtained (hemispheric lateralization, electroencephalographic changes) appears to represent new knowledge about the effects of cannabis on humans.

TABLE 6

PSYCHOLOGIC PARAMETERS

Days	1–11	12–75	76–82	83–91	92–94
Subjective high		daily			
Work assignments (language learning and number addition, alternating days)	XXXXXXXXXXXX	XXXXXXXXXXXXXXXXXXXXX			
Psychosocial adaptation	2				93
Psychological testing					
WAIS	2			88	
Trails and mazes	2	54		88	
Rod and frame	2			88	
Raven	2			88	
PRI	2			88	
Rotter	2			89	
ACL	2	33 68		89	
Beck inventory	2	33 68		89	
MMPI		54		89	
Brain hemisphere dominance		57 58	80 81		
	preintoxi- cation 11 days	intoxication period 64 days	nonin- toxica- tion 7 days	intoxi- cation 9 days	detoxi- fication 3 days

REFERENCES

1. COHEN, S., P. LESSIN, P. HAHN, et al. 1976. The 94 day marijuana study. In The Pharmacology of Cannabis. S. Szara & M. Braude, Eds. The Raven Press. New York, N.Y. In press.
2. TASHKIN, D. P., B. J. SHAPIRO & I. M. FRANK. 1974. Acute physiological effects of smoked marijuana and oral Δ-9-tetrahydrocannabinol in healthy young men. N. Engl. J. Med. 289: 336–341.
3. TASHKIN, D. P., B. J. SHAPIRO & I. M. FRANK. 1974. Acute effects of smoked marijuana and oral Δ-9-tetrahydrocannabinol on specific airway conductance in asthmatic subjects. Amer. Rev. Resp. Diseases 109: 420–428.
4. TASHKIN, D. P., B. J. SHAPIRO, Y. E. LEE, et al. 1975. Effects of smoked marijuana in experimentally induced asthma. Amer. Rev. Resp. Diseases 112: 377–386.
5. HEPLER, R. S. & I. M. FRANK. 1971. Marijuana smoking and introacular pressure. J. Amer. Med. Ass. 217 (10): 1392.
6. HEPLER, R. S., I. M. FRANK & R. J. PETRUS. 1976. Ocular effects of marijuana smoking. In The Pharmacology of Cannabis. S. Szara & M. Braude, Eds. The Raven Press. New York, N.Y. In press.
7. MATSUYAMA, S. & L. F. JARVIK. 1976. Chromosome studies before and after supervised marijuana smoking. In The Pharmacology of Cannabis. S. Szara & M. Braude, Eds. The Raven Press. New York, N.Y. In press.
8. SILVERSTEIN, M. J. & P. LESSIN. 1974. Normal skin test responses in chronic marijuana users. Science 186: 740, 741.
9. RACHELEFSKY, G. S., G. OPELZ, M. R. MICKEY, et al. 1976. Intact humoral and cell mediated immunity in chronic marijuana smoking. To be published.

10. KOLODNY, R. C., P. LESSIN, G. TORO, et al. 1976. Depression of plasma testosterone with acute marijuana administration. In The Pharmacology of Cannabis. S. Szara & M. Braude, Eds. The Raven Press, New York, N.Y. In press.

11. HARSHMAN, R. A., H. J. CRAWFORD & E. HECHT. 1976. Marijuana, cognitive style and "hemispheric dominance." In The Therapeutic Potential of Marijuana. S. Cohen & R. C. Stillman, Eds. Plenum Publishing Corporation. New York, N.Y. In press.

12. HANLEY, J., E. D. TYRELL & P. M. HAHN. 1976. Computer analyses of electro-encephalographic data from human users of Cannabis sativa. In The Therapeutic Potential of Marijuana. S. Cohen & R. C. Stillman, Eds. Plenum Publishing Corporation. New York, N.Y. In press.

13. GROSS, S. J., J. R. SOARES, S. R. WONG, et al. 1974. Marijuana metabolites measured by a radioimmune technique. Nature (London) 252(5484): 581, 582.

CLINICAL STUDIES OF CANNABIS TOLERANCE
AND DEPENDENCE *

Reese T. Jones, Neal Benowitz, and John Bachman

Department of Psychiatry
University of California, San Francisco
San Francisco, California 94143

INTRODUCTION

Statements like cannabis-related "tolerance and physical dependence do not occur" are commonly made in standard pharmacology texts.[1] The summary report of the National Commission on Marihuana and Drug Abuse, when discussing the "addiction potential" of marijuana concluded that "fact and fancy have become irrationally mixed regarding marijuana's physiological and psychological properties. Marijuana clearly is not in the same category as heroin insofar as its physiologic and psychological effects are concerned. In a word, cannabis does not lead to physical dependence."[2] A recent book that describes extensive chronic marijuana studies in man does not even mention the possibility of dependence.[3] Yet, after a comprehensive review of various aspects of cannabis tolerance and dependence, Wikler thinks the evidence indicates that both tolerance and dependence can develop in man.[4]

For some years, we and others have noted, in outpatient studies, that very frequent cannabis users show diminished drug effects when compared to less frequent users,[5, 6] though not all investigators agree.[7] Such indirect evidence of tolerance, of course, could be explained by several alternate hypotheses: personality or genetic differences, other drug use, and so on.

Clinical reports of an abstinence syndrome associated with cannabis use are rare. Occasionally, very frequent cannabis users tested in our laboratories have reported the sudden onset of irritability, restlessness, insomnia, and perspiration after cessation of regular use.[6] Other investigators have reported similar signs and symptoms in small groups of cannabis users [8] and in primates after prolonged high doses of cannabis.[9-12] Such reports from outpatients should be viewed with some skepticism because of the possibility that these symptoms represent withdrawal from other drugs or concurrent illness. Possible species differences in drug response make the animal data open to question. Williams *et al.* reported several years ago that experimental subjects given frequent doses of cannabis or synhexyl compound reported a jittery feeling, insomnia, decreased appetite, weight loss, and autonomic symptoms when the experimental drug administration was suddenly stopped.[13]

In more recent studies of chronic marijuana smoking, Mendelson *et al.*'s experimental subjects experienced rapid weight loss, decreased appetite, tremor, increased urine specific gravity, and irritability after a 21-day period of frequent marijuana smoking. However, the signs and symptoms were not interpreted

* Supported by Grants DA00033 and DA4RG012 and Contract HSM–42–73–181 from the National Institute on Drug Abuse and National Institute of Mental Health Career Scientist Award KO2MH32904 to R.T.J.

by those investigators as withdrawal symptoms or evidence of physical dependence.[3, 14]

Some of the inconsistency in the preceding reports might be explained by considering what we know about other more well-studied drugs. In a general review of the determinants of tolerance and dependence, Seevers and Deneau make a simple but important point often overlooked or forgotten when discussing cannabis tolerance and dependence.[15] They point out that conditions for *optimal* development of dependence require "continual neuronal exposure" to the drug without interruption. Failure to recognize this requirement has led to "erroneous conclusions from poorly designed experiments." They were mainly discussing opiates, but the same might be said about cannabis. Other general reviews indicate that with a variety of sedative-hypnotic drugs and opiates continued "around the clock," chronic intoxication is necessary to most clearly demonstrate abstinence phenomena.[1, 15-19] Even with opiates, ordinary conditions of clinical or illicit administration are rarely adequate to produce maximal dependence.[15] For example, the standard stabilization dose of morphine in the Lexington studies was 200–400 mg per day in four equal doses.[1, 15] Nowadays, this dose sounds like a rather large one, but in the Lexington studies, it yielded only a midgrade intensity of dependence.[1]

There appears to be a "safe interval" between doses of opiates and other psychoactive drugs at which tolerance and dependence are not exhibited. This interval may vary from hours to days, depending on the drug, its disposition, and kinetics.[1, 16] With any psychoactive drug, there appears to be a certain dose level below which measurable physical dependence does not develop, even after prolonged and repeated administration, and below which tolerance, if evident at all, is minimal. On the other hand, there is virtually no psychoactive drug that has been experimentally tested in what Seevers and Deneau would term "adequate experiments" that does not produce dependence and show tolerance.[1, 15, 16]

We designed cannabis experiments with optimal conditions for the development of tolerance and dependence. The dosage *range* was selected to produce a level of intoxication similar to that experienced in the outside world. But, at the same time, and in contrast to previous research, the dosage *schedule* maintained this level of intoxication for prolonged periods of time. Other studies reported at this Conference used equivalent cannabis doses.[20] For example, the smoked dose consumed by Mendelson et al.'s subjects was in some cases in excess of equivalent oral doses given to our subjects. Though Mendelson et al.'s study used an adequate *dose* for a well-designed experiment on tolerance and dependence, they used an inappropriate *dose schedule*.[15] The subjects in that study tended to distribute their self-selected dosage, so that for fairly long periods of time each day, the "continual neuronal exposure to the drug" was probably lacking.

With proper attention to the factors that produce optimal conditions for the development of tolerance and dependence to cannabis,[1, 15, 16] it should not be surprising that both occur quite predictably in man.

METHODS AND MATERIALS

Subjects

This report is based on experience with 53 male volunteer subjects tested at various times from 1973 through 1975. The subjects were hospitalized for

21–42-day periods on the Clinical Research Ward of the Langley Porter Neuropsychiatric Institute. All were experienced cannabis users recruited through newspaper advertisements. An extensive screening process, including informational meetings, pretesting, and appropriate clinical and laboratory examinations, enabled us to accept only fully informed subjects thought to be in good physical and emotional health. We considered and rejected three to four subjects for every one finally accepted. The low subject dropout rate (two of 55) indicated that we were successfully informing potential subjects what the study involved.

The volunteers' ages ranged from 21 to 31 years, with a mean of 25 years. The mean education level was 14 ± 1.9 years. All had extensive past experience with cannabis. All smoked it at least twice weekly. The average subject used cannabis regularly for 5 ± 2.3 years. Most used marijuana daily. They drank beer or wine three to four times weekly. The individuals selected had only minimal past use of opiates or stimulants.

Subjects were paid $25 per day during the period of hospitalization.

The study had the approval of the Committee on Human Experimentation at the University of California, San Francisco.

Setting

Groups of two or four subjects were studied while living full time on a 21-bed general psychiatric unit planned and staffed for a variety of clinical research activities. The other patients living on the unit represented the gamut of acute psychiatric illnesses. Always under direct staff supervision, the research subjects had access to the facilities of a 100-bed psychiatric hospital and participated in many of the activities with the regular patients. Laboratory research testing occupied most weekday daytime hours. The usual recreational facilities (e.g., television, records, games, books, swimming, recreational therapy, and shop) were available at other times. They slept in two- or four-bed rooms. They were fed a regular hospital diet but could supplement it with additional foods or snacks if they wished.

Experimental Design and Drug Schedule

Subjects served as their own control in a double-blind crossover design that compared placebo conditions with various doses of tetrahydrocannabinol (THC) or crude cannabis extract. Both the effects of relatively pure THC and a crude cannabis extract were investigated with similar research protocols. Eleven subjects were given the crude extract, and 42 subjects were given pure THC. The differences in the effects of the two treatments were small and inconsistent, so that for the purposes of this report, results from all subjects will be lumped together.

The oral doses of marijuana were similar to those used in outpatient investigations in several laboratories.[21] However, we administered the drug every 4 hr, because the major effects of such doses generally last for about 4 hr.[21] Because of ethical and medical considerations, doses acceptable to most of our volunteer subjects were selected. As is the case with any psychoactive drug, certain individuals found the dose to be in excess of what they preferred. On the other hand, as many or more subjects felt that the doses we administered were less than desired.

Drugs

Subjects received either delta-9-tetrahydrocannabinol (Δ^9-THC) or crude cannabis extract that contained the same amount of THC plus other naturally occurring cannabinoids. Four were switched from THC to crude extract during the experimental phase; the rest received one drug or the other. The THC was administered orally in capsules that contained 10–30 mg of THC in sesame oil. Crude cannabis extract was administered orally in gelatin capsules that contained the equivalent of 10–30 mg of THC with the extract dissolved in 0.2–0.4 cm^3 of 95% ethanol solution. Identical-looking placebo gelatin capsules contained only sesame oil or ethanol.

During the entire period of hospitalization, the subjects received, every 4 hr, capsules of either placebo, THC, or crude extract under double-blind conditions. The exact number of days that a subject received the placebo or a drug varied slightly, but we always provided for a drug-free drying out period prior to beginning THC or crude extract administration, followed by doses of the drug given so as to produce mild to moderate degrees of continuous intoxication and followed again at unpredictable times by another placebo period. Six subjects were switched from drug to placebo, back to drug, and back to placebo again to examine the interaction between prolonged hospitalization and the onset and cessation of various symptoms. Two subjects had their THC dose doubled at the time when they appeared to have developed maximum tolerance.

In general, after a 3–7-day period of receiving placebo under double-blind conditions, the THC or crude extract was started at a dose of 10 mg every 4 hr. The dose level was increased to 30 mg every 4 hr over a 1–5-day interval. Twenty-one subjects received an additional 30-mg dose at bedtime. Thus, the maximum dose level was 210 mg per day. On a per kilogram basis, the total 24-hr maximum dose varied from 2.2 to 4.2 mg/kg, with a mean of 3.1 mg/kg. The fixed dose of 180–210 mg per day then continued for an 11–21-day interval, followed by an abrupt switch to placebo for a 5–9-day interval. The individual doses were usually given at 8 AM, 12 PM, 4 PM, 8 PM, midnight, and 4 AM. In the rare event of unpleasant or unacceptable drug effects, a dose was omitted or decreased temporarily. This action was necessary with six subjects over only 23 occasions among the almost 4500 drug doses administered.

Neither patients, ward staff, nor research staff were aware of the exact sequence of drug and placebo. An attempt was made to vary the drug dose change points by a few days. Pairs of subjects were on the same dose schedule, but the schedule would vary for the groups of four. At the doses used, there was seldom any question in the subject's mind as to when the placebo stopped and the drug was started. There was usually very little question when the drug was stopped because of the rapid disappearance of both subjective and physiologic effects.

The crude cannabis extract was an ethanol extract that contained 29% Δ^9-THC, 1.5% cannabinol, and 2.8% cannabidiol. The pure THC contained 96% THC, with the remainder being trace amounts of other cannabinoids, including Δ^8-THC, cannabichromene, and other unidentified substances. The drugs were obtained from the National Institute on Drug Abuse. Assays for THC content were repeated throughout the study by use of gas chromatographic techniques.

At various stages of the study, some subjects smoked, under standard conditions at a single daily session, varied numbers of machine-rolled 1-g marijuana cigarettes that contained 2.2% THC.

Because of the slight variations in the exact dose increase schedules for certain subjects, much of the data in this report are grouped according to the phase of study so as to allow for easier comparison between subjects. Each stage referred to consisted of 3 days. For any given measure, the mean values from each individual over 3 days were treated as a single observation, and changes were examined for statistical significance, generally by use of repeated measures analysis of variance. The stages of the study were defined as follows:

Stage	Definition
Predrug	3 days immediately preceding onset of THC administration. This stage began 2–4 days after admission. Placebos were given from the time of admission.
Acceleration	first 3 days of THC administration. All patients started on 10 mg every 4 hr, but some had their dose increased to the maximum 30 mg every 4 hr at a faster rate than others. Thus, the total acceleration stage could vary from 2 to 5 days.
Maximum dose 1 (max dose 1)	first block of 3 days after the acceleration stage, where 30 mg of THC was given every 4 hr
Maximum dose 2 (max dose 2)	second block of 3 days after max dose 1
Maximum dose 3 (max dose 3)	last 3 days on the 30 mg every 4 hr dose schedule. Note that 4 to 10 days could intervene between the last day of max dose 2 and the first day of max dose 3. All patients were on a fixed dose of 30 mg of THC every 4 hr during the max dose 1–3 stages.
Postdrug 1 (post 1)	first 3 days on placebo after the last THC dose
Postdrug 2 (post 2)	next 3 days on placebo after post 1

Examination of individual-day data plots was done with all subjects and showed either no change between max dose 2 and max dose 3 or, with most subjects and most measures, a monotonic change consistent with the development of tolerance. Subjects returned to the laboratory for interviews and testing 1 week after discharge. A majority have remained in contact with us for up to 2 years after testing.

A great variety of behavioral, subjective, physiologic, and biochemical measures were obtained prior to, during, and after the period of THC administration.[22–26] Details as to exact methodology and results cannot be given here because of lack of space.

Subjects were involved in testing of various types from approximately 7 AM to 5 or 6 PM every weekday. Many measures were also obtained on weekends. When scheduling the repeated testing, attention was paid to the drug dose schedule and to the possibility of diurnal variations. We attempted to pay close attention to even the small details of making simple measurements. For example, body weight measures were always obtained between 7 and 8 AM with the subject wearing the same clothing. Oral body temperature was determined before the subject smoked his morning cigarettes or drank liquids. Vital signs were obtained after a fixed period of inactivity so as to attempt to obtain truly resting levels. Both supine and standing blood pressure measures were obtained. Specimens for biochemical measures were taken at 7 AM before the subjects left their beds. The skin temperature was measured in a temperature-controlled room at the fingertip by use of a digital thermocouple. Salivary flow was total unstimulated flow collected over a 5-min period at about 10 AM each day. Intraocular pressure was measured twice daily with an American Optical Company noncontact tonometer. Hand tremor was measured each morning with a Grass accelerometer and was quantified with computer power spectrum analysis.

The subjects used several pencil and paper self-report questionnaires to report aspects of mood and subjective state, including the Profile of Mood States, the Symptom Checklist-90, and the Subjective Drug Effects Questionnaire (SDEQ). The results of the testing with the SDEQ are described in some detail in this report.

The SDEQ is a 271-item symptom checklist. It was developed to describe the effects produced by a variety of psychoactive drugs, particularly psychedelic drugs.[27] In our study, the SDEQ was slightly modified to allow subjects to rate intensity of each symptom on a five-point scale of intensity, instead of using yes-no responses. Zero was "not present"; and five was "extremely intense." The SDEQ was administered every third day approximately 1 hr after the 4-PM dose of medication. Subjects were instructed to rate the presence or absence and intensity of any symptoms experienced during the preceding 3 days. Their normal nondrugged state was to be the basis of comparison. The patterns of SDEQ responses from 26 subjects were examined. The 89 most commonly experienced symptoms (those responded to by more than 40% of the subjects) were selected for further analysis. A principal components factor analysis of these 89 items with a Varimax rotation generated seven factors whose cumulative proportion of the total variance equaled 48%. Only the first three rotated factors contained more than 12 items with loadings of more than 0.35. The three sets of SDEQ items derived from the factor analysis and making up factors I–III were scored by use of the five-point scale of intensity as scales I–III. The responses to each item in a particular set were summed to yield a scale score.

The patient's ward behavior was rated at the end of each day during the evening shift by two members of the Research Ward nursing staff by use of the Nurse's Observation Scale for Inpatient Evaluation (NOSIE-30). This was a 30-item scale that allows for measurement of both positive and negative shifts in ward behavior.

Details about these and some of the other measures have been described in a series of publications.[22-26]

RESULTS

Each subject made an estimate of his level of intoxication hourly when awake. Zero was defined as sober, and 100 was defined as a level of intoxication as intense as that ever experienced after smoking or ingesting cannabis. The average ratings made at 10 AM are shown in FIGURE 1. This was a time of day when most subjects appeared to be maximally intoxicated. After receiving placebo capsules for 5 days, the slow dose increase group was given 10 mg of THC or crude cannabis extract every 4 hr for 4 days, then abruptly was switched to 30 mg at 8 AM on Day 6. That dose continued through Day 24. After the initial placebo period, the rapid dose increase subjects were given 10 mg of THC or crude cannabis extract every 4 hr for a 24-hr period on Day 6, then abruptly were started on 30 mg every 4 hr on Day 7.

Several important aspects of the development of tolerance to cannabis are illustrated by these simple subjective "high" ratings. Tolerance develops rapidly. The level of intoxication 2 hr after the first 30-mg dose is much less ($p < 0.01$) in the group previously exposed to only 96 hr of minimal but continuous intoxication. By Day 12, there was no difference in level of intoxication between the

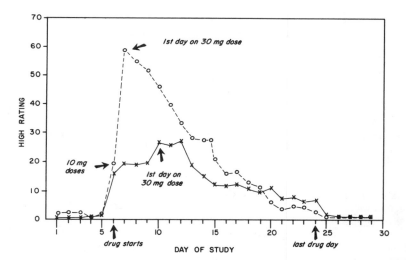

FIGURE 1. Daily self-reports of level of intoxication ("high") made by subjects treated with a rapid and a slower increase in dose of THC. Zero was defined as non-intoxicated, and 100 was defined as the maximal intoxication ever experienced after cannabis. Points are mean values for 10-AM ratings. Doses prior to the indicated first 30-mg dose of THC were 10 mg given orally every 4 hr. ×, Slow dose increase ($n = 12$); ○, rapid dose increase ($n = 10$).

two subject groups. When the drug was stopped on Day 24 (usually at 4 or 8 PM) and placebo capsules were substituted, all subjects quickly lost any feelings of intoxication.

The average intensity of intoxication produced by these oral doses of THC or cannabis extract was not greater than most subjects' past experience with the drugs outside of the laboratory. The degree of intoxication was similar to that experienced by subjects smoking marijuana at self-selected doses in the Boston chronic smoking studies.[3, 14, 20] Most subjects reported significant decreases in level of intoxication prior to each 4-hr dose. The high ratings are consistent with those made by outpatient research subjects given similar oral doses by other investigators.[21]

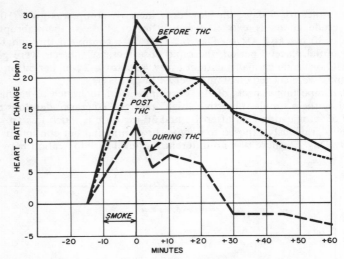

FIGURE 2. Mean heart rate increases after smoking a marijuana cigarette that contained 20 mg of THC. Smoking occurred before chronic oral THC doses were begun, during oral THC administration, when clinical evidence of tolerance was just becoming apparent, and 20–48 hr after the last oral dose of THC. Time after the 10-min period of controlled smoking is indicated. The mean values are for eight subjects.

A similar pattern of decreased drug effect over time was evident on a variety of drug-induced physiologic alterations (salivary flow, heart rate, blood pressure, intraocular pressure). Thus, the pattern of change in subjective high ratings probably does not simply reflect different criteria adopted by the slow dose increase group of subjects because of more experimental drug experience before first receiving the initial 30-mg dose.

Evidence of cross tolerance between the effects of smoked marijuana and the oral THC doses is shown on FIGURE 2. The mean heart rate increase after smoking a 1-g marijuana cigarette that contained 20 mg of THC was measured three times during the study. The "before THC" session was during the first placebo period. The "during THC" smoking session occurred between Days 9 and 12, when the six subjects were beginning to show evidence of tolerance to the oral doses, as judged by the subjective high ratings. The "post-THC" marijuana smoking session was during the final placebo phase 20–48 hr after the last oral dose of THC. The diminished heart rate increase and shortened duration of change after smoking a marijuana cigarette during the oral THC administration are significant ($p < 0.001$). The rapid loss of this aspect of tolerance is illustrated by the almost normal heart rate increase induced by smoking only 20–48 hr after the last oral THC dose. Skin temperature decreases after smoking show a similar pattern of change. Thus, with this dose schedule, tolerance, as measured by both subjective and physiologic changes, is quickly acquired and quickly lost.

Tolerance developed to many physiologic effects. The changes followed a time course similar to that of subjective intoxication judgments. The magnitude of some of the changes listed in TABLE 1 are small, but all are statistically significant when carefully measured under controlled conditions. The cardiovascular changes have been reported in detail elsewhere.[25, 26] It is important to note that tolerance does *not* develop to blood pressure decreases measured in the supine position. Thus, one can see tolerance or not on a blood pressure measure, depending on the recording conditions. The finger skin temperature decrease initially is 4–7° C, probably due to peripheral vasoconstriction. This explanation could account for the common complaint of cold extremities and the skin pallor sometimes seen during cannabis intoxication. The initial body temperature increase is only 0.3° C when carefully measured by oral morning temperatures on awaking, but the drug-related increase and subsequent return to predrug levels as the THC or cannabis is continued are significant (p < 0.001). When THC is begun, the initial salivary flow decrease returns to predrug levels more slowly than do the other measures, as does the initial 2–3-mm intraocular pressure decrease.

The initial cannabis-induced electroencephalographic (EEG) alpha slowing and auditory-evoked potential amplitude decreases are no longer evident after 10 days on continued 30-mg doses. The drug-related sleep EEG eye movement decreases are of very large magnitude and have been described in detail elsewhere.[24] The initial increases in sleep duration and improved quality (both as judged by the subjects' self-reports and by nursing staff observations) gradually disappear as the drug is continued and return to predrug levels by the end of 15–20 days of chronic cannabis ingestion. The ability to visually track a moving target and to perform on cognitive and psychomotor tasks shows initial drug-related impairments and then returns to baseline or even better than predrug performance levels, despite continuous drug dosage. The nursing staff's observations of drug-related motor and cognitive retardation and decrements in general ability to function reflect a similar pattern best explained by the development of tolerance.

A temporary increase in dose level was associated with the temporary reappearance of the drug effects. Six subjects were tested over a 6-week hospitalization period, when the active drugs were alternately started and stopped to separate the effects of prolonged hospitalization and repeated testing from specific drug effects. The pattern of response was more consistent with both rapid acquisition of and loss of tolerance rather than with just the effects of hospitalization, repeated testings, and the simple passage of time.

As is the case with almost all other drugs, tolerance does not develop to all drug effects.[1, 15, 16] For example, there was no tolerance to the cannabis-related weight gain or the hematocrit and hemoglobin decreases. This is probably due to the sustained increase in plasma volume. The increased plasma volume probably accounts for the appearance of tolerance to the orthostatic blood pressure drops. More puzzling is a serum bilirubin decrease and a plasma testosterone

TABLE 1

TOLERANCE DEVELOPS TO CANNABIS-INDUCED

Mood changes	EEG slowing
Tachycardia	EEG evoked potential alterations
Orthostatic hypotension	sleep EEG changes
Skin temperature decrease	sleep time and quality
Body temperature increase	eye tracking
Salivary flow decrease	psychomotor task performance
Intraocular pressure decrease	ward behavior alterations

decrease, which persist unchanged during the period of THC administration. Of course, with higher doses or longer periods of drug administration, tolerance may be evident with these measures.

A more detailed description of self-reported subjective drug effects is provided in TABLE 2, which lists SDEQ items that comprise factors I–III derived

TABLE 2

SUBJECTIVE DRUG EFFECTS QUESTIONNAIRE ITEMS
THAT COMPRISE FACTORS I–III

Factor I: Sedation
  Thinking seemed fuzzier
  Thoughts moved slower
  Can't hold onto thoughts as well
  Harder to concentrate
  Losing sense of time
  Speech sounded slower and more slurred
  Felt like it's harder to talk
  Liked to talk less
  Harder than usual to describe present feelings
    in words
  Movements seemed slower
  Whole body and arms, legs and head, especially,
    felt heavier, more sluggish, and stuffier
  Body felt more unsteady and less under control
  Arms or legs felt weaker
  Stomach felt heavier
  Mouth and throat felt drier
  Lips felt numb
  Eyesight worse and more blurred than usual
  Eyelids felt as if they were closing
  Felt sleepier, dreamier, dopey, high, and dizzy

Factor II: Good Feelings
  Felt more at peace with the
    world
  Had a greater feeling of love
    for others
  Liked having people around
    more
  Felt more relaxed
  Felt extreme well-being
  Thinking seemed clearer
  Felt it's easier to talk
  Liked to talk more
  Noticing things around you
    more
  Seeing the comical side of
    things more
  Felt happier and sillier
  Liked answering these ques-
    tions

Factor III: Tension-Arousal
  Body felt worse and more
    tense than usual
  Felt more nervous and tense
  Felt worse than usual
  Noticing bodily feelings more
    than usual
  Body more energetic
  Body felt hotter
  Skin felt more perspiring
  Stomach felt more jittery
  Less hungry than usual
  Had more things on your mind
  Noticing feelings more than
    usual
  Felt more irritable

from a factor analysis of the 271 items in the SDEQ. The items in Factor I, "sedation," include symptoms commonly reported by individuals intoxicated by cannabis. Factor II is a collection of what might be termed "good feelings." Factor III includes some symptoms not commonly thought to be associated with cannabis intoxication and describes a "tense and aroused state."

The intensity and differing time courses of the symptoms that comprise the three factors are given in TABLE 3. The symptoms in factor I were most intense

TABLE 3

MEANS AND STANDARD ERRORS OF SDEQ SCORES AT VARIOUS STUDY STAGES

Items in:	Stages of Study (3 days/stage)					
	Predrug	Max Dose 1	Max Dose 2	Max Dose 3	Postdrug 1	Postdrug 2
Factor 1, sedation Score range: 0–130	7.7±0.9	38.9±1.6 *	31.3±2.4 * †	18.3±1.1 * †	7.9±0.8 †	7.0±0.9 †
Factor II, good feelings Score range: 0–52	5.8±0.9	6.9±1.3	6.6±1.2	9.7±1.6 *	8.3±1.3	10.0±1.4 *
Factor III, tension-anxiety Score range: 0–56	4.0±0.8	8.5±1.2 *	7.2±1.1	5.3±0.6	11.9±1.0 *	12.0±1.5 *
Number of subjects	24	22	26	23	19	22

* Significant difference (p <0.05) when compared to predrug.
† Significant difference (p <0.05) when compared to max dose 1.

when the maximum dose of THC was started. As the THC or crude cannabis extract was continued, there was a progressive lessening of their intensity. Note that by this measure of drug effects, the subjects were nowhere near a maximum intoxication level. Ratings of "extremely intense" on the 30 SDEQ items that comprise factor I would result in a total score of 120. The average score of 39 reflects only modest levels of symptom intensity.

The cluster of symptoms included in factor II is more difficult to interpret. Their intensity was never great (average of 10 on a possible 52-point scale) and gradually increased during the study independently of the beginning or cessation of drug administration. The symptoms may represent drug effects to which tolerance does not develop but, more likely, may simply be evidence of adaptation to the study and the hospital. The absence of a clear change in intensity when the drug was started and stopped makes the interpretation of the symptoms in factor II difficult without a drug-free comparison group.

The time course of the symptoms that comprise factor III illustrates some of the subjective aspects of the withdrawal syndrome after a period of prolonged cannabis intoxication. The feelings of tension, irritability, and other symptoms were mild (only a score of 12 on a 56-point scale) but appeared in a significantly greater intensity during the postdrug period ($p < 0.05$). The increase in "tension-arousal" in the max dose 1 drug stage probably is a reflection of a biphasic action of cannabis, particularly evident when the dose is increased rapidly.

All subjects had a morning interview when inquiry was made as to any unusual symptoms or complaints. TABLE 4 lists the percentages of subjects who complained of various symptoms during the different stages of the study. "Predrug" refers to the first placebo period; "early drug" is the first and "late drug" is the last half of the THC administration phase. "Postdrug" is the placebo

TABLE 4

SYMPTOMS DURING PHASES OF DRUG ADMINISTRATION
(47 SUBJECTS)

	Predrug (%)	Early Drug (%)	Late Drug (%)	Postdrug (%)
Disturbed sleep	28	6	4	89
Decreased appetite	6	9	9	81
Restlessness	4	11	6	89
Irritability	15	23	9	62
Sweating	2	4	6	55
Chills	4	4	6	40
Feverish feeling	2	6	2	38
Nausea	9	23	4	34
Muscle spasm	0	17	0	17
Tremulousness	2	15	2	21
Loose stools	2	0	2	23
Abdominal distress	0	9	2	36
Stuffy nose	2	2	2	11
Hiccups	0	0	2	17
Wild dreams	0	0	0	19

TABLE 5

SIGNS AND SYMPTOMS OF ABSTINENCE AFTER ABRUPT CESSATION
OF PROLONGED CANNABIS INTOXICATION

Mood changes	hyperactivity
Disturbed sleep	hiccups (rare)
Decreased appetite	nasal congestion (rare)
Restlessness	weight loss
Irritability	hemoconcentration
Perspiration	salivation
Chills	tremor
Feverish feeling	loose bowel movements
Nausea	body temperature increase
Abdominal distress	sleep EEG eye movement rebound
Tremulousness	waking EEG changes
	intraocular pressure increase

period, beginning at 8 AM on the day after cessation of THC. The drug was usually stopped at 4 or 8 PM. The Table lists the percentages of subjects who complained of at least one occurrence of a given symptom during each period. The intensity of complaints varied. The tolerance that develops to some of the initial drug effects is reflected in the diminished complaints of irritability, nausea, and tremulousness as the drug was continued.

A summary of physiologic and psychologic changes that follow abrupt cessation of THC or cannabis administration appears in TABLE 5. The weight loss and hemoconcentration occur mainly in the first 48 hr of abstinence and may amount to 6 kg in some cases. The marked sleep EEG changes, which consisted of eye movement and rapid eye movement sleep increases with little change in stage-4 sleep, begin as soon as 4 hr after the last drug dose. Increases in salivary flow (100%), fine hand tremor, and body temperature (0.3° C) peak at 24–48 hr after the drug is stopped. Hyperactivity is always noted by both ward nursing and research staff, particularly during the first 24 hr off the drug. The waking EEG changes are inconsistent but when present consist of mildly paroxysmal records with enhanced photic driving and buildup of amplitude during hyperventilation. The intraocular pressure increase is small (2–3 mm) but consistent. Most of the changes have reverted to baseline by 96 hr. All can be reversed by administration of smoked or oral doses of cannabis or THC. The withdrawal syndrome appeared to run its course in 72–96 hr, although sleep disturbances that lasted at least 7 nights were reported by a few subjects.

DISCUSSION

When administered according to a schedule that produces continuous intoxication, modest oral doses of THC or cannabis extract produce rapid and profound tolerance to many psychologic and physiologic effects. A predictable pattern of signs and both physical and psychologic symptoms followed cessation of drug ingestion. The 10–30-mg oral doses administered in this study are well within the range used in many outpatient studies, where only mild clinical effects are noted.[21] If allowance is made for the difference in potency between oral and smoked marijuana, the doses and levels of intoxication are quite comparable to those self-selected by similar subjects in the Boston chronic studies.[14, 20]

The period of intoxication produced by an oral dose of THC lasts approximately 4 hr. Thus, the doses administered every 4 hr, in effect, "bathe the neuronal pool constantly." This maximizes the degree to which tolerance and dependence develop to a variety of psychoactive drugs.[15] The subjects in Mendelson et al.'s studies developed less tolerance but did demonstrate some withdrawal symptoms, even though intoxicated for only a portion of each waking day during the 21-day study.[3, 14, 20] Subjects in those studies showed evidence of tolerance on cardiovascular measures, caloric intake, and weight gain. They demonstrated some aspects of a mild abstinence syndrome, particularly anorexia, weight loss, and tremor. As with short-acting opiates like meperidine, ultra short-acting barbiturates, and rapidly metabolized minor tranquilizers, frequent dosage is probably necessary to best demonstrate a tolerance and dependence to cannabis.

We can only speculate about the mechanisms by which tolerance develops. Some of our results provide indirect evidence that the tolerance is not mainly metabolic or dispositional in origin. If it were, the rapid administration of cannabis by smoking, which is virtually identical to an intravenous injection, should produce similar maximal effects during the time of maximal tolerance but with a shorter time course of effects.[1] We found that smoking a marijuana cigarette at a time when a subject is maximally tolerant produces no measurable effects. Thus, there is probably a large functional component to cannabis tolerance. Indirect mechanisms that produce tolerance, for example, the homeostatic changes that involve increased plasma volume and disappearance of orthostatic blood pressure drops, continue well after tolerance develops, as measured by other indices. This pattern of change would be unlikely if there were marked reductions in ambient drug levels because of metabolic or dispositional changes. As with other psychoactive drugs, there is probably a combination of metabolic, dispositional, and functional changes that account for tolerance, with the functional changes accounting for a greater portion of the change.

Other explanations for the pattern of change that we see should be briefly considered. Rather than using a separate placebo-treated comparison group, subjects were used as their own control throughout the period of hospitalization. We elected to use the latter control rather than a comparison group because of a need to deal with small samples and to minimize the problem of individual differences in response. In each and every case, characteristic changes were noted when the placebo was stopped and the drug started or when the drug was stopped and the placebo started, regardless of whether this changeover occurred on Day 4, 5, or 6 or Day 15, 20, or 30. These physiologic and subjective changes, always time-locked precisely with the beginning and cessation of drug administration or change in dose, argue against the patterns of change in signs or symptoms that represent the simple sequence effects, habituation, or adaptation that stems from the prolonged testing and hospitalization.

The issue of observer and subject bias is important, because the effects of the doses used made much of the double blind not so blind. The bias on the part of the subjects was clearly in the direction of believing that tolerance could not develop to cannabis and believing even more strongly that dependence would not develop. Thus, we expected the subjects to minimize the evidence for tolerance and dependence. Most of the subjects were aware that evidence for dependence on cannabis might be misinterpreted or misused by forces that attempted to control or suppress the drug. That they reported accurately and reliably even minimal symptoms speaks well for the volunteer subjects' integrity and involvement in the study. For most subjects, little could be gained by such reports, but they could lose much in the sense that many subjects had a deep personal involvement and belief in the desirability and safety of cannabis use. The bias of the research staff directly responsible for data collection was probably on the side of being slightly "pro" rather than "anti" cannabis, assuming such global distinctions can be made.

Following the doses used in our studies, the intensity of the abstinence syndrome was mild, and it was relatively short-lived. Although it is risky to compare intensity of withdrawal symptoms across classes of drugs without testing in the same population, we have the impression that the symptoms and their intensity were similar to those produced in the Lexington studies by 400 mg per day of barbiturates administered in divided doses.[17-19, 28] In those studies, none of the 18 subjects who received 400 mg daily had a seizure or delirium, and only one subject developed minor withdrawal symptoms of a significant degree. The minor symptoms included tremulousness, anorexia, nausea, insomnia, and temperature elevation. Two patients who received 200 mg of pentobarbital nightly for 1 year showed no significant evidence of withdrawal from the drug.[18] In discussing the Lexington barbiturate studies, Fraser makes the point that the development of a high degree of physical dependence requires that "the dosage be sufficiently elevated to maintain *continuous* definite impairment of motor coordination."[17] Practically no physical dependence to barbiturates developed in patients given doses low enough to permit them to acquire tolerance. In contrast, in our cannabis studies, patients had impairment of motor coordination only during the first few days (if at all) and were given doses such that most developed rather marked tolerance. Thus, an appropriate comparison of barbiturate withdrawal and cannabis withdrawal should probably consider only the effects of relatively low doses of barbiturates.

Subjects in our study reported many symptoms similar to those experienced during opiate withdrawal.[1, 15, 29] If one applied Himmelsbach's rating scale, some of our subjects would receive withdrawal symptom scores from 20 to 30.[29] Such scores are similar to those experienced during abstinence by opiate addicts studied at Lexington after receiving 100 mg of morphine daily for several weeks.[1, 15, 29]

Many subjects in our study showed abstinence symptoms of a similar intensity as subjects given 0.5 liter of 95% ethanol in divided daily doses for 1 month.[30] Subjects given this dose of alcohol in the Lexington studies developed only a slight tremor, anorexia, irritability, and sleep disturbance when the alcohol was discontinued. Although not commonly appreciated, a far greater dose and/or duration of alcohol treatment is necessary to produce the dramatic delirium tremens, seizures, and so on often associated with marked alcohol dependence. Thus, the intensity and pattern of withdrawal symptoms experienced by subjects given cannabis for 21 days are similar to those produced by moderate doses of opiates or sedative-hypnotic drugs administered for about the same duration. With cannabis, as with other psychoactive drugs, there seems to be a relationship between the dose administered during the period of the development of dependence and the intensity of the subsequent withdrawal syndrome.

If a cannabis withdrawal syndrome appears so predictably in the laboratory setting, one might legitimately ask why is it not more evident in the real world? The answer is that it is reported in clinical situations if careful clinical inquiry is made.[6, 8] Because drug users intend to interpret symptomatology partially according to culturally determined expectations, the appearance of a set of symptoms, such as that seen in our laboratory population, is probably often interpreted as a mild case of influenza or a hangover from the alcohol consumed along with the cannabis. Some of our subjects likened the symptoms to the flu and commented that they had experienced them before but never considered their onset in the context of any drug use pattern. At the doses and intermittent dose schedules currently used in our society, more severe withdrawal symptoms are not likely.

When trying to understand certain aspects of drug dependence, there is much to suggest that common and ordinary clinical data can be misleading. A mistaken impression persisted for almost 50 years that physical dependence did not develop to barbiturates.[1, 19] No marked degree of tolerance and dependence develop to ethanol as it is commonly used by most people.[1, 16] Until relatively recently, the etiology of the ethanol withdrawal syndrome was disputed.[1, 16, 30] So, perhaps we should not be surprised if there are differences in marijuana data from controlled laboratory experiments as contrasted with those from the real world.

Experience with many drugs that were initially introduced or popularized as nondependence producing suggests that clinical impressions are as often initially wrong as they are correct.[1, 16, 31] Just a few examples are the substitution of heroin as a treatment for morphine dependence, the overly optimistic interpretation of experimental data and misleading advertising that contribute to the long lag between introduction to clinical use and recognition of the dependence liability of meperidine, the generally ignored scientific articles in the 1930s that suggest the possibility of amphetamine dependence, and the widespread use of many minor tranquilizers (meprobamate, diazepam, methaqualone) before clinical evidence of dependence became clear-cut.

Of course, an important variable needed to predict the likelihood of dependence is the dose commonly used. The "usual" or common dose of any recreational drug depends on several uncontrolled, unpredictable, and poorly understood variables. For example, consider the relatively large doses of lysergic acid diethylamide, amphetamine, or phencyclidine used in a recreational setting. The increase in popular illicit dose seems to parallel increased availability and would not have been predicted from prior laboratory or clinical experience.

With those who would argue that laboratory experimentation with higher doses of cannabis is irrelevant to *present-day* patterns of use, we would have to agree. What the future holds is the question. What a "relevant" dose would be if availability of the drug changes in the marketplace cannot be accurately estimated. The absolute numbers of users and drug availability determine many of the consequences of recreational drug use and determine the range of doses used. For example, those who use alcohol at reasonably safe, prudent doses seem to be on the same continuum as those who use excessive doses to their own and to society's detriment.[32] With both alcohol and cannabis, it appears that users and "abusers" are not two separate populations. There are some indications that doses of cannabis used follow the same positive skewed normal dose distribution as alcohol doses, which suggests that as cannabis becomes more readily available and more people use it, greater numbers of people will be using higher doses.

Approximately 20% of our subjects gave evidence of already using higher dosage levels in their ordinary social use than were administered as part of this study. Approximately the same percentage showed signs of a mild withdrawal syndrome on admission to the study during the placebo-drying out phase. These signs, of course, could be a result of their concurrent alcohol use but certainly suggest the possibility that there are substantial numbers of people already using cannabis at dosage and dose schedules that lead to some degree of physical dependence.

No less speculative but perhaps more relevant is the issue of the clinical significance of drug dependence as manifested by a mild, transient abstinence syndrome. The relationship between such syndromes and drug-seeking behavior is not a simple one.[1, 16, 31] There is much to suggest that dependence and drug-seeking behavior do not necessarily always go together. Drug-seeking behavior is shaped by a multitude of social, economic, psychologic, and other factors. If we better understood the role of the relatively mild withdrawal symptoms from tobacco as a determinant of tobacco-seeking behavior, and if we understood why the relatively mild abstinence syndrome associated with the low-potency doses of illicit heroin generally available in this country should be associated with heroin-seeking behavior, we could better answer the question about the significance of a mild abstinence syndrome after cannabis administration. Of course, we do not have the information to answer such questions. Therein lies my main concern about speculating too much about the social implications of our data.

The findings of our study do have practical significance for such things as determining time of testing in studies of chronic users. For example, in the Costa Rica chronic user study described at this Conference, much of the laboratory testing was performed at a time when the subjects might well have been in a withdrawal state.[33] This situation could lead to erroneous conclusions as to marijuana effects. The observed increases in rapid eye movement sleep time or the fairly high testosterone levels might more reflect the consequences of the withdrawal of cannabis rather than the effects of its current use. The somewhat inconsistent data from outpatient studies of cannabis tolerance can be partially explained by the surprisingly rapid disappearance of tolerance.[5-7] Cannabis resembles lysergic acid diethylamide or nitrites in the rapidity with which most of the evidence of tolerance disappears. Thus, Perez-Reyes *et al.*[7] and others who found no evidence of tolerance in otherwise well-controlled outpatient studies of drug users might well consider when their users last engaged in sustained marijuana use. For example, in many outpatient test situations, we used to ask our subjects not to smoke cannabis for a few days before coming into the laboratory. This stipulation may be of no consequence with intermittent, infrequent users who have no great degree of tolerance developed anyway but could allow sufficient time to pass so that the very frequent, daily cannabis user may lose a substantial portion of his tolerance before the time of laboratory testing.

For those who would be tempted to shape social policy concerning cannabis with our findings in mind, a few parting reminders may be useful. Our studies do not indicate that the use of cannabis *will* lead to measurable physical dependence or drug-seeking behavior in any given individual. The data only indicate that cannabis *can* produce physical dependence after certain doses and dose schedules in certain situations. We can say nothing very definitive about drug-seeking behavior as it might relate to the dependence. One could make and defend exactly the same conclusion when discussing opiates, alcohol, and other sedative-hypnotics and, indeed, probably all psychoactive drugs. The serious mistakes scientists have made in the past regarding predictions of the dependence liability of a variety of new and old drugs leads us to be rather cautious when making predictions about the ultimate dependence potential of cannabis if it should become available for widespread, uncontrolled use. Great care and caution are indicated in interpreting findings such as ours, so that some people will not be needlessly alarmed nor others be falsely reassured about the possible consequences of cannabis use.

REFERENCES

1. GOLDSTEIN, A., L. ARONOW & S. M. KALMAN. 1974. Principles of Drug Action: The Basis of Pharmacology. 2nd edit. John Wiley & Sons, Inc. New York, N.Y.
2. NATIONAL COMMISSION ON MARIHUANA AND DRUG ABUSE. 1972. First report. Marihuana: A Signal of Misunderstanding. United States Government Printing Office. Washington, D.C.
3. MENDELSON, J. H., A. M. ROSSI & R. E. MEYER. (Eds.) 1973. The Use of Marijuana: A Psychological and Physiological Inquiry. Plenum Publishing Corporation. New York, N.Y.
4. WIKLER, A. This monograph.
5. JONES, R. T. 1971. Marihuana-induced "high": influence of expectation, setting and previous drug experience. Pharmacol. Rev. 23: 359–369.
6. JONES, R. T. 1971. Tetrahydrocannabinol and the marijuana-induced social "high" or the effects of the mind on marijuana. Ann. N.Y. Acad. Sci. 191: 155–165.
7. PEREZ-REYES, M., M. C. TIMMONS & M. E. WALL. 1974. Long-term use of marijuana and development of tolerance or sensitivity to delta-9-tetrahydrocannabinol. Arch. Gen. Psychiat. 31: 89–91.
8. KIELHOLZ, P. & G. LADEWIG. 1970. Uber Drogenabhangigkeit bei Jugendlichen. Deut. Med. Wochschr. 95: 101–105.
9. KAYMAKCALAN, S. & G. A. DENEAU. 1971. Some pharmacologic effects of synthetic Δ⁹-tetrahydrocannabinol (THC). Pharmacologist 13: 247.
10. DENEAU, G. A. & S. KAYMAKCALAN. 1971. Physiological and psychological dependence to synthetic Δ⁹-tetrahydrocannabinol (THC) in rhesus monkeys. Pharmacologist 13: 246.
11. KAYMAKCALAN, S. 1973. Tolerance to and dependence on cannabis. Bull. Narcotics 25: 39–47.
12. SASSENRATH, E. N. & L. F. CHAPMAN. 1975. Tetrahydrocannabinol-induced manifestations of the "marihuana syndrome" in group-living macaques. Fed. Proc. 34: 1666–1670.
13. WILLIAMS, E. G., C. K. HIMMELSBACH, A. WIKLER, D. C. RUBLE & B. J. LLOYD. 1946. Studies on marihuana and pyrahexyl compound. Publ. Health Rep. 61: 1059–1083.
14. BABOR, T. F., J. H. MENDELSON, I. GREENBERG & J. C. KUEHNLE. 1975. Marijuana consumption and tolerance to physiological and subjective effects. Arch. Gen. Psychiat. 32: 1548–15552.
15. SEEVERS, M. H. & G. A. DENEAU. 1963. Physiological aspects of tolerance and physical dependence. Review. In Physiological Pharmacology: A Comprehensive Treatise. W. S. Root & F. G. Hofmann, Eds. : 565–640. Academic Press, Inc. New York, N.Y.
16. KALANT, H., A. E. LE BLANC & R. J. GIBBONS. 1971. Tolerance and dependence on some non-opiate psychotropic drugs. Pharmacol. Rev. 23: 135–191.
17. FRASER, H. F. 1968. Discussion of C. F. Essig's Report. Res. Publ. Ass. Res. Nervous Mental Disease 46: 197, 198.

18. ESSIG, C. F. 1968. Addiction to barbiturate and nonbarbiturate sedative drugs. Res. Publ. Ass. Res. Nervous Mental Disease **46:** 188–196.
19. ISBELL, H., S. ALTSCHUL, C. H. KORNETSKY, A. J. EISENMAN, H. G. FLANARY & H. F. FRASER. 1950. Chronic barbiturate intoxication: an experimental study. Arch. Neurol. Psychiat. **64:** 1–28.
20. MENDELSON, J. H., T. F. BABOR, J. C. KUEHNLE, A. M. ROSSI, J. G. BERNSTEIN, N. K. MELLO & I. GREENBERG. This monograph.
21. TINKLENBERG, J. R., W. T. ROTH & B. S. KOPELL. 1976. Marijuana and ethanol: differential effects on time perception, heart rate, and subjective response. Psychopharmacologia. In press.
22. LAU, R., D. TUBERGEN, E. DOMINO, N. BENOWITZ & R. JONES. 1976. Phyto-hemagglutinin-induced lymphocyte transformation in humans receiving delta-9-tetrahydrocannabinol. Science **192:** 807.
23. BENOWITZ, N., C. LERNER & R. T. JONES. 1976. Depression of growth hormone and cortisol response to insulin-induced hypoglycemia after prolonged oral delta-9-tetrahydrocannabinol. J. Clin. Endocrinol. Metab. **42:** 938–941.
24. FEINBERG, I., R. JONES, J. M. WALKER, C. CAVNESS & J. MARCH. 1975. Effects of high dosage delta-9-tetrahydrocannabinol ingestion. Clin. Pharmacol. Ther. **17:** 458–466.
25. BENOWITZ, N. L. & R. T. JONES. 1975. Cardiovascular effects of prolonged delta-9-tetrahydrocannabinol ingestion. Clin. Pharmacol. Ther. **18:** 287–297.
26. JONES, R. T. & N. BENOWITZ. 1975. The 30-day trip—clinical studies of cannabis tolerance and dependence. *In* The Pharmacology of Marihuana. M. C. Braude & S. Szara, Eds. : 627–642. The Raven Press. New York, N.Y.
27. KATZ, M. M., I. E. WASKOW & J. OLSSON. 1968. Characterizing the psychological state produced by LSD. J. Abnormal Psychol. **73:** 1–14.
28. WIKLER, A. & C. F. ESSIG. 1970. Withdrawal seizures following chronic intoxication with barbiturates and other sedative drugs. *In* Modern Problems of Pharmacopsychiatry. E. Niedermeyer, Ed. Vol. **4:** 170–184. S. Karger. Basel, Switzerland.
29. HIMMELSBACH, C. K. 1942. Clinical studies of drug addiction: physical dependence, withdrawal and recovery. Arch. Intern. Med. **69:** 766–772.
30. ISBELL, H., H. F. FRASER, A. WIKLER, R. E. BELLEVILLE & A. J. EISENMAN. 1955. An experimental study of the etiology of "rum fits" and delirium tremens. Quart. J. Studies Alc. **16:** 1–33.
31. LACOURSIERE, R. B., H. E. SPOHN & K. THOMPSON. 1975. Medical effects of abrupt neuroleptic withdrawal. Comp. Psychiat **17:** 285–294.
32. LE BLANC, A. E. 1975. Perspectives in drug abuse with particular reference to sedative-hypnotics. *In* Hypnotics, Methods of Development and Evaluation. F. Kagan, T. Harwood, K. Rickles, A. D. Rudzik & H. Sorer, Eds. : 201–219. Spectrum Publications. New York, N.Y.
33. COGGINS, W. J., E. W. SWENSON, W. W. DAWSON, A. FERNANDEZ-SALAS, J. HERNANDEZ-BOLANOS, C. F. JIMINEZ-ANTILLON, J. R. SOLANO, R. VINOCOUR & F. FAERRON-VALDEZ. This monograph.

EFFECTS OF CANNABIS AND ALCOHOL ON AUTOMOBILE DRIVING AND PSYCHOMOTOR TRACKING

R. W. Hansteen

Addiction Research Foundation
Palo Alto, California 94304

R. D. Miller

Vancouver Society for Total Education
Vancouver, British Columbia, Canada

L. Lonero

Driver Vehicle Operations Research
Ministry of Transportation and Communication
Toronto, Ontario, Canada

L. D. Reid

Institute for Aerospace Studies
University of Toronto
Toronto, Ontario, Canada

B. Jones

Vancouver General Hospital
Vancouver, British Columbia, Canada

This paper is a final report on the driving and psychomotor tracking studies conducted by the Canadian Commission of Inquiry into the Non-Medical Use of Drugs (LeDain Commission). Preliminary reports of these studies appeared in the commission's cannabis report.[28]

The effects of cannabis on psychomotor performance have been studied for a variety of psychomotor tasks, including skills involved in automobile driving [12] and simulated driving.[4, 8, 16, 22] Psychomotor abilities that have been shown to be impaired by cannabis under certain conditions include pursuit tracking accuracy,[9, 12, 13, 18, 26] hand and body steadiness,[5, 9, 11] braking stop time,[12, 16] and start time.[16]

Other abilities that are of likely importance in the complex skill of automobile driving that also have been shown to be adversely affected by cannabis at certain doses are short-term memory,[15] vigilance and signal detection,[20, 23] and performance on divided attention tasks.[2]

Additional areas of interest regarding driving ability and traffic safety and possible adverse or beneficial effects due to cannabis include judgmental faculties, such as the perception of danger, driver attitudes, risk taking, susceptibility to distraction or stress, and experience in driving while "high," that is, state-dependent learning.[7, 10, 24]

The effects of cannabis on psychomotor abilities have frequently been shown to be related to dosage. At low dosages, effects are generally not observed, but with larger dosages, effects become apparent and progressively larger with increased dosage.[3] The dosage relationship is complicated by the finding that tolerance and/or tachyphylaxis can develop to certain effects of cannabis,[6] although the rate and extent of tolerance development and the behaviors effected have not yet been fully specified.

Researchers have also been investigating the possibility that heavy, long-term cannabis usage has permanent effects on psychomotor and other types of performance,[19, 21, 22] but so far, the findings are inconclusive.

Very little research has been performed on the possible interactional effects of cannabis and other drugs. In one study, an additive effect of cannabis and alcohol was found for some pursuit tracking patterns and for heart rate.[14]

The following two studies add to the growing, yet still incomplete, body of knowledge regarding the effects of cannabis on psychomotor performance and automobile driving ability. In both studies, alcohol conditions were included in the design, because certain effects of alcohol on behavior are known. Also, because blood alcohol level is directly related to automobile crashes,[1] there is concern regarding possible similar effects due to cannabis. However, the results of the present and similar studies cannot answer the question of whether cannabis does or will contribute to highway crashes and fatalities.[25]

Such a hypothesis must be answered by direct testing, for example, by comparing drug levels in persons involved in crashes with drug levels in persons having similar backgrounds, driving under similar environmental conditions, but not involved in crashes, as was done in the case of alcohol. Nevertheless, the present studies do show that cannabis can adversely affect psychomotor performance and driving ability, and these results, together with other evidence, suggest that until further conclusive data are available, driving under the influence of cannabis, like alcohol, should be avoided.

Experiment A: Effects of Cannabis and Alcohol on Some Automobile Driving Tasks

Procedure

This project was divided into two separate but related studies. In the main experiment, 16 licensed drivers (four females and 12 males) each attended four weekly experimental sessions, in addition to a preliminary no-drug practice session. The four experimental conditions, given to all subjects in a double-blind Latin square design, were placebo (extracted marijuana and a nonalcoholic drink), two levels of National Institute of Mental Health marijuana [21 and 88 μg of Δ^9-tetrahydrocannabinol (Δ^9-THC) per kilogram of body weight, producing average doses of 1.4 and 5.9 mg of Δ^9-THC], and one dose of ethanol (producing an average blood alcohol level of 0.07% 20 min after finishing drinking, the equivalent of about three cocktails). Subjects always received a standard drink, followed by a 0.4-g cigarette, each with or without drug, as appropriate to the condition.

The drinks were mixed with commercial carbonated "bitter lemon," well chilled, and were drunk from stoppered bottles by a straw to reduce cues as to the amount of alcohol being administered. The subjects took an average of 27 min to consume the alcoholic drink. Blood alcohol level was measured with a Breathalyzer four times during each session.

The smoking technique employed was standardized and closely controlled. A 5-sec smoke inhalation was followed by a brief air inhalation period, and the smoke was retained in the lungs for a total of 25 sec. A 20-sec rest period followed exhalation. This cycle was repeated until the entire cigarette, including the butt, was consumed, smoked in a pipe when necessary. On the average, this procedure took about 10 min. On the basis of the available evidence, it would appear that with our standard administration technique, nearly all of the THC delivered in the smoke was absorbed. Subsequent to the pharmacologic studies, 24 cigarettes, comparable to those used in the main experiment, were smoked by machine with the same timing schedule. This experiment suggested that the actual THC delivered to the subjects in the smoke was 53% of that originally in the marijuana cigarettes.

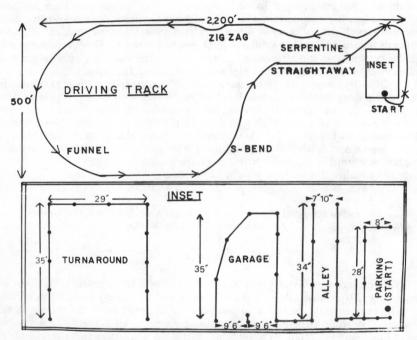

FIGURE 1. Diagram of the automobile driving track. The inset shows the dimensions of the sections that involved slow forward and backward maneuvering.

Subjects began the first driving trial, which consisted of six course laps (about 6 min each), within 5–10 min after smoking. Each lap involved driving through a 1.1-mile course that included both slow forward and backward maneuvering and higher-speed (about 25 mph) straight and curved sections, marked out with wooden poles and plastic cones. The driving course, constructed on an abandoned airplane landing strip at Rockcliffe Air Force Base in Ottawa, is diagrammed in FIGURE 1. In one part of the course, the subjects were asked to maintain their speed at 25 mph. For the other parts, the subjects were instructed to drive as quickly as possible without making too many hits or awkward movements and without exceeding 30 mph at any time. A second trial (three laps) began 3 hr after smoking. The subject's driving was scored on hits of cones and poles (recorded by observers stationed along the driving course), rough handling (superfluous and/or awkward movements, recorded by an in-car observer), and driving time (measured by stopwatch and speedometer checks). The automobiles used were mid-1960s vintage, full-sized, four-door Chevrolets with automatic transmissions but without power steering or power brakes.

Supplementary physiologic and psychologic parameters were measured during each session. Included in the test battery were heart pulse rate, visual imagery (visual impressions reported after a 1-min period with eyes blindfolded), Clyde's Mood Scale [3] (a questionnaire that measures six different mood dimensions), Royal Highness inventory (a multiple-choice questionnaire designed to assess some subjective effects of cannabis), how high scale (a rating form on which the subject rates his or her usual "high" and how "high" he or she currently is on a scale between "not high" and the "highest you have ever been"; successive points are recorded by the subject at several times throughout the experimental session, with one graph for the cannabis "high" and another for the alcohol "high"), driving high inventory (a multiple-choice questionnaire on which the subject rates his or her attitudes and experiences regarding driving while "high"), postsession questionnaire (a multiple-choice questionnaire given at the end of each session on which the subject rates how much of each drug was received and its effects), morning-after questionnaire (on which subjects answer questions regarding possible aftereffects of the experimental drugs).

The 16 subjects in the study were all paid volunteers, aged 21–30 years, and were mostly university students. The subjects were psychiatrically screened, and no individuals with detectable pathology were included. Subjects were all experienced with alcohol and cannabis and had used cannabis a minimum of 1 year or a maximum of 4 years (median of 3). Before the study began, four of the subjects reported using cannabis daily, 10 were using the drug between one and four times per week, and two subjects were using cannabis once per month or less. Thirteen of the 16 subjects reported that they were experienced in driving in normal traffic after both smoking cannabis or drinking alcohol, while three had never done so. The subjects had minimal experience with other psychoactive drugs, and no heavy tobacco smokers were included.

A separate sample of 12 subjects (three females and nine males), experienced with alcohol but not cannabis, were given only the alcohol and placebo drink conditions and were tested on only one trial that consisted of six laps. Course and rating conditions and practice trials were the same as described for the main study.

Results

Both the alcohol dose and the higher dose of cannabis were found to result in poorer car handling performance. FIGURE 2 shows the mean number of hits per lap during the first and second driving trials after administration of cannabis, alcohol, or placebo. During the first trial, significantly more hits (of cones and poles) resulted when subjects received alcohol or the higher dose of cannabis than when they received only the placebos (Dunnet's *t* statistic,[27] $\alpha = 0.05\%$). The mean numbers of hits per lap were 13.2 in the placebo condition, 16.8 in the higher-cannabis condition, and 17.4 in the alcohol condition (i.e., mean increases of 27 and 32% for cannabis and alcohol, respectively). There was

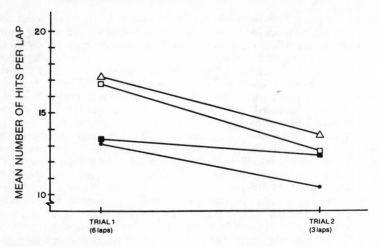

FIGURE 2. Mean number of hits per lap during the first and second driving trials after administration of cannabis (■, 21 μg/kg; □, 88 μg/kg), alcohol (△, 0.07% blood alcohol level), or placebo (●).

no difference between the number of hits made in the low-cannabis and placebo conditions.

In the second trial, given 3 hr after smoking, the numbers of hits in the alcohol and higher-marijuana conditions continued to be somewhat higher than in the placebo condition: 11 of 16 subjects made more hits on trial 2 after receiving alcohol or the higher cannabis dose than placebos (with the lower cannabis dose, 10 of the 16 subjects made more hits on trial 2 than with placebos).

Rough handling during the first trial tended to be greater after drug treatment than in the placebo condition, although only the alcohol scores were statistically significant. The mean numbers of occurrences of rough handling, that is, superfluous or awkward movements, per lap during the first trial were 1.7 for placebo, 1.9 for the lower cannabis dose, 2.2 for the higher cannabis dose, and 2.7 for alcohol.

Driving time was affected by the higher dose of cannabis. FIGURE 3 shows the mean number of seconds taken to complete each lap during the first and second driving trials after administration of cannabis, alcohol, or placebo. In the first trial, subjects required significantly longer time to complete both the slower maneuvering and the higher-speed sections of the course after receiving the higher cannabis dose than after placebo. The differences were small but consistent. In the second trial, differences in driving time among the four experimental conditions were not statistically significant.

TABLE 1 shows the results of the driving high inventory (presession) administered to subjects in the car just before driving on trial 1 (about 15 min after finishing smoking). The Table shows that the higher marijuana dose resulted in a "high" that was usually reported to be less than the *highest* the subjects had ever experienced (item 1) but about the same as or a little greater than the *average* "high" experienced (item 2). In contrast, for most subjects, the lower cannabis dose generally resulted in a "high" that was reported to be less than their average "high." The alcohol dose resulted in an alcohol intoxication that was generally rated as less than the most severe intoxication experienced outside the experiment (item 4) but about the same as or more than their average intoxication (item 5). The subjects were also asked if they had ever driven when feeling as "high" or intoxicated as they did at that moment (items 3 and 6). Although data for all subjects are presented, three of the 16 subjects reported that they had never driven in normal traffic after smoking cannabis or drinking alcohol. Thus, of the 13 experienced subjects, all except one reported having driven when feeling at least as "high" as they felt when receiving the lower cannabis dose, whereas seven reported having driven when feeling at least as "high" as they did after receiving the higher cannabis dose. Eleven of the 13 subjects had driven when feeling as "high" as they felt after being administered the alcohol dose.

TABLE 2 shows the results of the driving high inventory (postsession) administered in the car just after completing the final lap in trial 2 (about 3.5 hr after smoking). Under the higher cannabis dose, about 75% of the subjects thought their driving performance was worse than on the practice day, that driving required more effort, and that they were not likely to drive when feeling as they did at the beginning of the driving session. After receiving the lower cannabis dose, the responses to these items were similar to those given after receiving the placebo.

TABLE 3 shows the results of the postsession questionnaire administered at the end of the session. These data supplement TABLE 1 in showing the subjects' subjective estimates of quantities and effects of drugs received. It is interesting to note that while subjects were generally able to judge the type and relative amount of drug received, such was not always the case. For example, three subjects responded "moderately" and four subjects responded "quite a bit" to the question, "How high did the marijuana make you feel?," even though on that day, they received alcohol but no active cannabis.

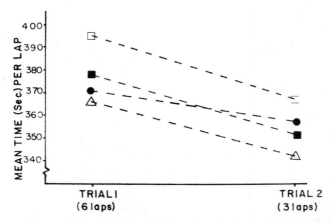

FIGURE 3. Mean time (seconds) per lap during the first and second driving trials after administration of cannabis (■, 21 µg/kg; □, 88 µg/kg), alcohol (0.07% blood alcohol level), or placebo (●).

TABLE 1

NUMBER OF SUBJECTS WHO RESPONDED TO EACH RESPONSE CATEGORY IN THE DRIVING HIGH INVENTORY (PRESESSION) FOLLOWING ADMINISTRATION OF PLACEBO (P), THE LOWER CANNABIS DOSE (M1), THE HIGHER CANNABIS DOSE (M2), OR ALCOHOL (A)

1. Compared to the *highest* you have ever been on cannabis (marijuana or hashish) outside the experiment, how would you rate the way you feel *now*?

	P	M1	M2	A
Much higher now	0	0	0	1
A little higher now	0	1	2	1
About the same	0	0	2	0
A little less high now	1	6	8	7
Much less high now	10	9	4	7
Not high at all now	5	0	0	0

2. Compared to the *average* high you have experienced from cannabis outside the experiment, how would you rate the way you feel *now*?

Much higher now	0	0	1	0
A little higher now	0	2	7	1
About the same	0	2	6	6
A little less high now	3	7	2	8
Much less high now	8	5	0	1
Not high at all now	5	0	0	0

3. Outside the experiment, have you ever driven a car when you were as *high* or *higher* on cannabis than you are now?

Yes	12	11	7	10
No	3	4	9	5
Missing responses	1	1	0	1

4. Compared to the *most alcohol intoxication* you have experienced outside the experiment, how would you rate the way you feel *now*?

Much more intoxicated now	0	0	1	2
A little more intoxicated now	0	0	0	1
About the same	0	0	1	2
A little less intoxicated now	1	1	2	8
Much less intoxicated now	5	6	6	3
Not intoxicated at all now	10	9	6	0

5. Compared to the *average* amount of intoxication you have experienced when drinking alcohol, how would you rate the way you feel now?

Much more intoxicated now	0	0	2	4
A little more intoxicated now	0	0	0	3
About the same	0	1	0	4
A little less intoxicated now	2	2	2	3
Much less intoxicated now	5	4	6	2
Not intoxicated at all now	9	9	6	0

6. Outside the experiment, have you ever driven a car when you were as *intoxicated* or more *intoxicated* by *alcohol* than you are now?

Yes	13	15	9	11
No	3	1	7	5

7. Compared to your last couple of laps on practice day, how well do you think you will be able to drive today?

Much better	1	0	0	0
A little better	4	1	2	0
About the same	7	7	4	6
A little worse	4	7	4	6
Much worse	0	1	6	4

TABLE 1—*Continued*

8. Outside the experiment, how likely are you to drive when feeling the way you do now?

Certain to drive	6	4	2	2
Quite likely	4	4	2	4
Undecided	3	5	2	2
Quite unlikely	2	1	4	4
Certain not to drive	1	2	6	4

9. Would you normally prefer to miss an event of moderate importance to you (say a movie, or a visit to friends) rather than drive when feeling the way you do now?

Yes	2	3	9	7
No	14	13	7	9

TABLE 2

NUMBER OF SUBJECTS WHO RESPONDED TO EACH CATEGORY IN THE DRIVING HIGH INVENTORY (POSTSESSION) FOLLOWING ADMINISTRATION OF PLACEBO (P), THE LOWER CANNABIS DOSE (M1), THE HIGHER CANNABIS DOSE (M2), OR ALCOHOL (A)

1. Compared to your last couple of laps on practice day, how well do you think you drove today?

	P	M1	M2	A
Much better	1	1	0	1
A little better	4	2	2	2
About the same	6	8	2	4
A little worse	3	4	4	5
Much worse	1	0	8	4
Missing responses	1	1	0	0

2. In order to achieve the level of driving performance that you did today, how much effort did you have to make, compared to your last couple of laps on practice day?

Much more effort today	0	0	6	2
A little more effort	3	4	4	3
About the same	9	9	5	11
A little less effort	1	2	1	0
Much less effort	2	0	0	0

3. Outside the experiment, how likely are you to drive when feeling the way you did at the beginning of today's driving session?

Certain to drive	6	5	2	2
Quite likely	4	3	3	4
Undecided	3	4	0	3
Quite unlikely	2	2	5	3
Certain not to drive	0	1	6	4

4. Compared to your practice day, how did you enjoy driving today?

Much more	2	2	2	3
A little more	2	3	3	6
About the same	9	5	2	5
A little less	2	4	2	0
Much less	0	1	7	2

TABLE 3

NUMBER OF SUBJECTS WHO RESPONDED TO EACH RESPONSE CATEGORY IN THE
POSTSESSION QUESTIONNAIRE FOLLOWING ADMINISTRATION OF PLACEBO (P),
THE LOWER CANNABIS DOSE (M1), THE HIGHER CANNABIS DOSE (M2),
OR ALCOHOL (A)

	P	M1	M2	A
1. How much alcohol do you think was in your drink?				
None	7	8	6	1
Very little	9	8	4	1
Moderate amount	0	0	6	5
Quite a bit	0	0	0	7
Very large amount	0	0	0	2
2. How much marijuana do you think was in the material you were given?				
None	3	0	0	0
Very little	11	7	0	7
Moderate amount	1	7	5	7
Quite a bit	1	2	9	2
Very large amount	0	0	2	0
3. How drunk did you feel?				
Not at all	12	11	10	2
Very little	4	5	3	2
Moderately	0	0	3	7
Quite a bit	0	0	0	4
Very much	0	0	0	1
4. How high did the marijuana make you feel?				
Not at all	6	0	0	2
Very little	9	8	0	7
Moderately	1	7	4	3
Quite a bit	0	1	8	4
Very much	0	0	4	0

FIGURE 4 shows mean subjective cannabis "high," determined from the how high scale points plotted by each subject during each session. Although the successive points have been connected by dotted lines to facilitate viewing, a more accurate time course of the cannabis "high" would have been obtained if estimates had also been made at intermediate points. This contention is particularly likely during the first hour after smoking the higher cannabis dose. The first point was plotted immediately after smoking, and the subjective feeling of "high" may have subsequently increased and then declined by the time the second estimate was made 1 hr after smoking. Item 2 of TABLE 1 supports this contention, because 13 of the 16 subjects are shown to have rated their "high" as being "about the same" or "a little higher" than average at the start of trial 1 of driving, after the how high scale ratings were made.

Other subjective measures were also found to be sensitive to cannabis. The Royal Highness inventory (RHI) scores, measured immediately and 1 hr after smoking, increased as a function of cannabis dose. The alcohol condition also resulted in an increase in RHI scores compared to placebo but to a lesser extent than occurred with the higher cannabis dose. Three and one-half to 4.5 hr after smoking, the RHI scores obtained in the higher cannabis dose condition were slightly, but significantly, elevated compared to the placebo condition. The Clyde Mood Scale scores, measured about 1.5 hr after smoking, showed a decrease in "clear thinking" due to alcohol and the higher dose of cannabis. Also, alcohol resulted in a decrease in the factor "unhappy" and an increase in the "friendly" score. An obvious increase in eyes-closed visual imagery was found with the higher cannabis dose compared to placebo, both in the questionnaire totals and in the subjects' drawings of their visual images. In contrast, a decrease in imagery was suggested with alcohol.

FIGURE 5 shows mean pulse rate for the four experimental conditions, measured over the course of each session. The Figure shows a clear dose-related increase in heart rate due to cannabis and a small increase due to alcohol.

In the morning-after questionnaire, subjects were asked how they felt after leaving the experiment. After the placebo condition, the subjects usually reported feeling "about average" between the time they left the experiment and when they went to bed that evening, whereas after cannabis sessions, there were more reports of feeling "very well" during the same period. After the alcohol session, there were more reports of feeling "not very well." No indications of prolonged drug effects were found regarding difficulty in getting to sleep, awakening during the night, feeling unrefreshed the next morning, increased or decreased sexual activity, or gastrointestinal problems.

The subjects in the second study, who were given only the alcohol and placebo conditions, showed alcohol effects that were similar to those found in the main experiment.

EXPERIMENT B: EFFECTS OF CANNABIS AND ALCOHOL ON PSYCHOMOTOR TRACKING PERFORMANCE

Procedure

Twenty-two male subjects each attended six weekly experimental sessions in addition to two preliminary no-drug practice sessions. The six experimental

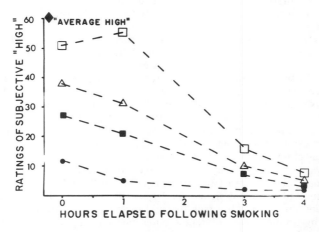

FIGURE 4. Ratings of subjective cannabis "high," determined from responses to the how high scale after administration of cannabis (■, 21 μg/kg; □, 88 μg/kg), alcohol (0.07% blood alcohol level), or placebo (●). Rating values refer to percentage of distance between "not high" and "highest ever."

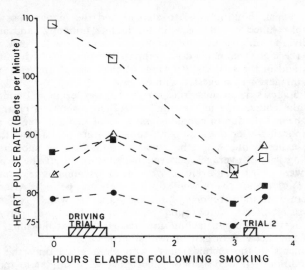

FIGURE 5. Heart pulse rate after administration of cannabis (■, 21 μg/kg; □, 88 μg/kg), alcohol (0.07% blood alcohol level), or placebo (●).

conditions (given to all subjects in a double-blind Latin square design) were placebo (extracted cannabis and a nonalcoholic drink), two levels of cannabis (21 and 88 μg of Δ^9-THC/kg, which gave average doses of 1.6 and 6.8 mg of Δ^9-THC), two levels of alcohol (0.07 and 0.03% of the blood alcohol level), and the low cannabis and low alcohol doses combined. Again, subjects always received a standard drink followed by a 0.4-g cigarette, each with or without drug as appropriate to the condition. Subjects followed the same smoking schedule as described in experiment A.

After smoking, subjects began the first trial, which consisted of six tracking runs (3 min each). A 20-min break occurred between the third and fourth runs, during which supplementary measures were taken. In the tracking task,[17] the subject sat in front of an 8 × 10-in. screen that displayed a fixed central horizontal target line and a small circle that continuously moved up and down in a random fashion when the tracking control was at rest. Forward and backward movements of a hand-operated "joy stick" changed the rate and direction of the circle movement in proportion to the stick deflection. By such deflections, the subject would compensate for the signal fluctuations and was asked to keep the circle as close to the target line as possible. The distance between the circle and line was the *error,* and a score was calculated for each 3-min run, based on the integral of the square of the error, divided by the integral of the square of the amplitude of the input signal; the larger the error, the higher the score. In addition, for simple tracking (see below), the subjects' dynamic responses were described by simple linear differential equations, called "describing functions." [17]

In four of the six tracking runs, the subject was required only to perform the compensatory tracking (simple tracking). In the other two runs (complex tracking), two additional complications were added to the task. (1) Three times in each run, the control dynamics between the "joy stick" and the circle were reversed unexpectedly (that is, it became necessary to push to get the circle to move in the direction that had earlier been achieved by pulling, and vice versa). Performance on this task was measured by the speed of reaction and adaptation to the polarity change. (2) Four other times in each run, the number 1, 2, or 3 appeared without warning on an electronic tube above the target screen. The subject was required to push a left or right pedal or continue pushing a middle pedal with his foot, depending on which of the three numbers appeared. Performance on this task was measured by the speed of foot choice reaction and by the number of times the subject either failed to respond to cue (false negatives) or responded when he should not have (false positives).

A second trial, which involved two simple tracking runs and one complex run, was started 4 hr after drug administration.

Supplementary physiologic and psychologic measures were collected during each session. Variables included in the test battery that were also measured in experiment A were blood alcohol level (measured with a Breathalyzer), heart pulse rate, visual imagery, Clyde's Mood Scale, and postsession questionnaire. In addition, the following parameters were measured: blood pressure, palmar tonic skin conductance, conjunctival injection (redness of eyes), depth perception and visual acuity (measured with a Keystone Diagnostic apparatus), and time estimation.

Results

FIGURE 6 shows mean error scores for simple tracking after administration of cannabis, alcohol, a combination of cannabis and alcohol, or placebo. In trial 1, alcohol resulted in a clear dose-related increase in errors in simple

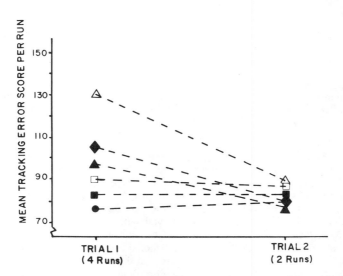

FIGURE 6. Mean tracking error score per run for simple tracking during the first and second trials after administration of cannabis (■, 21 μg/kg; □, 88 μg/kg), alcohol (▲, 0.03% blood alcohol level; △, 0.07% blood alcohol level), low alcohol plus low cannabis (◆), or placebo (●).

tracking compared to placebo. The higher cannabis dose, but not the lower dose, also resulted in a significant increase in error scores. The combination of low cannabis and low alcohol produced error scores that were not significantly different from those obtained in the low alcohol alone condition. In trial 2, given 4 hr after drug administration, there were no consistent drug effects on error scores.

Interpretation of the subjects' "describing functions" obtained on simple tracking runs indicated that alcohol resulted in an increase in "effective reaction delay time" in the subjects' continuous tracking performances and an increase in "random output uncorrelated with input." These effects increased with dose. Examination of the "describing functions" for cannabis revealed a dose-dependent increase in "random output uncorrelated with input," with the effect due to the higher cannabis dose roughly equivalent to that of the lower alcohol dose.

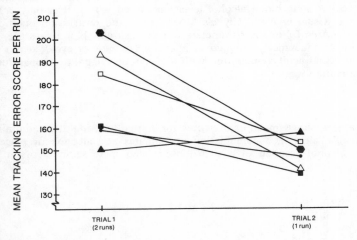

FIGURE 7. Mean tracking error score per run for complex tracking during the first and second trials after administration of cannabis (■, 21 μg/kg; □, 88 μg/kg), alcohol (▲, 0.03% blood alcohol level; △, 0.07% blood alcohol level), low alcohol plus low cannabis (⬡), or placebo (●).

Cannabis did not result in a change in "effective reaction delay time" or other aspects of the "describing functions." The combination of alcohol and marijuana resulted in an increase in "random output uncorrelated with input" that was not substantially greater than that found with the same low doses of each drug separately. "Effective reaction delay time" in the combination condition was not noticeably different from that observed with the alcohol dose given alone.

FIGURE 7 shows mean error scores for complex tracking. In trial 1, only the higher cannabis dose, the higher alcohol dose, and the combination of low cannabis and low alcohol produced increased error scores for complex tracking compared to placebo. Moreover, the combination of low cannabis and low alcohol produced greater error scores in complex tracking than those that resulted from the corresponding doses of each drug given alone. In trial 2, the differences between the placebo and drug conditions were not significant.

Foot choice reaction time was faster in the placebo condition than in any of the drug conditions; however, only the decrement due to the higher alcohol dose was significant. Neither cannabis nor alcohol, nor the combination of the two, resulted in a tendency to miss signals or to respond at the wrong time on this secondary attention and reaction time task. Reaction time to tracking control polarity reversals was reliably longer with the higher dose of alcohol compared to placebo, but no significant effects were seen in the other drug conditions. No major drug effects on these measures were observed on the later trial, which was given 4 hr after drug administration.

The how high scale ratings of intoxication during the period of the first trial indicated that the higher doses of alcohol or cannabis typically made the subjects slightly "higher" than they usually become when using these drugs. The lower cannabis or alcohol doses made them feel somewhat less "high" than they typically become. The combined alcohol-cannabis treatment resulted in alcohol ratings that were similar to those obtained when the low alcohol dose was given alone and in cannabis ratings that were similar to those obtained when only the low cannabis dose was given. Clyde's Mood Scale self-ratings indicated a decrease in "clear thinking" and "unhappy" for all drug conditions. The alcohol-cannabis combination did not result in scores on these factors that were different from those of either the low-alcohol or low-cannabis conditions. The higher cannabis dose resulted in an increase in the factor "friendly," whereas the other drug conditions were not different from placebo in this respect. Also, the higher alcohol dose resulted in an increase in the factor "dizzy," whereas the other conditions did not. No significant drug differences were found in the factors "aggressive" and "sleepy." The RHI scores increased with cannabis and alcohol, as described in experiment A. There was no evidence of an additive effect on the RHI in the combined alcohol-cannabis condition. Four and one-half hours after the higher cannabis dose was administered, RHI scores were still significantly elevated, whereas drug differences on other subjective self-report measures had largely disappeared.

Within 1.5 hr after cannabis administration, visual imagery was increased as in the other experiment. The alcohol conditions resulted in a slight decrease in imagery, as was the case in the driving study. The combined alcohol-cannabis dose resulted in a degree of imagery that was intermediate to the low alcohol and low cannabis doses. There was a suggestion that accuracy of depth perception decreased slightly due to the higher cannabis dose but not with the other drug conditions. Visual acuity measures were not affected by the drugs. Time estimations of the intervals spent tracking in trial 1 were longer for the cannabis conditions compared to the placebo condition. However, the time spent tracking was underestimated in the placebo condition, and in this study, the time estimates in the cannabis conditions were more accurate. Three to 4.5 hr after drug administration, there was a negligible drug effect on these measures.

Pulse rate and conjunctival injection increased with administration of cannabis. Increases in pulse rate and conjunctival injection also resulted from consumption of alcohol, and the combined alcohol-cannabis condition resulted in a greater increase in these measures than was observed with each dose separately. Within 15 min after smoking the higher cannabis dose, diastolic blood pressure (while sitting) was an average of 14% higher than in the placebo condition. The difference did not appear when measurements were made 45 min after drug administration. There were no reliable changes in this measure under the other drug conditions. No significant drug differences were found in systolic blood pressure, although there was a tendency for an increase in the higher cannabis condition. No consistent effects on tonic skin conductance were found in any of the drug conditions.

Blood alcohol level was measured (with a Breathalyzer) three times during each session. Estimates obtained after the administration of the low alcohol dose alone were not different from the corresponding measures in the low alcohol-cannabis combination condition. This finding suggests that at the low doses studied, cannabis does not have a significant effect on the rate of alcohol appearance in and disappearance from the blood.

DISCUSSION

Both the driving study and the psychomotor tracking study show ways in which cannabis can affect performance. In both studies, similarities and differences between the effects of cannabis and alcohol were apparent.

The results of the tracking study indicate that alcohol, cannabis, and the combination of these drugs can result in decreased psychomotor tracking performance. The clearer and more pronounced performance decrement in complex tracking that resulted from the combination of alcohol and cannabis (compared to the same low doses of each drug separately) suggests that the effects of the drugs combine on this measure. Effects of the two drugs also appear to be additive on some of the supplementary variables (for example, pulse rate and conjunctival injection) but appear to not interact on others (for example, the RHI and Clyde's Mood Scale) and were possibly antagonistic on visual imagery. None of the drug conditions caused subjects to miss signals or respond at the wrong time in the choice reaction test, which suggests a lack of drug effect on the level of attention required to perform this simple task. The high alcohol dose did result in an increase in choice reaction time, in reaction time to tracking control polarity reversals, and in "effective reaction delay time" during continuous tracking. No similar consistent changes in reaction time measures were found with the doses of cannabis employed.

The mechanism for the interaction of alcohol and cannabis effects is not clear. It would appear that cannabis can enhance certain alcohol effects in the absence of discernible alteration of alcohol absorption, metabolism, or excretion. We were not, of course, able to assess the possible effects of alcohol on blood levels of THC and its metabolites. The differential pattern of effects of the alcohol, cannabis, and combination conditions suggests that these drugs do not interact solely by one simply enhancing the general effects of the other. Other doses and conditions of administration must be explored to elucidate the mechanism manifested here.

The results of the driving study show a decremental effect of both the higher cannabis dose and the alcohol dose on car handling performance. The fact that there were no major drug differences in the rough handling score, rated by the observer in the car, suggests that the drug effects on performance, at the doses used here, are not dramatic. It would be premature to predict from these results whether cannabis does or will have serious effects on traffic safety. This initial study only measured car handling in rather artificial circumstances. For example, the difficulty and risk involved in traffic were not represented in the test situation, and there was no explicit penalty for making errors, unlike normal driving conditions. In addition, subjects were always aware that they were performing and under observation. These results do serve to point out the possibility that cannabis may adversely affect traffic safety and to underline the urgent need for extensive research into this question.

REFERENCES

1. BORKENSTEIN, R. F., R. F. CROWTHER, R. P. SHUMATE, W. B. ZIEL & R. ZYLMAN. 1964. The Role of the Drinking Driver in Traffic Accidents. Department of Police Administration, Indiana University. Bloomington, Indiana.
2. CASSWELL, S. & D. MARKS. 1973. Cannabis induced impairment of performance of a divided attention task. Nature (London) **241:** 60, 61.
3. CLYDE, D. J. 1963. Manual for the Clyde Mood Scale. University of Miami Press. Coral Gables, Fla.
4. CRANCER, A. J., JR., J. M. DILLE, J. C. DELAY, J. E. WALLACE & M. D. HAYKIN. 1969. The effects of marihuana and alcohol on simulated driving performance. Science **164:** 851–854.
5. EVANS, M. A., R. MARTZ, D. J. BROWN, B. E. RODDA, G. F. KIPLINGER, L. LEMBERGER & R. B. FORNEY. 1973. Impairment of performance with low doses of marihuana. Clin. Pharmacol. Ther. **14:** 936–940.
6. JONES, R. T. & G. C. STONE. 1970. Psychological studies of marijuana and alcohol in man. Psychopharmacologia **18:** 108–117.
7. KALANT, H. 1969. Marihuana and simulated driving. Science **166:** 640.
8. KIELHOLZ, P., L. GOLDBERG, V. HOBI, D. LADEWIG, G. REGGIANI & R. RICHTER. 1972. Cannabis and simulated car driving: an experimental study. Deut. Med. Wochschr. **97:** 789–794.
9. KIPLINGER, G. F. & J. E. MANNO. 1971. Dose-response relationships to cannabis in human subjects. Pharmacol. Rev. **23:** 339–347.
10. KLEIN, A. W., J. H. DAVIS & B. D. BLACKBOURNE. 1971. Marijuana and automobile crashes. J. Drug Issues **1:** 18–26.
11. KLONOFF, H., M. LOW & A. MARCUS. 1973. Neuropsychological effects of marijuana. Can. Med. Ass. J. **20:** 150–156.
12. KLONOFF, H. 1974. Marijuana and driving in real-life situations. Science **186:** 317–324.
13. MANNO, J. E., G. F. KIPLINGER, S. E. HAINE, I. F. BENNETT & R. B. FORNEY. 1970. Comparative effects of smoking marihuana or placebo on human motor and mental performance. Clin. Pharmacol. Ther. **11:** 808–815.
14. MANNO, J. E., G. F. KIPLINGER, N. SCHOLZ & R. B. FORNEY. 1971. The influence of alcohol and marihuana on motor and mental performance. Clin. Pharmacol. Ther. **12:** 202–211.
15. MILLER, R. D., R. W. HANSTEEN, C. ADAMEC & H. E. LEHMANN . 1972. A comparison of delta-9 THC and marijuana effects in humans. *In* Cannabis: A Report of the Commission of Inquiry into the Non-Medical Use of Drugs. Information Canada. Ottawa, Ontario, Canada.
16. RAFAELSEN, O. J., P. BECH, J. CHRISTIANSEN, H. CHRISTRUP, J. NYBOE & L. RAFAELSEN. 1973. Cannabis and alcohol: effects on simulated car driving. Science **179:** 920–923.
17. REID, L. D. 1970. An investigation into pursuit tracking in the presence of a disturbance signal. Can. Aeronaut. Space Inst. Trans. **3:** 35–44.
18. ROTH, W. T., J. R. TINKLENBERG, C. A. WHITAKER, C. F. DARLEY, B. S. KOPELL & L. E. HOLLISTER. 1973. The effect of marihuana on tracking task performance. Psychopharmacologia **33:** 259–265.
19. RUBIN, V. & L. COMITAS. 1975. Acute effects of ganja smoking in a natural setting. *In* Ganja in Jamaica. : 63–79. Mouton. The Hague.
20. SHARMA, S. & H. MOSKOWITZ. 1974. Effects of two levels of attention demand on vigilance performance under marihuana. Percept. Motor Skills **38:** 967–970.

21. SOUEIF, M. I. 1971. The use of cannabis in Egypt: a behavioural study. Bull. Narcotics 23: 17–28.
22. SZARA, S. 1974. Effects in man. In Marihuana and Health, Fourth Report to the U.S. Congress. R. C. Petersen, Ed. : 93–127. United States Government Printing Office. Washington, D.C.
23. THEODOR, L. & R. D. MILLER. 1972. The effects of marijuana on visual signal detection, and the recovery of visual acuity after exposure to glare. In Cannabis: A Report of the Commission of Inquiry into the Non-Medical Use of Drugs. Information Canada. Ottawa, Ontario, Canada.
24. WALLER, J. A. 1965. Chronic medical conditions and traffic safety: review of the California experience. N. Engl. J. Med. 273: 1413–1420.
25. WALLER, J. A. 1971. Drugs and highway crashes. J. Amer. Med. Ass. 215: 1477–1482.
26. WEIL, A. T., N. E. ZINBERG & J. M. NELSON. 1968. Clinical and psychological effects of marihuana in man. Science 162: 1234–1242.
27. WINER, B. J. 1962. Statistical Principles in Experimental Design. : 89. McGraw-Hill Book Company. New York, N.Y.
28. ANONYMOUS. 1972. Cannabis and its effects. In Cannabis: A Report of the Commission of Inquiry into the Non-Medical Use of Drugs. : 11–165. Information Canada. Ottawa, Ontario, Canada.

GENERAL DISCUSSION

Reese T. Jones, *Moderator*

Department of Psychiatry
University of California, San Francisco
San Francisco, California 94143

DR. A. WIKLER: Dr. Cohen, you mentioned that the marijuana smokers were "stoned." Could you be more specific than that? Could you describe by what measurements you judged that they were "stoned"? Specifically, I would like to ask whether you analyzed a speech sample. Also, you mentioned that tolerance developed to the euphoric effects of marijuana. After tolerance had developed to the euphoric effects, was this tolerance replaced by dysphoria and irritability?

DR. S. COHEN: By "stoned" I meant what the "heads" called "stoned." It was a feeling of relaxation, perhaps a little reverie, a pleasant subjective feeling that we did not measure, except in response to the question of how "stoned" are you on a scale of one to seven, with seven being the most "stoned."

DR. WIKLER: You did not analyze a speech sample. You did not ask the subjects to take 5 minutes to describe an interesting experience they had in the past and analyze their speech production for coherency and so on.

DR. COHEN: No, we didn't do that.

Your second question was with regard to dysphoria and irritability after tolerance to the initial euphoric effects. No, it was not dysphoria that replaced the euphoria. Rather, it was nonphoria. Let me give you an example by relating what happened after one individual took 23 joints in one day. He found that after the first dozen or so, he wasn't getting high at all; nothing was happening. He continued to smoke merely to get a record.

DR. WIKLER: No, I mean the group as a whole. Was their behavior characterized by irritability, by complaints, grumpiness, and so on?

DR. COHEN: There was a certain amount of that. We considered these effects to be due more to the restraints they were under, not prison-like but certainly a hospital-like atmosphere, rather than to the marijuana. As I said in my talk, the placebo group were more irritable. In fact, I might try to make a contribution to this strange issue of the fact that in Jamaica, people work better with marijuana, although other tasks are done poorer, like some of the tasks we proposed to them. It may be that done under the influence of a minor tranquilizer, a boring task is easier and perhaps performed even better, whereas a highly skilled cognitive task is not performed as well. This explanation may account for some of the divergence in work activity that seems to occur under the influence of marijuana.

DR. M. FINK: I would like to add something to the tolerance issue. You mentioned, Dr. Cohen, that there was tolerance to behavioral and cardiovascular effects. Did you also see changes in response time to any of the other measures? Also, did you have dropouts, that is, people leaving your clinic or leaving your laboratory after the second or third week, for example?

DR. COHEN: There was some tolerance to bronchodilation, but it wasn't complete, although it is possible that it could become complete. We didn't see tolerance to the reduction in intraocular pressure, so tolerance is apparently a variable phenomenon for some items and not for others. Tolerance was in fact, more than complete for the tachycardia. Eventually, we were seeing pulse rates in the chainsmokers that were lower than their baseline pulse rate.

DR. FINK: Specifically, were there changes in the EEG over time?

DR. COHEN: There was no tolerance to the EEG changes.

DR. FINK: Did you have dropouts?

DR. COHEN: Yes. In those who came on the ward for 94 days, there were two dropouts, one of whom developed acute appendicitis. The other person was discharged from the study because he became extremely paranoid.

DR. REGINA RUMSTEIN (*Pace University, Pleasantville, N.Y.*): What was the nonverbal task that seemed to improve under the influence of marijuana?

DR. COHEN: It wasn't a nonverbal task. One of the psychomotor tasks was to add a column of six-digit numbers on an electronic calculator, for which the subject received a dime for the right answer. The other task involved learning a foreign language to which they had never been exposed and answering correctly the questions in the back of the book, which was part of the learning process. The subject received a dime for each correct answer to that task also.

The nonverbal task I think you are referring to is the hemispheric dominance test. I have no samples of these tests, but they are alleged to discriminate between right and left hemispheric thought processes.

QUESTION: In an earlier report, there were some dose-related elevations of alkaline phosphatase in your group. Have those observations been extended? Also, what about glucose metabolism throughout the course of the study?

DR. COHEN: Initially, the first year we thought we saw an increase in alkaline phosphatase. This increase was not confirmed during further studies, and we can't report on anything like that now. We found no change from baseline in blood glucose studies, although I am aware of the literature, which indicates possible elevations in glucose tolerance.

DR. G. G. NAHAS (*College of Physicians and Surgeons, Columbia University, New York, N.Y.*): In your cytogenetic studies, Dr. Cohen, did you study the incidence of micronuclei and of abnormal patterns during metaphase and anaphase? During your immunity studies, other than studies of incorporation of radioactive thymidine during phytohemagglutinin-stimulated blastogenesis, did you look for incorporation of any other precursors? Did you also investigate other parameters of cell-mediated immunity, such as phagocytic motility and rosette formation?

DR. COHEN: Dr. Nahas, I'd like to send you the papers involved rather than tell you what our immunologists found, and because you are an expert immunologist, I would rather not delve into it.

DR. W. J. COGGINS: Dr. Jones, regarding the effects of THC on blood pressure, I was intrigued by your data but do not agree with your interpretation. As I understand it, the postural effects drop out over the 21 days of use. The supine effects remain present over the 21 days. If I understand you correctly, you suggested that this effect was due to increased fluid retention and intravascular volume.

DR. JONES: That's one speculation based on the effects of other hypotensive drugs.

DR. COGGINS: I feel a little uncomfortable with that interpretation. I would expect the effect to go in the opposite direction, because one usually sees postural changes due to ganglionic blocking effects and not due to intravascular volume increases.

Also, if you look at the supine effects, which disappear as intravascular volume increases due to fluid retention effects of the drug, you have to invoke still another mechanism to explain why those pressures aren't staying the same or increasing rather than dropping.

DR. JONES: I simply speculated about the postural mechanisms because I think this is a case where there are some testable hypotheses about mechanisms of drug effects, which doesn't happen very often in this business. Dr. Benowitz, would you like to comment on the blood pressure changes?

DR. N. BENOWITZ: The supine blood pressure changes were relatively modest and were associated with a decrease in heart rate. It may be that the blood pressure changes over the prolonged period of time were due to heart rate changes. The postural effects as related to hypotension, which was quite severe in the beginning, as the data showed, became somewhat less. It was our feeling that perhaps since the subjects were upright during the day most of the time, volume expansion was not compensating for this postural effect on hypotension; basal blood pressures, which were taken at rest in the morning, perhaps represented merely the heart rate-slowing effect. Therefore, in a functional context perhaps, we could explain these two different phenomena. And although the effect has not been well characterized with other antihypertensive drugs, I think that there is some evidence of volume expansion, which can affect both postural and supine changes with guanethidine used as a prototypic drug.

DR. J. MENDELSON: I would like to make one brief comment on the relationship between volume expansion and blood pressure changes. In our studies, we measured caloric intake and weight, but we did not initially measure plasma volume with acceptable techniques, namely, the use of deuterium. Dr. Benowitz did measure plasma volume with the dye dilution technique, which I think he probably would acknowledge is not the best method. Benowitz and coworkers didn't do calorie counts. At least some of you leave with the feeling that a group of investigators are pursuing a rather esoteric area that may be of interest to cardiovascular physiologists in a weird sense, perhaps.

There is more to this aspect. It involves the nature of consumatory behavior as associated with substance use. As many of you in medicine know, probably the greatest bane that one sees in clinical practice in substance use as it relates to alcohol is the concurrence of the toxic effects of ethanol superimposed on the decrement of nutritional intake that most alcoholics have. In other words, most of the intercurrent illness that we see in people who have alcohol problems is associated not only with the fact that they are drinking a lot of alcohol but also with the fact that they are taking in a relatively small amount of food.

For some time, we thought that the food decrement problem was due to the fact that one can get 7 cal/g from ethanol, so why get the calories from food. There is therefore a satiation effect. That, in fact, is probably not the case. Alcoholics probably eat less when they are drinking to get a bigger bang for their buck from ethanol, because as a function of decrement in food intake, the rate of ethanol metabolism is slowed; higher blood alcohol levels are therefore maintained.

If one is thinking about potential health hazards of a substance, I think it is very important to ask a derivative question, namely: What effect does the use of that substance have on consumption of, for instance, food, and how might the interactional effects of consumatory behavior on substance use produce either an adverse or even possibly a beneficial health consequence?

DR. J. SCHONEBERG SETZER (*Metropolitan New York Synod, Lutheran*

Church in America, New York, N.Y.): My clinical observations of regular use of marijuana, by which I mean daily or near-daily usage, has left me with concern over a deleterious effect of cannabis that has hardly been mentioned here, although Dr. Wikler came the closest to pointing it out. And before I am lumped with the antidrug crowd, I wish to say that I am a parapsychologist of religion and have been very interested and active in the study of altered states of conciousness by use of psychoactive substances. The Old Testament priests used cannabis, the Brahmans still do, and a lot of other people in this country are using it quite differently from the way I understand it is being used in Jamaica and Costa Rica. I am in favor of its legalization and regulation.

Now, that being said, our physiologic and sociologic studies here are obviously very sophisticated, and I am very appreciative of that. Our psychologic studies are still somewhat crude, however. Think of the analogy of going after a horsefly with a sledgehammer. And I think that is why we have ignored this very subtle effect of reality orientation deterioration that several of us have observed. It is very subtle. The closest analogy to it that I know is getting nibbled to death by a duck.

Let me illustrate this point by a most unusual case. I have noticed this effect in a disturbingly high proportion of my regular cannabis users among students, but I will just mention a case that is the most interesting one I know.

A Shaman friend of mine lives with the bears on a mountaintop in New England. This man is very sophisticated in his buddhist psychologic orientation. He has a clandestine psychedelic drug therapy program by which he takes drugs with his clients; he uses ketamine hydrochloride, THC, and a very broad panoply of psychopharmaceutical substances. This man had noticed that regular use of cannabis substances caused a deterioration in his reality testing. And this man, with the possible exception of a few yogis, has spent more time being concerned about his moment-to-moment state of consciousness than anyone else I know.

This effect concerned me enough, but over several years, I observed in him that though he himself voluntarily dried out periodically to overcome the effects of cannabis, he deteriorated in his overall ability to reality test in a rather distressing way that was very subtle, that he himself couldn't see.

So, I would like to see psychologic tests of a sophistication that would deal with these very subtle aspects of reality testing in the coming years.

DR. JONES: For the past three days, we have heard the results of many sophisticated psychologic tests that have not demonstrated what you are saying. We haven't proved that the things you describe are not happening; we have just proved that certain things don't happen, as measured by those tests. What you're saying may very well be true.

DR. SETZER: I'm not making these comments as a criticism. I am simply saying that our research has some distance to go.

DR. LOREN MILLER (*University of Kentucky, Lexington, Ky.*): Concerning the measurement of subjective states, I don't see why independent measurements of mood or reality testing can't be made by another observer along with the patient's own subjective interpretations.

DR. JONES: I think that's what we did in our study and what Dr. Mendelson did also.

DR. MENDELSON: I didn't describe the work performed by Dr. Thomas Babor, a social psychologist who attempted to look at not only what subjects reported but also at how they behaved and interacted through a series of rather good behavioral ratings. And these data are presented in detail.

I am sure you all recognize that the state of the art of assessment of human behavior and feeling states is certainly not as accurate as measurements of standing and supine blood pressures. The instruments that are available are not as accurate, and we can only hope that work in drug abuse or substance use-related areas will improve as our colleagues in the basic scientific disciplines and in behavioral science develop better and more sophisticated instruments.

DR. MILLER: Dr. Jones, in one curve you showed that during the withdrawal state after cannabis administration, tension-anxiety increased, yet euphoria didn't seem to change, as measured on your other curve. Is that correct?

DR. JONES: The "euphoria" measure can be misleading, because none of those changes are interpretable. This is a good example of a measure where to interpret the pattern of change, we would need a placebo control group kept in the hospital for the entire 4–6 weeks.

The scale may not really represent "euphoria" in the sense you are using it. Rather, it described good feelings that progressively increased during the period of hospitalization, because I think people became more comfortable, better acquainted with us, and got to like the people they were working with. The tension-anxiety increase is one very predictable concomitant of what happens in abstinence, an increase in tension-anxiety that you don't see during other phases, except in the high-dose, rapid-initiation phase when cannabis does produce an arousal-type phenomenon, but it's transient.

DR. MILLER: I thought that those mood states might be correlated to some extent, tension-anxiety along with euphoria; if one would change, the other would change.

DR. JONES: They're correlated in the opposite direction. It is a negative correlation.

DR. MILLER: But it didn't seem to occur in your data.

DR. ALVIN B. SEGELMAN (*Rutgers University, New Brunswick, N.J.*): I have three major questions. First, being neither an anthropologist nor a social or psychologic scientist, one problem concerns me, and I would like to direct these questions to Drs. Comitas, Knight, Carter—indeed, most of the people who have given papers. That is, how does one establish, particularly in the foreign studies, that a person is smoking or using hashish, marijuana, and other drugs? I think the only answer to this question is determination of blood levels, and that leads me to my second question: Why hasn't a single study mentioned blood levels of THC metabolites? I am well aware that precise techniques in this area have recently been employed by Kale and others. I am simply asking this question, because no one has tied these things together, and the press is undoubtedly here and has undoubtedly already made some comments.

I think that all of the conclusions that have been made and will be made here should be suffixed with "in the absence of suitable blood levels of THC metabolites, no definite conclusions can be made at this time." I think that is terribly important. If anyone would like to argue against this point, I wish they would do so now.

DR. JONES: We can't answer your first question, because we're not the right panel to ask.

With respect to your second question, we have refrigerators full of serum just waiting for somebody who can perform adequate blood assays. We have looked at urinary levels of several cannabinoids by use of thin-layer chromatography and, indeed, find that the spots appear when you administer the drug and disappear promptly when the drug is withdrawn.

You had a third question.

DR. SEGELMAN: I think there is another point to be made; namely, there have been attempts with such techniques as gas chromatography, gas liquid chromatography, and radioimmunoassays in our work to measure these parameters. The more important question, however, is what do these blood levels mean. If one is working with a substance like ethanol, which enters all tissues and organs as a function of its water concentration, there is no protein binding. The rate of catabolism, or clearance, is well known. I am sure that you recognize that this is not the case with THC or its metabolites.

In other words, a blood level of THC may not bear any relationship to the properties that the drug has in tissue-binding sites where it is acting. I agree with the principle involved in simple measurements, but there is a caveat. The caveat is that if you measure these levels, they may not, in fact, relate to the pharmacologic action of the compound in crucial tissue sites in the central nervous system.

There is no question about what you just said. I am simply asking why these measurements haven't been made, and you say that they have been done. Why weren't they mentioned?

DR. JONES: The precision and reproducibility of these assays are poor. I can't say much more.

DR. SEGELMAN: With the present state of the art, I think we have the techniques for measuring these things; it just seems that it wouldn't be difficult to at least pull blood samples.

DR. JONES: You'd be surprised. I would urge you to publish if you have refined such analytic techniques.

DR. SEGELMAN: I would appreciate it if some of the anthropologists would respond to my other question. How does one determine if the subjects are smoking or using marijuana? I am mentioning this point because of a personal experience I recently had with a friend who is one of our major investigators, not with marijuana but with some other drugs. He has found many individuals who have lied simply to get in this program for a variety of reasons, possibly financial, and I would suspect that in these foreign studies, having been conducted in societies in which the social income of these individuals is rather low, people might distort the facts to gain some monetary reward.

COMMENT: We anthropologists are certainly not gods. We can't determine without a shadow of a doubt the level of usage or whether, indeed, people are users. This point was a great concern to me, and I was also afraid that some subjects might be lying. The only way that we could safeguard against these "put-ons" was to spend prolonged periods of time with people in their natural settings, observing them smoking. We spent over two years with three anthropologists working with the 82 subjects that we have reported on for the Costa Rican study. We had clear records of many smoking sessions with each individual. We also took some blood samples in conjunction with the sleep EEG. These data have not been reported yet, but we have no doubt that these people were heavy chronic users.

QUESTION: Dr. Cohen gave some evidence that the right hemisphere of the brain showed more activity, and recent reports have shown that the right hemisphere is associated with intuitive activity. Could I assume, then, that cannabis elicits intuitive activity in the subject? And could we use that effect as subjective evidence for proving subjective responses?

DR. JONES: I think all those left-right measures are intriguing but still pretty messy ones to use yet. There are lots of methodologic problems, but your question is certainly appropriate.

DR. JAMES HALIKAS (*Washington University, St. Louis, Mo.*): How are we to reconcile the Costa Rican testosterone data, because those results were negative? We also have positive data from Dr. Jones, from the original studies of Kolodny, and from Dr. Cohen. We can reconcile Dr. Mendelson's data by saying that they were obtained too early, before 5 or 6 weeks out in the field. The Costa Rican data stand out, however.

DR. JONES: Dr. Coggins, when were the testosterone specimens drawn in the Costa Rican study?

DR. COGGINS: The specimens were drawn at about 7:30–8:00 AM. The last marijuana smoking was at midnight or earlier the night before.

DR. JONES: I think Dr. Mendelson's data would suggest that by then they are back to normal. Certainly, our data suggest that.

DR. HALIKAS: There's a rebound; they're clearly back to normal. I am suggesting, however, that after 20 years of heavy use, perhaps it is suppressed on a long-term basis.

DR. MENDELSON: If I were reviewing the adequacy of techniques, knowing what we know now, and there is a lot of information on variants in plasma testosterone levels, I would feel that one would have to use the best techniques available. There is a dual variation in plasma testosterone levels, but less than 20% of the variants can be explained by the dual cycle. And if you look at the variants, 80% of them occur as a function of episodic secretory pulses.

We do know something about these pulse rates; we do know something about the biologic half-life of plasma testosterone. Most of the changes that are reported fall within the degree of variance that you would ordinarily expect to occur in any healthy young or middle-aged adult. So until data are generated that can show specific changes in episodic secretory rates, testosterone production rates, or testosterone degradation rates, I think this area remains a matter of conjecture.

DR. JONES: I agree entirely with Dr. Mendelson's statements. I think it is a curious and interesting finding but to try to make more of it than that seems premature.

DR. CANNIE ADAMEC (*Dalhousie University, Halifax, Nova Scotia, Canada*): I would like to make a general comment about all of the data that have been presented in the last three days concerning the lack of information on women who smoke. Dr. Carter mentioned that most Costa Rican smokers are men, and it was disadvantageous to add another variable to the study. Dr. Soueif mentioned that very rarely do women smoke, or at least get arrested for smoking, in Egypt.

In North America, a smaller proportion of women smoke, but there is a proportion of women who do smoke. Dr. Perez-Reyes mentioned that the rate and pattern of metabolism of a contraceptive are unaffected in women who have smoked marijuana, and the LeDain Commission included a few women in their samples. I am making a request for more information on female cannabis smokers.

DR. JONES: Dr. Szára will give the Food and Drug Administration male chauvinist position.

DR. S. SZÁRA: We at the National Institute on Drug Abuse are very much interested in women and also in women smoking marijuana. But we are constrained in our efforts of trying to get more data on female smokers. The Food and Drug Administration has very strict regulations that would hamper our efforts of going into female populations on an experimental basis. We are allowed to study females in a natural setting but are not able to administer drugs because of these regulations.

DR. JONES: Your point is well taken, though I think it is long overdue to include the other half of the world.

DR. NAHAS: I am sorry that I was not given the opportunity to present the results of the Columbia University study that took place last year on chronic marijuana users studied in a hospital environment. Some of the results could give an answer to the question asked by Dr. Adamec.

The general results we observed are consistent with many of those reported here, especially in relation to testosterone levels; after one month of heavy smoking, we did not observe any changes. However, one of the most clear-cut observations in this study was that after one month of smoking five to 10 marijuana cigarettes (2% THC, 1 g), we observed in nine of 10 of them a marked decrease in their sperm counts, which averaged 52% and ranged from 30 to 70%. This decrease in sperm count was associated with a significant increase in abnormal, immature sperm, in all subjects.

As I mentioned, there was no change in testosterone levels. There were also alterations in immunity levels and creatinine phosphokinase. These data would indicate that it is possible, as Dr. Kolodny first reported, but not in a controlled environment, that heavy marijuana smoking is associated with oligospermia. All of these observations have already been made on animals, but, of course, this is irrelevant to man at present. The significance of these findings thus far is that women have in their ovaries only 400,000 eggs, while men have 300 million sperm per ejaculate. This is quite a difference.

DR. JONES: I might add that we found no evidence of abnormal sperm or decreased sperm counts in our subjects. Of course, we were depending on their drug history data to account for this information, but they were very heavy users, and they had normal sperm counts.

DR. O'BRIEN (University of Connecticut, Storrs, Conn.): After listening for the past few days, I still have some reservations and concern about the other cannabinoids in marijuana that we're not considering. Cannabinol and cannabidiol may either antagonize or enhance the effects that we are seeing and may change the data various investigators are getting. I don't think this factor has been considered.

Dr. Mendelson, would you care to comment on the development of tolerance and how it relates to drug-seeking behavior with respect to quantity, quality, or potency of the drug either to obtain the desired response or to prevent withdrawal?

DR. MENDELSON: I think it is a very complicated matter and well beyond the time available to discuss it.

DR. R. W. BAIRD (Hayden Clinic, New York, N.Y.): It is time we analyzed the kids in their real environment. Come up, Dr. Jones, for a year to Harlem and spend time with your anthropological friends and observe the patient in his own environment, not where he is going to Harvard and the old man is giving him money for college, paying the rent, and giving him a car. Observe the individual in his environment and explain to me why he is "stoned."

DR. JONES: You are quite correct. Many of us are studying the handpicked, selected, successful survivors, if that's the case. The average IQ of our subjects is 120; the average education is 18 years. We wouldn't take kids from Harlem because they wouldn't make very good subjects: they're not cooperative; they're not smart enough or too smart to perform simple laboratory tests and so on. So you don't get any data on what the drug might do in that population, which might be quite different than in my Berkeley graduate student population.

DR. MENDELSON: I think biological scientists do the best job they can in the situations in which they are working. There is always a certain degree of what's called indeterminacy introduced when you attempt to do control studies. But, by and large, I think many of us in medicine feel that this is a reasonable pathway. I am not discounting the astute clinical observations that are made in realistic life settings. Nevertheless, the progress of science is dependent in some ways on constructing studies that are scientifically adequate and valid.

I don't think any of us pretend to have the final answers. On the other hand, I don't think any of us should allow an emotional didactic approach to supersede a more rational attempt to find the facts and report them as we find them.

DR. BAIRD: In your paper, did you observe any psychologic changes in subjects who were taking marijuana under controlled situations? Can you give me a yes or no answer, or are you going to give me an indifferent in the middle? I just want to know, yes or no, did you observe firsthand any adverse reactions to the active consumption of marijuana when the subject was taking it?

DR. MENDELSON: Of course, we observed reactions, but the only way one can answer that is like when they asked Willie Sutton, "Why do you rob banks?" And he says, "That's where the money is." People do take psychoactive drugs to get a central effect. They use alcohol, they use marijuana, a variety of things.

NEUROPSYCHOLOGIC STUDIES

NEUROPSYCHOLOGIC, INTELLECTUAL, AND PERSONALITY CORRELATES OF CHRONIC MARIJUANA USE IN NATIVE COSTA RICANS*

Paul Satz and Jack M. Fletcher
Department of Clinical Psychology
University of Florida
Gainesville, Florida 32611

Louis S. Sutker
Department of Psychology
University of Victoria
Victoria, British Columbia, Canada

Problem

Despite more than four decades of marijuana research, considerable controversy still exists concerning the acute and/or chronic effects of this drug on human adaptive functions, particularly on cognition, attention, and personality. This uncertain state of affairs could have tragic long-term health implications if marijuana usage, which is increasing radically in this country, were shown to cause transient or irreversible damage to the brain or personality.[1-3] By the same token, if no relationship exists between marijuana use and brain dysfunction, adverse legal, psychologic, and social consequences may needlessly result due to misinformation about the health effects of this drug. The potential abuses of such misinformation are reflected in the recent personal conclusions of Senator James O. Eastland, who chaired the Senate Internal Security Committee on Marihuana:

(1) If the cannabis (marihuana) epidemic continues to spread . . . we may find ourselves with a large population of semi-zombies—of young people acutely afflicted by the amotivational syndrome. . . .

(2) We may also find ourselves saddled with a partial generation of young people —people in their teens and early twenties—suffering from irreversible brain damage. . . .

(3) The millions of junior high school and grade school children who are today using marihuana may produce another partial generation of teen-agers who have never matured, either intellectually or physically, because of hormonal deficiency and a deficiency in cell-production during the critical period of puberty. . . . We may witness the phenomenon of a generation of young people who have begun to grow old before they have even matured.

(4) . . . there is the possibility . . . that we may develop a large population of youthful respiratory cripples. And there is the possibility—which can only be confirmed by epidemiological studies—that marihuana smokers are producing far more than their quota of malformed and genetically damaged children. . . .

The preceding comments illustrate some of the abuses and risks that can ensue when controversy and misinformation prevail concerning scientific knowl-

* Supported by National Institute on Drug Abuse Contract NO1-MHE-0233.

edge, particularly when some of these facts conflict with legal and social systems. Nevertheless, as long as controversy exists concerning the effects of marijuana usage on human health, people have a right to be informed about possible long-term risks.

Brain Function

Let us first examine the evidence for these long-term risks on brain function. A review of the literature reveals that this evidence is based largely on laboratory studies that have evaluated the *acute* short-term effects of natural (hemp) or synthetic [Δ^9-tetrahydrocannabinol (Δ^9-THC)] administrations, on a few motor and perceptual learning tasks, employing naive and/or experienced users as subjects. Most of these studies, moreover, have failed to assess quantitatively the broad range of neuropsychologic adaptive skills (e.g., intelligence, memory, perception, language, attention, judgment) that are known to be altered selectively after lesions form in the cerebral cortex.[4-8] In addition, many of these studies, particularly the earlier ones, have failed to control for dosage level and quality of marijuana; in fact, no control groups were used in most early studies.[9-11] Subsequent laboratory studies were additionally marred by the use of small samples and by reliance on subjective reports concerning personality variables, such as mood, motivation, and inhibition. Finally, many of these studies were conducted in unnatural laboratory settings in which anticipatory sets of the subjects were not systematically controlled for. Two excellent reviews of this laboratory research can be found in Weil *et al*.[12] and Hollister.[1] While these reviews conclude that marijuana smoking may have an immediate depressing effect on some cognitive or attentional tasks (within 15–30 min), the effects are neither severe nor replicable between studies.[13] More puzzling, however, is the finding that the interference effects are more commonly seen in naive subjects than in experienced drug users.[1, 12] For example, in the Weil *et al*. study,[12] the chronic users performed as well or better on most of the cognitive-attentional tasks after smoking marijuana than before. This high performance level, however, was inversely related to their judgmental reports on performance, which contradicts the false sense of improvement that is sometimes reported by chronic users.

But, again, what are the long-term effects on brain function, if any, of marijuana usage, especially in chronic smokers? This is precisely the area of our greatest ignorance at the present time.[1, 14] If marijuana usage produces immediate interference effects in some aspects of attention and cognition, whether systematic or not, are these effects reflective of corresponding changes in brain function, and, if so, are they permanent? Preliminary answers to these questions can only come from systematic study of individuals who have smoked marijuana extensively for many years. To date, only one such study, the Jamaica Project,[15] has been conducted with appropriate control groups. The results, which will be presented below, have unfortunately been overshadowed by three earlier studies, each of which has reported evidence of severe and irreversible brain damage in cases of chronic marijuana usage.[16-19] Each of these studies, however, is grossly marred in terms of design and methodology. The Campbell *et al*. study,[16] for example, based its conclusions on the results of air encephalograms that were given to 10 patients (with no controls) in a neurology ward in England. According to Kolodny (Brecher [20] p. 147),

In the 10 cases reported, all 10 men had used LSD—many of them over 20 times—as well as cannabis, and nine of the 10 had used amphetamines. One subject had a previous history of convulsions, and a number had used sedatives, barbiturates, heroin, or morphine. On the basis of these facts, speculative connection between cannabis use and brain damage is highly suspect. Unfortunately, this type of report is typical of much of the research done in this field.

Similar criticisms have been leveled at the Heath study,[17] which reported abnormal brain wave changes after marijuana inhalation in six rhesus monkeys, two of which, after autopsy, were shown to have microscopic changes in the septal region of the brain. It was shown, however, that the dosage levels used by Heath were extremely toxic and would be equivalent to a person smoking 30 marijuana cigarettes three times per day for 6 months![20] At this dosage level, one is undoubtedly seeing the effects of toxicity rather than of the drug per se.

The third study, which reported organic changes in the brains of chronic marijuana smokers, was based largely on subjective psychoanalytic interviews of *psychiatric* patients who were chronic marijuana smokers.[18, 19] The authors identified a separate clinical syndrome, which they referred to as an "amotivational syndrome." The symptoms included disturbed awareness of self, apathy, confusion, poor reality testing, sleep disturbances, memory defects, and impairment of time sense. The authors also noted that many of their patients ($N = 51$) were physically thin and presented with much of the fatiguability and weariness characteristic of some of the aged. These symptoms were interpreted as a profound disturbance in personality due to an underlying biochemical and structural defect in the central nervous system. Support for this "amotivational syndrome" was based on the fact that most of the symptoms were believed to vary as a function of temporal onset or termination of the drug.[19] However, the fact that the symptoms cleared after cessation of drug would contradict the authors' hypothesis of a structural, and therefore *irreversible,* defect in brain function. More serious methodologic problems exist in this study, however. The use of subjective patient reports, which often lack objectivity and validity, is extremely hazardous in this type of clinical research. Moreover, to assume that these subjective reports and impressions reflect symptoms that correspond to underlying brain functions is not warranted by the data. Furthermore, no control group of psychiatric patients who were nonsmokers was employed for comparison purposes. Finally, the selection of patients referred to a psychiatric hospital may produce a significant bias in sampling that would not be representative of the general population of chronic marijuana smokers.

Personality

The latter point is vividly illustrated when we turn to studies in the personality sphere. A recent large-scale longitudinal survey investigated the life histories, adjustment, and academic achievement of marijuana users (mild and heavy) and controls at the University of California at Los Angeles for several years.[3] They found that the frequency and duration of marijuana use had no correlation with academic achievement, which presumably reflects motivation. They did find, however, that "chronic users more frequently dropped out of school one or more times, but after their return they performed as well as their peers" (p. 134). Other differences in life history and social pattern were found between the chronic users and controls. The chronic users more often grew up in suburban areas, the frequency of their religious practice was much lower, they more often left home to get away from their parents for school, their sexual experiences began earlier, they saw themselves as more sexually experienced and liberal than nonusers, and they suffered more venereal disease. However, no differences in overall adjustment or achievement were found between the chronic smokers and their controls, a result that does challenge the Kolansky and Moore theory of an "amotivational syndrome." [19] Also, the Hochman and Brill [3] study was recently replicated on a large group of students at the State University of New York at Stony Brook. [21]

Nevertheless, it should be pointed out that the UCLA study did reveal subtle differences in life-style and personality of the chronic users, which were not, however, interpreted as abnormal. The chronic users appeared more rebellious, independent, reckless, questioning, and antiauthoritarian than the nonusers. More direct support for these findings was reported recently in a quantitative assessment of personality patterns in adolescent drug users in two Southern schools. [2] The authors used the 16 Personality Factor Questionnaire, [22] which measures 16 major dimensions of the normal adult personality. Krug and Henry [2] demonstrated that the adolescent drug user ($n = 171$), in contrast to the control group ($n = 392$), was more dominant, more impulsive, morally expedient, socially uninhibited, unconventional, less skilled in analyzing the motives of others, and more radical. The authors speculated that these distinctive personality patterns of drug users had antecedents in their child-rearing practices during the formative stages of development. They concluded that "the pattern suggests child-rearing practices which uncritically reward independence and the development of social skills and ignore training or education in prevailing societal or ethical standards" (p. 444). Thus, these data suggest that personality differences between adolescent drug users and nonusers arise not so much because of drug use but because of differences in upbringing. These differences, however, may serve to make contact with the drug culture more probable but at the same time cannot be attributed to marijuana use alone. Indeed, marijuana consumption was found to be independent of the use of other drugs, many of which are known to produce changes in brain function and personality.

Another recent study [23] employed the 16 Personality Factor Questionnaire (16 PF), along with a Motivational Analysis Test, to a college group of marijuana users. This study was addressed to possible personality differences within groups of users and, for this reason, used no control group. Despite this shortcoming, the authors found no distinctive personality type within their marijuana user group, as had been suggested by other reports. [18, 24] In fact, this study [23] found four distinctive groups that accounted for most of the variance in their users: an antisocial norm group, a frustrated upper-middle-class group, a hostile rebel group, and a follower group. The authors concluded that none of these factors were indicative of pathology and that these personality patterns might be found in any adolescent group, regardless of drug use.

The Krug and Henry study, [2] along with the UCLA [3] and SUNY reports, [21] do provide evidence for subtle differences in social and personality patterns of adolescent drug users. These differences, however, apparently emerge long before the adolescent begins using drugs. Furthermore, these controlled studies provide no support for the rather speculative hypotheses for an irreversible defect in brain function and personality (amotivational syndrome) of chronic marijuana smokers. [18, 19] In fact, the college studies suggest that the motivational and scholastic achievement records of marijuana users are homogeneous and probably no different from nonsmoking controls. This similar performance level of drug users would not be predicted if an underlying defect in brain function existed.

Chronic Studies

More direct assessment of higher brain functions in chronic marijuana users has been reported in three recent neuropsychologic studies. Each of these studies is noteworthy for its use of control groups and the administration of special neuropsychologic tests designed to measure higher cortical brain functions in man. Grant et al.[14] administered a brief neuropsychologic test battery ($n = 8$) to a highly selected group of medical students (moderate users) who had smoked marijuana on an average of three times per month for at least 3 years and to a control group of students matched for intelligence. No differences between groups were found. These results are in agreement with those obtained in an earlier study by Mendelson and Meyer[25] that employed similar tests with a small group of casual ($n = 10$) and heavy users ($n = 10$). The main problem, particularly in the Grant et al. study,[14] concerns the use of medical students as the drug user group; the rigorous selection procedures already used for admission into medical school would probably mask or decrease the chances of observing any performance differences between groups. Another limitation in these two studies concerns the small sample sizes, the restricted number of tests, and the short duration and frequency of usage for their marijuana groups.

If an underlying defect in brain function is postulated to occur with chronic marijuana usage, an investigation should be addressed to users who have smoked marijuana consistently for many years. Infrequent usage for a few years, by individuals highly selected for intelligence and motivation, may mask more incipient long-term cortical and personality deficits. Only one study to date has been addressed to this particular question, the Jamaica Project on Ganja,[15] which was alluded to earlier. The neuropsychologic phase of this project[26] comprised the administration of 19 specialized neuropsychologic tests that were standardized in North America to assess changes in higher adaptive functions that occur after selective brain lesions have been produced in adults.[27, 28] The personality phase of this project[29] included the Lowenfeld Mosaic Test, a nonverbal *projective* measure in which the subject is encouraged to make designs by use of differently colored and shaped wood blocks without any time or choice constraints in the task. A modified Eysenck Personality Inventory was also administered as part of the psychiatric phase to examine extraversion and neuroticism traits in chronic users.

The overall tests were administered to a group of approximately 30 smokers and 30 controls; the user group had a history of regular *ganja* smoking that ranged from 7 to 37 years, with a mean of 17.5 years. Heavy users, who comprised part of the ganja group, smoked on the average of eight or more cigarettes per day. The results of this study revealed no major differences in neuropsychologic or personality functions between chronic smokers and matched controls. Nor were there any differences between groups in terms of intellectual function.

This study represents the most comprehensive effort to date to determine the long-term effects, if any, on higher adaptive brain functions in *chronic* marijuana smokers. These negative results, moreover, are compatible with the studies cited earlier that examined various neuropsychologic or personality characteristics in groups of *moderate* smokers with appropriate control groups.[2, 3, 14, 21, 25]

However, because of the potential health and legal implications associated with long-term chronic marijuana usage, some reservations should be directed to the neuropsychologic and personality phase of this project. First, no attempt was made to standardize the neuropsychologic test battery on a group of Jamaican residents *prior* to the experimental study. The test battery, which was standardized on North Americans, contained many items that were culturally biased against native Jamaicans. In fact, the authors revealed that some of the subtests of the Wechsler Adult Intelligence Scale had to be omitted because of obvious cultural bias.[26] Yet other tests, with equal bias, were not excluded. Knights [26] explained his reasoning as follows:

These tests are not culture free, but since the primary concern was to determine differences between the smokers and non-smokers, this was not considered a limiting factor, on the assumption that any cultural bias in the test items would be similar and consistent for both groups (p. 11).

This reasoning would not follow, however, if a floor effect occurred on several of the tests. In other words, if the tests were too difficult for both groups, which might be expected for rural disadvantaged groups from either culture, depressed performance levels would mask possible differences between groups. The fact that Knights reported no means or performance levels for either group prevents a determination of this problem. Nevertheless, the possibility of a floor effect must be considered.

Second, virtually no attempt was made to include measures of short-term memory, under distraction, for verbal and perceptual functions in the neuropsychologic test battery. In fact, this criticism could be leveled at the vast majority of acute and chronic studies that have used human subjects. This omission is particularly significant in view of possible attentional deficits that occur after the immediate use of marijuana in inexperienced subjects,[1, 12, 13] and there have been reports of memory and time disturbances in some cases of chronic marijuana usage, especially in the "amotivational syndrome." [18, 19] Also, disturbances in short-term memory have long been known to occur as primary symptoms after lesions have occurred in different structures and systems of the brain.[30]

Third, the analytic methods employed in the Jamaica Project [26] were essentially univariate *t* and *F* tests; such tests present certain statistical problems when multiple measures and significance tests are computed.[31] The use of multivariate extensions of these univariate tests, followed by separate univariate *t* tests (for matched-pair variables), would have been advised. The importance of the multivariate tests cannot be sufficiently emphasized. Multivariate procedures have at least two advantages over more well-known univariate tests. The first advantage is that multivariate tests take into account the dependent structure that prevails among several correlated measures, as in the neuropsychologic battery, for example. Groups that are not significantly different when considered in the univariate context *may actually differ* in the multivariate context. Thus, the multivariate tests ensure that all possible sources of variance will be considered. The second advantage of multivariate tests is that they provide a check on type-1 error rates by adjusting the α level across repeated tests and by reducing the likelihood of chance differences between groups.[31]

Fourth, no attempt was made to evaluate the long-term neuropsychologic effects between light users (one to four spliffs/day) and heavy users (eight spliffs/day). This evaluation would have helped to identify possible within-group differences in the chronic smokers.

Fifth, the personality examination consisted largely of a projective test, the validity of which is equivocal at best and which purports to measure vastly different clinical syndromes simultaneously. For example, on the basis of this test, it was concluded that there were no major personality differences between smokers and nonsmokers. Still later, it was concluded that "there is no evidence of organic brain damage or schizophrenia among the subjects, based on the results of the Lowenfeld Mosaic Test" [26] (p. 118). A study of this magnitude should have included a more objective and quantitative assessment of personality structure, especially since previous work had indicated some interpretive difficulties because of the way native Jamaicans responded to the test.[32, 33]

Despite the preceding reservations, the Jamaica Project stands as a landmark study on the long-term effects of chronic cannabis usage. However, because of the potential health and legal implications associated with marijuana usage [1] and the reservations already cited above, it seems mandatory that a replication study be conducted, in an additional culture in which cannabis has long been used and in which particular attention is focused on problems of cultural bias in the selection and standardization of an appropriate neuropsychologic and personality test battery. This paper is addressed to this problem.

PREEXPERIMENTAL PHASE

Introduction

Whenever an attempt is made to conduct cross-cultural psychologic research, the problem arises of interpreting test results independently of cultural bias. Because of cultural differences, tests developed and standardized in one culture may not measure the identical phenomena in another culture. While this problem was noted in the psychologic portions of the Jamaica Project,[26] no direct attempts to deal with cultural bias in the tests were made. Rather, it was argued that because the focus of the Jamaica Project concerned differences between groups, sources of variance that stemmed from cultural bias would be the same for both groups. Furthermore, because the neuropsychologic tests assessed abilities (motor, somatosensory-perceptual, and so on) that are primarily "nonverbal," these tests generally conformed to traditional approaches to "culture fairness." The flaw in the latter argument should be obvious.

Our initial approach to test selection in Costa Rica was similar to that employed in the Jamaica Project. We wanted a battery of neuropsychologic tests that assessed abilities less susceptible to the effects of cultural bias. Thus, we selected initially a battery of tests somewhat similar to that employed in Jamaica. However, as our planning progressed, we became concerned about additional problems not considered in the Jamaica Project. To reiterate, the first, and most obvious, problem concerned the possible existence of ceiling and floor effects. If the tests selected were either too easy (ceiling effect) or too difficult (floor effect) for the Costa Rican sample, important differences between marijuana users and nonusers might be masked. A second problem concerned the nature of the neuropsychologic tests themselves. The battery utilized in the Jamaican study comprised virtually no measures of short-term memory, particularly those that employ distraction retrieval procedures. Measures of this sort, that is, memory and learning tasks, are more susceptible to linguistic and educational differences between North American and Latin American cultures. It is also true that deficiencies in these abilities are likely to be associated with very subtle deficits in brain function. Indeed, one of the primary disturbances in any organic brain syndrome is a memory deficit. Therefore, it was deemed of vital importance to employ in our study measures sensitive to minor deficits in memory and learning.

Measures of this sort are available and have been employed extensively at the University of Florida. Their inclusion into the neuropsychologic and intelligence battery, however, necessitated translation into Spanish. This translation created the problem of whether the tests would measure in Costa Rica the same functions or operations that they purported to measure in the United States. Thus, to deal with the problem of ceiling and floor effects, and to ensure the appropriateness of the neuropsychologic and intelligence tests, a preexperimental psychologic study was conducted in Costa Rica. This preexperimental phase was designed to help in the final selection of a modified test battery that could be used in the experimental (matched pair) phase of the study. Furthermore, redundant or inappropriate measures could be discarded. Summarily, we hoped to derive a set of valid and representative measures, sufficiently similar to those employed in the Jamaica Project for comparison and replication and that would also be sensitive to very subtle differences in brain function between marijuana users and nonusers.

Method

Sample

The sample for the preexperimental phase consisted of 86 Costa Rican males (mean age, 31.3; range, 16–64). In general, these Ss were members of the lower-middle class (mean educational level about eighth grade) applying for services with the Ministry of Health in San José. None of the Ss were considered for inclusion into the experimental phase. Thus, this sample constituted a separate group of native Costa Ricans.

Tests

The following list of 17 neuropsychologic tests was designed to measure a variety of functions, including immediate and short-term memory (for verbal and nonverbal materials), learning, and somatosensory-perceptual motor abilities. All of these tests have been used extensively in clinical practice and research at the University of Florida Neuropsychology Laboratory and at the Psychology Service of the Gainesville Veterans Administration Hospital.

Four tests were selected from the Williams Scale for the Measurement of Memory.[34] This particular battery of memory tests is not well known in the United States but has been used widely in clinical and experimental studies in England. It has also proved to be effective in this country in detecting memory disturbance that occurs after relatively mild unilateral brain damage in temporal lobe disorders.[35, 36] A brief description follows.

Williams Memory Scale. (1) Digit span is a measure of digit recall traditionally used to assess immediate recall in clinical practice. It consists of a set of trials in which the subject is required to remember a list of digits of gradually increasing length. Two conditions, for digits forward and digits backward (repeating digits in the opposite direction of presentation), are given. The digit span consists of the sum total of digits forward and digits backward.

(2) The Rey-Davis is a test of "nonverbal learning" and is a good measure of visuospatial ability. In this test, four square boards are laid out in front of the subject. On each board, eight pegs are inserted loosely in the board; a ninth peg is fixed. The modified version used in Costa Rica consists of asking the subject to find and remember the location of the fixed peg on each board. On each of the five trials that comprise the test, the subject must go to each board and point to the fixed peg. If the subject points to the wrong peg, he must find it before going on to the next board. Score consists of the total number of errors across all five trials.

(3) Word learning is a verbal learning task that consists of five trials with a set of Spanish words of extremely low frequency of use not in the subject's vocabulary. These words are read along with a definition to the subject. On each trial, the subject is required to recall the appropriate definition for the stimulus word. Each miss is corrected before going to the next word. A score is obtained that consists of the total number of errors committed across five trials.

(4) Delayed recall is a measure of retention. A subject is shown a card with nine line drawings of common objects. After a 10-min delay, he is asked to name the objects. For each picture not recalled spontaneously, a prompt, or clue, is given for the object. Should the subject still fail to name the correct picture, he is shown a sheet with the original nine drawings and six others. Failure to select the appropriate drawing is labeled an error of recognition. Scoring consists simply of the total number of errors in the three recall conditions.

The Wechsler Memory Scale,[37] one of the first standardized memory tests, was also given. It has proved effective in detecting both mild and severe signs of organic brain damage and consists of seven subtests. All verbal tests were translated into Spanish appropriate for Costa Rica.

Wechsler Memory Scale. (5) Personal and current information consists of six simple questions that relate to current information (e.g., How old are you?). It is intended as part of a simple orientation interview.

(6) Orientation is designed to test a subject's immediate orientation, asking questions like "What is today's date?," "Where are you?," and so on.

(7) Mental control consists of three subitems that require careful attention (counting backward from 20 to 1, repeating the alphabet, and counting forward by 3s). With measures 5 and 6, it functions as a guide to the Ss current mental status.

(8) Logical memory consists of two short paragraphs of a narrative nature devised by a consulting psychologist in San José (Dina Krauskopf) by use of material that was culturally homogeneous for the population to be examined. The subject is read the paragraphs (one at a time) in his native language and is asked to relate to the examiner the content of the passage immediately upon hearing it for the first time. Scores are based on the number of phrases correctly remembered or approximated for each of the two paragraphs. After a 90-min interpolated delay, the subjects are again asked to repeat to the examiner the

content of the two paragraphs that he heard earlier. Thus, two scores are obtained: one for immediate short-term verbal memory and one for delayed short-term memory.

(9) Digit span conforms to standard clinical tests of forward and backward recall for digits as described in measure 1.

(10) Visual reproduction is a test composed of three geometric designs that the subject must draw from memory. Each figure is viewed for 10 sec.

(11) Associate learning is a verbal learning task that consists of 10 paired word associates. Some of the pairs are easily associated (e.g., north-south), whereas others are difficult to associate (e.g., obey-inch). The score consists of the total number of difficult associates recalled plus one-half of the easy paired associates.

(12) The Facial Recognition Memory Test [38] is a test of memory for non-verbal stimuli (faces). The subject is presented a card that contains 12 photographs of unfamiliar men and women, which he is asked to study for 45 sec. At the end of this time period, the photograph is removed, and an interpolative task of approximately 90 sec is presented. The subject is then presented a photograph of 25 pictures of unfamiliar men and women and asked to identify the 12 that appeared in the first photograph. This task is a measure of non-verbal memory (short term); scores are reported in terms of number of photographs correctly identified. This test is an excellent measure of memory for nonverbal stimuli and represents an analog to the Logical Memory Test.

(13) As a measure of fine manual ability, the Finger Oscillation Test [39] was given. A version of this test was also given in Jamaica. In our version of this task, the subject is required to rapidly depress a key for 10 sec with his index finger. A Veeder-Root counter records the frequency with which the key is depressed during the time interval. Four 10-sec trials per hand are administered; scores are summed and averaged over trials for each hand. Difference scores between hands are used to determine the degree of manual laterality.[40]

Two well-known cognitive measures of somatosensory-perceptual ability were also given. Similar versions of these tasks were given in Jamaica.

(14) The Halstead Tactual Performance Test,[41] as modified and administered in the Satz Neuropsychology Laboratory, is designed to test unilateral tactile learning and central nervous system integrity. It provides an indirect measure of transfer capabilities from the dominant to the nondominant cerebral hemispheres. By eliminating all visual and auditory cues, the subject is required to pick up 10 wooden geometric shapes and place them in a formboard in a 15-min interval, first by use of the preferred hand and then by use of the nonpreferred hand. Evidence of the transfer of learning from the dominant cerebral hemisphere to the nondominant cerebral hemisphere is demonstrated by a significant reduction in the time required to perform the task with the nonpreferred hand.

(15) The Finger Localization Test [42] is composed of three parts that, when combined, measure the subject's ability to integrate and report sensory stimulation. Part I measures unilateral and bilateral differentiation between digits, which should be an easy task in the absence of cortical dysfunction. The fingers of each hand are numbered one to five, beginning with the thumb: stimulation by touching the finger in question with the tip of a pen or pencil, out of the subject's range of vision, is reported by number. Part II requires the subject to identify the finger stimulated by pointing to the same finger represented on a diagram of each hand. Part III requires the subject to identify

a letter of the alphabet that is traced on his fingertip. Scores are reported in terms of the task and are combined for total errors in terms of right and left sides.

(16) The Benton Visual Retention Test [43] is a measure of reproduction memory. The subject is shown a drawing of a common geometric figure that he views for 10 sec. The figure is then removed, and, after a 5-sec delay, the subject is asked to reproduce the figure graphically. Reproductions are either correct or incorrect, with a correct reproduction receiving a score of one. The total score is the number of correctly reproduced figures. It has proved to be a useful task in detecting mild disturbances in writing ability (agraphia) and voluntary movements (apraxia) that occur after brain injury.

(17) The measure of intelligence chosen was the IPAT Culture Fair Intelligence Test.[44] This measure was developed by Raymond B. Cattell for use with children and adults and is designed as a measure of general intelligence (g). In an attempt to make the instrument "culture fair" (i.e., minimally contaminated by differences in cultural patterns of motivation, achievement, social status, and so on), Cattell employed nonsense material, presumably universally unfamiliar, in addition to some commonplace material. The test, though heavily concentrated on perception, taps such categories as progressions, analogies, and abstract reasoning. A visual mode of stimulus presentation is used with a multiple choice response mode. In general, the major reviews of the instrument raise some doubt as to its universal applicability.[45] However, it has come closer to meeting such standards than any other test that purports to be "culture fair." Furthermore, it does appear to be a reasonably good measure of g. In lieu of a test designed specifically to measure g within a particular culture, the Culture Fair Intelligence Test would appear to be an appropriate instrument to employ. Split-half and test-retest reliability coefficients exceed 0.80 in most samples, and the validity coefficients (i.e., as a measure of g) have ranged from 0.56 to 0.85 with the Stanford-Binet, 0.73 with the Otis Group Intelligence Test, and 0.84 with the Wechsler-Bellevue.[44]

Procedure

The 86 Ss (preexperimental) were administered this battery of tests in Costa Rica by native Latin Americans (Dina Krauskopf and Miriam Gutierrez). These examiners were experienced in psychologic assessment and were trained on location in administration of the neuropsychologic battery by two of the authors (L. S. S. and P. S.). The tests were individually administered in the order described above in a single session of about 2 hr. Testing took place in separate rooms at a small apartment in San José rented specifically for the purposes of test administration.

Results (preexperimental)

Neuropsychologic Data

TABLE 1 presents means, standard deviations, and ranges for each of the 17 neuropsychologic tests for the 86 Costa Rican subjects. In addition, minimum and maximum possible scores are reported for each test. As the Table indicates, the performance of this standardization sample is generally well within the range of possible scores. Only orientation and personal information demonstrate a ceiling effect, which suggests that these subtests can be discarded. No tests show evidence for a floor effect. Indeed, performance of this sample is adequate, even on the verbal tests that require translation (e.g., logical memory), and approximates performance of North American subjects. Two sets of rather similar tests were found to be highly correlated, visual reproduction and the Benton Visual Retention ($r = 0.72$) and associate learning and word learning

TABLE 1

MEANS, STANDARD DEVIATIONS, RANGES, AND MINIMUM-MAXIMUM SCORES ON NEUROPSYCHOLOGIC BATTERY IN COSTA RICAN STANDARDIZATION SAMPLE

Test	Mean	SD	Range	Min.-Max.
Williams Memory Scale				
Digit span	8.81	1.97	2–14	0-15
Rey-Davis	6.29	4.11	0–20	0-20
Word learning	20.28	12.41	0–49	0-50
Delayed recall	6.98	4.87	0–24	0-27
Wechsler Memory Scale				
Personal and current information	5.38	.88	3–6	0-6
Orientation	4.85	.47	2–5	0-5
Mental control	4.73	2.39	0–9	0-9
Logical memory, immediate	10.61	3.58	2–19	0-23
Logical memory, delayed	8.08	3.36	2–15	0-23
Digit span	8.17	2.08	0–12	0-15
Visual reproduction	8.31	4.07	1–14	0-14
Associate learning	13.5	4.22	3–22	0-30
Facial recognition	8.08	1.42	4–11	0-12
Finger oscillation, right hand	49.28	10.56	20–109	—
Finger oscillation, left hand	45.05	9.26	30–105	—
Tactual performance	18 min 17 sec	6 min 55 sec	4 min 43 sec to 30 min	0-30 min
Tactual performance (errors)	2.00	3.83	0–14	0-20
Finger localization (total errors)	5.71	4.17	0–21	0-30
Benton visual retention	6.18	2.51	0–10	0-10

($r = 0.56$), which suggests that either one of these correlated tests could be excluded. In general, however, the battery of neuropsychologic tests were quite appropriate for use in Costa Rica.

Intelligence Data

In analyzing the data obtained with the Culture Fair Intelligence Test (CFIT), several problems became evident. The first was that the mean deviation IQ for this group (76) was quite low, even though the standard deviation (15.9) approximated that of the standardization population. Closer inspection of this data suggested the presence of a floor effect with the CFIT. The distribution of scores was positively skewed and the lowest score (57) was also the mode of the distribution. We found this extremely puzzling and led us to question whether the CFIT was adequately assessing the intelligence of this Costa Rican sample.

In an attempt to resolve these questions and to obtain a measure of intelligence suitable for use in Costa Rica, additional intelligence tests were given to 30 Ss randomly selected from the standardization group of 86. Two additional intelligence tests were administered, Raven's Colored Progressive Matrices (CPM)[46] and a Spanish version of the Wechsler Adult Intelligence Test (WAIS).[47]

The CPM was chosen because it is widely cited as a measure of intelligence

TABLE 2

DESIGN OF SHORT-FORM SCALE *

Subtest	Items Used	Multiple Score By
Information (I) †	every third item	3
Comprehension (C)	odd items only	2
Arithmetic (A)	odd items only	2
Similarities (S)	odd items only	2
Digit span (D)	unchanged	1
Vocabulary (V)	every third item	3
Digit symbol (DS)	unchanged	1
Picture completion (PC)	every third item	3
Block design (BD) †	odd items only	2
Picture arrangement (PA)	odd items only	2
Object assembly (OA)	odd items only	2

* For further scoring details, consult the authors.
† Subtract one point from obtained scaled score.

free of cultural bias and comparable to the CFIT. The task consists of designs that the subject is required to complete with multiple-choice options of the design part that best fits. No verbal responses are required. Answers may complete a pattern, complete an analogy, systematically alter a pattern, introduce systematic permutations, or systematically resolve figures into parts. Scores are reported in terms of the number of items correctly solved and may be converted to percentile ranks.

A Spanish version of the WAIS [47] was administered because of its traditional use as a measure of intelligence in the United States and other countries. It has also been widely used with brain-damaged populations.[48] Because of restrictions on the amount of testing time, the WAIS was administered according to the Satz-Mogel Short-Form Procedure.[49] This procedure, outlined in TABLE 2, was chosen because it uses all 11 WAIS subtests and scales in a variety of settings.[49-51]

The results of this preliminary study have been summarized in another

TABLE 3

DESCRIPTIVE ASPECTS OF THE IQ SCORES FOR THE COLORED PROGRESSIVE MATRICES,
CULTURE FAIRNESS SCALE, WECHSLER ADULT INTELLIGENCE SCALE,
AND SATZ-MOGEL RESCORING OF THE WAIS

Test	Mean	SE	SD	Range
CPM (raw)	26.27	1.12	6.12	12–36
CF (normal)	72.17	2.74	14.99	57–118
WAIS (FSIQ)	112.57	1.76	9.63	95–135
Satz-Mogel (FSIQ)	112.0	1.76	9.64	94–133

paper.[52] The basic descriptive results are contained in TABLE 3. Examination of this Table shows that the sample ($N = 30$) obtained a full-scale WAIS IQ of 113 with a standard deviation of 9.6. This IQ score, while somewhat inflated because of the small sample size, probably reflects cultural and sampling differences between Puerto Rico and Costa Rica. Costa Rica is currently experiencing a push toward literacy that is more intensive than that found in other Latin American cultures.[53] The standard deviation for the WAIS is smaller than that of the standardization population. However, scores were symmetrically distributed around the mean, and the range of scores was entirely adequate.

The results of the CPM on this additional sample are also presented in TABLE 3. Inspection reveals that the CPM produced a restricted range of scores and a surprisingly low mean raw score (26.27). This problem, previously noted by Johnson *et al.*,[54] is compounded by the fact that the CPM yields no deviation IQ. Thus, direct comparisons among the CFIT, WAIS, and CPM are difficult to make.

TABLE 3 also reveals that the mean (112) and standard deviation (9.6) obtained for the Satz-Mogel rescoring of the WAIS are virtually identical. This fact, coupled with the high intertest correlations between original and rescored WAIS protocols (TABLE 4), suggests that the WAIS could be administered in accordance with the Satz-Mogel Short-Form Procedure.

To determine whether the CFIT provides a valid and culture-fair measure of intelligence for this Costa Rican sample, TABLE 5 is helpful. This Table

TABLE 4

CORRELATIONS AMONG THE SATZ-MOGEL SHORT-FORM SCALE AND WAIS SUBTESTS,
VERBAL IQ, PERFORMANCE IQ, AND FULL-SCALE IQ

Subtest	r *	Subtest	r
Information	0.86	Digit symbol	1.00
Completion	0.92	Picture completion	0.87
Arithmetic	0.87	Block design	0.93
Similarities	0.83	Picture arrangement	0.89
Digit span	1.00	Object assembly	0.87
Vocabulary	0.85	Performance IQ	0.90
Verbal IQ	0.94	Full-scale IQ	0.97

* For all rs, p $<$0.001.

contains correlation coefficients among the three tests for this sample. The most interesting correlation is between the WAIS and CFIT (0.86). The strength of this correlation suggests, of course, that the two tests have common variances. Thus, the problem with the CFIT probably reflects the absence of a Latin American standardization rather than any inherent problem in test construction. In the end, because the WAIS had been standardized in a Spanish-speaking culture, did not produce a floor effect, and yielded scores that were not misleading, it is probably the most useful measure of intelligence for the experimental phase of this project.

EXPERIMENTAL PHASE

Introduction

This phase of the psychologic studies constitutes the primary thrust of this project. The purpose of this phase was to determine whether chronic use of marijuana is associated with any disturbances in neuropsychologic, intellectual, and personality spheres.

TABLE 5

PEARSONIAN INTERTEST CORRELATIONS FOR THE COLORED PROGRESSIVE MATRICES, CULTURE FAIRNESS SCALE, AND THE WECHSLER ADULT INTELLIGENCE SCALE

Test	CPM	CFIT	WAIS (FSIQ)
Colored progressive matrices			
Culture fairness scale	0.63 *		
Wechsler Adult Intelligence Scale (FSIQ)	0.68 *	0.86 *	

* $p \leq 0.001$.

We felt that the preexperimental phase provided some evidence to support the use of this modified neuropsychologic and intellectual battery in this culture. The only deletions from the neuropsychologic battery were the subtests of the Wechsler Memory Scale, saving only the logical memory subtest. As indicated under PREEXPERIMENTAL PHASE, these subtests were felt to be largely redundant. It was also determined that the WAIS, administered by the Satz-Mogel Short-Form Procedure, provided an appropriate and valid measure of intellectual functioning.

One problem not yet discussed concerns selection of a personality test. In the Jamaica Project, a projective test, the Lowenfeld Mosaic Test,[33] was employed. Initially, we also planned to use a projective measure of personality. However, during planning, issues arose concerning the reliability and validity of personality tests. Projective tests are entirely appropriate in small, individualized settings when carefully administered and interpreted by experienced clinicians. However, projective tests are also notorious for their low reliability and lack of construct validity.[55, 56] To administer a projective measure in another culture for the purpose of describing *group* differences would merely compound the problem. This problem was apparent from previous attempts to use the Lowenfeld Mosaic Test [32, 33] in Jamaica. These data indicated that native Jamaicans performed quite *differently* from North American subjects. To employ this test in such a context would imply acceptance of the universality of psychoanalytic theory and interpretations in explaining differences in test performance; it would further imply that the test was a valid measure of these universal constructs. We found these assumptions psychometrically unpalatable.

Because of these concerns, we began to examine more objective types of tests. One test considered, which has been translated into Spanish, is the MMPI.[57] This test, however, is designed to measure clinical psychiatric disorders. Its use also requires an experienced clinician for interpretation, especially in view of the fact that the construct validity of the items and scales of the MMPI are low. Finally, as a test, the MMPI is apparently more sensitive to *state* rather than *trait* variables, which lowers its test-retest reliability.[58] We wished to describe more basic traits of personality than would have been permitted by the MMPI.

It should be apparent that in deciding on a personality test, we wanted one that was objective, reliable, and with reasonable construct validity. In addition, we wanted a test sensitive to basic personality traits in the normal adult personality, over and above clinical pathology. A test of this type should therefore be sensitive to very subtle differences in the personality structure of marijuana users and nonusers.

The test finally selected was form E of the IPAT 16 PF.[22] The 16 PF is a personality test constructed on the basis of factor analyses of literally thousands of questionnaire items, self-ratings, and behavior ratings. The 16 basic personality factors that comprise the 16 PF constitute a portion of the 24–30 primary factors discovered from the factor analytic studies and that presumably form the basic dimensions of the normal adult personality. TABLE 6 lists the factors that comprise the 16 PF along with a brief description of each factor.

In general, studies report that the reliability of the test is high, around 0.90.[22] Because the 16 primary factors were constructed according to factor analytic techniques and are factor pure, it can be presumed that construct validity is high. The strength of its construct validity has been demonstrated in many prediction studies in which the test is used to predict actual behavioral criteria.[22] Furthermore, most tests created from a construct point of view apparently measure more basic underlying constructs of personality, in the sense that predictions made on the basis of multiple regression techniques are more likely to be cross-validated in another sample. This finding is in contrast with the low cross-validity of both projective measures and tests constructed along the lines of the MMPI.[58]

In general, the 16 factors that comprise the 16 PF can be found in the MMPI, though in a more deviant direction. Thus, the test is somewhat sensitive to clinical disorders in personality.[59] Furthermore, the 16 primary factors of the test can be reduced to a set of eight second-order factors. These factors, identified and described in TABLE 7, correspond to aspects of personality more generally recognized. Two of the three second-order factors (neuroticism and extraversion) are represented in the Eysenck Personality Inventory. A modified version of the Eysenck scales, composed of items that make up the neuroticism and extraversion scales, was administered in Jamaica.[26] Thus, conversion of the primary factors into secondary factors makes possible a direct comparison of results obtained with the 16 PF with those obtained in Jamaica with the modified Eysenck Personality Inventory.

TABLE 6

16 PF PRIMARY FACTORS

Factor	Low Sten Score Description (1–3)	High Sten Score Description (8–10)
A	Reserved, detached, critical, aloof, stiff (sizothymia)	Outgoing, warmhearted, easygoing, participating (affectothymia)
B	Dull, low intelligence (crystallized, power measure)	Bright, high intelligence (crystallized, power measure)
C	Affected by feelings, emotionally less stable, easily upset, changeable (lower ego strength)	Emotionally stable, mature, faces reality, calm (higher ego strength)
E	Humble, mild, easily led, docile, accommodating (submissiveness)	Assertive, aggressive, competitive, stubborn (dominance)
F	Sober, taciturn, serious (desurgency)	Happy-go-lucky, gay, enthusiastic (surgency)
G	Expedient, disregards rules (weaker superego strength)	Conscientious, persistent, moralistic, staid (stronger superego strength)
H	Shy, timid, threat-sensitive (threctia)	Venturesome, uninhibited, socially bold (parmia)
I	Tough-minded, self-reliant, realistic (harria)	Tender-minded, sensitive, clinging, overprotected (premsia)
L	Trusting, accepting conditions (alaxia)	Suspicious, hard to fool (protension)
M	Practical, "down-to-earth" concerns (praxernia)	Imaginative, bohemian, absent-minded (autia)
N	Forthright, unpretentious, genuine but socially clumsy (artlessness)	Astute, polished, socially aware (shrewdness)
O	Self-assured, placid, secure, complacent, serene (untroubled adequacy)	Apprehensive, self-reproaching, insecure, worrying, troubled (guilt proneness)
Q_1	Conservative, respecting traditional ideas (conservativism of temperament)	Experimenting, liberal, free-thinking (radicalism)
Q_2	Group dependent, a "joiner" and sound follower (group adherence)	Self-sufficient, resourceful, prefers own decisions (self-sufficiency)
Q_3	Undisciplined, self-conflict, lax, follows own urges, careless of social rules (low self-sentiment integration)	Controlled, exacting will power, socially precise, compulsive, following self-image (high strength of self-sentiment)
Q_4	Relaxed, tranquil, torpid, unfrustrated, composed (low ergic tension)	Tense, frustrated, driven, overwrought (high ergic tension)

Form E of the test, developed by Herbert Eber, requires a lower literacy level (about fifth grade) from alternative forms of the test. Like all forms of the 16 PF, it can be adapted for cross-cultural purposes. Unfortunately, the Spanish version of some items of form E did not conform to language conventions in Costa Rican Spanish. However, in conjunction with Dr. Carter and Dina Krauskopf, and with the cooperation of IPAT, a suitable version of the test for use in Costa Rica was devised.

Because of time constraints, it was not possible to carry out a preexperimental standardization of the 16 PF. However, the test has proved satisfactory in many other countries.[22] Furthermore, the fact that the problem of culture fairness has been one of the principal concerns of Dr. Cattell and IPAT from its inception provided some rational basis for using this test without a preexperimental evaluation.

TABLE 7

16 PF SECOND-ORDER FACTORS

Symbol	Technical Title	Popular Label
Q_I	Exvia vs invia	extraversion vs introversion
Q_{II}	Adjustment vs anxiety	low anxiety vs high anxiety
Q_{III}	Pathemia vs cortertia	sensitivity, emotionalism vs tough poise
Q_{IV}	Subduedness vs independence (promethean will)	dependence vs independence
Q_V	Discreetness	—
Q_{VI}	Prodigal subjectivity	—
Q_{VII}	Intelligence (same as factor B)	—
Q_{VIII}	Superego strength (similar to factor 6)	—

Method

Sample

The sampling procedures used for the experimental phase of this project have been described extensively in other chapters of the final report of this massive project. In general, a sample of 84 chronic marijuana users and 156 potential controls were identified by the anthropologists on the field team. Minimal criteria for chronic marijuana use were defined as consumption of at least one marijuana cigarette three times per week for at least 10 years. Users in the final sample actually consumed much more marijuana than this figure, at a *daily* rate of about nine marijuana cigarettes for an average of about 17 years.

An experimental group of 41 users was finally selected and matched on an individual basis with 41 nonusers. Matching criteria included age within 4 years, level of education, marital status, occupation, frequency and duration of tobacco use, and alcohol consumption. Potential Ss were excluded if there was any question of their ability to cooperate over a period of 2 years or if a clear-cut disease entity emerged on medical examination that might confound the effects of marijuana use. None of the 41 users and 41 nonusers participated in the preexperimental phase of the psychologic studies.

Procedure

TABLE 8 outlines the tests used in the experimental phase and their order of administration, which was constant. As before, the psychologic battery was administered individually by experienced native Latin Americans (Dina Kraus-

TABLE 8

FINAL TEST BATTERY IN ORDER OF ADMINISTRATION FOR EXPERIMENTAL PHASE

1. Logical memory
2. Finger oscillation test
3. Halstead Tactual Performance Task
4. Digit span
5. Word learning
6. Rey-Davis
7. Delayed recall
8. Facial recognition test
9. Finger localization
10. Benton visual retention

11. Wechsler Adult Intelligence Scale
    a. Information
    b. Comprehension
    c. Arithmetic
    d. Similarities
    e. Digit span
    f. Vocabulary
    g. Digit symbol
    h. Picture completion
    i. Block design
    j. Picture arrangement
    k. Object assembly

12. 16 Personality Factors Test

kopf and Miriam Gutierrez) in quiet, separate rooms at a rented apartment. Testing was divided into two sessions of about 2 hr each, with a break for coffee separating the sessions. This break was to counteract the possible effects of fatigue on the test results and occurred at the same time for each subject.

Statistical Analysis

A description of statistical procedures by which this vast array of data were analyzed precedes the description of results. All data were subjected to a multivariate extension of the t test (Hotelling's T^2), followed by separate univariate *t* tests (for matched pairs) for each variable. As stated earlier, the importance of the multivariate tests cannot be sufficiently emphasized. One problem with multiple univariate tests is that a certain proportion of these tests will be significant because of chance (depending on the confidence level chosen). Several studies [31] have shown that the most efficient way of controlling type-I error without being overly conservative is to conduct an initial multivariate test, followed by separate univariate analyses. If the multivariate test on the variable set as a whole is significant, significant differences obtained with the univariate analyses can be attributed to real differences that exist between the groups. This procedure is recommended for any analysis of multiply dependent continuous variables normally distributed. In the data described below, all assumptions for the multivariate tests (except for that of randomness) were met, including that of homogeneity of covariance matrices. As in the case of a univariate analysis of variance, the sampling distribution of a multivariate analysis of variance is sufficiently robust, so that deviations from the assumption of randomness are minimal.[60]

Results (experimental)

Neuropsychologic Data

TABLE 9 presents the means, standard deviations, ranges, and results of the univariate *t* test for each of the 16 major variables that comprise the neuropsychologic analysis. These variables were also used for the multivariate test. In general, there were no significant univariate differences on any test. This finding is reinforced by the failure to find a significant multivariate difference between the user and nonuser groups (Hotelling's $T^2 = 0.67$; 16 and 65 df; $p \leq 0.82$).

Closer inspection of the data merely highlights the similarity in performance between users and nonusers. Where possible, performance is documented visually to show differences in learning between the two groups. TABLE 10 presents the descriptive statistics and univariate *t* tests for the Williams Scale for the Measurement of Memory. This Table is interesting in that it reveals a tendency for the user group to perform more poorly than the nonuser group on word learning, delayed recall, and Rey-Davis subtests. FIGURE 1 plots the mean number of errors in word learning for each group across the five trials included in the test. Though there is a trend for the user group to perform more poorly, it is also obvious that both groups showed similar learning curves on this memory task. A similar finding is evident on the other test of verbal memory, logical memory. Although there was a nonsignificant trend for the user group to perform more poorly, FIGURE 2 shows that the two groups actually responded similarly to the immediate and delayed conditions of the test. Similar findings were apparent on the Rey-Davis subtest. Referring back to TABLE 10, one can see a nonsignificant trend for the user group to perform more poorly. However, FIGURE 3, which plots mean errors for each group across the five trials of the task, shows that learning curves are quite similar for the two groups. Because the Rey-Davis subtest presumably measures a nonverbal aspect of memory (spatial), it is interesting to compare performance on this task with the facial recognition task (see TABLE 9). Again, there was a slight though nonsignificant trend for users to perform more poorly. In general, the results of the memory

TABLE 9

MEANS, STANDARD DEVIATIONS, AND TESTS OF SIGNIFICANCE FOR NEUROPSYCHOLOGIC
BATTERY FOR USER (U) AND NONUSER (N) GROUPS

		Mean	SD	Range	t Value	$p > t$
Age	U	30.24	7.30	19–47		
	N	30.61	7.26	18–50		
Logical memory, immediate	U	9.29	3.90	3–18	0.53	0.60
	N	9.66	3.61	4–17		
Logical memory, delayed	U	7.38	3.65	1–15	0.32	0.75
	N	7.56	3.47	0–14		
Finger oscillation, right hand	U	45.54	8.14	26–60	0.32	0.75
	N	46.02	5.72	29–58		
Finger oscillation, left hand	U	43.54	6.50	29–54	0.80	0.43
	N	42.39	5.83	32–58		
Tactual performance	U	17 min 03 sec	5 min 01 sec	7 min 13 sec to 30 min	0.66	0.51
	N	17 min 45 sec	6 min 13 sec	8 min 36 sec to 30 min		
Tactual performance (total errors)	U	1.24	2.79	0–11	0.61	0.55
	N	0.93	2.45	0–10		
Digit span	U	8.46	1.35	6–11	0.39	0.70
	N	8.59	1.41	5–12		
Word learning (errors)	U	25.80	11.79	3–48	0.77	0.45
	N	24.00	10.16	3–42		
Delayed recall (errors)	U	9.56	6.79	0–29	1.48	0.15
	N	7.63	5.03	0–25		
Facial recognition test	U	7.90	1.56	4–11	0.34	0.74
	N	8.00	1.16	5–10		
Finger localization (total errors)	U	6.10	3.35	0–16	0.68	0.50
	N	5.59	3.53	1–16		
Benton visual retention	U	5.70	2.26	1–10	0.12	0.91
	N	5.66	1.93	0–9		
Rey-Davis	U	7.17	3.69	0–17	1.75	0.09
	N	5.76	3.10	0–16		
WAIS verbal IQ	U	111.07	10.64	85–139	0.58	0.57
	N	109.98	9.54	88–136		
WAIS performance IQ	U	106.59	7.68	90–117	0.28	0.78
	N	107.17	11.57	84–132		
WAIS full-scale IQ	U	109.22	8.09	88–124	0.05	0.98
	N	109.12	9.89	92–133		

TABLE 10

MEANS, STANDARD DEVIATIONS, AND TESTS OF SIGNIFICANCE FOR
WILLIAMS MEMORY BATTERY FOR USER (U) AND NONUSER (N) GROUPS

	Mean	SD	Range	*t* Value	p > *t*
Word learning	U 25.80	11.79	3–48	0.77	0.45
	N 24.00	10.16	3–42		
Delayed recall	U 9.56	6.97	0–29	1.48	0.15
	N 7.63	5.03	0–25		
Rey-Davis	U 7.17	3.69	0–17	1.75	0.09
	N 5.76	3.10	0–16		
Digit span	U 8.46	1.35	6–11	0.39	0.70
	N 8.59	1.41	5–12		

tests, across different stimulus materials, show no significant differences in memory and learning between users and nonusers.

In looking more closely at the results for the somatosensory-perceptual tasks, the absence of significant univariate differences is even more dramatic. TABLE 11 reports the descriptive statistics and univariate *t* tests for the different components of the Halstead Tactual Performance Task. On the six different scores

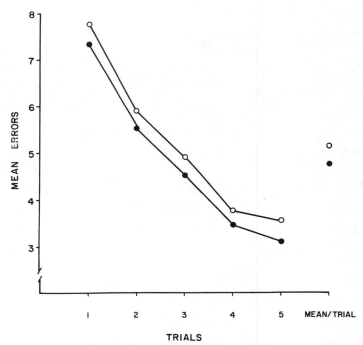

FIGURE 1. Mean error recall × trials and groups on word learning test. Maximum errors was 10 per trial. ●, Nonuser; ○, user.

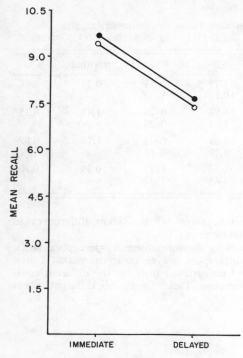

FIGURE 2. Mean correct recall for immediate and delayed conditions × groups on logical memory test. Maximum score was 22. ●, Nonuser; ○, user.

obtained for this task, no significant group differences emerged. Instead, as FIGURE 4 (time) and FIGURE 5 (errors) show, transfer of learning from right hand to left hand is clearly present and similar for both groups. TABLE 12 presents descriptive statistics and univariate t tests for the different portions of the finger localization test. Differences between the groups, none of which are significant, occur inconsistently, with no general trends appearing.

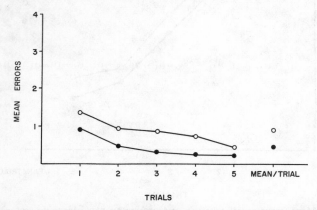

FIGURE 3. Mean recognition error (location) × trials and groups on Rey-Davis (nonverbal learning) test. Maximum score was 4 per trial. ●, Nonuser; ○, user.

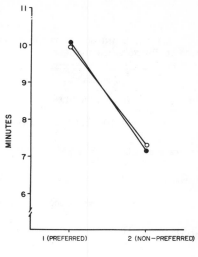

FIGURE 4. Mean transfer of learning (minutes) between hands on tactual performance test × groups. Maximum time per hand was 15 min. ●, Nonuser; ○, user.

Considering trends in the data on the 16 major variables in the neuropsychologic battery, it appears that on 11 of these variables, the user group performed more poorly. This finding, however, merely highlights the importance of the multivariate test on all 16 variables. The fact that this test was not significant should lend even more caution to interpreting trends that may appear in the data.

Intelligence Data

The purpose of this analysis was to compare performance of the two groups on the subtests and scales that comprise the WAIS. TABLE 13 presents the means, standard deviations, ranges, and univariate *t* tests for each of the WAIS subtests ($n = 11$) and scales ($n = 3$). These 14 variables were also combined for a multivariate test, which was not significant (Hotelling's $T^2 = 0.88$; 14 and 67 df; p ≤ 0.58). Similarly, the univariate *t* tests were not significant. The user group had a higher though nonsignificant mean subtest performance on six of the 11 subtests and a slightly higher verbal and full-scale IQ. Once again, performance of the two groups was quite similar on this aspect of the psychologic studies. This finding is clearly illustrated in FIGURE 6, which plots mean subtest scatter for both groups. The difference in scatter, particularly in the

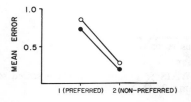

FIGURE 5. Mean transfer of learning (errors) between hands on tactual performance test × groups. Maximum errors per hand was 10. ●, Nonuser; ○, user.

TABLE 11

MEANS, STANDARD DEVIATIONS, AND TESTS OF SIGNIFICANCE FOR
TACTUAL PERFORMANCE SUBTESTS FOR USER (U) AND NONUSER (N) GROUPS

		Mean	SD	Range	t Value	$p > t$
RH time	U	9 min 48 sec	3 min 20 sec	3 min 11 sec to 15 min	0.15	0.88
	N	10 min 04 sec	3 min 12 sec	5 min 16 sec to 15 min		
RH errors	U	0.83	1.91	0–7	0.24	0.81
	N	0.73	1.88	0–8		
LH time	U	7 min 06 sec	2 min 37 sec	3 min 07 sec to 15 min	0.35	0.73
	N	7 min 14 sec	3 min 13 sec	3 min 20 sec to 15 min		
LH errors	U	0.26	1.11	0–6	0.36	0.72
	N	0.20	0.72	0–3		
Total time	U	17 min 03 sec	5 min 01 sec	7 min 13 sec to 30 min	0.66	0.51
	N	17 min 45 sec	6 min 13 sec	8 min 36 sec to 30 min		
Total errors	U	1.24	2.79	0–11	0.61	0.55
	N	0.93	2.46	0–10		

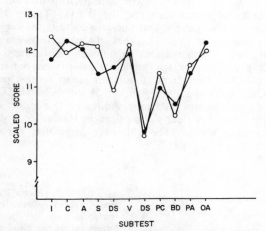

FIGURE 6. Mean subtest performance on WAIS × groups. Maximum scaled score per subtest was 19. For abbreviations, see TABLE 2. ●, Nonuser; ○, user.

TABLE 12

MEANS, STANDARD DEVIATIONS, AND TESTS OF SIGNIFICANCE FOR FINGER
LOCALIZATION SUBTESTS FOR USER (U) AND NONUSER (N) GROUPS

	Mean	SD	Range	*t* Value	p > *t*
Part I					
LH errors	U 0.02	0.16	0–1	1.14	0.26
	N 0.10	0.37	0–2		
RH errors	U 0.29	0.75	0–4	1.65	0.11
	N 0.07	0.35	0–2		
Bilateral LH errors	U 0.93	1.06	0–2	0.10	0.92
	N 0.90	1.22	0–4		
Bilateral RH errors	U 1.00	0.95	0–3	0.22	0.83
	N 0.95	1.07	0–4		
Total part-I errors	U 2.24	2.06	0–9	0.49	0.63
	N 2.02	2.02	0–7		
Part II					
LH errors	U 0.12	0.40	0–2	0.24	0.81
	N 0.15	0.57	0–3		
RH errors	U 0.34	0.53	0–2	0.78	0.44
	N 0.46	0.78	0–3		
Total part-II errors	U 0.46	0.74	0–3	0.71	0.48
	N 0.61	1.09	0–5		
Part III					
LH errors	U 1.37	1.22	0–5	0.11	0.92
	N 1.39	1.14	0–4		
RH errors	U 1.85	1.48	0–5	0.79	0.44
	N 1.61	1.11	0–4		
Total part-III errors	U 3.22	2.32	0–10	0.46	0.65
	N 3.00	1.87	0–7		
Total RH errors	U 3.68	2.23	0–11	1.29	0.20
	N 3.05	2.02	0–8		
Total LH errors	U 2.41	1.51	0–6	0.34	0.74
	N 2.54	2.06	0–8		
Total RH and LH errors	U 6.10	3.35	0–16	0.68	0.50
	N 5.58	3.53	1–16		

TABLE 13

MEANS, STANDARD DEVIATIONS, AND TESTS OF SIGNIFICANCE FOR
WAIS SUBTESTS AND SCALES FOR USER (U) AND NONUSER (N) GROUPS

		Mean	SD	Range	t Value	p > t
Information	U	12.34	2.58	8–17	1.22	0.23
	N	11.76	2.56	8–17		
Comprehension	U	11.88	2.70	2–16	0.74	0.46
	N	12.22	2.10	8–17		
Arithmetic	U	12.20	1.91	9–15	0.39	0.70
	N	12.00	2.42	6–18		
Similarities	U	12.05	2.22	4–16	1.44	0.16
	N	11.32	2.62	2–17		
Digit span	U	10.89	2.12	7–16	1.08	0.29
	N	11.46	2.68	6–18		
Vocabulary	U	12.34	2.60	7–19	0.95	0.35
	N	11.83	2.65	7–17		
Digit symbol	U	9.66	2.08	7–17	0.32	0.75
	N	9.78	1.99	6–15		
Picture completion	U	11.32	2.83	6–18	0.51	0.61
	N	10.93	4.03	0–19		
Block design	U	10.21	2.36	4–15	0.49	0.63
	N	10.46	2.46	6–14		
Picture arrangement	U	11.49	2.89	5–17	0.21	0.83
	N	11.37	3.60	1–19		
Object assembly	U	11.90	1.32	10–16	0.73	0.47
	N	12.15	1.74	7–16		
Verbal IQ	U	111.07	10.64	85–139	0.58	0.57
	N	109.98	9.54	88–136		
Performance IQ	U	106.59	7.68	90–117	0.28	0.78
	N	107.17	11.57	84–132		
Full-scale IQ	U	109.22	8.09	88–124	0.05	0.96
	N	109.12	9.89	92–133		

performance subtests, is not remarkable; further, as FIGURE 7 shows, verbal, performance, and full-scale IQs are quite similar for both groups.

Personality Data

TABLE 14 presents the means, standard deviations, ranges, and univariate t tests for each of the 16 personality factors. Only one t test was significant, that for factor Q_1 ($t = 2.35$; $p \leq 0.02$), a factor associated with a conservatism-liberalism personality dimension. However, the fact that the multivariate test for all 16 variables was not significant (Hotelling's $T^2 = 0.57$; 16 and 65 df; $p \leq 0.89$) minimizes this finding. The fact that the two groups endorsed very similar behavior in responding to the test items is quite evident in FIGURE 8,

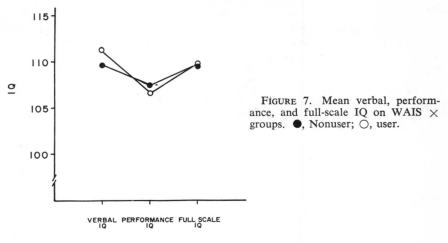

FIGURE 7. Mean verbal, perform-ance, and full-scale IQ on WAIS × groups. ●, Nonuser; ○, user.

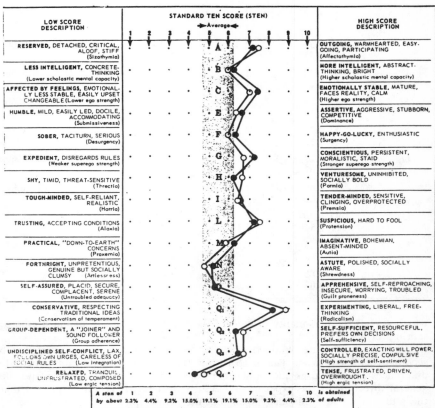

FIGURE 8. Mean 16 PF test profile × groups. ●, Nonuser; ○, user.

TABLE 14

MEANS, STANDARD DEVIATIONS, AND TESTS OF SIGNIFICANCE FOR 16 PF
PERSONALITY TEST FOR USER (U) AND NONUSER (N) GROUPS

Factor	Mean	SD	Range	t Value	$p > t$
A	U 7.10	1.73	4–10	0.83	0.41
	N 7.41	1.75	4–10		
B	U 6.00	1.40	3–10	0.13	0.90
	N 6.05	1.69	1–9		
C	U 7.00	1.98	2–10	0.28	0.78
	N 7.10	1.61	2–10		
E	U 6.41	1.58	4–10	0.41	0.68
	N 6.53	1.40	4–10		
F	U 5.90	1.18	4–10	0.73	0.47
	N 6.10	1.70	2–10		
G	U 6.76	1.98	1–9	0.81	0.42
	N 7.07	1.71	4–10		
H	U 6.39	1.86	2–9	0.83	0.41
	N 6.02	1.89	3–10		
I	U 6.51	2.01	2–10	0.00	1.00
	N 6.51	1.73	2–10		
L	U 7.20	1.71	4–10	0.08	0.94
	N 7.17	1.73	2–10		
M	U 5.88	2.29	1–10	0.53	0.60
	N 6.15	2.13	3–10		
N	U 4.98	2.22	1–9	0.33	0.75
	N 5.12	2.02	1–9		
O	U 5.22	2.01	1–10	0.44	0.67
	N 5.02	1.82	1–8		
Q_1	U 8.88	1.62	4–10	2.35	0.02
	N 8.20	1.91	2–10		
Q_2	U 6.90	2.22	2–10	0.81	0.42
	N 6.54	2.13	2–10		
Q_3	U 6.63	1.88	1–9	0.12	0.91
	N 6.68	1.60	3–9		
Q_4	U 4.85	1.61	2–9	0.07	0.92
	N 4.83	1.84	2–9		

which reveals the personality profiles of the two groups on the standard clinical scoring form.

Similar results were obtained when the primary factors were converted into second-order factors. As TABLE 15 shows, there were no significant univariate differences between user and nonuser groups. In view of this finding and the general direction of the experimental results thus far, it is not surprising that the multivariate test was also nonsignificant (Hotelling's $T^2 = 0.36$; 8 and 73 df; $p \leq 0.95$). The personality profile of the two groups is similar for both the 16 primary factors and the eight second-order factors.

POSTEXPERIMENTAL PHASE

Introduction

Postexperimental analyses of the experimental data were conducted to ensure that subtle changes in brain function or personality attributable to marijuana use were not overlooked. These analyses took the form of divisions of the user group according to different dimensions of marijuana use and life-style. The first of these divisions split the user group in terms of *frequency* of marijuana use, thus creating a *low-user* group and a *high-user* group. Formation of these groups ensured that marijuana effects would not be missed because of the substantial heterogeneity in frequency of marijuana use of the user group. Furthermore, if the findings of the experimental phase could be replicated in the high-user group, the results of the experimental phase would be strengthened.

The second dimension along which the user group was investigated was formulated and described by Carter and Doughty.[61] This dimension involves the marijuana typology devised by the anthropologists on the basis of their anthropologic field work in Costa Rica. Three types of marijuana users are described in Costa Rica. The first type, termed "Pastoralist-Escapist," described a pattern of use designed to "escape reality." This marijuana life-style is similar to patterns of use common in North America, that is, the use of marijuana to escape social and personal responsibilities. "Street movers," the second type, are characterized by mobile patterns of use. This type usually smokes in a group, often at "established" bistros that permit the use of marijuana. Smoking is very much a social convention and street movers freely admit their use of marijuana.

TABLE 15

MEANS, STANDARD DEVIATIONS, AND TESTS OF SIGNIFICANCE FOR 16 PF
SECOND-ORDER FACTORS FOR USER (U) AND NONUSER (N) GROUPS

Factor	Mean	SD	Range	t Value	$p > t$
Q_I	U 6.07	1.29	3.3–9.4	0.31	0.76
	N 6.17	1.48	3.6–10.0		
Q_{II}	U 4.73	1.39	1.9–8.7	0.17	0.87
	N 4.69	1.42	1.8–7.2		
Q_{III}	U 3.92	1.78	1.0–7.9	0.52	0.60
	N 3.74	1.67	1.0–7.7		
Q_{IV}	U 7.53	1.18	3.8–9.7	0.71	0.48
	N 7.35	1.10	5.4–9.9		
Q_V	U 4.35	1.41	1.0–7.4	0.61	0.55
	N 4.19	1.19	1.0–6.5		
Q_{VI}	U 6.62	1.41	3.2–8.9	0.36	0.72
	N 6.72	1.19	4.8–9.6		
Q_{VII}	U 6.00	1.40	3.0–10.0	0.13	0.90
	N 6.05	1.69	1.0–9.0		
Q_{VIII}	U 6.77	1.34	4.2–10.0	1.32	0.20
	N 6.38	1.32	3.4–9.5		

As a consequence, they are more likely to be in trouble with the police. They are less likely to subsist in relatively permanent familial relationships and to hold a particular job for any length of time.

In contrast, "stable users" are often happily married with a stable and enduring familial relationship. Job patterns are also generally stable. Stable users are more likely to smoke alone and to avoid use in social settings. Similarly, stable users generally avoid areas in which marijuana use is common and therefore avoid difficulty with the police.

This marijuana typology is quite interesting, particularly as it relates to personality. From the anthropologic studies,[61] it is evident that these patterns of use relate principally to family practices in child upbringing. An attempt was therefore made to determine whether a relationship existed among these anthropologic typologies, the neuropsychologic battery, and the factorial dimensions of the 16 PF test.

Method

Level of Use Groups

The two user groups were formed by dividing marijuana users according to the median number of cigarettes consumed daily. These estimates were obtained from electroencephalographic log reports and the nutritional surveys. The median estimate was 7.7 cigarettes per day. The subject at the median was discarded, leaving 20 users who smoked on an average less than seven cigarettes daily (low users) and 20 users who smoked more than seven cigarettes per day (high users).

Marijuana Typology Groups

Two groups were formed for this postexperimental analysis. The first group, termed here street movers, consisted of 16 actual street movers and two pastoralist-escapists identified from the 41 users. Because there were only two pastoralist-escapists in the user group, they were combined with the street movers for these analyses. The remaining users ($n = 23$) conformed to the life-style attributed to the stable user type of marijuana consumer.

Results (postexperimental)

Level of Use Groups

Three comparisons were made for this analysis, between high users and their matched controls, low users and their matched controls, and high users and low users. The results of these comparisons are presented in TABLE 16. For the purpose of brevity, TABLE 16 reports only probability levels (i.e., probability of rejecting the null hypothesis of no group differences) and direction of group differences for any significant univariate results. There were *no* significant multivariate differences in any of the comparisons, which suggests that these specific univariate results must be interpreted cautiously.

TABLE 16

UNIVARIATE PSYCHOLOGIC ANALYSES × USER GROUPS

Group	Neuropsychologic			Intelligence (WAIS)			16 PF (personality)		
	Variable	p > t	Direction	Variable	p > t	Direction	Variable	p > t	Direction
High user (H) vs control (C), $n_H = n_C = 20$	left hand tapping	0.04	H faster	(none)			(none)		
Low user (L) vs control (C), $n_L = n_C = 20$	(none)			information object assembly	0.05 0.04	L higher C higher	Q_1 (radicalism)	0.03	L more radical
High user (H) vs low user (L), $n_H = n_L = 20$	(none)			(none)			(none)		

In comparing high users versus their matched controls, only the finger oscillation task (left hand) produced a significant univariate difference ($t = 2.27$; 19 df; p $\leq$ 0.04). The direction of the results indicates that high users tap faster with their left hand than do their control counterparts. This finding is probably due to the fact that two members of the high user group were left-handed. There were no significant differences on the WAIS and 16 PF test.

Similarly unimpressive were the results obtained by comparing low users versus their matched controls. There were no significant differences on the neuropsychologic test battery. On the WAIS, the low user group performed higher on the information subtest ($t = 2.12$; 19 df; p $\leq$ 0.05), whereas the control group had a higher object assembly score ($t = 2.24$; 19 df; p $\leq$ 0.14). These results probably reflect a trend for users to perform better on the verbal subtests and for the controls to perform better on performance subtests.

The 16 PF produced one rather ubiquitous finding: low users were found to be more extreme on factor Q_1, associated with a conservatism-radicalism personality dimension ($t = 2.43$; 19 df; p $\leq$ 0.03). This was also the only significant univariate difference between users and nonusers. The difficulties in interpreting this difference were alluded to under EXPERIMENTAL PHASE.

The most important comparison in this section is between high users and low users. As TABLE 16 shows, there were *no* significant univariate (or multivariate) differences between high users and low users on the neuropsychologic, intelligence, or personality tests. This finding merely strengthens the negative results of the experimental phase and suggests that level of marijuana use has little influence on the overall results of the experimental phase.

Marijuana Typology Groups

This portion of the postexperimental phase was conducted in the same manner as for the user groups. Thus, univariate and multivariate significance tests were computed between street movers and their matched controls, stable users and their matched controls, and street movers and stable users. TABLE 17 presents the results of these comparisons.

Results for the comparison between street movers and their matched controls are easily summarized. There were no significant univariate (or multivariate) differences between these groups on the neuropsychologic, intellectual, or personality tests.

Comparing stable users and their matched controls produced no significant group differences on the neuropsychologic and intellectual battery. However, there was a significant multivariate difference between stable users and their matched controls on both the 16 PF primary factors (Hotelling's $T^2 = 2.45$; 16 and 29 df; p $\leq$ 0.02) and the second-order factors (Hotelling's $T^2 = 2.21$; 16 and 29 df; p $\leq$ 0.05). Furthermore, significant univariate differences were found on factors H ($t = 2.61$; 22 df; p $\leq$ 0.02), L ($t = 2.40$; 22 df; p $\leq$ 0.03), L_1 ($t = 2.42$; 22 df; p $\leq$ 0.02) and the second-order factor Q_{VIII} ($t = 2.40$; 22 df; p $\leq$ 0.02). Stable users, in comparison with their matched controls, are more venturesome (H+), suspicious (L+), radical (S+), and conscientious (Q_{VIII}+). Interpretation of this finding is reserved for the DISCUSSION.

When street movers and stable users are compared, several interesting differences arise. On the neuropsychologic test battery, stable users are slower than street movers on the tactual performance task ($t = 4.04$; 39 df; p $\leq$ 0.05) and

TABLE 17

UNIVARIATE PSYCHOLOGIC ANALYSES × TYPOLOGY GROUPS

Group	Neuropsychologic			Intelligence (WAIS)			16 PF (personality)		
	Variable	$p > t$	Direction	Variable	$p > t$	Direction	Variable	$p > t$	Direction
Street mover (SM) vs control (C), $n_{SM} = n_C = 18$		(none)			(none)			(none)	
Stable (S) vs control (C), $n_S = n_C = 23$		(none)			(none)		H (venturesomeness)	0.02	S more venturesome
							L (suspiciousness)	0.03	S more suspicious
							Q (radicalism)	0.02	S more radical
							Q_{VIII} (conscientiousness)	0.02	S more conscientious
Street mover (SM) vs stable (S), $n_{SM} = 18$, $n_S = 23$	form board (total time)	0.05	S slower	picture-completion	0.002	S lower	H (venturesomeness)	0.01	SM more venturesome
	finger localization (total errors)	0.06	S more errors	performance IQ	0.02	S lower			

make more errors on finger localization ($t = 3.66$; 39 df; $p \leq 0.06$). The multivariate test, which comprises the 16 neuropsychologic variables, was *not* significant (Hotelling's $T^2 = 0.82$; 13 and 27 df; $p \leq 0.63$)!

The WAIS also revealed some interesting univariate differences. The stable users were significantly slower than the street movers on the picture completion subtest ($t = 11.64$; 1 and 39 df; $p \leq 0.002$), and they had a lower performance IQ ($t = 5.54$; 1 and 39 df; $p \leq 0.02$). Once again, however, the multivariate test on all 14 variables was not significant (Hotelling's $T^2 = 1.50$; 14 and 26 df; $p \leq 0.18$).

In the personality sphere, only one significant difference emerged. Street movers obtained a higher mean score on factor H, a factor associated with venturesomeness ($t = 6.45$; 1 and 39 df; $p \leq 0.01$). This finding is interesting in view of the fact that stable users scored higher on factor H than did their matched controls. On this basis, one might expect a difference on factor H between users and nonusers. Such a finding, however, was not obtained and merely highlights the folly of interpreting single univariate differences when so many dependent significant tests are computed. Thus, it is not surprising that no significant multivariate difference between street movers and stable users was found on the 16 PF primary factors (Hotelling's $T^2 = 1.54$; 16 and 24 df; $p \leq 0.16$) and second-order factors (Hotelling's $T^2 = 1.45$; 8 and 32 df; $p \leq 0.22$). Nevertheless, the fact that so many differences emerged in the marijuana typology portion of the postexperimental phase, especially in the personality area, certainly suggests that there is some substance to the typology.

Discussion

The present study represented an additional attempt to examine the effects of chronic marijuana use on higher brain function and personality. Particular efforts were made to avoid some of the methodologic problems found in previous acute and chronic drug studies, as cited under PROBLEM. In this respect, subject selection was rigorous, with care taken to control for the level of marijuana use. Variables confounded in other studies, including socioeconomic class, use of other drugs, and educational level, were carefully controlled. The size of the sample in the experimental phase ($N_U = N_N = 41$) was sufficiently large to permit the use of multivariate statistical procedures, which ensured that subtle differences between marijuana users and nonusers were not overlooked. Concerning the measures themselves, the problem of culture fairness was addressed as a primary issue. Attempts at standardization were made with a Costa Rican sample to ensure an absence of ceiling and floor effects in the tests. This procedure permitted the use of measures (e.g., verbal memory tasks) that are commonly considered to be culturally biased. These measures, which pertain to verbal and nonverbal information consolidation and retrieval abilities, are vital in the assessment of higher adaptive cognitive functions. Altogether, the preexperimental phase helped to rule out the presence of psychometric artifacts that might have masked between-group differences. Finally, variables that relate to level and pattern of intake were investigated. Postexperimental analyses of these variables ensured that subtle effects attributable to marijuana use were not masked because of the heterogeneity of these variables within the user group.

Despite the preceding considerations concerning data analysis, sample, and test selection, the results of the experimental phase failed to detect any differences between the user and nonuser groups on the neuropsychologic, intellectual, or personality tests, even when intake was as high as an average of eight or more cigarettes per day for more than 10 years. In the neuropsychologic and intellectual spheres, these negative findings are further buttressed by the fact that similar findings have been reported in several other chronic marijuana studies.[14, 25, 26] These studies, each of which involved different sampling and geographic groups, by use of additional neuropsychologic and intellectual tests, lend additional support for the findings of the present study. Thus, on the basis of these studies, one might conclude, with caution, that chronic marijuana use is not associated with permanent or irreversible impairment in higher brain functions or intelligence. Nevertheless, it must be recognized that more direct measures of molecular brain structure and chemistry in humans were not employed in any of these studies, and for good reason! Consequently, the final word concerning the question of brain damage in humans cannot be given at the present time. However, the present results do not favor hypotheses that postulate brain damage as a consequence of marijuana intake. Nor is there any strong evidence in the human literature to warrant such a hypothesis, the Campbell *et al.* study [16] notwithstanding.

More difficult to explain is the apparent discrepancy in neuropsychologic performance between the present study and the acute laboratory studies.[1, 12, 13] These studies, though still controversial and limited in the administration of neuropsychologic procedures, have, nevertheless, demonstrated instances of interference in attentional and perceptual tasks after marijuana use. But, again, the results have varied as a function of dosage level, anticipatory sets, and experience usage of the subjects, to name but a few of the relevant independent variables.[1, 12] More important, however, is the fact that no follow-up studies have been conducted on these subjects over time to determine whether these interference effects, if real, are permanent or just transient. Nor is there evidence as to whether these behavioral effects reflect corresponding changes in brain functions. Although answers to these questions cannot be determined at the present time, the present results, nevertheless, suggest that if the effects were permanent (in these acute studies), they should have been found in the chronic studies. The fact that they have not certainly does not support the conclusion that marijuana use produces permanent and irreversible brain damage in humans.

With regard to the personality area, the present study was essentially similar to previous large-scale controlled studies that have likewise failed to demonstrate any significant personality disturbance in chronic marijuana users.[2, 3, 21] In fact, the profiles of the user and nonuser groups in the present study were virtually identical when plotted for each of the 16 PF traits (cf. FIGURE 8). No abnormal or deviant personality traits emerged for either group, whether analyzed by univariate or multivariate techniques. The latter finding lends no support to the recent speculations concerning an amotivational syndrome or organic brain defect after chronic marijuana usage.[18, 19] It was earlier shown that this hypothesis lacked scientific credibility anyway, by virtue of its reliance on subjective interview reports, sampling bias (psychiatric patients), and the absence of a control group. The present results are further strengthened by the fact that the 16 PF possesses respectable reliability and validity and that the factors provide quantitative assessment of both normal and abnormal dimensions of personality that are applicable to Costa Rican adults (see PREEXPERIMENTAL PHASE).

The present results, however, should not be taken to mean that marijuana use may be an insignificant social or personal event with no influence on individual behavior. We have only to examine the carefully collected anthropologic data for contraindicative evidence. This evidence revealed the presence of at least three different marijuana life-styles in Costa Rica. Comparing users in terms of these patterns revealed some interesting differences in personality, presumably as a function of attitudes and concerns about marijuana use. Thus, users characterized by stable family and work histories (stable users) are also apparently more venturesome, liberal, suspicious, and have more superego strength than do their control counterparts. These personality findings can be related to marijuana use in Costa Rica. For example, to use marijuana in a country where such behavior is illegal and often associated with irresponsibility, such personality traits as liberality and venturesomeness would assist in adapting marijuana use into one's behavioral repertoire. Furthermore, to engage in this behavior successfully, that is, while maintaining good family and job relations and without police harassment, one would have to be conscientious at work and sufficiently aware of the social and legal complications to avoid behavior that would jeopardize a "stable" pattern of use. Thus, at least in the stable user group, marijuana use was related to a set of fairly coherent response styles reflected as personality traits in the 16 PF.

A final comment should be made concerning the issue of personality differences as it relates to chronic marijuana usage. Although some North American studies have disclosed subtle differences in personality and attitudinal traits of marijuana users, the results have uniformly failed to support an amotivational or defect hypothesis.[2, 3, 21, 23] The question to be answered, however, is whether these subtle differences in personality reflect factors that *precede* marijuana use and lead a person to engage in drugs or whether they reflect changes in personality that are a *consequence* of such usage. The study by Krug and Henry[2] suggested that certain antecedent child-rearing practices during the formative stages of development might account largely for these differences. In the present study, the patterns of marijuana usage in Costa Rica likewise seemed related to earlier formative child-rearing practices in some of the users that may have increased the probability of contact with marijuana. These precursor events were reflected in the personality findings of the postexperimental phase, particularly between the stable users and their matched controls. Although these differences were found only for certain subgroups of chronic users in the present study, the point is that these differences were *not abnormal* and, furthermore, may have reflected differences in personality *prior* to marijuana usage. If true, failure to control for precursor variables would explain, in part, the findings of Kolansky and Moore[18, 19] concerning an amotivational disturbance in their "psychiatric patients."

The present findings, in summary, provide an additional, but not final, chapter on the long-term effects of chronic marijuana usage on higher adaptive brain functions and personality in man. The results, though unremarkable, are, nevertheless, compatible with other controlled studies that have examined the effects of chronic marijuana usage. It is hoped that the additional methodologic controls employed in the present study, by investigators with no vested interest in the results, will buttress what is clearly becoming a majority finding, namely, that chronic marijuana usage does not irreversibly damage the brain or personality. However, the final chapter is not yet at hand, and future studies might benefit from some of the limitations in the present study. Time constraints and available resources did not permit the use of behavioral reaction time measures that would have focused more directly on attention and distractibility phenomena. This omission is unfortunate because it would have permitted more direct comparison with some of the acute laboratory studies.[1, 12, 13] Another limitation concerns the use of behavioral measures in the assessment of higher brain functions. Despite and sophistication and validity of these tests, they do not represent direct measures of higher cortical functioning. Consequently, the final part of this chapter must await developments in the neurosciences concerning brain metabolism and chemistry. Finally, it is hoped that future studies will consider the use of prospective and retrospective longitudinal designs in their research. There is no substitute for having repeat observations on the same subjects over time, preferably *before* and *after* exposure to marijuana. This type of design would settle, once and for all, the delicate issue concerning precursor variables in personality and subtle brain changes, if any, after chronic marijuana usage.

SUMMARY

The present cross-cultural study investigated the effects of chronic marijuana usage on higher adaptive brain functions and personality in native Costa Ricans. After extensive standardization in Costa Rica, a battery of neuropsychologic, intelligence, and personality tests was administered to two carefully matched groups of marijuana users and controls ($N_U = N_C = 41$). Multivariate analyses of multiple combinations of variables, followed by separate univariate tests on each measure, revealed essentially no significant differences between users and nonusers on any of the neuropsychologic, intelligence, or personality tests. Furthermore, no relationship was found between level of daily use (high vs low) and test performance. These findings were discussed in terms of previous chronic and acute studies of changes in adaptive brain functions and personality as a function of marijuana intake.

ACKNOWLEDGMENTS

The authors gratefully acknowledge the prolonged and intensive efforts of Dina Krauskopf and Miriam Gutierrez in test selection and administration and in maintaining subject interest so that the project could be completed. We also thank Ms. Gleanor Carrol of the National Institute on Drug Abuse for her interest and support in planning and assisting in the completion of this study.

REFERENCES

1. HOLLISTER, L. 1971. Marihuana in man: three years later. Science **172:** 21–29.
2. KRUG, S. & T. HENRY. 1974. Personality, motivation, and adolescent drug use patterns. J. Counsel. Psychol. **21:** 440–445.
3. HOCHMAN, J. & N. BRILL. 1973. Chronic marihuana use and psychosocial adaptation. Amer. J. Psychiat. **130:** 132–140.
4. REITAN, R. 1967. Psychological assessment of deficiencies associated with brain damage in subjects with and without subnormal intelligence. *In* Brain Dam-

age and Mental Retardation: A Psychological Evaluation. J. L. Khana, Ed. : 32. Charles C Thomas. Springfield, Ill.

5. SATZ, P. 1966. Specific and non-specific effects of brain lesions in man. J. Abnormal Psychol. **71:** 65–70.

6. COSTA, L. & H. VAUGHN. 1962. Performance of patients with lateralized cerebral lesions: verbal and perceptual tests. J. Nervous Mental Disease **134:** 162–168.

7. TEUBER, H. 1964. The riddle of frontal lobe function in man. *In* The Frontal Granular Cortex and Behavior. J. Warren & K. Albert, Eds. : 410–444. McGraw-Hill Book Co. New York, N.Y.

8. MILNER, B. 1962. Laterality effects in audition. *In* Interhemispheric Relations and Cerebral Dominance. V. B. Mountcastle, Ed. : 177–195. The John Hopkins Press. Baltimore, Md.

9. SILER, J., W. SHEEP, L. BATES, G. CLARK, G. COOK & W. SMITH. 1933. Marihuana smoking in Panama. Military Surg. **73:** 269–280.

10. MAYOR'S COMMITTEE ON MARIHUANA. 1944. The Marihuana Problem in The City of New York. Jaques Cattell Press. Tempe, Ariz.

11. WILLIAMS, E., C. HINNELSBACH, A. WIKLER, D. RUBIE & B. LLOYD. 1946. Studies of marihuana and pyrahexyl compounds. Public Health Rep. **61:** 1059–1083.

12. WEIL, A., N. ZINBERG & J. NELSON. 1968. Clinical and psychological effects of marihuana in man. Science **162:** 1234–1242.

13. MANNO, J., G. KIPLINGER, N. SCHOLZ & R. FORNEY. 1971. The influence of alcohol and marihuana on motor and mental performance. Clin. Pharmacol. Ther. **12:** 202–211.

14. GRANT, I., J. ROCHFORD, T. FLEMING & A. STUNKARD. 1973. A neuropsychological assessment of the effects of moderate marihuana use. J. Nervous Mental Disease **156:** 278–280.

15. RUBIN, V. & L. COMITAS (Eds.). 1975. Ganja in Jamaica. Mouton. The Hague, The Netherlands.

16. CAMPBELL, A., M. EVANS & J. THOMPSON. 1971. Cerebral atrophy in young cannabis smokers. Lancet **1:** 1219–1224.

17. HEATH, R. 1973. Marihuana: effects on deep and surface electroencephalograms on rhesus monkeys. Neuropharmacology **1:** 1–14.

18. KOLANSKY, A. & W. MOORE. 1971. Effects of marihuana use on adolescent young adults. J. Amer. Med. Ass. **216:** 486–492.

19. KOLANSKY, A. & W. MOORE. 1975. Marihuana: can it hurt you? J. Amer. Med. Ass. **232:** 923, 924.

20. BRECHER, E. 1974. Marihuana: the health questions. Consumer Rep. : 143–149.

21. GOODE, E. 1971. Drug use and grades in college. Nature (London) **234:** 225–227.

22. CATTELL, R., H. EBER & M. TATSOUKA. 1970. Handbook for the 16 P.F. IPAT. Champaign, Ill.

23. BURDSAL, C., G. GREENBERG & R. TIMPE. 1973. The relationship of marihuana usage to personality and motivational factors. J. Psychol. **85:** 45–51.

24. KLECHNER, J. 1968. Personality differences between psychedelic drug users and non-users. Psychology **5:** 66–71.

25. MENDELSON, J. & R. MEYER. 1972. Behavioral and biological concomitants of chronic marihuana smoking by heavy and casual users. Technical Papers of the First Report of the National Committee on Marihuana and Drug Abuse. : 68–246. United States Government Printing Office. Washington, D.C.

26. KNIGHTS, R. 1975. Psychological test results. *In* Ganja in Jamaica. V. Rubin & L. Comitas, Eds. : 111–120. Mouton. The Hague, The Netherlands.

27. KNIGHTS, R. & A. MOULE. 1968. Normative data on the motor steadiness battery for children. Percept. Motor Skills **26:** 643–650.

28. REITAN, R. 1966. A research program on the psychological effects of brain lesions on human beings. *In* International Review of Research on Mental Retardation. N. R. Ellis, Ed. Vol. 1: 153–218. Academic Press, Inc. New York, N.Y.

29. ABEL, T. 1975. Report on the Lowenfeld mosaic test. *In* Ganja in Jamaica. V. Rubins & L. Comitas, Eds. : 118–120. Mouton and Co. The Hague, The Netherlands.

30. LURIA, A. 1973. The Working Brain. Basic Books, Inc., Publishers. New York, N.Y.

31. HUMMEL, T. & J. SLIGO. 1971. Empirical comparisons of univariate and multivariate analyses of variance. Psychol. Bull. **76**: 49–57.

32. KERR, M. 1952. Personality and Conflict in Jamaica. University Press. London, England.

33. LOWENFELD, M. 1954. The Lowenfeld Mosaic Test. Newman-Neame. London, England.

34. WILLIAMS, M. 1968. The measurement of memory in clinical practice. Brit. J. Social Clin. Psychol. **7**: 19–24.

35. REYNOLDS, G. 1974. Memory functions in temporal lobe epileptics: comparison between groups with right and left foci. Unpublished Doctoral Dissertation. University of Florida. Gainesville, Fla.

36. FLETCHER, J. 1975. Memory functions in temporal lobe seizure patients: Laterality effects in memory. Unpublished Master's Thesis. University of Florida. Gainesville, Fla.

37. WECHSLER, D. 1945. A standardized memory scale for clinical use. J. Psychol. **19**: 87–95.

38. MILNER, B. 1968. Visual recognition and recall after right temporal lobe excision in man. Neuropsychologia **6**: 191–209.

39. REITAN, R. 1969. Manual for Administration of Neuropsychological Test Batteries for Adults and Children. Privately published by the author. Indiana University Press. Bloomington, Ind.

40. SATZ, P., K. ACHENBACH & E. FENNELL. 1967. Correlations between assessed manual laterality and predicted speech laterality in a normal population. Neuropsychologia **5**: 295–310.

41. REITAN, R. 1964. Psychological deficits resulting from cerebral lesions in man. *In* The Frontal Granular Cortex and Behavior. J. Warren & K. Albert, Eds. : 295–312. McGraw-Hill Book Co. New York, N.Y.

42. BENTON, A. 1959. Right-Left Discrimination and Finger Localization: Development and Pathology. Hoeber. New York, N.Y.

43. BENTON, A. 1963. The Revised Visual Retention Test. 3rd edit. The Psychological Corporation. New York, N.Y.

44. INSTITUTE OF PERSONALITY AND ABILITY TESTING. 1973. Technical Supplement for the Culture Fair Intelligence Tests Scales 2 and 3. IPAT. Champaign, Ill.

45. BUROS, O. (Ed.). 1965. The Sixth Mental Measurements Yearbook. : 718–723. Gryphon Press. Highland Park, N.J.

46. RAVEN, J. 1965. Guide to the Standard Progressive Matrices, Sets A,B,C,D, and E. H. K. Lewis. London, England.

47. WECHSLER, D. 1968. Escalar de Inteligencia Wechsler para Adultos. R. F. Green & J. H. Martinez, Transl. The Psychological Corporation. New York, N.Y.

48. MATARAZZO, J. 1973. Wechsler's Measurement and Appraisal of Adult Intelligence. 5th edit. The Williams & Wilkins Co. Baltimore, Md.

49. SATZ, P. & S. MOGEL. 1962. An abbreviation of the WAIS for clinical use. J. Clin. Psychol. **18**: 77–79.

50. MOGEL, S. & P. SATZ. 1963. Abbreviation of the WAIS for clinical use: an attempt at validation. J. Clin. Psychol. **19**: 289–300.

51. GOEBAL, R. & P. SATZ. 1975. Profile analysis and the abbreviated WAIS: a multivariate approach. J. Consult. Clin. Psychol. **43:** 780–785.
52. FLETCHER, J., J. TODD & P. SATZ. 1975. Culture-fairness of 3 intelligence tests and a short-form procedure. Psychol. Rep. **37:** 1255–1262.
53. CARROL, E. E. 1975. Personal communication.
54. JOHNSON, D., C. JOHNSON & D. PRICE-WILLIAMS. 1967. The draw-a-man test and Raven progressive matrices performance of Guatemalan Maya and Ladino children. Rev. Interamer. Psycol. **1:** 143–157.
55. HARRIS, J. 1960. Validity: the search for a constant in a universe of variables. *In* Rorschach Psychology. M. Rickers-Ovsiankina, Ed. : 380–439. John Wiley & Sons, Inc. N.Y.
56. HOLZBERG, J. 1960. Reliability re-examined. *In* Rorschach Psychology. M. Rickers-Ovsiankina, Ed. : 361–379. John Wiley & Sons, Inc. New York, N.Y.
57. CASTRO, G. & M. QUESADA. 1971. Mini-mult: una forma abreviada del inventario de multifasico de la personalidad de Minnesota, MMPI. Acta Psiquiuat. Psicol. Amer. Lat. **17:** 12–17.
58. WIGGINS, J. 1973. Personality and Prediction: Principles of Personality Assessment. Addison-Wesley Publishing Co., Inc. Reading, Mass.
59. CATTELL, R. & L. BOLTON. 1969. What pathological dimensions lie beyond the normal dimensions of the 16 P.F.? A comparison of MMPI and 16 P.F. factor domains. J. Consult. Clin. Psychol. **33:** 18–29.
60. HARRIS, R. 1975. A Primer of Multivariate Statistics. Academic Press, Inc. New York, N.Y.
61. CARTER, W. & P. DOUGHTY. This monograph.

PROBLEMS IN STUDYING THE EFFECTS OF CHRONIC CANNABIS USE ON INTELLECTUAL ABILITIES

Robert M. Knights and Mary L. Grenier

Department of Psychology
Carleton University
Ottawa, Ontario K1S 5B6, Canada

The theme of this Conference illustrates the general social concern regarding the use of cannabis. Within this context, the focus of this paper is on the effects of the long-term use of marijuana on the cognitive functioning of humans. The literature reviewed may be grouped into three general categories: laboratory studies that examine the acute effects in regular users, surveys of the characteristics of long-term users, and comparisons of heavy chronic users versus nonuser controls.

In the laboratory studies of regular users, volunteers are usually required to perform tasks that require complex attentional and short-term memory tasks. These investigations generally find that the acute cannabis intake impairs these abilities in a dose-related fashion. In addition, the degree of impairment has been shown to increase with task complexity and novelty.[1]

Surveys of long-term users have included clinical observations and uncontrolled studies of various populations in the world. The magnitude of the effects of cannabis use on intellectual skills reported has been dependent on the society surveyed. For example, the history of cannabis usage in South America has been reviewed by Wolff [2] and Cordeiro de Farias,[3] and these writers conclude that cannabis contributes heavily to mental and physical deterioration. Reports from India [4, 5] conclude that moderate use of the drug does not produce injurious effects on the mind but that excessive use does. Surveys in North America on the intellectual functioning of chronic users of high-potency cannabis all report that, generally, no evidence of cognitive impairment can be attributed to cannabis.[1, 6] Several clinical and interview reports suggest that impairment of intellectual functioning may be associated with chronic cannabis use in North America.[7-9]

The comparisons of heavy chronic users with nonuser controls include studies that involve both experimental and natural settings. In some of the experimental studies, a consistent problem with respect to the evaluation of results has been the fact that the subjects are often atypical or deviant groups or are multiple drug users. For example, Marcovitz and Meyers [10] employed army delinquents, Hekimian and Gershon [11] used psychiatric patients, and Robins *et al.*[12] used multiple drug users. Other studies have employed more typical nonusers in experimental settings. For example, performance on a cognitive task was examined by Jones [13, 14] and Jones and Stone,[15] who compared the performance of infrequent users (less than two cigarettes per month) to that of chronic users (more than seven cigarettes per week) on a digit substitution test. In agreement with other similar studies, the naive subject was shown to be more variable and unpredictable than the experienced user. In addition, the infrequent users were impaired on the cognitive task after smoking 1 g of marijuana, whereas the frequent users were not affected compared to the placebo controls.

Three studies have compared the abilities of heavy chronic cannabis users with controls in their natural setting. Fink and Dornbush [16] studied smokers in Greece who had used marijuana for more than 10 years. Forty users were compared with 40 nonuser controls on tests of physiologic, cognitive, sensory, and perceptual performance, in addition to medical and psychiatric measures. There were no significant differences in mood, thought, or behavior between the two groups.

A second study conducted in Jamaica [17] also found no indication of intellectual impairment in chronic heavy users when contrasted to appropriate matched controls. Chronic users included subjects with at least 10 years of daily consumption of very potent cannabis. Controls from the same environment who had never used the drug were matched in terms of social class, alcohol use, and general intelligence. The testing battery included measurement of physiologic, sensory, and perceptual-motor functioning, memory, concept formation, abstract reasoning ability, and cognitive style. There was no evidence of significant differences on any of the numerous psychologic tests.

The present authors participated in a third study of users and nonusers in a natural setting in Jamaica. Because a detailed description of the psychologic testing conducted in this study has been presented elsewhere,[18] only a brief summary will be included here. In Jamaica, the potent cannabis preparation of ganja has a long history of widespread and frequent use. The estimated incidence of cannabis use for normal adult males is in excess of 50%,[19] and one religious group has ritualized ganja smoking. Subjects were selected from four of seven localities studied by anthropologists involved in a survey of ganja use in Jamaica. These localities included two coastal communities with economies based on fishing and agriculture, a farming settlement in southeastern hill country, and the incorporated area of Kingston. It is important to note that random sampling techniques were not possible because of the illegality of ganja and the lack of statistics dealing with the use of the drug. Thus, the smoking or nonsmoking status of the subjects was known to the researchers, and the assessments could not be concluded blind. The design included 30 ganja smokers and 30 nonsmokers matched for age, socioeconomic status, and residence. The mean age was 34 years, and the mean educational level was third grade.

As a result of the pervasiveness of ganja smoking among working-class males, user subjects were not difficult to locate. Identifying adequate controls, however, was difficult, and they were defined as confirmed nonsmokers who may have had some limited experience in the past, in the form of a few experimental attempts at ganja smoking. Smokers were defined as chronic users if they had been smoking a minimum of three cigarettes daily for a minimum of 10 years. All subjects were admitted to University Hospital in Jamaica for 6 consecutive days of examination. On admission, the user subjects were asked to supply a sample of the ganja they usually smoked, and the mean percentage by weight of Δ^9-tetrahydrocannabinol ranged from 0.7 to 10.3. Thus, after having been selected as known smokers or nonsmokers, their participation was on a completely voluntary basis. All subjects were offered financial compensation for 1 week's stay in the hospital, guaranteed confidentiality, and round-trip transportation from their home community to the University Hospital. Smokers were asked to abstain from the use of ganja while they were in the hospital.

An in-depth interview was conducted before admission to collect life history data for each subject, including family background, occupational patterns, property holdings and income, marital history, religious and political affiliation, ganja smoking history, experience, and attitudes, alcohol patterns, and possible charges for law violation.

The 19 psychologic tests selected for the study included one personality measure (Lowenfeld Mosaic Test), three intelligence measures (eight subtests from the Wechsler Adult Intelligence Test, the Ammons Full Range Picture Vocabulary Test, and selected items from an aphasia screening test), and 15 neuropsychologic tests. The neuropsychologic tests included six motor and psychomotor tests (dynamometer, finger tapping, maze steadiness, graduated holes, pegboard, and tactual performance test), four sensory perception tests (tactile stimulation, auditory stimulation, tactile form recognition, and finger tip writing recognition), four tests of memory and attention (tactual performance memory and location scores, time-sense-memory, and seashore rhythm), and one concept formation test (Indiana-Reitan Category Test). These tests had a total of 47 subtest scores. Scores on these tests were not examined for level of performance but were studied for differences between ganja smoker an nonsmoker groups.

The data were analyzed in a variety of ways, including 47 analyses of variance. The fact that only three statistically significant effects were obtained can be attributed to chance. In an attempt to determine if there was even a general trend for one group to perform better than the other, mean scores for each subtest variable were compared. The smoker group scored better on 29 variables, and the nonsmoker group scored better on the remaining 18 variables. These frequencies did not differ from chance expectations.

In an effort to determine the reliability of the results, two types of comparisons were made between the Jamaican and North American scores. One comparison examined the similarity of pattern of intratest correlations, and the second compared the magnitude of correlations between performance with the right and left hands. In both types of review, the general pattern of relationship was similar in both regions. On the basis of this demonstration of reliability, it was concluded that long-term cannabis use did not produce observable intellectual or specific ability deficits.

There are several factors that may have contributed to the findings of this study. These factors include subject assessment, time of testing, potential tolerance effects, and age of the subject. The Jamaican test administrator usually knew which group the subject was in because of his dress or conversation. Although it is conceivable that this knowledge could influence test scores, it is difficult to explain how it might influence performance on the simple motor tests or on the variety of tests in which a high score was sometimes good while on others it was a poor score.

Testing of the subjects occurred at least 48 hr after admission to the hospital, where no ganja was available. It is known that Δ^9-tetrahydrocannabinol (THC) has a two-phase biologic half-life, in which the rapid phase lasts about 30 min and the slow phase about 56 hr.[20] It is likely that the men in this study had very little THC in their body when they were tested. Other observations of these subjects when they were not in the hospital revealed acute effects of ganja, and the test results obtained when they were not under the influence of ganja provide evidence against any gross chronic impairment.

Another factor to be considered is that of drug tolerance. The smokers had used ganja for an average of 17.5 years, and the development of tolerance has been reported.[21] The results of this study are consistent with this idea, because smokers and nonsmokers obtained similar results.

An interesting point to consider in the interpretation of these data is the influence of the age of the subjects. It is also applicable to the studies of Fink and Dornbush [16] and Bowman and Pihl [17] in Greece and Jamaica. It is known that intellectual abilities in humans peak in the early 20s and decline thereafter, especially in nonverbal skills. Because these men were in their middle 30s, it may be that the decrement in general abilities for both smokers and nonsmokers is greater than any subtle impairment produced by ganja smoking. The implication of this suggestion is that if impairment of cognitive skills is the result of heavy ganja use, it might be more readily detected during adolescence, when intellectual growth is still occurring.

This brief review of the laboratory, survey, and chronic heavy user studies generally indicates that long-term cannabis usage is not associated with major impairment of intellectual function. In fact, this general conclusion has been consistently stated in the recent literature.[22] Further research of the type reviewed will not advance the state of knowledge about long-term marijuana use for three reasons.

First, findings from studies conducted outside North America may not be relevant to this society. Fundamental differences in potency, form, and mode of administration of cannabis exist, and the user populations bear little resemblance to one another. Dornbush [23] has pointed out that the user in the United States is usually under 30 years of age and is found among the most achievement-oriented social classes, in contrast to users in foreign countries, who come from the lowest, least productive strata and are well over 30. One of the basic differences that inhibits a generalization is a sociocultural one. Bowman and Pihl [17] discuss their lack of group differences in Jamaica in terms of expectations of the users. Unlike the "amotivational syndrome" [24] often reported in North American literature, the Jamaican subjects consider marijuana a stimulant and smoke to provide energy and strength in order to accomplish particularly heavy tasks. As Jones [13] notes, the effect of the mind on marijuana is a significant factor.

A second issue that complicates the interpretation of the effects of chronic cannabis use in North America is that of personality factors. On this continent, long-term marijuana users are frequently classified as deviant with respect to the rest of the culture. Studies of prisoners, delinquents, and psychiatric patients are common sources of data, but they do not represent the general population. Because marijuana possession and use has been generally illegal, it is exceedingly difficult to find a normal sample of chronic users. As a result, the effects of marijuana use on personality and the effects of personality on marijuana are related in such a complex fashion that separation of specific contributing factors is beyond current research techniques.

Third, many chronic marijuana users in North America are multiple drug users. The majority of cannabis users studied in North America have had experience with alcohol and tobacco; in addition, the use of heroin, amphetamines, and lysergic acid diethylamide is much more common among cannabis users than in the general population.[1] Several survey studies have reported that those who use alcohol are much more likely than teetotalers to use cannabis and that most cannabis users still drink alcohol. Furthermore, heavy users of cannabis tend to drink more alcohol than do light or infrequent users. Similarly, tobacco use has been traditionally associated with marijuana use in North

America, and most regular cannabis users initially learned the technique of inhaling smoke from experience with tobacco cigarettes.

An interesting approach to sorting out the complexities of the effects of multiple drug use has been suggested by Kandel.[25] She identified stages in adolescent involvement in drug use and found that drug use does not begin with marijuana but, rather, first with legal drugs, beer, or wine and with cigarettes or hard liquor subsequently. Patterns of drug use were defined in terms of a seven-step Guttman scale classification in which legal drug use was found to be a necessary step between nonuse and illegal drug use, with a progression from nonuse to illegal drug use seldom occurring. In attempting to assess changes in intellectual functioning or other possible results of cannabis use, the identification of stages in drug use has important implications. Studies should examine drug users as they progress through the stages in order to attempt to evaluate the cumulative effects as they occur.

The problems of relevance, personality factors, and multiple drug use tend to limit the value of studies that examine long-term effects. There are, however, three approaches that have not been fully exploited. Although studies of animals have investigated the physiologic effects of marijuana administration, the evaluation of behavioral change and problem-solving ability after prolonged cannabis use merits detailed attention. A unique use of animals is illustrated in the findings of Fried.[26] He forced pregnant rats to smoke and found that the offspring showed a lasting reduction in weight gain and activity level.

A second approach yet to be exploited and requiring long-term study is based on the disease model, as illustrated in the study of the relationship between tobacco smoking and lung cancer. Future studies should be able to determine the association between the frequency and amount of marijuana use and the cause of disease or death. It would be an important finding if there was a differential rate of brain lesions between user and nonuser groups.

A third type of study that may contribute to new knowledge about cannabis is rigorous investigations of the clinically reported therapeutic effects for the reduction of seizures and migrane headaches.

In conclusion, there is little doubt from the studies of long-term and heavy users that marijuana does not appear to have destructive effects of great magnitude that impair intellectual skills. This is not to say, however, that the drug does not have any subtle deleterious effects. It should be remembered that the human brain is a very plastic and durable organ with a great capacity for adaptation.

REFERENCES

1. LE DAIN COMMISSION. 1972. A Report to the Commission of Inquiry into the Non-Medical Use of Drugs. Information Canada. Ottawa, Ontario, Canada.
2. WOLFF, P. O. 1949. Marijuana in Latin America. Linacre Press. Washington, D.C.
3. CORDEIRO DE FARIAS, R. 1955. Use of Maconha (cannabis sativa L.) in Brazil: control by health and police authorities. Bull. Narcotics 7(2): 5–19.
4. CHOPRA, I. C. & R. N. CHOPRA. 1957. The use of cannabis drugs in India. Bull. Narcotics 9: 4–29.
5. INDIAN HEMP DRUGS COMMISSION, 1893–1894. Report on Indian Hemp. Vol. 1–7. Government Central Printing Office. Simla, India. Primary volume reprinted 1969. Thomas Jefferson. Silver Spring, Md.

6. MAYOR's COMMITTEE ON MARIJUANA. 1944. The Marijuana Problem in the City of New York. Jaques Cattell Press. Tempe, Ariz.

7. BRILL, N. Q., E. CRUMPTON, I. M. FRANK, J. S. HOCHMAN, P. LOMAX, W. H. McGLOTHLIN & L. J. WEST. 1970. The marijuana problem. Ann. Intern. Med. 73(3): 449–465.

8. FARNSWORTH, D. L. & H. K. OLIVER. 1968. The drug problem among young people. Rode Island Med. J. 51: 179–182.

9. KING, A. B. & D. L. COWEN. 1969. Effect of intravenous injection of marijuana. J. Amer. Med. Ass. 210(4): 724, 725.

10. MARCOVITZ, E. & H. J. MEYERS. 1944. The marijuana addict in the army. War Med. 6: 382–391.

11. HEKIMIAN, L. J. & S. GERSHON. 1968. Characteristics of drug abusers admitted to a psychiatric hospital. J. Amer. Med. Ass. 205: 125–130.

12. ROBINS, L. N., H. S. DARVISH & G. E. MURPHY. 1970. The long-term outcome for adolescent drug users: a follow-up study of 76 users and 146 non-users. In The Psychopathology of Adolescence. J. Zubin & A. M. Freedman, Eds. : 159–180. Grune & Stratton, Inc. New York, N.Y.

13. JONES, R. T. 1971. Tetrahydrocannabinol and the marijuana-induced social "high," or the effects of the mind on marijuana. Ann. N.Y. Acad. Sci. 191: 155–165.

14. JONES, R. T. 1971. Marijuana-induced "high:" influence of expectation, setting and previous drug experience. Pharmacol. Rev. 23: 359–369.

15. JONES, R. T. & G. C. STONE. 1970. Psychological studies of marijuana and alcohol in man. Psychopharmacologia 18: 108–117.

16. FINK, M. & R. L. DORNBUSH. 1972. Chronic hashish use in Greece. Unpublished report.

17. BOWMAN, M. & R. PIHL. 1973. Cannabis: psychological effects of chronic heavy use. Psychopharmacologia 29: 159–170.

18. RUBIN, V. & L. COMITAS. 1975. Ganja in Jamaica. Mouton & Co. Paris, France.

19. PRINCE, R., R. GREENFIELD & J. MARRIOTT. 1972. Ganja: the benevolent alternative? Bull. Narcotics 24(1).

20. HOLLISTER, L. E. 1971. Marijuana in man: three years later. Science 172: 21–29.

21. DORNBUSH, R. L., G. CLARKE, A. ZAKS, P. CROWN, J. VOLAVKA & M. FINK. 1972. 21-Day administration of marijuana in male volunteers. In Current Research in Marijuana. M. F. Lewis, Ed. : 115–128. Academic Press, Inc. New York, N.Y.

22. TINKLENBERG, J. R. (Ed.). 1975. Marijuana and Health Hazards: Methodological Issues in Current Research. Academic Press, Inc. New York, N.Y.

23. DORNBUSH, R. L. 1975. Marijuana and the central nervous system. In Marijuana and Health Hazards: Methodological Issues in Current Research. J. R. Tinklenberg, Ed. Academic Press, Inc. New York, N.Y.

24. McGLOTHLIN, W. H. & L. J. WEST. 1968. The marijuana problem: an overview. Amer. J. Psychiat. 125(3): 126–134.

25. KANDEL, D. 1975. Stages in adolescent involvement in drug use. Science 190: 912–914.

26. FRIED, P. 1975. Behavioural and electroencephalographic correlates of the chronic use of marijuana. Mimeograph. Carleton University. Ottawa, Ontario, Canada.

ACUTE EFFECTS OF CANNABIS ON COGNITIVE, PERCEPTUAL, AND MOTOR PERFORMANCE IN CHRONIC HASHISH USERS *

Rhea L. Dornbush †

Department of Psychiatry
New York Medical College
New York, New York 10029

Anna Kokkevi

Department of Psychiatry
Athens University Medical School
Eginition Hospital
Athens, Greece

Many tasks have been used to assess cognitive, perceptual, and motor effects of marijuana consumption. Their diversity, in addition to their differences in procedure, samples, and experimental conditions, has led to seemingly inconsistent reports of the changes in these functions.

Anecdotally, the most consistent changes are in time sense and in short-term memory, and these measures are most frequently included in batteries of mental functioning. While subjects report that time passes slowly, the effect has been difficult to demonstrate experimentally by use of the conventional methods of measurement. These methods include reproduction (the subject is asked to reproduce a time period that was previously indicated), estimation (the subject is asked to estimate the length of a given time period), and production (the subject is asked to define a period of time). These methods yield different data.[1]

Reproduction is the easiest method and requires the subject to count during an interval to be reproduced. Regardless of what he is counting, he merely has to repeat the procedure. Reproduction is insensitive to cannabis effects.[2,3] Karniol et al.[4] and Tinklenberg et al.[5] found that the production task resulted in underjudgments; Jones and Stone[6] did not obtain this result.

In contrast to an expected underestimate of time by production, estimation methods should result in overjudgments. Clark et al.,[7] and Jones and Stone[6] obtained overestimations; Weil et al.[8] did not. The outcome of time sense measures varied with the interval used. Shorter intervals, as seconds, are generally overjudged; longer intervals, as minutes, are underjudged. Marijuana studies have used intervals that varied from 1 sec to 5 min.[2,5,9] Further, time sense measures differ when the intervals are filled or empty and when instructions emphasize subjective or objective time.[1]

The effects of marijuana on memory are more consistent. Subjects report that they cannot remember the beginning of a sentence or the word that immediately precedes the one they are speaking. Among the most sensitive tests of memory change are those that involve a delay of recall, even as short as a

* Supported by Grant HSM 42–70–98 from the National Institute on Drug Abuse.
† Present address: Reproductive Biology Research Foundation, St. Louis, Mo. 63108.

313

few seconds.[2, 10] These tests permit us to more precisely define the locus of marijuana effects in the memory process. Recall is always nearly perfect, if not perfect, when it is immediate, that is, when the item must be repeated without any intervening delay or interpolated task. From this fact, it is assumed that perception, registration, and retrieval of the item are correct. These processes are not affected by marijuana. On the other hand, when a delay occurs between item presentation and recall, retention falls off, and a deficit ensues. The interval between presentation and recall is the time when the item must be stored or coded for later retrieval. It is, therefore, assumed that marijuana affects storage processes.[2, 10-12]

A simple digit span, which is an immediate recall task and in which there is minimal involvement of storage processes, is usually not sensitive to marijuana effects.[13]

Other categories of mental functioning have not been as extensively or consistently explored as time sense and memory. There is little uniformity in test selection from study to study; no two studies have used the same methodologic procedures. For example, Weil et al.[8] measured sustained attention with a continuous performance task (CPT), alertness by use of the digit symbol substitution test (DSST), and muscular coordination by employing a pursuit rotor apparatus. Caldwell et al.[14] measured auditory and visual acuity and sensory thresholds. The LeDain Commission[15] examined short-term serial position memory and general alertness (DSST). Meyer et al.[16] measured field dependence, attention, alertness, time perception, task focusing, and muscular coordination. Hosko et al.[3] measured reaction time and time sense by use of the method of reproduction. Jones and Stone[6] measured field dependence with a rod and frame apparatus, time sense by use of methods of estimation and production, and general alertness with DSST. Kiplinger et al.[17] examined motor performance, delayed auditory feedback, and stability of stance.

In each study, a smoking route of administration was used. An oral route has been used by others, including Hollister and Gillespie,[18] Melges et al.,[13] Tinklenberg et al.,[5] Waskow et al.,[19] and Darley et al.[12]

In addition to the type of task and route of administration, cannabis effects are related, but not limited, to time of testing, type of cannabis preparation, characteristics of the user, set, and setting. However, when differences in experimental procedures are evaluated, a general pattern of marijuana effect does emerge. The effects of marijuana on cognitive, perceptual, and motor functions are temporary. Complex tasks, those that require simultaneous and coordinated mental operations, such as the goal-directed serial alternation task (GDSA) or serial sevens, memory tasks with a delayed recall, or multisignal reaction time, are more consistently affected than simple tasks, such as digit span, single-signal reaction time, or time reproduction tasks.[13, 20, 21] Performance impairment is related to dose: complex tasks are usually affected by higher doses, less so or not at all by lower doses. Simple tasks are not affected by low doses but may be by higher doses.[1, 15]

Thus, the acute effects of marijuana in users with limited cannabis experience have been well documented. The effects in chronic users are still unclear. Because American populations of long-term users (10 years or more) are not available, data on long-term effects were obtained from users in other countries. A small group of chronic hashish users was identified in Greece. What is unique about this sample is that they have restricted themselves to cannabis preparations. There is virtually no abuse, or even use, of other substances, except for tobacco and social use of alcohol. The acute effects of various cannabis preparations were observed in these subjects to determine differences and similarities in performance between American short-term users and Greek long-term users.

To assess mental functioning in chronic hashish users in Greece, we selected tests that were similar to those used on American populations and that were as free of cultural limitations as possible. These tests sampled several different functions, namely, memory, alertness, time sense, mental coordination, and motor performance.

METHODS AND MATERIALS

Subjects

Twenty subjects were used. Their mean age was 43.5 years (SD 10.4); mean years of hashish use was 25.8 (SD 10.2). These subjects were a subsample of a group of users who had been previously identified and whose characteristics have been defined.[24, 25]

Drugs

Subjects received five cannabis preparations (four active substances and one placebo) on 5 different days. The preparations were 0 mg of Δ^9-tetrahydrocannabinol (Δ^9-THC, American THC-free marijuana leaf), 78 mg of Δ^9-THC (American marijuana leaf), 90 mg of Δ^9-THC (Greek hashish), 100 mg of Δ^9-THC (liquid infused on placebo), and 180 mg of Δ^9-THC (Greek hashish). These preparations were mixed with tobacco and rolled into large cigarettes of identical appearance to those the subjects usually smoked.

Procedures

The testing occurred on 5 days; 4 days were consecutive, and the fifth day occurred after an interruption of at least 1 day. This sequence was prompted by the delayed arrival of THC at the Athens laboratories. The order of drug administration was only semirandom for the same reason: marijuana, hashish, and placebo were completely randomized, but THC was always the last preparation given. These orders were considered in the statistical analysis.

The smoking period was 15 min. The postsmoking evaluation was approximately 90 min in duration. Psychophysiologic, mood, and other continuously measured variables were assessed for the first 30 min and again from 60 to 70 min. Psychologic tests were presented twice: 30–50 min postsmoking and again at 70–90 min postsmoking. Performance during each time period was assessed separately.

Tasks

The psychologic test battery included the following five items.
Digit Span,‡ Forward and Backward. This task is a subtest of the Wechsler

‡ Despite the fact that this test is usually not sensitive to marijuana effects in American users, we included it in this battery to observe the differences and similarities in performance between American short-term users and Greek long-term users.

Adult Intelligence Scale (WAIS) and was administered as specified in the WAIS. The subject is asked to repeat ascending lengths of digits both forward and backward. The maximum length is nine.

Barrage de Signe. This task is an alertness test, similar to the DSST. Subjects are given a sheet with rows of symbols. Three symbols at the top of the page serve as standards. Subjects are required to cross out the symbols on the sheet that are the same as the three standards. There is a 3-min limit on this task. The score is the number correct minus the number incorrect.

Time Estimation. Subjects are required to estimate the length of time of the *barrage de signe* task, that is, 3 min.

Serial Sevens. The subject is given a number and is required to subtract seven from that number until he reaches a designated goal. The time to complete the task and the number of errors are combined to yield a fault index.

Star Tracing. The test consists of a six-point star of about 20 cm in diameter formed with dots. The subject is asked to draw the star by following the dots, as quickly as possible, without lifting the pencil or turning the paper around. Two scores are obtained: the time required for completion of the test and the errors or number of dots excluded by the line drawn by the subject.

Data Processing

Data were analyzed by multiple linear stepwise regression, comparing each drug against placebo. If the main effect of the drug was significant, posthoc *t* tests were performed among the various substances.

Separate analyses were performed at each of the two testing periods, that is, at 30 and 70 min. No statistical comparison of changes in performance between the two time periods was undertaken.

Results

Of the five psychologic tests presented, three resulted in significant drug effects at one or both time points. Figure 1 shows performance on these five tests as a function of quantity of Δ^9-THC smoked. Table 1 gives the means and standard deviations of performance on each of the tests and the p values for the drug effect and for the comparisons among drugs that were significant.

Differences between Placebo and Active Substances

In the *barrage de signe* task, at 30 min, all drug conditions, except THC (100 mg), resulted in impaired performance. Only hashish (180 mg) and marijuana (78 mg) were significantly different from the placebo. At 70 min, hashish (180 mg) was still significantly worse than placebo.

All active drug preparations, except THC (100 mg), in the time estimation task, at 30 min, caused overestimations of the 3-min task. THC (100 mg) produced a mean exact estimate of the task, and the placebo caused an underestimation. Only hashish (180 mg) and marijuana (78 mg) were significantly different from the placebo. At 70 min, the same pattern of under- and overestimations was observed as at 30 min. However, the differences were not significant.

In the serial sevens task at 30 min, performance was impaired significantly in the hashish (180 mg) condition compared to the placebo. At 70 min, however, this difference was no longer significant.

No differences in the digit span and star tracing tasks were observed compared to the placebo at either 30 or 70 min.

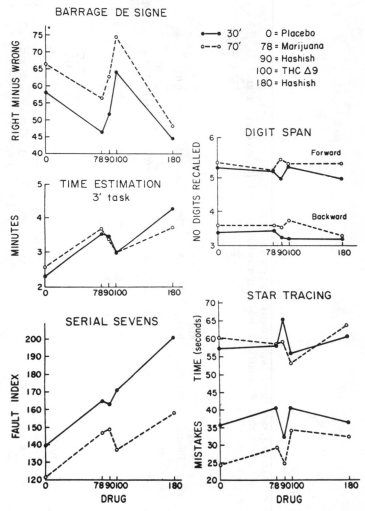

FIGURE 1. Psychologic test performance in chronic Greek hashish users as a function of Δ^0-THC administered.

Differences among the Active Substances

In the *barrage de signe* task, at 30 and 70 min, performance was significantly better in the THC (100 mg) condition than with the other three active preparations.

TABLE 1

MEANS (FIRST LINE) AND STANDARD DEVIATIONS (SECOND LINE) FOR THE FIVE TESTS OF MENTAL PERFORMANCE AS A FUNCTION OF DOSE (THC QUANTITY SMOKED)

Task	Time	Drug Effect	Drug					Drug Comparisons *	
			0 Placebo	78 mg Marijuana	90 mg Hashish	100 mg THC	180 mg Hashish	0.01	0.05
Barrage de signe	30	0.01	58.05 23.51	46.25 23.13	51.85 27.43	64.16 25.40	44.35 25.94	H4 <THC MJ <THC	H4 < placebo MJ < placebo H2 < THC
	70	0.01	66.95 22.15	56.45 23.80	62.85 28.72	74.95 24.97	48.10 23.37	H4 < placebo H4 <THC H4 < H2 H2 <THC MJ <THC	
Time estimation	30	0.05	2.50 2.18	3.55 1.80	3.48 1.85	3.00 1.81	4.30 2.32	H4 > placebo	MJ > placebo H4 > THC
	70	ns	2.58 2.06	3.70 1.37	3.40 1.91	3.00 1.82	3.75 2.52		
Serial sevens	30	0.05	139.70 64.55	165.75 73.62	163.60 71.78	171.68 73.12	201.50 85.53	H4 > placebo	H4 > H2

	70	ns	121.20 / 69.20	146.80 / 62.73	148.55 / 64.18	137.89 / 63.24	158.30 / 81.88
Digit span (forward)	30	ns	5.30 / 0.95	5.20 / 0.93	4.95 / 1.07	5.32 / 0.80	5.00 / 0.84
	70	ns	5.45 / 0.92	5.20 / 1.12	5.55 / 1.07	5.42 / 0.88	5.40 / 0.80
(backward)	30	ns	3.40 / 1.07	3.45 / 0.97	3.25 / 0.89	3.21 / 0.89	3.05 / 0.92
	70	ns	3.60 / 0.86	3.60 / 1.02	3.55 / 0.86	3.74 / 0.64	3.30 / 0.90
Star tracing (time)	30	ns	57.30 / 20.30	58.05 / 20.68	65.65 / 24.44	56.00 / 21.54	60.85 / 21.42
	70	ns	60.45 / 20.73	58.90 / 19.80	59.25 / 18.96	53.16 / 18.05	64.35 / 34.44
(mistakes)	30	ns	35.35 / 21.74	40.50 / 24.15	32.20 / 16.35	40.26 / 21.43	36.10 / 20.02
	70	ns	24.60 / 15.35	29.40 / 17.49	24.60 / 25.15	34.05 / 18.07	32.15 / 15.90

* MJ, marijuana.

In time estimation, at 30 min, hashish (180 mg) produced greater over-estimations of time than did THC (100 mg). This difference disappeared at 70 min.

In serial sevens, at 30 min, hashish (180 mg) performance was significantly impaired compared to that after a lower dose of hashish (90 mg). This difference was not present at 70 min.

There were no statistically significant differences among the active substances in the digit span and star tracing tasks at either 30 or 70 min.

While no statistical comparisons were undertaken between the two time points, performance always improved during the second testing period, especially in the placebo condition (FIGURE 1). This finding suggests that improvement reflects an interaction of practice effect and the drug's lessening effect with time.

DISCUSSION

There was no simple dose-response relationship for cannabis substances in the tasks on which there was a drug effect. Hashish (180 mg) with the largest quantity of THC usually resulted in the greatest impairment. However, differences in performance were most prominent and most frequent not only with hashish (180 mg) but also with marijuana (78 mg). Hashish (180 mg) was significantly different from the placebo in *barrage de signe,* time estimation, and serial sevens. Marijuana (78 mg) was significantly different from the placebo in *barrage de signe* and time estimation. Why hashish (90 mg) and THC (100 mg) conditions, which both contained greater THC quantities than did marijuana, were not different from the placebo is difficult to explain. It may be that hashish (90 mg) was most similar to the dose and quality of material that subjects typically used. Although the marijuana (78 mg) contained only 12 mg less THC than did hashish (90 mg), it had a different combination of cannabinoids. Assays of American marijuana and Greek hashish indicated that marijuana contained less cannabidiol and cannabinoids than did hashish.[22]

Recent evidence indicates that different combinations of cannabinoids may result in different effects. Karniol *et al.*[4] found that THC caused deficits in time estimation; the effect was blocked when THC and cannabidiol were consumed together. Therefore, marijuana may represent a qualitatively different and new substance for Greek subjects.

The data from the THC condition are more complex. In the *barrage de signe* condition, performance was actually better than that with the placebo. There are two possible explanations for this result.

THC has a very short shelf life. It is affected by light and air and deteriorates rapidly. However, studies of heart rate[23] indicate that THC was as potent as the other cannabis products and caused heart rate increases as great as those produced by hashish (180 mg).

It was noted under METHODS AND MATERIALS *that the order of drug presentation was only semirandom.* THC was always the last drug presented, whereas the order of the other drugs was randomized. In the *barrage de signe* task, there was a clear order or practice effect (FIGURE 2). When each drug was the first to be administered, correct performance was lowest; performance increased steadily when the drug was administered on the second, third, and fourth days of the series. Thus, superior performance in the THC condition may be a result of its order of occurrence, that is, always the last day. This finding suggests a practice effect. However, that a practice effect was possible with these large doses is itself noteworthy.

The time estimation data correlate with anecdotal reports. Users indicate that time passes slowly. To be consistent with these reports, experimental methods of estimation should produce overestimations, as did occur. Under nondrug conditions, time sense is usually underestimated, as was the case with placebo. In this framework, then, the mean exact estimate of the task, namely, 3 min, found in the THC condition may also be considered a deviation from what would be expected under nondrug conditions.

After an average of 25 years of cannabis use, Greek subjects evidenced a similar pattern of response on these tests of mental functioning after administration of doses that ranged from 78 to 180 mg of Δ^9-THC, as did American short-term users who consumed up to 25 mg of THC. That is, performance on

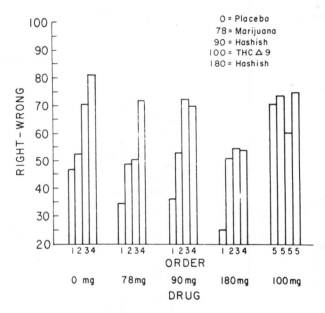

FIGURE 2. Performance on the *barrage de signe* task as a function of its order of presentation within each drug condition.

simple tasks, such as digit span and star tracing, was unaffected. Performance on more complex tasks, such as *barrage de signe*, serial sevens, and time estimation, was affected. The heavy long-term use of cannabis does not qualitatively change the general patterns of response in acute use that are exhibited by, as yet, occasional short-term users.

REFERENCES

1. BECH, P., L. RAFAELSON & O. RAFAELSON. 1974. Cannabis: a psychopharmacological review. Danish Med. Bull. **21:** 106–120.
2. DORNBUSH, R. L., M. FINK & A. M. FREEDMAN. 1971. Marijuana, memory and perception. Amer. J. Psychiat. **128:** 194–197.

3. HOSKO, M., M. KOCHAR & R. WANG. 1973. Effects of orally administered delta-9-tetrahydrocannabinol in man. Clin. Pharmacol. Ther. **14:** 344–352.
4. KARNIOL, I. G., I. SHIRAKAWA, N. KASINSKI, A. PFEFERMAN & E. A. CARLINI. 1974. Cannabidiol interferes with the effects of delta-9-tetrahydrocannabinol in man. Eur. J. Pharmacol. **28:** 172–177.
5. TINKLENBERG, J. R., B. S. KOPELL, F. T. MELGES & L. E. HOLLISTER. 1972. Marijuana and alcohol: time production and memory functions. Arch. Gen. Psychiat. **27:** 812–815.
6. JONES, R. & G. STONE. 1971. Psychological studies of marijuana and alcohol in man. Psychopharmacologia **18:** 108–117.
7. CLARK, L. D., R. HUGHES & E. N. NAKASHIMA. 1970. Behavioral effects of marijuana. Experimental studies. Arch. Gen. Psychiat. **23:** 193–198.
8. WEIL, A., N. ZINBERG & J. NIELSEN. 1968. Clinical and psychological effects of marijuana in man. Science **162:** 1234–1242.
9. DORNBUSH, R. & A. KOKKEVI. 1976. The acute effects of various cannabis substances on cognitive, perceptual and motor performance in very long-term hashish users. *In* Pharmacology of Marihuana. The Raven Press. New York, N.Y.
10. DORNBUSH, R., G. CLARE, A. ZAKS, P. CROWN, J. VOLAVKA & M. FINK. 1972. 21-Day administration of marijuana in male volunteers. *In* Current Research in Marijuana. M. Lewis, Ed. Academic Press, Inc. New York, N.Y.
11. ABEL, E. 1971. Marihuana and memory. Science **173:** 1038–1040.
12. DARLEY, C., T. TINKLENBERG, L. HOLLISTER & R. ATKINSON. 1973. Marihuana and retrieval from short-term memory. Psychopharmacologia **29:** 231–238.
13. MELGES, F. T., J. R. TINKLENBERG, L. E. HOLLISTER & H. K. GILLESPIE. 1970. Marihuana and temporal disintegration. Science **168:** 1118–1120.
14. CALDWELL, D., S. MYERS, E. DOMINO & P. MERRIAM. 1969. Auditory and visual threshold effects of marijuana in man. Percept. Motor Skills **29:** 755–759.
15. LEDAIN, G. 1972. Cannabis. A Report of the Commission of Inquiry into the Non-medical Use of Drugs. Information Canada. Ottawa, Ontario, Canada.
16. MEYER, R., R. PILLARD, L. SHAPIRO & S. MIRIN. 1971. Administration of marijuana to heavy and casual marijuana users. Amer. J. Psychiat. **128:** 198–204.
17. KIPLINGER, G., J. MANNOM, B. RODDA & R. FORNEY. 1971. Dose-response analysis of affects of tetrahydrocannabinol in man. Clin. Pharmacol. Ther. **12:** 650–657.
18. HOLLISTER, L. E. & H. K. GILLESPIE. 1970. Marihuana, ethanol and dextroamphetamine: mood and mental function alteration. Arch. Gen. Psychiat. **23:** 199–203.
19. WASKOW, I., J. OLSSON, C. SALTZMAN, M. KATZ & C. CHASE. 1970. Psychological effects of THC. Arch. Gen. Psychiat. **22:** 97–107.
20. CASSWELL, S. & D. F. MARKS. 1973. Cannabis and temporal disintegration in experienced and naive subjects. Science **179:** 803–803.
21. RAFAELSON, L., H. CHRISTRUP, P. BECH & O. J. RAFAELSON. 1973. Cannabis and alcohol: effects on psychological tests. Nature (London) **242:** 117, 118.
22. VOLAVKA, J. 1975. Acute EEG effects of cannabis preparations in long-term users of hashish. Unpublished report.
23. CROWN, P., R. DORNBUSH & J. VOLAVKA. 1976. Intercorrelations between physiological and psychological effects of marijuana, hashish, and THC-Δ-9 in long-term hashish users. *In* Hashish! A Study of Long-Term Use. C. Stefanis, R. Dornbush & M. Fink, Eds. The Raven Press. New York, N.Y. In press.
24. BOULOUGOURIS, J. C., A. LIAKOS & C. STEFANIS. This monograph.
25. STEFANIS, C., A. LIAKOS & J. C. BOULOUGOURIS. This monograph (first paper).

DIFFERENTIAL ASSOCIATION BETWEEN CHRONIC CANNABIS USE AND BRAIN FUNCTION DEFICITS

M. I. Soueif

Psychology Department
Cairo University
Cairo, Egypt

INTRODUCTION

In a series of papers, we have reported on progressive stages of a study of long-term cannabis consumption among Egyptian males.[1-9] The study included the following main parts:

(a) The administration of standardized interviewing schedules, of which the reliabilities were established, to 204 cannabis consumers and 115 controls, all living in the city of Cairo, and to 40 consumers and 40 controls drawn from rural areas of Upper Egypt.

The findings obtained in part a enabled us to formulate several hypotheses concerning specific function deficits expected to be associated with chronic cannabis usage. Accordingly, a battery of 12 objective psychologic tests that generated 16 test variables was constructed with the intention of including it among our investigation procedures.

(b) In part b, the entire battery together with the interviewing schedules were administered to 850 consumers and 839 controls. This time our subjects were prison inmates (in contrast to the volunteers we studied in part a, who were free citizens). The 850 users included practically all of the male population convicted exclusively for hashish use incarcerated in Egyptian prisons from June 1967 to March 1968.

Detailed descriptions of all groups of subjects, of the prevalent methods of drug consumption, and of the tools of investigation have been reported elsewhere.[3, 4] Statistical analyses of the interview responses and test scores that underlined various patterns of regularities have also been provided in two reports.[7, 8] This paper will attempt to bestow form and meaning to our main test results. A theoretical framework is suggested, with the following specific aims:

To account for the level of functioning revealed through test scores obtained by chronic users compared with nonusers.

To integrate apparently discrepant findings within our study.

To suggest points of convergence among seemingly conflicting reports by various investigators.

To generate hypotheses that may aid in collecting new data and raising new questions.

Procedure

Subjects

A very brief account of the subjects and the battery of tests will be given to guarantee reasonable communication.

In our sample, users' ages ranged from 15 to about 50, with an average of 39 years (±10.5). All 460 consumers were detained in prisons situated in big cities and intended for urban offenders, while 390 subjects were incarcerated in rural prisons. Sixty percent were illiterate, and the remaining 40% were distributed among various levels of education, with only six subjects having received high school diplomas; 26% were classified as skilled laborers. The majority of our users (89%) had been taking hashish regularly for long periods before they were arrested, periods that ranged from slightly over 5 years to approximately 30 years. About two-thirds of the whole group of users had been taking the drug more than once daily. They took an amount that ranged from 0.54 to 1.08 g per sitting. Smoking, by means of a water pipe, was the prevalent route of administration (89.4% of the group). The estimated Δ^9-tetrahydrocannabinol (Δ^9-THC) content of the stuff used by the group ranged from 1.9 to 3.6%, averaging 3.04% by weight.* Though there were rumors to the effect that hashish and other narcotic substances were smuggled into the prisons and clandestinely traded among inmates, to the best of our information our subjects were not under the effect of any such substance when they were examined.

Controls were defined as subjects who had never taken hashish or any other narcotic substance, as specified in Act 182 passed in June 1960 by the Egyptian Government as to the prohibition and/or regulation of the use of narcotic substances.[3] Their ages were between 15 and about 50 years, with an average of 33 (±9.75). A total of 454 subjects were selected from urban prisons and 385 from rural ones. Fifty-five percent were illiterate; the remaining 45% were literate or semiliterate, with 44 subjects holding high school diplomas and nine others university graduates. The group included 26% who were classified as skilled laborers.

Controls were, thus, almost equated to users with respect to age range and variance but were slightly younger with respect to average age. The former group also included slightly more literates than did the latter. On the other hand, however, drug takers had a higher average monthly income than did nonusers. They included a higher percentage of individuals reared in an urban environment than did controls.

Tests

Our battery of tests included the following:

Tool Matching. A test designed to assess speed and accuracy of form perception.

---

* We are grateful to Drs. Z. I. El-Darawy and Z. M. Mobarak, who, at our request in 1971, carried out the quantitative determination of Δ^9-THC content in seven samples of hashish seized at different places on the illicit market. The analysis was performed at the laboratories of the National Centre for Social and Criminological Research in Cairo.

H Marking. A test constructed to assess aiming combined with motor speed.

Speed. A test that measures motor speed.

Mark Making. This test assesses aiming combined with motor speed.†

Trail Making Test (part A). The test is scored for speed of complex psychomotor performance that requires recall and shifts of orientation in space.[10, 11]

Initial Reaction Time. A test designed to assess speed of verbal response to an ambiguous visual stimulus.

Distance Estimation. Subject was required to estimate length of each of three standardized sticks shown to him one at a time.

Time Estimation. A period of 3 min was a criterion, during which time the subject was instructed to rest but not to leave the testing situation nor to get engaged in conversation. By the end of the period, the subject is asked to estimate the length of time that has elapsed since he received instructions.

Digits Forward. A test constructed to assess immediate memory for the digits forward.

Digits Backward. A test designed to assess immediate memory for digits backward.‡

Bender Gestalt (copy). The test involves copying simple designs by drawing.

Bender Gestalt (recall). Subjects are required to produce, out of immediate memory, the same designs mentioned under *copy.*

It should be noted that all tests were administered under standardized conditions. It should also be mentioned that most of these tools were already used on various Egyptian groups (psychiatric and nonpsychiatric) and proved to be of clinical value.[13-15]

Findings

Analysis of variance based on $3 \times 3 \times 2$ factorial design was the statistical method of choice. The following comparisons and interactions were, thus, supplied for each test variable: comparisons between drug takers and controls irrespective of literacy and residence, between levels of literacy irrespective of drug consumption and residence, and between residence positions on a continuum of "urbanism-ruralism" regardless of drug behavior and literacy; interactions between drug consumption and literacy, between drug consumption and residence, between literacy and residence, and among drug consumption, literacy, and residence.

TABLE 1 presents the outcome of an analysis of variance that compared users with controls, irrespective of literacy and residence, on 16 test variables.

Cannabis users were significantly differentiated from nonusers on 10 of 16 test variables. Controls as a whole obtained better scores than did drug takers on almost all variables; the difference sometimes reached a very high level of statistical significance.

Cannabis users proved to be decidedly slower than controls on all speed tasks. This finding is illustrated by the results obtained on the first six tests. Even on mark making and initial reaction time, where acceptable statistical

---

† The four tests cited so far were selected from among the objective tools included in the General Aptitude Test Battery.[23]

‡ These last two tests form part of the Weschsler Scale for Intelligence.[12]

significance failed to emerge (for reasons that will be discussed later), users tended to perform more slowly than nonusers.

This finding is in agreement with the self-descriptions our subjects gave when they were interviewed.[4] When asked about the usual quantity of their output during work, our users were differentiated from nonusers at a very high level of significance ($\chi^2 = 40.82$; 2 df; $p > 0.001$); the difference favored the controls. A similar result was obtained with nonprisoner interviewees ($\chi^2 = 7.02$; 2 df; $p > 0.05$).[3]

The importance of tests that examine speed and accuracy of performance, in general, and of psychomotor activity, in particular, is well documented abundantly in the literature of validation studies of such tests. Examples are reports

TABLE 1

F RATIOS BETWEEN CANNABIS USERS AND CONTROLS IRRESPECTIVE
OF LITERACY AND RESIDENCE

Test Variable	F	p
Tool matching	13.23	0.001
H marking	76.26	0.001
Speed	30.40	0.001
Mark making	2.71	ns
Trail making, part A	7.13	0.01
Initial reaction time	2.36	ns
Distance overestimation	4.75	0.05
Distance underestimation *†	5.54	0.05
Distance estimation, discrepancy †	0.73	ns
Time estimation ‡	0.56	ns
Time estimation, discrepancy *†	5.78	0.05
Digits fordward	3.70	ns
Digits backward	27.70	0.001
Digits forward and backward	3.04	ns
Bender gestalt, copy	11.51	0.001
Bender gestalt, recall	9.34	0.001

* Controls made more mistakes than did users.
† Analysis of discrepancy irrespective of direction.
‡ For technical reasons, we could not perform two different analyses, one for over-estimation and one for underestimation.

on the validation of such tests for a wide variety of jobs,[16-19] for psychiatric diagnoses,[13, 14, 20, 21] and of other tests to establish factorial validity.[22, 23]

In estimating (rather short) distances, hashish users showed a tendency to err more than controls in the direction of overestimation, a finding in agreement with the verbal responses we were given by both convicted and unconvicted users.[7-9] Contrary to popular notion, the average size of error made by users in time estimation proved to be smaller than that made by controls. In both cases, however, our findings should be accepted with caution, because the degree of statistical significance was rather modest. We know from the literature on time perception studies in normals and abnormals that the estimation of a certain period of time is very sensitive to the techniques utilized in testing, to the duration of the intervals to be estimated, and to other experimental conditions.[24–26]

Memory span for digits distinguished between consumers and controls at a very high level of significance on one modality only, digits backward. Again, this finding is congruent with the self-report data we obtained from detainees and from free interviewees. In responding to our relevant questions, the convicted users were significantly weaker than their control prison mates ($\chi^2 = 13.73$; 2 df; p > 0.01), and the free users were also reliably differentiated from their controls ($\chi^2 = 8.17$; 2 df; p > 0.02).

The Bender Gestalt Test for visuomotor coordination differentiated, at a very high level of confidence, between users and nonusers on the two versions that required copying and recall. In both cases, users gave less accurate performance than controls.

Obviously, therefore, most of our objective tests differentiated, reliably, between chronic users and nonusers, showing the latter to give superior performance in speed and/or accuracy tasks. In addition, we could establish a reasonable amount of agreement between such findings and outcome of analysis of interview data reported by both prison and nonprison groups.

DISCUSSION

There is an appalling dearth of information concerning objective test behavior of chronic cannabis users when not under the immediate influence of the drug. Without such information, which should permit comparisons across various social sectors (e.g., prisoners vs nonprisoners or males vs females), across nations and/or cultures (e.g., Egyptians vs Indians or Americans), and across designs of research (retrospective vs prospective), the methodologic approach adopted in the present study does not allow determining what is specific and what is open to generalization in our results.

An additional difficulty is that our users had been taking the drug on a regular basis for very long periods of time, from 5 to 30 years. Under such conditions, comparisons between our findings and the results reported under such titles as "effects of long-term consumption," by which authors usually refer to a few months, seem unconvincing.

To compare test behavior of chronic users while not under an immediate drug condition with performance by naive subjects under such an influence raises other problems of methodology that should themselves be investigated. It is tempting, however, to underline some congruencies. For example, Melges et al.[27] found that the span of immediate memory digits significantly deteriorated under the effect of Δ^9-THC. Tinklenberg et al. stated that the poorest mean scores on a "running memory span" test were obtained during peak of the drug's action, although the differences did not reach significance.[28] Weil and Zinberg[29] reported on the phenomenon of "temporal disintegration," which "has two principal manifestations: simple forgetting of what one is going to say next, and a strong tendency to go off on irrelevant tangents because the line of thought is lost." Weil et al.[30] demonstrated significant decrements in performance on pursuit rotor of subjects while under the effect of the drug. Manno et al.[31, 32] reported similar impairment of performance on pursuit tracking.

Extrapolation from acute effects to behavior correlates established in chronic users, though, should be exercised with great caution. From a purely methodologic viewpoint, although studies of acute effects of the drug may provide useful information about cumulative effects, such studies cannot be treated, implicitly or explicitly, as criteria for cross-validation of research on chronicity. This is particularly so when points of disagreement between findings in the two kinds of research emerge.

ELABORATION

Meaning of Interactional Effects

Introduction

One of the findings that kept recurring throughout our analyses of test results was that certain combinations among drug consumption, level of literacy, and residence revealed the main drug effect better than others. We may have here a pointer to a fundamental rule that regulates the emergence of a significant association between cannabis usage and function deficit.

A Working Hypothesis

The following is proposed as a working hypothesis: The size of any psychologic deficit likely to be associated with chronic cannabis usage in an individual is a function of his general level of proficiency when not under the influence of the drug (presumably ascertainable through comparable nonusers). Other conditions being equal, the lower the nondrug level of proficiency, the smaller the deficit.

Expected Moderators

Before proceeding to examine empirically this broad hypothesis, several research findings that relate to some "ordinary moderators" (or partial determinants) of the level of proficiency have to be mentioned. Three such moderators will be discussed: literacy, residence, and age. Similar moderators may be determined by future investigators. The expectation, then, is that such moderators will yield patterns of results that resemble what will be presented in this report.

A well-documented finding about psychologic testing is that the majority of tests constructed to assess psychomotor and/or cognitive abilities are highly correlated with the level of literacy. Wechsler puts it clearly: "Practically all studies show that educational attainment and intelligence ratings (as measured by test scores) correlate to a relatively high degree." [33] What is true of intelligence ratings can, with due qualification, be extended to tests of general abilities. The Wechsler Intelligence Scale for adults includes several subscales that assess various aspects of perceptual and motor functioning. It follows that the level of literacy can be considered a predictor of the level of proficiency on tests of abilities. Therefore, the amount of deficit (as defined by such tests) expected to be associated with cannabis usage would be a function of the individual's level of literacy.

While conducting our research, we were struck by what may be labeled the "underresponsiveness" of our rural subjects (prisoners and nonprisoners) in contrast with their urban counterparts. In a country like Egypt, with a wide cultural gap between town and country, such contrasting effects could be more impressive than in most Western countries.[34] The underresponsiveness of our villagers could be detected in various aspects of their behavior; examples are slowness of gross and fine motor activity, such as walking and handling equipment used in various crafts; long reaction time in starting to answer questions; a tendency to repeat a single word or a few words every few sentences; long intervals of silence between phrases or small units of discourse; and slow utterance of single words. These observations are in agreement with various findings made by cultural anthropologists who studied nonurban societies.[35] Another type of research finding that we found compatible with our remarks was work on identical twins reared apart. A definite association has been established between low scores on various tests of abilities and being brought up in rural areas.[36, 37] Commenting on that finding, Shields maintained the following: "Of course, if one were to study only selected pairs of twins where the environment of one was grossly 'enriched' and that of the other grossly 'restricted' it would be surprising if they were still found to be alike."[38] Relevant, also, is the famous study conducted by Klineberg early in this century. Klineberg could establish a very high correlation between scores obtained on the National Intelligence Test by 425 12-year-old black boys and the duration of their stay in the city.[39] § Guided by such findings, the suggestion is made that the level of urbanism should be taken as a predictor of the level of proficiency on tests of psychomotor and cognitive abilities. Urban subjects would be expected to earn high scores, rurals low scores, and semirurals would fall in between. Therefore, the magnitude of deficit expected to be associated with cannabis usage would be positively correlated with the person's level of urbanism.

Chronologic age has always been a concern for students of human behavior whenever administering tests of abilities to adults.[40] There is considerable evidence that speed and accuracy of psychomotor performance decline with age.[41] A negative correlation between immediate and short-term memory efficiency, on one hand, and old age, on the other, has also been recognized.[42] Basing our opinion on such information and relevant extrapolations, the suggestion is made that age be considered a predictor of proficiency on tests of psychomotor and cognitive abilities. It would, therefore, follow that the size of deficit shown to be associated with cannabis intake would vary with age. Young adult users would be expected to show more deficit than old ones.

Specific Predictions

Six specific predictions were formulated:

We would expect performance on psychomotor and cognitive tests to be significantly correlated with the position the subject occupies on a continuum of "literacy-illiteracy." The lower the level of literacy, the smaller the size of function deficit associated with cannabis usage.

§ It is possible that such linear correlation would remain true only for IQs below average. In all probability, the relationship would level off for above-average. IQs.

We would expect performance on psychomotor and cognitive tests to be significantly correlated with the position occupied by the subject on the continuum of "urbanism-ruralism." The nearer the subject's position to the ruralism pole, the smaller the size of function deficit associated with cannabis usage.

We would expect performance on our psychomotor and cognitive tests to be significantly (but inversely) correlated with age. The older the subject, the smaller the function impairment associated with cannabis consumption.

TABLE 2

F RATIOS ON 16 TEST VARIABLES AMONG THREE LEVELS
OF LITERACY REGARDLESS OF DRUG USE

Test Variable	F *
Tool matching	243.00
H marking	240.00
Speed	1036.10
Mark making	268.00
Trail making, part A	50.92
Initial reaction time	10.89
Distance overestimation	0.35
Distance underestimation	62.14
Distance estimation, discrepancy	37.98
Time estimation	6.29
Time estimation, discrepancy	11.55
Digits forward	156.80
Digits backward	1778.00
Digits forward and backward	232.60
Bender gestalt, copy	357.00
Bender gestalt, recall	267.00

* Except for distance overestimation, p was greater than the 0.001 level of significance in all cases.

Testing of Specific Predictions

TABLE 2 presents the outcome of the analysis of variance of scores obtained on the tests by our subjects classified as representing three levels of literacy regardless of drug usage. Except for "distance overestimation," all test variables differentiated at a very high level of statistical significance between subjects. Subjects high on literacy obtained the best scores, illiterates the worst, while semiliterates tended to fall in between.[7-9] TABLE 2 confirms our first prediction.

TABLE 3 presents t tests between median scores obtained by users and non-users within each position on the literacy continuum. We have used medians, instead of means, as measurements of central tendency, to avoid the possibility of capitalizing on any deviations of the distributions of test scores from normality. Inspection of TABLE 3 shows a trend toward less significant differences between users and nonusers, the nearer we move from the literate to the illiterate groups.

The same finding is presented graphically in FIGURE 1. In the literate groups, 10 test variables differentiated between consumers and controls, mostly at very

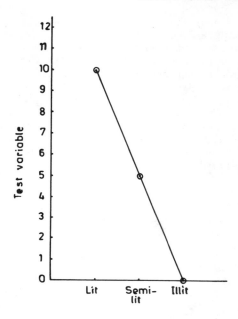

FIGURE 1. The lower is the level of literacy, the less detactable is the psychologic impairment associated with cannabis usage.

TABLE 3

t TESTS * BETWEEN MEDIAN TEST SCORES OBTAINED BY USERS AND NONUSERS WITHIN EACH ONE OF THE THREE LEVELS OF LITERACY

Test Variable	Literates	Semiliterates	Illiterates
Tool matching	3.19 †	3.78 †	1.10
H marking	4.27 †	1.97 ‡	1.61
Speed	1.84 §	1.70 §	1.11
Mark making	3.22 †	1.50	1.42
Trail making, part A	2.80 †	1.38	2.60 ‡
Initial reaction time	0.44	1.05	1.30
Distance overestimation	0.90	0.40	0.54
Distance underestimation	2.68 †	1.55	1.54
Distance estimation, discrepancy	1.40	0.76	1.36
Time estimation	0.53	1.19	3.00 ‡
Time estimation, discrepancy	0.36	0.06	1.53
Digits forward	2.71 †	0.17	2.41 §
Digits backward	2.37 ‡	0.44	0.21
Digits forward and backward	3.38 †	0.05	1.17
Bender gestalt, copy	1.41	5.81 †	0.43
Bender gestalt, recall	2.60 †	5.17 †	1.09

* One-tailed test (in the illiterates, p was based on a two-tailed test because the difference was in the unexpected direction).
† p=0.001.
‡ p=0.01.
§ p=0.05.

high levels of statistical significance. Among the illiterates, the number of reliable differentiators was reduced to three. And in the semiliterates, five variables discriminated significantly between users and nonusers.

One could, therefore, conclude that no function deficit was correlated with cannabis consumption in the illiterate groups. This finding supports our second prediction.

TABLE 4 shows the results of an analysis of variance of test scores obtained by our subjects classified as representing three positions on the continuum of urbanism irrespective of drug taking. In all cases, F ratios were highly significant (for the direction of the differences, see Soueif [7-9]). Other conditions being equal, urbans tend to earn high scores, rurals low scores, and semirurals scores in between. This result confirms our third prediction.

TABLE 4

F RATIOS ON 16 TEST VARIABLES AMONG URBAN, SEMIRURAL, AND RURAL SUBJECTS IRRESPECTIVE OF DRUG USE

Test Variable	F *
Tool matching	73.30
H marking	120.00
Speed	81.90
Mark making	193.60
Trail making, part A	17.86
Initial reaction time	16.46
Distance overestimation	9.99
Distance underestimation	13.91
Distance estimation, discrepancy	18.29
Time estimation	6.43
Time estimation, discrepancy	18.44
Digits forward	33.56
Digits backward	5.20
Digits forward and backward	24.60
Bender gestalt, copy	18.65
Bender gestalt, recall	47.60

* $p = 0.001$ in all cases.

TABLE 5 presents t tests between median scores obtained by users and controls within each category along the urbanism continuum. The reader can readily detect a trend toward less significant disparities between cannabis users and nonusers, the more we move from urban through rural groups. The same fact is displayed graphically in FIGURE 2. In urban groups, consumers were differentiated, mostly at high levels of statistical significance, along eight test variables, in the rurals the number of differentiators was reduced to three, while in the semirurals the number was seven. This finding confirms our fourth prediction.

To test our fifth and sixth predictions, we decided to limit relevant comparisons to two age groups: those below 25 years vs those above 35 years. This decision was made to permit optimum clarity of the contrast effect between groups compared.

TABLE 5

t Tests * between Median Test Scores Obtained by Users and Nonusers Within Each One of Three Positions on the "Urbanism-Ruralism" Continuum

Test Variable	Urbans	Semirurals	Rurals
Tool matching	2.11 †	3.08 ‡	0.63
H marking	4.01 ‡	3.49 ‡	0.42
Speed	1.73 §	2.89 ‡	1.98 †
Mark making	4.13 ‡	2.59 ‡	0.93
Trail making, part A	0.45	2.49 †	1.19
Initial reaction time	2.24 †	0.87	0.06
Distance overestimation	0.24	0.34	0.66
Distance underestimation	1.46	0.60	3.93 ‡
Distance estimation, discrepancy	2.60 †	0.36	0.07
Time estimation	0.73	0.19	0.27
Time estimation, discrepancy	0.98	0.03	0.44
Digits forward	0.24	1.21	1.59
Digits backward	0.70	0.70	0.57
Digits forward and backward	1.50	1.00	1.00
Bender gestalt, copy	1.42	1.86 §	2.05 †
Bender gestalt, recall	3.46 †	1.84 §	2.33 †

* One-tailed test (except in the third test in rurals, because the observed difference was in the unexpected direction).

† $p = 0.01$.

‡ $p = 0.001$.

§ $p = 0.05$.

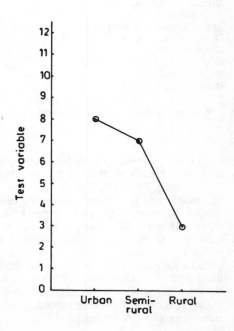

Figure 2. The nearer the subjects are to ruralism, the less detectable is the psychologic impairment associated with cannabis usage.

TABLE 6 presents tests of significance between median scores obtained by young and old controls. On all of the variables, the young subjects earned better scores than did the old ones. Differences between the two groups reached a satisfactory level of statistical significance on nine of the 16 test variables, thus substantiating our fifth prediction. We did not make a similar comparison within users because it proved rather difficult to find two sizable subgroups that would differ in age and remain equivalent in duration of cannabis consumption.

To test our sixth prediction, we had to accept the fact that we could not equate the users (who represented two age groups) regarding duration of drug taking. Longer duration was almost automatically contingent with older age. This difficulty, however, did not impede our comparisons, nor did it confuse the conclusion drawn therefrom. And, incidentally, the two groups of consumers were equated with respect to frequency of drug use.

TABLE 6

t TESTS BETWEEN MEDIAN TEST SCORES OBTAINED BY YOUNG (BELOW 25 YEARS)
AND OLD (35–50 YEARS) NONUSERS

Test Variable	t *
Tool matching	6.04
H marking	6.03
Speed	4.86
Mark making	5.06
Trail making, part A	2.75
Initial reaction time	0.95
Distance overestimation	0.37
Distance underestimation	0.40
Distance estimation, discrepancy	1.38
Time estimation	0.23
Time estimation, discrepancy	0.45
Digits forward	3.46
Digits backward	1.26
Digits forward and backward	2.33
Bender gestalt, copy	3.49
Bender gestalt, recall	6.77

* To reach the 0.05 level of confidence (one-tailed test), t should be at least about 1.70.

TABLE 7 presents t tests between median scores obtained by users and nonusers within each of two age groups: below 25 and above 35 years.

We should note that in the younger group of users, the duration of drug experience was less than 5 years, whereas the older users had an average consuming duration of at least 20 years. In both groups, frequency of cannabis usage was above 30 times per month. Inspection of TABLE 7 reveals a definite trend toward less statistically significant differences between users and controls in the older group of subjects. In other words, less function deficit was associated with drug consumption in the older group, despite the fact that the older users had a much longer duration of drug use than did the younger users. Whereas seven tests differentiated significantly between young users and controls, the older groups were reliably differentiated on four tests only. The same trend is graphically presented in FIGURE 3.

TABLE 7

t TESTS * BETWEEN MEDIAN TEST SCORES OBTAINED BY USERS AND NONUSERS WITHIN EACH OF TWO "AGE AND DURATION" GROUPS (FREQUENCY: MORE THAN 30 TIMES PER MONTH)

Test Variable	Users (age, <25 yr; duration, <5 yr; frequency, 30+ per month) vs Controls (age, < 25 yr)	Users (age, 35–50 yr; duration 20 yr; frequency, 30 per month) vs Controls (age 35–50 yr)
Tool matching	2.44 †	1.16
H marking	4.99 ‡	0.82
Speed	2.83 ‡	2.11 †
Mark making	2.54 †	0.27
Trail making, part A	0.17	0.29
Initial reaction time	0.21	0.22
Distance overestimation	0.24	0.44
Distance underestimation	4.04 ‡	0.27
Distance estimation, discrepancy	4.08 ‡	0.05
Time estimation	0.44	0.02
Time estimation, discrepancy	0.60	0.29
Digits forward	1.36	2.13 †
Digits backward	0.62	0.20
Digits forward and backward	0.99	2.87 ‡
Bender gestalt, copy	1.54	1.91 §
Bender gestalt, recall	2.44 †	1.23

* One-tailed test.
† $p = 0.01$.
‡ $p = 0.001$.
§ $p = 0.05$.

FIGURE 3. The older are the subjects, the less detectable is the function deficit associated with cannabis usage (frequency of drug consumption: >30 times per month).

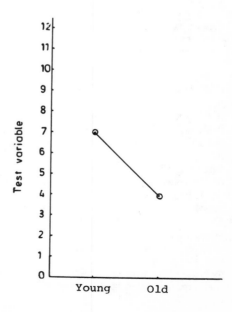

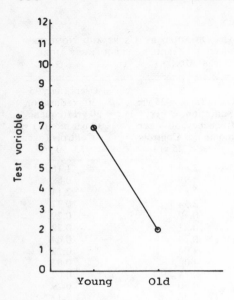

FIGURE 4. The older are the subjects, the less detectable is the function deficit associated with cannabis usage (frequency of drug consumption: <30 times per month).

The data in TABLE 8 are similar to those in TABLE 7, except for the frequency of drug consumption, which in this case is below 30 times per month for the two groups of users. TABLE 8 shows the same trend revealed in TABLE 7: less statistically significant differences between older consumers and controls (only on two test variables) than between younger equivalent groups (on seven test variables). FIGURE 4 graphically represents this finding. TABLES 7 and 8 substantiate our sixth prediction.

The general conclusion is that all of our predictions were confirmed. This conclusion lends substantial support to our initial working hypothesis, to the effect that the lower the nondrug level of proficiency, the smaller the function deficit to be associated with drug consumption.

Discussion

Obviously, our conclusion is based on the detection of a trend that manifests itself faintly, though consistently and persistently, through our analyses. Perhaps the trend could have made a more impressive appearance, had we been willing to delete the groups of semiliterates and semirurals when testing our second and fourth specific predictions, thus restricting our comparisons to the extreme poles of the relevant continua (as we did in testing our sixth prediction).

It has, justly, been said, "that no single experiment can establish the absolute proof of any result, however significant the results may happen to be." [43] The gist of such dictum is that research workers should be wary of imprudently accepting, as a fact, what may turn out, on careful replication, to be just an illusion, a mistake that methodologists used to call "Type-I error." It is not a less serious flaw, however, to make a "Type-II error," namely, to brush aside, as chimera, a true regularity that may reveal an important fact or a basic relationship, if we continue to examine closely the conditions of its emergence.

The differential association between the size of function deficit and chronic cannabis consumption, which we have been trying to delineate, seems to be one of those low relief regularities that may prove generously rewarding. At the present stage of its development, however, our hypothesis seems to generate more questions than answers. First, it would be foolish to generalize such a formula to other groups of subjects (e.g., females) and other cultural settings on an a priori basis. Cross-validation studies are needed to define the limits beyond which the formula should not be extended. And would the hypothesis stand a direct empirical examination? Supposing a prospective study was conducted on a cohort of subjects who were followed up until they became differentiated into confirmed cannabis users and nonusers. Would it be possible to establish the same relationship between the magnitude of psychomotor and cognitive function deficit they display, then, and their predrug level of proficiency? A third question would concern the possibility of a transposition of the hypothesis to the domain of inquiry into the acute effects of cannabis consumption. The working hypothesis should read, then, as follows: The amount of impairment that is likely to be effected by the drug, as defined by objective psychologic test scores, is a function of the level of predrug proficiency; other conditions being equal, the lower the initial level, the less the impairment.

TABLE 8

t Tests * between Median Test Scores Obtained by Users and Nonusers within Each One of Two "Age and Duration" Groups
(frequency: 30 times per month)

Test Variable	Users (age, <25 yr; duration, <5 yr; frequency, $\leq$30 per month) vs Controls (age, <25 yr)	Users (age, 35–50 yr; duration,, >20 yr; frequency, $\leq$30 per month) vs Controls (age 35–50 yr)
Tool matching	1.91 †	2.44 ‡
H marking	1.95 †	0.96
Speed	1.71 †	0.20
Mark making	1.61	1.75 †
Trail making, part A	4.70 §	1.11
Initial reaction time	0.34	0.28
Distance overestimation	0.50	0.05
Distance underestimation	0.92	0.48
Distance estimation, discrepancy	2.13 ‡	0.44
Time estimation	0.26	0.04
Time estimation, discrepancy	0.76	0.03
Digits forward	1.04	1.37
Digits backward	0.58	0.72
Digits forward and backward	0.91	1.29
Bender gestalt, copy	4.14 §	0.90
Bender gestalt, recall	3.35 §	0.41

* One-tailed test.
† $p=0.05$.
‡ $p=0.01$.
§ $p=0.001$.

It is tempting, at this juncture, to present a tentative neuropsychologic explanation of the regularity we have been tracing, a step beyond mere statistical description. The following question arises: What is the common psychologic (or central) denominator beyond the three demonstrated moderators: literacy, urbanism, and young age? We propose that "level of arousal" could be the key process. Therefore, our illiterates, rurals, and old-age subjects are believed to have low levels of arousal compared with their counterparts.

Martin [44] gives the following definition: "When we speak of an individual's *arousal* level we refer to some allegedly stable characteristic level of organismic activity." And Brodal [45] describes the same process but in more physiologic terms, as follows: "Following high frequency electrical stimulation of the brain stem in chloralosane-anesthetized cats, the synchronized discharges of high voltage slow-waves in the electroencephalogram (EEG) are replaced by low voltage fast activity, closely resembling the corresponding changes observed in the human EEG on transition from a relaxed or drowsy sate to attention or alertness. These changes are generally referred to as *desynchronization, activation or the arousal reaction*. They occur diffusely over the entire cortex." Though one cannot equate the concepts of "arousal level" and "arousal reaction," yet one can think of a prevailing pattern of electrical activity in the cortex to characterize a more or less stable level of alertness or arousal. In trying to differentiate between arousal reaction and arousal level, Martin [44] states: "When we measure an orienting reaction, we are measuring relatively transient psychophysiological events in response to simple stimuli, superimposed on an ongoing level of arousal. This kind of work examines the way in which information is perceived, attended to, and processed . . . ." The idea has been extensively investigated in relation to psychiatric disorder.[46] Several objective psychologic tests have been suggested for the indirect measurement of the level of arousal. Examples are the continuous performance test, critical flicker fusion, spiral after effect, level of skin potential, and sedation threshold.[47]

Some measurements of speed of performance have also been suggested for the assessment of cortical arousal.[48] To account for several inconsistencies that emerge from use of such tests, Claridge proposed a model for two functionally related mechanisms of arousal, "which he terms the *tonic arousal system* and the *arousal modulating system*. The function of the former tonic system is to maintain the individual's overall level of arousal while the second modulating system regulates the activity level of the tonic arousal system and guards the central nervous system from overstimulation. Apart from this homeostatic role, the modulating system also filters incoming information to facilitate the reception of relevant and inhibit the reception of irrelevant data." [47] It might be the case that illiteracy, ruralism, and old age exert their influences through the tonic arousal system; they keep it at a low level of activity or they set a low ceiling for its arousability. Because of the multiplicity of questions that still await to be solved regarding the anatomic basis of the activating system, we are deliberately using "arousal" and "arousal systems" as functional concepts.[45]

One of the merits of the kind of field research presented here is that the investigator can cope with a large number of subjects, a fact that, more often than not, permits discriminating important, though subtle, patterns of regularity. Because human laboratory experiments are performed under many constraints, such experiments cannot handle large numbers of subjects. Field work, therefore, might do a scouting job that can provide laboratory studies with useful insights into the optimum conditions for an experimental design that gives meaningful results.

It might be a good exercise in the methodology of cannabis research to speculate on what kind of results we might have obtained had we been concentrating on a group of subjects who were all illiterates, rurals, and/or rather old. "No significant differences between users and nonusers" would have been, in all probability, the main finding. On the other hand, had we selected our subjects from among literates, urbans, and/or young adults solely, the opposite finding would have been reported without a hint about the other part of the story. It is possible that this is the case for some empirical reports that have appeared in the last few years.

Bowman and Pihl used a whole battery of objective tests in two field studies conducted in Jamaica. In the first study, they administered the tests to 16 users and 10 controls who were drawn from rural or semirural areas. In the second study, the investigators gave the tests to 14 users and 14 controls derived from the slum areas of one city. The results of both studies showed nonsignificant differences between users and controls.[49] It should also be noted that the majority of the examinees in the two studies were either illiterate or semiliterate, and their average age was 30 ± 5 years. In the light of our broad perspective amplified by our empirical findings, Bowman and Pihl were bound to obtain negative results.

It is interesting to note that some conflicting reports on the acute effects of cannabis usage can be reconciled logically with each other through our broad hypothesis (if we use the transposed version suggested for the area of short-term effects). The two reports, one by Waskow et al.[50] reporting no significant differences and the other by Melges et al.[27] reporting reliable differences between users and nonusers, provide almost a classic example for the hypothesis we are presenting. What is truly instructive about those two studies is that both used a double-blind experimental approach, yet they obtained mutually contradictory results. Obviously, the double-blind approach did not automatically provide protection against all sources of bias. Underlined here is the kind of bias that emerges from the sample of subjects studied in each experiment. The fact is that the two groups of researchers experimented on two different types of subjects. Waskow et al. examined 32 men who were all criminal offenders with an average IQ of 95 and average eighth-grade educational level. Melges et al. tested eight normal male graduate students (whose range of IQs could be estimated at >110). Because tests of cognitive abilities of the kind used in the two studies are known to be significantly correlated with the level of education and with the intelligence quotient, too, it is conceivable that the subjects' levels of predrug proficiency would differ in the two studies; it would be appreciably lower in the Waskow et al. than in the Melges et al. study. Following our working hypothesis, the discrepancy between the findings reported in the two studies would, naturally, be expected; subjects with a low predrug level of proficiency (in the Waskow et al. study) displayed minimal function deficit contingent with Δ^9-THC consumption, whereas those with a high predrug ability level (in the Melges et al. study) showed impairment of a sizable magnitude. The two studies thus complement (rather than negate) each other, in showing the role of some organismic variables in moderating the effects of cannabis usage in man.

Other studies that testify to the validity of the same conclusion can be cited. An example is another study performed by Melges et al. in which they obtained a result that was in disagreement with what they themselves had reported in

1970. By way of comment, those investigators stated the following: "The group of subjects used in this experiment were not as proficient on their initial baseline cognitive tests as the subjects we used in a previous study of marijuana intoxication."[28]

It is tempting to draw the reader's attention here to a group of studies that obtained results that appear to substantiate our main finding, though such studies belong to another field of investigation. Reviewing the work performed from 1960 to 1970 on intellectual deterioration under conditions of mental illness, Payne found that he was faced with two types of investigations: type A, which concentrated on patients who had originally an above-average or average IQ; those patients showed significant deterioration. And type B, which studied patients who were initially subnormal; those patients displayed very little deterioration. Commenting on the divergence between the two kinds of reports, Payne made the following remark: "It is possible to speculate that the dull who had become psychotic deteriorate little intellectually."[48] The same basic paradigm seems to account for possible function impairment contingent with mental illness and with cannabis consumption.

Stretching the paradigm to account for the social history of the drug, would it be the case that cannabis usage was believed to be benign (or not really harmful) throughout its past, not only because rigorous scientific research was lacking then, but also because the drug was mainly taken by the illiterate and the rural within the context of truly debilitating sociocultural conditions? (One has only to think of the social conditions prevalent in countries like Egypt, India, and South Africa until the nineteenth century.) This might explain why the famous Indian Hemp Drugs Commission (1894) came to the conclusion that, "In respect to the alleged effects of the drug . . . the moderate use of hemp drugs produces no injurious effects on the mind."[51]

SUMMARY

To summarize, 12 objective tests that generated 16 test variables were administered to 850 male regular cannabis users and 839 nonusers. The tests were designed to assess various modalities, including speed of psychomotor performance, distance estimation, time estimation, immediate memory, and visuomotor coordination. Most of the test variables differentiated significantly between consumers and controls. At the same time, a significant second-order interaction emerged in most cases. This interaction meant that, under certain conditions that relate to the two dimensions "literacy-illiteracy" and/or "urbanism-ruralism," the superiority of controls over cannabis users became impressive, whereas under other conditions it almost disappeared.

To account for this complex pattern of results, a working hypothesis was presented to the effect that "other conditions being equal, the lower the nondrug level of proficiency on tests of cognitive and psychomotor performance the smaller the size of function deficit associated with drug usage." For an empirical examination of the hypothesis, six predictions were formulated. Three predictions defined specific relationships between level of performance, on one hand, and each of three organismic variables, on the other: literacy, urbanism, and age. The remaining predictions delineated relationships to be expected between size of function deficit and the three organismic variables. All our predictions were confirmed, showing less function impairment to be contingent with cannabis usage among the illiterates, rurals, and older subjects.

Level of cortical arousal was suggested as the central process associated with the three organismic variables.

Because the version of our working hypothesis was formulated with reference to chronic material, the possibility of a transposition of the paradign to research on the acute effects of the drug was discussed. The suggestion was made that our working hypothesis, in either version, is capable of establishing genuine integration between reports that present conflicting results on possible function deficits contingent with cannabis consumption.

REFERENCES

1. COMMITTEE FOR THE INVESTIGATION OF HASHISH CONSUMPTION IN EGYPT. 1960. Hashish Consumption in Egypt: Research in Progress, Report I: The Interviewing Schedule: Construction, Reliability and Validity. National Centre for Social and Criminological Research. Cairo, Egypt (in Arabic).
2. COMMITTEE FOR THE INVESTIGATION OF HASHISH CONSUMPTION IN EGYPT. 1964. Hashish Consumption in Egypt: Research in Progress. Report II: Hashish Users in Cairo City: A Pilot Study. National Centre for Social and Criminological Research. Cairo, Egypt (in Arabic).
3. SOUEIF, M. I. 1967. Hashish consumption in Egypt, with special reference to psychosocial problems. Bull. Narcotics 19(2): 1–12.
4. SOUEIF, M. I. 1971. The use of cannabis in Egypt: a behavioural study. Bull. Narcotics 23(4): 17–28.
5. SOUEIF, M. I. 1972. The social psychology of cannabis consumption: myth, mystery and fact. Bull. Narcotics 24(2): 1–10.
6. SOUEIF, M. I. 1973. Cannabis ideology: a study of opinions and beliefs centering around cannabis consumption. Bull. Narcotics 25(4): 33–38.
7. SOUEIF, M. I. 1975a. Chronic cannabis users: further analysis of objective test results. Bull. Narcotics 27(4): 1–26.
8. SOUEIF, M. I. 1975b. Chronic cannabis takers: some temperamental characteristics. Drug Alc. Depend. 1(2): 125–154.
9. SOUEIF, M. I. 1975c. Some economic implications entailed by psychosocial correlates of regular cannabis consumption in Egypt. Paper presented at the International Conference on Alcoholism and Drug Addiction, Bahrain, November 29 to December 5 (mimeographed).
10. PARTINGTON, J. E. & R. G. LEITER. 1949. Partington pathways test. Psychol. Serv. Center Bull. 1: 9–20.
11. REITAN, R. M. 1955. The relation of the trail making test to organic brain damage. J. Consult. Psychol. 19: 393, 394.
12. WECHSLER, D. 1944. The Measurement of Adult Intelligence. 3rd edit. The Williams & Wilkins Co. Baltimore, Md.
13. SOUEIF, M. I. & A. METWALLY. 1961. Testing for organicity in Egyptian psychiatric patients. Acta Psychol. 18: 285–296.
14. SOUEIF, M. I., S. ABDEL-NABY & A. Q. HELMY. 1964. Objective assessment of psychiatric changes produced by reserpine in Egyptian schizophrenics. Acta Psychol. 22: 85–99.
15. ASHOUR, A. M., M. I. SOUEIF & A. H. HASSAN. 1976. Clinical and electroencephalographic validation of psychometric tests of organicity in Egyptian psychiatric patients. Unpublished report.
16. CRONBACH, L. J. 1960. Essentials of Psychological Testing. 2nd edit. Harper & Row, Publishers. New York, N.Y.

17. ANASTASI, A. 1968. Psychological Testing. 3rd edit. : 345. Macmillan. London, England.
18. BEMIS, S. E., 1968. Occupational validity of the general aptitude test battery. J. Appl. Pyschol. **52:** 240–244.
19. ABDEL-QUADER, M. 1971. Standardization of the General Aptitude Test Battery in Egypt. National Centre for Social and Criminological Research. Cairo, Egypt (in Arabic).
20. YATES, A. 1973. Abnormalities of psychomotor functions. *In* Handbook of Abnormal Psychology. H. J. Eysenck, Ed. 2nd edit. : 261–283. Pitman Med. London, England.
21. PAYNE, R. & J. H. G. HEWLETT. 1960. Thought disorder in psychotic patients. *In* Experiments in Personality. Vol. II. Psychodiagnostics and Psychodynamics. H. J. Eysenck, Ed. : 3–104. Routledge and Kegan Paul. London, England.
22. EL-SHEIK, A. 1971. Personal tempo and the metric tempo in preferred poetry: a correlational study. Unpublished M.A. Thesis. Cairo University. Cairo, Egypt.
23. UNITED STATES EMPLOYMENT SERVICE. 1962. Guide to the Use of the General Aptitude Test Battery: III. Development. United States Government Printing Office. Washington, D.C.
24. BINDRA, D. & H. WAKSBERG. 1956. Methods and terminology in studies of time estimation. Psychol. Bull. **53:** 155–159.
25. ORME, J. E. 1962. Time studies in normals and abnormal personalities. Acta Psychol. **20:** 285–303.
26. WALLACE, M. & A. I. RABIN. 1960. Temporal experience. Psychol. Bull. **57**(3): 213–236.
27. MELGES, F. T., J. R. TINKLENBERG, L. E. HOLLISTER & H. K. GILLESPIE. 1970. Marihuana and temporal disintegration. Science **168:** 1118–1120.
28. TINKLENBERG, J. R., B. S. KOPELL, F. T. MELGES & L. N. HOLLISTER. 1972. Marijuana and alcohol. Arch. Gen. Psychiat. **27:** 812–815.
29. WEIL, A. T. & N. E. ZINBERG. 1969. Acute effects of marihuana on speech. Nature (London) **222:** 434–437.
30. WEIL, A. T., N. E. ZINBERG & J. M. NELSEN. 1968. Clinical and psychological effects of marihuana in man. Science **162:** 1234–1242.
31. MANNO, J. E., G. F. KIPLINGER, S. E. HAINA, I. F. BENNETT & R. B. FORNEY. 1970. Comparative effects of smoking marihuana or placebo on human motor and mental performance. Clin. Pharmacol. Ther. **11:** 808–815.
32. MANNO, J. E., G. F. KIPLINGER, N. SCHOLTZ & R. B. FORNEY. 1971. The influence of alcohol and marihuana on motor and mental performance. Clin. Pharmacol. Ther. **12:** 202–211.
33. WECHSLER, D. 1954. The Measurement of Adult Intelligence. : 103. The Williams & Wilkins Co. Baltimore, Md.
34. BERGER, M. 1964. Arab World Today. Chap. 3. Doubleday & Company, Inc. New York, N.Y.
35. HALLOWELL, A. I. 1949. Acculturation processes and personality changes. *In* Personality in Nature, Society and Culture. C. Cluckhohn & H. A. Murray, Eds. : 340–346. Alfred A. Knopf, Inc. New York, N.Y.
36. NEWMAN, H. H., F. N. FREEMAN & K. J. HOLZINGER. 1937. Twins: A Study of Heredity and Environment. University of Chicago Press. Chicago, Ill.
37. NEWMAN, H. H. 1947. How differences in environment affected separated one-egg twins. *In* Readings in Social Psychology. T. M. Newcomb & E. L. Hartley, Eds. Holt, Rinehart & Winston, Inc. New York, N.Y.
38. SHIELDS, J. 1973. Heredity and psychological abnormality. *In* Handbook of Abnormal Pyschology. H. J. Eysenck, Ed. : 540–603. Pitman Med. London, England.

39. MURPHY, G., L. B. MURPHY & T. M. NEWCOMB. 1937. Experimental Social Psychology. 2nd edit. : 64. Harper & Row, Publishers. New York, N.Y.
40. BROMLEY, D. B. 1966. The Psychology of Human Aging. Penguin Books. Harmandsworth, England.
41. SAVAGE, R. D. 1973. Old age. In Handbook of Abnormal Psychology. H. J. Eysenck, Ed. : 645–688. Pitman Med. London, England.
42. HULICKA, I. M. 1966. Age differences in Wechsler memory scores. J. Genet. Psychol. 109: 135–145.
43. EDWARDS, A. 1956. Experimental Design in Psychological Research. : 30. Holt, Rinehart & Winston, Inc. New York, N.Y.
44. MARTIN, I. 1973. Somatic reactivity: interpretation. In Handbook of Abnormal Psychology. H. J. Eysenck, Ed. : 333–361. Pitman Med. London, England.
45. BRODAL, A. 1969. Neurological Anatomy in Relation to Clinical Medicine. 2nd edit. Chap. 6: 304. Oxford University Press. Oxford, England.
46. CLARIDGE, G. S. 1967. Personality and Arousal. A Psychological Study of Psychiatric Disorder. Pergamon. London, England.
47. McGHIE, A. 1969. Pathology of Attention. Penguin Books. London, England.
48. PAYNE, R. W. 1973. Cognitive abnormalities. In Handbook of Abnormal Psychology. H. J. Eysenck, Ed. : 420–486. Pitman Med. London, England.
49. BOWMAN, M. & R. O. PIHL. 1973. Cannabis: psychological effects of chronic heavy use. Psychopharmacologia 29: 159–169.
50. WASKOW, I. E., J. E. OLSSON, C. SOLZMAN, M. KATZ & C. CHASE. 1970. Psychological effects of tetrahydrocannabinol. Arch. Gen. Psychiat. 22: 97–107.
51. INTERIM REPORT OF THE COMMISSION OF INQUIRY INTO THE NON-MEDICAL USE OF DRUGS. 1970. Information Canada. Ottawa, Ontario, Canada.

GENERAL DISCUSSION

Max Fink, *Moderator*

Department of Psychiatry
State University of New York at Stony Brook
Stony Brook, New York 11794

QUESTION: There has been considerable literature on disorganization of recent memory. Have any of your tests been able to measure that variable?

DR. P. SATZ: As I tried to point out, I've been somewhat dismayed, in looking at the literature, that most studies have not used distraction techniques, which are really a more valid measure of recent memory and retrieval. We used several tests along that dimension and could not find any defects or differences. In other words, the results were not in abnormal ranges, nor were there differences between groups.

MR. D. LEFF (*Medical World News*): When, where, and on how many subjects were these trials conducted in Greece?

DR. R. L. DORNBUSH: These studies were conducted in Athens, Greece at Eginition Hospital, which is part of the University of Athens. The study was carried out between 1971 and 1974 and was multifaceted. This aspect was concerned with the effects of acute use in chronic smokers and was done in the summer of 1972. There were 20 subjects. The tests were given twice after each drug administration, 30 and 70 min after smoking.

MR. LORIN MILLER: The digit span performance seemed generally low; when you give a drug under those conditions, it is difficult to evaluate the effect due to lack of a good baseline. That lack even occurs for the acute studies, like in the American literature. There is a lot of variability in the results obtained; if you examine them, there doesn't seem to be any one variable that you can pick out, except that control performance is sometimes low. When that occurs, you get no differences. When performance under control conditions is good, if you give a drug, you get a deficit. How often does this type of effect occur in these kinds of studies?

DR. DORNBUSH: We don't know whether performance on the other tests administered was good. It's easier to come to a conclusion with digit span, because we know that the average North American adult digit span or memory span is seven items plus or minus two. We don't know whether performance of these men on the other tasks is also generally low, because there are no established baselines.

MR. MILLER: The point I am trying to make is that the effect of the drug may vary as a function of general intellectual ability.

DR. DORNBUSH: There is no question of that. These people were generally lower class. The mean educational level was third grade. I believe, though, that the Costa Rican level was higher. It was about an eighth-grade level of literacy in Costa Rica.

DR. W. E. CARTER: It was around sixth grade.

DR. DORNBUSH: We were looking at a population that is not particularly sophisticated. When we talk about our typical North American user, we mean the college or graduate student, and marijuana effects on performance levels may be different. The point is that the accumulated evidence suggests that the effects may be very similar.

DR. R. T. JONES: I'm impressed by the doses that your subjects were able to handle without falling down. Our laboratory has been accused of giving rather large doses, but your doses were four or five times higher than ours on a daily basis. The effect seems to be relatively modest, yet you say that 25 years' use of cannabis doesn't seem to modify the response. Somehow these statements don't all seem to fit together.

DR. DORNBUSH: Very briefly, the fact that these individuals did consume 180 mg of Δ^9-THC indicates that there is some kind of tolerance being manifested. I don't think it is the traditional tolerance. We should have given these men 20 mg of Δ^9-THC, which is the dose given in many American laboratories. I think we could, then, say a lot more.

DR. A. WIKLER: The first question I was going to ask has been partially answered. It seems to me that your data indicate that your Greek subjects certainly have residual tolerance to marijuana. I believe that this tolerance is the same kind we consider ordinarily. But what we consider tolerance ordinarily is learned tolerance. The other question I wanted to ask is more pertinent to your data. Did you include analysis of a speech sample?

DR. DORNBUSH: No.

DR. WIKLER: I think that's extremely important. Did you administer the goal-directed serial alternation task?

DR. DORNBUSH: No.

DR. WIKLER: That's also important. These two parameters, the goal-directed serial alternation task and analysis of a speech sample for internal consistency and logical sequence of thoughts, are both very important. Weil, Zinberg, and Nelson showed a very clear-cut deficit in formerly heavy users of marijuana who smoked cigarettes with a presumably high content of Δ^9-THC. Those tasks should have been administered. These tests measure the important effects of marijuana, which are not determined by digit symbol substitution tests and that sort of thing. I use a little poem I invented in a paper published several years ago: The drunkard staggers only when he walks, and the pothead forgets only when he talks. You have to measure the pertinent variables.

DR. DORNBUSH: Regarding speech samples, we have to be very cautious in evaluating data from other countries. One of the problems with speech samples, and, in fact, with the entire psychologic test battery, was that these subjects were Greek and spoke only Greek. I don't know whether we could have understood the meaning of speech analyses in these subjects.

DR. SATZ: Dr. Soueif, I am very intrigued by your finding that the differences between groups attenuated as a function of sex, age, and literacy factors, but then you invoked the possibility of some kind of arousal level. Now this explanation is more of an inferential one. I would like to go back to possibly a more basic methodologic explanation. I said earlier about this kind of research that one should always be on the alert in behavioral studies for the possibility of floor effects. In looking at your variables, you relied a lot on perceptual speed reaction times, measures that we know from North American studies to vary as a function of these three variables. In other words, if you are less literate, or if you are older or more rural, having less opportunity for certain educational opportunities, there is a tendency to perform poorer on these perceptual speed reaction time measures. If, indeed, that was the case in your data, it would account for the effect without having to resort to more explanatory arousal mechanism possibilities. It might be wise, if you haven't done it already, to look at those correlations both within and between groups. Also, if you have many variables, by chance you are going to see some significance, and you should watch out for type-1 error, therefore the need for multivariate analysis.

DR. M. I. SOUEIF: When I was thinking of the concept of arousal level, I was merely considering it as a common denominator for the three variables of age, literacy, and urbanism-ruralism. I am just toying with this idea; I'm presenting you with the whole thing just to get a reaction.

DR. SATZ: You may be correct, but I am bothered when you find such robust differences in your institutional population. What about the use of poly-drugs? Was there much use of other kinds of drugs?

DR. SOUEIF: In this group, about 31% of the subjects were taking opium over and above the cannabis, and about 25% were taking alcohol, again over and above cannabis. But when I examined the differences on these tests between those who smoked opium plus cannabis and those who used only cannabis, to my astonishment I found that those who used opium plus cannabis performed better. I can't explain this finding; it may be just an empirical effect.

DR. SATZ: Where were they from? You probably want to look at that finding as a function of sex, age, and literacy, too.

DR. SOUEIF: Well, they were from the same type of group.

DR. SATZ: That's intriguing.

DR. W. J. COGGINS: Dr. Soueif, just for clarity, were you studying these subjects while they were acutely intoxicated or simply with a history of intoxication in the drug-free state?

DR. SOUEIF: The subjects were not actually under the influence of the drug when they were examined, but they had a drug history and were taking it on a regular basis before being imprisoned. There was a rumor that some of the stuff was smuggled into the prison. However, regardless of whether they were taking the drug while in prison during the testing situation, they were intoxicated.

DR. COGGINS: Were these people being tested while they were under long jail sentences, or were they in and out of prison for 3 days, 3 weeks, and so forth?

DR. SOUEIF: When we examined their criminal records, as an offshoot of the study, comparing them with the records of the controls, we found that they had fewer criminal offenses and less aggressive crimes. However, almost all of them received sentences of 6 months to more than 4 years. I don't know whether you would call this a short period or not.

DR. COGGINS: I suppose we would both agree that it would be long if we were in there.

DR. CANNIE ADAMEC (*Dalhousie University, Halifax, Nova Scotia, Canada*): Dr. Dornbush, on your time estimation task, were the men asked to state how much time they felt had passed, or was it an accurate estimation of time that you were looking for, or was the distinction even made?

DR. DORNBUSH: The distinction was not made.

DR. S. COHEN: I would like to ask the people who spoke about the Costa Rican, Jamaican, and Greek studies whether the subjects who were so mentally dilapidated were excluded as nontestable. In other words, was an important part of the sample eliminated simply because of their serious mental deterioration?

DR. V. RUBIN: No one was excluded from the study in Jamaica. Ganja is illegal. People there are arrested and put in jail for its use, as they are in Egypt, India, and in this country, and participation had to be on a voluntary basis. The subjects were invited to participate. Their health status was not taken into consideration, and there was no exclusion at any point of any of the subjects.

DR. COHEN: That's not what I meant. Were they self-excluded because they were so deteriorated? Or did you exclude them because they couldn't be tested?

DR. RUBIN: We didn't exclude anyone who was willing to be tested, smoker or nonsmoker. As Dr. Knights pointed out, it is much more difficult to find nonsmokers than to find smokers. These men were all between the ages of 23 and 53 and seemed to be representative of the society in which they lived. They were all matched with respect to sex, age, socioeconomic status, education, and all of the other usual variables. There was no evidence of mental deterioration, as there apparently is in Egypt and India.

DR. SATZ: That question has bothered me all along. That phase of the selection process, of course, was the responsibility of our competent anthropologists, but it is possible that there was another group of heavy smokers in Costa Rica who may have died in past years or were so deteriorated that they couldn't become volunteers. We've discussed that at length, and I seriously doubt that possibility.

DR. DORNBUSH: As I mentioned, the group in Greece was a subsample of a larger group. For the selection of the larger group, the only reasons for exclusion were use of drugs other than hashish, alcoholism, or an age older than 58 years. These were our reasons for exclusion. There was no exclusion due to inadequate performance. In fact, users were selected first, simply because they were users and met the criteria employed.

QUESTION: In view of the nonsignificance of the data, I wonder if Dr. Dornbush would comment on the experimental set-up and the situation in which the subjects were tested. In Greece, cannabis smokers are not used to smoking cannabis in a laboratory environment. Might not the effects on those tests have been very different than those obtained with a little Bouzouki music in the dark?

DR. DORNBUSH: I think the best answer that I can give is that we were faced with the dilemma six years ago over how to undertake this study with the best possible controls and how to give reasonable answers to questions that were at that time plaguing us as scientists. We did the best we could.

DR. FINK: I think that it is easy to criticize the scientist and say, "Why didn't you do it with Bouzouki music, or why didn't you do it with rabbinical students?" It is a very difficult task that these groups have accepted and have carried out. I think the remarkable thing at the moment is the consistency of the findings over four different cultures, four different populations. Dr. Wikler criticized, correctly perhaps, the selection of certain tasks, an excellent suggestion. Perhaps that could be done in another study. It was not included in this one for a variety of reasons.

SLEEP ELECTROENCEPHALOGRAPHIC-ELECTROOCULOGRAPHIC CHARACTERISTICS OF CHRONIC MARIJUANA USERS: PART I *

I. Karacan,† A. Fernández-Salas,‡ W. J. Coggins,§
W. E. Carter,§ R. L. Williams,† J. I. Thornby,†
P. J. Salis,† M. Okawa,† and J. P. Villaume †

† Department of Psychiatry
Baylor College of Medicine
and Veterans Administration Hospital
Houston, Texas 77030
‡ Hospital Mexico
San José, Costa Rica
§ Department of Community Health and Family Medicine
University of Florida
Gainesville, Florida 32610

INTRODUCTION

The sleep electroencephalogram-electrooculogram (EEG-EOG) is increasingly recognized as a particularly sensitive tool for evaluating the effects of drugs, especially drugs that affect the central nervous system. Use of the waking or sleep EEG is one of the few reasonably direct, nonintrusive methods of monitoring central nervous system activity in man. The sleep EEG-EOG has several advantages over the waking EEG in evaluations of drugs. First, there are at least two distinct states of consciousness during sleep, rapid eye movement (REM) sleep and non-REM (NREM) sleep, and they make possible the assessment of drug effects under a greater variety of natural conditions than is true during wakefulness. Second, the sleep EEG-EOG is more clearly organized than the waking EEG, and sleep brain wave patterns can be easily and reliably categorized as belonging to one of five distinct stages of sleep: NREM stages 1, 2, 3, and 4 and stage-1 REM. Again, the natural variety in the sleep EEG-EOG permits a more extensive evaluation of drug effects on brain activity. Furthermore, the relatively clear organization of the characteristic sleep stage patterns allows easier detection of anomalies than does the mixed-frequency activity of the waking EEG. Third, the sleep EEG-EOG is characterized by the periodic occurrence of several distinct wave forms, such as α, β, and δ waves, sleep spindles, K complexes, and eye movements, that can be examined for subtle changes. Fortunately, there now exist automated methods for detailed quantitative description and analyses of these fundamental sleep EEG-EOG wave forms.

Marijuana and its major active constituent tetrahydrocannabinol (THC) are presumed to affect the central nervous system because of their effects on certain physical and mental functions. Present knowledge concerning the short- and long-term effects of these agents in humans is incomplete and confusing. Studies

* Performed pursuant to Contract NO1–MHE–0233 with the National Institute on Drug Abuse.

that use the sleep EEG-EOG might be expected to at least promote a better understanding of the drugs' neurophysiologic effects. Anecdotal, survey, and clinical evidence [1-12] suggests that these agents have hypnotic properties, and this possibility provides an additional reason for sleep laboratory studies.

Several sleep laboratory studies of effects of marijuana and THC in humans have been described. Unfortunately, the promise of increased understanding has not been fulfilled by these studies. In many instances, confusion has resulted because of methodologic problems in the studies or inadequacies in the study reports. To examine the studies, we have classified them according to the length of the drug administration period, the subjects' past experience with marijuana, and the subjects' health status. We have called studies that involved one or two consecutive drug administration nights short-term studies; studies that involved more than two consecutive drug administration nights have been called longer-term studies. Subjects have been labeled either naive or experienced with respect to marijuana. Naive subjects were those so labeled in the report or those whose described past experience with the drug was virtually nil; experienced subjects were those so labeled in the report or those whose past experience was described or implied. Health status of the subjects has been indicated by the labels normal and patient. Normal subjects were those described as such in the study report or those for whom no pathologies were described. Patients were subjects for whom pathologies were described. Only changes that were revealed to be statistically significant at the 0.05 level or better have been labeled significant. Other changes have been called tendencies, if they appeared large enough to warrant the term.

There are no known short-term studies that used naive normal subjects or experienced patients. Bobon *et al.*[13] have presented the only report of a short-term study that involved a relatively naive patient. The single patient was an anxious and depressed insomniac who was resistant to increasing doses of sedatives. She had smoked marijuana at least once in a previous experiment conducted an unstated time before the one described, but because of the patient's age (56 years), we have assumed that her previous use of marijuana was minimal. The patient slept a total of 24 consecutive nights in the laboratory, but the report considered only eight consecutive nights: one placebo, two drug, two placebo, two drug, and one placebo. The authors did not state whether the first placebo night was also the first laboratory night. (Significant changes in sleep patterns are associated with adjustment to sleeping in a laboratory.[14, 15]) The drug was Δ^8-THC (20 mg). Both drug and placebo were administered in spansule form 90 min before bedtime. A statistical procedure that assumed independent observations [16] was applied to the data. The assumption of independence was not valid for this study. Furthermore, by use of their procedure on the data, we have been unable to replicate their statistical findings. They described a significant increase in wakefulness (percentage of stage 0) and number of shifts from stage to stage on drug nights, in addition to a significant increase in time from sleep onset to the onset of REM sleep (REM latency) that was tempered by a significant linear trend for REM latency to increase over the 8 study nights. The authors also reported a tendency for REM percentage to decrease and percentage of movement time to increase on drug nights. Our analyses suggested a significant change only for number of stage shifts and tendencies only for REM percentage and movement time percentage. This study suggests that THC may change certain aspects of the sleep EEG-EOG. However, generalizations are limited because it was a case study, and the apparent inappropriateness of the statistical procedures prevents proper assessment of the nature and extent of the changes.

Short-term studies of experienced normal subjects are relatively more plentiful. Hosko et al.[17] performed a two-dose study of the effects of Δ^9-THC in seven healthy young-adult males. Five subjects were marijuana users (one, three times per week; three, one time per week; one, three times in 3 years). Two subjects denied any previous use of marijuana. All subjects reported abstaining from marijuana during the 2 weeks prior to the study. Over 9 consecutive nights, subjects received the drug on two occasions (200 μg/kg on night 3 or 4, 300 μg/kg on night 8 or 9 for six subjects; 400 μg/kg on night 8 for one subject), had 2 nonlaboratory nights (nights 5 and 6), and received placebo on the remaining 5 nights. The drug, in alcoholic solution, was administered single-blind in flavored corn oil vehicle 3–5 hr before bedtime. The vehicle alone served as the placebo. A battery of neurologic and psychophysiologic evaluations was administered hourly between drug administration and bedtime. No statistical analyses of the sleep data were described. The authors observed no consistent drug-related changes in the group as a whole. They noted a reduction in REM percentage on drug nights for two subjects, an increase in REM percentage on nights following some drug nights in four subjects, and no change in REM percentage in three subjects. In two subjects, they also noted an increase in percentage of stages 3 and 4 on some drug nights. A prime consideration in comparing the results of this study with those from other studies is the long interval between drug administration and bedtime. The number of subjects was reasonably adequate, but the wisdom of using subjects with such varying degrees of previous experience with marijuana may be questioned. The lack of reported statistical analyses prevents the study results from having more than suggestive value.

Two studies of experienced normal subjects were performed in our laboratory.[18] (Portions of the data had previously been described in abstract form.[19]) Both were considered pilot or preliminary in nature. The first was a short-term study designed to assess the effect of smoking marijuana to a "high" at bedtime. It involved 10 experienced young-adult normal males and 10 age- and sex-matched normal controls. The experienced subjects had been using marijuana at least five times per week for 3 months or more. Controls did not use marijuana. Each subject spent 2 consecutive nights in the laboratory. Before bedtime each night, the "smokers" smoked marijuana cigarettes until they reached a subjective "high." Each subject provided his own marijuana. Controls simply reported to the laboratory for the 2 nights of sleep. Data from the first night were not used in the analyses. Values for 19 conventional sleep EEG-EOG variables were compared with independent sample t tests. The only immediate effect of bedtime smoking in the "smokers" was a significant reduction in percentage of stage-4 sleep in comparison to control levels.

In the second study, we assessed the short-term effects of abstention from marijuana by frequent users. Twenty experienced normals (same age range and use patterns as in our first study) and 20 age- and sex-matched normal controls slept 2 or 3 consecutive nights in the laboratory. The experienced subjects had abstained from using marijuana during a 24–36-hr period prior to the second sleep night. The controls simply reported for the 2 or 3 sleep nights. Again, data from the first night were excluded from the analyses. There were no significant differences (independent sample t tests) between "abstainers" and controls on any of the 19 variables examined.

In a cross-study analysis, we compared the data from the study-1 "smokers" with data from the study-2 "abstainers." The "smokers" exhibited a significantly lower percentage of stage-4, higher percentage of stage-2, and longer stage-2, stage-3, and stage-4 latencies. In contrast to most other studies of marijuana or THC, our studies revealed no changes in the subjects' REM sleep. Instead, the drug seemed to affect slow-wave sleep (stages 3 and 4), especially stage-4 sleep.

There were, of course, several shortcomings in our studies. For several reasons, it was necessary to have the experienced subjects supply their own marijuana in study 1, and this requirement obviously prevented adequate control of the quality of the material. The criterion for the dose was the attainment of a "high" rather than some specified number of cigarettes or amount of material. No placebo was administered to control subjects, and therefore the effect of bedtime smoking itself was not controlled. Study 2 would have been improved if an abstention period of standard length had been used. In all studies, independent sample *t* tests were used, because we felt the matching procedure for controls was rudimentary. This, of course, elevated the degrees of freedom in comparison to matched-pair *t* tests. Some may question the propriety of our decision. In the cross-study analyses, some of the differences may simply have reflected the fact that there were twice as many "abstainers" as "smokers."

Pivik *et al.*[20] have also performed a series of short-term studies. (Portions of the data were initially described in abstract form,[21] and the full report has been reviewed in *Sleep Research*.[22]) Although the wording of the report suggests that the subjects were experienced in marijuana use (i.e., they were described as not having used drugs for 2 months prior to initial study), their actual status in this respect is unknown. Because the short-term evaluations were called "normative," it is assumed that the subjects were normal. All were young-adult males. Four subjects underwent an initial study that consisted of 8 consecutive nights: four placebo baseline, one drug, and three placebo recovery. On the drug night, marijuana extracts of known Δ^9-THC content were administered orally at bedtime. The dose was 16 mg, or 196–268 μg/kg. At 2-month intervals, one of these subjects underwent two additional studies of similar design. On drug nights, the doses were 13 mg (150 μg/kg) and 17 mg (196 μg/kg). Two other of the four original subjects were studied a second time at least 2 months after the initial study. The protocol involved 14 consecutive nights: six placebo baseline, one drug, three placebo recovery, one drug, and three placebo recovery. On the first drug night, 4.3 mg of marijuana extract (61 or 68 μg/kg) was administered at bedtime. On the second drug night, 6.8 or 8.6 mg (135 or 123 μg/kg) of the extract was given. For all subjects, a placebo was administered orally on nondrug nights. It consisted of an extract derived from marijuana from which all cannabinoids had previously been removed, and it resembled the drug extract in color and taste.

In analyzing their data, Pivik *et al.* treated all of the drug nights as if they had arisen from different subjects, even though three subjects each contributed 3 of the nights. The assumption of independence was invalid and therefore casts doubt on all of the results. Except for three comparisons, the statistical procedures were not made clear. It was often difficult to discern whether drug nights were compared to averages of baseline or recovery nights or to only the final baseline and the initial recovery nights. A ranking procedure was used to demonstrate a significant reduction in REM percentage on drug nights in comparison to the average of baseline and the average of recovery nights. The average reduction for all 10 drug nights, relative to the last baseline night, was

2.1%. Apparently, a one-tailed test was used. A two-tailed test would have been more appropriate. By use of the procedure they described, we have been unable to obtain the probabilities they reported. Other analyses (at least one of which was a matched-pair t test) indicated the following significant changes on drug nights in comparison to baseline nights: decreased REM amount during the second half of the night for the 13- and 17-mg doses, decreased minutes of stage 2 in the first half of the night and increased minutes in the second half for the 17-mg dose, decreased time awake after sleep onset, and increased total sleep time. There was a tendency for minutes of stage 4 to be increased during the first half of the night, especially for the 17-mg dose, and for REM amount to be decreased during the second half of the night for all doses. In comparison to baseline nights, recovery nights were characterized by the following significant changes: increased percentage of REM for the night as a whole (all doses together) and for the first half of the night (17-mg dose only), decreased REM latency, decreased percentage of stage 1 for the 17-mg dose, decreased minutes of stage 1 during the first half of the night for the 17-mg dose, shift of stages 3 and 4 from the first to the second half of the night, and increased total sleep time. There was a tendency for the minutes of stage 1 to be reduced in the second half of the night with the 17-mg dose. The only result reported for the drug versus recovery comparison was the lack of a significant change in total sleep time. It is unclear why results for other parameters were not reported. The authors summarized their findings by stating that THC had two main effects on "undisturbed sleep: increase in Stage 4 sleep and reduction in REM sleep." It should be noted that the conclusion concerning stage-4 sleep rested only on a tendency for minutes of stage 4 to be increased during the first half of the drug nights. As we have discussed, the method of determining the significance of the REM reduction was suspect.

In a second experiment, Pivik *et al.* investigated the supposed REM suppressant effects of THC and synhexyl, a semisynthetic Δ^{6a-10}-THC homolog. They took advantage of the fact that on undisturbed recovery nights that follow nights of experimental REM sleep suppression, REM percentage typically is higher than on baseline nights. This phenomenon is called an REM rebound. Two additional young-adult males underwent three separate series of sleep nights. Each series consisted of 2 nights of experimental REM deprivation and 5 recovery nights. Five baseline nights preceded the first series of deprivation and recovery nights. The amount of time between each series was not stated. In one of the series, the subects received 20 mg (244 or 259 μg/kg) of Δ^9-THC orally on the morning after the second night of REM deprivation. In another series, they received 60 mg (733 or 777 μg/kg) of synhexyl orally at the same time. The third series served as a control. Order of drug administration varied for the two subjects. A two-way analysis of variance with repeated measures was used to compare the baseline nights and the recovery nights from each series. The tabulated degrees of freedom for the analysis indicate that the analysis was inappropriate for the study (e.g., an error term with 15 degrees of freedom from a study that involved *two* subjects run under *four* conditions). Among other things, it appears that for the "subjects within groups" term, with five degrees of freedom, "groups" actually referred to "nights," and the subjects were treated as different subjects for each of the five "groups." A follow-up Tukey test revealed only one significant difference: REM percentage was higher on the control recovery nights than on baseline nights. This difference is evidence of a typical REM rebound on control recovery nights. The lack of significant elevation in REM percentage on recovery nights that followed administration of the drugs was interpreted by the authors as evidence of the REM suppressant effect of the two drugs. This conclusion rested only on a failure to reject the null hypothesis. In summary, the small number of subjects in these two studies, the inappropriateness of several of the statistical procedures, and the lack of clarity in describing certain comparisons necessitate caution in interpretation of the results.

Reports of six longer-term studies of marijuana and THC have appeared. Kales *et al.*[23] have presented the only report of a longer-term study of naive subjects, and it is a very brief abstract. We assume that the subjects were normal, because no pathologies were described. Four subjects spent 16 consecutive nights in the laboratory: four placebo baseline, three drug, four placebo recovery, three drug, and two placebo recovery. On drug days or nights, marijuana was smoked. On placebo days or nights, some unspecified other material was smoked. No statistical analyses were described in the abstract, but the authors concluded that initial smoking of marijuana produced a decrease in REM sleep, that REM sleep quickly returned to baseline levels and above on subsequent drug nights, and that there was a moderate REM rebound on recovery nights. The usefulness of this report is very limited because of the small number of subjects, the lack of reported statistical analyses, and the report's brevity and lack of specificity.

An abstract by Gillin *et al.*[24] describes the only known longer-term study of naive patients. Three male psychiatric inpatients, ages 46–61, served as subjects. The patients' past histories of marijuana use were not stated, but, due to their ages, we assume that use was minimal. Two patients were manic depressives, and one was a psychotic depressive. The authors did not describe the current status of the patients with respect to antidepressants or other medication. After two adaptation nights, the patients underwent three placebo baseline, five to seven drug, and two placebo recovery nights. We assume that the nights were consecutive. It is not clear whether first-night data were excluded from analyses. On drug days, the patients received 300 μg/kg of Δ^9-THC at 9 AM and 10 PM. Presumably, the placebo was administered in the same fashion. The following variables were examined across conditions: total sleep time, minutes of NREM sleep, minutes of REM sleep, REM percentage, REM latency, and sleep latency. The only significant change was a reduction in minutes of REM sleep on the first drug night (matched-pair t test, one-tailed). It is noteworthy that this change was not significant when REM amount was expressed as a percentage. This study is suggestive, but the results should be interpreted cautiously because of the small number of patients, the patients' unknown drug status, and the use of a one-tailed test. In addition, the possibility of REM disturbances related to depressive illness itself [25, 26] should temper comparison of the results to those from nondepressed individuals.

In the same abstract cited earlier, Kales *et al.*[23] reported the results of a longer-term study of experienced subjects. The subjects were described as "chronic users," but their degree of experience was not stated. Four subjects spent 9 consecutive nights in the laboratory: 4 nights following days of continued marijuana smoking and 5 recovery nights. Two of these subjects spent an additional 9 (presumably consecutive) nights in the laboratory: four recovery, three drug, and two recovery. No statistical analyses were described, but the conclusions were the same as those listed earlier for the longer-term study of naive subjects. In addition, the authors noted that there was no evidence in the experienced subjects of an increase in REM sleep as they continued to use marijuana. This report, like the earlier one, is only of suggestive value because of the small number of subjects, the lack of reported statistical analyses, and the report's brevity.

A third longer-term study has been described by Freemon.[27] (Portions of the data had been described previously.[28]) Six young-adult subjects (at least two were female[28]) participated. Previous experience with marijuana was limited to "occasional social use" for five subjects, and these subjects had not used other illegal drugs. The remaining subject had used marijuana "almost daily" between ages 16 and 18 and had also used lysergic acid diethylamide at that time. No subjects had used marijuana during the 6-week to 1-year period prior to the study. Two subjects slept 8 consecutive nights in the laboratory: two placebo baseline, four drug, and two placebo recovery. Three subjects slept 14 consecutive nights: three placebo baseline, six drug, and five placebo recovery. The sixth subject slept 14 consecutive placebo baseline nights. At bedtime on drug nights, subjects received 20 mg of Δ^9-THC, dissolved in 20 ml of prune juice or flavored corn oil. The vehicle alone served as the placebo. First-night data were excluded from the analyses. Data beyond the first 6 hr of sleep were not considered in calculating stage percentages.

Statistical analyses were described only for the REM percentage values. One-tailed sign tests indicated a significant reduction in REM percentage on the first drug night as compared to baseline nights. A two-tailed test would have been more appropriate, and use of it would not have resulted in a significant statistic. A chi-square analysis failed to show a significant difference for this same effect, but it is not clear how the data could be analyzed with this procedure. Nine out of 10 of the subjects' two lowest REM percentage values occurred on drug nights. Probability analyses indicated a probability of less than one in 1000 for this result. This analysis was invalid, because the 10 observations were not independent.

Statistical analyses of other data were not described, but the author noted that in three subjects, REM percentage was depressed at least through the fourth drug night. In the other two subjects, it gradually returned to baseline levels or above after the first 2–4 drug nights. There was no apparent rebound of REM percentage on recovery nights. Some subjects exhibited increased sleep latency and time awake after sleep onset on recovery nights relative to baseline. This study suggests an REM suppressant effect of THC, but the effects were not large and were assessed inappropriately. Other changes were not exhibited by all subjects and were not described statistically. The study is therefore only of suggestive value.

In their longer-term study of experienced subjects, Barratt et al.[29] utilized a 10-day drug administration period. (A previous report of data from this study had appeared elsewhere.[30]) The 12 subjects were young-adult white males. It is assumed that they were normal. The extent of their experience with marijuana was not described. They had abstained from the drug for 3 days to 2 months prior to the study. Four similar subjects were studied for up to 8 nights and were then rejected from the study. Two of them were rejected because they had no stages-3 and -4 sleep on baseline nights. The protocol consisted of 1 adaptation, 3 baseline, 10 drug, and 7 recovery nights. Presumably, the nights were consecutive. During the recovery period, data were collected only on the first, fourth, and seventh nights. At an unspecified time within 2 hr of bedtime on drug nights, eight subjects each smoked a total of 200 μg/kg of Δ^9-THC in two marijuana cigarettes, according to a carefully standardized and supervised procedure. On their "drug" nights, the remaining four subjects smoked alfalfa, which they were told was marijuana. These subjects served as a control group.

Statistical analyses were described as including one-sample runs tests for direction of changes in drug and recovery night sleep stage percentages from baseline values, chi-square one-sample tests of the number of changes in sign, and Wilcoxon tests for nonpaired replicates for comparison of actual percentages on baseline nights and each drug and recovery night. The one-sample runs test is actually a test of randomness (i.e., a test of the number of changes in direction), a fact the authors seemed to realize later in reporting the results, and it assumes independent observations. Sleep characteristics on successive nights for a given subject are not independent, and therefore the runs test was invalid. A similar disregard for the assumption of independent observations was apparent in the description of the chi-square procedure: eight subjects who had 10 study nights each were converted to 80 subjects. Possibly, this disregard resulted from the realization that a chi-square analysis is valid only for large samples. In any case, later in the report it became apparent that the chi-square analysis was not the procedure actually used, because results were presented for comparisons of individual drug and recovery nights to baseline. Because of this discrepancy, the actual method of analyzing the number of changes in sign and its appropriateness are unknown. We are not familiar with the Wilcoxon test for nonpaired replicates, and no reference was provided for it. The name implies a test that assumes independent observations, and this assumption would not be valid for these data.

The runs tests revealed that seven of eight experimental subjects exhibited significantly fewer changes in direction of slow-wave sleep time during drug and recovery periods, as compared to baseline, than would be expected by chance. Tests for other stages in the experimental subjects and for all stages in controls failed to reveal "comparable changes." By use of the two other statistical procedures, the authors determined that, in the control group, the only significant change from baseline was a reduction in total sleep time on the first "drug" night. The experimental subjects also exhibited this significant change. In addition, their combined stages-3 and -4 percentage increased, relative to baseline, over the first 4 drug nights and decreased over the last 3 drug nights and during the recovery period. These changes were significant for drug nights 3, 4, 8–10, and for all three recovery nights. Stage-2 percentage typically changed in the opposite direction, but this change (increase) was significant only on the last drug night. Total body movements were significantly reduced in the experimental group on drug nights 3–5 and on the 3 recovery nights; they were significantly increased on drug night 8. Various measures of REM sleep, including REM density, showed no significant changes.

Conclusions regarding these significant changes are limited because of the inappropriateness of the statistical procedures. Furthermore, it will be recalled that two of four subjects were rejected from the study because they had no stages-3 and -4 sleep on baseline nights. Because the final sample contained eight experimental and four control subjects, we might infer that these two subjects were originally scheduled as control subjects. Elimination of them may have introduced a selection factor that contaminated the stages-3 and -4 data for controls.

Given these problems, we, nevertheless, note that this study suggests an interesting biphasic response of slow-wave sleep to marijuana smoking at bedtime. The decrease in stages-3 and -4 sleep on later drug nights would seem to agree with our finding [18] of reduced stage 4 in current users who smoked at bedtime. In addition, in both our study and that of Barratt et al., marijuana was smoked at bedtime, and there were no apparent changes in characteristics of REM sleep. Studies in which THC was administered at or before bedtime have generally suggested at least a slight decrease in REM percentage and possibly an increase in the amount of slow-wave sleep. Slow-wave sleep is normally concentrated in the first half of the night, whereas REM sleep is concentrated in the second half. Perhaps the differences in results from THC and marijuana studies reflect the fact that oral administration produces effects somewhat later than does smoking.[10]

A study by Feinberg et al.[31] is the most recently reported longer-term study of experienced subjects. The seven physically and mentally healthy young-adult males had used one or two marijuana cigarettes per day on an average for the month prior to the study. Their average duration of use was 4 years. The sleep study was one aspect of a larger project that required hospitalization on a psychiatric ward for 21–30 days. Four subjects were studied for 3 nights of placebo baseline, 3 initial drug nights, 3 drug nights at the end of a 12–16-day period of high drug dosage, and 3 initial placebo recovery nights. The remaining three subjects were studied only during the late high-drug and initial recovery periods. Apparently, the baseline and initial drug nights were consecutive, as were the high-drug and recovery nights. On initial drug days, subjects received capsules that contained 10 mg of THC in sesame oil at 8 AM, 12 AM, 6 PM, 9 PM, and 4 AM, and 20 mg prior to sleep at 10–11 PM, for a total of 70 mg/day. On high-drug days, the bedtime dose was 60 mg, and the other doses were each 30 mg, for a total of 210 mg/day. Placebo capsules contained sesame oil and were administered in the same fashion as drug capsules. First-night data were apparently not excluded from analyses. The authors stated that baseline data may have been contaminated by effects due to adaptation to hospitalization and some degree of withdrawal from prestudy marijuana and alcohol use and that both baseline and recovery data were contaminated by the fact that some subjects smoked a marijuana cigarette on 1 or more days. Data from all nights should be interpreted in light of the fact that subjects were awakened each morning at 4 AM to receive drug or placebo.

Results of statistical analyses (matched-pair t tests) were presented both for the data from the four subjects studied under all four conditions and for the total seven subjects studied during high-drug and initial recovery conditions. There were numerous significant differences for an extensive list of variables. Among the major findings for the four subjects who underwent the complete protocol were significant decreases in measures of REM amount and eye movement activity during drug periods and increases in combined stages-2–4 sleep. In comparison to baseline nights for these subjects, recovery nights were characterized by significantly longer awakenings, shorter REM latency, greater REM activity, and less stage-3 sleep. For the total seven subjects, the recovery nights, in comparison to high-drug nights, were characterized by longer sleep latency, shorter total sleep time, shorter REM latency, more REM sleep and eye movement activity, and fewer epochs of stages-2–4 sleep.

This study is the best yet described, and the analyses of the data seemed appropriate. The small sample size for the full protocol limits the possibility of making inferences with respect to the population, but the sample size for the partial protocol was sufficient to allow cautious generalizations. The contaminants of baseline and recovery data mentioned by the authors should be recalled. In addition, the acute effect of the 4-AM awakening and the possible cumulative effects of such awakenings over a 3-week period should be considered. As we have mentioned, REM sleep is normally concentrated in the latter part of the night, and Feinberg *et al.* did not present any data that suggested a change in this pattern in their subjects. It is likely that many of the 4-AM awakenings interrupted REM sleep, and this procedure might have resulted in continued partial REM deprivation in the subjects. Admittedly, the deprivation, if it occurred, was probably very slight, but the possibility exists that some of the recovery changes in REM sleep reflected the effects of previous, consistent partial REM deprivation.

The foregoing represents the sum of our knowledge about the effects of marijuana and THC on human sleep. Much of the work in this area is marred by serious methodologic problems. Investigators' failure to use adequate numbers of subjects and appropriate statistical procedures has severely hindered intelligent interpretation of results and drawing of conclusions. Common to most studies has been a lack of completeness in the characterization of the study subjects with respect to such parameters as physical and mental status, past experience with marijuana and other drugs, and duration and frequency of use of marijuana. In no case were drug screens performed to determine the current drug status of subjects. Nevertheless, interpreted cautiously, the existing studies suggest that marijuana and THC *may* affect both REM and slow-wave sleep when administered at or near bedtime. Whether effects are observed and the direction of effects probably depend on both the form (marijuana or THC) and the quality of the material administered and the time of administration. Subjects' past marijuana use patterns (naive or experienced) and, for users, subjects' current use patterns (abstainer or continuing user) may also be important determinants of response. All of these factors must be examined before the contradictions and inconsistencies in the sleep literature can be resolved. And, finally, there has been no clear evidence from sleep laboratory studies that either marijuana or THC has hypnotic effects, but such effects have not been assessed in a sample of subjects with sleep difficulty who might be most sensitive to the effects.

The present study represents a departure from the philosophy of most previous sleep studies, which have been concerned with the rather acute effects of marijuana or THC administered at or near bedtime to naive subjects or subjects with varying degrees of experience with the drug. In this study, our objective was to describe the sleep patterns of chronic long-term users during a period when they maintained their normal daytime use patterns. We were therefore more interested in effects present after years (10–27) of use than in acute effects. The study was one part of a larger project designed to assess the physical, nutritional, mental, and social effects of long-term marijuana use. Because of this project, it has been possible to develop a complete characterization of the subjects. Of special importance, in our opinion, was the fact that we were able to study a large number of marijuana users and carefully matched control subjects, and this fact maximized the likelihood of making reliable conclusions.

METHOD

Thirty-two long-term, chronic male marijuana users, ages 20–48 (mean, 30.3 years), and their matched male controls served as subjects. All subjects were residents of San José, Costa Rica. The marijuana users smoked 2.5–23.3

marijuana cigarettes per day (mean, 9.2 cigarettes; median, seven cigarettes) and had used the drug for 10–27 years. Analyses of 13 street samples of Costa Rican marijuana revealed a Δ^9-THC content that ranged from 1.27 to 3.72% by weight. The standard Costa Rican cigarette contains approximately 200 mg of marijuana. The control subjects, ages 21–47 (mean, 30.4 years), were not marijuana users, nor did they use other illegal drugs. They were matched with users with respect to age (within 5 years), level of education, marital status, occupation, tobacco smoking frequency and duration, and alcohol use. All subjects were selected from an original sample of 84 users and 156 nonusers. Prior to selection, a medical history, a physical and neurologic examination (including a test of mental status), and a series of clinical and laboratory tests had revealed that all subjects were free of gross pathologies. A specific attempt was made to select subjects from all socioeconomic levels. Potential subjects above age 50 were rejected so as to minimize the influence of brain deterioration associated with aging. Descriptions of the project procedures, the neuropsychologic, health, and social characteristics of subjects, and the sociocultural aspects of marijuana use in Costa Rica have appeared elsewhere.[32-34] Pertinent characteristics of subjects are summarized in TABLE 1. All subjects were paid $80 to participate in the sleep study.

Several procedures and facts increased our confidence that subjects were, in fact, what they claimed to be (i.e., users or nonusers) and that the data on duration of use among users were accurate. Each subject's reported smoking behavior was validated by questioning individuals in the person's social network, and the dispersion of networks over the city of 400,000 inhabitants made collusion to provide false data unlikely. Two subjects who claimed to be users and one who claimed to be a nonuser were determined by this procedure to be misrepresenting their past marijuana use and were eliminated from the study. Many subjects were directly observed smoking marijuana by the project field research team, and some were observed more than once over an 18-month period. The levels of observed smoking were inconsistent with casual use. Subjects suffered many inconveniences to participate in the project. They were repeatedly contacted and required to submit to interviews over 18–24 months. Not the least inconvenience for users was the risk of being identified as a user by police, despite preventive measures taken by the project staff. Incentives for misrepresentation of use to participate were low. Aside from the $80 paid for participation in the sleep study, subjects were paid only for any time lost from work, at a rate comparable to that paid in San José for blue-collar work. Independent information from the police revealed that some subjects had been known to local narcotics police for years as regular users of marijuana. Users' estimates of age of onset of marijuana smoking were obtained twice during the study, at times separated by at least several months. The estimates were highly consistent from time to time, and it would be unlikely that such consistency could have been maintained if the information were false.

The sleep study consisted of 8 consecutive nights of sleep in the modern, modified clinical EEG laboratory of the Hospital Mexico in San José. Marijuana users were encouraged to continue their usual daytime pattern of use. To minimize acute effects of smoking at or before bedtime, we made every attempt to prevent the users from smoking marijuana at any time while they were in the hospital building. We were generally successful, but laboratory technicians reported suspicions of a few violations. Approximately 2 hr before his usual bedtime, each subject was transported to the hospital. Before entering the laboratory, he described his marijuana consumption during the previous 24 hr to a project staff member who was not involved in sleep EEG-EOG data collection or processing. On entering the laboratory, the subject was wired for EEG-EOG and heart rate recordings. He then completed a presleep questionnaire concerning his daytime activities and feelings. Five-minute heart rate samples, with the subject lying in bed relaxed, were taken 90, 60, and 30 min before bedtime. The subject retired at his usual bedtime. EEG-EOG patterns and heart rate were monitored continuously throughout each night. Recording began at "lights out" and was terminated when the subject arose in the morning. The subject was awakened and/or arose at his usual arising time in the morning, completed a postsleep questionnaire concerning the quality of his sleep, was unwired, and left the hospital for the remainder of the day. We systematically attempted to keep total time in bed constant across nights for a given subject. For all except two subjects, we were reasonably successful. A Costa Rican technician helped illiterate subjects complete the pre- and postsleep questionnaires. Laboratory personnel were ignorant of the names of subjects (every subject was assigned and referred to by an identification number) and of their group (user or control) membership.

Sleep EEG-EOG recording procedures have been described previously.[35] Heart rate was monitored by means of Beckman electrodes placed at V5 and on the left shoulder. For 10 of the users and their matched controls, all data were simultaneously recorded on magnetic tape by a Sangamo tape recorder. During the sleep study period, at least one prebedtime blood sample was obtained from most subjects for later determination of THC levels.

To keep procedures in Costa Rica consistent with those used in our Houston laboratory, three experienced Costa Rican EEG technicians received training in the Houston laboratory prior to initiation of the study. They returned to Costa Rica and performed the night technician duties under the immediate supervision of a senior technician from Houston. Overall supervision of data collection was the responsibility of one of the authors (A. F.-S.), who is an American-trained neurologist and electroencephalographer and who also received training in our Houston procedures. The senior author made periodic visits to Costa Rica to assure that data collection was proceeding satisfactorily and maintained frequent telephone communication with personnel in Costa Rica.

Three users and one control subject did not sleep 8 *consecutive* nights. Two of the users and the control failed to report to the laboratory on 1 night. For the third user, the break in the run was 32 days in length. For all four subjects, data from the first laboratory night after return were discarded from the analyses. In three cases, subjects slept at least 1 extra night to make up for the lost data. Data from the initial adjustment night and from postadjustment nights were analyzed separately because of the well-known first-night effect.[14, 15]

Our prestudy instructions to subjects included prohibitions against taking daytime naps, drinking alcoholic beverages, drinking coffee or tea after 5 PM, taking any drugs or medicine (other than marijuana for the users), and eating meals after 9 PM. It soon became apparent that these prohibitions were unenforceable in Costa Rica. Of particular concern was the fact that many subjects napped and drank alcoholic beverages at least occasionally. Some also took medicines (aspirin, laxatives, cold tablets, antacids). (Items on the daily presleep questionnaire provided information on these matters.) We discarded from analysis the data from nights when a drug was taken after 4 PM. We also discarded the data from nights contaminated by daytime naps of the following

TABLE 1

CHARACTERISTICS OF 32 MARIJUANA USERS AND 32 MATCHED CONTROLS

Pair No.	Marijuana Users						Matched Controls	
	Age (years)	Duration of Use (years)	Average Drug Use: 3-Day* (cig./day)	Average Drug Use: During Study† (cig./day)	Life-style Type‡	Sleep Difficulty§	Age (years)	Sleep Difficulty§
1	32	17	2.9	2.2	SP	0	31	0
2	20	10	8.6	10.7	SP	0	23	0
3	43	23	17.5	7.6	SP	0	43	1
4	28	10	14.3	12.1	SP	0	28	0
5	30	12	20.9	20.9	SS	1	32	1
6	28	12	6.0	3.7	SS	0	24	0
7	27	10	23.3	23.2	SS	0	24	1
8	34	10	21.9	21.9	SS	0	35	0
9	30	12	10.0	10.7	SP	0	32	2
10	28	12	10.8	10.8	SS	0	31	0
11	39	17	2.7	9.0	SS	0	34	0
12	27	15	17.7	10.2	SP	0	22	0
13	27	14	2.5	1.4	SS	0	30	0

14	31	15	8.7	1.9	SS	1	34	0
15	22	10	3.7	2.1	SP	0	22	1
16	33	16	3.1	2.6	SP	0	34	0
17	22	10	15.2	?	SP	0	23	1
18	41	25	20.0	7.5	SS	1	41	1
19	22	11	6.0	6.2	SS	0	21	1
20	35	20	4.4	7.5	SS	0	35	0
21	39	20	2.7	2.8	SS	0	36	1
22	45	25	6.0	?	SP	0	44	0
23	31	16	10.9	8.0	SS	1	29	0
24	30	17	2.5	2.5	SS	0	32	1
25	29	11	12.5	6.2	SS	1	27	0
26	24	14	5.2	6.2	SS	0	24	0
27	26	11	3.0	3.1	SP	1	28	1
28	24	10	6.0	8.6	SS	0	25	0
29	48	27	7.1	9.8	SP	0	47	1
30	22	10	4.2	4.9	SP	0	22	0
31	29	18	7.7	8.8	SP	1	31	1
32	24	11	7.0	6.8	SP	1	29	0

* Determined by interview on 3 consecutive days prior to sleep study.
† Determined by questioning each night before subject entered sleep laboratory; information was not obtained for two subjects (?).
‡ SP, "street person"; SS, "stable smoker."
§ Determined by interview prior to sleep study: 0, never; 1, sometimes; 2, always.

types: naps 2 hr or more in length and that began between 12 AM and 2:59 PM and naps 1 hr or more in length and that began between 3 PM and bedtime. Decisions to discard data were made by the senior author before he had examined the sleep EEG-EOG data and were therefore not influenced by the sleep pattern characteristic of the night. Because users and their controls were originally matched with respect to alcohol use, for this analysis we decided not to discard data contaminated by alcohol consumption. Most drinks were taken at the noon or evening meal time, and in only one case was the drink consumed after 7 PM (one beer at 8 PM in a control subject; the data were included). Technical difficulties resulted in the loss of data for 7 nights in users and 4 nights in controls. TABLE 2 summarizes the study with respect to all of these factors. Data were collected for a total of 516 nights. For each group, about 90% of the data was used in the statistical analyses.

Data were actually collected on 39 subjects in each group. Three pairs of subjects were discarded because controls took naps on a majority of study days. Two pairs were discarded because users took naps on a majority of the days. One pair was discarded because both subjects took naps on a majority of days and because the user took an antibiotic on all 8 days. One user and one control were discarded because no data were obtained on their pairmates. Again, the decisions to discard these subjects were made before EEG-EOG data had been examined. The fact that most of these subjects were discarded because one or both of the subjects in a pair took naps on a majority of days does not mean that each nap would have resulted in the deletion of a night according to the rules stated in the previous paragraph. Rather, it was related to the consistency of the napping pattern and our feeling that consistent nappers might be more different from nonnappers than are occasional nappers.

Sleep EEG-EOG recordings were scored minute-by-minute according to criteria described elsewhere.[35] The records were scored randomly, and the scorers were ignorant of subjects' group membership. The scoring data were processed by an IBM 370 computer program that generated descriptors of various sleep characteristics for the night as a whole and for specified segments of the night. For each subject, all usable postadjustment night data were averaged, and the resultant subject means were averaged to provide group means. Data on heart rate, wave form characteristics of the EEG-EOG, blood levels of THC, and pre- and postsleep questionnaire items are being analyzed and will be described in the future.

The main analyses of the data consisted of comparisons of users and their matched controls with respect to the variables described in TABLE 3. For the comparisons of adjustment night data, 27 pairs of subjects were usable. The remaining five pairs were discarded because of naps (2), medicine (1), or technical difficulty (1) on one subject's first night. All 32 pairs of subjects were usable for comparisons of postadjustment night data. In both analyses, t tests for matched pairs were used. Because the main analyses revealed so few differences between groups, we performed several other analyses designed to assess more subtle differences. The results of these analyses will be described briefly.

RESULTS

Differences between Group Means

TABLE 4 shows the results of between-group comparisons for adjustment night data. Marijuana users exhibited a slightly (average increase of 3.1%)

TABLE 2

SUMMARIZATION OF EEG-EOG SLEEP STUDY NIGHTS AND THEIR CONTAMINANTS
FOR 32 MARIJUANA USERS AND 32 MATCHED CONTROLS

	Marijuana Users	Matched Controls
General		
No. of nights recorded	258	258
No. of nights used	233	234
No. of nights recorded/subject	7–9	8–9
No. of nights used/subject	5–8	6–8
Naps Preceding Sleep Nights		
No. of subjects taking naps during study	14	19
No. of nights "with naps"	29	30
No. of nights "with naps"/subject	1–3	1–4
No. of nights "with naps" and discarded due to naps	14	15
No. of nights "with naps" and discarded for other reasons	2	1
No. of nights "with naps" and used	13	14
Medicine Preceding Sleep Nights		
No. of subjects taking medicine during study *	5	8
No. of nights "with medicine"	8	13
No. of nights "with medicine"/subject	1–2	1–2
No. of nights "with medicine" and discarded due to medicine	1	4
No. of nights "with medicine" and discarded for other reasons	1	1
No. of nights "with medicine" and used	6	8
Alcohol Preceding Sleep Nights		
No. of subjects drinking alcohol during study	14	17
No. of nights "with alcohol"	20	36
No. of nights "with alcohol"/subject	1–4	1–7
No. of nights "with alcohol" and discarded due to alcohol	0	0
No. of nights "with alcohol" and discarded for other reasons	4	7
No. of nights "with alcohol" and used	16	29
Median (and range) of alcohol use for nights "with alcohol" and used:		
Beer, glasses	2 (1–10)	2.5 (1–10)
Cane alcohol (*guaro*), shots	4 (1–6)	2 (1–15)
Gin, shots	0	0.75 (0.5–1)
Readjustment to Laboratory After Break in Run: no. of nights discarded	7	4
Technical Difficulties: no. of nights unusable	3	1

* Medicines were aspirin, laxatives, cold tablets, and antacids.

TABLE 3

STANDARD EEG-EOG SLEEP VARIABLES

Variable	Definition
Time in bed	minutes from record start ("lights out") to record end (arising)
Sleep period time	minutes from sleep onset, whatever the stage (stage 1 for most nights), to final awakening
Total sleep time	sleep period time less stage-0 time (wakefulness)
Sleep efficiency index	ratio: (total sleep time/time in bed) × 100
Sleep latency	minutes from record start to sleep onset, whatever the stage
Sleep latency 1	minutes from record start to onset of first stage 1
Sleep latency 2	minutes from record start to onset of first stage 2
Number of stages	number of stage occurrences during the sleep period
Number of stage-1 shifts	number of entries to and exits from stage 1
Number of awakenings	number of awakenings, including the final morning awakening
REM period length	average duration (minutes) of REM periods (REM periods interrupted by final morning awakening excluded from calculations)
REM interval length	average time (minutes) from the end of one REM period to the beginning of the next
Number of REM periods	number of REM periods during the sleep period
Stage percentages	for each stage, minutes as a proportion of sleep period time
Stage latencies	for each stage, minutes from sleep onset, whatever the stage, to onset of the stage in question (sleep period time substituted if stage was absent; stage-1 latency $=0$ unless another sleep stage occurred first)

but significantly greater REM percentage than did controls. The increase was apparently entirely due to the significantly longer average duration of REM periods, because there was no difference in the number of REM periods. There were tendencies for users to exhibit longer time in bed, sleep latency, sleep latency 1, and sleep latency 2. There were no other trends or significant differences between groups.

TABLE 5 presents the results for between-group comparisons of postadjustment night data. Again, the users exhibited a slight (average increase of 2.4%) but significant elevation in REM percentage in comparison to controls, and this increase was due to significantly greater REM period lengths. On postadjustment nights, the users' sleep latency 1 was significantly greater than that of controls. There were tendencies for users to exhibit a lower sleep efficiency index, longer sleep latency 2, and longer stage-1 latency (from sleep onset). There were no other significant differences or tendencies between groups.

Differences in Night-to-Night Variability

We assessed night-to-night variability for users and controls in a second analysis. Gaps in the data for certain subjects (caused by our discarding data for certain nights or by losses due to technical difficulties) allowed us to use only 22 pairs of subjects and four consecutive postadjustment nights per subject. Nights 2–4 were used for 17 pairs, nights 4–7 for two pairs, and nights 5–8 for three pairs. For each parameter listed in TABLE 3, a standard deviation was calculated for each subject. The Wilcoxon signed-ranks test was used to compare groups with respect to these standard deviations. Only for sleep latency 1 was there a significant difference ($p < 0.05$): marijuana users showed greater variability than their matched controls. Median estimates of each group's standard deviation were derived from Hodges and Lehmann contrast estimators.[36] The estimate for users (9.8) was twice as great as that for controls (5.0). A similar trend ($p < 0.10$) was apparent for sleep latency (8.0 vs 4.8), but it was not significant. It seems probable that these effects were at least partially related to the higher average values for the measures of sleep latency in the users, because higher mean values typically imply higher variances. Worthy of note is the fact that use of a parametric procedure (derivation of a

TABLE 4

ADJUSTMENT NIGHTS: COMPARISONS BETWEEN 27 CHRONIC MARIJUANA USERS AND 27 MATCHED CONTROL SUBJECTS FOR SLEEP EEG-EOG VARIABLES

Variable	Marijuana Users (mean ± SD)	Matched Controls (mean ± SD)	p Value *
Time in bed	420 ± 49	390 ± 68	<0.10
Sleep period time	390 ± 53	372 ± 65	
Total sleep time	381 ± 51	362 ± 64	
Sleep efficiency index	90.8 ± 8.4	93.0 ± 6.0	
Sleep latency	25.5 ± 27.8	15.2 ± 9.1	<0.10
Sleep latency 1	25.9 ± 27.7	15.2 ± 9.1	<0.10
Sleep latency 2	32.7 ± 31.6	21.2 ± 10.3	<0.10
Number of stages	38.3 ± 15.5	32.6 ± 12.6	
Number of stage-1 shifts	21.2 ± 11.9	18.6 ± 9.2	
Number of awakenings	3.81 ± 3.51	3.15 ± 2.92	
REM period length	28.6 ± 7.3	23.0 ± 7.3	<0.05
REM interval length	76.0 ± 29.8	72.2 ± 20.6	
Number of REM periods	3.44 ± 1.01	3.41 ± 0.84	
Percentage of stage 0	2.4 ± 3.2	2.6 ± 5.7	
Percentage of stage 1	7.4 ± 4.2	7.1 ± 3.8	
Percentage of stage 1 REM	23.5 ± 5.2	20.4 ± 6.1	<0.05
Percentage of stage 2	55.9 ± 7.0	56.7 ± 10.8	
Percentage of stage 3	5.3 ± 4.0	7.4 ± 7.9	
Percentage of stage 4	5.4 ± 6.6	5.8 ± 7.8	
Latency to stage 0	189 ± 172	216 ± 137	
Latency to stage 1	0.4 ± 1.7†	0.0 ± 0.0	
Latency to stage 1 REM	104 ± 56	102 ± 50	
Latency to stage 2	7.2 ± 6.7	6.0 ± 4.3	
Latency to stage 3	115 ± 154	115 ± 160	
Latency to stage 4	178 ± 177	194 ± 176	

* Established with two-tailed matched-pair *t* tests.
† Stage 2 occurred first for two subjects.

mean estimate that equaled the square root of the average of the subject's night-to-night variances) to analyze these data produced obviously misleading results for several variables because of a few highly variable subjects.

TABLE 5

POSTADJUSTMENT NIGHTS: COMPARISONS BETWEEN 32 CHRONIC MARIJUANA
USERS AND 32 MATCHED CONTROL SUBJECTS FOR SLEEP EEG-EOG VARIABLES

Variable	Marijuana Users (mean ± SD)	Matched Controls (mean ± SD)	p Value *
Time in bed	428 ± 54	406 ± 71	
Sleep period time	409 ± 50	394 ± 67	
Total sleep time	404 ± 47	390 ± 65	
Sleep efficiency index	94.7 ± 4.8	96.3 ± 2.5	<0.10
Sleep latency	16.1 ± 16.7	10.2 ± 7.6	
Sleep latency 1	21.9 ± 19.1	11.1 ± 8.0	<0.01
Sleep latency 2	23.5 ± 19.2	15.9 ± 10.2	<0.10
Number of stages	32.4 ± 9.2	32.6 ± 6.8	
Number of stage-1 shifts	16.8 ± 7.7	17.0 ± 5.5	
Number of awakenings	2.70 ± 1.99	2.29 ± 1.60	
REM period length	29.5 ± 4.6	26.8 ± 5.3	<0.05
REM interval length	68.8 ± 12.6	66.6 ± 8.2	
Number of REM periods	3.99 ± 0.58	3.92 ± 0.78	
Percentage of stage 0	1.2 ± 2.2	0.9 ± 1.2	
Percentage of stage 1	6.4 ± 3.3	6.1 ± 2.2	
Percentage of stage 1 REM	27.5 ± 3.6	25.1 ± 4.1	<0.05
Percentage of stage 2	54.3 ± 6.8	54.9 ± 7.9	
Percentage of stage 3	5.5 ± 3.0	6.3 ± 3.7	
Percentage of stage 4	5.1 ± 4.7	6.7 ± 5.9	
Latency to stage 0	274 ± 106	268 ± 108	
Latency to stage 1	5.8 ± 14.3†	0.9 ± 3.8‡	<0.10
Latency to stage 1 REM	82 ± 22	82 ± 28	
Latency to stage 2	7.4 ± 4.4	5.7 ± 3.8	
Latency to stage 3	94 ± 118	86 ± 118	
Latency to stage 4	176 ± 152	153 ± 144	

* Established with two-tailed matched-pair *t* tests.
† Stage 2 occurred first on 9 nights from seven subjects; stage-1 REM occurred first on 1 night from one subject.
‡ Stage 2 occurred first on 2 nights from two subjects.

Differences Due to Life-style Pattern and Marijuana Use Level

Evaluation of the life patterns of the marijuana users indicated that there were two main types of users [32]: one type, called "street people," had continued to exhibit adolescent patterns of behavior in adulthood; "stable smokers" had adopted the adult pattern of a stable family life, income, and occupation. Interviews with users on 3 consecutive days before the sleep study yielded an estimate of typical daily marijuana use level. Use was categorized as follows: low, 0–5; medium, 5+–10; and high, 10+–24 marijuana cigarettes per day. In a third analysis, we attempted to determine whether sleep patterns of users differed according to life-style or use level. The data were the same as those used for the analysis of postadjustment night differences in mean values (32 subject pairs). A multivariate general linear hypothesis model was constructed and applied to the data for all parameters listed in TABLE 3, by use of computer program BMDX63.[37] Subject-pairs' values for a parameter were used as dependent vectors in the analysis. Independent variables consisted of the overall mean, the life-style type ("street person" or "stable smoker"), and two variables that reflected use level ("low" or "high" and "low" or "medium"). Five hypotheses were tested: differences in mean values between users and controls (replication of the main analyses); differences in mean values between life-styles, within the user group; interactions between life-style and group (user or control); differences in mean values among the three use levels, within the user group; and interactions between use level and group. Tests of the first hypothesis supported the main analysis; users exhibited a significantly longer sleep latency 1 ($p < 0.01$) and a greater REM percentage ($p < 0.05$) than did their matched controls, and they tended ($p < 0.10$) to have a longer REM period length. There were no other significant differences, but the users tended ($p < 0.10$) to have a longer time in bed, lower sleep efficiency index, longer sleep latency and sleep latency 2, and longer stage-2 latency. Tests of the third hypothesis indicated that *controls* of "stable smokers" had a longer time in bed, sleep period time, and total sleep time, more sleep stages and REM periods, and lower percentage of stage 3 than did *controls* of "street people," whereas for the users, the differences between "stable smokers" and "street people" tended in the opposite direction. The interactions for the first three parameters were significant at $p < 0.01$; for the latter three parameters, they were significant at $p < 0.05$. The meaning of the interactions is unclear. On the basis of the available evidence, we conclude that they were due to chance factors in the subject selection, especially because there is no apparent reason why particular subgroups of control subjects should differ in their sleep characteristics. Tests of the remaining hypotheses revealed no significant differences.

Correlation between Daytime Use Level and Sleep Variables

A final analysis was designed to evaluate the correlation between marijuana use on a particular day and sleep characteristics that night. For convenience, we examined the data used in the analysis of night-to-night variability (minus one subject, for whom we did not obtain daily smoking information). The values for daily use were obtained from the questioning of the subjects each night just before they entered the sleep laboratory. A correlation coefficient was calculated for each parameter listed in TABLE 3, for each subject. Wilcoxon signed-ranks tests were used to test statistical significance. There were no significant correlations. We hesitate to draw conclusions from these correlation analyses, because, by design, smoking behavior and other factors were uncontrolled in the study. Careful research under more controlled conditions is needed to adequately assess any possible relationships between amount of daytime marijuana smoking and sleep patterns at night.

Discussion

The most impressive result of this study, in our opinion, was the lack of evidence of major disturbances of EEG-EOG sleep patterns in our user subjects studied *in situ*. The only significant differences observed in the users were a moderate elevation in sleep latency and slight elevations in REM percentage and REM period length. Five aspects of the study, and their interactions, must be considered in interpreting the results: the users had smoked marijuana chronically for at least 10 years; the users continued their usual marijuana smoking during the day; the users were generally prevented from smoking marijuana during at least the 2 hr before going to bed, and this condition might have resulted in the occurrence of acute withdrawal effects; levels of both chronic and current daytime marijuana use varied among users and daytime use varied from day to day, and therefore drug dosage was uncontrolled; the intended "naturalism" of the study resulted in the occurrence of contaminating events, such as naps and alcohol use. Even if the last three factors could be discounted as causes of the findings, it would be difficult with our data to determine conclusively whether "true" drug effects were due to chronic use, current daytime use, or both.

For each effect observed, whether positive (i.e., a significant difference) or negative (i.e., no difference), there exist several possible explanations. Two general explanations might pertain to any effect. First, it is possible that the difference or lack of difference represented a "true" result. This conclusion is, of course, the most desirable one, but it must necessarily be accepted only after all other explanations have been reasonably rejected. Second, although great efforts were made to assure that users were indeed users and had been so for at least 10 years, and that controls were nonusers and well matched with users, there exists the possibility that some unknown and uncontrolled aspect of the subject selection procedure produced an effect. There is no way to eliminate this possibility, but in future analyses we will explore it to some degree by comparing the Costa Rican data with normative data [35] collected in the United States.

In addition to these explanations, several other factors might explain the apparent normality of our users' sleep patterns. First, it is possible that there are positive "true" drug effects in individuals such as our users but that the sleep EEG-EOG is not sensitive to the effects. We are reluctant to accept this explanation, however, because sleep EEG-EOG patterns show clear changes as a function of age,[35] are abnormal in many physical and mental diseases,[35] and are typically altered by drugs.[38] Moreover, as noted in the Introduction, previous studies of bedtime administration of marijuana and THC have suggested the occurrence of drug-related changes in the sleep EEG-EOG. Another possibility is that sleep-related changes in chronic and current users occur primarily during the daytime in the form of increased napping. This explanation is suggested by Kay's study [39] of individuals taking chronic stable doses of methadone. Although there were few major changes in the subjects' nighttime sleep patterns, there were reports of increased daytime napping. The data in Table 2 indicate that during our study, fewer users (14) than controls (19) took naps but that in users naps occurred on about the same number of days (29) as in controls (30). The high rate of napping in both groups was at least partially due to the Latin American custom of taking siestas, but in future analyses we will explore the napping patterns and amounts in greater detail.

Still other alternative explanations for our subjects' apparent normality relate to their drug use levels. It may be that the amount of drug used by our subjects was insufficient to produce noticeable changes in the brain function monitored by the sleep EEG-EOG. Or, perhaps the variability in the amount of marijuana smoked among users and from day to day was sufficient to obscure effects that would be apparent under more controlled conditions. For example, for the average marijuana use rate (9.2 cigarettes per day), subjects might have absorbed from 2.34 to 34.2 mg of Δ^9-THC per day [9.2 cigarettes per day times 200 mg of marijuana per cigarette, times 1.27 or 3.72% Δ^9-THC content by weight, times 10 or 50% absorbed in the lungs (with maximal smoking efficiency, no more than 50% may be absorbed [40])]. If subjects absorbed only 2.34 mg, the average daily dose at the average use rate was very much lower than bedtime doses used in previous studies that suggested drug-related changes in sleep patterns.[13, 20, 27, 29] If subjects absorbed as much as 34.2 mg, it was at least comparable to the bedtime doses examined. However, it will be recalled that Hosko *et al.*[17] administered up to about 28 mg of Δ^9-THC 3–5 hr before bedtime and observed no consistent changes in sleep patterns. As a result, it is quite likely that for some subjects in the study, regular dose levels during the day were too low to be expected to produce changes in sleep patterns attributable directly to immediate daytime drug use, and the normality of these subjects' sleep patterns should therefore not be surprising. On the other hand, the analyses of data from subgroups formed according to use level failed to reveal any significant interactions between use level and group (user or control), so subjects whose high regular doses (20 cigarettes or more) might have led us to expect effects on EEG-EOG sleep characteristics were not distinguishable with respect to the essential normality of the characteristics from those who took lower regular doses. In addition, the lack of significant correlations between daily use levels and values for sleep variables provides some tentative evidence against the possibility that the variability in daily usage obscured effects.

Another explanation relates to the prebedtime abstinence period. It seems arguable that marijuana use may have certain effects on sleep brain mechanisms and that the abstinence period was sufficient to allow either normal functioning to be reattained or acute withdrawal processes that produce apparent normality to become operative. This explanation might plausibly pertain to effects due to current daytime use of marijuana, but it seems unlikely that residual effects of long-term chronic use would be so immediately reversible. On the other hand, a distinct possibility is that the brain, when exposed chronically to a centrally acting substance, such as marijuana, has sufficient plasticity to readjust its function so as to give the appearance of normality (i.e., develop tolerance). Our data do not allow us to choose between this explanation and the others. Only further research can demonstrate which explanation is closer to the truth.

Another set of alternative explanations must be examined for the positive findings of elevated sleep latency, REM percentage, and REM period length in the users. On the average, the users' sleep latency 1 was twice as long on post-adjustment nights as that of controls. Many sleep researchers would argue that the appropriate measure of time to fall asleep is what we call sleep latency 2. Values for this parameter showed a tendency to be larger in users than in controls on both adjustment nights and postadjustment nights. It is doubtful that this effect was the result of preexisting differences between users and controls, because, as the data in TABLE 1 show, the user group actually contained fewer subjects who reported any sleep difficulty before the study than the control group. More likely is the possibility that the elevated sleep latency was part of an acute withdrawal process associated with the prebedtime abstinence from marijuana. Data from previous studies of THC administered at bedtime [24, 27, 31] suggest that increased sleep latency may characterize withdrawal from use for 4–20 days. However, in the two fully reported studies of marijuana smoking,[18, 29] there were no apparent changes in sleep latency during the recovery period. On the psychologic level, it may be that the enforced abstinence interfered with established habits of use sufficiently to create difficulty in falling asleep. Or, perhaps anxiety associated with sleeping in the laboratory delayed sleep onset in the users. Use of marijuana is illegal in Costa Rica, and the sleep study was conducted in a government hospital. Several users verbally expressed great concern as to whether their anonymity would be preserved, and all users may have felt this concern to a greater or lesser extent. However, one of the first-night effects of sleeping in a laboratory is a reduction in the amount of REM sleep.[14, 15] This reduction has been attributed to anxiety concerning the strangeness of the sleeping environment and the recording procedures. If anxiety were present prior to sleep onset in our user subjects, it was not sufficiently strong after sleep onset to reduce REM percentage below control levels.

The users' elevations in REM percentage and REM period length were statistically significant but very small on the average and would not usually be considered clinically significant. A normal subject may show larger changes from just one night to the next. On the other hand, the fact that the significant differences in the REM characteristics were observed on both the adjustment and the postadjustment nights indicates that they were probably not spurious. It will be noted that on the average, the users spent more time in bed and more time asleep than did controls on all study nights. Because REM sleep occurs predominantly during the latter part of the night and successive REM periods tend to be longer, the extra sleep in users probably contained relatively high amounts of REM sleep. This explanation might account for the users' slight elevation in REM percentage and REM period length. In future analyses, we will examine the data again after reducing all nights to a standard length. If the differences between groups in REM percentage and REM period length disappear, the extra sleep in users can be considered the cause of the present results for these two parameters. If the differences persist, we will then examine the successive individual REM periods to determine whether particular ones were more affected by the drug than others. Whatever the outcome of the procedure for standardizing length of the sleep period, in future analyses we will also explore various portions of the night to determine whether changes in the distribution of REM sleep or of other stages occurred in the marijuana users.

Another possible contributor to the users' elevated REM percentage might have been the 2-hr prebedtime abstention from smoking. As documented in the INTRODUCTION, previous studies of bedtime THC administration suggest that it has an REM suppressant effect, whereas two of three studies of bedtime marijuana smoking revealed no changes in REM sleep. These discrepancies may relate to the time course of the two drugs' effects. Presumably, the brain mechanisms that are acutely affected by bedtime THC, and whose altered functioning determines the observed changes in nighttime REM sleep, may also be sensitive to the THC in marijuana smoked during the day. Perhaps the 2-hr abstinence period was sufficient to allow these mechanisms to switch to an REM rebound mode of operation and thereby produce the slightly elevated REM percentage. REM rebound is typically characterized by elevated REM percentage, shortened REM latency, and elevated eye movement activity (REM density). In their study of subjects recovering from 12–16 days of 210 mg of THC per day, Feinberg *et al.*[31] observed greater REM sleep amount, shorter REM latency, and more eye movement activity in comparison to previous nights under the high-drug condition. This finding indicates that REM rebound may occur during withdrawal from THC. In our users, there was no evidence of reduced REM latency (see TABLES 4 & 5), which suggests that the elevated REM percentage in our user subjects was not due to an REM rebound. Nevertheless, in future analyses, by use of an automated detection system,[41] we will examine the density of eye movements to explore this matter further. Although one explanation of greater eye movement activity in users would be that the subjects were experiencing REM rebound, another might be that increased eye movement activity is a "true" effect of long-term marijuana smoking and current daytime smoking. It will probably be impossible to determine which explanation applies to the present data. On the other hand, if we fail to find greater eye movement activity in the users, we may reasonably conclude that REM rebound did not occur in our subjects. The possibility that the slight elevation in REM percentage was a "true" effect of long-term smoking and/or current daytime smoking would then gain support. An explanation of the mechanism that controls such an REM elevation would have to await future clarification of the relationships between marijuana and the biogenic amines, which are crucial in the regulation of REM sleep.[42]

Although marijuana may not dramatically change the quantitative aspects of EEG-EOG sleep reflected in the conventional parameters we have examined, the qualitative aspects of the EEG-EOG wave forms should also be considered. Waking EEG studies of brain activity with marijuana or THC administration have suggested few if any remarkable changes,[43–45] although Heath[46] observed slow-wave activity in the septal area of one man with electrodes implanted in several deep nuclear structures. In none of the previous sleep EEG-EOG studies of marijuana or THC have any abnormal wave forms been described. Feinberg *et al.*[31] specifically examined their recordings visually for the presence of precentral fast activity (15–25 Hz) and detected none. For our data, five experienced sleep-stage scorers visually examined samples of the recordings without knowledge of the subjects' group membership. Later, after learning which subjects were users and which were controls, they examined the recordings again. No abnormal wave forms were seen. Before we make final conclusions on this matter, however, we will submit our tape-recorded data to analysis by an automated system[47] that describes various characteristics of sleep EEG-EOG wave forms (e.g., incidence, frequency, amplitude, and duration).

Discrepancies between the results of this study and those of previous ones are not at all surprising. Our study was a reasonably naturalistic study of very long-term marijuana users. Daily marijuana use by the subjects continued as usual during the study, except that smoking was typically stopped at least 2 hr before bedtime. Any "true" drug effects demonstrated by our study were a mixture of effects due to chronic marijuana use and current daytime use. In most other studies, the interest was in the more immediate effects associated with bedtime drug administration. It is likely that our future analyses of the REM sleep data will indicate that in our user subjects, REM amount was either no different from control levels or slightly elevated and that this effect was not due to REM rebound. These results would differ from those of previous studies.

The discrepancies concerning the REM sleep effect would conceivably be attributable to the length of marijuana use, the form of the drug, or the schedule by which it was administered.

In interpreting our results, it should be kept in mind that in the interest of naturalism, the study was intentionally less controlled than an experimental study should be. As a result, contaminants, such as naps, alcohol, and medicine, were present, even after we discarded the most seriously contaminated data. Although we asked subjects not to nap, drink, or take medicine, we intentionally did not pressure them on these matters. We felt that it was better to remain cordial and at least learn what they were doing than to be condemnatory and risk their not reporting their actions to us. Other researchers contemplating cross-cultural studies should be forewarned by our experience, for they may also find that precision is not critical to members of other cultures.

Although the meaning of our results is not yet clear, we believe that our data are reliable. The sample was the largest ever described for a sleep study of marijuana or THC, and carefully selected control subjects were used. Of course, one problem, common to all studies in which many variables are examined statistically, is that the making of large numbers of statistical tests may result in false-positive significances by chance alone. There is no satisfactory solution for this problem, but in the present study, our confidence in the results is strengthened by the fact that most differences were detected on both the adjustment and the postadjustment nights. Still another problem concerns the appropriateness of parametric procedures for sleep data. We have become convinced that for many parameters, and especially for latency measures, for which extreme values may occur, nonparametric procedures may be more appropriate in studies with small or moderate numbers of subjects. In the present study, however, the relatively large number of nights for each subject and the large sample size would tend to counteract the usual problems associated with parametric procedures.

Previous sleep laboratory studies of marijuana and THC administered at bedtime have represented one type of moderately controlled experimentation on naive or mildly to moderately experienced subjects. Our study was designed to describe *in situ* the sleep patterns of very long-term marijuana users who continued their usual daytime smoking. It would seem that future research should proceed along two paths. First, carefully controlled work with both marijuana and THC should establish firmly the effects of bedtime administration and the importance of such factors as the degree of subjects' previous experience, the form of the drug, and the time of administration. Second, a systematic program of study of the effects of chronic use and withdrawal should be undertaken. The program might well follow that developed in the study of other psychoactive drugs used chronically.[48] A series of studies of chronic users should examine sleep patterns when the users are chronically taking a stable drug dose, withdrawing from a chronic stable drug dose, and being administered other drugs during withdrawal (to study cross-tolerance). Other studies should explore sleep patterns in "clean" subjects during a predrug baseline period, a period when a stable drug dose is taken chronically, and a withdrawal period when placebo is administered. We may note that study of users during withdrawal and abstinence would probably indicate whether the apparent normality of our users' sleep patterns was due to the development of tolerance. Change in sleep patterns during this period would provide support for the "tolerance" hypothesis, whereas the lack of change would tend to support the "no effect" hypothesis.

Ideally, such a study would be conducted over several months, because there is evidence that some drug withdrawal and abstinence effects may not appear in the sleep EEG-EOG until long after discontinuation of the drug.[39]

In conclusion, we have presented data that suggest a slight increase in sleep latency, REM percentage, and REM period length among long-term marijuana users who continued their daytime marijuana smoking but did not smoke during the 2 hr or so before bedtime. The source and the meaning of these changes remain unclear, and an understanding of these results must await further analyses of our data and future experimental work.

ACKNOWLEDGMENTS

We extend special thanks for assistance with this study to Dr. F. Faérron-Valdez, Director, *Hospital Mexico;* R. Weaver, Houston laboratory manager; G. McCoy, J. Moseley, and G. Vardiman, Houston senior technicians; and C. Achi Campos, L. Mesén de Chaves, and M. Berrocal de Jiménez, *Hospital Mexico* technicians.

REFERENCES

1. SILER, J. F., W. L. SHEEP, L. B. BATES, G. F. CLARK, G. W. COOK & W. A. SMITH. 1933. Military Surg. **73:** 269–280
2. BROMBERG, W. 1934. Amer. J. Psychiat. **91:** 303–330.
3. ALLENTUCK, S. & K. M. BOWMAN. 1942. Amer. J. Psychiat. **99:** 248–251.
4. GASKILL, H. S. 1945. Amer. J. Psychiat. **102:** 202–204.
5. WILLIAMS, E. G., C. K. HIMMELSBACH, A. WIKLER & D. C. RUBLE. 1946. Public Health Rep. **61:** 1059–1083.
6. JOHNSON, R. D. 1968. Rhode Island Med. J. **51:** 171–178, 187.
7. HAINES, L. & W. GREEN. 1970. Brit. J. Addictions **65:** 347–362.
8. TART, C. T. & H. J. CRAWFORD. 1970. Psychophysiology **7:** 348 (abs.).
9. WASKOW, I. E., J. E. OLSSON, C. SALZMAN & M. M. KATZ. 1970. Arch. Gen. Psychiat. **22:** 97–107.
10. HOLLISTER, L E. 1971. Science **172:** 21–29.
11. COUSENS, K. & A. DiMASCIO. 1973. Psychopharmacologia **33:** 355–364.
12. ROSSI, A. M., J. G. BERNSTEIN & J. H. MENDELSON. 1974. *In* The Use of Marijuana. A Psychological and Physiological Inquiry. J. H. Mendelson, A. M. Rossi & R. E. Meyer, Eds. : 161–174. Plenum Publishing Corporation. New York, N.Y.
13. BOBON, D. P., H. SCHULZ, D. J. MATTKE & O. SIMONOVA. 1973. *In* The Nature of Sleep. U. J. Jovanović, Ed. : 89–92. Gustav Fischer Verlag. Stuttgart, Federal Republic of Germany.
14. RECHTSCHAFFEN, A. & P. VERDONE. 1964. Percept. Motor Skills **19:** 947–958.
15. AGNEW, H. W., JR., W. B. WEBB & R. L. WILLIAMS. 1966. Psychophysiology **2:** 263–266.
16. COX, D. R. 1951. Biometrika **38:** 312–323.
17. HOSKO, M. J., M. S. KOCHAR & R. I. H. WANG. 1973. Clin. Pharmacol. Ther. **14:** 344–352.
18. PRANIKOFF, K., I. KARACAN, E. A. LARSON, R. L. WILLIAMS, J. I. THORNBY & C. J. HURSCH. 1973. J. Florida Med. Ass. **60:** 28–31
19. KARACAN, I., K. PRANIKOFF & A. LARSON. 1972. Psychophysiology **9:** 95 (abs.).
20. PIVIK, R. T., V. ZARCONE, W. C. DEMENT & L. E. HOLLISTER. 1972. Clin. Pharmacol. Ther. **13:** 426–435.

21. PIVIK, T., V. ZARCONE, L. HOLLISTER & W. DEMENT. 1969. Psychophysiology 6: 261 (abs.).
22. COLASANTI, B. & N. KHAZAN. 1973. In Sleep Research. M. H. Chase, W. C. Stern & P. L. Walter, Eds. Vol. 2: 307, 308. Brain Information Service/ Brain Research Institute, University of California. Los Angeles, Calif.
23. KALES, A., J. HANLEY, W. RICKLES, N. KANAS, M. BAKER & P. GORING. 1972. Psychophysiology 9: 92 (abs.).
24. GILLIN, J. C., J. KOTIN, R. POST, R. J. WYATT, F. SNYDER & F. K. GOODWIN. 1972. In Sleep Research. M. H. Chase, W. C. Stern & P. L. Walter, Eds. Vol. 1: 44 (abs.). Brain Information Service/Brain Research Institute, University of California. Los Angeles, Calif.
25. MENDELS, J. & D. R. HAWKINS. 1972. In Recent Advances in the Psychobiology of the Depressive Illnesses. T. A. Williams, M. M. Katz & J. A. Shield, Jr., Eds. : 147–170. United States Government Printing Office. Washington, D.C.
26. SNYDER, F. 1972. In Recent Advances in the Psychobiology of the Depressive Illnesses. T. A. Williams, M. M. Katz & J. A. Shield, Jr., Eds. : 171–192. United States Government Printing Office. Washington, D.C.
27. FREEMON, F. R. 1974. Psychopharmacologia 35: 39–44.
28. FREEMON, F. R. 1972. J. Amer. Med. Ass. 220: 1364, 1365 (letter to editor).
29. BARRATT, E. S., W. BEAVER & R. WHITE. 1974. Biol. Psychiat. 8: 47–54.
30. BARRATT, E., W. BEAVER, R. WHITE, P. BLAKENEY & P. ADAMS. 1972. In Current Research in Marijuana. M. F. Lewis, Ed. : 163–193. Academic Press, Inc. New York, N.Y.
31. FEINBERG, I., R. JONES, J. M. WALKER, C. CAVNESS & J. MARCH. 1975. Clin. Pharmacol. Ther. 17: 458–466.
32. CARTER, W. E. & P. L. DOUGHTY. This monograph.
33. COGGINS, W. J., E. W. SWENSON, W. W. DAWSON, A. FERNANDEZ-SALAS, J. HERNANDEZ-BOLANOS, C. F. JIMINEZ-ANTILLON, J. R. SOLANO, R. VINOCOUR & F. FAERRON-VALDEZ. This monograph.
34. SATZ, P., J. M. FLETCHER & L. S. SUTKER. This monograph.
35. WILLIAMS, R. L., I. KARACAN & C. J. HURSCH. 1974. The Electroencephalogram (EEG) of Human Sleep: Clinical Applications. John Wiley & Sons, Inc. New York, N.Y.
36. HOLLANDER, M. & D. A. WOLFE. 1973. Nonparametric Statistical Methods. John Wiley & Sons, Inc. New York, N.Y.
37. DIXON, W. J. (Ed.) 1972. BMD. Biomedical Computer Programs. X-Series Supplement. University of California Press. Berkeley, Calif.
38. KAY, D. C. 1973. Psychosomatics 9: 108–118.
39. KAY, D. C. 1975. Electroencephalogr. Clin. Neurophysiol. 38: 35–43.
40. JAFFE, J. 1975. In The Pharmacological Basis of Therapeutics. L. S. Goodman & A. Gilman, Eds. : 307. Macmillan Publishing Co., Inc. New York, N.Y.
41. SMITH, J. R., M. J. CRONIN & I. KARACAN. 1971. Comput. Biomed. Res. 4: 275–290.
42. JOUVET, M. 1972. Ergeb. Physiol. Biol. Chem. Exp. Pharmakol. 64: 166–307.
43. WIKLER, A. & B. J. LLOYD, JR. 1945. Fed. Proc. 4: 141, 142 (abs.).
44. DELIYANNAKIS, E., C. PANAGOPOULOS & A. D. HUOTT. 1970. Clin. Electroencephalogr. 1: 128–140.
45. RODIN, E. A., E. F. DOMINO & J. P. PORZAK. 1970. J. Amer. Med. Ass. 213: 1300–1302.
46. HEATH, R. G. 1972. Arch. Gen. Psychiat. 26: 577–584.
47. SMITH, J. R. & I. KARACAN. 1971. Electroencephalogr. Clin. Neurophysiol. 31: 231–237.
48. KAY, D. C. 1976. Personal communication.

PSYCHOPHYSIOLOGIC EFFECTS OF ACUTE CANNABIS SMOKING IN LONG-TERM USERS *

Aris Liakos, John C. Boulougouris, and Costas Stefanis

Department of Psychiatry
Athens University Medical School
Eginition Hospital
Athens, Greece

INTRODUCTION

A variety of psychophysiologic measures have been used in cannabis research. The most important of these measures is pulse rate, which appears to be a reliable index of cannabis effects. Pulse rate increases that follow cannabis administration are dose related and closely associated to Δ^9-tetrahydrocannabinol (Δ^9-THC) content of the material used.[1-3] In addition to the immediate drug effect, cannabis users have been reported to have a slow pulse rate,[4] and it appears that bradycardia may occur at a later stage after the administration of cannabis.[5]

The effects of cannabis on body temperature, pupil size, plethysmography, respiration rate, and galvanic skin responses have also been investigated, with inconsistent results. Some authors report a fall in body temperature after cannabis administration,[6, 7] whereas others report no change,[8] and early workers in the field reported that temperature rose after use.[9] The same inconsistency in the results obtained has been reported for pupillary changes. Some authors report a dilating effect of cannabis on pupil size,[10, 11] whereas others report no change.[8, 12-14] A constriction effect has been recently reported.[15] Similarly, Rickles et al.[16] report no changes in forearm blood flow, while Beaconsfield et al.[17] reported increased blood flow after cannabis administration. While the irritating effect of cannabis on the lung is well documented, no changes in respiration rate relative to placebo conditions have been reported.[12, 13] Finally, galvanic skin responses (GSR) were studied after cannabis administration, and some authors report decreased GSR responses after cannabis,[18, 19] while others report no change.[8]

In the majority of the above-mentioned studies, the psychophysiologic changes were investigated after the administration of small doses of the drug in subjects of limited to average marijuana experience. There is a lack of systematic investigations of the psychophysiologic effects of cannabis on very experienced chronic cannabis users who tolerate and consume large doses of the drug. In this paper, we report on the results of such an investigation on a sample of very-long-term Greek cannabis users.

* Supported by National Institute of Mental Health Contract HSM 42–70–98 through the International Association for Psychiatric Research.

MATERIALS AND METHODS

Subjects

Twenty long-term male users were studied. They all had at least 10 years of experience of cannabis use. Subjects who gave a history of usage of other drugs or who suffered from incapacitating physical or neurologic illnesses were excluded. Their mean age was 43 years (SD 10 years), and they reported smoking cannabis for a mean of 25 years (SD 10 years) at an average amount of 5 g of hashish per day.

Subjects received, under double-blind experimental conditions and according to a randomized block design, the following preparations: 2 g of marijuana, provided by the National Institute of Mental Health (NIMH, 2.6% Δ^9-THC), 4 g of hashish of Greek origin (4–5% Δ^9-THC), 3 g of the same hashish as the above, and 3 g of marijuana placebo provided by NIMH (THC free).

In addition, the subjects received 100 mg of pure THC provided by NIMH injected into 3 g of a marijuana placebo, on the last day of the testing sequence.

TABLE 1

CONTENTS OF THE MATERIALS ADMINISTERED

Doses Administered	Δ^9-THC (mg)	Cannabinol (mg)	Cannabidiol (mg)
Hashish, 4 g	180	66	74
Hashish, 2 g	90	33	37
Marijuana, 3 g	78	12	3
THC plus placebo	100	0	0

TABLE 1 shows the contents of Δ^9-THC, cannabinol, and cannabidiol at each dosage schedule employed.

The materials were mixed with tobacco, as is the custom for Greek users, rolled into large cigarettes identical in appearance, and were administered to each subject on 4 successive days, except for THC.

The following psychophysiologic parameters were measured before and after smoking: pulse rate, plethysmography, pupil size, GSR, respiration, and body temperature.

Measurement Techniques

Pulse Rate

The pulse rate was continuously monitored for a 10-min presmoking period, a 10-min smoking period, and a 30-min postsmoking period. There was a testing interval of 25 min after which time another 20 min of recording followed. The analyses were performed on 10-min averages.

Finger Plethysmography

This parameter was also monitored as described above for pulse rate. A photoelectric plethysmograph was applied to the subject's left index finger, which rested in a horizontal position on the arm of a chair. The average height of six consecutive waves comprised the score; wave heights were measured every 10 min of the recording. Only the height of the waves was analyzed, and 11 min of deflection is equivalent to a 1-mm^3 flow volume.

Pupil Size

Color slides were taken with a reflex camera from a distance of 45 cm under the standard bright illumination of two 300-W bulbs fixed 1 m away from and at a 45° angle to the subject's face. The subject's head was positioned on a headrest, and light and distance adaptation effects were standardized. Slides were projected to a 5-cm horizontal iris diameter, and the horizontal pupillary diameter was measured in millimeters. Iris size varies from subject to subject, and a positive correlation between iris and pupil sizes in subjects of the same age and sex has been previously demonstrated.[20] By standardizing the iris diameter, we partially eliminated intersubject pupillary variability. Pupil size is expressed in this way in artificial units, designated in FIGURE 3 as "enlarged pupil." The actual pupil diameter (in millimeters) may be calculated according to the equation $p = (i/I)P$, where P denotes the artificial pupil size (millimeters), i is the actual iris size (millimeters), and I represents the artificial iris size (50 mm). In a previous study,[20] iris diameter was found to vary between 11 and 12.4 mm (mean 11.7). From these data, we may calculate the function i/I to vary from 0.22 to 0.25. This means that our artificial units are approximately four to five times larger than the actual ones.

Three pupillary measurements were taken: before and 30 and 75 min after smoking.

GSR Measurements

Two parameters were measured: basal skin conductance, or the baseline skin conductance reading obtained after 2 min of resting, and GSR to shock, in which two shocks (identical for each subject) were administered, in each instance preceded by a 2-min rest interval. The intensity of the shocks delivered was determined for each subject by administering several sample shocks. Two measurements were taken: before and 75 min after smoking.

Respiration and Temperature

These parameters were monitored for the same periods as for plethysmography, and the analysis was performed on samples taken every 10 min.

Data Analysis

A stepwise linear regression analysis was used. The order in which the independent variables were entered into the regression was predetermined. This procedure makes linear regression analysis almost identical to analysis of co-variance.[21] In all analyses, the effects of intersubject variance were accounted for before testing the effect of the active substances. These effects were assessed by dummy coding the subjects and entering them as covariates.[21]

The variance of presmoking values was also accounted for by entering into the regression the presmoking averages before testing the effects of the active substances. Partial r (correlation coefficients) in the tables show the relationship between dependent and independent variables. The effects of the drugs as a group and of each one individually were tested against the placebo condition. The r^2 increments show the proportion of variance contributed to the dependent variable by the independent variable. The effects of intersubject variance that were accounted for before testing the effects of the drugs are not shown in the tables. Separate regression analyses are performed at each postsmoking time period.

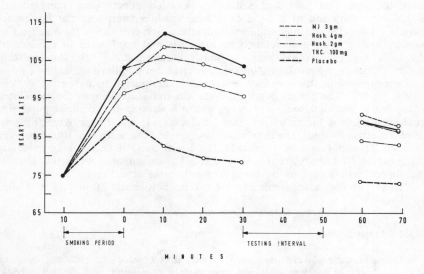

FIGURE 1. Effects of cannabis on heart rate ($n=20$).

RESULTS

Heart Rate

There was an increase in heart rate after administration of all four active preparations (FIGURE 1). This increase was significantly different from the placebo condition at all time periods tested, during and after smoking, times that extended to 70 min postsmoking. The effects were more prominent 20–30 min after smoking. The average maximum heart rate increase was 38 beats per minute, and it appeared 10 min after smoking as a result of pure THC administration. Placebo administration produced a maximum average increase of 17 beats per minute, and this increase appeared during the smoking period. Detailed results of the analysis are shown in TABLE 2.

TABLE 2
EFFECTS OF CANNABIS ON HEART RATE

Independent Variable	df	During Smoking 15 Min			Time After Smoking 10 Min			20 Min			30 Min			60 Min			70 Min		
		r_p	r^2 inc.	$F*$	r_p	r^2 inc.	$F*$	r_p	r^2 inc.	$F*$	r_p	r^2 inc.	$F*$	r_p	r^2 inc.	$F*$	r_p	r^2 inc.	$F*$
Heart rate, presmoking	1/79	0.45	0.07	20.17	0.36	0.07	11.77	0.42	0.09	16.88	0.45	0.10	20.33	0.53	0.13	30.80	0.55	0.14	34.64
THC, 100 mg	1/78	0.62	—	46.87	0.76	—	100.45	0.77	—	108.73	0.75	—	97.93	0.61	—	45.29	0.59	—	39.90
Hashish, 21 g	1/77	0.32	—	8.76	0.56	—	33.57	0.61	—	43.75	0.60	—	41.19	0.46	—	20.79	0.45	—	19.10
Hashish, 4 g	1/76	0.62	—	46.92	0.66	—	59.16	0.70	—	73.64	0.71	—	76.41	0.63	—	50.38	0.62	—	46.81
Marijuana, 3 g	1/75	0.48	0.13	22.50	0.71	0.30	76.84	0.76	0.29	104.46	0.75	0.26	97.20	0.68	0.17	63.35	0.64	0.15	51.65

$*$ In all cases, $p < 0.01$.

TABLE 3

EFFECTS OF CANNABIS ON PLETHYSMOGRAHY HEIGHT

Independent Variable	df	10 Min			20 Min			30 Min			60 Min			70 Min		
		r_p	r^2 inc.	F	r_p	r^2 inc.	F	r_p	r^2 inc.	F	r_p	r^2 inc.	F	r_p	r^2 inc.	F
Plethysmography, presmoking	1/79	0.402	0.081	15.246 *	0.375	0.068	12.973 *	0.541	0.167	32.71 *	0.199	0.024	3.271	0.111	0.007	0.986
THC, 100 mg	1/78	−0.125		1.20	−0.298		7.34 *	−0.33		8.96 *	−0.016		0.02	0.069		0.359
Hashish, 2 g	1/77	−0.186		2.71	−0.258		5.39 †	−0.17		2.24	−0.194		2.956	−0.174		2.358
Hashish, 4 g	1/76	−0.176		2.387	−0.146		1.64	−0.26		5.68 †	−0.139		1.498	−0.114		1.002
Marijuana, 3 g	1/75	−0.211	0.024	3.516	−0.240	0.046	4.59 †	−0.29	0.053	6.86 †	−0.165	0.037	2.120	−0.031	0.041	0.075
"Drug group"	4/75		0.024	1.121		0.046	2.353		0.053	2.826 †		0.037	1.253		0.041	1.411

* p <0.01.
† p <0.05.

Finger Plethysmography

A significant decrease in blood flow, as shown by the diminution in height of the plethysmography waves, was present 30 min after smoking (FIGURE 2). TABLE 3 shows that there is a significant overall drug effect at this time period and significant differences from placebo with all active drug preparations, except 2 g of hashish. At 20 min postsmoking, significant differences from placebo were also found with THC and 2 g of hashish, but there was no overall drug effect at this time (TABLE 3).

Pupil Size

There was a significant dilatation effect of the drugs as a group at both 30 and 75 min after smoking (TABLE 4). This effect was also significant when each preparation was contrasted individually to placebo conditions, except for

TABLE 4

EFFECTS OF CANNABIS ON PUPIL SIZE

Independent Variable	df	Time After Smoking					
		30 Min			70 Min		
		r_p	r^2 inc.	F	r_p	r^2 inc.	F
Pupil, presmoking	1/79	0.50	0.05	26.76 *	0.29	0.02	7.24 *
THC, 100 mg	1/78	0.30	—	7.25 *	0.45	—	19.57 *
Hashish, 2 g	1/77	0.03	—	0.75	0.12	—	1.03
Hashish, 4 g	1/76	0.23	—	4.06 †	0.37	—	12.02 *
Marijuana, 3 g	1/75	0.31	0.02	7.76 †	0.36	0.06	11.40 *
"Drug group"	4/75	—	0.02	3.557 †	—	0.06	6.969 *

* p <0.01.
† p <0.05.

2 g of hashish. FIGURE 3 shows these changes in artificial units of pupil diameter (millimeters of pupillary enlargement), which, as pointed out under MATERIALS AND METHODS, are four- to fivefold larger than actual pupil diameter. The changes are small, and that this was the case can also be seen in the amounts of pupillary variance contributed by the drugs (TABLE 4).

GSR Measurement

"Basal" skin conductance was decreased in comparison to the placebo condition. TABLE 5 shows that there was an overall drug effect and a significant difference between 3 g of marijuana and placebo. As can be seen in FIGURE 4, however, this decrease was not apparent, because presmoking and postsmoking values were similar when active preparations were administered, and the difference is due to the elevation in basal skin conductance with placebo administration. There were no significant differences in GSR to electric shock.

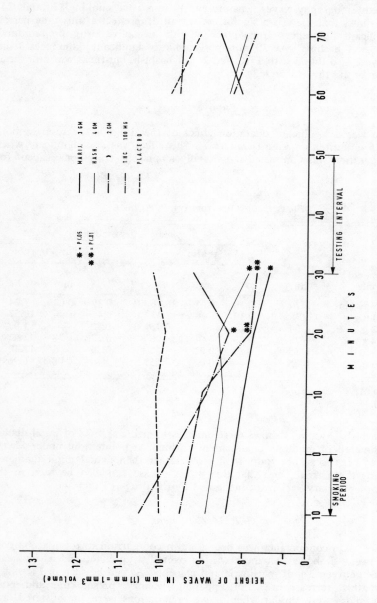

FIGURE 2. Effects of cannabis on finger plethysmography (*n*=20).

TABLE 5

EFFECTS OF CANNABIS ON "BASAL" SKIN CONDUCTANCE

Independent Variable	df	r_p	75 Min Postsmoking r^2 inc.	F
Basal skin conductance, presmoking	1/79	0.71	0.43	60.51 *
Hashish, 2 g	1/78	0.19	—	2.09
Hashish, 4 g	1/77	0.22	—	3.00
Marijuana, 3 g	1/76	0.36	0.06	8.38 *
"Drug group"	4/75	0.36	0.06	2.838 †

* $p < 0.01$.
† $p < 0.05$.

Temperature and Respiration

No significant changes relative to the placebo condition were found.

DISCUSSION

The pulse rate changes described in the present study are similar to those observed in less experienced subjects after administration of smaller doses of materials. This finding provides further evidence that very-long-term users

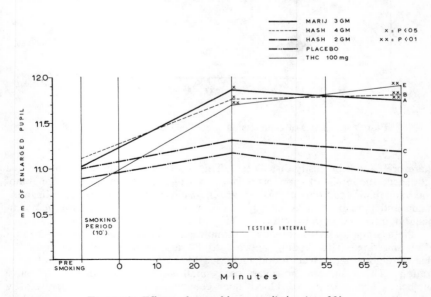

FIGURE 3. Effects of cannabis on pupil size ($n=20$).

tolerate large doses of cannabis. However, in many previous studies with less experienced users, it has been demonstrated that pulse rate changes are closely related to the Δ^9-THC content of the materials.[14, 15, 20] In the present study, 2 and 4 g of hashish produced pulse rate changes that were less pronounced than what was expected due to their THC content as compared to marijuana and pure THC. The explanation for this finding may be complex. The difference in the quality of materials and the experimental design may be responsible. Pure THC was not randomly administered and was the last drug given, after at least a 1-day interval. In addition, marijuana can be more evenly distributed in a mixture with tobacco than can hashish, which has a lumpy appearance and

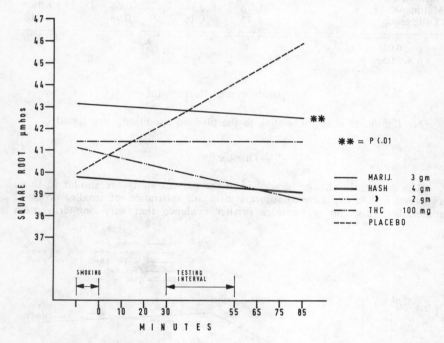

FIGURE 4. Effects of cannabis on "basal" skin conductance ($n=20$).

therefore cannot be easily distributed. This difference in appearance may have influenced the intake of cannabis during smoking. Furthermore, the cannabinol and cannabidiol contents of hashish are higher in comparison to those in marijuana and pure THC (TABLE 1), and Karniol et al.[22] have shown that cannabidiol interferes with the effects of THC on pulse rate.

Plethysmography results show a diminution in finger blood flow 20–30 min after smoking. This finding appears to be at variance with the result of Beaconsfield et al.,[17] who found increased blood flow after cannabis administration. These authors, however, used small amounts of cannabis in naive subjects. The absence of blood flow changes after cannabis reported by others [16] may also be explained by the low doses of materials used. A 2-g dose of hashish, which caused the least significant effects in this experiment, produced insignificant changes.

Our results show a small but significant dilatation of pupil size. This effect persists for 75 min after smoking and is evident only with large doses of materials. Older reports described a dilatating effect of cannabis on the pupil.[10, 11, 23] These reports, however, were noncontrolled descriptions of case histories. Recent systematic and controlled investigations of the effects of cannabis on pupil size, except for animal studies,[24] failed to demonstrate pupillary changes.[12-14] Small doses of cannabis were used in these older experiments, and the light conditions were not specified. We have measured the pupil under bright illumination and after administration of relatively high doses. We may therefore conclude that small pupillary dilatation occurs under bright illumination after administration of large doses of cannabis in long-term users.

"Basal" skin conductance showed a significant decrease in relation to the placebo condition. This finding is in agreement with those of Low *et al.*,[19] who found a significant decrease in baseline GSR activity after cannabis administration. This finding suggests an effect of cannabis on the level of arousal. Other authors have pointed out that cannabis effects may be related to impairment of vigilance.[25]

No changes were observed in GSR responses to shock. Similar findings have been reported by Rickles *et al.* after administration of moderate doses of marijuana.[20] Finally, there were no changes in respiration rate and temperature in our long-term users. These results concur with those obtained in other studies of less experienced cannabis users.[8, 12, 13]

REFERENCES

1. KIPLINGER, G. F., J. E. MANNO, B. E. RODA & R. B. FORNEY. 1971. Dose-response analysis of the effects of tetrahydrocannabinol in man. Clin. Pharmacol. Ther. **12:** 650–657.
2. RENAULT, P. F., C. R. SCHUSTER, R. HEINRICH & D. X. FREEDMAN. 1971. Marihuana: standardised smoke on heart rate in humans. Science **174:** 589–591.
3. JOHNSON, S. & E. F. DOMINO. 1971. Some cardiovascular effects of marihuana smoking in normal volunteers. Clin. Pharmacol. Ther. **12:** 762–768.
4. PEREZ-REYES, M., M. A. LIPTON & M. C. TIMMONS. 1973. The clinical pharmacology of orally administered D-9-Tetrahydrocannabinol. Clin. Pharmacol. Ther. **14:** 48–55.
5. JONES, R. T. & N. BENOWITZ. 1976. The 30 day trip—clinical studies of cannabis tolerance and dependence. *In* The Pharmacology of Marihuana. M. C. Braude & S. Szara, Eds. Vol. **2:** 627–642. The Raven Press. New York, N.Y.
6. HOLLISTER, L. E., R. K. RICHARDS & H. K. GILLESPIE. 1968. Comparison of tetrahydrocannabinol and synhexyl in man. Clin. Pharmacol. Ther. **9:** 783–791.
7. WASKOW, I. E., J. E. OLSSON, C. SALZMAN, M. M. KATZ & C. CHASE. 1970. Psychological effects of tetrahydrocannabinol. Arch. Gen. Psychiat. **22:** 97–107.
8. ISBEL, H., C. W. GORODETZSKY, D. JASINSKI, U. CLAUSSEN, F. SPULAK & F. KORTE. 1967. Effects of delta 9 trans-tetrahydrocannabinol in man. Psychopharmacologia **11:** 184–188.
9. WILLIAMS, E. G., C. K. HIMMELSBACH, A. WIKLER, D. C. RUBLE & B. J. LLOYD. 1946. Studies in marihuana and pyrahexyl compound. Publ. Health Rep. **61**(29): 1059–1083.
10. ALLENTUCK, S. & K. M. BOWMAN. 1942. The psychiatric aspects of marihuana intoxication. Amer. J. Psychiat. **99:** 248–251.

11. MARCOVITZ, E. & H. J. MYERS. 1944. The marihuana addict in the army. War Med. **6:** 382–391.
12. WEIL, A. T., N. E. ZINBERG & J. M. NELSEN. 1968. Clinical and psychological effects of marihuana in man. Science **162:** 1234–1242.
13. ISBEL, H. & D. R. JASINSKI. 1969. A comparison of LSD-25 with D–9–trans-tetrahydrocannabinol (THC) and attempted cross tolerance between LSD and THC. Psychopharmacologia **14:** 115–123.
14. DOMINO, E. 1971. Neuropsychopharmacologic studies of marihuana. Some synthetic and natural THC derivatives in animal and man. Ann. N. Y. Acad. Sci. **191:** 166–191.
15. HELPER, R. S., I. M. FRANK & R. PETRUS. 1976. Ocular effects of marihuana smoking. *In* The Pharmacology of Marihuana. M. C. Braude & S. Szara, Eds. Vol. **2:** 815–824. The Raven Press. New York, N.Y.
16. RICKLES, W. H., M. J. COHEN & R. S. NEIMARK. 1973. Marihuana and physiological reactivity to stress. Paper presented at the Annual Meeting of the American Psychiatric Association in Honolulu, Hawaii, May 1973. Summary in Marihuana and Health. 4th Report to the Congress (1974).
17. BEACONSFIELD, P., J. GINSBURG & R. RAINSBURY. 1972. Marihuana smoking. Cardiovascular effects in man and possible mechanism. N. Engl. J. Med. **287:** 109–212.
18. FERNANDEZ-GUARDIOLA, A., A. SALGADO, C. M. CONTRERAS, M. CONDES, T. GONZALEZ-ESTRADA, H. SOLIS, J. M. CALVO & F. AGALA. 1976. Multiunit and polygraphic recordings of the pharmacological effects of Δ^9-tetrahydrocannabinol. *In* The Pharmacology of Marihuana. M. C. Braude & S. Szara, Eds. Vol. **1:** 335–343. The Raven Press. New York, N.Y.
19. LOW, M. D., H. KLONOFF & A. MARCUS. 1973. The neurophysiological basis of the marihuana experience. Can. Med. Ass. J. **108:** 157–165.
20. LIAKOS, A. 1969. Comparison of drug induced pupillary changes in normal and neurotic subjects. Unpublished Ph.D. Thesis. London University. London, England.
21. COHEN, J. 1968. Multiple regression as a general data-analytic system. Psychol. Bull. **70:** 426–443.
22. KARNIOL, I., I. SHIRAKAWA, N. KASINSKI, A. PREFERMAN & E. CARLINI. 1974. Cannabidiol interferes with the effects of D-9-tetrahydrocannabinol in man. Eur. J. Pharmacol. **28:** 127–177.
23. BAKER-BATES, E. T. 1935. A case of Cannabis indica intoxication. Lancet **1:** 811.
24. PERRIN, R. G. & H. KALANT. 1971. Electroencephalographic and behavioural alterations produced by D^9-tetrahydrocannabinol. Science **172:** 968–970.
25. CLARK, L. D., R. HUGHES & E. N. NAKASHIMA. 1970. Behavioural effects of marihuana. Arch. Gen. Psychiat. **23:** 193–198.

EFFECTS OF ACUTE AND CHRONIC INHALATION OF HASHISH, MARIJUANA, AND Δ9-TETRAHYDROCANNABINOL ON BRAIN ELECTRICAL ACTIVITY IN MAN: EVIDENCE FOR TISSUE TOLERANCE *

Max Fink

Department of Psychiatry
State University of New York at Stony Brook
Stony Brook, New York 11794

INTRODUCTION

Cannabis and its many derivatives and products contain psychoactive substances of high potency and rapid onset. The widespread effects, which involve cerebral, cardiovascular, pulmonary, and neuroregulatory systems, may be seen on inhalation of burned material, on ingestion, and after intravenous administration of purified extracts and synthetic analogs. Two types of questions arise with regard to the cerebral effects.

What are the effects of cannabis substances on brain functions? What are their durations and pharmacodynamics? How do these drugs relate to other psychoactive substances in activity and potency?

Is repeated use of cannabis substances associated with deleterious cerebral effects? The question becomes popularly stated, "Does marijuana use cause brain damage?"

The effects on brain function are readily studied. In addition to examining changes in behavior, language, and psychologic tests, which provide indirect measures of brain functions, the changes in the scalp-recorded electroencephalogram in the alert (waking) state, in response to sensory stimuli, and during sleep, are direct indices of brain effects. Our focus in this report is on the changes in brain electrical activity.

Few studies of cannabis and brain electrical activity prior to 1970 are definitive, because the quality of the cannabis available for research was poor, and controls for duration and rate of inhalation were lacking. Also, the electroencephalographic (EEG) recording and analytic techniques were nonquantitative. The legal proscription of studies and the difficulties in obtaining permission to obtain and hold drug supplies also severely handicapped these studies.

In the earliest EEG reports, marijuana was compared to synhexyl compound in volunteer postaddicts.[32, 33] Wikler *et al.* described decreases in EEG α activity and an increase in the fast frequencies. The EEG changes were seen for 4–6 days and were no longer apparent in drug trials up to 39 days. Similar changes were reported by Ames, who administered single oral doses of cannabis sativa extract.[2]

Rodin *et al.* reported a slowing of the center frequency from 11 to 9–11 Hz in 10 volunteers who smoked marijuana until they achieved their usual "high." [21]

* Supported in part by Grants MH-13358 and 18172 to New York Medical College and Grant HSM 42-70-98 from the National Institute of Mental Health to the International Association of Psychiatric Research, Inc.

The EEG frequency change was carefully quantified by power density spectral analysis. Jones and Stone,[15] Hollister et al.,[14] Deniker et al.,[7] and Seyfeddini-pur,[24] however, failed to find consistent EEG changes in volunteers after oral administration of marijuana or Δ^9-tetrahydrocannabinol (Δ^9-THC) in similar studies. Hollister et al. reported increases in α activity, increased synchronization, and occasional paroxysmal activity, which they ascribed to relaxation and the setting and not to a drug effect.[14]

Single high doses of marijuana (0.7–1.0 mg/kg) in naive volunteers elicited severe toxic reactions, including ataxia, hypersomnia, increased deep tendon reflexes, tremor, and myoclonus. In the EEG, Tassinari et al.[29] reported increases in α amplitudes, a reduced reactivity to eye opening, and no change in fast activity when subjects were not grossly toxic.

There have been few studies of chronic cannabis use. Miras presented sample records from chronic hashish users in Greece.[19a] The records exhibited increased slowing and decreased fast activity, presumably related to hashish smoking. Deliyannakis et al. reported increased α activity in three, decreased slowing in three, and α blocking and desynchronization in 11 of their 25 chronic hashish users.[6a] They ascribed these effects to smoking hashish and not to tobacco and compared the changes to those reported after use of D-lysergic acid diethylamide (LSD) and mescaline.

Some authors have studied the effects of cannabis on the sleep EEG and in response to sensory stimulation. Barratt et al. observed the effects of daily smoking of marijuana (0.2 mg/kg) by experienced marijuana users.[3] They reported slow-wave sleep to increase during the first four nights and then to progressively decrease until the amount of slow-wave sleep was below baseline, remaining depressed in the postdrug period. Jones and Benowitz[16] noted initial rapid eye movement (REM) sleep and eye movement (EM) suppression during chronic (30-day) daily oral administration of 210 mg of Δ^9-THC in volunteers, with a marked rebound of REM and EM during withdrawal. Slow-wave sleep was relatively unchanged, remaining at baseline or increasing slightly. (A more complete review of the effects of cannabis on the sleep EEG will be found in Karacan et al.[17])

Lewis et al.,[18] in a study of the effects of oral Δ^9-THC on auditory (AER) and somatosensory evoked responses (SER) in occasional and frequent marijuana users, reported increases in latency of the AER and SER but no changes in their amplitudes. Their doses were equivalent to 0.2, 0.4, and 0.6 mg/kg, and testing was performed 4 hr after ingestion. These data differ from those of Roth et al.,[22] who studied the effects on the AER of smoking marijuana (equivalent to 10 mg of Δ^9-THC), Δ^9-THC (10 mg), or a placebo in 12 male cannabis users. They found decreased amplitudes of the AER, especially immediately after inhalation of cannabis, that persisted for up to 30 min. The differences in the results may reflect differences in route, dose, and particularly time after drug intake.

Differences between cannabis and alcohol were reported in studies of the contingent negative variation (CNV) by Kopell et al.[17a] The amplitudes of the CNV were enhanced by 26 mg of Δ^9-THC (20–29 mg, orally), whereas 43 g of alcohol (27–52 g) depressed the amplitudes in normal volunteers. Braden et al.[4] failed to confirm the increase in the CNV in experienced users who smoked 9.9 mg of Δ^9-THC, but they reported that the changes in CNV were negatively correlated with self-ratings of their "high."

To answer the question whether brain damage occurs after cannabis use is more difficult, because the definition of "damage" varies with the observer. For structural damage of a neuropathologic variety, samples are unavailable, because cannabis inhalation is not associated with mortality. Some authors have examined pneumoencephalograms and have suggested that enlargement of the ventricles may reflect an effect on brain structure. Some have observed a "ganja psychosis" and interpreted this psychopathologic syndrome as evidence of brain damage,[5a, 16b] while others have "read" EEG recordings and interpreted some patterns in cannabis users as evidence of brain damage.

In using EEG measures as an index of "damage," clinical EEG recordings are subjectively categorized as "normal" or "abnormal." Miras noted that chronic hashish users exhibited extensive EEG slow-wave activity, which could reflect cerebral dysfunction.[19a] A careful review of the EEG records of 40 severe long-term hashish users and 40 matched controls from the same population studied by Miras failed to show evidence of EEG abnormality.[8] Similarly, Rubin and Comitas [23] failed to find abnormal EEG records, either in waking or sleep records, in chronic ganja users in Jamaica. Campbell [5] reviewed EEG records obtained in psychiatric consultation with 11 young psychotic patients (aged 16–22 years) who smoked cannabis and retrospectively compared these records to those of schizophrenic and neurologic patients. He reported a greater amount of recurrent sharp and θ waves and moderately slow dysrhythmia in those who had used marijuana.

Almost all of the early studies of the resting EEG after cannabis use, except those of Rodin et al.,[21] relied on visual analysis of the EEG, a technique that is usually inadequate to measure the subtle dose-related effects of cannabis. To amplify these observations, my associates and I undertook two related programs. At New York Medical College, the EEG effects of marijuana, Δ^9-THC, and hashish were studied in young male volunteers who were occasional users of cannabis for at least 2 years.[8, 13, 30, 31] At the University of Athens, similar studies were performed in long-term chronic high-dose hashish users.[26, 27]

MATERIALS AND METHODS

Volunteers in New York were young male college and medical students who admitted to the social use of marijuana for at least 1 year at a frequency of once weekly. Subjects were free from mental illness and exhibited a normal resting EEG with at least 50% α activity. Marijuana, Δ^9-THC, and a marijuana placebo were obtained from the National Institute of Mental Health. The hashish was supplied by Dr. C. Miras of the University of Athens and was assayed for THC and other cannabinoids by the National Institute of Mental Health. Cigarettes were freshly prepared for each experiment, smoking rate was controlled, and each study followed a systematic design with controls of placebo (extracted marijuana leaf).

The EEG was recorded with eyes closed under laboratory conditions, with subjects maintaining alertness by continuous performance tasks, eye openings, and inquiries every 5 min. The EEG was recorded on paper and on FM magnetic tape and was analyzed by digital computer programs with an IBM 1800. Programs were based on period analysis, power density spectral analysis, and amplitude integration. The EEG was sampled at 320 sps, filtered at 1.1–35 Hz, with epoch lengths of 10–20 sec. Statistical processing was based on quadratic regression analysis or stepwise linear regression analysis.[12, 13a, 25, 30]

In the studies in Athens, the subjects were chronic hashish users between the ages of 26 and 58, with an average reported use of hashish of 23 years, and a recent daily use of 3.3 g of hashish/day. At the rated content of hashish, the amount smoked was equivalent to 100–200 mg of Δ^9-THC. EEG data were collected on FM magnetic tape under controlled laboratory conditions, and the tapes were processed in New York by means of computer programs identical to those used for the United States' subjects.[8, 13a]

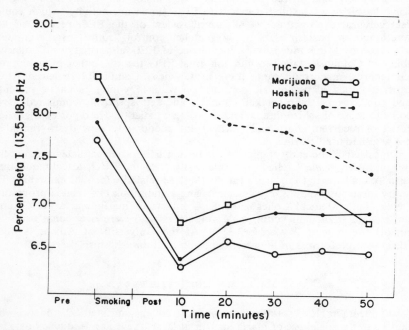

FIGURE 1. Decreased EEG β activity after inhalation of cannabis ($\cong$ 20 mg of Δ^9-THC).[30]

OBSERVATIONS

Occasional Users

During smoking, and increasing to a peak about 10 min after smoking onset, there are well-defined changes in brain electrical activity. There is an increase in EEG α activity, a decrease in β activities, and no changes in θ/δ activities or amplitudes. The average α frequency decreases by 0.15–0.20 Hz, a change that is associated with a decrease in the 11–12-Hz activity and an increase in the 9–10-Hz activity (FIGURES 1 & 2). These EEG changes are accompanied by sharp increases in heart rate (FIGURE 3).[30, 31]

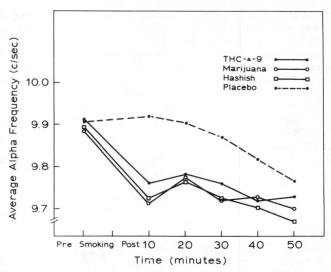

FIGURE 2. Decrease in average EEG α frequency after inhalation of cannabis ($\cong$ 20 mg of Δ^9-THC).[30]

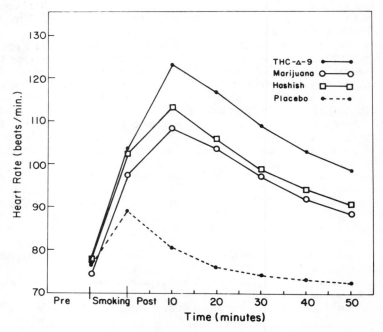

FIGURE 3. Increase in heart rate with inhalation of cannabis ($\cong$ 20 mg of Δ^9-THC).[30]

These changes are dose related within the range of 7.5–22.5 mg of Δ^9-THC and are found with all cannabis preparations. The intensity and duration of the EEG change vary with the dose. The EEG measures return to baseline within 20–30 min for the 7.5-mg dose but persist for at least 50 min, and occasionally up to 2 hr, after inhalation for 20 and 22.5 mg of Δ^9-THC.

Samples of marijuana, Δ^9-THC impregnated on extracted marijuana, and hashish equated for amounts of Δ^9-THC show an equivalence in their effects on EEG measures. In one study, however, there was a shorter duration for the effects of hashish, as if the dose were lower than that estimated from its Δ^9-THC content.[28]

A dose-dependent increase in heart rate and in the degree of mood change (known euphemistically as the "high") is observed. In the statistical analyses of one study, EEG, mood, and heart rate were found to be dependent on drug dosage and not on each other.[28]

Chronic Users

These acute studies were performed in young United States' volunteers whose use of cannabis could best be described as "occasional," "social," or "moderate." Similar acute administration studies were undertaken in long-term hashish users, who were older and whose use of cannabis could best be described as "chronic" and "heavy." † In the initial acute administration studies, there was little effect after the inhalation of doses of Δ^9-THC below 80–100 mg (or of equivalent marijuana or hashish). At these and higher doses, the subjects reported changes in mood and physiologic measures similar to the effects of the 10–22.5-mg doses in the United States' occasional users.

In a systematic crossover study, 20 chronic hashish users inhaled 2 and 4 g of hashish (90 and 180 mg of Δ^9-THC), 3 g of marijuana (78 mg), and 3 g of a placebo with 100 mg of Δ^9-THC infused or without infusion. After smoking, the EEG α activity increased, β activities decreased, and the mean EEG frequency decreased. These effects were dose dependent, with greater effects for hashish (4 g) and marijuana (3 g) than for hashish (2 g) or Δ^9-THC extract. Accompanying these EEG changes were dose-related increases in heart rate, changes in mood ("mastura"), and in the price (drachma) the subjects were willing to pay for the experience. The drug effects persisted for at least 75–90 min after inhalation.

Two studies of the effects of daily inhalation of cannabis were done.[8, 31] In one study, four postheroin users between 21 and 39 years of age smoked marijuana twice daily for 22 days. Each marijuana cigarette contained 6.5 mg of Δ^9-THC and was smoked in 40 min. During the initial days, postsmoking euphoria was present. Dysphoria appeared during the third to the sixth days and persisted, so that the two subjects withdrew after 10 and 17 days. The EEG records (on visual assessment only) showed increased synchronization of frequencies, with increased amplitudes and slowing of α activity. In one subject, who exhibited θ/δ activity before cannabis administration, the records showed distinct paroxysmal discharges.[31]

In a second experiment, six medical student volunteers who were occasional

---

† For characteristics of this population, see reports by Stefanis et al.,[27a] Liakos et al.,[18a] and Boulougouris et al.[3a, 3b]

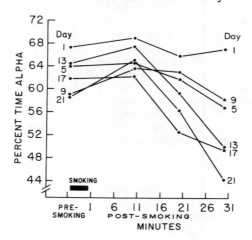

FIGURE 4. Progressive changes in EEG α activity with daily administration of inhaled cannabis for 21 days in volunteers. Progressive change in degree of post-smoking α activity after repeated administration.[9]

cannabis users smoked cigarettes that contained 1 g of marijuana (equivalent to 14 mg of Δ^9-THC) in 21 daily sessions. EEGs were recorded before smoking and continuously for 30 min after smoking. Heart rate increased after each smoking of marijuana, but the amount of increase was progressively less with each week's smoking (FIGURE 4). The EEG showed increased α activity and decreased β activity immediately after smoking. Initially, the α enhancement persisted for 20–30 min, but by the second and third weeks, the postsmoking record showed lesser amounts of α activity and greater amounts of θ activity (FIGURE 5).[9]

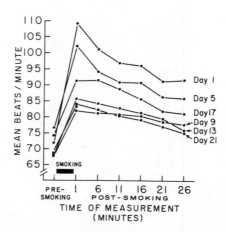

FIGURE 5. Progressive decrease in the degree of heart rate increase with smoking cannabis for 21 days by volunteers ($n = 5$).[9]

In examining the group of long-term hashish users in Greece, special attention was paid to tests of brain damage. Users and controls were examined in an extensive neurologic, neuropsychologic, and electrophysiologic test battery.[26] The clinical EEG records of 46 users and 40 matched controls were examined independently by four qualified neurologist-electroencephalographers. In hashish smokers, records were taken at least 3 hr after smoking. As reflected in TABLE 1, there were no differences in the incidence of abnormal EEG records in users and controls.[26] This finding was corroborated by the absence of significant differences in neurologic examinations and in echoencephalograms and by the absence of the diagnosis of organic psychosis (organic dementia) among the users.[27]

DISCUSSION

The inhalation of burned cannabis substances has rapid and sustained effects on brain functions, characterized for the alert EEG by enhanced α activity and a slowing of the mean frequency. The changes are dose dependent; higher doses

TABLE 1

EEG CLASSIFICATION

	Hashish Users ($n=46$)	%	Controls ($n=40$)	%
Normal	16	34.7	13	32.5
Within normal limits	20	43.5	15	37.5
Borderline	6	13	6	15
Abnormal	4	8.8	6	15

show a greater degree of change and for a longer period after smoking. Chronic users show the same changes as occasional users, but the quantity of Δ^9-THC necessary to elicit the cerebral, some of the behavioral, and the heart rate effects is significantly increased, clearly indicating the development of physiologic tolerance to cannabis on long-term use. Tolerance is rapidly developed, as demonstrated by the EEG and heart rate measures in the 21-day daily administration study in occasional users. The changes in EEG and heart rate with ingested cannabis are similar to those seen after smoking.[16]

The degree of the cerebral effect of a cannabis preparation is related to the Δ^9-THC content, the frequency of use by the subject, and time of measurement in relation to smoking. The EEG effects are short-lived at social doses, but with higher doses, the effects on physiologic indices may persist up to at least 4 hr. These factors alone provide reasonable explanations for the differences reported in the studies cited in the INTRODUCTION.

For more than a decade, the effects of compounds on the alert human EEG have provided an independent method of classifying psychoactive drugs.[11, 12] Cannabis substances are clearly distinguishable from sympathomimetic stimulants and hallucinogens, deliriants, thymoleptics, anxiolytics, and antipsychotic drugs. The effects are similar to those seen with low doses of alcohol and monoamine oxidase inhibitors on chronic administration. This classification of cannabis suggests that clinical trials in depressed patients should be considered, particularly if the high oral doses (to 210 mg/day) reported by Jones and Benowitz are to be used.[16] This suggestion differs from that made by Ablon and Goodwin,[1] who found a high incidence of dysphoric reaction with cannabis in hospitalized patients with unipolar depressive illness. The effects were mainly seen with the first doses, and factors of dosage, set, and expectation may be relevant.

The observations that Greek chronic hashish users smoked more than 100 mg of Δ^9-THC without the toxicity reported by Tassinari et al.[29] or by others who used lower doses indicated clearly that tolerance developed in these subjects.[26] The decrease in heart rate and in the EEG α response in our acute 21-day inhalation studies also suggests tolerance development. Cohen,[6] Jones et al.,[16a] and Mendelson et al.[19] each report a reduction in response in behavioral, cardiovascular, and electrophysiologic measures on repeated smoking or ingestion of cannabis substances in United States' volunteers who received daily dosages for 21–94 days. Those observations, and our own, are compelling evidence in man that tolerance develops rapidly if exposure is repeated and persistent for at least 7–21 days. Even the recent negative reports may be interpreted in the light of these experiences. Stillman et al.[28] failed to observe tolerance in volunteers who smoked 7.5 mg of Δ^9-THC in a marijuana cigarette when sessions were held twice weekly, and Perez-Reyes et al.[20] failed to observe tolerance in groups of frequent and infrequent marijuana users who received intravenous infusions of Δ^9-THC. The number and frequency of the doses in these studies were too low for the development of a degree of tolerance measurable by their tests.

"Reverse tolerance," the increased responsivity to smaller doses of cannabis on repeated administration, has been reported, particularly in the popular and anecdotal literature. In our experiments, by use of doses that elicit measurable physiologic effects (>5 mg of Δ^9-THC equivalent), we have not observed this increased sensitivity to cannabis and believe that the reports of such findings may represent the effects of expectation and setting in users who received insignificant amounts of centrally active material.

These studies provide direct evidence that cannabis inhalation affects brain function. For further localization of the site of action, the evidence from animal data suggests that these substances exert their action on limbic structures, particularly the hippocampus, which may be involved in memory and recall functions. In their review, Drew and Miller[9] cite studies to support this view and then go on to assert that the effects may be of an anticholinergic nature. In human material, anticholinergic drugs exert characteristic changes in the alert EEG: decreased α abundance and increased θ and β frequencies.[10] These changes are distinguishable from the EEG effects of cannabis preparations. Further support for the anticholinergic hypothesis will have to come from more systematic human studies than those that are cited in their report.

We also find that chronic hashish users respond to inhaled cannabis in the same ways as new users, albeit with evidence of tolerance, requiring higher dosages for equivalent drug effects. Further, the comparison of resting EEG patterns between chronic users and controls shows no evidence of chronic brain damage, a finding that is consistent with the neurologic and psychopathologic data in these men. From these observations, we can conclude that cannabis is a potent psychoactive substance, with well-defined cerebral pathophysiologic effects. These effects bear a time course that parallels the behavioral, psychologic, and other physiologic measures. Cerebral adaptation to repeated intoxication is rapid, and tolerance does occur. "Brain damage," as ordinarily defined in anatomic, pathologic, or psychopathologic terms, has not been defined in these studies, and the type and incidence of such damage will have to await more extensive population sample studies and more refined techniques.

SUMMARY

An EEG profile for cannabis preparations equated for Δ^9-THC activity has been defined in occasional cannabis users in New York and in long-term, high-dose hashish users in Athens. The EEG effects of enhanced α activity, decreased β activity, and decreased mean frequency are dose dependent, both in intensity and in duration. The behavioral measures, particularly self-ratings of euphoria ("high" or "mastura") and heart rate, are also dose dependent and interrelated with the EEG measures.

Tolerance to the cerebral, heart rate, and behavioral effects of repeated inhalations of Δ^9-THC are demonstrable in chronic users and also in short-term (21-day) experimental administration studies.

Δ^9-THC and cannabis preparations are distinguishable from opiates, hallucinogens, and deliriants by their EEG effects.

No differences in incidence of abnormal EEG records were found between long-term heavy hashish users and controls. Taken in conjunction with the neurologic, echo-EEG, and psychopathologic data in these men, we failed to define a syndrome of persistent brain damage as a result of hashish use, although persistent adaptational changes are noted in the development of tissue tolerance.

ACKNOWLEDGMENTS

I am indebted to Drs. R. Dornbush, P. Crown, J. Volavka, C. P. Panayiotopoulos, and C. Stefanis for their collaboration in the studies at New York Medical College and the University of Athens.

REFERENCES

1. ABLON, S. & F. K. GOODWIN. 1974. High frequency of dysphoric reactions to tetrahydrocannabinol in depressed patients. Amer. J. Psychiat. **131**: 448–453.
2. AMES, F. 1958. A clinical and metabolic study of acute intoxication with cannabis sativa and its role in the model psychoses. J. Mental Sci. **104**: 972–999.
3. BARRATT, E. S., W. BEAVER & R. WHITE. 1974. The effects of marijuana on human sleep patterns. Biol. Psychiat. **8**: 47–54.
3a. BOULOUGOURIS, J. C., A. LIAKOS & C. STEFANIS. This monograph.
3b. BOULOUGOURIS, J. C., C. P. PANAYIOTOPOULOS, E. ANTYPAS, A. LIAKOS & C. STEFANIS. This monograph.
4. BRADEN, W., R. C. STILLMAN & R. J. WYATT. 1974. Effects of marijuana on contingent negative variation and reaction time. Arch. Gen. Psychiat. **31**: 537–543.
5. CAMPBELL, D. R. 1971. The electroencephalogram in cannabis associated psychoses. Can. Psychiat. Ass. J. **16**: 161–165.

5a. CHOPRA, G. S. & B. S. JANDU. This monograph.

6. COHEN, S. This monograph.

6a. DELIYANNAKIS, E., C. PANAGOPOULOS & A. D. HUOTT. 1970. The influence of hashish on the human EEG. Clin. Electroencephalogr. **1:** 128–140.

7. DENIKER, P., J. R. BOISSIER, P. ETEVENON, D. GINESTET, P. PERON-MAGNAN & G. VERDEAUX. 1974. Etude de pharmacologie clinique du delta 9 tétra-hydrocannabinol chez des sujets volontaires sains avec contrôle polygraphique. Therapie **29:** 185–200.

8. DORNBUSH, R., G. CLARE, A. ZAKS, P. CROWN, J. VOLAVKA & M. FINK. 1972. 21-Day administration of marijuana in male volunteers. *In* Current Research in Marijuana. M. F. Lewis, Ed. : 115–128. Academic Press, Inc. New York, N.Y.

9. DREW, W. G. & L. L. MILLER. 1974. Cannabis: neural mechanisms and behavior —a theoretical review. Pharmacology **11:** 12–32.

10. FINK, M. 1958. Effect of anticholinergic compounds on post-convulsive electroencephalogram and behavior of psychiatric patients. Electroencephalogr. Clin. Neurophysiol. **12:** 359–369.

11. FINK, M. 1969. EEG and human psychopharmacology. Annu. Rev. Pharmacol. **9:** 241–258.

12. FINK, M. 1974. EEG profiles and bioavailability measures of psychoactive drugs. *In* Psychotropic Drugs and the Human EEG. T. Itil, Ed. : 76–98. S. Karger. Basel, Switzerland.

13. FINK, M., J. VOLAVKA, R. DORNBUSH & P. CROWN. 1973. Effects of cannabis on human EEG and heart rate—evidence of tolerance development on chronic use. *In* Psychopharmacology, Sexual Disorders and Drug Abuse. T. A. Ban, J. R. Boissier & C. J. Gessa, Eds. : 703–704. North-Holland. Amsterdam, The Netherlands.

13a. FINK, M., J. VOLAVKA, C. P. PANAYIOTOPOULOS & C. STEFANIS. 1976. Quantitative EEG studies of marijuana, Δ^9-tetrahydrocannabinol, and hashish in man. *In* The Pharmacology of Marihuana. M. C. Braude & S. Szara, Eds. Vol. **2:** 383–391. The Raven Press. New York, N.Y.

14. HOLLISTER, L., S. SHERWOOD & A. CAVASINO. 1970. Marijuana and the human electroencephalogram. Pharmacol. Res. Commun. **2:** 305–308.

15. JONES, R. & G. STONE. 1970. Psychological studies of marijuana and alcohol in man. Psychopharmacologia **18:** 108–117.

16. JONES, R. & N. BENOWITZ. 1976. The 30-day trip: clinical studies of cannabis tolerance and dependence. *In* The Pharmacology of Marihuana. M. C. Braude & S. Szara, Eds. Vol. **2:** 627–642. The Raven Press. New York, N.Y.

16a. JONES, R. T., N. BENOWITZ & J. BACHMAN. This monograph.

16b. KNIGHT, F. This monograph.

17. KARACAN, I., A. FERNÁNDEZ-SALAS, W. J. COGGINS, W. E. CARTER, R. L. WILLIAMS, J. I. THORNBY, P. J. SALIS, M. OKAWA & J. P. VILLAUME. This monograph.

17a. KOPELL, B. S., J. R. TINKLENBERG & L. HOLLISTER. 1972. Contingent negative variation amplitudes. Arch. Gen. Psychiat. **27:** 809–811.

18. LEWIS, E. G., R. E. DUSTMAN, B. A. PETERS, R. C. STRAIGHT & E. C. BECK. 1973. The effects of varying doses of Δ^9-tetrahydrocannabinol on the human visual and somatosensory evoked response. Electroencephalogr. Clin. Neurophysiol. **35:** 347–354.

18a. LIAKOS, A., J. C. BOULOUGOURIS & C. STEFANIS. This monograph.

19. MENDELSON, J. H., T. F. BABOR, J. C. KUEHNLE, A. M. ROSSI, J. G. BERNSTEIN, N. K. MELLO & I. GREENBERG. This monograph.

19a. MIRAS, C. J. 1969. Experience with chronic hashish smokers. *In* Drugs and Youth. R. Wittenborn, H. Brill, J. P. Smith & S. A. Wittenborn, Eds. Charles C Thomas. Springfield, Ill.

20. PEREZ-REYES, M., M. C. TIMMONS & M. E. WALL. 1974. Long-term use of

marihuana and the development of tolerance or sensitivity to Δ^9-tetrahydro-cannabinol. Arch. Gen. Psychiat. **31:** 89–91.

21. RODIN, E. A., E. L. F. DOMINO & J. P. PORZAK. 1970. The marijuana-induced "social high." J. Amer. Med. Ass. **213:** 1300–1302.

22. ROTH, W. T., M. GALANTER, H. WEINGARTNER, T. B. VAUGHAN & R. J. WYATT. 1973. Marijuana and synthetic Δ-trans-tetrahydrocannabinol: some effects on the auditory evoked response and background EEG in humans. Biol. Psychiat. **6:** 221–234.

23. RUBIN, V. & L. COMITAS. 1975. Ganja in Jamaica. Mouton, The Hague, Paris.

24. SEYFEDDINIPUR, N. 1975. Klinische und elektroenzephalographische Beobach-tungen bei akuter Haschisch-Wirkung. Muench. Med. Wochschr. **117:** 447–482.

25. SHAPIRO, D. M. & M. GLASSER. 1974. Measurement and comparison of EEG-drug effects. *In* Psychotropic Drugs and the Human EEG. T. Itil, Ed. : 327–349. S. Karger. Basel, Switzerland.

26. STEFANIS, C., R. DORNBUSH & M. FINK. 1976. Hashish! A Study of Long-Term Use. The Raven Press. New York, N.Y. In press.

27. STEFANIS, C., A. LIAKOS, J. BOULOUGOURIS, M. FINK & A. M. FREEDMAN. 1976. Chronic hashish use and mental disorder. Amer. J. Psychiat. **133:** 225–227.

27a. STEFANIS, A., A. LIAKOS & J. C. BOULOUGOURIS. This monograph (first paper).

28. STILLMAN, R. C., H. WEINGARTNER, R. J. WYATT, J. C. GILLIN & J. EICH. 1974. State-dependent (dissociative) effects of marihuana on human memory. Arch. Gen. Psychiat. **31:** 81–85.

29. TASSINARI, C. A., M. R. PERAITA-ADRADOS, G. AMBROSETTO & H. GASTAUT. 1974. Effects of marijuana and Δ9-THC at high doses in man. Electroencephalogr. Clin. Neurophysiol. **36:** 94.

30. VOLAVKA, J., P. CROWN, R. DORNBUSH, S. FELDSTEIN & M. FINK. 1973. EEG heart rate and mood change ("high") after cannabis. Psychopharmacologia **32:** 11–25.

31. VOLAVKA, J., R. DORNBUSH, S. FELDSTEIN, G. CLARE, A. ZAKS, M. FINK & A. M. FREEDMAN. 1971. Marijuana, EEG and behavior. Ann. N.Y. Acad. Sci. **191:** 206–215.

32. WIKLER, A. & B. J. LLOYD. 1945. Effect of smoking marijuana cigarettes on cortical electrical activity. Fed. Proc. **4:** 141, 142.

33. WILLIAMS, E. G., C. K. HIMMELSBACH, A. WIKLER, D. C. RUBLE & B. J. LLOYD. 1946. Studies on marijuana and pyrahexyl compound. Public Health Rep. **61:** 1059–1083.

GENERAL DISCUSSION

Stephen I. Szára, *Moderator*

Biomedical Research Branch
National Institute on Drug Abuse
Rockville, Maryland 20852

DR. SZÁRA: I would like to start out with a statement and a question. With the papers presented today, we should keep in mind that the Costa Rican study reported by Dr. Karacan took place in a naturalistic setting and examined chronic heavy marijuana users, without administration of cannabis, except that which the subjects took on their own outside the laboratory. On the other hand, in the Greek study, not only did the researchers study chronic heavy hashish users, but they also administered various strengths and varieties of cannabis preparations to the chronic users; they compared their observations with the reactions of moderate users in a New York study. In the Jamaican study, the major emphasis was on the mental status and the psychologic and physiologic reactions of chronic marijuana users. In the latter study, however, there was no acute administration of the drug.

Drs. Fink and Liakos, you have shown that the effect of acute administration of cannabis is, in some cases, identical in chronic users and normals and that there was some variability. With regard to Campbell's data obtained in 1971 concerning brain damage in cannabis users, have you tried to identify potential brain dysfunction that may be associated with chronic heavy cannabis use but that may not be apparent during the immediate influence of the drug?

DR. M. FINK: Dr. Szára, part of our data will be presented later this week in the medical review, but, effectively, both the users and their controls underwent neurologic examinations and EEG recordings of various kinds. In the two populations, we could not find gross neurologic deficits that could not be ascribed to incidental events. There was one user with evidence of brain damage, but he had been involved in a motorcycle accident one year before in which he suffered a concussion and was hospitalized. We believed that there was a more direct relationship between that trauma and his neurologic status than between the trauma and his use of drugs. Our EEG studies were performed very carefully, largely because the EEG was a principal tool for our studies in Athens. In 1969, Professor Miras of Athens had presented EEG data in this country that were suggestive of brain damage. In the present study, the resting EEG, a very good index of brain damage, was perfectly normal in users and controls. Psychologic tests were also done and will be reported this afternoon. An echo EEG was also done to assess brain damage in a sample of users and of the control population. The echo EEG is a more recent method, and we are not sure how sensitive it is for brain damage, but the echo EEG findings between the two populations were not significantly different. On each of these criteria, on medical, psychologic, neurologic, EEG, and echo EEG findings, there was no evidence of a prolonged brain damage effect. One criticism could be that the users were selected from those who were functioning in the community, that is, those users with brain damage after many years of hashish use, who were in mental hospitals or had died, or were no longer available for other reasons. That is an objection that is difficult to answer. But, as Dr. Stefanis will demonstrate, this study was based on an extensive survey of the population, and the sample selected is characteristic of the sample of hashish users in Greece defined by other criteria. For these reasons, we came to the conclusion that there is no evidence of brain damage in the long-term user. In addition, in the acute administration studies of hashish, THC, and marijuana, neurologic, psychologic, and behavioral assessments were made, and these long-term users performed, acted, and reacted in the same way as did our New York population of non-chronic users.

DR. SZÁRA: Dr. Fink, you mentioned that the clinical EEG was not abnormal and that you obtained practically identical EEG responses in chronic heavy users and nonusers. We know from the literature that chronic heavy alcohol use does produce changes in brain function that are reflected by neuropsychologic tests, but apparently the EEG is not always sensitive enough to detect brain damage that was clearly shown in neuropsychologic tests.

DR. FINK: The sensitivity of the EEG has been a question for 40 years, since electroencephalography in man was first described in 1929. Early workers were very enthusiastic about the EEG, claiming that it could classify mental illness. The early style of classification was purely visual and descriptive, visual meaning that the reader examined the record. This method led to disappointment, and that disappointment persists even today among many workers who claim that the EEG is an inadequate tool. However, beginning with the conference in 1961 at UCLA on quantitative EEG analysis (only 14 years ago), there has been an explosive development of quantitative applications of the EEG. Such techniques as power spectral analyses, averaged evoked response, contingent negative variation, and sleep EEG are examples. With quantitative EEG methods, it is possible to find subtle and small differences in the EEG. I think the study of cannabis is a good example, for here we can see the differences between modern methods and older descriptions. Alcohol effects are greater than those of cannabis and should be much easier to describe. Chronic alcoholic patients uniformly have gross EEG changes. A fine example are the studies by Romano and Engel (published in 1937 and 1939), who found that chronic alcoholics have EEG changes that parallel their delirium and psychosis. They used one of the first frequency analyzers for their measurements. If one measures changes in frequency, amplitude, and variability patterns, differences due to drugs become clear. At present, few alcohol studies have used quantitative EEG methods, and that is why you seem disappointed.

DR. I. KARACAN: The effect on sleep of the chronic alcoholic is clear. Several studies have been performed, and if you look at sleep EEGs, you will find significant differences between alcoholics and controls. When chronic alcoholics stop drinking for 6 months, disturbances remain. This is also true for morphine addicts, who show effects in the sleep EEG up to 6 months after withdrawal. However, our data with marijuana did not show persistent effects on the sleep EEG. I think that our technique is probably sensitive enough to detect changes, but marijuana does not show these changes.

DR. FINK: Dr. Karacan, you presented the interesting findings of four observations of 25 variables studied for the effects of cannabis on sleep recordings. What other drugs act in the same way as cannabis on the sleep EEG? Also, in the hierarchy of drugs that have been studied for the treatment of the mentally ill or for effects on brain function, where does cannabis stand? Can one classify cannabis by using the sleep EEG? And can one estimate its potency?

DR. KARACAN: These questions are obviously important. There are no easy answers. What drugs show the kind of reactivity that cannabis gives after somebody has taken it for a long enough period? A barbiturate, LSD, or maybe some other drug? There are only a few studies on this subject. Sleep research, its clinical applications, and their relations to pharmacology are a new field. There are very few dose-response curves for drugs in the sleep research literature, because the methods are new. We now have, in our laboratory and in others, appropriate techniques to determine amounts of REM and non-REM sleep, α, β, and δ frequencies, K complexes, power spectral and REM density, and other measures. These parameters are difficult to quantify visually. With such techniques, we were able to show a dose response in the β-activity increase to a barbiturate. For the classification of cannabis, I do not have the answer yet; we do have data for potency, but the answer will require further study.

DR. FINK: I have just been reminded that Dr. E. Hartmann of Boston State Hospital has made a table of compounds that affect sleep, and, as I recall, only reserpine increased REM period. All other compounds reduced REM sleep. Is that not true?

DR. KARACAN: I think that Hartmann's observation with reserpine is true. I think the first observation on reserpine was made in Canada, even before sleep was studied. A patient in psychotherapy reported increased dreaming. I believe LSD also increases REM sleep, but the problem with LSD is that the dose is so critical. If one give too little LSD, REM does not change; if one gives too much, the subject becomes aroused and can't fall asleep. LSD also increases REM sleep.

DR. FINK: Would it be fair to say that opiates do not increase REM sleep?

DR. KARACAN: Yes.

DR. FINK: I think it may be important to emphasize that in the politics of cannabis, this drug is always equated with opiates in legal references. Opiates and cannabis are often joined in legal jargon. Both in the sleep studies and in the quantitative EEG studies in Athens and New York, I think it's clear that there are distinct physiologic differences between the effects of opiates and cannabis. Cannabis is a distinct pharmacologic substance that belongs to a separate physiologic or pharmacologic class.

DR. KARACAN: Dr. Fink, have you carried out studies on cannabis beyond 15 min? Have you looked at the effects after a few hours?

DR. FINK: No. In one study, we went to 4 hr, and the effects had disappeared by that time. That is a deficiency in our acute inhalation studies: we may not have extended them long enough.

DR. KARACAN: May we assume that the effects of acute smoking disappear in 4 hr?

DR. FINK: Yes.

DR. R. T. JONES: Dr. Karacan, the only way you can interpret the significance of your findings would be to know the last time your subject smoked marijuana prior to that sleep night. If you gave those data, I didn't hear them.

DR. KARACAN: The subjects came to our sleep lab about 2–3 hr before bedtime. We asked them to smoke their usual daily dose but not to smoke just before they came to the lab, because we did not want to see acute effects in a chronic smoker; we wanted to see the effects without this last smoking of ganja. As a rule, their last smoking occurred 2–3 hr before bedtime.

DR. JONES: If they smoked their last "joint" 2–3 hr before bedtime, probably the increase in REM sleep time and the delay in sleep onset represent an effect of the withdrawal of cannabis rather than of chronic use. Such results are quite consistent with those reported by Feinberg. In Feinberg's study, the subjects received their last dose prior to the withdrawal period at 4 PM. Already by that night, only 4 hr after the last oral dose, the subjects were showing increases in REM sleep time as opposed to the decreased REM that one sees during the acute period of administration. One has to distinguish between drug effects and withdrawal effects.

DR. KARACAN: In my published report, you will see that I also mentioned this point as one possibility, but I don't think it is the most likely. In our studies, when there was a withdrawal effect, REM sleep time increased, as did the latency to the first REM period. The first REM appearance from going to sleep takes about 90 min in the normal subject. During withdrawal, latency will shorten. In, our subjects, however, this latency did not decrease. In the rebound, we also expected the REM density to increase, as Feinberg reported. Unfortunately, we have not yet examined the data for these effects. I believe the latency is not shortened, so I doubt the possibility you raise. If I find the REM density to be increased, I will find your suggestion more agreeable.

DR. E. B. TRUITT, JR. (*George Washington University Medical Center, Washington, D.C.*): There is an important difference in the work of Drs. Fink and Liakos concerning the effects of THC as contrasted with those of whole marijuana or hashish. One of you had more effects with THC alone and one less, and I think it's important to establish whether THC alone is comparable to whole marijuana in these measures. Can you comment on the differences?

DR. A. LIAKOS: As I said in the discussion, our design may have affected the results for THC. Due to technical difficulties, we didn't have THC in time to rotate its administration. We had to administer it on a separate occasion at the end of the experiment. That's one possibility. The other one is that the substances used, marijuana and hashish, contained different quantities of THC and other possibly active constituents. There is some evidence that the effects of THC may be inhibited by CBN or CBD. Another possibility is that the dose-response curve may not be straight when one gives high doses. We do not know the THC dose-response curve at very high doses; it's possible that when you give a very high dose of THC, the relationship between dose and effect decreases.

DR. FINK: Dr. Truitt raised a very interesting question that has puzzled us. Our data do manifest confusion over the fact that different samples had differen amounts of CBN, CBD, and THC. We rated the samples on the basis of the Δ^9-THC, because at the time were doing this experiment, THC content seemed to be the principal parameter that we could use to compare the samples. In looking at the data, some effects were lower with high doses of hashish, which may be related to their high content of CBD.

MR. W. NELSON (*City College of The City University of New York, New York, N.Y.*): Dr. Karacan, is your contention, then, that marijuana or cannabis increases REM sleep? You offered a lot of alternative explanations, and I wasn't sure which one you were really promoting.

DR. KARACAN: Our design raises some questions, but chronic smokers compared to controls did exhibit an increase of 14–15 min per night on the average, and the increase was about 2.4%.

MR. NELSON: In 1964, Oswald measured REM sleep in chronic amphetamine addicts and found normal amounts of REM sleep that rapidly increased when the amphetamines were removed. That may be what you were seeing here also. Since you have recently surveyed the literature, did you find reports of REM sleep percentage after termination of cannabis? Is there a REM rebound, and how far has it been looked for?

DR. KARACAN: I think one of the better studies was published by Feinberg in 1975. He studied subjects for up to 3 days. On the first night, there was a significant rebound, but not on the other two nights.

MR. NELSON: Some of the earlier studies failed to find a REM rebound. Vanergy and Snyder recently reported that cannabinoids prevent reuptake of norepinephrine, a mechanism of action of the tricyclic antidepressants. In the REM sleep data from studies of the tricyclic antidepressants, the initial reports also failed to show a REM rebound. However, when the subjects were examined 2 weeks after the termination of the drug, a REM rebound was detected. Obviously, to answer the question for cannabis, subjects must be followed for a long period after termination of cannabis use.

DR. KARACAN: I agree. Another good study was performed by Kay in Kentucky, who examined morphine addicts up to 6 months but did not find a REM rebound. There are many factors that affect REM rebound, such as the organism, the time after withdrawal, and the time of drug administration. It is a very complex issue, really.

DR. M. PEREZ-REYES: I want to make a comment about the interaction of cannabidiol and Δ^9-THC. We administered cannabidiol intravenously and then administered Δ^9-THC in a crossover fashion. We found that cannabidiol administration does not change the action of Δ^9-THC. I think that Dr. Truitt referred to the studies of Karniol, who administered Δ^9-THC and cannabidiol orally. I think cannabidiol may interfere with gastrointestinal absorption of Δ^9-THC. In that sense, it might act as an antagonist when the only thing it is doing is reducing absorption. Intravenously, we found no interaction.

DR. FINK: Are you saying that there is no interaction by smoking, only after oral administration?

DR. PEREZ-REYES: Karniol demonstrated the interaction by giving oral cannabidiol with oral THC. He has not studied inhalation. I have studied the intravenous administration of these two compounds, and found no interaction.

DR. FINK: However, the question is: when cannabis is chiefly used by smoking, is there evidence for an interaction between cannabidiol and Δ^9-THC by the smoking route?

DR. PEREZ-REYES: I think intravenous administration gives a more accurate answer than oral. I think the likelihood that CBD might interfere with THC by inhalation is not too high. When you give the drugs orally, I'm sure they compete.

DR. J. R. TINKLENBERG: I find it very useful, as Dr. Fink has done, to compare the effects of cannabis with those of other psychoactive drugs about which perhaps more is known. I would like to ask two questions in that regard. First, it was mentioned that cannabis differs significantly from drugs that have central anticholinergic effects on quantitative EEG measures. Can that point be elaborated further? Second, it was mentioned that studies of people who use alcohol chronically indicate that there are significant changes, again on quantitative measures. Were those studies conducted after a sufficient period of drying-out, for example, 3–4 months, to remove the compounding effects of ongoing toxicity, rebound, and so forth?

DR. FINK: The first question is easier to answer than the second. In the cannabis studies reported here, we have examined the EEG changes under acute administration by inhalation in a large number of experiments, in a variety of subjects. The changes are quite consistent, in that α activity is consistently increased, β activity is decreased, and the mean α frequency decreased. These characteristic signs of cannabis must be contrasted with the effects of anti-cholinergic drugs. In the 1950s, atropine and scopolamine were found to have few direct effects on the central nervous system, except at very high doses. Studies of diethazine, benactyzine, and JB329 (Ditran®) followed. The latter compounds are characterized as potent anticholinergics with high penetrance in the central nervous system in animals. In EEG studies that employed a methodology similar to that used for cannabis, we found a decrease in α activity, a marked increase in the β bands, particularly in the bands from 18 to 30 Hz, and a significant increase in the θ bands, from 4 to 7 Hz. Drew and Miller, in a recent report, hypothesized that cannabis must have anticholinergic effects; as their model, they used the peripheral nervous system, where the cholinergic activity is well known. I believe that the EEG is a more direct measure of central nervous system activity, and from the cannabis data, it is clear that cannabis is not anticholinergic in the central nervous system. I think Drew and Miller will have to reexamine their data as applied to man. The question about alcoholism is unclear. A problem in the study of alcoholism is the definition of conditions, similar to the problem of cannabis. There is chronic alcohol use and its effects on brain function, measurement by EEG, psychologic tests, and so on. There is also the problem of the acute administration of alcohol, the single dose given to a new subject, or the single dose given to a chronic user.

DR. TINKLENBERG: I guess I'm focusing on the chronic alcoholic. You hospitalize him for 3–4 months and are relatively sure he's not continuing to ingest alcohol. You then use the quantitative EEG techniques, and what do you expect to find?

DR. FINK: The findings will depend almost exclusively on whether the individual has recovered from the cerebral dysfunction that he exhibited at the time of admission, when he will likely exhibit gross manifestations of cerebral dysfunction, revealed by neurologic examination, psychologic tests, personality variables, memory tests, and by the EEG, perhaps even spinal fluid changes. If one waits 4–6 months, and if the individual has recovered, the EEG will show a parallel recovery. It may show no persistent changes during recovery from chronic alcoholism. However, in cases where there is no recovery or poor recovery from chronic alcoholism, where the changes in behavior persist, these changes will be accompanied by differences on EEG tracings. Such studies are not performed very often, because the quantitative EEG is usually not made in clinical settings. When the EEG is taken, it will show effects of persistent slowing, dysrhythmia, and asymmetries. A very good study is that of Romano and Engel, who examined patients during recovery from alcoholic delirium and showed that some patients had a normal EEG at the time they left the hospital and some had an abnormal EEG, depending on the state of recovery.

EFFECTS OF DECRIMINALIZATION OF MARIJUANA IN OREGON

Paul H. Blachly

Department of Psychiatry
University of Oregon Health Sciences Center
Portland, Oregon 97201

Mariquana was not a problem in Oregon when our state legislature enacted the Uniform Narcotic Act in 1935. Indeed, there was no legislative discussion of marijuana at the time; it was simply included with narcotics as a package. Since then, the use of marijuana has expanded here, as it has elsewhere in this country. Believing that the result of the legislation that controls marijuana was counterproductive, the Oregon legislature in 1973 enacted a bill that abolished criminal penalties for simple possession of marijuana and replaced it with a maximum civil fine of $100.00. What has been the result?

With regard to evaluating marijuana legislation, we can speak of measurable parameters, such as the number of arrests, convictions, hours of police investigation, time spent in jail, and dollar cost to the taxpayers for maintaining the police-judicial-penal-probation system. We can also speak of intangible parameters, such as fear, suspicion, freedom, respect for law, interest of students in their studies, or the excitement and games in outwitting authorities. Judgment regarding the validity of legislative treatment must rest both on measurable data and on opinion regarding intangibles.

A public opinion poll commissioned by the Drug Abuse Council [1] conducted one year after the law went into effect revealed that 58% of Oregon residents favored the elimination of criminal penalties for possession of small amounts of marijuana. On the basis of their 802 personal interviews, they also found that three of every 10 people interviewed favored the new state law that made possession a civil offense, akin to a parking ticket. An additional 26% favored changes that made the sale and/or possession of small amounts legal. Nineteen percent of the respondents indicated "yes" to "had they ever used," a percentage that ranged from 46 in the 18–29-year-old group to 2% in the over 60 age group. Ten percent currently used the drug, with 40% reporting a decrease in use in the past year and only 5% reporting increased use. Only 4% of those not currently using marijuana indicated the possibility of legal prevention as a reason, and 2% stated unavailability. Lack of interest (53%) and health dangers (23%) were the primary reasons for nonuse. Replication of the poll in 1975 [2] showed little change, except that 35% of users reported decreased usage in the past year, and only 9% reported increased usage.

A study prepared by the State Office of Legislative Research one year after implementation of the new law concluded that the law removes small users or possessors from the criminal justice machinery without relaxing criminal penalties for pushers or sellers of the drug and permits the law to concentrate on other matters without precipitating major negative effects. [3] Since passage of the law, there have been no efforts to repeal it. In only one political race was the new law criticized, and that person was defeated.

To sample the opinions of those who deal most frequently with the issue of marijuana laws, I mailed an opinionnaire on October 30, 1975 to 186 persons in our police-judicial-parole system. (See copy of opinionnaire in APPENDIX I.) It was sent to all 36 district attorneys in the state of Oregon, all police chiefs in cities with a population greater than 5000, all district and circuit court judges, and to the five members of the Oregon State Parole Board. A somewhat modified opinionnaire (APPENDIX II) was sent to 157 educators, who included all principals of high schools in the state that had an attendance greater than 500 and presidents of all colleges and universities in the state.

To sample medically significant aspects of marijuana use,[4] we compared the number of admissions to Dammasch State Hospital directly due to marijuana in 1971, before the new legislation, with the number admitted for this reason in 12 months preceding the writing of this paper (November 1974 to October 1975).

You will find that the responses give not only an idea of current opinion but also, and more intriguingly, an explanation of why there is such vehement divergence of opinion on this matter.

RESULTS

The number of admissions to Dammasch State Hospital directly due to marijuana use decreased from 23 in 1970 to seven during 1975. In the same time, the number of admissions for drug abuse of all types, except alcohol, decreased from 343 to 284. Thus, the percentage of drug abuse admissions due primarily to marijuana was 6.7% in 1970 and 2.5% in 1975.

Opinionnaires were returned from 61% (113) of persons in the legal (police-judicial) system and 71% (111) of educators within 2 months. In addition to checking preferences, many volunteered comments, and several wrote detailed letters. The questionnaire could be answered anonymously, but persons were requested to indicate their name, address, and phone number if they did not feel constrained to be anonymous. Fortunately, many chose to give their name and affiliation, which helped us to compare subgroups within the legal system. The number of parole board members was too small to list separately.

Comments regarding each of the questions will be made after the results of each question rather than repeating them in DISCUSSION AND COMMENTS. TABLE 1 compares perceptions of drug problems related to marijuana versus drug problems of all kinds. The majority do not feel that the problems have decreased, but there is a wide divergence of opinion. Police (86%) feel that marijuana problems have increased, but only 24% of judges share this view. Only 9% of police feel marijuana problems have decreased, whereas 43% of judges feel they have decreased. Educators and district attorneys have an intermediate view. Police (74%) feel that drug problems of all kinds have increased, but this opinion is true of only 25% of educators. Only 13% of police and 8% of district attorneys feel that drug problems of all kinds have decreased, whereas this opinion is true of 42% of educators.

TABLE 2 samples what has happened to respect for the law and the police. None of the police felt that respect for the law had increased, but 20% of judges and 21% of educators felt that it had. Sixty-eight percent of the police felt that it had decreased, whereas only 35% of judges and 23% of educators felt that it had decreased. Five percent of the police felt that respect for the police had increased, but 60% felt that it had decreased. Fifteen percent of judges

TABLE 1

PROBLEMS FROM MARIJUANA VERSUS OTHER DRUGS

Question	n	Category	In-creased (%)	De-creased (%)	No Change (%)	Don't Know (%)
1. Problems related to						
marijuana have	112	legal, all	49	25	18	8
	23	police	86	9	5	0
		district at-				
	13	torneys	61	15	15	8
	21	judges	24	43	14	19
	110	educators	41	28	25	6
2. Drug problems of all						
kinds have	113	legal, all	60	8	24	7
	23	police	74	13	13	0
		district at-				
	13	torneys	54	8	31	8
	21	judges	52	10	29	10
	111	educators	25	42	22	11

and 19% of educators felt that such respect had increased, but only 20% of judges and 19% of educators felt that it had decreased. Judge Don Sanders volunteered:

> To answer items 3 and 4, it is necessary to understand the effect of changes in laws relating to possession of marijuana and alcoholic beverages.
> Under recent Oregon law, the maximum (and only) penalty for possession of less than an ounce of marijuana (and also for the offense of minor in pos-

TABLE 2

RESPECT FOR THE LAW AND THE POLICE

Question	n	Category	In-creased (%)	De-creased (%)	No Change (%)	Don't Know (%)
3. Respect for the						
law has	109	legal, all	9	43	35	13
	22	police	0	68	32	0
		district at-				
	12	torneys	17	25	42	17
	20	judges	20	35	30	15
	109	educators	21	23	42	14
4. Respect for the						
police has	109	legal, all	7	36	42	16
	20	police	5	60	30	5
		district at-				
	13	torneys	8	23	54	15
	20	judges	15	20	50	15
	108	educators	19	19	49	13

session of alcoholic liquors) is $100 fine. As you no doubt know, recent U.S. Supreme Court opinions provide, in substance and effect, that the detention of a juvenile in foster care, childrens' home or ranches or state institutions may not exceed the maximum time an adult could be sentenced for a like offense. There can be no quarrel with these holdings. It must also be noted that both literally, and as a practical matter juveniles cannot be fined.

It is true these offenses can be said to constitute conduct inimical to the best interest of the juvenile under ORS 419.476(a)(c). However, under the limitations literally imposed by law, no matter what label is attached to the activity, it appears the juvenile cannot be made a ward on account of this conduct. Moreover, the same conduct cannot be the basis of taking further or different action as to a juvenile already a ward of the court for other causes. It would seem to follow irrespective of whether these laws are or are not as they should be as to adults, they have made more problems than they solved in dealing with juveniles. No one more quickly learns the peculiar status juveniles occupy by reason of these laws than the juveniles themselves.

TABLE 3

PROSECUTION VERSUS CONVICTION OF MARIJUANA OFFENDERS

Question	n	Category	In-creased (%)	De-creased (%)	No Change (%)	Don't Know (%)
5. Number of persons prosecuted for marijuana of-fenses has	113	legal, all	30	54	11	4
	22	police district at-	36	50	9	5
	13	torneys	61	23	15	0
	21	judges	14	71	10	5
6. Number of persons convicted for marijuana of-fenses has	113	legal, all	32	50	14	4
	22	police district at-	45	36	9	9
	13	torneys	54	23	23	0
	21	judges	14	62	19	5

TABLE 3 compares prosecution versus conviction of marijuana offenders. Thirty-six percent of police indicated that prosecution had increased and 50% that it had decreased, whereas only 14% of judges felt that it had increased and 71% that it had decreased. Forty-five percent of police and 50% of district attorneys felt that convictions had increased, whereas only 14% of judges felt that convictions had increased. In contrast, 36% of the police felt that convictions had decreased, and 62% of judges felt that they had decreased.

TABLE 4 compares prosecution versus conviction of other drug offenders. Sixty-four percent of police felt that prosecution of other drug offenders had increased, and 55% of judges felt that it had increased. Twenty-five percent of district attorneys felt that prosecutions had decreased, as opposed to only 10% of judges. Greater consistency was seen regarding convictions of other drug offenders. Fifty percent of police, 33% of district attorneys, and 57% of judges felt that convictions had increased. Twenty-five percent of district attorneys felt that it had decreased, as opposed to 5% of the judges.

TABLE 4

PROSECUTION VERSUS CONVICTION OF OTHER DRUG OFFENDERS

Question	n	Category	In-creased (%)	De-creased (%)	No Change (%)	Don't Know (%)
7. Number of persons prosecuted for other drug offenses has	112	legal, all	55	17	25	4
	22	police district at-	64	18	14	5
	13	torneys	46	23	31	0
	20	judges	55	10	30	5
8. Number of persons convicted of other drug offenses has	111	legal, all	50	18	27	5
	22	police district at-	50	18	22	9
	13	torneys	38	23	38	0
	21	judges	57	5	33	5

TABLE 5 indicates that most educators feel that more students are involved with marijuana but that fewer are involved in other drug problems. Question 10 for legal persons attempted to sample the same opinion as question 7 to educators. Clearly, the legal persons (49%) see an increase in drug problems in the schools, whereas only 19% of educators see such an increase. Only 5% of legal persons see a decrease of drug problems in the schools, whereas 42% of educators see a decrease in disruption due to drugs.

TABLE 6 reveals that more educators see drug education as increasing, whereas legal persons tend to see it as decreasing.

TABLE 5

SCHOOL PROBLEMS RELATED TO DRUGS

Question	n	Category	In-creased (%)	De-creased (%)	No Change (%)	Don't Know (%)
5. Number of students involved in mari-juana problems has	109	educators	47	23	17	13
6. Number of students involved in other drug problems has	110	educators	29	40	15	15
10. School problems re-lated to drugs have	106	legal, all	49	5	14	32
	21	police district at-	76	14	5	5
	13	torneys	46	0	23	30
	21	judges	38	5	14	43
7. Amount of school disruption related to drug problems has	108	educators	19	42	36	3

TABLE 6

DRUG EDUCATION

Question	n	Category	In-creased (%)	De-creased (%)	No Change (%)	Don't Know (%)
8. & 11. Interest and ef-	110	legal, all	25	31	23	21
forts at drug	22	police	32	36	32	0
education		district at-				
have	12	torneys	17	58	17	8
	20	judges	30	10	15	45
	107	educators	40	19	36	5

TABLE 7 suggests that police do not see themselves doing any less work in drug cases than in the past, whereas district attorneys think police are putting in less effort on drug cases.

The same questions regarding current and future legislation regarding marijuana were asked of legal-police persons and educators. TABLE 8 shows that to the statement "we should return to the former law regarding marijuana __ __ __," a "no" was given by 29% of police, 58% of educators, 62% of district attorneys, and 72% of judges.

"We should liberalize the law further, but not make marijuana legal . . ." was answered "no" by 100% of police, 83% of educators, 75% of district attorneys, and 69% of judges, with an additional 13% of judges undecided.

To the proposition "we should tax, control, and sell marijuana like we do alcohol and cigarettes," "no" was checked by 90% of police, 77% of educators, 61% of district attorneys, and 53% of judges. Interestingly, 23% of judges said "yes," and an additional 24% indicated "no opinion." The comments of Judge Edwin Allen help us to understand the considerations reflected in the divergence of opinion:

> I am of the opinion that the change in Oregon's marijuana laws has made a complete farce out of certain aspects of the criminal justice system. For example, the possession of three-fourths of an ounce of marijuana subjects an individual to a $100.00 fine. Possession of one and one-half ounces of marijuana subjects a person to a possible sentence of ten years' imprisonment and

TABLE 7

POLICE EFFORT SPENT ON DRUG CASES

Question	n	Category	In-creased (%)	De-creased (%)	No Change (%)	Don't Know (%)
9. The proportion of	110	legal, all	27	29	22	22
police effort spent	21	police	38	29	33	0
on drug cases has		district at-				
	13	torneys	23	54	15	8
	18	judges	17	25	19	39

a fine of $2,500.00. Also, cultivation, transportation and furnishing of the original three-fourths of an ounce mentioned above, subjects a person to the same penalties as would sale of the one and one-half ounces. I am completely at a loss as to how the foregoing is supported by any logic.

I have been advised by law enforcement officials that, in regard to small amounts of marijuana, if that is the only contraband taken in a search, then no action whatsoever is taken and the violation ignored, and I cannot say that I blame them. To issue citations, process reports and come into court when they know that that individual, at a maximum, will be fined $100.00 seems pointless. And, of course, under Oregon Revised Statutes 161.645 the court must consider the financial resources of the defendant in ascertaining fines, and the burden that payment of a fine would impose with due regard to the other obligations of the defendant; and as opposed to the procedure in force before

TABLE 8

OPINIONS REGARDING LEGISLATION

Question	n	Category	Yes (%)	No (%)	No Opinion (%)
1. We should return to	109	legal, all	28	61	10
former law regard-	21	police	67	29	5
ing marijuana	13	district attorneys	23	62	15
	18	judges	17	72	11
	108	educators	35	58	6
2. We should liberalize	103	legal, all	14	81	6
the law further but	21	police	0	100	0
not make marijuana	12	district attorneys	25	75	0
legal	16	judges	19	69	13
	103	educators	8	83	10
3. We should tax, control	105	legal, all	12	75	12
and sell marijuana	20	police	0	90	10
like we do alcohol	13	district attorneys	23	61	15
and cigarrettes	17	judges	23	53	24
	105	educators	11	77	11

the adoption of the new Criminal Code, that failure to pay a fine resulted in imprisonment, now one must proceed by contempt to secure the payment of a fine. I know of no instances where contempt proceedings were instituted either for fines for possession of less than an ounce, or fines for any other offenses.

I believe that the only use now being made of the Oregon statutes concerning possession of less than an ounce of marijuana by the criminal justice system, is a reason to conduct a thorough search of a person or property, or as a convenient vehicle whereby a drug offense involving other drug charges can be negotiated down to a violation.

The people of this state and this country must make an intelligent decision instead of the illogical decisions they have been making. Either treat marijuana as a drug, the use of which will not be sanctioned by society, and return to the penalties we once had, or remove all penalties concerning marijuana, place it under government control and tax it to the highest level, consistent with making it more attractive to possess through legal channels rather than illegal channels.

Many educators volunteered the statement that whereas marijuana was much less of a problem now than in the past, alcohol was an increasing problem and that it was not unusual to see drunken students in school. The volunteered comments from educators that follow paint the picture more vividly than do the cold statistics:

A "problem" with marijuana is distinct from marijuana "use," and I'm not confident that answers to the above opinionnaire allow us to make that distinction.

We should not be more liberal and we should not make marijuana legal; rather, we should continue with a variety of instruments (including opinion polls) to measure the effect of the present legislation.

The more marijuana is legalized the more it seems OK to kids. The same with booze. I work closely with this crap (booze and drugs) and the passive attitude our society has adopted doesn't help my job or the kids that are having their lives wrecked.

Legalize and sell with stipulations.

It is becoming very difficult to sit back and watch bright young minds blown by an assortment of pills and pot. The light penalty for possession of marijuana makes the whole situation a big joke. THE USERS ARE LAUGH-ING!!!

It's good to see the hysteria decrease in U.S. about marijuana; it's sad we still talk about marijuana but do little about alcohol abuse.

It's time society got off their back side, stood up on their hind legs and said *no* to this legalized garbage.

Respect for law and police has not declined just because of change in marijuana laws.

I see young people being critically destroyed through use of marijuana, from observations and work with a great number of students, students attitudes seem to be changed from positive actions to negative actions toward home, school, and respect for authority—clarity of thought seems to be lost— they seem to be unable to judge the loss of their own normal functioning. By no means should laws be relaxed regarding use and possession for marijuana— a great way to destroy a nation (continued use/sanction).

Until conclusive research gives us reliable information on marijuana, we run a risk of making decisions without full knowledge of consequences— neither should we make "outlaws" of those using it.

The present law was the final blow "which caused parents to give up." Parents now tell me that they have little or no support from juvenile authorities and that police actions are most limited.

I feel marijuana is a much less harmful "drug" than either alcohol or cigarettes, both of which are condoned by the FDA and the government. There has been no evidence of marijuana abuse causing crime, etc., whereas the list of alcohol related abuses grows daily.

The use of marijuana has simply become a part of the culture and like smoking, some do and some don't. Previously many smoked because it was a challenge to try it. The faddish aspect has worn off. In my estimation, alcohol (which I indulge in myself on occasion) is a much more insidious and deadly form of indulgence. Obesity is not far behind.

Drugs—"pot" students are now so cool that they present no problem in school. Alcohol—serious problem—presents many problems in all aspects of school life.

Many students justify marijuana usage because it is to this generation what alcohol was to prior generations. I cannot recall such excessive use of alcohol while the student was attending classes in school in the prior generations. It *was* common to see "beer busts" at evening parties and some school-related events, but it was uncommon to see students under the influence of alcohol during the school day. It is common to see students under the influence of drugs during the school day.

I did not agree with the passing of the new law on marijuana. Our experience leads us to believe that marijuana is only a stepping stone to the use of other drugs—harder ones.

The "problems" are fewer but there still seem to be more students using it. Students are heavily involved with alcohol.

Marijuana users do not exhibit aggressive behavior, therefore we don't have discipline problems with this type of individual. However, they become very passive and unmotivated which means they usually become attendance problems and grades are usually affected.

Although I favor Oregon's marijuana legislation, I don't think the changes noted above are consequences of that legislation.

Parents no longer appear shocked when faced with the news that the youngster is using it. A large percentage of our fights and assaults are rooted in marijuana usage/sale/thefts.

Drug problems are "people problems," we should work on people. There will always be a drug of one kind or another.

The law *really* hasn't changed things much—people just smoke it more openly.

Taxing marijuana would presumably: 1) create more revenue and 2) reduce the attractiveness of it (no longer contraband). But I do not think it should be generally available—since reports of long-range effects are yet scanty in conclusions.

Representative Comments from the Police-Legal System

The problem has not changed, but our internal priorities in law enforcement have as a result of the legislature's action. The use of marijuana is now much more open and thus routine detection particularly with regard to routine traffic stops have maintained a similar level of prosecution in this area.

The biggest weakness in the marijuana law is that it does not effectively prohibit youngsters (16, 15—down to 10 or 11) from using marijuana—at least our alcohol laws make an effort to.

A spreading use of alcohol and an apparent decrease in interest in drug activities among young people in this area is the cause for the decreases noted. I doubt that the law change was responsible. I feel that the problem just ran its course. It's still with us but not to the degree that it was. If alcohol related activity was included in the total appraisal of the problem we would have to show an increase in involvement at all levels—schools and after school.

Little consideration has been given to the problem of contiguous state lines. In this jurisdiction people from the State of Washington find Oregon a haven for their illegal activities.

. . . but the young public are users of marijuana and know we can't do much about their use or possession, so they taunt the police. They no longer attempt to try to hide their use, but since it is illegal, they force police to either not perform their duty and ignore it or waste their time and make an arrest. Let's either legalize it or make it a crime that carries some penalties.

The decrease in penalty for what I consider probably the most dangerous of all drugs because it does not appear to be simply convinces our real young people it is *all right*.

(We should return to the former law regarding marijuana) Not without additional manpower! We are finding marijuana use spreading into the adult community. We are also experiencing increasing community pressure to spend more time on marijuana and other drug enforcement.

Use of marijuana has reached epidemic proportions. Decriminalization is *not* the answer, if you legalized burglary, you would have no more burglaries. It is a very effective way for the courts and DA's to reduce their caseloads. Also a very good way to discourage sincere police officers.

We seem only to deal with the drug abusers and "followers"—not those who really financially benefit from illegal sales. It really seems a waste to take up criminal justice systems time with "drug abuse." There seems to be a total lack of facilities to deal with individual problems.

I don't know where their heads are, I mean the people who passed the new marijuana law. I don't think they have really researched the problem. They probably just talked to the users and not any law enforcement people who work the street and really see the problem. I think they should get their heads on straight and find out the real truth.

I believe that the stigma of illegality attached to marijuana for so many years would hinder any efforts to control and tax it in the manner that alcohol and tobacco are presently controlled. In other words, the black market would be too strong for adequate control.

The Legislature only hid from the truth when they changed the law. "If you can't whip them, join them." Many of them had personal family problems and they may have felt they would protect their kids.

It is difficult to assess the situation in that all drug cases have increased in number, but not necessarily related to the change in the marijuana laws. I believe the police have a tendency to ignore the cases involving less than an ounce.

All drug problems and related crime seems on the increase. Excluding pot has probably allowed more police time for heavier drug offenses.

My opinion is these new laws are like all laws which impose arbitrary standards. Less than an ounce of marijuana equals $100 fine. Two ounces means a 10 year maximum. One must be right and the other wrong. Both cannot be correct.

DISCUSSION AND CONCLUSIONS

We must avoid jumping to the conclusion that any changes in attitudes here discussed result directly from changes in the marijuana law as opposed to spontaneous changes of a cyclical nature that occur in matters of public attitudes.

I had always assumed that an unenforceable law was worse than none at all, believing that it only bred contempt for the law. From a substantial number of the comments, I found that many do not share my belief. They seem to equate ethics with law. At any rate, this body of opinion cannot be ignored by legislators.

The following conclusions seem warranted: medically significant problems from use of marijuana have decreased coincident with decriminalizing marijuana, and there is extreme divergence of opinion regarding the marijuana law and drug problems. Policemen often see it in an entirely different light than do judges and district attorneys. The policeman's job is to enforce the law. An unenforceable law will frustrate, anger, or corrupt him. Educators tend to see it more like judges in some respects and like policemen in others. Educators tend to feel that marijuana and especially other drug problems have decreased among students, whereas policemen feel that the same problems have increased. But educators tend to see the successful students, police the failures.

With regard to existing and further legislative changes, only the police prefer to return to the former law. The majority do not wish to now liberalize the law further. Likewise, the majority do not wish to tax, control, and sell marijuana like alcohol and cigarettes, although it is of interest that 23% of the judges favor this idea, and an additional 24% are undecided. (Seventeen percent of the district attorneys are in favor of this idea, and 17% are undecided.) While relegalization is not an entirely unreasonable possibility in the future, great opposition to relegalization and taxation would be brought to bear in the name of morality by those who now sell marijuana.

REFERENCES

1. DRUG ABUSE COUNCIL. 1974. Survey of Marijuana Use—State of Oregon. Washington, D.C.
2. DRUG ABUSE COUNCIL. 1975. Survey of Marijuana Use– State of Oregon. Washington, D.C.
3. BISHOP, B. 1974. Effects of the Oregon laws decriminalizing possession and use of small quantities of marijuana. Vol. **74**: 96. Legislative Research. Salem, Oregon.
4. BLACHLY, P. H. & B. J. BLACHLY. 1974. Sampling technique for medically significant drug abuse. Int. J. Addictions **9**: 885–890.

DISCUSSION PAPER: TOWARD A RATIONALLY BASED SOCIAL POLICY ON MARIJUANA USAGE

Robert C. Petersen

Division of Research
National Institute on Drug Abuse
Rockville, Maryland 20852

By now, after three days of marijuana discussion, you may feel a little like the little girl who wrote the book report on a book about penguins that she had just read. She wrote, "This book told me more about penguins than I ever really wanted to know."

More seriously, I would like to comment on three areas with special emphasis on a research perspective. They are decriminalization, the principal social policy change now taking place in the United States, the researchers' potential role in determining drug use social policy, and, finally, I would like to comment, if only briefly, on the limitations of our present knowledge and some areas in which we need additional research.

With respect to decriminalization, it might be useful at the outset to acknowledge that the health consequences of marijuana use have only limited relevance to the question of decriminalizing the possession of marijuana for personal use. Much more relevant are the social and material costs associated with alternative law enforcement strategies. To what extent do we wish to further burden an already overburdened legal system with perpetrators of a victimless crime? Just how influential are the laws concerning possession on drug usage behavior? What are the behavioral implications of changing them? What is the social cost of diverting law enforcement efforts from other activities? The legislators of six states (Oregon, Maine, California, Alaska, Ohio, and Colorado) have thus far elected to remove criminal sanctions for the possession of small amounts of marijuana for personal use.

While the decision to decriminalize possession ultimately represents a value judgment, research and the researcher can make a modest contribution to that decision. As new states alter their laws, they provide potential sites for studies of marijuana use before and after the enactment of new laws and for comparisons with areas that have similar demographic characteristics in which more restrictive policies continue to apply. Blachly's report on the Oregon experience is one example of this kind of study.[1] If use patterns are not significantly altered by less restrictive policies, the arguments for continuing harsher criminal penalties, even if a drug is dangerous, are something less than compelling.

It must, of course, be remembered that laws and law enforcement policies exist in a larger social context. Marijuana policy is no exception. For those who like to think in terms of statistical norms, 1975 represented a significant turning point in patterns of marijuana use. For the first time in our history, a majority (53%) of an entire age group, young adults aged from 18 to 25, have used the drug one or more times. Moreover, use rates once higher among better educated youth are now virtually identical for similarly aged youth regardless of educational background.[2] By contrast, in 1967, when large-scale drug surveys first began, only one of 20 college students had ever used the drug; a large majority of them have now done so. Clearly, the legal dictum "prevalency of a crime is no excuse for legalizing it" cannot be literally applied when we are speaking of recreational drug use that affects such large numbers. The impact of a legal prohibition is significantly eroded when a majority of a socially significant group chooses to ignore it.

Given the obvious limitations of law, it is important to consider alternative social control strategies. Although it may be difficult to prove conclusively, there is good reason for believing that the social controls represented by custom, patterns of usage in one's social reference group, and the like are much more significant than are legal restraints in governing use of recreational drugs. Alcohol provides an apt model. The extent to which alcohol constitutes a problem drug in a society is related to the ways in which its consumption is "regulated" by customs that discourage its abuse. It is, I think, generally conceded that societies in which alcohol consumption occurs in a family context as a dietary adjunct have fewer problems that those in which drinking is an end in itself. Societies in which immoderate drinking is an important mode of escape, a demonstration of manhood, or in which heavy drinking is an acceptable pattern have greater problems than do societies in which such patterns are not encouraged or acceptable.[3] One of the explanations for the problem of the American Indian in coping with alcohol is that he had no customs to discourage its abuse. Moreover, the prevailing frontier cultural models with which he came into contact were characterized by abuse.[4]

Several of the cannabis studies reported in this monograph illustrate the importance of examining the social context of use. Beaubrun has suggested that well-entrenched Jamaican lower-class use may have different, less disruptive consequences than it does in upper-class Jamaican youth without well-defined methods of coping with such use.[5] Carter et al.'s distinctions between "street movers" and "stable smokers" in Costa Rica similarly emphasize the importance of examining cannabis use in context.[6] Nepal was reported as having stable and nondisruptive cannabis use locally, a picture that was changed by the influx of outsiders with a different use orientation.

Use patterns and expectations are clearly complex, even in cultures in which patterns are established by many years of use. Even in societies in which cannabis use is endemic, new patterns of use may be introduced that have quite different consequences that are difficult to anticipate from examining more traditional use. In our society, predicting future trends is obviously made more difficult by the fact that past patterns are changing, sometimes rapidly.

While use among American youth, those under 18 years of age, has increased substantially since 1972, usage among individuals older than 18 has increased much less. If we limit ourselves to current use, defined as use within the last month, it has increased in all age groups of youth. A similar increase has not been found among adults, however. There is also evidence that as people go on to adult life, taking on traditional vocational and marital responsibilities and roles, use drops.[7] Thus, it is at present difficult to know just how much of experimentation will become more regular use and, in turn, how much of regular use will become clearly persistent use.

Our American experience has largely been confined to relatively small amounts of low-potency material used by the healthiest segment of our population for limited periods of time. It's a bit like trying to predict the future of alcohol use in a society in which there has been mainly occasional use of recently introduced 3.2% beer over a short period of time.

When we turn to the research evidence concerning the implications of longer-term heavier use, those data have some serious limitations. It is possible that some of the tasks employed to measure performance have had only limited relevance and that a low level of motivation has resulted in a diminished performance in both experimental and control groups, thus masking drug-related differences. With respect to other measures of functioning, there may be important differences in the demands made in a highly industrialized culture from those of a less industrially complex one. The limited size of the samples thus far studied is also a decided limitation to broader interpretation. Similarly sized samples of cigarette smokers would almost certainly have missed some of the most serious health implications of heavy smoking. These implications include lung cancer, heart disease, and emphysema. Even in our culture, research has largely been defined to healthy, highly motivated subjects often eager to demonstrate unimpaired performance under the influence of marijuana. One can only speculate on what would occur under more typical motivational conditions were use more completely accepted.

My purpose in outlining these concerns is not to argue that the misgivings mentioned are necessarily critical in fact. It is rather to stress that our picture of marijuana is still quite incomplete and that there is a very real danger in developing a rational social policy, of leaping to unwarranted conclusions uncritically.

Here are a few of the questions that seem to me both important and as yet unanswered or inadequately answered:

What are the implications of regular cannabis use for adolescents, especially those experiencing more than the usual difficulties in achieving firm identity or acquiring necessary social and intellectual skills? Surely many of us have misgivings based on some clinical contact with such youngsters for whom marijuana use may complicate an already difficult problem in coping. On this issue, we have only limited data, and our overseas studies are largely irrelevant. We obviously need to know more.

Apart from the young, what are the implications of regular and possibly heavy cannabis use for the more marginal members of our society, those with low motivation, poorer functioning, or otherwise disadvantaged? The concerns of some minority leaders that marijuana use may be more insidious for members of their groups than for highly motivated members of the majority may have a basis in fact that should be more carefully examined. As Mellinger et al. have indicated, conclusions based on well-motivated, bright middle-class students in a highly selective academic environment may not be relevant to other less selected groups.[8]

We know little about the implications of marijuana use for the less healthy physically. We are, after all, an underexercised and overfed people. The implications of a drug-induced tachycardia may be quite different for a population with those characteristics than for a rural population of farm workers long accustomed to hard work. There is evidence that marijuana use results in more rapid onset of chest pain (angina pectoris) in cardiac patients after exercise than does cigarette smoking.[9-11] Thus, the implications of cannabis use may be quite different in physically impaired groups from those in normals. Little work has been done in this area.

In this country, multiple drug use, often concomitantly, rather than the use of cannabis alone, is the rule rather than the exception. We need to know more about the implications of the use of alcohol and other drugs in conjunction with marijuana use. Combinations may have more serious implications than cannabis use alone.

In trying to examine the marijuana issue as objectively as possible, it is important to study those who use cannabis without apparent ill effects and how they may differ from others who do not.

We are especially concerned about the young, children and younger adolescents who are now using in large numbers. We need larger-scale epidemiologic studies with special emphasis on this group to guide us in determining how restrictive to be. I might add parenthetically that most epidemiologic research on marijuana to date has looked simply at *frequency* of use rather than the actual *quantity* consumed and the circumstances of its consumption. Just as daily use of alcohol is not necessarily hazardous, although heavy Saturday night drinking may be, it is vital that we look at use in more sophisticated terms that are better related to possible hazard than is frequency per se.

I am intrigued by Dr. Campbell's admittedly subjective and clinical observation of a decline in the quality of abstracting and synthesizing in essay examinations of Canadian college students who used cannabis four or more times per week.[12] While admittedly a "soft sign" that might not be confirmed under conditions of blind judging, it suggests a method of subtle evaluation that may prove useful and relevant. With a bit of ingenuity, systematic research could be performed free from the obvious limitations of his preliminary observation.

The possible value of animal studies of learning performance after chronic cannabis use is underscored by the work of Kalant *et al.* in Canada.[13] Such work could also be usefully extended by use of levels of cannabis consumption that bear some realistic relationship to likely human levels, should heavier use become more common. Work should certainly include younger animals because of our concern with possible learning disabilities in children and adolescents that may be drug related.

If the large numbers who have elected to experiment with cannabis in the United States and Canada do, in fact, go on to regular use in future years, it seems virtually inescapable that our society will have to make some accommodation to that use. Whatever one's personal preferences, it may be important to come to terms eventually with cannabis use by reducing the likelihood of ill effects rather than eliminating use entirely. If this is so, it is essential that we know more about the parameters of use and the implications of different patterns of use. Cost-benefit modeling of the various alternative strategies of control may be a useful way of arriving at more rational social policy as patterns of use become more stabilized.

Having been involved in the American marijuana research program virtually from its inception, I hope I may be forgiven some concluding observations based on that experience, namely:

We need a wiser, more consistent social policy regarding all recreational drug use. Our present policies are a patchwork of inconsistency in which there is encouragement of some types of clearly hazardous drug use along with harsh treatment of other types of drug usage, no more, and possibly less, dangerous. For example, we might well consider outlawing the advertising and promotion of all recreational drugs, as we have done with the television advertising of cigarettes.

There is a continued need to examine the problem of cannabis usage in perspective. It continues to be an arena in which our worst fears too often interfere with clear thinking. As researchers, we can help others to recognize the essential complexity of drug issues and to think more subtly about solutions. We can discourage the type of simplistic thinking that seizes upon isolated findings without respect for their limitations to establish a "case" for or against marijuana. We can encourage awareness of the absurdity of some of our thinking, which insists on classifying our socially accepted drugs as "good" drugs and others, less familiar, as "bad."

We need to think about new and better ways to encourage wiser behavioral choices, more judicious decisions regarding substance use. Often we have seen our efforts in the past as failures, when, in fact, they may more accurately be regarded as partial successes. While we have not, for example, eliminated cigarette smoking, we have probably significantly reduced its hazards. This reduction of hazards has occurred in several ways. The type of cigarette now being consumed is less hazardous than that marketed formerly. By encouraging better recognition of the rights of the majority who do not smoke, through the provision of nonsmoking areas and outright smoking prohibition in some areas, we have caused many to become more thoughtful about the implications of their behavior. In some groups in which a majority were formerly smokers, physicians are an example, few now continue to smoke. Thus, drug use patterns can be shifted in more benign directions, even if use cannot altogether be eliminated.

There are few societies that have been utterly lacking in mind-altering recreational substances. The challenge in developing a rationally based social policy regarding such substances is not to eliminate them but to develop policies that minimize the individual and societal risks that they pose.

REFERENCES

1. BLACHLY, P. This monograph.
2. ABELSON, H. I. & R. B. ATKINSON. 1975. Public Experience with Psychoactive Substances, A Nationwide Study among Adults and Youth. Response Analysis Corporation. Princeton, N.J.
3. FOX, R. 1966. Aspects of Alcoholism. J. B. Lippincott Co. Philadelphia, Pa.
4. MacANDREW, C. & R. B. EDGERTON. 1969. Drunken Comportment. A Social Explanation. Aldine Publishing Company. Chicago, Ill.
5. BEAUBRUN, M. H. 1973. Drug abuse in different cultural groups in Jamaica, Paper presented at ANZCP/WA Meeting, Sydney, Australia, October 15–19.
6. CARTER, W. E., J. COGGINS & P. L. DOUGHTY. 1976. Chronic cannabis use in Costa Rica, Report by the Center for Latin American Studies of the University of Florida to the National Institute on Drug Abuse.
7. O'DONNELL, J. A., H. L. VOSS, R. R. CLAYTON, G. T. SLATIN & R. G. W. ROOM. 1976. Young Men and Drugs—A Nationwide Survey, NIDA Research Monograph 5. National Institute on Drug Abuse. Rockville, Md.
8. MELLINGER, G., R. H. SOMERS, S. T. DAVIDSON & D. I. MANHEIMER. This monograph.
9. ANGELICO, I. & J. BROWN. 1974. Marihuana and angina pectoris. N. Engl. J. Med. 191(15): 800.
10. ARONOW, W. S. & J. CASSIDY. 1975. Effect of smoking marihuana and of a high nicotine cigarette on angina pectoris. Clin. Pharmacol. Ther. 17(5): 549–554.

11. PRAKASH, R., W. S. ARONOW, M. WARREN, W. LAVERTY & L. A. GOTTSCHALK. 1975. Effects of marihuana and placebo marihuana smoking on hemodynamics in coronary disease. Clin. Pharmacol. Ther. **18**(1): 90–95.
12. CAMPBELL, I. This monograph.
13. FEHR, K. A., H. KALANT, A. E. LeBLANC & G. V. KNOX. 1975. Permanent learning impairment after chronic heavy exposure to cannabis or ethanol in the rat. Unpublished paper.

GENERAL DISCUSSION

Alfred M. Freedman, *Moderator*

Department of Psychiatry
New York Medical College
New York, New York 10029

Ms. Barbara Orlowski (*City University of New York, New York, N.Y.*):
I am a firm believer in individual freedom. In this bicentennial year, everybody
is throwing up individual freedom, but it doesn't really exist. Some people do
not drink alcohol and do not smoke cigarettes, and there should definitely be
an alternative. Some people like to change their state of awareness, their state
of consciousness, and it is up to them to do it. It has nothing to do with
anybody else.

Also, cigarette filters might be getting better, and the person who is smoking
them might be less prone to getting cancer, but what about the people who are
being subjected to the cigarette smoke around them and are being polluted in that
way? If you are going to talk about tobacco and alcohol, these drugs contribute
to a lot of problems for nonsmokers who don't like having smoke blown in their
faces and for nondrinkers who don't like people driving who are all over the
road. Now, this might be true of people who smoke "grass" and drive cars, too,
but I think the major factor is that "grass" should be legalized. I think making
it less of a crime is ridiculous. I think that maybe making 1 oz. a misdemeanor
and 1.5 oz. a 10-year sentence is ridiculous. The drug should be legalized and
controlled by the government. Some people are making $50 or more off each
ounce of marijuana, which should cost much less. New York City wouldn't be
in its present condition if it could tax marijuana.

Dr. P. H. Blachly: Perhaps New York City might consider marijuana as
another source of bailing itself out of its difficulties. I use the term relegalization, of course, because marijuana was grown in this country for many years.
It only became illegal about 40 years ago. I think your points are basically very
well taken. I don't have a lot of argument.

Dr. Robert C. Petersen (*National Institute on Drug Abuse, Rockville,
Md.*): I'm not sure that passive inhalation of marijuana is necessarily any better
and that maybe we should restrict it all between consenting adults.

Dr. Harry Powers (*Cambridge, Mass.*): Dr. Blachly, what does the law
in Oregon say about the difference between marijuana and Δ^9-THC?

Dr. Blachly: It doesn't say anything.

Dr. Powers: At this meeting, we have heard an awful lot about marijuana
and the various chemical, pharmacologic, and primarily sociologic and clinical
effects of marijuana. We also heard about Δ^9-THC, and I submit that there
might be a difference between those two substances.

Dr. Petersen: The only obvious point, of course, is that THC is not
actually used by anyone, except in experimental settings. As far as I know,
there is no THC on the market.

Dr. Powers: That's true, but if it's not mentioned in the law, it may not
be differentiated by the people who enforce the law.

Dr. Petersen: It can easily be added to the law, if you choose to do so.

Dr. Gordon Fowler: What about the implications for science? I think

422

that there are major implications, because we are getting to a point now where we can't discuss technical and physiologic things anymore, and we are getting very much into the subjective area with mood-altering and consciousness-altering drugs. There have to be ways to measure subjective experience. This would be a major change in science, because for the last 200 years, science has been very rational in dealing with objective findings, but there has been nothing subjective in science since, I'd say, Newton. And this subjectivity is a change that is taking place. Would you agree?

DR. FREEDMAN: I think to say that science has totally ignored subjective phenomena really ignores a tremendous amount of work that has been done in the whole field of psychology over the last century. Better methods of studying and making objective studies of fantasy could be developed. However, the notion that science has been involved in objective tasks and has ignored subjective experience is erroneous in my opinion.

DR. FOWLER: Haven't we heard a lot of that in this meeting? Everybody is trying to be very objective about their findings, and every time someone says something about subjective moods, they mention the mind-body dualism as if it is a very controversial thing, which it may be.

DR. FREEDMAN: My impression would be that such dualism was not put forward strongly, rather the notion that there is a synthesis between the objective and subjective states.

QUESTION: Dr. Blachly, you mentioned that people were hospitalized in Oregon directly as a consequence of marijuana use. Could you be more explicit as to why they were hospitalized?

DR. BLACHLY: I can't be more specific. I think those figures are highly suspect. We receive monthly reports from the hospital; we have been getting these reports for years. The reports just say that so many were hospitalized for LSD, so many for heroin, and so many for marijuana and glue, and so on. That is just the way the figures break down. It could well be that a different person is screening them, and I suspect that marijuana probably is not one of the main reasons that they were hospitalized. I suspect that the person who was interviewing was more concerned in 1970 than they have been recently.

MS. ANNA STERN (*Canarsie Youth Center, Brooklyn, N.Y.*): What are the implications of the current findings and current trends toward decriminalization for funding of adolescent drug abuse prevention and treatment programs in which the clients primarily abuse marijuana? Many use other drugs, but the primary drug abused is marijuana.

DR. PETERSEN: I actually haven't followed the provisions for services to teenagers. I think that the obvious concern is that the implications of use by adolescents may be quite different. The implications for young people in adolescent development crises may be quite different. We should remember that we are talking about marijuana; we are talking about a particular segment of the population when we are talking about the younger people who may be terribly vulnerable.

MS. STERN: We see totally different patterns in the kids whom we see in our program versus kids who are making it in school. I was just curious whether the change in the research would wipe out these programs.

DR. PETERSEN: I hope not. I think your concern is very reasonable.

DR. DENNIS ROGERMAN (*New York Medical College, New York, N.Y.*): A few of the speakers this afternoon have made the comment that marijuana smoking is no longer a cause celebre and that there has been a general slackening of interest. Has this change been translated through a concomitant disinterest in foundation support for continuing research on marijuana and through less scientific interest in the field? And, if so, regarding the increased number of people who are using marijuana, how could this situation be overcome?

DR. BRYANT: Most of the money and other resources that are available to support scientific research in this country on the properties of marijuana and the effects of its use come from the federal government, taxpayer's dollars. I am sure Dr. Petersen is more familiar with the details of the new federal budget, but my understanding is that part of the dollars for research in the drug field is earmarked for marijuana-related research. My understanding is that the total amount for such research is about the same.

As I indicated, I think that only a small amount of dollars comes from foundations for the support of basic research. For the most part, foundations are more involved and active in the support of what I would call socioeconomic demographic research rather than basic research. We still get inundated with requests, so I am sure that the interest is still there.

DR. EDMUND BRAUN (*Metropolitan Hospital, New York, N.Y.*): I have been very impressed over the past three days with the care used, the exhaustive nature of these studies, and the restraint in interpretation of the results. I think that these points emphasize very strongly a conclusion that many of you may have already reached, namely, that the whole issue of marijuana in many respects has been grossly exaggerated and even vulgarized.

There is a major problem in many of our cities, and it exists in people who are using or abusing drugs. I think that we can be diverted and we have been diverted, both by the proponents of drug restrictions and the opponents of drug restrictions, into making drug use the major issue. I think that this conference has been extraordinarily good in the sense that it puts the facts in their proper perspective. However, we do have to make use of that perspective in realizing that there is a problem, that the problem of the young people, particularly in places like East Harlem, needs a solution. We should not be diverted into making a major argument over drug use. To that end, I think these conferences are extremely useful in putting all of the information in a proper perspective, and I think research on the various short-term and long-term effects of the drugs should be continued.

DR. BLACHLY: I think that is a very important concept, and we should bear in mind that the abuse of marijuana or of any of the other drugs is a problem-solving behavior exhibited by the individual. The real challenge is to provide more constructive or less destructive problem-solving activities for these people.

MR. MICHAEL SONNENREICH, ESQ.: The point you are making about East Harlem is very legitimate. We should continue research; we probably should increase research—not because it is going to do anything social policy-wise, simply because we should know as much as possible about these substances for a variety of reasons. The most important is that when you break down these drugs and synthesize them, they may have tremendous properties that are of great value.

With respect to the social issue, however, regardless of whether there is marijuana in East Harlem, it is not a priority from a social-planning point of view. As Dr. Blachly said, there are so many alternatives. The drug actually is a way of coping with a situation, and the situation will not be solved by dealing with any part of the drug abuse problem; the only result will be transferance. I don't think we should predicate our research, or our concern as scientists on conducting research, on whether we're going to solve a problem in East Harlem.

DR. BLACHLY: I think every problem has solutions, which, in themselves, create more problems. The major question is have we set up, with these laws about marijuana, a solution that is more destructive than the original problem for which it was designed to cure. With regard to marijuana, I think the evidence is quite clear that the cure was worse than the original evil. Now, that's not necessarily true with laws for other drugs. But we have to look at that cost to benefit ratio with each decision.

DR. COOPER (*National Institute on Drug Abuse, Rockville, Md.*): Dr. Bryant, would you elaborate on a statement you made (and I am paraphrasing it) as to the fact that in the next couple of years it is inevitable that we are going to move toward a policy of decriminalization. Is this change going to occur through public opinion or through state by state action? Polls taken in Congress indicated exactly the opposite of what you are saying.

DR. T. BRYANT (*Drug Abuse Council, Washington, D.C.*): I think it will be a state by state action, and my predictions are like almost anyone else's— take them with a big grain of salt. But, based on the work that we are doing with about 25 states, I think that there is a chance that decriminalization legislation will be introduced and discussed. It seems now that this decriminalization stands a reasonable chance of passage.

Many of these states are going to wait one or two years for further study or they are going to take a look at the experience of other states that have decriminalized the drug, in particular, California.

My reading of the Congress is exactly the same as yours. I don't think that there is a large body of support for decriminalizing marijuana in the Congress. On the other hand, this is a very iffy question in the State of California in terms of public opinion, particularly in the state legislature. In Oregon, you had three or four well-organized congressional legislative leaders who were really quite courageous because they took an awful lot of flack and were able to work within the legislative process, in terms of compromise or this or that committee's interest. If you have people who are willing to stick their necks out on the issue and work with state legislators and public opinion, I think you can do something.

MR. SONNENREICH: Remember that the marijuana laws and all of our drug laws first start at the state level. When the federal government controlled marijuana through the Marijuana Tax Act in 1937, almost all of the states had already controlled marijuana. So what's happening here is not a unique process. The states will act first.

When California went, 10% of the population of the United States went with it, and as the population increases, whatever your poll of the federal government, the federal government is very conservative in changing laws, taking laws off the books and penalties. The result will be that as more states act positively, suddenly the congressmen in each state will vote for decriminalization. They are going to mold the federal law to the state law. In that respect, I think Dr. Bryant is 100% correct.

We said that when the Commission was finished, it would take 3–5 years, and I think that estimate will be correct.

DR. COOPER: Do you think, though, if something negative happened, in other words, as more big states like California enact such legislation, if certain negative consequences arise, that these results may change public opinion the other way?

MR. SONNENREICH: It is possible but would be quite difficult. I sense that unless something dramatic happens that everybody in this room in three days has really missed, and these surveys that have been conducted have just totally missed, I don't think you will see a dramatic change. You may have somebody yelling and screaming; you may have somebody throw up his hands like Rockefeller did in New York. The reality is, though, that you will see another state and then another state enact this legislation. It will then become very difficult, not for the senators but for the congressmen, to get reelected by consistently saying we're going to vote against something like that. The federal law will change when about 30–35 states have decriminalized usage of the drug.

CONFERENCE SUMMARY

Max Fink

Department of Psychiatry
State University of New York at Stony Brook
Stony Brook, New York 11794

Concerns about the usage of cannabis are its potentiality for physical and psychologic harm in users, namely, psychosis, loss of motivation, brain damage, withdrawal from society, and physical damage. Fears that cannabis usage leads to use and dependence on other addicting substances and to criminality, sexual assault, and unrestrained aggression are less commonly voiced today. Reports that cannabis usage was increasing in the 1960s led some scientists, with governmental support and encouragement, to undertake systematic studies of these concerns. To find populations of long-term users, not available in the United States or Western Europe, scientists went to countries where cannabis use had only recently been proscribed, which provided the possibility that some subjects had used cannabis for many years. Such populations were found in Costa Rica, Greece, and Jamaica. Concurrent studies in India and Egypt and some long-term experimental studies in the United States and Canada provide a wealth of experience to assess the role of cannabis in syndromes of concern.

The goals of this Conference were to answer specific questions: Is long-term cannabis use associated with brain damage and cerebral dysfunction? Is cannabis use associated with psychosis and/or an amotivational syndrome? Is cannabis use accompanied by physical or mental defects? Does cannabis use elicit tolerance, dependence, or withdrawal?

Subjects were carefully selected from among cooperative long-term male users of ganja or hashish, who reported no more than occasional use of alcohol and the nonuse of other dependence-producing drugs. All users smoked tobacco, as did the control subjects, who were selected from the same social class, community of origin, education, and work experience as the users. Controls professed not to use drugs other than alcohol, socially.

The numbers of long-term users studied in Costa Rica, Greece, and Jamaica were 84, 47, and 30, with 156, 40, and 30 subjects as controls. In the acute assessments in Costa Rica, a smaller sample of 41 users and 41 controls was examined. In India, the subjects were 275 users seen in their homes or at work; in Egypt, the sample consisted of 850 males convicted of hashish offenses during one year and detained in prison. Of these 850, 577 were rated as "heavy" and 273 as "moderate" users.

The duration of cannabis use averaged 16.9 years in the Costa Rican sample, 23 years in the Greek, and 17.5 years in the Jamaican. The amount of cannabis smoked daily, as assayed for its content of Δ^9-tetrahydrocannabinol, was large by United States' and Canadian standards: 20–160 mg in Costa Rica, 120–200 mg in Greece, and 20–90 mg in Jamaica.

The total sample of long-term users studied intensively was small, no more than 118 users in the controlled studies,[3, 5, 9] and 1125 in the studies in India[6] and Egypt.[24, 25] A cannabis-related defect that occurred with a frequency less than 20/1000 would probably not be detectable in these samples. Nevertheless, the data are consistent among the experimental studies, and their observations bear on the questions of major concern.

The users were examined in a variety of life situations but also in laboratory settings to measure the acute effects of cannabis substances on behavior, mental and psychologic performance, and on physiologic tests. The subjects smoked various quantities of ganja/hashish, marijuana, and Δ^9-THC infused in tobacco. Cannabis inhalation has direct dose-related effects on heart rate,[8, 12, 23] brain functions,[12, 16] and psychologic test performance.[11, 18, 23] The effects are not persistent, and the reactions of long-term users on mood, performance tests, heart rate, and EEG are similar in direction and degree to the effects of smoking these substances demonstrated by the more casual users ordinarily studied in acute trials in the United States and Canada[4, 8, 12–15, 19] and in the "long-term" experimental studies in the United States.[8, 13, 15, 19]

Brain damage, as defined by physiologic (EEG),[12, 16] neurologic,[3, 7, 10] echo EEG,[3] psychologic tests,[7, 11, 18, 18a, 23] was not demonstrated. While each inhalation of cannabis is accompanied by defined changes in the EEG,[3, 12] sleep EEG,[15, 16] and performance tests,[11, 18, 23] these changes do not persist beyond the 2–4 hr of immediate drug effect.

Cerebral dysfunction, as evidenced by an organic mental syndrome or organic psychosis, is not observed clinically or with experimental inhalation.[4, 8, 11, 17, 26] Psychiatric evaluations present a mixed picture, with psychopathy prominent in one sample.[26] Psychosis is also not present, and its absence may, in part, reflect such subjects' inability to volunteer for these studies, their exclusion from the samples, or their natural absence from the population of users. The sampling methods do not permit a resolution of this ambiguity.

There is no evidence of an amotivational syndrome[4, 5, 9, 18, 20, 26]; in contrast, in two studies the users seem to augment their work output, to relieve the monotony of dull, repetitive, laborious work by smoking cannabis.[5, 9] Comitas[9] makes an exceptionally strong refutation of the concept of a drug-related amotivational syndrome. While the work output of lower-class workers may be enhanced, there is some concern that cannabis may inhibit the output of workers who have more complex tasks or who come from higher social classes, for whom mental operations usually predominate.[17, 18] In some studies, cannabis use is associated with a reduction in aggression and assaultiveness.[20, 28]

The naturalistic observations of Chopra and Jandu[6] and Soueif[24, 25] reflect different views of long-term cannabis use, defining incidences of psychosis, an amotivational syndrome, and organic mental syndromes that contrast sharply with those observed in comparison studies in Costa Rica, Jamaica, and Greece and with the long-term experiments in the United States and Canada. In one report from Jamaica, however, a significant number of mental hospital admissions was related to ganja use.[17]

In these samples of cannabis users, no consistent medical defects as a consequence of such use are defined.[3, 7, 10] Users have body weights lower than those of the controls in two studies.[7, 10] The effects on chromosomes were examined, with negative findings.[8, 10] Some discussants, accepting the negative findings with regard to brain damage, psychosis, the amotivational syndrome, and dependence, raised new concerns that cannabis may be associated with impaired spermatogenesis and lowered testosterone levels, issues that were not addressed by the studies and reported at this Conference only tangentially.[7, 8, 19, 21]

Tissue tolerance is observed. Long-term users who inhale large quantities of cannabis exhibit the same effects that occasional users demonstrate to much lower doses. Tolerance is seen in measures of heart rate [3, 12] and in EEG effects.[12] Tolerance develops rapidly and may be demonstrated within 2 weeks [12] and is not accompanied by defined withdrawal symptoms when usage ceases.[27]

Some observers have examined the subjects' drug-seeking behavior as evidence for dependence, but the data are not well defined, either in long-term users [27] or in experimental laboratory subjects.[8, 15]

The experimental studies of daily cannabis usage for periods of up to 3 months in young adult male volunteers show responses in mood, heart rate, EEG, and performance tests similar to those obtained in trials in long-term users. [8, 13, 15, 19] Evidence for tolerance is defined,[15, 19] and one study finds evidence for a withdrawal syndrome.[15] The studies also document well-defined effects of cannabis on pupillary size and intraocular pressure but do not demonstrate any physical side effects.[8, 13, 15, 19]

Concerns that long-term cannabis use is associated with individual or social toxicity are not confirmed. In the discussion of the significance of these findings for social policy, the recommendations for decriminalization of cannabis use made by both the United States' and Canadian commissions were supported, with predictions that as cannabis use increased and individual states in the United States relaxed their proscriptions, national relegalization would probably become public policy within this decade (see comments by Bryant and Sonnenreich in the final General Discussion and the Discussion Paper by Petersen). In reflecting on the Oregon experience with relaxed regulations, Blachly [1] reported wide discrepancies in opinions among different segments of the population sampled.

A principal caveat in these studies is the sample size and the methods of sampling, which may fail to document damage that occurs infrequently. The discrepancies between the controlled and experimental studies, on the one hand, and the open, naturalistic studies, on the other, are great, and further attention will be required for their resolution. Nevertheless, these carefully designed studies in Canada, Costa Rica, Jamaica, Greece, and the United States fail to define evidence for brain or systemic damage, for either an organic or psychogenic psychosis, or for an amotivational syndrome. The studies demonstrate evidence for tolerance but not for dependence or withdrawal, and they fail to find a link between cannabis use and that of narcotics or alcohol. While these concerns may be allayed, the studies do not bear on the problem of interference with motor coordination or sensory perception associated with cannabis use,[14] functions that may have a significant effect on such common tasks as driving, machine tool operation, flying, or instrumental monitoring (as in flight controllers). The studies reported here provide substantive data for the continuing assessment of social policy for marijuana use.

REFERENCES

1. BLACHLY, P. H. Effects of decriminalization of marijuana in Oregon.
2. BOULOUGOURIS, J. C., A. LIAKOS & C. STEFANIS. Social traits of heavy hashish users and matched controls.
3. BOULOUGOURIS, J. C., C. P. PANAYIOTOPOULOS, E. ANTYPAS, A. LIAKOS & C. STEFANIS. Effects of chronic hashish use on medical status in 44 users compared with 38 controls.
4. CAMPBELL, I. The amotivational syndrome and cannabis use with emphasis on the Canadian scene.

5. CARTER, W. E. & P. L. DOUGHTY. Social and cultural aspects of cannabis use in Costa Rica.
6. CHOPRA, G. S. & B. S. JANDU. Psychoclinical effects of long-term marijuana use in 275 Indian chronic users. A comparative assessment of effects in Indian and USA users.
7. COGGINS, W. J., E. W. SWENSON, W. W. DAWSON, A. FERNÁNDEZ-SALAS, J. HERNANDEZ-BOLANOS, C. F. JIMINEZ-ANTILLON, J. R. SOLANO, R. VINOCOUR & F. FAERRON-VALDEZ. Health status of chronic heavy cannabis users.
8. COHEN, S. The 94-day cannabis study.
9. COMITAS, L. Cannabis and work in Jamaica: a refutation of the amotivational syndrome.
10. CRUICKSHANK, E. K. Physical assessment of 30 chronic cannabis users and 30 matched controls.
11. DORNBUSH, R. L. & A. KOKKEVI. Acute effects of cannabis on cognitive, perceptual, and motor performance in chronic hashish users.
12. FINK, M. Effects of acute and chronic inhalation of hashish, marijuana, and Δ^9-tetrahydrocannabinol on brain electrical activity in man: evidence for tissue tolerance.
13. GREENBERG, I., J. H. MENDELSON, J. C. KUEHNLE, N. MELLO & T. F. BABOR. Psychiatric and behavioral observations of casual and heavy marijuana users in a controlled research setting.
14. HANSTEEN, R. W., R. D. MILLER, L. LONERO, L. D. REID & B. JONES. Effects of cannabis and alcohol on automobile driving and psychomotor tracking.
15. JONES, R. T., N. BENOWITZ & J. BACHMAN. Clinical studies of cannabis tolerance and dependence.
16. KARACAN, I., A. FERNÁNDEZ-SALAS, W. J. COGGINS, W. E. CARTER, R. L. WILLIAMS, J. I. THORNBY, P. J. SALIS, M. OKAWA & J. P. VILLAUME. Sleep electroencephalographic-electrooculographic characteristics of chronic marijuana users: part I.
17. KNIGHT, F. Role of cannabis in psychiatric disturbance.
18. KNIGHTS, R. M. & M. L. GRENIER. Problems in studying the effects of chronic cannabis use on intellectual abilities.
18a. LIAKOS, A., J. C. BOULOUGOURIS & C. STEFANIS. Psychophysiologic effects of acute cannabis smoking in long-term users.
19. MENDELSON, J. H., T. F. BABOR, J. C. KUEHNLE, A. M. ROSSI, J. G. BERNSTEIN, N. K. MELLO & I. GREENBERG. Behavioral and biologic aspects of marijuana use.
20. MELLINGER, G. D., R. H. SOMERS, S. T. DAVIDSON & D. I. MANHEIMER. The amotivational syndrome and the college student.
21. PEREZ-REYES, M., D. BRINE & M. E. WALL. Clinical study of frequent marijuana use: adrenal cortical reserve metabolism of a contraceptive agent and development of tolerance.
22. PETERSEN, R. C. Discussion paper: toward a rationally based social policy on marijuana usage.
23. SATZ, P., J. M. FLETCHER & L. S. SUTKER. Neuropsychologic, intellectual, and personality correlates of chronic marijuana use in native Costa Ricans.
24. SOUEIF, M. I. Cannabis-type dependence: the psychology of chronic heavy consumption.
25. SOUEIF, M. I. Differential association between chronic cannabis use and brain function deficits.
26. STEFANIS, C., A. LIAKOS & J. C. BOULOUGOURIS. Incidence of mental illness in hashish users and controls.
27. STEFANIS, C., A. LIAKOS, J. C. BOULOUGOURIS, R. L. DORNBUSH & C. BALLAS. Experimental observations of a 3-day hashish abstinence period and reintroduction of use.
28. TINKLENBERG, J. R., W. T. ROTH, B. S. KOPELL & P. MURPHY. Cannabis and alcohol effects on assaultiveness in adolescent delinquents.
29. WIKLER, A. Aspects of tolerance to and dependence on cannabis.